CENSUS OF INDIA 1931

Census of India 1871-1951, 9 Sets In 384 Bindings (9788121258876) Rs. 700000

Census of India 1931, 28 Vols. In 52 Bindings (9788121271233) Rs. 102000

1. India - Report (9788121276153) Rs. 2820 (Vol. I, Pt. 1)
2. India - Imperial Tables (9788121276139) Rs. 3210 (Vol. I, Pt. 2)
3. India - Ethnographical and Administration Report (9788121276115) Rs. 2900 (Vol. I, Pt. 3 & 5)
4. The Andaman And Nicobar Islands - Report, Tables (9788121276078) Rs. 720 (Vol. II, Pt. 1, Pt. 2)
5. Assam - Report (9788121276054) Rs. 1340 (Vol. III, Pt. 1)
6. Assam - Tables and Administrative Report (9788121276030) Rs. 1830 (Vol. III, Pt. 2 & 3)
7. Baluchistan - Report, Imeprial and Provincial Tables and Administrative Report (9788121276016) Rs. 2320 (Vol. IV, Pt. 1 & 2 & 3)
8. Bengal & Sikkim - Report (9788121275972) Rs. 2860 (Vol. V, Pt. 1)
9. Bengal & Sikkim - Tables (9788121275958) Rs. 1660 (Vol. V, Pt. 2)
10. Calcutta (9788121275910) Rs. 960 (Vol. VI, Pt. 1 & 2)
11. Bengal, Sikkim And Calcutta - Administrative Report (9788121275934) Rs. 580 (Vol. V & VI, Pt. 3)
12. Bihar And Orissa - Report (9788121275897) Rs. 1780 (Vol. VII, Pt. 1)
13. Bihar And Orissa - Tables and Administrative Report (9788121275873) Rs. 1190 (Vol. VII, Pt. 2 & 3)
14. Bombay Presidency - General Report (9788121275835) Rs. 3620 (Vol. VIII, Pt. 1)
15. Bombay - Statistical tables (9788121275811) Rs. 3060 (Vol. VIII, Pt. 2)
16. Bombay Presidency Aden - report and tables and Administrative report (9788121275798) Rs. 520 (Vol. VIII, Pt. 3 & 4)
17. Cities of the Bombay Presidency Report & Statistical tables (9788121275750) Rs. 2020 (Vol. IX, Pt. 1 & 2)
18. The Western India States Agency, In Two Parts - The Report & The Statistical Tables (9788121275736) Rs. 2560 (Vol. X, Pt. 1 & 2)
19. Burma - Report (9788121275712) Rs. 1860 (Vol. XI, Pt. 1)
20. Burma - Tables and Administrative Report (9788121275699) Rs. 1690 (Vol. XI, Pt. 2 & 3)
21. Central Provinces & Berar - Report (9788121275651) Rs. 2340 (Vol. XII, Pt. 1)
22. Central Provinces & Berar - Tables and Administrative Report (9788121275637) Rs. 3120 (Vol. XII, Pt. 2 & 3)
23. Coorg - Report And Tables and Madras - Report (9788121275613) Rs. 2680 (Vol. XIV, Pt. 1)
24. Madras - Imperial And Provincial Tables and The Administration Report (9788121275576) Rs. 1950 (Vol. XIV, Pt. 2 & 4)
25. North - West Frontier Province - Report & Tables (9788121275538) Rs. 2300 (Vol. XV, Pt. 1 & 2)
26. Delhi - Report & Tables (9788121275514) Rs. 1180 (Vol. XVI, Pt. 1 & 2)
27. Punjab - Report (9788121275491) Rs. 2070 (Vol. XVII, Pt. 1)
28. Punjab - Tables (9788121275477) Rs. 1690 (Vol. XVII, Pt. 2)
29. United Provinces of Agra And Oudh - Report (9788121275453) Rs. 3380 (Vol. XVIII, Pt. 1)
30. United Provinces of Agra And Oudh - Imperial And Provincial Tables and Administrative (9788121275439) Rs. 3600 (Vol. XVIII, Pt. 2 & 3)
31. Baroda - Report (9788121275415) Rs. 2800 (Vol. XIX, Pt. 1)
32. Baroda - Tables (9788121275392) Rs. 730 (Vol. XIX, Pt. 2)
33. Baroda - Administrative (9788121275378) Rs. 780 (Vol. XIX, Pt. 3)
34. Central India Agency - Report (9788121275354) Rs. 1690 (Vol. XX, Pt. 1)
35. Central India Agency - Tables and Administrative Volume (9788121275330) Rs. 2260 (Vol. XX, Pt. 2 & 3)
36. Cochin - Report & Tables (9788121275293) Rs. 2460 (Vol. XXI, Pt. 1 & 2 - A & B.)
37. Gwalior - Report (9788121275279) Rs. 1470 (Vol. XXII, Pt. 1)
38. Gwalior - Tables (9788121275255) Rs. 980 (Vol. XXII, Pt. 2)
39. H. E. H. The Nizam's Dominions (Hyderabad State) - Report (9788121275231) Rs. 1540 (Vol. XXIII, Pt. 1)
40. H. E. H. The Nizam's Dominions (Hyderabad State) - Tables (9788121275217) Rs. 1510 (Vol. XXIII, Pt. 2)
41. Jammu & Kashmir State - Report (9788121275194) Rs. 2060 (Vol. XXIV, Pt. 1)
42. Jammu & Kashmir State - Imperial & State Tables (9788121275170) Rs. 1940 (Vol. XXIV, Pt. 2 & 3)
43. Mysore - Report (9788121275156) Rs. 1950 (Vol. XXV, Pt. 1)
44. Mysore - Tables (9788121275132) Rs. 1380 (Vol. XXV, Pt. 2)
45. Ajmer-Merwara - Report And Tables (9788121275118) Rs. 780 (Vol. XXVI)
46. Rajputana Agency And Ajmer-Merwara - Report and Tables and Administrative (9788121275095) Rs. 2380 (Vol. XXVII, Pt. 1 & 2)
47. Travancore - Report (9788121276092) Rs. 2960 (Vol. XXVIII, Pt. 1)
48. Travancore - Tables & Administrative (9788121275996) Rs. 1360 (Vol. XXVIII, Pt. 2 & 4)
49. Jaipur State- Report (9788121275859) Rs. 1280 (Pt. 1)
50. Jaipur State- Tables (9788121275774) Rs. 2030 (Pt. 2)
51. Mayurbhanj state- Report (9788121275675) Rs. 3180 (Pt. 1)
52. Mayurbhanj state- Tables (9788121275552) Rs. 3070 (Pt. 2)

Owing to the antiquity and rarity of this book, certain pages are regrettably absent, and readability is compromised due to the blurring of the original text. If you possess any insights regarding the availability of these missing sections, kindly inform us. Your assistance is crucial in ensuring the completion of this significant work for the benefit of future generations.

CENSUS OF INDIA, 1931

BOOK - 17: VOLUME - IX

CITIES OF THE BOMBAY PRESIDENCY

PART I - REPORT
PART II - STATISTICAL TABLES

H.T. SORLEY

GYAN

Published by

Gyan Publishing House
5, Ansari Road
Daryaganj, New Delhi-110002
Phone: 011-47034999, 9811692060
E-mail: books@gyanbooks.com

Distribution Network
gyanbooks.com
India, USA, Canada, UK, Australia

ISBN: 978-81-212-7123-3 (Set) 28 Vols. In 52 Bindings

ISBN: 978-81-212-7575-0 (PB) Vol. IX, Pt. I, II

First Published, 1933

2nd Impression 2024

Printed at: Gyan Press, Delhi.

CENSUS OF INDIA 1931

CENSUS OF INDIA, 1931

VOLUME IX

THE
CITIES OF THE BOMBAY PRESIDENCY

IN TWO PARTS

PART I—REPORT
PART II—STATISTICAL TABLES

BY

H. T. SORLEY, M.A.

INDIAN CIVIL SERVICE

PROVINCIAL SUPERINTENDENT OF CENSUS OPERATIONS
BOMBAY PRESIDENCY

BOMBAY
PRINTED AT THE GOVERNMENT CENTRAL PRESS
1933

TABLE OF CONTENTS

Part I—Report

A. POPULATION STATISTICS.

CHAPTER I—INTRODUCTORY.

	Page
1. Scope of the Report	1
2. Statistics of the Cities	1
3. Nature of statistics	1
4. Cost of the Census in Cities	2
5. Comparison of Bombay City with other cities outside India	3
6. Comparison of Bombay City with cities in India	3
7. Number of Cities in different provinces in India	3
8. The Census City	3
9. Variation in the population of the Cities in the Presidency	4

CHAPTER II—BOMBAY CITY.

1. Definition of Bombay	6
2. Taking of the Census	6
3. Wards, sections and density of population	6
4. Area of the Island and area of the Sections	6
5. Changes in the population figures and accuracy of the Census enumeration ..	7
6. Vital statistics	8
7. Density	9
8. Religion	11
9. Birthplace	14
10. Europeans and Anglo-Indians	24
11. Age	25
12. Sex	31
13. Civil condition	34
14. Literacy	35
15. Language	37
16. Bilingualism	37
17. Caste	38
18. Infirmities	44
19. Occupation	45

CHAPTER III—KARACHI CITY.

1. Introductory	57
2. Enumeration and its results	57
3. Units for which the figures are presented	58
4. Birthplace	59
5. Religion	60
6. Age, sex and civil condition	61
7. Literacy	63
8. Occupation and Industries	64

CHAPTER IV—OTHER CITIES.

I—Poona.

1. Introductory	66
2. Birthplace	67
3. Age, sex and civil condition	68
Religion	69
Occupation	70

II—Sholapur.

		Page
1.	Introductory	70
2.	Birthplace	71
3.	Religion	71
4.	Age, sex and civil condition	72
5.	Literacy	72
6.	Occupation and industry	73

B. HOUSING STATISTICS.

CHAPTER V—HOUSING IN BOMBAY CITY.

1.	Introductory	75
2.	System of enumeration and compilation	75
3.	Instructions	75
4.	Difficulties encountered	75
5.	Statistical Tables of Housing	76
6.	Definition of building and standards of overcrowding	76
7.	Total number of buildings	77
8.	Buildings per acre	77
9.	Housing Table I	79
10.	Housing Table II	82
11.	Housing Table III	84
12.	Housing Table IV	85
13.	Housing Table V	85
14.	Housing Table VI-A	88
15.	Housing Table VI-B	91
16.	Housing Table VII	92

CHAPTER VI—HOUSING IN KARACHI.

1.	Introductory	93
2.	Definition of building	93
3.	Pressure of population on Housing	93
4.	The Housing Tables	93
5.	Housing Table I	94
6.	Housing Table II	95
7.	Housing Tables III, IV and V	95
8.	Housing Tables VI-A and VI-B	96
9.	Housing Table VII	97

CHAPTER VII—HOUSING IN SHOLAPUR.

1.	Introductory	98
2.	Housing Tables	98

CHAPTER VIII—HOUSING CONDITIONS AND ECONOMIC WELFARE IN CITIES.

1.	Special Economic enquiries held during the decade	100
2.	Correlation with the Census statistics	100
3.	The types of city population considered in special enquiries	100
4.	Chief heads of examination	101
5.	Housing available	101
6.	Family budgets, expenditure on food and rent	103
7.	Mortality rates amongst working and non-working mothers in Bombay.	105
8.	Chief defects in existing housing	106
9.	Overcrowding in cities	107

MAPS AND DIAGRAMS.

	Facing page
1. Proportional changes in the population of the seven cities of the Bombay Presidency 1881-1931	4
2. Map of Bombay Town and Island showing divisions used in the Census and the density of each section 1931	6
3. Actual number of births and deaths (in thousands) and excess of deaths over births in Bombay City	8
4. Variation in the population by main religions	10
Maps showing distribution of population by Religion—	
5. Hindu	12
6. *Muslim*	12
7. Christians	12
8. Zoroastrians	12
9. Distribution of every 1,000 persons by age-periods—Bombay City, Karachi City and the Presidency compared	26
10. Distribution of every 1,000 persons by age-groups—Bombay City and Presidency compared, 1921 and 1931	26
11. Diagram showing the distribution of 1,000 of each sex in each religion by civil condition	35
12. Diagram showing the distribution of the working population by occupation ..	53
13. Map of Karachi City showing the boundaries of each quarter	57
14. Map of Greater Poona showing units adopted in the Census Tables, 1931 ..	66
15. Buildings per acre by sections, Bombay City	76
16—Actual number of buildings with different numbers of floors, Bombay City since 1901	76
17. Percentage distribution of buildings according to number of floors, Bombay City since 1901	76
18. Percentage distribution of tenements in sections, Bombay City, 1931 ..	76
19. Percentage distribution of total population of each religion, occupying each class of tenements with one room, two rooms, etc.	93

APPENDICES.

	Pages
Appendix A—Report from the Executive Health Officer, Bombay Municipality, on Preliminary Census Operations	109–127
Appendix B—Report of the Chief Officer, Karachi Municipality, on Preliminary Census Operations	128–129
Appendix C—Part I—Children aged 4 to 15 by individual age-groups, Bombay City ..	131–135
Part II—Distribution of children in Bombay City aged 4 to 15 by main languages and wards	136
Appendix D—Distribution of children aged 6 to 11 by religion, Karachi City ..	137–152

Part II—Statistics

A—CITY TABLES.

Serial No.	Table.		Pages
		1. ALL CITIES.	
1.	II.	Variation in Population since 1881	154–155
		2. BOMBAY.	
2.	I.	Area, Houses and Population	156
3.	II.	Variation in Population since 1881	157–159
4.	III.	Religion	160–166
5.	IV.	Age, Sex and Civil Condition	167–169
6.	V.	Part I—Literacy by Religion and Age—Bombay City	170
7.	V.	Part II—Literacy by Religion and Age by Sections	171–177
8.	VI.	Part I—Birthplace	178–181
9.	VI.	Part II—Special Statistics regarding Birthplace combined with Age, Caste and Occupation	182–193
10.	VII.	Part I—Occupation or Means of Livelihood—Total earners and by Classes and Orders	194–199
11.	VII.	Part II—Occupation or Means of Livelihood by Religion	200–225
12.	VIII.	European and Allied Races and Anglo-Indians by Age	226–227
		3. KARACHI.	
13.	I.	Area, Houses and Population	228
14.	II.	(See the General City Table for All Cities).	
15.	III.	Religion	229–231
16.	IV.	Age, Sex and Civil Condition	232–238
17.	V.	Part I—Literacy by Religion and Age—Karachi City	239
18.	V.	Part II—Literacy by Religion and Age by Quarters	240–248
19.	VI.	Part I—Birthplace	249–250
20.	VI.	Part II—Selected Birthplaces combined with Age and Selected Occupations	251
21.	VII.	Part I—Occupation or Means of Livelihood	252–257
		4. POONA.	
22.	I.	Area, Houses and Population	258
23.	II.	(See General Table for All Cities).	
24.	III.	Religion	259–260
25.	IV.	Age, Sex and Civil Condition	261–265
26.	V.	Part I—Literacy by Religion and Age	266–269
27.	VI.	Part I—Birthplace	270–271
28.	VII.	Part I—Occupation or Means of Livelihood	272–277
		5. SHOLAPUR.	
29.	I.	Area, Houses and Population	278
30.	II.	(See General Table for All Cities).	
31.	III.	Religion	279
32.	IV.	Age, Sex and Civil Condition	280–281
33.	V.	Part I—Literacy by Religion and Age	282
34.	VI.	Part I—Birthplace	283
35.	VII.	Part I—Occupation or Means of Livelihood	284–288
		6. POONA AND SHOLAPUR.	
36.	VIII.	European and Allied Races and Anglo-Indians by Age	289

B—HOUSING TABLES.

SERIAL NO.	TABLE.		PAGES
		1. BOMBAY TOWN AND ISLAND.	
37.	I.	General Classification of Buildings by Uses	290–294
38.	II.	Classification of Buildings by the Number of Floors contained in each	295–299
39.	III.	Residential Buildings Classified according to the Number of Tenements contained in each	300–304
40.	IV.	Classification of Residential Buildings by the Number of Occupants	305–312
41.	V.	Distribution of Persons by Rooms in Residential Buildings ..	313–317
42.	VI-A.	Tenements by Rooms and Population	318–322
43.	VI-B.	Details of One-Roomed Tenements containing more than one family	323
44.	VII.	Tenements by Rooms and Population by Religion	324–333
		2. KARACHI.	
45.	I	General Classification of Buildings by Uses	335–337
46.	II	Classification of Buildings by the Number of Floors contained in each	338
47.	III.	Residential Buildings by the Number of Tenements ..	339
48.	IV.	Residential Buildings by the Number of Occupants	340
49.	V.	Distribution of Persons by Rooms in Residential Buildings ..	341
50.	VI-A.	Tenements by Rooms and Population	342–346
51.	VI-B.	Details of One-Roomed Tenements containing more than one family	347
52.	VII.	Tenements by Rooms and Population by Religion	348–355
		3. SHOLAPUR.	
53.	I.	General Classification of Buildings	356
54.	II.	Classification of Buildings by the Number of Floors ..	356
55.	III.	Distribution of Buildings by the Number of Rooms ..	357
56.	IV.	Classification of Buildings by the Number of Families ..	357

CHAPTER I—INTRODUCTORY.

CITIES OF THE BOMBAY PRESIDENCY—POPULATION STATISTICS.

1. Scope of the Report.

This volume deals with only four cities of the Bombay Presidency, namely Bombay, Karachi, Poona and Sholapur. In the corresponding volume of the 1921 Census there were three additional cities dealt with, namely Ahmedabad, Surat and Hubli. For various reasons, however, connected chiefly with the non-co-operation movement the statistics available in respect of these three cities are so unreliable and incomplete that the exclusion of them from the present Report was inevitable. The present volume is divided into two parts : Part I The Report and Part II The Tables. Part I is divided into a portion dealing with population statistics and a portion dealing with housing statistics.

2. Statistics of the Cities.

In Part II the various tables given are of two kinds. The first, which are called City Tables, present certain population statistics of a kind similar to those presented in the Imperial Tables given in Volume VIII, Part II, of the 1931 Census Report for the Bombay Presidency. But they refer to cities only. The second kind of tables are called Housing Tables. They present statistics of house accommodation, pressure of population on tenements and the like. These statistics which were first given for Bombay City in 1901 have been compiled on the present occasion for the cities of Bombay, Karachi and Sholapur.

3. Nature of the Statistics.

As it is desirable at this stage to indicate the nature of the statistical material available in regard to the population of the cities dealt with in the present report a list of the tables for the three cities is given here.

List showing City Tables prepared and printed in Part II of this Volume.

Table I—Area, Houses and Population ..	Bombay, Karachi, Poona and Sholapur.
Table II—Variation in population since 1881 ..	One for Bombay alone by sections and one for all the four cities combined.
Table III—Religion	All the four cities.
Table IV—Age, sex and civil condition ..	All the four cities.
Table V, Part I—Literacy by religion and age.	All the four cities.
Table V, Part II—Literacy by sections, religion and age.	Bombay and Karachi.
Table VI, Part I—Birthplace	All the four cities.
Table VI, Part II—Special statistics regarding birthplace combined with age, caste and occupation.	Bombay and Karachi.
Table VII, Part I—Occupation or means of livelihood.	All the four cities.
Table VII, Part II—Occupation or means of livelihood by religion.	Bombay.
Table VIII—Europeans and allied races and Anglo-Indians.	Separate for Bombay by wards, and combined for Poona and Sholapur.

The tables compiled in respect of housing will be described in their proper place in the portion of Part I of this volume dealing with housing (see page 75 below).

4. COST OF THE CENSUS IN CITIES.

The original system was that the cost of enumeration should be borne by the municipalities of the cities concerned and the cost of abstraction and compilation by Government. Following the practice however observed at last Census, Government bore half the enumeration costs incurred by the municipalities of Bombay and Karachi and recovered from these bodies half of the costs of abstraction and compilation. In the case of other municipalities there was no such arrangement and the costs of abstraction and compilation were recovered by Government from them on a basis of Rs. 100 per 10,000 of the population. Forms were supplied free and the costs of enumeration were borne by the municipalities. The following statement (No. 1) shows the costs incurred for Census Operations in the cities of Bombay and Karachi.

STATEMENT NO. 1.

City.	Cost of enumeration.		Cost of abstraction and compilation.		Total costs.	
	1921	1931	1921	1931	1921	1931
	Rs.	Rs.	Rs.	Rs.	Rs.	Rs.
Bombay	28,204	37,828	43,896	22,963	72,000	60,791
Karachi	39,000	19,691	10,020	4,515	49,020	24,206
Total ..	67,204	57,519	53,916	27,478	121,020	84,997

As explained above, these costs were shared, half and half, by Government and the municipalities.

As compared with 1921, the cost of enumeration in Bombay was 34 per cent. higher and the cost of abstraction and compilation was 47·7 per cent. lower. The increased cost of enumeration in Bombay was the result of the civil disobedience movement which caused a general apathy of the public towards the Census and necessitated the employment of a hired staff of enumerators and supervisors. The decreased cost of abstraction and compilation was due to economical administration. The abstraction office was moved from Bombay to Ahmednagar, a place of decidedly cheaper living, and the office was run with a smaller staff who were paid at lower rates of pay. The work was also completed within a shorter period than in 1921. As a result of these measures of economy the saving in cost amounts to about 50 per cent. of the costs incurred in 1921 for abstraction and compilation. As regards the Karachi City Census it was found possible to achieve it at half the cost of the 1921 Census. In 1921 the Karachi Municipality spent a considerable amount of money on house-numbering, by fixing metal sheet numbers to the houses. On the present occasion approval was not given to this practice. The municipality was advised to paint the numbers on the houses. This was done and the cost considerably reduced.

Despite the increased costs of enumeration in Bombay the work was found to be most unsatisfactory. The greatest difficulty was experienced by the Deputy Superintendent of Census in getting the work done at all. Some of the difficulties encountered are dealt with more fully in Chapter II of this volume.

5. COMPARISON OF BOMBAY CITY WITH OTHER CITIES OUTSIDE INDIA.

The population of Bombay is compared with that of the other great cities of the world in the statement (No. 2) given below.

STATEMENT NO. 2.

Population of Bombay City ..		1,161,383
Cities beyond India—		
Cities having population over 7 millions.	Greater London.	8,202,818
Cities having population over 6 millions.	New York ..	6,930,446
Cities having population over 3 millions.	Berlin ..	4,000,000
	Chicago ..	3,376,438
Cities having population over 2 millions.	Paris ..	2,871,039
	Osaka ..	2,590,000
	Tokio ..	2,300,000
	Buenos Aires.	2,100,000
Cities having population 1 million and over.	Philadelphia.	1,950,961
	Vienna ..	1,886,000
	Moscow ..	1,600,000
	Detroit ..	1,568,662
	Rio de Janeiro	1,500,000
Cities having population 1 million and over—*contd.*	Canton ..	1,370,000
	Nankin ..	1,300,000
	Peking ..	1,300,000
	Sydney ..	1,238,660
	Los Angeles	1,238,048
	Hamburg ..	1,130,000
	Warsaw ..	1,110,000
	Glasgow ..	1,088,000
	Cairo ..	1,060,000
	Melbourne ..	1,020,000
	Birmingham.	1,002,000
Cities having population 1 million.	Budapest ..	1,000,000
	Leningrad ..	1,000,000
	Montreal ..	1,000,000
	Rome ..	1,000,000
	Shanghai ..	1,000,000

6. COMPARISON OF BOMBAY CITY WITH CITIES IN INDIA.

In the statement (No. 3) given below the population of Bombay City is compared with the population of other cities in India.

STATEMENT NO. 3.

	Bombay	1,161,383	18.	Madura	182,018
1.	Greater Calcutta	1,485,582	19.	Srinagar	173,573
	Calcutta proper	1,196,734	20.	Patna	159,690
2.	Madras	647,230	21.	Mandalay	147,932
3.	Hyderabad (Deccan)	466,894	22.	Jaipur	144,179
4.	Delhi	447,442	23.	Bareilly	144,031
5.	Lahore	429,447	24.	Trichinopoly	142,843
6.	Rangoon	400,415	25.	Dacca	138,518
7.	Ahmedabad	313,789	26.	Meerut	136,709
8.	Bangalore	306,470	27.	Sholapur	135,574
9.	Lucknowr	274,659	28.	Indore	127,327
10.	Amritsai	264,840	29.	Jubbulpore	124,382
11.	Karach	263,565	30.	Peshawar	121,866
12.	Greater Poona	250,187	31.	Ajmer	119,524
13.	Cawnpore	243,755	32.	Multan	119,457
14.	Agra	229,764	33.	Rawalpindi	119,284
15.	Nagpur	215,165	34.	Baroda	112,862
16.	Benares	205,315	35.	Moradabad	110,562
17.	Allahabad	183,914	36.	Salem	102,179

7. NUMBER OF CITIES IN DIFFERENT PROVINCES IN INDIA.

The province in India with the largest number of cities having a population of one hundred thousand and over is the United Provinces, which has nine such cities. Bombay, the Punjab and Madras have four each, Bengal has three and Burma and the Central Provinces have two each. Bombay City is the fourth largest city in the British Empire, the second largest city in India, and, as far as the statistics of other countries can be relied upon, is the twenty-first city in size in the whole world.

8. THE CENSUS CITY.

Towns with a population of 100,000 and over and towns which, though falling below this standard of population, have been declared by the Local Government to be " Cities " are treated as cities for Census purposes. Ahmedabad, Surat and

Hubli are all cities for Census purposes but, as explained above, statistics in respect of them find no place in the present volume. The population enumerated in Surat at this Census proved to be under 100,000, namely 98,936, which would remove it from the " City " class in the absence of orders from the Local Government that it should be regarded as a Census " City ". Surat is not a growing town but there is little doubt that its present Census enumeration is an understatement. It seems likely that the population should be about the 1921 figure, as many persons must have escaped enumeration on account of the opposition to the Census caused by the non-co-operation movement in Gujarat. There is no reason to think that Surat has failed to maintain its population at a stationary level and the Census figures must be regarded as only partially accurate. Hubli has returned a population of 89,982. It was also affected by the non-co-operation movement against Census enumeration and probably the population enumerated is understated. It does however show a substantial increase in population over 1921 when it was first included in the category of Census " Cities ".

9. Variation in the Population of Cities in the Presidency.

The statement (No. 4) given below shows the population of places classed at one time or another as " Cities " for the last four Censuses.

STATEMENT No. 4.

City	1901	1911	1921	1931
Bombay	776,006	979,445	1,175,914	1,161,383
Ahmedabad	199,609	232,777	274,007	313,789
Surat	119,306	114,868	117,434	98,936
Greater Poona	175,463	188,701	214,796	250,187
Sholapur	75,288	61,345	119,581	135,574
Karachi	116,663	151,903	216,883	263,565
Hyderabad	64,790	69,140	73,951	96,021
Hubli	60,214	61,440	69,206	89,982
Belgaum	26,237	31,451	38,306	41,204
Broach	42,896	43,403	42,648	34,276
Nasik	21,490	33,463	42,756	48,703
Sukkur	31,316	35,294	42,759	69,277

In 1901 all the above were treated as " Cities ". In 1911 only Bombay, Ahmedabad, Karachi, Surat, Poona and Sholapur were treated as " Cities ". In 1921 Hubli was added to the 1921 list. In 1931 these seven towns remain as " Cities " but the population statistics and the report are confined to Bombay, Karachi, Poona and Sholapur only. The population of cities and of towns once classified as " Cities " at one time or another has been given in the statement above. The population of towns with a population of over 50,000 is set out here for comparison :—

Kolhapur	69,860
Shikarpur	62,505

The statement (No. 5) given below shows the comparative growth of the various cities of the Bombay Presidency since 1872.

STATEMENT No. 5.

City	1872	1881	1891	1901	1911	1921	1931
Bombay	644,405	773,196	821,764	776,006	979,445	1,175,914	1,161,383
Ahmedabad	128,505	137,041	159,366	199,609	232,777	274,007	313,789
Karachi	56,753	73,560	105,199	116,663	151,903	216,883	263,565
Poona	125,613	144,340	182,099	175,463	188,701	214,796	250,187
Surat	107,855	109,844	109,229	119,306	114,868	117,434	98,936
Sholapur	53,403	59,890	61,915	75,288	61,345	119,581	135,574
Hubli	37,961	36,677	52,595	60,214	61,440	69,206	89,982

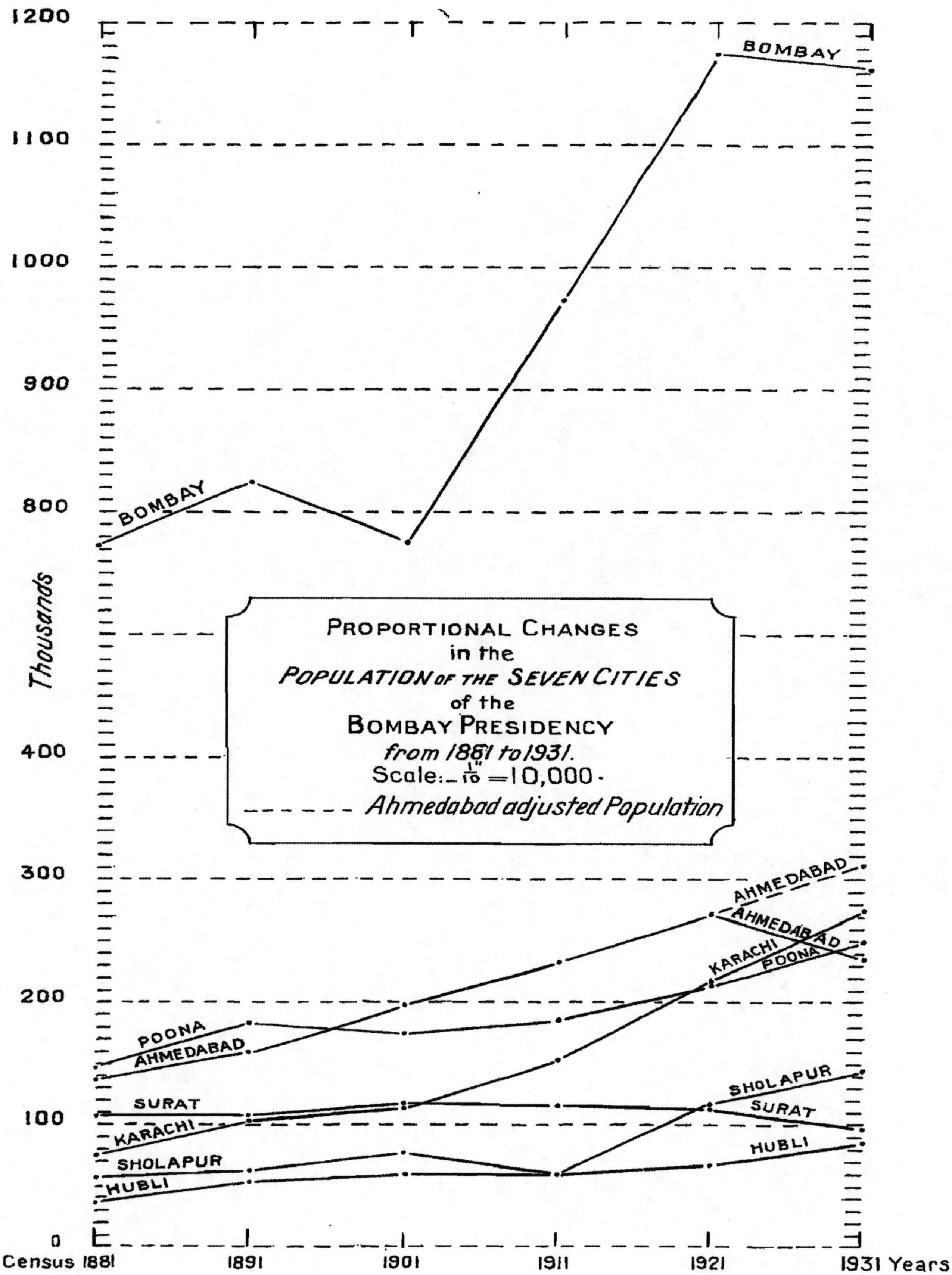

PROPORTIONAL CHANGES
in the
POPULATION OF THE SEVEN CITIES
of the
BOMBAY PRESIDENCY
from 1881 to 1931.
Scale:- 1/10" = 10,000.
Ahmedabad adjusted Population
Thousands
1200
1100
1000
900
800
400
300
200
100
0
Census 1881
1891
1901
1911
1921
1931 Years
BOMBAY
POONA
AHMEDABAD
SURAT
KARACHI
SHOLAPUR
HUBLI
G P Z.O. POONA, 1932

The enumerated population of Ahmedabad in 1931 was 234,265. This figure was known to be much too low as the city was badly affected by the non-co-operation movement which greatly hampered Census Operations. This matter has been discussed at some length in another volume of the Bombay Presidency Census Report, Vol. VIII, Part I. The Census authorities did not accept the enumerated population as correct and by estimate raised the population figure from 234,265 to 313,789 ; of which 310,000 was estimated as the population of the City and 3,789 as the population of Ahmedabad Cantonment. The Municipality of Ahmedabad have recently taken a Census of their own in July 1932 and have found the population to be 382,768. Though this cannot be recognised officially as the Census figure, there is no reason to doubt its substantial accuracy. Ahmedabad has certainly been flourishing in the last decade and it is certain that the general increase in population found throughout the Presidency has not omitted Ahmedabad.

The statement (No. 6) given below shows the variation in the population of the cities since 1872, of which the Census figures are taken as equivalent to 100 in each case.

STATEMENT No. 6.

Variation in population of Cities since 1872.

—	Proportionate population of each city at each succeeding Census taking population of 1872 as 100.						
	1872	1881	1891	1901	1911	1921	1931
Bombay ..	100	120	128	120	152	182	180
Ahmedabad ..	100	107	124	155	181	213	244
Karachi ..	100	130	185	206	268	382	464
Poona ..	100	115	145	140	150	171	199
Surat ..	100	102	101	112	107	109	92
Sholapur ..	100	112	116	141	115	224	254
Hubli ..	100	97	139	159	162	182	237

The great increase in the population of Karachi is worthy of note. The stationary nature of the population of Surat is also remarkable. Sholapur showed a great increase in the decade 1911 to 1921 but the increase has since slowed down. Hubli shows a large increase this Census.

CHAPTER II—BOMBAY CITY.

1. Definition of Bombay.

Bombay City as a Census unit includes the main Island (town) with the area reclaimed from the sea within the last decade, 1921 to 1931, and four islands in the Harbour, namely Cross Island, Middle Ground, Oyster Rock and Butcher Island. This means that the definition of Bombay remains the same as in the Census of 1921. In the 1921 Cities Report there is a very long and detailed discussion of the area of the Island and the areas of sections. The conclusions at which the Superintendent of Census Operations (Mr. Sedgwick) arrived are stated on page 8 of the Cities Report for 1921 and have been accepted here. There is no need for going into difficult questions of disputed areas in this Report. The definition of the Bombay Census area is now sufficiently clearly established.

2. Taking of the Census.

The Census of Bombay City was taken by the Executive Health Officer of the Bombay Municipality under the general supervision of the Provincial Superintendent of Census Operations, Bombay Presidency. The manner in which the Census was taken in 1931 has been fully described in the excellent report of the Executive Health Officer, Dr. J. S. Nerurkar. That report has been printed as Appendix A to the present volume. Particular attention should be directed to the description of the difficulties encountered, especially in consequence of the civil disobedience movement.

3. Wards, Sections and Density of Population.

A map has been prepared of Bombay Town and Island showing the boundaries of the various wards and sections, and the density of population by sections. This map will be found opposite page 6.

4. Area of the Island and Areas of Sections.

The following statement (No. 1) shows the area in acres of each section at this Census and in 1921.

Statement No. 1.

Ward and Section.	*Area, 1921*	*Area, 1931*	Increase (+) Decrease (—)
A Ward	**1,443·81**	**1,768·49**	**+324·68**
Upper Colaba	162·64	409·51	+246·87
Lower Colaba	279·74	279·74	
Fort South	133·11	133·11	
Fort North	158·68	158·68	
Esplanade	709·64	787·45	+ 77·81
B Ward	**637·65**	**637·65**	
Chakla	47·02	47·02	
Mandvi	187·33	187·33	
Umerkhadi	100·64	100·64	
Dongri	302·66	302·66	
C Ward	**460·60**	**550·60**	**+ 90·00**
Market	85·21	85·21	
Dhobi Talao	118·27	208·27	+ 90·00
Fanaswadi	98·44	98·44	
Bhuleshwar	73·46	73·46	
Kumbharwada	44·08	44·08	
Khara Talao	41·14	41·14	

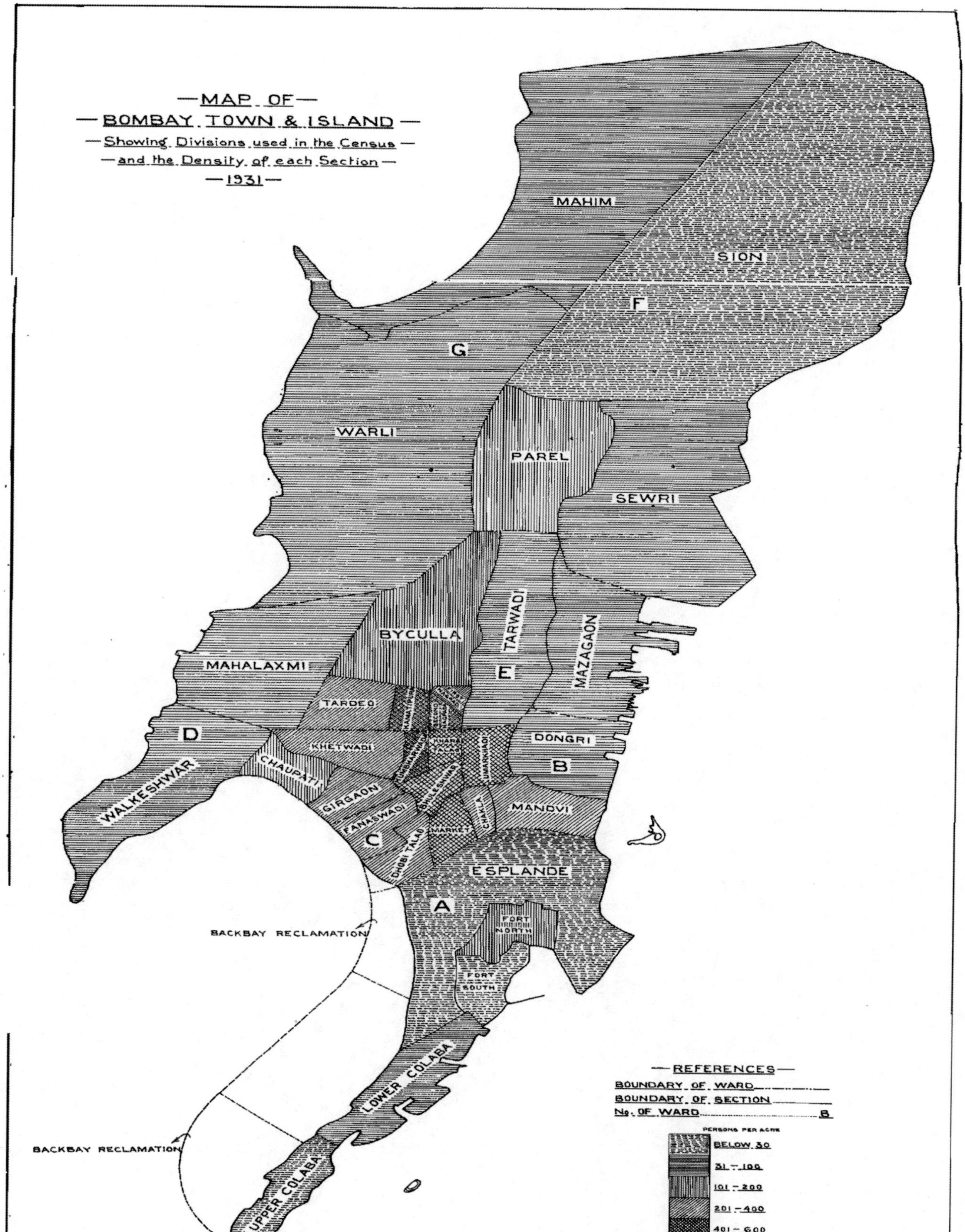
—MAP OF—
—BOMBAY TOWN & ISLAND—
—Showing Divisions used in the Census—
—and the Density of each Section—
—1931—
MAHIM
SION
F
G
WARLI
PAREL
SEWRI
BYCULLA
TARWADI
MAZAGAON
MAHALAXMI
E
TARDEO
D
KHETWADI
DONGRI
CHAUPATI
B
WALKESHWAR
GIRGAON
FANASWADI
MANDVI
MARKET
CHAKLA
C
DHOBI TALAO
ESPLANDE
A
FORT NORTH
BACKBAY RECLAMATION
FORT SOUTH
LOWER COLABA
BACKBAY RECLAMATION
UPPER COLABA
—REFERENCES—
BOUNDARY OF WARD
BOUNDARY OF SECTION
No. OF WARD B
PERSONS PER ACRE
BELOW 30
31 – 100
101 – 200
201 – 400
401 – 600
601 – 727

STATEMENT No. 1—*contd.*

Ward and Section.	Area, 1921	Area, 1931	Increase (+) Decrease (—)
D Ward	**1,624·53**	**1,624·53**	
Khetwadi	155·00	155·00	
Girgaum	112·40	112·40	
Chaupati	108·72	108·72	
Walkeshwar	589·90	589·90	
Mahalaxmi	658·51	658·51	
E Ward	**2,416·59**	**2,416·59**	
Tardeo	149·86	149·86	
Kamathipura	62·44	62·44	
First Nagpada	29·38	29·38	
Second Nagpada	33·05	33·05	
Byculla	567·57	567·57	
Tarwadi	498·81	498·81	
Mazagaon	1,075·48	1,075·48	
F Ward	**4,698·05**	**4,698·05**	
Parel	561·25	561·25	
Sowri	577·70	577·70	
Sion	3,559·10	3,559·10	
G Ward	**3,784·38**	**3,784·38**	
Mahim	1,511·00	1,511·00	
Worli	2,273·38	2,273·38	
Grand Total ..	15,065·61	15,480·29	+ 414·68

The total area of the Island at each of the previous Censuses and at this Census after rounding off the acres thus comes to :—

1872	11,930 acres.
1881	14,229 ,,
1891	14,080 ,,
1901	14,342 ,,
1906	14,386 ,,
1911	14,576 ,,
1921	15,066 ,,
1931	15,480 ,,

The total increase in area in Upper Colaba, Esplanade and in Dhobi Talao is due to the Back Bay reclamation.

5. CHANGES IN THE POPULATION FIGURES AND ACCURACY OF THE CENSUS ENUMERATION.

The population of Bombay in 1921 was 1,175,914. The population enumerated in the present Census is 1,161,383, a decrease of 14,531. If the figures of recorded births and deaths are taken for the intercensus period of 120 months the enumerated population in 1931 would show a deficiency of 108,130. The statement (No. 2) which follows will make the point clear.

STATEMENT No. 2.

Year.	Births and deaths in Bombay between 1921–1931.		
	Births.	Deaths.	Excess of deaths over births.
1st April 1921 to 1st January 1922	14,523	36,716	22,193
Do. 1922 do. 1923	20,452	37,297	16,845
Do. 1923 do. 1924	20,995	37,959	16,964
Do. 1924 do. 1925	21,838	38,774	16,936
Do. 1925 do. 1926	20,268	31,968	11,700
Do. 1926 do. 1927	21,068	31,991	10,923
Do. 1927 do. 1928	21,685	27,632	5,948
Do. 1928 do. 1929	24,017	27,312	3,295
Do. 1929 do. 1930	24,220	26,555	2,335
Do. 1930 do. 1931	25,329	27,552	2,223
1st January 1931 to 1st April 1931	6,447	5,215	—1,232
120 Months ..	220,842	328,972	108,130

Thus there is a difference in population of 108,130 (excess of deaths over births in ten years) *minus* 14,531 (difference in population enumerated in 1921 and 1931) to be accounted for. Were the figures of births and deaths accurate this would give the exact number of immigrants.

6. VITAL STATISTICS.

The figures of births and deaths cannot be regarded as accurate and the birth figures are undoubtedly less satisfactory than the death figures. If the population be reduced to thousands and the figure 93,599 reduced to 9·4 per annum, the following calculation can be made (statement No. 3).

STATEMENT No. 3.

Year.	Population in thousands.	Deduct for excess of deaths over births.	Results.	Add constant for immigrants (9·4).	Result, being population at the end of each year.
1	2	3	4	5	6
1921 ..	1,175·9	22·2	1,153·7	9·4	1,163·1
1922 ..	1,163·1	16·8	1,146·3	9·4	1,155·7
1923 ..	1,155·7	17·0	1,138·7	9·4	1,148·1
1924 ..	1,148·1	16·9	1,131·2	9·4	1,140·6
1925 ..	1,140·6	11·7	1,128·9	9·4	1,138·3
1926 ..	1,138·3	10·9	1,127·4	9·4	1,136·8
1927 ..	1,136·8	5·9	1,130·9	9·4	1,140·3
1928 ..	1,140·3	3·3	1,137·0	9·4	1,146·4
1929 ..	1,146·4	2·3	1,144·1	9·4	1,153·5
1930 ..	1,153·5	2·2	1,151·3	9·4	1,160·7
1931 ..	1,160·7	1·2	1,161·9	9·4	1,171·3

ACTUAL NUMBER OF BIRTHS & DEATHS (IN THOUSANDS) AND EXCESS OF DEATHS OVER BIRTHS IN BOMBAY CITY DURING THE DECADE 1921–30

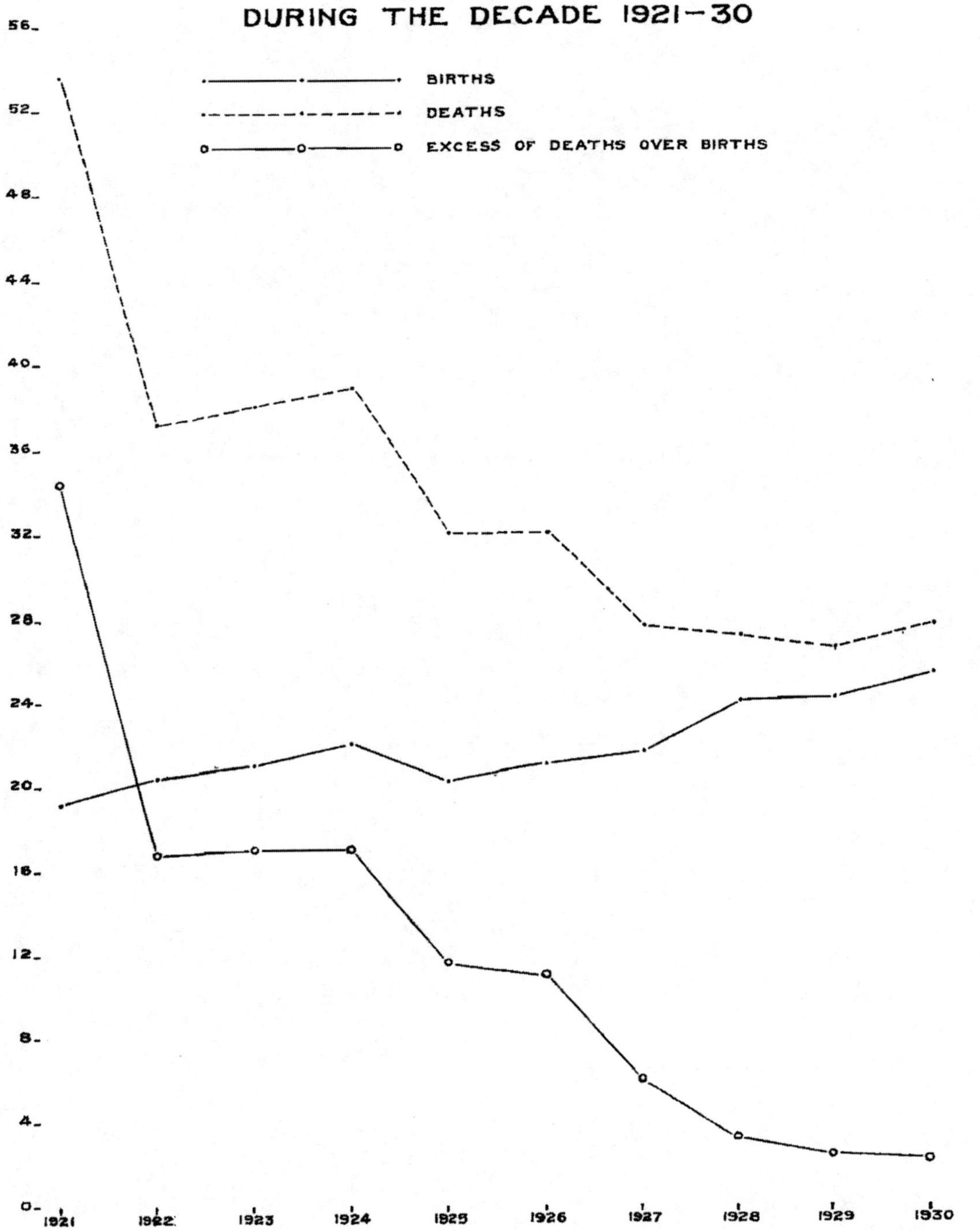

G.P.Z.O. Poona, 1932.

By this calculation the population in 1931 would be expected to be 1,171,300 whereas it was actually enumerated as 1,161,383, a deficiency of 9,917, which would show that the vital statistics are not accurate.

The remarks quoted below from the report of the Executive Health Officer, Bombay Municipality show that the expected population of Bombay City in 1931 was between one million three hundred thousand and one million five hundred thousand, but that several influences were at work which prevented these expectations from being fulfilled.

"Having regard to the extensions and developments made in the city and to the increased activities and developments in traffic since 1921, the population that was expected to be in the city was between 13 to 13½ lakhs. For statistical purposes the population for the successive years was obtained by adding 1/10 of the difference between the population figures of 1921 and 1911 to the estimated population of the previous year. Thus the estimated population would be for the Year 1922 :— 1,220,473
Year 1923 :— 1,220,120
Year 1924 :— 1,239,767
Year 1925 :— 1,259,414
Year 1926 :— 1,279,061
Year 1927 :— 1,298,708

There was, however, reason to believe that the increase which occurred in the years 1911 to 1920 did not continue at a uniform rate and hence the estimated population for 1927 was retained unaltered for the subsequent years. Thus the population that was expected in the City was somewhere about 1,300,000.

In 1931 the final count of the population of the Bombay City that was declared was 1,157,851. This was at a time when there was trade depression all over necessitating the exodus of the unemployed to their native villages. This exodus is estimated at nearly two lakhs. In respect of the mill industry alone, it was officially ascertained from the Millowners' Association that five mills were closed between April and August 1930 throwing thereby out of employment 12,669 persons who could not have been absorbed in any other industry and must have therefore left the city for their villages with their families which, if calculated at four members in a family would disclose the figure of 50,000 as the exodus for the mill industry alone. Although there are no data for estimating the exodus due to other industries, the figure of 150,000 would not be an exaggeration. Owing to the movement of non-cooperation, it can roughly be estimated that about 10,000 persons must have escaped enumeration altogether. This figure of exodus when added to the actual figure obtained after enumeration would make the population figure over 1,300,000 that was expected and under the normal conditions this expectation would perhaps have proved true."

The enumerated population of Bombay is probably not very far from the final truth. The population has certainly not been standing still during the past decade. But there have been severe epidemics, a heavy business slump and several years of bad trade, which have combined to depress the figures for the last years of the decade.

7. DENSITY.

Density of population in cities is an important criterion of congestion and overcrowding. The crude figures are, however, liable to misconstruction unless the topographical conditions of the various sections are adequately allowed for. What really matters of course is the density of population in those areas where population congregates, as in most sections there are usually some areas that are comparatively open. The density figures are therefore to be used with caution. Mr. Sedgwick drew attention to this point in his 1921 Cities report. He remarked "It is particularly important to remember that, in the peripheral sections, dock basins, salt pans, etc., are included in the total area. This means that the density per acre of occupiable dry land is really higher than the figure shown. This particularly applies to Esplanade, Mandvi and Dongri with their large dock basins and to Sion with its salt pans and lakes. Secondly, it must be remembered that the boundaries of Mahalaxmi, Byculla, Parel, Mahim and Worli were almost certainly different in 1881 from what they were in 1901. Thirdly, the uncertainty regarding areas of sections in 1901 and 1911 has to be remembered. And lastly it must be remembered that the 1901 densities were calculated on a population thinned out by plague emigration and by plague losses not yet refilled."

The density of Bombay Town and Island as a whole in 1931 was 75 persons per acre. The density of population in 1921 on the then reported area was 78 ; in 1911 the figure was 64. The particular circumstances prevailing at the time of the Census in 1931 must be taken into account. Bad trade conditions have undoubtedly had some effect in lowering population in particular areas. If this be remembered it will be safe to conclude that there has been no great improvement in a lowering of the density in overcrowded localities.

The statement (No. 4) given below shows the density of population per acre for six Censuses. A map showing density will be found opposite page 6.

STATEMENT No. 4

Section.	Number of persons per acre.					
	1881	1891	1901	1911	1921	1931
1	2	3	4	5	6	7
Upper Colaba	20	30	27	11	23	1·1
Lower Colaba	56	52	49	70	72	71·3
Fort South	27	30	25	26	31	26
Fort North	258	247	171	158	195	163
Esplanade	21	16	16	26	22	18
Chakla	726	624	473	470	489	384
Mandvi	261	227	191	202	206	223
Umerkhadi	526	498	460	434	469	413
Dongri	118	106	90	95	60	43
Market	558	502	319	339	412	454
Dhobi Talao	402	401	296	338	357	213
Fanaswadi	189	192	131	219	306	326
Bhuleshwar	508	506	390	481	471	478
Kumbharwada	778	699	598	602	737	727
Khara Talao	700	649	556	552	582	565
Khetwadi	175	169	159	188	256	254
Girgaum	206	217	119	247	320	345
Chaupati	100	103	60	102	131	149
Walkeshwar	21	24	19	20	31	39
Mahalaxmi	17	46	28	41	58	56
Tardeo	90	83	92	121	213	212
Kamathipura	438	442	404	556	714	602
First Nagpada	323	376	357	218	260	246
Second Nagpada	482	552	547	638	699	636
Byculla	29	51	113	147	161	162
Tarwadi	31	44	38	59	82	81
Mazagaon	49	59	45	41	34	40
Parel	17	26	60	82	107	113
Sewri	13	14	21	38	50	46
Sion	4	5	6	7	16	19
Mahim	19	10	21	24	32	33
Worli	10	17	25	49	53	50

The density of population has changed altogether in some sections, chiefly Upper Colaba, Esplanade, Dhobi Talao and Fanaswadi. In the first three of these the Back Bay reclamation, which has added some uninhabited land, is the chief cause

VARIATION IN THE POPULATION BY MAIN RELIGIONS IN THE BOMBAY CITY TAKING THE FIGURE FOR 1881 FOR EACH RELIGION AS 100

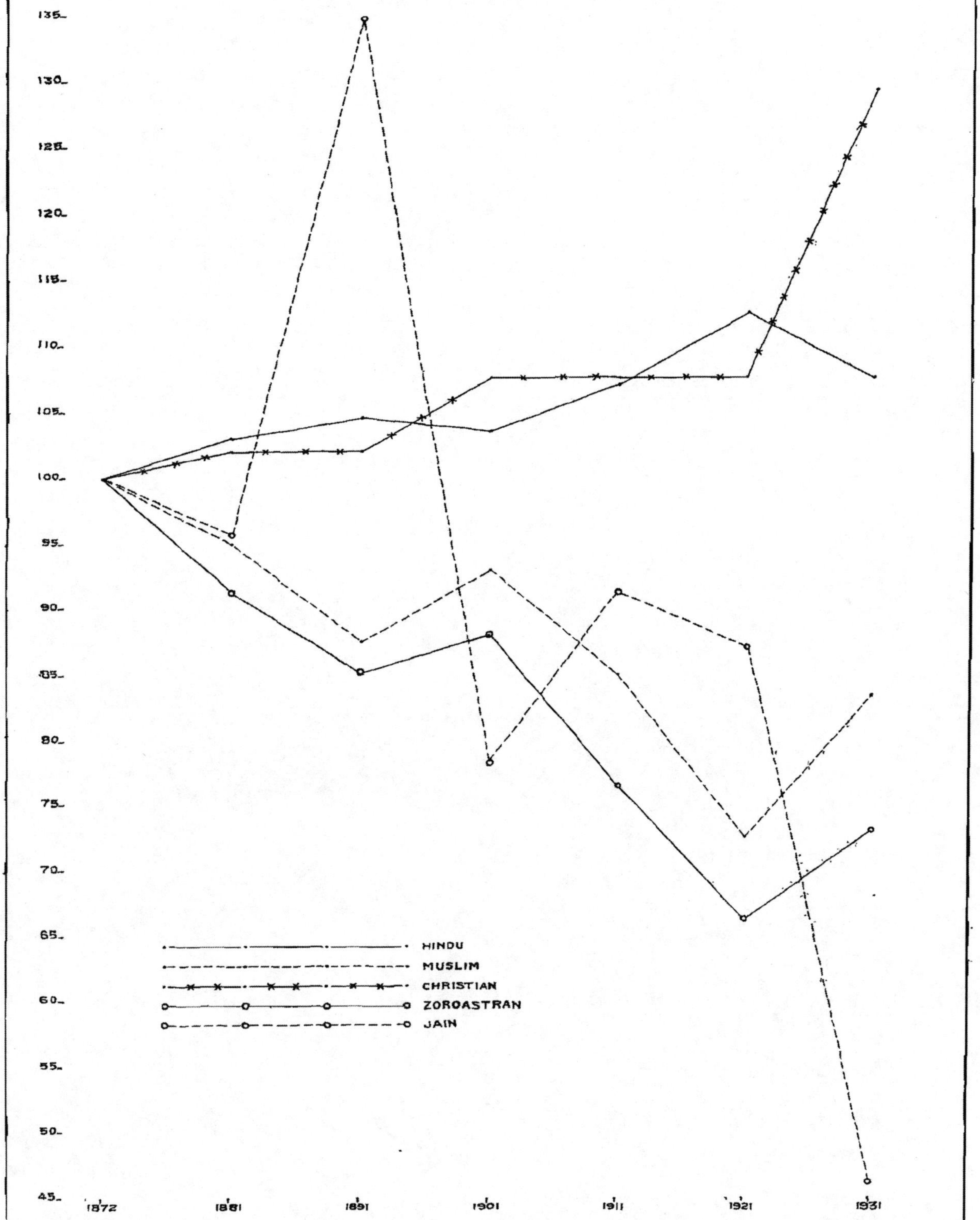

G.P.Z.O. POONA, 1932.

of the fall in density. But this does not mean that the actual density per occupied acre has fallen. In Fanaswadi an increase in area has proceeded simultaneously with an increase in density of population. This would seem to show that in Fanaswadi congestion is becoming worse. In Kamathipura the density has fallen considerably. This area is inhabited by labourers. Many of these have left Bombay owing to the trade slump and the density has fallen from 714 to 602. Changes in the density in other sections are not noteworthy. It was pointed out in 1921 that the central portions of the city declined in density after 1881 and had begun to fill up again. " Undeniably ", it was remarked, " the central portions of the city are far more densely crowded than is compatible with sanitation and if it is true, as seems to be the case, that they are now increasing in density after temporarily thinning out, the fact is very deplorable ". This may be admitted. There is no sign this Census of any improvement in this respect though the densities of some of the most thickly populated parts of the city have fallen a little. The departure of labourers and of traders from Cutch and Kathiawar, and non-cooperation may however account for this slight decrease.

8. RELIGION.

The actual numerical changes in the different religions since 1921 are shown in the table which appears later in this section. All religions except Hindu and Jain have increased their figures at this Census. In respect of Jains it is always doubtful whether the numbers recorded are really accurate as many return themselves as Hindus. Sometimes there is no uniformity about this practice so that the comparative figures of Jains and Hindus are always liable to a certain amount of disturbance by influences which cannot be gauged statistically. The figures recorded must therefore be taken for what they are worth and this phenomenon borne in mind. As regards Hindus, the disturbance is of course not nearly so great as in the case of the Jains, who are a very much smaller community. The present Census shows that the number of Jains enumerated has decreased by 11,460 and the number of Hindus by 47,829. The decrease may, however, be more apparent than real as these sections of the Bombay population were affected considerably by the non-cooperation movement. In the case of the Jains in particular the numerical effect of this was probably quite important. The disturbance caused by non-cooperation can be shown indirectly from several facts. If the figures of immigration from important areas which usually supply numbers of Hindu and Jain immigrants into Bombay be examined it will be hard to resist the conclusion that they are unduly low. For instance the number of immigrants recorded from Ahmednagar district this Census is only 17,467 against 48,501 in 1921. Satara district provides only 53,211 as against 65,953, in 1921 ; Kolaba district 32,666 as against 43,160 ; Cutch 20,029 as against 37,480 and Kathiawar 53,288 as against 72,435. As has been pointed out already, bad trade and the business slump have almost certainly led to some decrease in the number of these immigrants but it is quite impossible that the decrease can be as large as the Census enumeration shows. The main cause must be the civil disobedience movement which led many Hindus and Jains to evade enumeration or to make false returns.

The statement (No. 5) now given shows the actual increase or decrease in each religion for 1931 as compared with 1921.

STATEMENT No. 5.

Religion.	Persons.	Males.	Females.
Hindu	— 47,829	— 41,730	— 6,099
Muslim	+ 24,561	+ 16,607	+ 7,994
Jain	— 11,460	— 8,589	— 2,871
Zoroastrian	+ 5,531	+ 2,647	+ 2,884
Christian	+ 12,559	+ 5,824	+ 6,735
Jew	+ 1,073	+ 543	+ 530
Total population ..	— 14,531	— 23,951	+ 9,420

The increase in the Muslim and the Christian population is worthy of note. The loss in the numbers of Hindus and Jains affects mostly the male population which contributes more than the female to an area of immigration like Bombay with its accessive characteristics.

In the Table (No. 6) which follows the percentage distribution of the population by religion is shown for six Censuses. The percentage of Hindus increased steadily from 1881 to 1921 but this Census it has fallen from 71·2 to 68. The percentage of Muslims, which showed a decline from 1901 to 1921, has risen this Census from 15·7 to 18 per cent. The percentage of Christians in the Bombay population has been remarkably constant on the whole but this Census it shows a rise from 5·8 to 7. The percentage of Zoroastrians shows little variation from the 1911 figure. It has not recovered the percentages which were prevalent prior to 1911. The percentage of Jews shows little variation over forty years. The Jain percentage figures are subject to capricious fluctuations for the reasons already explained. The majority of the population of Bombay City consists of Hindus and Muslims. These together form more than three quarters of the total. Up to the present Census Hindus were gaining and Muslims losing. But this time the order has been reversed. Four maps are attached which show the distribution of the Hindu, Muslim, Christian and Zoroastrian communities.

STATEMENT NO. 6.

Religion.	1881	1891	1901	1911	1921	1931
Hindu ..	65·2	66·1	65·5	67·8	71·2	68·0
Muslim ..	20·5	18·9	20·1	18·3	15·7	18·0
Jain ..	2·2	3·1	1·8	2·1	2·0	1·0
Zoroastrian ..	6·2	5·8	6·0	5·2	4·5	5·0
Christian ..	5·5	5·5	5·8	5·8	5·8	7·0
Jew ..	0·4	0·6	0·8	0·7	0·6	0·8
Others ..	....	....	....	0·1	0·2	0·2

The statement (No. 7) which follows shows the regional distribution of religions.

STATEMENT NO. 7.

No.	Sections	*Percentage Table of the population of sections of Bombay by religion, 1931.*						
		Hindu.	Muslim.	Jain.	Zoroastrian.	Christian.	Jew.	Others.
1	2	3	4	5	6	7	8	9
	City as a whole ..	68	18	1·1	5	6·9	0·7	0·2
1	Upper Colaba ..	67	10·8	..	5·2	16·5	0·5	..
2	Lower Colaba ..	55·6	8·7	0·4	6·0	27·3	1·8	0·2
3	Fort South ..	48·4	12·8	..	1·5	34·0	3·1	0·2
4	Fort North ..	54·2	17·3	0·4	23·0	10·7	0·2	0·2
5	Esplanade ..	54·9	23·3	0·1	4·2	16·0	0·6	0·9
6	Chakla ..	32·0	66·6	0·9	0·2	0·2	..	0·1
7	Mandvi ..	78·3	20·1	0.6	0·0	0·4	0·4	0·2
8	Umarkhadi ..	25·0	69·2	1·1	0·0	1·6	3·1	0·0
9	Dongri ..	68·5	22·8	4·2	0·1	1·5	2·8	0·1
10	Market ..	78·9	9·3	7·8	0·2	3·8	0·0	0·0
11	Dhobi Talao ..	58·7	2·7	0·6	16·0	22·0	0·0	0·0
12	Fanaswadi ..	87·6	1·3	0·2	5·1	5·8	..	0·0
13	Bhuleshwar ..	60·7	34·2	4·5	0·6	0·0	..	0·0

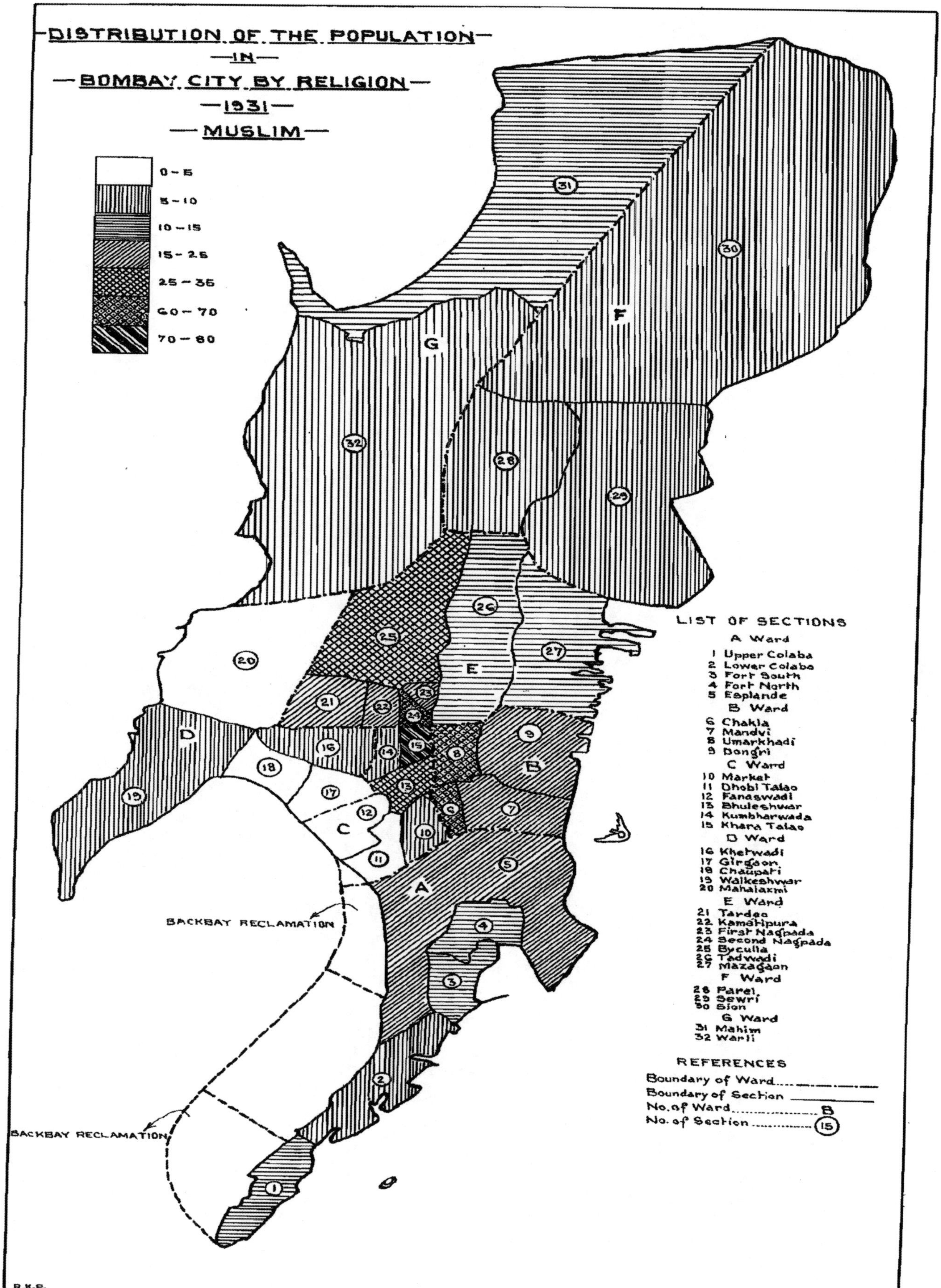

G.P.Z.Q. POONA, 1936.

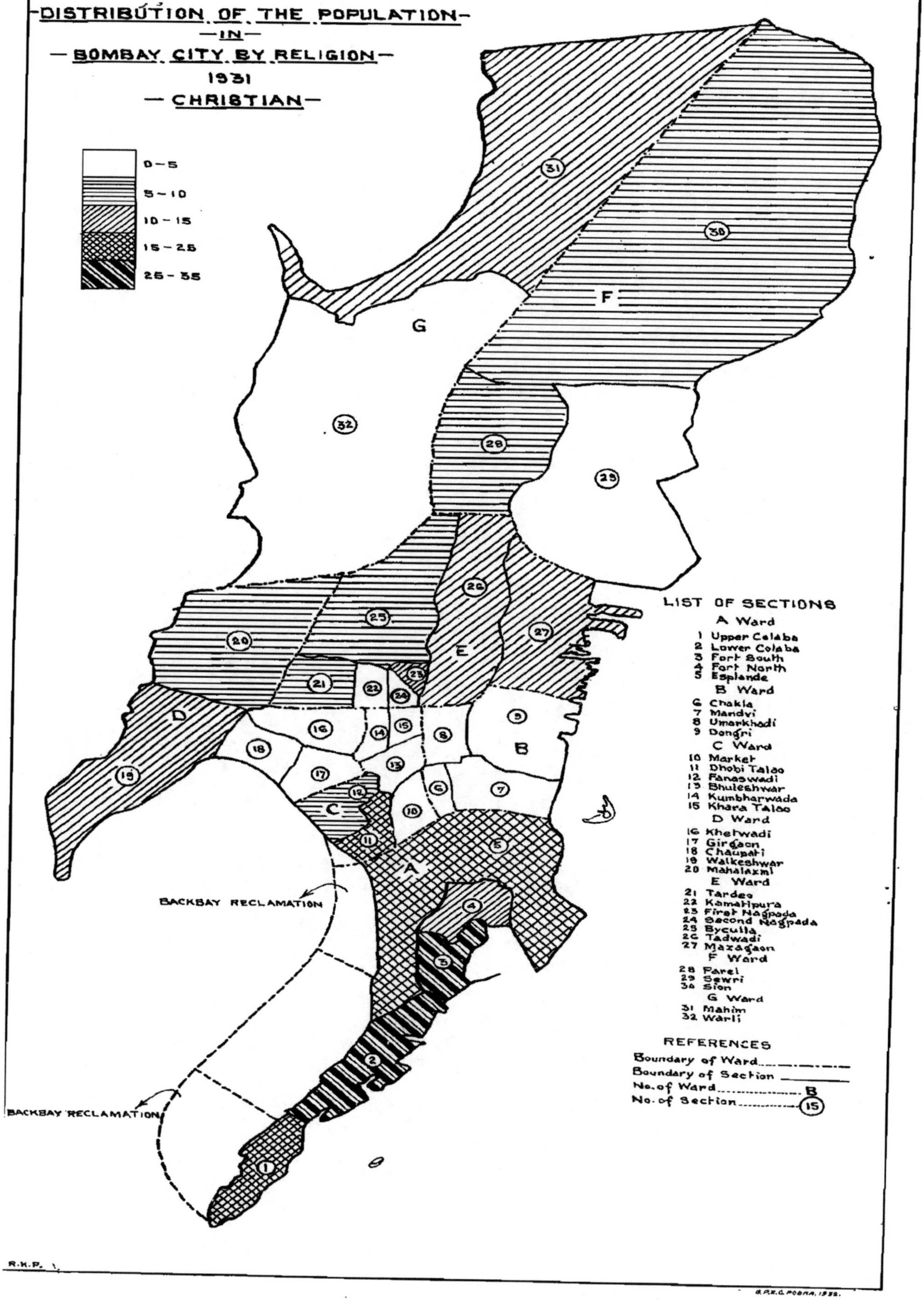
DISTRIBUTION OF THE POPULATION
IN
BOMBAY CITY BY RELIGION
1931
CHRISTIAN
0–5
5–10
10–15
15–25
25–35
G
F
E
D
C
B
A
BACKBAY RECLAMATION
BACKBAY RECLAMATION
LIST OF SECTIONS
A Ward
1 Upper Colaba
2 Lower Colaba
3 Fort South
4 Fort North
5 Esplande
B Ward
6 Chakla
7 Mandvi
8 Umarkhadi
9 Dongri
C Ward
10 Market
11 Dhobi Talao
12 Fanaswadi
13 Bhuleshwar
14 Kumbharwada
15 Khara Talao
D Ward
16 Khetwadi
17 Girgaon
18 Chaupati
19 Walkeshwar
20 Mahalaxmi
E Ward
21 Tardeo
22 Kamathipura
23 First Nagpada
24 Second Nagpada
25 Byculla
26 Tadwadi
27 Mazagaon
F Ward
28 Parel
29 Sewri
30 Sion
G Ward
31 Mahim
32 Warli
REFERENCES
Boundary of Ward
Boundary of Section
No. of Ward B
No. of Section 15
R.K.P. 1

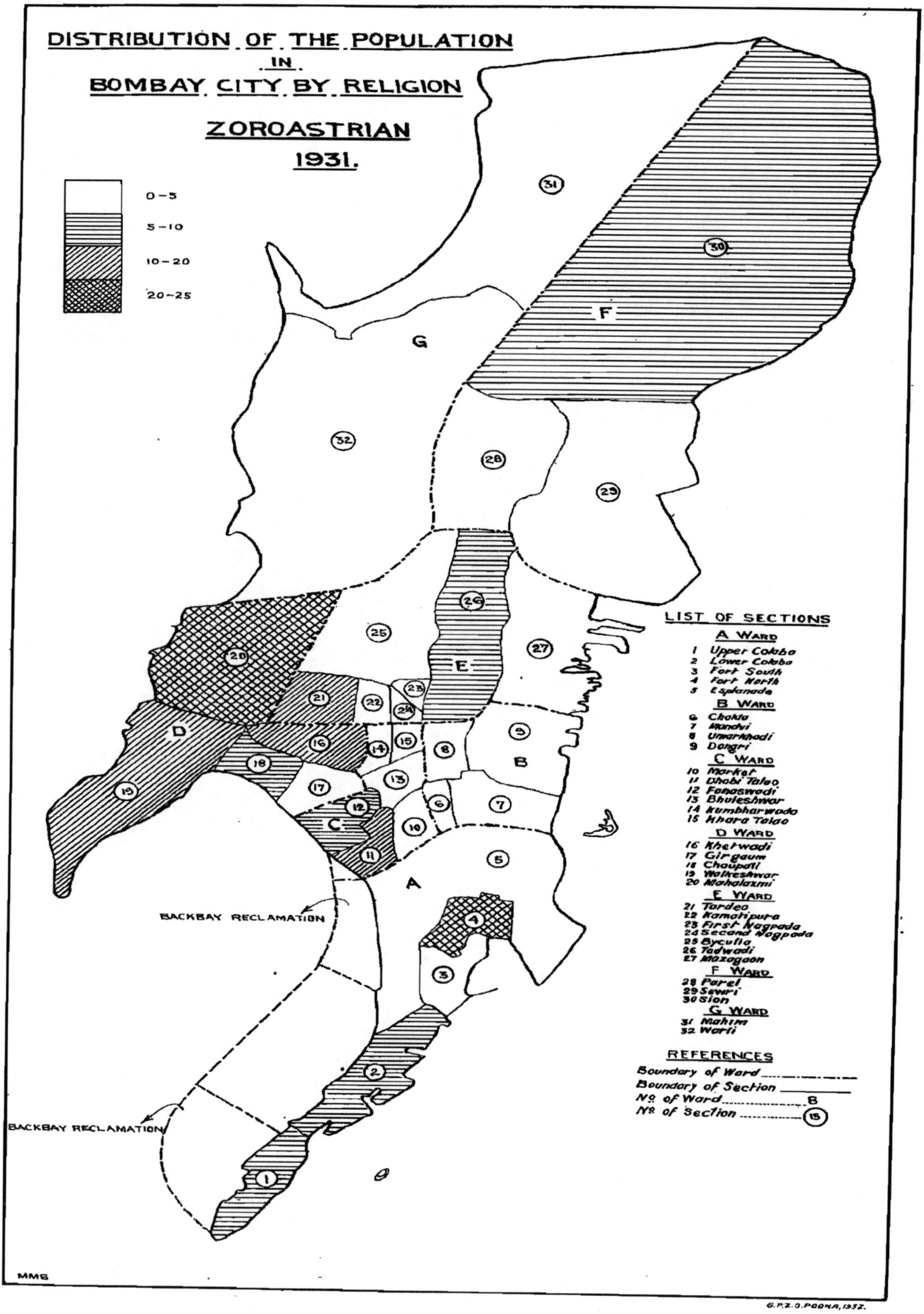

G.P.Z.O.POONA, 1932.

STATEMENT No. 7—*contd.*

No.	Sections.	Percentage Table of the population of Sections of Bombay by religion 1931.						
		Hindus.	Muslims.	Jain.	Zoroastrians.	Christians.	Jews.	Others.
1	2	3	4	5	6	7	8	9
14	Kumbharwada ..	92·8	5·9	1·0	0·1	0·2	0·0	0·0
15	Khara Talao ..	22·8	76·7	0·4	0·0	0·1	..	0·0
16	Khetwadi ..	69·0	9·1	0·5	18·7	2·7	0·0	0·0
17	Girgaum ..	94·4	0·9	0·9	1·0	2·8	0·0	0·0
18	Chaupati ..	84·2	3·0	1·2	6·4	4·9	0·2	0·1
19	Walkeshwar ..	60·6	9·4	1·6	14·5	13·1	0·2	0·6
20	Mahalaxmi ..	64·1	4·9	0·4	22·4	7·9	0·0	0·3
21	Tardeo ..	56·0	19·1	0·9	18·0	5·3	0·2	0·5
22	Kamathipura ..	71·8	24·0	1·1	0·1	1·0	0·6	1·4
23	First Nagpada ..	42·5	24·7	0·9	0·1	11·8	20·0	0·0
24	Second Nagpada ..	25·8	7·3	0·5	0·2	1·0	3·0	0·0
25	Byculla ..	57·4	29·0	1·0	1·0	9·0	2·0	0·2
26	Tarwadi ..	67·8	11·7	0·3	6·4	12·2	1·5	0·1
27	Mazagaon ..	67·8	14·7	0·2	2·6	14·1	0·4	0·2
28	Parel ..	82·8	5·8	0·7	4·4	5·7	0·5	0·1
29	Sewri ..	86·2	9·9	0·7	0·2	2·9	0·0	0·1
30	Sion ..	75·2	8·5	0·7	7·7	7·3	0·3	0·3
31	Mahim ..	74·2	13·6	0·7	0·8	10·5	0·1	0·1
32	Worli ..	87·9	6·3	0·6	1·1	3·7	0·4	0·0
33	Harbour etc. ..	51·2	27·9	0·5	1·1	16·8	0·2	2·3

It will be seen that the areas where Hindus are most predominant are Mandvi (78·3), Market (78·9), Fanaswadi (87·6), Kumbharwada (92·8), Girgaum (94·4), Chaupati (84·2), Parel (82·8), Sewri (86·2) and Worli (87·9). The areas in which Muslims are most predominant are Chakla (66·6), Umarkhadi (69·2) and Khara Talao (76·7). In no other section does the proportion of Muslims exceed 34·2 (in Bhuleshwar). Zoroastrians are most numerous proportionately in Fort North (23 per cent.), Dhobi Talao (10), Khetwadi (18·7), Mahalakshmi (22·4), Tardeo (18) and Walkeshwar (14·5). In no other section do they form more than 7·7 per cent. of the total population. The distribution of Christians is more diffuse than that of Zoroastrians. Christians are most numerous proportionately in Lower Colaba (27·3), Fort South (34), Dhobi Talao (22), Tarwadi (12·2), Mazagaon (14·1) and Mahim (10·5).

The following statement (No. 8) for 1921 and 1931 shows the comparative proportions of Muslims and Hindus in the sections in which these are most predominant respectively.

STATEMENT No. 8.

Section.	Proportion of Muslims per 100 Hindus.		Section.	Proportion of Muslims per 100 Hindus.	
	1931	*1921*		*1931*	*1921*
Khara Talao	336	221	Dongri	33	11
Umarkhadi	277	187	Fort South	26	11
Chakla	208	150	Mandvi	26	33
First Nagapada.. ..	58	47	Mazagaon	22	16
Bhuleshwar	56	42	Fort North	21	11
Byculla	51	31	Mahim	18	15
Esplanade	47	18	Tarwadi	17	14
Kamathipura	43	22	Upper Colaba	18	15
Tardeo	34	28			

The sex composition by religion is a matter of some interest since the sex proportions throw light upon the characteristics of the city population in respect of immigration and permanent settlement. For the City as a whole the proportion of females to males is 554 to 1,000. The following statement (No. 9) shows the proportion of females to males in each religion for six Censuses.

STATEMENT NO. 9.

Religion.	Number of females per 1,000 males in each religion 1881-1931					
	1881	1891	1901	1911	1921	1931
Hindu	664	571	610	521	531	562
Muslim	679	633	617	507	452	455
Christian	521	493	521	486	480	569
Zoroastrian	831	910	904	903	864	888
Jain	341	311	381	329	357	381
Jew	..	..	..	883	870	873

The 1931 returns show that the proportion of females to males has risen over the 1921 returns in every case. The reason for this is not very clear but the general increase of population and the absence of anything like the influenza epidemic in the decade may have something to do with it. Further if the number of male labourers leaving Bombay on account of the trade slump has been considerable it would tend to bring the total figures of the proportion of females to males a little nearer the figures found amongst the resident population, where the female proportion would be expected to be higher. The Jains show by far the lowest proportion of females to males. This is because they are largely a merchant and trading community with family ties elsewhere. The Zoroastrians show the highest proportion of females to males. They are the converse case to the Jains. They are permanently resident in Bombay which is in many ways their home town.

9. BIRTHPLACE.

Mr. Sedgwick remarked in 1921 "The fact that the Bombay population is largely immigrant, using that term of course in its Census sense, is well known. The percentage of the total population which has actually been born in Bombay has steadily declined at each Census, as is shown in the margin. We have now reached a condition of things possibly unexampled. Where the matter will end it is difficult to see." (Census of India, Vol. IX, page 16).

Census.	Per cent.
1872	31·1
1881	27·8
1891	25·0
1901	23·4
1911	19·6
1921	16·0
1931	24·6

Mr. Sedgwick forecasted that the proportion of the Bombay-born population in the Bombay City population was likely still further to decline. The Census figures of 1931 do not on the face of them bear out this forecast. It is perhaps possible, had the enumeration been accurate, that the forecast would have been fulfilled. But the figures as actually recorded do not bear this out. The percentage of the Bombay-born population steadily declined till 1921 from 31·1 in 1872 to 23·4 in 1901 to 16 in 1921. But this Census the figures show a rise to 24·6, which accords very closely with the figures of 1891. The enumeration at the present Census was not very satisfactory. In cases where birthplace was not filled in, that is, where the column in the enumeration book was returned blank, "Bombay" was shown as the birthplace, according to instructions which were issued. Very possibly this has affected considerably the final figures of the proportion of the Bombay-born population and also of the number of immigrants from various areas. The proportion of the Bombay-born population to the total city population per mille at each Census since 1872 is shown in the statement (No. 10) below :—

STATEMENT NO. 10.

Census.	Home-born per mille of total population.
1872	311
1881	278
1891	250
1901	234
1911	196
1921	160
1931	246

The following statement (No. 11) shows the distribution of every 1,000 of the population of Bombay by birth-place in 1921 and 1931.

STATEMENT No. 11.

Birth-place.	1931	1921
Bombay City	246	160
Ratnagiri	204	200
Kolaba	28	37
Thana and Bombay Suburban district	11	13
Central Division	142	206
Surat	50	34
Ahmedabad	18	15
Other districts of Gujarat	8	6
Belgaum, Bijapur, Dharwar and Kanara	9	9
Sind	3	6
Cutch	17	32
Kolhapur, S. M. C. States and Sawantwadi	14	13
Madras Presidency	18	13
Punjab, Delhi and North-West Frontier Province	13	11
United Provinces	72	60
Central Provinces and Berar	4	4
Bengal, Bihar, Orissa and Assam	3	4
Rajputana, Ajmer-Merwara	10	18
Hyderabad State	14	17
Baroda State	5	7
French and Portuguese possessions in India	33	29
Other Asiatic countries	7	8
Europe	6	9
Elsewhere (including Bombay unspecified)	19	27

The distribution of persons born in Europe is shown in the statement (No. 12) below. The distribution will be seen to be very irregular.

STATEMENT No. 12.

Ward.	Number of persons.	Ward.	Number of persons.
A	1,505	E	577
B	28	F	201
C	1,098	G	146
D	587	Harbour, etc.	2,523

Of these the following is the distribution of persons born in Great Britain and Ireland.

Ward.	Number of persons.	Ward.	Number of persons.
A	1,327	E	285
B	22	F	192
C	1,009	G	140
D	61	Harbour, etc.	2,252

The distribution of persons born in French and Portuguese possessions is shown below (statement No. 13). This population is almost entirely composed of persons from the Portuguese possessions on the West Coast of India, particularly Goa.

STATEMENT No. 13.

Ward.	Number of persons.	Ward.	Number of persons.
A	2,010	E	10,089
B	442	F	2,196
C	11,005	G	4,001
D	7,080	Harbour, etc.	1,279

In the following statement (No. 14) the actual number of immigrants into Bombay City from the more important districts of origin is shown for six Censuses.

STATEMENT No. 14.

Birth-place	1881	1891	1901	1911	1921	1931
1	2	3	4	5	6	7
Ahmedabad	7,004	9,439	9,594	16,298	17,557	20,470
Broach	1,763	1,537	1,226	1,660	2,272	4,497
Kaira	133	1,651	2,132	2,976	3,879	4,017
Surat	35,803	29,940	25,097	35,072	39,682	58,275
Thana including (Bombay Suburban district) ..	17,051	15,128	10,557	15,705	14,797	12,355
Kolaba	11,506	28,851	21,100	37,119	43,180	32,666
Ratnagiri	126,190	162,586	145,835	216,060	235,566	237,256
Nasik	7,142	6,352	7,939	9,863	24,451	17,347
Ahmednagar	8,274	9,543	15,100	14,611	48,501	17,467
Poona	69,004	54,543	64,791	71,185	89,231	66,999
Sholapur	8,749	4,420	8,812	8,528	11,816	7,367
Satara	45,404	37,864	60,387	56,754	65,953	53,211
Cutch	45,333	38,000	28,179	36,470	37,480	20,029
Kathiawar	32,568	39,050	45,531	58,775	72,435	53,288
Kolhapur	4,220	4,248	5,993	9,309	....	5,391
Baroda	3,906	8,357	5,625	4,501	6,349	6,027
Hyderabad State	8,525	9,518	7,431	9,302	19,602	15,914
Madras	6,075	8,276	6,005	8,278	15,156	21,415
Rajputana	9,381	12,907	10,461	12,453	19,722	8,389
Punjab, including Delhi ..	2,429	6,572	6,116	8,616	10,425	11,837
United Provinces	....	....	....	{ 50,682	{ 70,911	{ 83,323
Oudh	8,722	8,831	6,043			
Upper India	....	15,303	....	....	....	....
North-West Frontier Provinces	2,227	16,653	29,881	1,101	2,273	3,091
Central Provinces and Berar ..	2,391	1,950	4,330	3,843	5,046	4,814
Central India Agency ..	2,088	2,966	2,407	4,005	3,360	3,330
Portuguese and French possessions in India	21,938	21,399	18,794	32,106	34,111	38,702

These figures show considerable variation in the number of immigrants recorded in the 1931 Census as compared with the figures recorded in the 1931 Census. Ahmedabad, Broach, Kaira, Surat, Ratnagiri, Madras, the Punjab, the United Provinces, French and Portuguese settlements have shown an increase of 50,981 at this Census. On the other hand, other places of origin show a decrease of 146,596. This gives a net decrease of 95,615 in the number of immigrants. As compared with the 1921 figures the number of persons born in Bombay shows an increase of 97,943. The detailed statistics of immigration discussed later in this section show the nature of the decrease in the number of immigrants. The differences in the number of immigrants from Ahmednagar, Poona, Satara, Cutch, Kathiawar and Rajputana recorded at the 1921 and 1931 Censuses are certainly remarkable. Apart from differences caused by unsatisfactory enumeration already commented on, the cause of the variations must lie partly in the fact that large numbers of these persons must be labourers and traders who, coming to Bombay when trade is flourishing, depart therefrom in times of depression. This would explain a decrease in the numbers in 1931. Increases are harder to account for. Why the number of immigrants from the United Provinces should have risen from 70,911 in 1921 to 83,323 in 1931 is obscure. So is the increase recorded in the number of immigrants from Surat. As regards the immigrants from the United Provinces, the only probable reason that occurs is that the increase must be despite the fact that large numbers of United Provinces immigrants must have returned to their own province. It would seem to suggest that there was a considerable expansion in Bombay after 1921 up till the time of the slump and that some of this expansion has remained. The following statement (No. 15) shows the variation in the actual number of immigrants recorded at the Censuses of 1921 and 1931 :—

STATEMENT No. 15.

District.	Increase 1921 Immigrants. (+)	Decrease 1921 Immigrants. (—)	District.	Increase 1921 Immigrants. (+)	Decrease 1921 Immigrants. (—)
Ahmedabad ..	2,913	....	Thana ..	....	2,442
Broach ..	2,225	....	Kolaba ..	....	10,514
Kaira ..	138	....	Nasik ..	....	7,104
Surat ..	18,523	....	Ahmednagar ..	....	31,040
Ratnagiri ..	1,690	....	Poona ..	....	22,232
Madras ..	6,259	....	Sholapur ..	....	4,449
Punjab ..	1,412	....	Satara ..	....	12,742
United Provinces ..	12,412	....	Cutch ..	....	17,451
North West Frontier Province	818	....	Kathiawar ..	....	19,147
French and Portuguese Settlements.. ..	4,591	....	Kolhapur ..	....	3,870
			Baroda ..	....	322
			Hyderabad State ..	....	3,688
			Rajputana ..	....	11,333
			Central Provinces and Berar ..	....	232
			Central India Agency ..	....	30
	50,981				146,596

The extent to which the Ratnagiri district contributes to the population of Bombay City is remarkable. In 1931 no fewer than 237,256 persons were returned as born in Ratnagiri district. This is equivalent to 20·4 per cent. of the total population of the City. The other main contributors are Surat district 58,275, 5·0 per cent.; Kolaba district 32,666, 2·8 per cent.; Poona district 66,999, 5·8 per cent.; Satara district 53,211, 4·6 per cent.; Kathiawar, 53,288, 4·6 per cent.; Madras 21,415, 1·8 per cent.; United Provinces 83,323, 7·2 per cent.; and French and Portuguese possessions in India (actually only Portuguese possessions) 38,702, 3·3 per cent. The extent to which the various sources of immigration have grown or diminished in importance as contributors to the Bombay City population is

MO-III Bk Ra Cs 3—5

shown in the statement (No. 16) which follows. The proportions are based on the 1881 figures as equivalent to 100 in each instance.

STATEMENT NO. 16.

District.	1891	1901	1911	1921	1931
Ahmedabad	135	137	233	251	292
Broach	87	70	94	129	255
Kaira	1,241	1,603	1,937	2,917	3,020
Surat	84	70	98	111	163
Thana including Bombay Suburban district	84	59	87	82	72
Kolaba	225	184	323	375	284
Ratnagiri	129	116	172	187	188
Nasik	89	111	138	344	243
Ahmednagar	115	183	177	586	211
Poona	79	94	103	129	97
Sholapur	51	101	98	135	84
Satara	83	133	125	145	117
Cutch	84	62	81	83	44
Kathiawar	120	140	180	221	164
Kolhapur	100	142	221	220	128
Baroda	224	144	115	162	155
Hyderabad State	112	87	109	230	187
Madras	136	99	136	250	353
Rajputana	138	112	133	210	89
Punjab and Delhi	270	257	355	429	487
*North India	375	329	475	671	789
Central Provinces	82	182	161	211	201
Central India Agency	142	115	194	161	159
French and Portuguese Possessions	98	86	147	156	176

* Including the North West Frontier Provinces and United Provinces of Agra and Oudh.

These figures must be corrected by reference to the actual numbers of immigrants shown in statement No. 14 above. It is important to examine the ratio of females to males in each stream of immigration from the more important areas contributing to the population of Bombay City. The following statement (No. 17) gives the information for the 1931 Census, the ratio being expressed as relative to 1,000 males.

STATEMENT NO. 17.

Birthplace.	Per 1,000	Birthplace.	Per 1,000
Bombay City	728	Satara	545
Ahmednagar	738	Surat	595
Nasik	679	French and Portuguese Settlements	493
Poona	661	Punjab, Delhi and North West Frontier Provinces	238
Kolaba	619	Rajputana	228
Cutch	641	United Provinces	211
Hyderabad (Deccan)	443	Europe	407
Thana and Bombay Suburban district	613	Other Asiatic countries	211
Kathiawar	594		
Ratnagiri	541		

The statement affords some clue as to the extent to which the stream of immigration is composed of permanent or temporary immigrants. In Bombay Town and Island as a whole the ratio of females to males is 621 to 1,000. For the Bombay City-born population alone the ratio is 728 to 1,000. The ratio of females to males in the district of Ahmednagar is 785 to 1,000 ; of Nasik 765 to 1,000 and of Poona 716 to 1,000. From this it may be presumed that a large proportion of these immigrants do not take their families with them but consist of able-bodied adult males arriving at the city to find work.

Further light is thrown on the character of the immigration into Bombay City by the statements (Nos. 18 and 19) which follow. The first shows the percentage of actual workers, male and female, and of dependents at the 1921 and 1931 Censuses coming from various areas. The second statement shows the percentage of immigrants in three age-groups, namely 0 to 15, 15 to 40, and 40 and over, for the last two Censuses.

STATEMENT No. 18.

District of birth.	Percentage to total immigrants.					
	1931			1921		
	Actual workers.		Dependents.	Actual workers.		Dependents.
	Males.	Females.	Both sexes.	Males.	Females.	Both sexes.
1	2	3	4	5	6	7
Ahmednagar	43	26	31	42	18	40
Kolaba	49	10	41	47	10	43
Poona	44	16	40	46	12	42
Ratnagiri	51	12	37	52	12	36
Satara	52	12	36	56	10	34
Surat	48	17	35	56	5	39
Thana and Bombay Suburban district ..	38	18	44	48	5	47
Cutch	44	16	40	44	3	53
Kathiawar	53	7	40	49	6	45
Rajputana	62	4	34	76	3	21
United Provinces	68	3	29	76	3	21
French and Portuguese Possessions ..	55	11	34	57	10	33
The same for the total population of the City	44	5	51	52	9	39

STATEMENT No. 19.

District of birth.	Percentage to total immigrants.					
	1931			1921		
	0-15	15-40	40 and over	0-15	15-40	40 and over
1	2	3	4	5	6	7
Ahmednagar	33	46	21	29	53	18
Kolaba	18	64	18	22	59	19
Poona	29	57	20	26	55	19
Ratnagiri	21	63	16	22	62	16
Satara	20	54	26	22	61	17
Surat	33	49	18	19	63	18
Thana and Bombay Suburban district ..	18	58	24	23	58	19
Cutch	29	53	18	28	53	19
Kathiawar	19	54	27	23	59	18
Rajputana	26	60	14	13	72	15
United Provinces	11	71	18	13	69	18
French and Portuguese Settlements ..	15	69	16	61	63	21
The same for the total population of the City	25	61	14	21	62	17

These statements show that generally in 1931 there has been an increase in the number of female workers and also an increase in the number of dependents. This would appear to indicate a tendency for labour to settle in Bombay City in respect of the immigrants from the areas specified. They show also the extent to which the immigrant population from these areas consists of workers in the prime of working life. Where the figures for persons under 15 years are high it would suggest that settlement of a permanent or a semi-permanent type is taking place. Thus in the case of the Ahmednagar and Surat immigrants who show a substantial increase in the lowest age-group at this Census, it is fair to assume that numbers are máking a permanent home in the City, possibly helping to swell the mill population. City Table VI, Part II, gives special statistics of immigrants by caste and occupation. It has been compiled as far as possible on the lines followed in 1921. Statistics regarding castes immigrating from particular areas are compared for the 1921 and 1931 Censuses in the statement (No. 20) which follows.

There is no uniformity in these figures. It will be noted that while Dheds and Mahars have increased in numbers from some areas they have decreased from others. The same is true of Kunbi Marathas. There has been a large increase in the number of Goanese Christians.

STATEMENT NO. 20.

District and Caste.	Persons (Immigrants)	
	1931	1921
1	2	3
Ahmedabad	**20,470**	**17,557**
Bhangi	1,010	956
Brahman, others	1,205	1,138
Lohar	1,820	1,750
Vani (Hindu)	4,000	1,729
Broach	**4,497**	**2,272**
Zoroastrians	1,607	525
Vani (Hindu)	630	337
Kaira	**4,017**	**3,879**
Dhed or Mahar	400	392
Vani	600	545
Bohra	330	324
Surat	**58,275**	**39,682**
Brahman, others	2,519	2,219
Bhandari	982	252
Bhatia	754	372
Darji	740	620
Dhed or Mahar	4,540	3,490
Kharva	4,005	3,095
Koli	1,913	1,798
Kunbi Maratha	3,983	1,225
Lohana	1,803	339
Lohar	1,009	674
Sonar	840	251
Sutar	820	1,296
Bohra	2,302	1,384
Shaikh	2,076	1,184
Zoroastrian	2,803	2,761

STATEMENT No. 20—*contd.*

District and Caste.	Persons (Immigrants). 1931	1921
1	2	3
Thana	**11,865**	**14,797**
Bhandari	620	585
Brahman, others	591	671
Kayasth Prabhu	732	728
Kunbi Maratha	998	2,059
Kolaba	**32,666**	**43,180**
Agri	1,320	3,990
Bhandari	1,206	1,604
Brahman, Chitpavan	1,020	1,074
Brahman, others	976	731
Chambhar, Mochi	2,201	2,099
Dhed or Mahar	3,940	3,846
Kayasth Prabhu	1,203	1,381
Koli	1,124	1,339
Kunbi Maratha	14,993	14,655
Shaikh	555	799
Ratnagiri	**237,256**	**235,556**
Brahman, Chitpavan	2,218	3,693
Brahman, Deshastha	955	900
Brahman, Gaud Saraswat	1,644	1,589
Brahman, Saraswat	2,283	2,484
Brahman, others	3,360	3,385
Bhandari	14,797	20,849
Chambhar, Mochi	6,349	5,622
Dhed or Mahar	17,845	13,490
Dhobi	1,120	973
Gavli	1,307	1,604
Kayasth Prabhu	708	421
Koli	789	705
Kumbhar	1,027	1,310
Kunbi Maratha	135,899	124,488
Nhavi	1,720	1,610
Sonar	4,721	4,074
Sutar	2,789	2,431
Teli	1,937	2,615
Vani, others (Hindu)	5,985	6,063
Shaikh	6,945	7,773
Nasik	**17,347**	**24,541**
Brahman, others	880	827
Dhed or Mahar	6,349	9,342
Kunbi Maratha	6,092	6,391
Vanjari	511	1,681
Ahmednagar	**17,467**	**48,501**
Chambhar	1,002	2,561
Dhed or Mahar	6,109	16,235
Kunbi Maratha	4,800	12,833
Shaikh	1,201	1,889

STATEMENT No. 20—*contd.*

District and Caste.	Persons (Immigrants).	
	1931	1921
1	2	3
Poona	**66,999**	**39,231**
Brahman, Chitpavan	990	1,300
Brahman, Deshastha	728	880
Brahman, others	901	979
Chambhar	2,890	3,550
Dhed or Mahar	7,829	10,955
Kunbi Maratha	29,845	46,636
Nhavi	800	1,197
Shaikh	1,082	2,847
Sholapur	**7,367**	**11,816**
Chambhar	1,249	1,184
Dhed or Mahar	2,229	2,331
Maratha	2,998	3,390
Satara	**53,211**	**65,953**
Brahman, others	1,197	1,082
Chambhar, Mochi	3,050	4,561
Dhed or Mahar	11,816	13,335
Kunbi Maratha	20,817	30,776
Nhavi	792	1,070
Shaikh	619	1,321
Cutch	**20,029**	**37,480**
Bhatia	2,752	3,535
Brahman, others	957	966
Lohana (Hindu)	4,433	5,954
Vani, others (Hindu)	2,010	3,409
Khoja	1,827	1,976
Memon	1,507	1,674
Shaikh	1,560	1,644
Vani, others (Jain)	1,529	3,447
Kathiawar	**51,824**	**72,435**
Bhangi	805	791
Brahman, others	2,128	3,434
Chambhar, Mochi	1,295	1,259
Darji, Shimpi	2,821	2,064
Dhed or Mahar	2,804	3,784
Kharva	1,165	1,122
Kunbi Maratha	1,329	1,410
Lohar	845	976
Sonar	1,801	1,165
Vani, others	5,954	11,167
Bohra	2,697	2,671
Khoja	2,220	2,067
Memon	1,524	2,233

STATEMENT No. 20—*contd.*

District and Caste.	Persons (Immigrants).	
	1931	1921
1	2	3
Baroda	**6,027**	**6,349**
Brahman, others	521	541
Maratha	501	456
Vani, others	521	501
Zoroastrian	1,529	1,329
Hyderabad State	**15,914**	**19,602**
Koli	1,897	1,541
Kunbi Maratha	3,201	3,149
Shaikh	864	845
Madras	**21,415**	**15,126**
Brahman, Saraswat	915	903
Brahman, others	1,821	1,535
Kunbi Maratha	1,229	1,180
Shaikh	1,025	978
Rajputana	**8,389**	**19,722**
Rajput	550	525
Vani, others (Hindu)	894	927
Shaikh	1,426	1,391
Vani, Oswal (Jain)	876	864
Vani, others	899	876
Punjab	**8,517**	**7,692**
Pathan	1,009	955
Shaikh	1,890	1,730
United Provinces	**83,323**	**70,911**
Ahir	1,140	2,256
Brahman, others	4,550	4,111
Dhobi	1,240	1,330
Kunbi Maratha	4,003	4,164
Rajput	1,320	5,871
Thakur	2,103	2,409
Vani, others (Hindu)	1,002	990
Memon	1,320	1,225
Pathan	2,472	2,194
Shaikh	13,302	15,358
Sayyad	1,063	1,004
North West Frontier Province	**724**	**2,273**
Pathan	119	419

STATEMENT NO. 20—*concld.*

District and Caste,	Persons (Immigrants).	
	1931	1921
1	2	3
Central Provinces and Berar	**4,814**	**5,046**
Maratha	625	639
Central India Agency	**3,330**	**3,360**
Brahman, others	320	223
French and Portuguese Settlements in India	**38,702**	**34,111**
Brahman, Gaud Saraswat	710	671
Maratha	1,500	1,488
Goanese (Christian)	18,975	10,279

10. EUROPEANS AND ANGLO-INDIANS.

The number of Europeans (British subjects and others) shows a marked fall this Census from 13,544 in 1921 to 8,400. The reason is the smaller number of troops stationed in Bombay and a reduction in the number of Europeans, living mostly in Fort North and Esplanade. If the reduction in military strength be taken into account it will be seen that the decline in the number of Europeans as compared with the 1901 and 1911 figures is not very great. The 1921 figures were abnormally high. Anglo-Indians show a great increase. But it may be doubted whether the Census represents the facts correctly. It is more than likely that numbers of Indian Christians return themselves as Anglo-Indians. The population of "Others" is smaller than it has been since 1901. But the decline from the 1921 figure is trifling. The population of Europeans and Anglo-Indians taken together about equals the population of 1911 but is less than that of 1921 when special circumstances prevailed.

The following table (No. 21) gives statistics for four Censuses.

STATEMENT NO. 21.

Race.	1901	1911	1921	1931
Anglo-Indians	3,258	4,188	4,724	7,039
Europeans (British subjects)	10,707	10,131	13,544	8,400
Others	1,494	1,724	1,182	1,009
Total ..	15,459	16,043	19,450	16,448

The statement (No. 22) below shows the proportionate increase in the total population of Bombay and in the population of Europeans and Anglo-Indians in Bombay, the 1881 figures being taken as 100.

STATEMENT No. 22.

Class.	Proportion at each Census taking the 1881 figure in each case as 100.					
	1881	1891	1901	1911	1921	1931
Total Population	100	106·2	100·3	126·6	152·0	150·2
Eu opeans and Anglo-Indians	100	136·6	133·6	138·4	167·3	141·5

There is nothing very remarkable about this statement. The statement which follows (No. 23) shows the distribution over various nationalities of "Others" who number 1,009.

STATEMENT No. 23.

Belgian	99
Dutch	4
French	125
Greek	37
Italian	130
Portuguese (born in Europe)	89
German	146
Russian	20
Spanish	37
Swiss	50
Other Europeans (unspecified)	80
Chinese	14
Japanese	4
Persian	2
African	19
United States of America	30
American (unspecified)	112
Armenian	11
Total ..	1,009

The figures show a slight fall. In 1921 the number was 1,182. In 1901 and in 1911 the figures were 1,494 and 1,724 respectively. This shows that the reduction in the number of European foreigners occasioned by the war has continued. This is a very natural result in these days of keen trading competition when, a place once having been lost in the trading community, recovery of it is very difficult.

11. AGE.

The age distribution of the urban population usually differs considerably from the age distribution of the rural population. The reason is to be found in the different economic conditions prevailing. Cities are preeminently places where there is comparatively a smaller number of persons in the highest and the lowest age-groups. Thus children and aged persons tend to form a much smaller proportion of the population of a town or city than they do of a rural area. Cities have large numbers of persons in the active wage-earning periods of life and they are usually recruited from rural areas to which the workers return after their period of wage-earning is over. From this point of view cities may be regarded preeminently as places where able-bodied persons come to earn a living and not so much as places that are really typical of the whole series of grades of population from childhood to senile decay. Bombay City is par excellence a city of this working type with, comparatively, few children, old men and women, and, comparatively, a great preponderance of adults in the working stage. It also presents remarkable figures for the number of immigrants that make up its population. Only 24·6 per cent. of the Bombay City population is home-born. Of the non-home-born population the greater number do not reside in the city for the whole of their lives and a very large proportion of those who in early manhood or in adult life earn their living in the city leave it when they cease to be earners. Though the other cities in the Presidency dealt with in the present report show features similar to those presented by Bombay, none of them show these features in anything like so exaggerated a form, and in the case of Karachi, Sholapur and Poona it is easy to see the extent to which the basis of a rural distribution of population has been disturbed by the characteristic features of a city distribution. In Bombay City, on the other hand, the age distribution is so different from the general age distribution of the Presidency that it is obvious that quite extraordinary influences are in operation. In the table which follows this point is made quite clear. The statement (No. 24) shows the population per mille by age-groups for Bombay City, as compared with the general population of the Bombay Presidency and the other three cities of the Presidency dealt with in the present volume :—

STATEMENT NO. 24.

Age-group.	General population of the Presidency.	Bombay City.	Karachi.	Poona City Municipality.	Sholapur.
1	2	3	4	5	6
0—5	150	89	139	129	144
5—10	131	81	114	111	116
10—15	115	74	101	108	111
15—20	89	99	101	111	108
20—25	95	132	117	118	116
25—30	88	155	108	97	95
30—35	81	141	95	89	81
35—40	65	86	69	68	62
40—45	53	61	53	53	50
45—50	41	31	36	38	36
50—55	32	23	26	29	27
55—60	23	12	16	19	20
60—65	18	9	13	15	7
65—70	8	3	4	6	7
70 and over ..	11	4	8	9	10

The important fact which this statement discloses is that, while in the Presidency as a whole the number of persons per mille in the age-groups 20 to 25, 25 to 30, 30 to 35, and 35 to 40, are 95, 88, 81 and 65 respectively, in Bombay City the figures are 132, 155, 141 and 86. The other three cities show figures for these age-groups which are much nearer the general Presidency level.

In the Statement (No. 25) which follows there is shown the distribution per mille of the total population of each sex by age-groups in Bombay City and in the Presidency generally in 1921 and 1931. It will be noted that in 1931 the proportion of persons in the two lowest age-groups has risen considerably but that otherwise the distribution remains more or less in 1931 what it was in 1921. In fact on the whole the proportion of persons in the highest age-groups has fallen. The reason for the increase in the proportion of persons in the two lowest age-groups is not clear and cannot be fully explained except by reference to accurate vital statistics. Those which exist however, by their inaccuracy, do not permit of any really adequate explanation of the phenomenon. The general increase of

DISTRIBUTION OF EVERY 1000 PERSONS BY AGE PERIODS — BOMBAY AND KARACHI CITIES — COMPARED WITH THE GENERAL POPULATION OF THE PRESIDENCY 1931

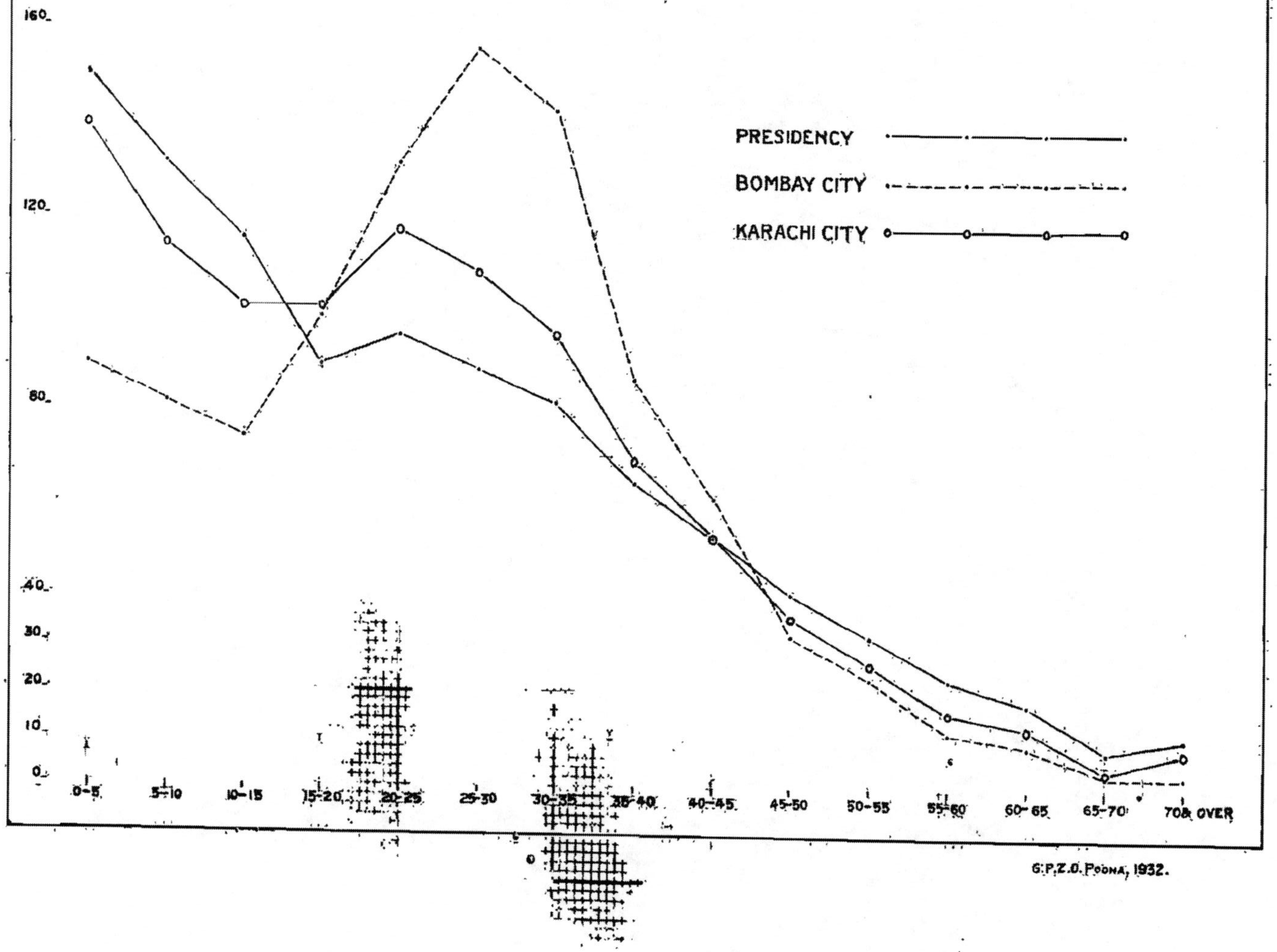

G.P.Z.O. Poona, 1932.

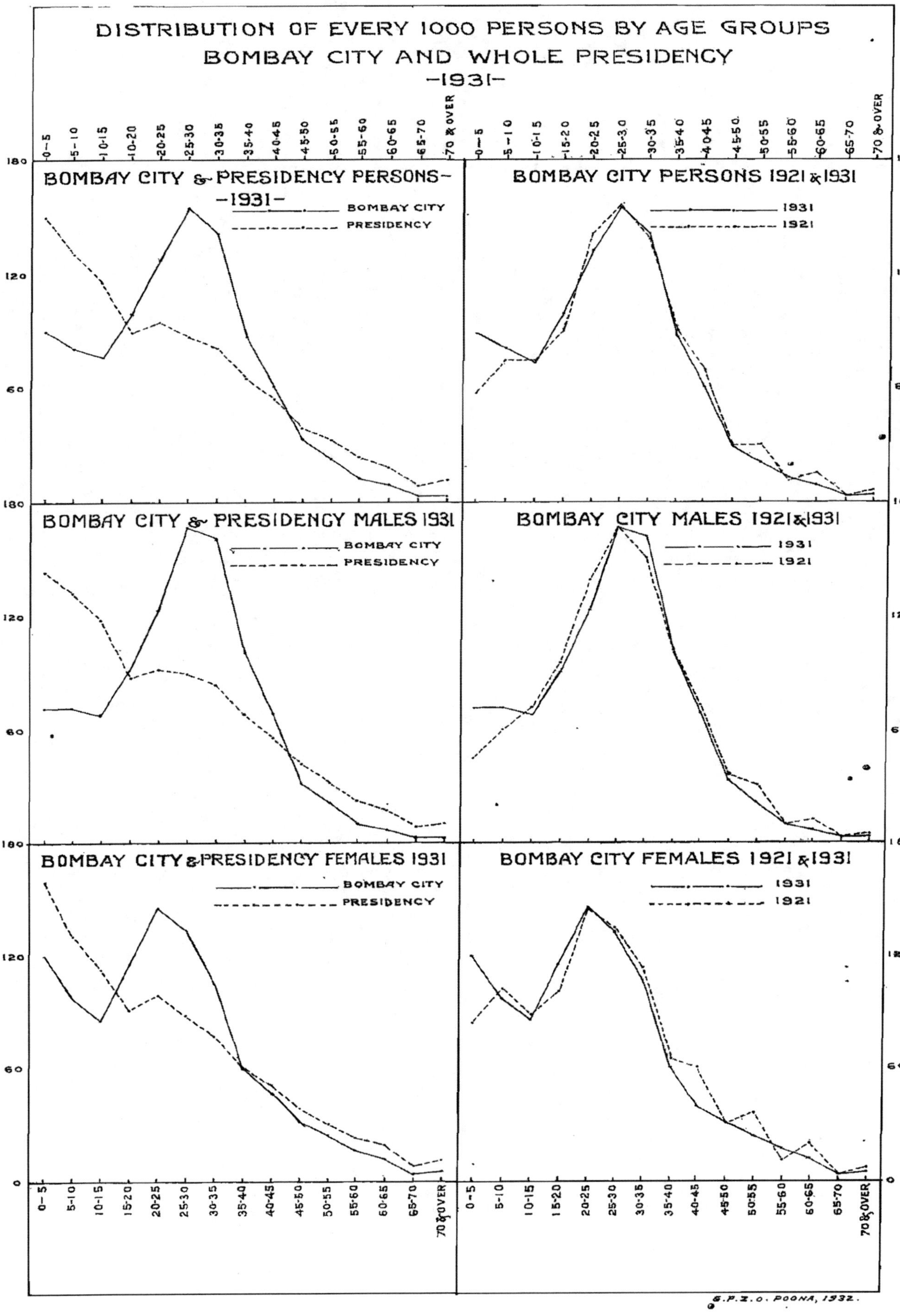
DISTRIBUTION OF EVERY 1000 PERSONS BY AGE GROUPS
BOMBAY CITY AND WHOLE PRESIDENCY
-1931-
BOMBAY CITY & PRESIDENCY PERSONS -1931-
BOMBAY CITY
PRESIDENCY
BOMBAY CITY PERSONS 1921 & 1931
1931
1921
BOMBAY CITY & PRESIDENCY MALES 1931
BOMBAY CITY
PRESIDENCY
BOMBAY CITY MALES 1921 & 1931
1931
1921
BOMBAY CITY & PRESIDENCY FEMALES 1931
BOMBAY CITY
PRESIDENCY
BOMBAY CITY FEMALES 1921 & 1931
1931
1921
180
120
60
0
0-5
5-10
10-15
15-20
20-25
25-30
30-35
35-40
40-45
45-50
50-55
55-60
60-65
65-70
70 & OVER
G.P.Z.O. POONA, 1932.

population in the Presidency in the last decade has probably meant more births in Bombay City and the fall in the total population of the city must be due chiefly to the bad trade and business conditions prevailing at the time the Census was taken. Thus it may be possible to explain an apparently contradictory phenomenon—a rise in the proportion of young persons and a fall in total population.

STATEMENT No. 25.

Age-group.	1921				1931			
	Presidency.		Bombay City.		Presidency.		Bombay City.	
	Males.	Females.	Males.	Females.	Males.	Females.	Males.	Females.
1	2	3	4	5	6	7	8	9
0—5 ..	118	133	45	84	143	159	72	120
5—10 ..	148	152	60	103	132	131	72	97
10—15 ..	74	107	72	88	118	112	68	85
15—20 ..	122	70	90	100	87	91	91	115
20—25 ..			140	144	92	99	123	145
25—30 ..	331	325	167	135	89	88	167	133
30—35 ..			151	113	84	77	161	106
35—40 ..			102	65	68	61	101	60
40—45 ..			74	59	56	51	69	46
45—50 ..	162	160	36	31	42	39	32	31
50—55 ..			31	36	32	31	21	25
55—60 ..			11	11	22	23	10	16
60—65 ..	..	..	13	20	17	19	7	12
65—70 ..	45	53	3	4	8	8	3	4
70 and over ..	..	..	5	7	10	11	3	5

The statement (No. 26) below shows the distribution per mille of the Bombay City population over the various age-groups for the last six Censuses. It demonstrates the manner in which the age distribution has altered as Bombay has grown in size. It will be obvious that when Bombay was a much smaller place than it is to-day its population was distributed by age more in the manner in which the population of places like Poona and Sholapur is distributed by age to-day. As it has got bigger the City has become less and less a place for children and old people. In this it presents the same features as are exhibited in present-day New York.

STATEMENT No. 26.

Age-group.	1931	1921	1911	1901	1891	1881
0—5	89	58	67	69	80	106
5—10	81	75	67	84	81	104
10—15	74	78	78	92	95	96
15—20	99	94	108	100	110	132
20—25	132	141	151	132	136	134
25—30	155	156	154	140	126	123
30—35	141	138	125	121	108	78
35—40	86	90	80	71	67	78
40—45	61	69	69	74	71	83
45—50	31	34	31	32	34	
50—55	23	33	32	40	42	18
55—60	12	11	11	13	14	26
60—65	9	15	17			
65—70	3	3	4	32	36	22
70 and over	4	5	6			

The rise in the proportion of children up to the age of 10 has already been noticed. The ratio for the age-groups from 10 to 15, to 40 to 45 years has fallen at this Census as compared with 1921 but the explanation is probably due to the number of the wage-earning classes which have left Bombay on account of the trade slump. It is interesting to compare the population in three age-groups, 0 to 15, 15 to 50, and 50 and over, for the last two Censuses for the Bombay Presidency and the four cities.

In the following statement (No. 27) this comparison is made.

STATEMENT No. 27.

Age-group.	Bombay Presidency.		Bombay City.		Karachi.		Poona.		Sholapur.	
	1921	1931	1921	1931	1921	1931	1921	1931	1921	1931
1	2	3	4	5	6	7	8	9	10	11
0—15 ..	39	40	21	24	33	35	33	35	35	37
15—50 ..	50	51	72	71	60	58	56	57	54	55
50 and over ..	11	9	7	5	9	7	11	8	11	8

From the above it will again be remarked how much more closely to the Presidency figures the figures for Karachi, Poona and Sholapur approximate than do the Bombay City figures. Judged by the Sundbarg formula Bombay City is distinctly accessive. Karachi, Poona and Sholapur have all clearly rural characteristics in their age distribution of population. This is due to these cities being the permanent residence of many of their inhabitants. In fact a fair analogy of the difference between Bombay and the other cities in this respect can be found in the difference seen between certain parts of the London area, as for instance between an industrial and commercial area like the City of London, or Southwark, and a residential area like Acton or Croydon. It will be noted that in 1931, despite the large numbers of wage earners who had left Bombay owing to trade and business depression, the proportion of persons aged between 15 and 50 has risen from 50 to 51. This has been accompanied by a fall in the proportion of persons aged 50 and over from 11 to 1921 to 9 in 1931. It will further be noted that both Poona and Sholapur show a rise in the proportion of persons in the 15 to 50 age-group and a fall in the proportion of persons aged 50 and over.

It is desirable to make still further examination of the age distribution of the population of Bombay City. This examination is carried out in the statement (No. 28) given below, which shows the distribution per mille of the population over four age-groups, namely 0 to 20, 20 to 40, 40 to 60, and 60 and over.

STATEMENT No. 28.

Age-group.	Distribution of ages per mille of the population.					
	1881	1891	1901	1911	1921	1931
1	2	3	4	5	6	7
0—20	438	366	345	320	345	343
20—40	413	437	464	510	525	514
40—60	127	161	159	143	147	128
60 and over	22	36	32	27	23	15

The four age-groups may be taken as a rough general measure of (1) the population of children and students, (2) two types of wage-earners, and (3) persons who have passed the wage-earning stage. The change in the proportions of the various groups indicates how the growth of business and factory development in Bombay has affected the population at various ages. It would seem to show that Bombay is becoming progressively a place for younger and younger workers as the figures for the 20 to 40 age-group show a tendency to rise, while the figures for the 40 to 60 age-group show a tendency to fall. Whether from this any reliable conclusion can be drawn as to a rise in the standard of living is perhaps doubtful. But *prima facie* the phenomenon would appear to suggest that a worker can retire from the factory to his village at an earlier age than used to be the case. It is a point that deserves the attention of sociologists.

The statement (No. 29) given below shows the distribution per mille of the Bombay City population by religion and age in 1931 :—

STATEMENT No. 29.

Age-group.	Distribution of 1,000 persons of each religion by age-groups, Bombay City, 1931.					
	Total population of the City.	Hindu.	Muslim.	Jain.	Zoroastrian.	Christian.
1	2	3	4	5	6	7
0—5	89	93	79	78	73	84
5—10	81	82	79	84	84	75
10—15	75	72	77	88	88	76
15—20	99	100	96	116	90	108
20—25	131	135	126	138	92	133
25—30	155	162	152	136	96	138
30—35	141	147	141	141	96	124
35—40	86	84	93	93	84	86
40—45	61	57	68	61	76	69
45—50	31	28	35	27	62	41
50—55	23	19	24	8	55	30
55—60	12	10	13	15	39	15
60—65	9	7	10	9	32	10
65—70	3	2	3	4	16	4
70 and over	3·7	2	4	2	17	4
Age unspecified	0·3	....	....	....	....	3

Conclusions from this table are liable to some error unless allowance is made for the different conditions affecting the residence of the persons following the various religions. Thus the longevity of the Zoroastrians, though an undoubted fact, is not to be gauged entirely by these figures. The Zoroastrians are town dwellers mostly concentrated in Bombay, while a large proportion of the Hindu population migrates back to its sources of origin. The figures here given for the higher age-groups can therefore hardly be taken as a fair basis for longevity by themselves. If the table be taken as it stands, it can be deduced therefrom that while in the population of the city as a whole there is one Parsi in every 21 persons, there is in the population aged over 65 years one Parsi to every two or three.

The age distribution by religions is examined more fully in the statements (Nos. 30 and 31) which follow. In these statements (1) the ratio per mille in each age-group for each religion in Bombay City is shown with reference to the

Presidency ratios and (2) the age distribution is given for Zoroastrians in Bombay City and the Presidency as a whole.

STATEMENT No. 30.

Age-group.	Hindu.		Muslim.		Jain.		Zoroastrian.		Christian.	
	Presidency Ratio per mille.	Bombay City per mille Ratio to Presidency.	Presidency Ratio per mille.	Bombay City per mille Ratio to Presidency.	Presidency Ratio per mille.	Bombay City per mille Ratio to Presidency.	Presidency Ratio per mille.	Bombay City per mille Ratio to Presidency.	Presidency Ratio per mille.	Bombay City per mille Ratio to Presidency.
1	2	3	4	5	6	7	8	9	10	11
0—5 ..	151	62	149	53	135	58	81	90	131	64
5—10 ..	132	62	130	61	119	71	91	92	117	64
10—15 ..	117	62	110	70	112	79	95	93	110	69
15—20 ..	89	112	87	110	96	121	92	98	102	106
20—25 ..	94	144	99	127	97	142	91	101	110	121
25—30 ..	86	188	97	157	85	150	89	108	99	139
30—35 ..	80	184	86	164	80	175	88	109	90	138
35—40 ..	64	131	66	141	67	139	78	108	69	125
40—45 ..	53	108	53	128	57	107	73	104	57	121
45—50 ..	41	68	37	95	45	60	61	102	39	105
50—55 ..	32	59	29	83	36	22	53	104	30	100
55—60 ..	23	43	21	62	27	56	39	100	19	79
60—65 ..	19	37	17	59	21	43	32	100	14	71
65—70 ..	8	25	7	43	10	40	17	94	6	67
70 and over.	11	18	12	33	13	15	20	85	7	57

STATEMENT No. 31.

(Zoroastrians per mille)

Age-group.	Presidency.	City.
0—5	81	73
5—10	91	84
10—15	95	88
15—20	92	90
20—25	91	92
25—30	89	96
30—35	88	96
35—40	78	84
40—45	73	76
45—50	61	62
50—55	53	55
55—60	39	39
60—65	32	32
65—70	17	16
70 and over	20	17

In the marginal statement (No. 32) the percentage of each religion found in Bombay City to the strength of the religion in the Presidency is shown. From this will be obvious the fallacy of computing comparative longevity from the Bombay City figures alone. While nearly two-thirds of the Zoroastrian community are resident in Bombay City less than one twenty-fifth of the Hindu community is so resident. This must be borne in mind while conclusions are being drawn from the four statements given above.

STATEMENT No. 32.

Religion.	Strength.
1	2
Zoroastrian	63·71
Christian	28·20
Muslim	4·33
Jain	4·33
Hindu	3·85

12. SEX.

The sex composition of the population of the Bombay Presidency has been very fully discussed in the 1931 Census Report for Bombay Presidency. Those who are interested in this matter are referred to the pages of that Report. Mr. Sedgwick remarked in 1921 : " It is inevitable that just as the age composition of the City is abnormal so will be the sex composition." The abnormality of the age composition has been shown clearly in the immediately preceding section of the present report. The extent of the abnormality of the sex composition will be realised if the figures discussed in the present section are compared with the Bombay Presidency figures discussed in the main report referred to above. The marginal statement shows the number of females per mille of males in Bombay City since 1872. This statement shows that there has been a rise in the female ratio at this Census and the ratio now stands higher than it has done since 1911. The reason why this is so is by no means clear. There may be several influences at work, as for instance the rise in the number of female births at this Census, the greater number of persons who may be making Bombay a permanent home (inevitable if the city grows in size) and the possibility of there being a larger number of women workers in the prime of life, which is a likelihood in a city where textile production plays so large a part in the industrial organisation. The reasons however cannot be stated categorically. It is for social and public workers to endeavour to explain the phenomenon revealed by the Census figures. The Census itself does not offer any complete explanation. Even with a rise in the female ratio this Census the characteristic feature of the Bombay City population, its very predominantly masculine character, remains little affected. The City is predominantly an area where males are out of all proportion in number to females. In this disparity Bombay City is unique in the Bombay Presidency and probably in all India. It exhibits a disproportion in the number of the sexes that can exist only as an abnormality which must be corrected in other areas. To a great extent the disparity in Bombay City is made up in the sources of immigration which feed the supply of Bombay residents. Students who are interested in this matter are advised to refer to the section on Birthplace in the present report. They should examine the sex proportions for those immigration supply areas by consulting the tables discussed in the general Census report of the Presidency for 1931. If this is done, some light will be thrown on the amazing deficiency of females prevalent in Bombay City. The whole problem is an interesting study on the effects of particular kinds of migration into cities from rural areas. Economically too the problem suggests conclusions of the most important character which need not be discussed here. It is sufficient to refer students to the statistics provided in the various volumes of the Bombay Presidency Census (see volumes VIII, Part I, 1921, pages 197 to 200 and volume VII, Part I, 1911, pages 41 to 47.) It has been mentioned in the general Census report of the Presidency that the sex proportions in Bombay City and the Ratnagiri district afford interesting complements of each other. Students can be strongly advised to study this subject in the detail which it deserves but which cannot be demonstrated fully in a Census Report.

Census.	Number of females.
1872	612
1881	664
1891	586
1901	617
1911	530
1921	525
1931	554

The statements (Nos. 33 and 34) which follow carry the examination of the sex ratio further along general lines. The first statement below shows the number of females per mille of males for the last six Censuses and the second statement shows for the last two Censuses the percentage of females to males in each section of the City.

STATEMENT No. 33.

Religion.	Number of females per 1,000 males in each of the main religions since 1881.					
	1881	1891	1901	1911	1921	1931
1	2	3	4	5	6	7
Hindu	664	571	610	521	531	562
Muslim	679	633	617	507	452	455
Jain	341	311	381	329	357	381
Zoroastrian	931	910	904	903	864	888
Christian	521	493	521	486	480	569

STATEMENT No. 34.

(Percentage of females to males)

Section.	1931	1921
1	2	3
Bombay City	55	52
Upper Colaba	51	33
Lower Colaba	46	46
Fort South	22	19
Fort North	54	58
Esplanade	46	34
Chakla	50	39
Mandvi	54	50
Umerkhadi	63	59
Dongri	61	65
Market	43	30
Dhobi Talav	61	51
Fanaswadi	63	53
Bhuleshwar	52	46
Kumbharwada	62	50
Khara Talav	55	49
Khetwadi	61	62
Girgaum	59	61
Chaupaty	61	61
Walkeshwar	57	58
Mahalaxmi	59	57
Tardeo	65	63
Kamathipura	60	63
First Nagpada	55	49
Second Nagpada	58	58
Byculla	56	56
Tarwadi	63	52
Mazagaon	52	59
Parel	57	58
Sewri	54	67
Sion	60	64
Mahim	64	64
Worli	56	53

It will be seen from the above that in no section of the city has the percentage of females to males been higher than 65 at the last two Censuses. In Fort South the percentage of females is only 22 though this represents an increase of 3 per cent. in 1931 over the 1921 figure. In Upper Colaba the female ratio has risen from 33 to 51. The reason for this is due to the fall in the military population at the 1931 Census and must not be taken as showing any considerable improvement in the conditions making for a higher ratio of females generally. The shortage of females is clearly seen if the population is considered over the age-groups as has been done in the statement (No. 35) given below.

STATEMENT NO. 35.

Age-group.	1931	1921	1911
0—5	93	98	99
5—10	75	90	92
10—15	69	64	58
15—20	70	58	55
20—25	65	53	53
25—30	44	42	42
30—35	36	39	39
35—40	33	34	35
40—45	37	42	45
45—50	54	44	51
50—55	64	60	63
55—60	68	56	64
60 and over	93	81	84
Unspecified	16	..	..

It will be noticed from the above the marked deficiency of females in the age-groups from 20 to 45 years. Only in the very lowest and the very highest age groups does the female ratio approach a normal reasonable distribution. It will be remarked that in the 1931 Census there has been some improvement in the female ratio in the 20 to 25 years age-group and also in the 45 to 50 years age-group. The reasons for this improvement are obscure. There has been no improvement in the intermediate age-groups as a whole. The unsatisfactory character of the age returns, especially for females, may account partially for these anomalies. The following two statements (Nos. 36 and 37) show (1) the percentage of males and females in each religion in Bombay City as compared with the total population of the City and (2) the corresponding figures for the Presidency as a whole.

These figures prove the extent of Zoroastrian and Christian concentration in Bombay City. The Muslim figures are interesting as showing that the Bombay City distribution is not very different from the Presidency distribution. This must be a pure coincidence because the Muslim population of the Presidency consists of two main classes, (1) the Sind population, which is predominantly rural and agricultural and (2) the Presidency proper population, which is predominantly urban and artisan, and petty trading. It is an arithmetical curiosity in these circumstances that the Muslim population of Bombay City should in its sex distribution approximate closely, both for males and females, to the general presidency figures.

STATEMENT NO. 36.

(Proportions, Bombay City)

Religion.	Males.	Females.
Hindu	67·5	68·7
Muslim	19·4	15·8
Jain	1·2	0·8
Zoroastrian	4·1	6·6
Christian	6·9	7·0
Other Religions	0·9	1·1

MO-III Bk Ra Cs 3—9

STATEMENT No. 37.

(Proportions, Bombay Presidency)

Religion.	Males.	Females.
Hindu	77·1	79·4
Muslim	19·4	17·3
Jain	1·1	1·1
Zoroastrian	0·3	0·3
Christian	1·3	1·2
Other Religions	0·8	0·7

13. CIVIL CONDITION.

There is very little change in the civil condition of the population of Bombay City as revealed by the 1931 Census. The following statement (No. 38) shows the percentages of persons unmarried, married and widowed in Bombay City in 1921 and 1931 respectively.

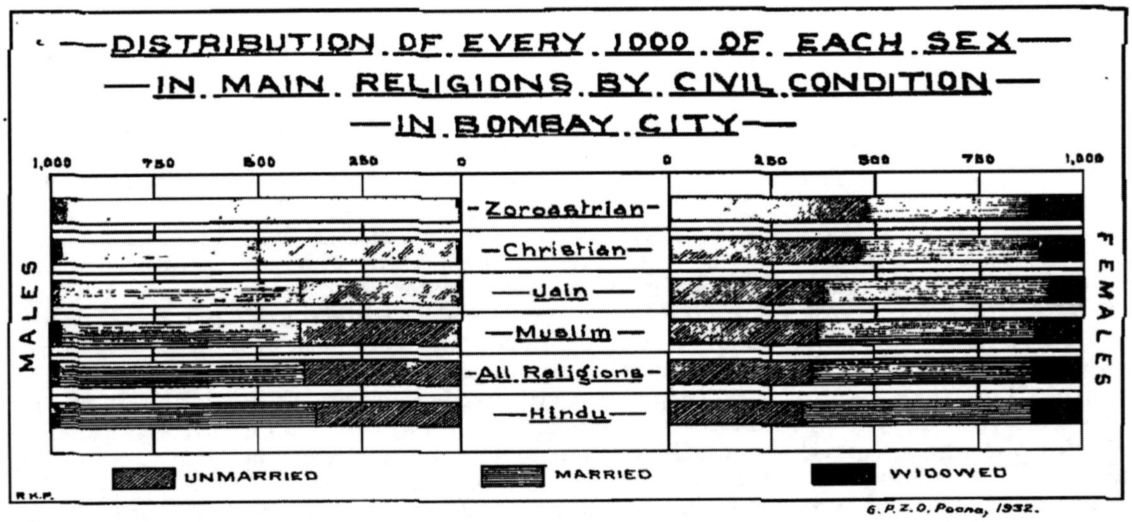

STATEMENT No. 38.

Population.	1921			1931		
	Unmarried.	Married.	Widowed.	Unmarried.	Married.	Widowed.
1	2	3	4	5	6	7
Whole population ..	35	58	7	37	58	5
Hindu	32	61	7	34	61	5
Muslim	37	57	6	38	57	5
Jain	37	58	5	39	58	3
Christian	51	44	5	49	46	5
Zoroastrian	51	41	8	52	41	7

The Christian population shows a little change. The percentage of unmarried has fallen this Census from 51 to 49 and the percentage of married has risen from 44 to 46. The Zoroastrians show by far the highest percentage of unmarried persons. In this community early marriage is practically unknown and the result is that the youthful section of the community is unmarried to an extent unparalleled in any of the other communities. The longevity of the Zoroastrians also accounts for the high percentage of widowed persons in that community. The long term changes in the civil condition of the population are shown in the following statement (No. 39).

STATEMENT No. 39.

Category.	1881	1891	1901	1911	1921	1931
Unmarried	336	349	354	345	345	372
Married	575	565	548	573	584	576
Widowed	89	86	98	82	71	52

The rise in the ratio of unmarried is probably in consonance with the statistics previously discussed as showing that Bombay City is becoming a place where the wage-earners are being drawn increasingly from the younger age-groups. The fall in the ratio of widowed persons is probably the converse side of the same phenomenon and is due to the smaller proportion of elderly persons in the population. Why, however, the ratio of widowed persons should have fallen so much in the 1931 Census is not clear.

In the statement (No. 40) given below the proportion per mille of the population in three age-groups is given for the last four Censuses.

STATEMENT No. 40.

Age-group	1901	1911	1921	1931
0—15	245	212	211	244
15—50	628	718	722	706
50 and over	85	70	67	50

To some extent this statement does not corroborate the previous one ; but it does not contradict it. The reason for the apparent discrepancy in respect of the proportions of unmarried in the former statement and the persons up to age 15 in the latter statement is that the age-group, 0 to 15, does not cover in any way adequately in Bombay City conditions the number of unmarried persons. In Bombay there is a considerable adult working population that is not married and the influence of Zoroastrian late marriages must not be forgotten. The fall in the proportion of widowed persons coincides with a fall in the ratio of the population aged over 50. There is a closer congruence between persons in this age-group and widowed persons than there is between persons aged up to 15 years and unmarried persons.

14. LITERACY.

The percentage of literacy in the population of Bombay City in 1931 was 24. The percentage of literacy in English in 1931 was 11·6. In 1921 the corresponding figures were 23 and 8. Thus the standard of literacy in general has remained almost stationary while the standard of literacy in English has risen, so that whereas in 1921 80 persons out of every thousand were literate in English in 1931 there were 116 such persons. It must however be borne in mind that the Census standard of literacy is mere ability to read and write an intelligible letter in any language and this standard is far below any effective standard of literacy such as would be required by an educational institution of any standing whatsoever. The following statement (No. 41) shows the amount of literacy in Bombay City by religions for the last three Censuses.

STATEMENT No. 41.

Religion.	Literate per 100 in each religion.				Literate in English per 100 in each religion.			
	1931	1921	1911	1901	1931	1921	1911	1901
1	2	3	4	5	6	7	8	9
Hindu	18·8	18·5	17·0	11	7·1	5·8	5·0	3
Muslim	19·3	18·3	16·0	13	4·9	3·2	3·0	2
Jain	25·4	60·1	57·0	52	6·8	8·1	6·C	2
Zoroastrian ..	74·2	77·0	74·0	67	53·0	44·4	39·0	31
Christian ..	51·0	53·3	50·0	51	42·5	44·2	40·0	46
Jew	45·6	..	..	..	31·6	..	..	..
Other religions ..	47·4	..	..	..	13·7	..	..	..

The high standard of literacy amongst Zoroastrians both in general and in English is very remarkable. It can be said of literacy in this community that the standard is actually far above the Census criterion. Of the Hindu community this is not by any means the case. The slight fall in the figures for Zoroastrian literacy in the 1931 Census does not reveal any falling-off in education. It is probably explained by differences in enumeration and by the greater increase in births shown in the 1931 figures; one result of which must be to increase the number of children below the literacy age. For the first time the Zoroastrian community showed in the 1931 Census an improvement in the numbers in the lowest age-groups, and this is bound to affect the literacy figures. The Muslim figures show a slight improvement over 1921 and the standard of literacy has been rising steadily since 1901. Progress in literacy amongst Hindus is of course slower because theirs is much the largest community and the Bombay population of Hindus is very largely recruited from classes that are very backward in education or in inclination towards attaining it. Still even so the figures show steady if slow progress. The apparent fall in the literacy of the Christian community may be due to causes similar to those operating in the case of the Zoroastrians, namely a sharp rise in the number of persons in the lowest age-groups. To some extent also the Christian community is recruited, like the Hindu, from classes that are backward in the matter of education and often resistant to it. In the general report for the Presidency it has been remarked how in many ways the Christian community conforms in its general statistical character to the Hindu community. This is of course due to the extent to which the Christian community consists of Indian Christians drawn from a backward class. The literacy figures for other Christians would be certain to give figures not much inferior to those shown by Zoroastrians. The great fall in literacy shown by Jains is unreal and must be attributed largely to civil disobedience and non-co-operation, though why non-co-operation with the Census should have taken this peculiar form is not readily explicable. Enumeration in this respect must have been much at fault. There is no reason whatever for thinking that Jains are less literate now than they were in 1921. In the marginal statement the distribution of each 100 literates by religion is shown. This statement is more useful for showing the religious composition of the Bombay City population than it is for showing standards of literacy. Indeed if any conclusions are to be drawn from it, they must be drawn after reference to the main tables showing the actual figures of the population by religion.

Religion.	*Strength.*
Hindu	53·0
Muslim	14·0
Jain	1·0
Zoroastrian	15·2
Christian	15·0
Jew	1·4
Other Religions	0·4

15. LANGUAGE.

No table has been prepared in the Census for Bombay City showing language by wards and sections. The figures which have been given below have been taken from Imperial Table XV, Part I, prepared for the whole Presidency and printed in Volume VIII, Part II, of the Bombay Presidency Census Report. The languages spoken in Bombay City according to that Table have been arranged according to numerical importance in statement (No. 42) given below.

STATEMENT No. 42.

Language (mother tongue).	Number of speakers.	Language (mother tongue).	Number of speakers.
Marathi	552,737	Eastern Hindi	3,438
Gujarati	242,443	Arabic	3,046
Western Hindi	197,029	Malayalam	2,474
Konkani	41,001	Bengali	1,721
Sindhi	25,708	Tulu	610
English (all speakers)	21,428	Hebrew	272
Telugu	17,142	Lahnda	127
Tamil	10,252	Balochi	27
Kanarese	8,300	Ahirani Khandeshi	22
Rajasthani	7,556	Bhili	6
Persian	7,156	Kachchhi	5
Pashto	3,540	Burmese	5
Punjabi	3,452	Brahui	2

It will be seen how predominant Marathi is. A glance at the birthplace statistics in paragraph 9 above will explain the reason for this predominance. The figures as they stand give some idea of the polyglot character of Bombay's population.

The statement (No. 43) below shows the percentage distribution over the city's population of the main languages for the last three Censuses.

STATEMENT No. 43.

Language.	Percentage.		
	1931	1921	1911
1	2	3	4
Marathi	47·6	51·4	50·9
Gujarati	20·9	20·1	20·9
Western Hindi	17·0	14·8	14·8
Konkani	3·5	2·8	2·8
Sindhi	2·2	0·2	4·2
English	1·8	2·1	2·0
Telugu	1·5	1·7	..

These figures tend to show a decline in the importance of Marathi. It is doubtful if this is really a fact. Defective enumeration, partly through non-co-operation and the departure from Bombay of many workers on account of trade depression, must have contributed towards the figures actually recorded. As language depends very largely on birthplace the language distribution does little more than record in another form the immigrant character of Bombay's population.

16. BILINGUALISM.

The statement (No. 44) given below shows the results of the Census enumeration of bilingualism. The table is so defective that it is useless making remarks upon it. Enumeration has plainly been most unsatisfactory. Checking statistics of this character in a city like Bombay is difficult at the best of times. When non-co-operation was in operation in addition to other difficulties the incomplete nature of the return can be easily understood. The number of speakers of subsidiary languages is plainly much underestimated. But no means exist of knowing the extent of the inaccuracy. The figures are given for what they may be worth.

STATEMENT No. 44.

Serial No.	Mother tongue.	Total, mother tongue.	Total, subsidiary languages.	Subsidiary Languages.								
				Marathi.	Western Hindi.	Gujarati.	English.	Kon-kani.	Telugu	Kana-rese.	Sindhi	Rajas-thani.
1	2	3	4	5	6	7	8	9	10	11	12	13
1	Marathi ..	552,737	20,886	..	11,215	1,476	8,112	..	..	83	..	..
2	Gujarati ..	242,443	32,652	3,010	16,192	..	13,223	..	..	3	207	17
3	Western Hindi ..	197,020	11,613	4,274	..	5,178	1,902	43	..	104	112	..
4	Konkani ..	41,001	14,206	2,108	3,124	367	8,512	..	..	95	..	..
5	Sindhi ..	25,708	8,134	1,056	2,657	3,997	424	..	..	..	..	..
6	English (all speakers) ..	21,428	7,303	288	6,675	136	..	201	..	..	..	..
7	Telugu ..	17,142	3,028	2,257	523	15	166	..	..	67	..	..
8	Kanarese ..	8,300	2,227	755	1,129	41	260	29	13	..	..	..
9	Rajasthani ..	7,856	1,562	171	844	543	..	..	..	3	1	..
10	Punjabi ..	3,452	1,555	21	1,345	29	160	..	..	..	..	..
	Total ..	1,117,096	103,166	13,940	43,704	11,782	32,759	276	13	355	320	17
		....	100	13·5	42·4	11·4	31·8	0·3	..	0·3	0·3	..

Out of the total population 1,117,096 speaking the important languages 9·2 per cent. are bilingual and 90·8 per cent. speak only mother tongue.

17. CASTE.

In the 1931 Census great efforts were made to tabulate every important caste of Hindus, Jains and Muslims. The enumeration was however faulty and perfunctory for reasons that have already been sufficiently explained. Not sufficient care was taken by enumerators to make detailed enquiry into sub-castes and the result has been that the number of persons returned as belonging to unspecified castes, sub-castes and sects is very large. Out of 75,946 Brahmans, only 22,104 have returned their sub-castes. Of 50,822 Hindu Vanis, only 2,762 have returned their sub-castes. 48,547 persons returned vague caste names, like names of geographical nature or names describing occupations or functions. A glossary of such unsatisfactory caste names has been given in the statistical table and this type of caste name has been classified under Intermediate Hindus. Of a Muslim population of 209,246 no fewer than 82,192 have failed to return their caste, race or tribe and 39,108 have omitted specifying whether they belong to the Sunni or Shia sect. While it is perfectly true that Muslims do not regard caste in the same way as Hindus, and indeed many of them maintain (contrary to Indian experience where Muslim conditions of life have been much influenced by centuries of Hindu environment) that there is no such thing as caste in Islam, there is no doubt that Muslims are divided into groups that do approximate in many ways to Hindu caste divisions. Most of these are undoubtedly due to racial and occupational differences. The carelessness of Muslims generally in describing these divisions has however produced an unsatisfactory result which is reflected in the census statistics. Much of the trouble, apart from the Islamic contempt for caste division, arises from the vague connotation of the term "caste" and no very satisfactory results will be obtained in respect of Muslims until caste for Census purposes is more carefully defined. At present the word "caste" covers distinctions due to racial differences, to topographical origin, to occupation, and to social custom. Until these various sources of equivocality are sorted out no substantial improvement is possible. It is obviously out of the question for a Census to do this kind of social and ethnographic enquiry, especially in an area so complex as Bombay City and the unsatisfactory nature of the caste returns must therefore be regarded as inevitable. In the case of the Jains there are still further difficulties. Many Jains do not know whether to regard themselves as Hindus or not. Some think themselves Hindus; others do not, and it appears to be left to individual caprice to make decisions on this question. In the case of the Jains there was an added complication caused by non-co-operation. The Jain community who are mostly traders, with some kind of Gujarat connection, were more affected by civil disobedience than any other community and the non-co-operation at times took very strange forms resulting in some columns of the Census forms being filled up while others were left blank. At this Census 12,424 Jains were enumerated in Bombay City. Of this number as many as 11,558 failed to state whether they belonged to the Digamber or the Swetamber sect, and 11,003 did not return their caste at all. For this the influence of a movement led by Mr. Gandhi, who is a Gujarati-speaking Bania from Kathiawar with a very special appeal to Gujarati and Kathiawari Hindus and Jains must be held primarily responsible.

In the statement (No. 45), which follows, some of the principal castes recorded at this Census have been compared in respect of numbers with the 1911 and the 1921 Census figures. The statement shows that with the exception of Brahmans (all castes), Kayasth Prabhus, Lohanas, Patani Prabhus, Sonars, Thakurs, Khojas and Memons, there has been a decrease this Census in the population of almost all castes. The chief reason for this, apart from non-co-operation, must be the fall in the number of immigrants caused by business and trade depression. There is not one entry of Jain Vanis (all castes). The rise in the number of Marathas may be attributable to the fall in the number returned as Kunbis. There is inextricable confusion over the use of the terms "Maratha" and "Kunbi" and no satisfactory statistics can be expected in this respect until the terms are better defined and understood.

STATEMENT No. 45.

Caste.	Population in		
	1911	1921	1931
1	2	3	4
Hindu.			
Bhandhari	28,846	30,058	23,671
Bhangi or Halalkhor	5,645	6,015	7,097
Bhatia	7,780	9,015	5,895
Brahman (all castes)	53,656	72,400	75,946
Chambhar or Mochi	21,305	27,589	23,449
Darji, Shimpi, Sai and Mirai	8,190	9,742	8,942
Dhobi, Parit, etc.	5,720	6,622	5,454
Gavli	5,962	5,065	3,014
Hajam, Nhavi, etc.	4,526	6,650	3,354
Kayasth Prabhu	5,090	5,964	6,380
Kharva and Kharvi	5,586	7,146	6,984
Kumbhar	3,798	4,405	2,517
Lohana	14,364	13,734	15,919
Lohar or Kammar	4,935	5,709	3,105
Mahar, Dhed and Holiya	57,855	92,481	67,360
Mali	6,480	7,742	3,799
Mang or Madig	4,247	9,549	5,227
Maratha	231,924	264,338	291,330
Kunbi	14,458	26,418	13,924
Patane Prabhu	2,359	3,515	3,511
Sonar, Soni, etc.	12,259	13,131	13,110
Sutar or Badig	6,950	8,451	3,783
Teli or Ghanchi	4,782	4,655	2,927
Thakur	2,822	3,390	4,300
Vani (all castes)	36,264	58,824	50,822

STATEMENT No. 45—*contd.*

Caste.	Population in		
	1911	1921	1931
1	2	3	4
Muslim.			
Arab	1,191	1,799	839
Bohra	13,272	16,886	16,069
Khoja	12,243	11,172	12,120
Memon	15,381	12,387	11,397
Pathan	11,106	10,371	10,067
Sayad	8,135	8,114	6,489
Shaikh	73,949	77,398	45,653

The long statement (No. 46) which follows shows the result of the Census enumeration of castes in Bombay City in 1931. The chief points may be stated here. The total number of Hindus recorded was 789,861, of which number 177,939 were returned as belonging to advanced castes; 497,873 as belonging to intermediate castes; 4,772 as belonging to primitive castes; 4,300 as belonging to other backward castes; and 104,977 as belonging to depressed castes. Muslims were returned at 209,246; Jains at 12,424, Christians at 80,728; Europeans and allied races at 9,409; and Anglo-Indians at 7,039. The Hindu community returned, amongst advanced castes, 75,946 Brahmans (all castes) and 50,822 Vanis (all castes). In the intermediate castes group the most numerous caste was Bhandari or Bari with 23,671 and Maratha and Kunbi with 305,254, or about one-third of the total population of Bombay City. In the primitive castes group the most numerous caste was the Thakur with 4,300 persons. In the depressed castes group the most numerously represented castes were Mahar, Holiya, Dhed and Wankar with 67,360 persons, and Chambhar with 23,449. Amongst Muslims the castes most numerously represented were Sheikh with 45,653 persons, Momin with 18,674, Bohra with 16,069 and Khoja with 12,120. Amongst Christians the most numerous divisions were Goanese (including Portuguese born in India) with 36,087 and Indian Christians with 28,193. The following statement gives details for all recorded castes. It will be seen that Marathas and Kunbis form the largest individual element in Bombay's mixed population. As these are a poorly educated section of the community and are largely employed in mills and general labour it will be obvious that the character of Bombay City, socially, politically and educationally, depends very largely on the nature of this large element in the city's population. No proper understanding of the city and its problems, and especially its problems of law and order which have been very insistent in recent years, can be reached without a study of the characteristics in city life shown by the Maratha Kunbi population. There is little doubt that the general unsettlement of mill and labouring conditions on a badly-educated and excitable population of this kind has contributed greatly to the serious communal disturbances which have caused the authorities so much anxiety in recent years. Further more the geographical distribution of the Hindu labouring population and the Muslim population, with its much greater concentration in particular quarters of the city (which can be studied from the maps opposite page 12 of this report), must be responsible for much of the extreme communalism which sweeps the city from time to time in a most aggravated form. It is a matter that deserves the closest attention of the authorities responsible for the maintenance of law and order. To what extent disturbances in the City are aided by unsettlement caused by bad housing conditions is not a subject which can be discussed in a Census Report. The housing statistics however which are discussed in a subsequent chapter of the present report merit the careful study of all who are jealous of the good management of an enormous city in which organised cotton-textile manufacture and general labour provide so much of the source of livelihood of a badly-educated and excitable multitude of persons following a low standard of living.

STATEMENT No. 46.

The following castes, tribes or races were recorded in the City among Hindus, Jains, Muslims and Christians.

Religion, caste, sub-caste, tribe or race.	Persons.	Males.	Females.
I. Total Hindus	**789,861**	**505,588**	**284,273**
(a) Advanced Castes	**177,939**	**110,636**	**67,303**
(i) Brahman, all castes	**75,946**	**49,496**	**26,450**
Brahman—Anavla	187	120	67
Do. Audich	272	175	97
Do. Chitpavan or Konkanastha	4,526	2,761	1,765
Do. Deshastha	3,422	2,191	1,231
Do. Devrukha	190	125	65
Do. Garud	3	2	1
Do. Havik	10	8	2
Do. Karhada	947	600	347
Do. Khadwal	33	9	24
Do. Kudaldeskar	528	319	209
Do. Mewada	18	9	9
Do. Modh	15	10	5
Do. Nagar	478	287	191
Do. Saraswat (proper)	6,379	3,702	2,677
Do. Gaud Saraswat	4,986	3,021	1,965
Do. Shri-gaud	20	15	5
Do. Shri-mali	80	64	16
Do. Tapodhan	10	8	2
Do. Sub-castes unspecified	53,842	36,070	17,772
(ii) Total, other advanced	**101,993**	**61,140**	**40,853**
Bhansali	741	435	306
Bhatia	5,895	3,450	2,445
Gujar	157	129	28
Kayasth	1,163	740	423
Kayasth Prabhu	6,380	3,528	2,852
Komti or Vaishya	2,555	1,493	1,062
Lohana or Luhana	15,919	9,135	6,784
Panchkalshi and Somvanshi Kshatriya	1,261	931	330
Panchal or Vishwa Brahman	479	280	199
Patane-Prabhu	3,511	1,819	1,692
Soni, Sonar, Aksali and Daivadnya Brahman	13,110	8,112	4,998
Vani, all castes	**50,822**	**31,088**	**19,734**
Vani—Agarwal	41	21	20
Do. Kapol	534	273	261
Do. Khadayata	1	1	....
Do. Lad	520	293	227
Do. Modh	219	110	109
Do. Nagar	979	557	422
Do. Oswal	401	255	146
Do. Porwal	16	11	5
Do. Shri-mali	44	24	20
Do. Sorathia	7	....	7
Do. Sub-castes unspecified	48,060	29,543	18,517
II. Intermediate	**497,873**	**326,419**	**171,454**
Agri	4,486	2,603	1,883
Ahir	2,313	2,211	102
Bhandari or Bari	23,671	14,510	9,161
Bhaiyya or Purbhaiyya	8,907	7,911	996
Bharwad, Dhangar or Kurub	836	562	274
Bhavsar or Chippa	299	156	143
Bhoi	510	370	140
Darji, Shimpi, Sai or Mirai	8,942	5,594	3,348
Dhobi, Parit, Agasa or Madiwal	5,454	3,803	1,651
Gavda	43	34	9
Gavli	3,014	2,238	776
Gavandi	55	23	32
Gurav	490	289	201
Gurkha	296	249	47
Hajam, Nhavi, Nadig or Kelasi	3,354	2,235	1,119
Jangam	124	67	57
Jath	30	26	4
Jaiswar	1,479	1,432	47
Kalal	57	40	17
Kamathi or Telugu	9,969	5,964	4,005
Kankalia	1,471	779	692
Kasar	1,948	1,087	861
Kharva	6,984	5,532	1,452
Khatri	7,946	4,945	3,001
Sonkoli	911	594	317

Religion, caste, sub-caste, tribe or race.	Persons.	Males.	Females.
II. Intermediate—*contd.*			
Koli—others (but not backward)	7,700	4,939	2,761
Koshti, Hutgar, Jed, Winkar or Devang	3,075	1,636	1,439
Kumbhar	2,517	1,524	993
Kurmi (Kunbi—Agriculturists—in Sind)	312	277	35
Lingayat or Veer Shaiva	347	222	125
Lohar, Luhar, Kammar	3,105	2,059	1,046
Lonari	27	20	7
Total, Maratta, Maratta-Kunbi, Kulwadi or Kanbi, Lewa or Rewa Kunbi of Khandesh	**305,254**	**196,469**	**108,785**
Kunbi, Kulwadi or Kanbi	12,905	9,413	3,492
Rewa or Lewa Kunbi	10	9	1
Maratta	291,330	186,355	104,975
Maratta-Kunbi	1,009	692	317
Mali	3,799	2,304	1,495
Nayar	303	235	68
Pardeshi	9,127	8,028	1,099
Pasi	1,920	1,763	157
Patidar	379	264	115
Rabari	17	17	....
Rajput	2,297	1,719	578
Sali, Padmasali	4,464	2,572	1,892
Shinde	46	26	20
Sutar	3,783	2,303	1,480
Tambat	38	27	11
Teli	2,927	1,814	1,113
Thakur	4,300	3,892	408
Other Intermediate	48,547	31,055	17,492
III. Total, Primitive (Aboriginal or Hill Tribes)	**4,772**	**4,241**	**531**
Barda	3	2	1
Bhil	24	19	5
Dhodia	13	8	5
Dubla	212	148	64
Gamit or Gamta	36	36	....
Gond	3	1	2
Koli-Mahadeo	37	34	3
Kokna	3	....	3
Nayak or Nayakda	139	99	40
Rajpardhi	1	1	....
Thakar	4,300	3,892	408
Vaswa	1	1	....
IV. Total, other backward	**4,300**	**2,728**	**1,572**
Bava or Bairagi	812	551	261
Beldar	74	46	28
Berad or Bedar	17	15	2
Bhampta	7	3	4
Bhavin and Devli	6	2	4
Bhisti	6	4	2
Bhute	12	9	3
Burud	260	142	118
Charan	14	5	9
Dasa	24	24	....
Garudi	7	4	3
Ghisadi	43	22	21
Gondhali	489	296	193
Gopal	1	1	....
Jogi	18	14	4
Johari or Javeri	2	1	1
Joshi	40	27	13
Kahar	488	446	42
Kaikadi	16	5	11
Kanjari	7	6	1
Khavas	10	8	2
Lamani	228	116	112
Mangela	543	298	245
Pangul	1	....	1
Ramoshi	135	99	36
Salat	3	....	3
Sangar	12	1	11
Takari	3	2	1
Vaidu	152	88	64
Vanjari	870	493	377
Total, Depressed	**104,977**	**61,564**	**43,413**
Bhangi or Halalkhor	7,097	4,299	2,798
Chambhar	23,449	13,464	9,985
Dhor	116	30	86
Mahar, Holiya, Dhed or Wankar	67,360	40,072	27,288
Mang or Madig	5,227	2,823	2,404
Mang Garudi	22	14	8
Meghwal	1,706	862	844

The following castes which are either territorial or functional names were returned among Hindus :—

Andhra, Bengali, Cutchi, Dakshini, Gujarati, Hindustani, Karwari, Kathewari, Kanadi, Multani, Marwadi, Madrasi, Malavni, Mahajan, Maheshwari, Mangalori, Nepali, Punjabi, Singh, Tamili, Telangi, Malwi, Sindhi, Deshawari, Dravidi, Desai, Patel, Baxi, Gadhwal, Upadhya, Tandel, Mistri, Kokni.

The population of these is :—

Persons.	Males.	Females.
48,547	31,055	17,492

Caste, tribe or race.	MUSLIM.								
	Total strength.			Shia.		Suni.		Sect unspecified.	
	Persons.	Males.	Females.	Males.	Females.	Males.	Females.	Males.	Females.
Arab	839	638	201	44	27	302	78	292	96
Baloch	78	75	3	6	..	58	1	11	2
Bohra	16,069	10,492	5,577	7,022	3,338	534	201	2,936	1,948
Bhangi	181	140	41	132	33	3	5	5	3
Hajam	235	193	42	1	4	148	30	44	8
Kasai or Khatik	768	426	342	1	..	221	222	204	120
Khatri	1,573	917	656	..	..	873	607	44	49
Khoja	12,120	6,693	5,427	3,120	2,598	662	329	2,911	2,500
Lohar	21	15	6	..	..	4	5	11	1
Makrani	13	10	3	6	2	4	1	..	..
Memon	11,397	7,143	4,254	53	5	6,265	3,741	825	508
Momin	18,674	12,436	6,238	23	7	11,762	5,814	651	417
Miana	3	3	..	..	..	3	..	..	..
Momna	95	77	18	..	..	33	17	44	1
Moghal or Mughal	1,165	902	263	335	96	339	83	228	84
Pathan or Afghan	10,067	8,254	1,813	111	9	7,323	1,601	820	203
Pinjari	453	287	166	73	27	119	78	95	61
Sayad	6,489	4,370	2,119	175	79	3,828	1,824	367	216
Sheikh	45,653	32,552	13,101	340	84	29,601	11,855	2,611	1,162
Sindhi Muhana	34	19	15	..	..	19	15	..	..
Sindhi Sumra	4	2	2	..	..	..	..	2	2
Teli	1,123	633	490	..	..	600	462	33	28
Caste etc., unspecified	82,192	57,641	24,551	5,596	2,694	37,905	16,432	14,140	5,425
Total, Population	209,246	143,918	65,328	17,038	9,003	100,606	43,491	26,274	12,834

Religion, caste, sub-caste, tribe or race.	Persons.	Males.	Females.
Total Jains	12,424	8,998	3,426
(a) Jain Digambar	213	146	67
(i) Mod	9	9	....
(ii) Madiwal or Oswal	11	5	6
(iii) Sorathia	9	7	2
(iv) Other castes and caste unspecified	184	125	59
(b) Jain Swetambar	653	537	116
(i) Madiwal or Oswal	72	46	26
(ii) Other castes and caste unspecified	581	491	90
(c) Sects unspecified	11,558	8,315	3,243
(i) Agarwal	7	6	1
(ii) Dehwal	16	15	1
(iii) Ladwani	3	3	....
(iv) Lohana	2	2	....
(v) Madiwal or Oswal	1,166	991	175
(vi) Porwal or Porwad	70	66	4
(vii) Sewak	36	36	....
(viii) Shetwal	18	15	3
(ix) Shri-mali Vani	2	2	....
(x) Caste unspecified	10,238	7,179	3,059

Religion, caste, sub-caste, tribe or race.	Persons.	Males.	Females.
Total Christians	**80,728**	**51,466**	**29,262**
I. Indian Christians	**64,280**	**41,490**	**22,790**
(*a*) Indian Christians	28,193	16,615	11,578
(*b*) Goanese, including Portuguese born in India	36,087	24,875	11,212
II. Europeans and Allied Races	**9,409**	**6,071**	**3,338**
(a) British Subjects	**8,400**	**5,394**	**3,006**
(i) English and British	7,345	4,630	2,715
(ii) Scotch	606	455	151
(iii) Welsh	90	67	28
(iv) Irish	278	181	97
(v) Australasian	48	34	14
(vi) Canadian	15	12	3
(vii) Newzealanders	5	5	....
(viii) South Africans	13	10	3
(b) Other Allied Races	**1,009**	**677**	**332**
(i) Belgian	99	45	54
(ii) Dutch	4	4	....
(iii) French	125	51	74
(iv) Greek	37	28	9
(v) Italian	130	111	19
(vi) Portuguese (born in Europe)	89	60	29
(vii) German	146	117	29
(viii) Russian	20	2	18
(ix) Spanish	37	34	3
(x) Swiss	50	29	21
(xi) Other Europeans and unspecified	80	53	27
(xii) Chinese	14	11	3
(xiii) Japanese	4	1	3
(xiv) Persians	2	2	....
(xv) Africans	19	9	10
(xvi) *United States of America*	30	30	....
(xvii) Americans and unspecified	112	82	30
(xviii) Armenians	11	8	3
III. Anglo-Indians	**7,039**	**3,905**	**3,134**

18. INFIRMITIES.

The statement (No. 47) below shows the actual number of recorded Census infirmities in Bombay City for the last three Censuses. The accuracy and the value of Census statistics of infirmities have been fully discussed in the Bombay Presidency Census Report for 1931. Students are advised to study chapter VII of that report before attempting to drawn conclusions from the crude Census figures. These figures as they stand show a rise in insanity and deaf-mutism since 1921 and a fall in blindness and leprosy. It is unlikely that the Bombay City figures can be very accurate. Nor can it be stated with any assurance that the accuracy of the statistics is growing. The Census figures for infirmities do continue to show certain similarities from Census to Census and this means that the figures recorded are probably in some kind of constant correlation with the truth. They have therefore considerable statistical value, which will rise as the reporting of these infirmities becomes better than it is to-day. It is however unsafe to generalise from the crude Census figures.

STATEMENT No. 47.

Category.	Number.								
	1931			1921			1911		
	Males.	Females.	Total.	Males.	Females.	Total.	Males.	Females.	Total.
1	2	3	4	5	6	7	8	9	10
Insane	135	77	212	52	27	79	152	73	225
Deaf-Mute	195	69	264	37	10	47	130	30	180
Blind	385	196	581	484	212	696	324	129	453
Leper	213	110	323	506	217	723	352	154	506

The following statement (No. 48) compares the incidence of the four Census infirmities in Bombay City with the incidence in Bombay Presidency for the last two Censuses.

STATEMENT No. 48.

Infirmity.	Number per ten thousand.			
	1921		1931	
	Bombay City.	Presidency,	Bombay City.	Presidency.
1	2	3	4	5
Insanity	0·7	4·2	1·7	4·8
Deaf-Mutism	0·4	5·3	2·3	7·8
Blindness	5·9	17·0	5·0	17·9
Leprosy	6·1	3·9	2·8	4·1

It will be noted that the City figures and the Presidency figures follow the same general lines. The fall in the incidence of leprosy in the city at this Census is the only exception and the reason why leprosy has fallen is not clear. Leprosy is notoriously one of the infirmities which the public hesitates to reveal and the number of lepers in Bombay is believed to be about 800, so that about 600 lepers have concealed their infirmity. Blindness, on the other hand, is not concealed to anything like the same extent. Many of the persons suffering from Census infirmities must belong to the beggar and vagrant class amongst whom enumeration is always very difficult. The incidence of blindness in Bombay City is much lower than in the Presidency. This is probably correct as conditions in many parts of the Presidency are much more inimical to the preservation of eye-sight than in Bombay. Deaf-mutism is an infirmity which, as shown in the Presidency report for 1931, shows peculiarities of local incidence, and Bombay City appears not to be one of these areas of high incidence. As regards insanity, the Bombay City figures are almost certainly far too low. This Census has recorded a rise in the incidence of insanity from 0·7 to 1·7 per 10,000 of the population. This may be due to better recording and to less concealment by the public. On the other hand, as Mr. Sedgwick pointed out in 1921, insanes would find city conditions unfavourable to them. There is not however sufficient evidence to warrant any dogmatic conclusions.

19. OCCUPATION.

In the 1931 Census only occupations returned in columns 9, 10 and 11 of the General Schedule have been tabulated. There was no separate industrial Census as in 1921. Column 12 of the General Schedule was however intended to supply information in respect of organised industries. This column was so badly filled up in the Bombay City enumeration books that no satisfactory statistics regarding industries could be compiled from it. The compilation of information from column 12 was, however, abandoned as a measure of economy. In the 1931 Census also the tabulation of the numbers of persons dependent for maintenance on each occupation was dispensed with. There have been no statements prepared in consequence showing, as in 1921, the numbers of non-working dependents. The absence of this information for each industry makes comparison with previous Censuses very difficult. The number of non-working dependents has however been compiled for the whole city in City Table VII, Part I, and for each religion in City Table VII, Part II, printed separately in volume IX, Part II, of the 1931 Census. The system adopted in the 1931 Census is to classify workers into two main classes, namely, principal earners and working dependents. In addition information has been compiled in respect of persons engaged in occupations subsidiary to their main occupations. For all practical purposes a " working dependent " is treated as a " worker ". The great difference in this Census classification of workers must be borne constantly in mind in making comparison between the 1931 Census results and those of previous Censuses. The point has been fully discussed in the Bombay Presidency report for 1931 and it is unnecessary to explain the position further here. As regards the returns for subsidiary occupation in Bombay City, it has to be pointed out that the returns are most unsatisfactory. Only 84 persons have been returned for the whole city as having subsidiary occupation. While it is true that a specialised modern city with organised industry must show less subsidiary occupation than is shown in occupational arrangements prevailing in the mofussil or in small towns and villages following a village or cottage system of industry, it is fantastic to think that there are in Bombay City only 84 persons with subsidiary occupations. The tables relating to subsidiary occupations in Bombay City must therefore be dismissed as worthless.

The statement (No. 49) below shows the occupational distribution of the Bombay City population between principal earners, working dependents and non-working dependents. This shows that one out of every two persons in the city is a "worker". Of the male population 693 persons out of every 1,000 are principal earners. Of the female population 128 out of every 1,000 are principal earners 868 females out of every 1,000 are non-working dependents ; and 316 males out of every 1,000 are in that category.

STATEMENT No. 49.

Category.	Persons.	Percentage to the total population.	Males.	Percentage to the population.	Females.	Percentage to the population.
1	2	3	4	5	6	7
Principal earners	563,042	48·5	510,120	68·3	52,922	12·8
Working dependents ..	2,861	0·2	1,096	0·1	1,765	0·4
Non-working dependents ..	595,480	51·3	236,165	31·6	359,315	86·8
Total ..	1,161,383	....	747,381	....	414,002	....

Bombay City can be characterised fairly as a city of workers ; and the occupational statistics fully corroborate in this respect the statistics of age and sex previously commented upon. A very large section of the population is actively employed in earning a living and the numbers of children and old people are correspondingly small. Of the principal earners shown in the statement above 2,541 males and 595 females returned themselves as earners but refused to specify their occupation. The figures for the 1911 and the 1921 Censuses, so far as they are capable of comparison, are given below in statement (No. 50).

STATEMENT No. 50.

Sex.	Actual workers.	
	1911	1921
1	2	3
Males	514,665	611,627
Females	81,445	105,672
	Dependents.	
	1911	1921
Both Sexes	383,325	458,945

The marginal statement shows the percentage to the total population of actual workers, male and female, for four Censuses. This statement would seem to show that the proportion of workers is falling, a fact which is not in consonance with conclusions available from other statistics. The fall must be only apparent. The reason for the apparent decline in the proportion of workers as compared with non-workers must lie in some of the following influences :—(*a*) perfunctory enumeration due to civil disobedience ; (*b*) differences in the Census classification of "principal earners" and "working dependents," and confusion at the time of enumeration as regards the meaning to be attached to the terms "working dependents" and "non-working dependents ;" (*c*) a fall in the number of immigrants from the districts of Kolaba, Nasik, Ahmednagar, Poona, Sholapur and Satara and from Cutch, Kathiawar, Kolhapur, Hyderabad and Rajputana, a fall which was not made up by a corresponding increase in the number of immigrants from Surat district, the United Provinces, Madras Presidency and from Portuguese India ; (*d*) the increased number of persons who have been enumerated in the lowest age-groups, due to the general increase of population typical of the Presidency as a whole. From the statement (No. 51) below a comparison is possible between workers and persons of working age for the last two Censuses.

Actual workers.	1931	1921	1911	1901
Males ..	44	53	52	48
Females ..	4·7	8	9	9
Dependents ..	51·3	39	39	43

STATEMENT No. 51.

Age-group.	1921			1931		
	Persons.	Males.	Females.	Persons.	Males.	Females.
1	2	3	4	5	6	7
0—15	248,047	136,826	11,220	283,290	158,071	125,219
15—20	110,281	69,822	40,459	115,323	67,890	47,433
20—40	617,031	431,894	185,137	596,546	412,647	183,899
40—50	121,114	84,966	36,148	107,602	75,708	31,894
50—55	38,708	24,171	14,537	26,227	15,953	10,274
55 and over	40,733	23,652	17,081	32,099	16,856	15,243
Unspecified	....	....	....	296	256	40
	1,175,914	771,332	404,582	1,161,383	747,381	414,002

The number of male workers in 1921 was 611,627, which was nearly equal to the total male population of the age-groups from 15 to 55. At the present Census the total male population in the same age-groups is 572,198. If allowance is made for the school-boy and student population, the number of male workers recorded in the 1931 Census seems to be not unreasonable. It may be fairly held that the whole male working-age population in Bombay City at present is actually employed in earning a living. This conclusion is corroborated in many ways by the Census statistics, as a careful study of the age statistics will prove.

The statement (No. 52), which follows, shows the distribution of workers in the classes and sub-classes of occupations according to the scheme followed in the

Census of 1931 and makes a comparison between the 1931 figures and the 1921 figures. At this Census detailed information in respect of beggars and prostitutes has not been compiled.

STATEMENT No. 52.

Class and Sub-Class.	1931		1921	
	Males.	Females.	Males.	Females.
1	2	3	4	5
Total	**511,216**	**54,887**	**611,297**	**105,672**
Class A—Production of Raw Materials	***10,580***	***1,841***	***6,961***	***2,025***
Sub-Class I—Exploitation of Animals and Vegetation	9,619	1,225	6,653	1,787
Sub-Class II—Exploitation of Minerals	961	116	308	238
Class B—Preparation and supply of material substances	**284,145**	**29,756**	**355,526**	**54,536**
Sub-Class III—Industry	154,466	21,867	188,619	42,348
Sub-Class IV—Transport	50,148	580	64,686	2,673
Sub-Class V—Trade	79,531	7,309	102,161	9,515
Class C—Public Administration and Liberal Arts	**57,236**	**4,079**	**31,680**	**4,485**
Sub-Class VI—Public Force	8,872	170	9,376	54
Sub-Class VII—Public Administration	30,834	1,452	8,141	2,232
Sub-Class VIII—Professions and Liberal Arts	17,530	2,457	14,163	2,199
Class D—Miscellaneous	**156,734**	**18,916**	**217,130**	**44,[illegible]**
Sub-Class IX—Persons living on their income	1,666	189	3,194	[illegible]86
Sub-Class X—Domestic service	34,117	6,180	33.695	8,860
Sub-Class XI—Insufficiently described occupations	115,814	10,186	175,173	30,297
Sub-Class XII—Unproductive	5,137	2,361	5,068	4,483
Occupation not returned	**2,521**	**595**	..	..

It will be noted that in 1931 almost all classes show a decline in numbers. This must be partly attributed to the change in Census classification. The class showing the greatest increase is Public Administration and the Liberal Arts in which male workers have increased from 31,680 to 57,236 though the female workers show a decrease. To this increase the chief contributors are Public Administration, which shows 30,834 male workers in 1931, as compared with only 8,141 in 1921; and Professions and Liberal Arts, which show 17,530 male workers in 1931, as compared with 14,163 in 1921. In Industry there has been a heavy, decline in numbers employed at this Census. The number of male workers is 154,466 and of female workers 21,867 in 1931, as compared with 188,679 and 42,348 respectively in 1921. The number of female workers in all clases and sub-classes together shows a decline of over 50 per cent. this Census. Difference in Census classification must be chiefly responsible for this result. The figures however must also be taken as reflecting to some extent the effect of the trade and business slump in the occupational incidence of the population. In the statement (No. 53) which follows the numbers of workers in the principal occupations are compared for 1921 and 1931. It is unnecessary to deal in detail with each order of occupation in the manner followed in the 1921 Report. There is little doubt that occupationally the distribution of the population in 1931 follows generally the distribution of 1921 and the declines in numbers are due to bad trade conditions.

There are no conspicuous examples of new types of occupation arising and creating new sources of employment.

STATEMENT No. 53.

Group, Order, Sub-Class, Class.	1931 workers.		1921 workers.	
	Males.	Females.	Males.	Females.
1	2	3	4	5
Sub-Class I—Exploitation of Animals and Vegetation	**9,619**	**1,325**	**6,653**	**1,787**
Order 1 (a)—Cultivation	2,308	423	2,831	1,210
Order 1 (b)—Cultivation of special crops, fruit, etc. (planters, managers, clerks and labourers)	2,015	103	1,842	265
Order 1 (c)—Group 18—Wood-cutters and charcoal burners	218	..	308	5
Order 1 (d)—Group 21—Cattle and buffalo breeders and keepers	3,103	53	112	3
Order 2—Group 27—Fishing, hunting and pearling	1,829	622	1,450	803
Sub-Class II—Exploitation of Minerals	**961**	**116**	**308**	**238**
Sub-Class III—Industry	**154,466**	**21,867**	**188,679**	**42,348**
Order 5—Textiles	99,709	16,825	102,516	31,472
Order 6—Hides, skins, and hard materials from the animal kingdom	1,266	88	2,875	187
Order 7—Wood	6,172	246	20,395	989
Order 8—Metals	3,125	88	10,530	277
Group 57—Smelting, forging and rolling of iron and other metals	74	2	2,583	43
Group 58—Makers of arms, guns, etc.	64	1	24	..
Group 59—Blacksmiths, other workers in iron, makers of implements	1,365	44	5,208	77
Group 60—Workers in brass, copper and bell metal	279	3	833	94
Group 61—Workers in other metals (except precious metals)	1,293	37	1,738	62
Order 10—Chemical products properly so-called and analogous	399	40	687	110
Order 11—Food industries	2,900	209	3,871	3,291
Group 73—Butchers	963	14	657	11
Group 75—Sweetmeat and condiment makers	528	5	294	4
Group 76—Toddy drawers	404	16	746	5
Order 12—Industries of dress and the toilet	22,730	2,049	24,440	2,363
Order 13—Furniture industries	1,177	2	282	5
Order 14—Building industries	3,387	35	7,916	881
Order 15—Construction of means of transport	643	128	341	13
Order 16—Production and transmission of physical force. (Heat, light, electricity, motive power, etc.)	1,184	21	980	21
Order 17—Miscellaneous and undefined industries	11,249	2,045	12,666	2,424
Group 95—Printers, engravers, bookbinders, etc.	2,096	75	3,237	123
Group 98—Makers of jewellery and ornaments	2,288	28	4,889	72
Group 100—Scavenging	4,475	1,529	4,060	2,172
Sub-Class IV—Transport	**50,148**	**580**	**64,686**	**2,673**
Order 18—Transport by air	39	6	11	..
Order 19—Transport by water	20,773	223	30,006	1,042
Groups 103, 104—Persons employed in harbours and docks, rivers, etc., including pilots and labourers	6,607	190	10,709	986
Group 102—Ship-owners, boat-owners and their employees, officers, mariners, etc., ships' brokers, boatmen and towmen	14,166	33	17,753	41
Order 20—Transport by road	14,808	174	13,134	278
Order 21—Transport by rail	13,106	148	18,384	1,207
Order 22—Post office, telegraph and telephone services	1,337	29	3,151	146
Sub-Class V—Trade	**79,531**	**7,309**	**102,161**	**9,515**
Order 23—Banks, establishments of credit, exchange and insurance	3,618	54	5,518	251
Order 24—Brokerage, commission and export	4,820	379	9,427	97
Order 25—Trade in textiles	963	20	4,758	163
Order 26—Trade in skins, leather and furs	81	10	559	12
Order 27—Trade in wood	309	37	723	37
Order 28—Trade in metals	375	10	1,759	31
Order 30—Trade in chemical products	586	43	441	5
Order 31—Hotels, cafes, restaurants, etc.	9,408	776	9,094	1,043
Order 32—Other trade in food stuffs	9,202	2,653	24,607	4,740
Order 33—Trade in clothing and toilet articles	1,782	365	4,978	167
Order 34—Trade in furniture	359	14	706	30
Order 35—Trade in building materials	12	..	295	18
Order 36—Trade in means of transport	362	22	217	16
Order 37—Trade in fuel	487	53	1,655	399
Order 38—Trade in articles of luxury and those pertaining to letters and the arts and the sciences	841	129	3,146	107
Order 39—Trade of other sorts	45,556	2,782	34,103	2,854

STATEMENT No. 53—*contd.*

Group, Order, Sub-Class, Class.	1931 workers.		1921 workers.	
	Males.	Females.	Males.	Females.
1	2	3	4	5
Sub-Class VI—Public Force	**8,872**	**170**	**9,376**	**54**
Order 40—Army	2,018	134	6,130	50
Order 41—Navy	672	2	14	..
Order 42—Air force	14	2	..	..
Order 43—Police	5,267	32	3,226	4
Sub-Class VII— Order 44—Public Administration	**30,834**	**1,452**	**8,141**	**2,232**
Group 159—Service of the State	4,784	270	858	5
Group 161—Municipal and other local (not village) service	27,673	1,175	6,982	1,950
Sub-Class VIII—Professions and Liberal Arts	**17,530**	**2,457**	**14,163**	**2,199**
Order 45—Religion	2,715	85	3,555	241
Order 46—Law	1,715	17	1,072	25
Order 47—Medicine	2,589	1,179	2,490	815
Order 48—Instruction	3,258	679	2,821	777
Order 49—Letters, arts and sciences (other than 44)	7,253	497	4,306	341
Sub-Class IX—Persons living on their income	**1,666**	**189**	**3,194**	**986**
Sub-Class X—Domestic Service	**34,177**	**6,180**	**33,695**	**8,860**
Sub-Class XI—Order 52 —General terms which do not indicate definite occupation	**115,814**	**10,186**	**175,173**	**30,297**
Group 188—Manufacturers, businessmen and contractors otherwise unspecified	6,288	343	2,717	742
Group 189—Cashiers, accountants, book-keepers, clerks and other employees in unspecified offices and warehouses and shops	50,017	2,411	43,271	1,695
Group 190—Mechanics otherwise unspecified	4,941	44	1,062	111
Group 191—Labourers and workmen otherwise unspecified	54,568	7,388	128,123	27,749
Sub-Class XII—Unproductive	**5,137**	**2,361**	**5,068**	**4,483**
Order 53—Inmates of jails, asylums and alms houses	956	4	533	121
Order 54—Beggars, vagrants, prostitutes	3,840	2,335	4,534	4,355
Group 193—Beggars and vagrants	3,826	1,199	4,430	1,360
Group 194—Procurers and prostitutes	14	1,136	104	2,995
Order 55—Group 195—Other unclassified non-productive industries	341	22	1	7

The chief individual sources of employment in Bombay City are explained below and numbered with Roman numerals :—

(I) Textiles, which means cotton textiles manufactured in large scale organised factories, employ 116,534 persons. Of these 99,709 are males and 16,825 are females. There has not been much decrease in the number of male workers. But the figure of female workers shows a heavy decline from 31,472 in 1921 to 16,825 in 1931.

(II) Industries of the dress and toilet employ 22,730 males and 2,049 females, as compared with 24,440 males and 2,363 females in 1921.

(III) Transport by water employs 20,773 males and 223 females, as compared with 30,006 males and 1,042 females in 1921.

(IV) Trade, "other sorts" (which includes the majority of the petty shop-keeping class), employs 45,556 males and 2,732 females as compared with 34,103 males and 2,354 females in 1921.

(V) Municipal and other local service employs 27,673 males and 1,175 females as compared with 6,982 males and 1,950 females in 1921. The explanation of this great increase in the number of municipal and other local service employees from 8,932 to 26,848 appears to be a difference in the method of enumeration. In 1931 daily labourers employed by the Bombay Municipality seem to have been included under this head. In 1921 the number of "labourers and workmen otherwise unspecified" was 155,872. In 1931 the number is 61,956. It is therefore more than probable that the total of "municipal servants" has been swollen by the inclusion in it of "municipal casual labourers."

(VI) Domestic service employs 34,117 males and 6,180 females, as compared with 33,695 males and 8,860 females in 1921.

(VII) Cashiers, book-keepers, clerks and other employees in unspecified offices are 50,017 males and 2,411 females, as compared with 43,271 males and 1,695 females in 1921. This category of employment is in a sense a measure of Census inefficiency of classification. Were it possible to classify this kind of employment more satisfactorily, much of this employment would be relegated to many different orders.

(VIII) Labourers and workmen otherwise unspecified are 54,568 males and 7,388 females as compared with 128,123 males and 27,749 females in 1921. The great decrease in the numbers under this occupational group is accounted for partly by better Census methods of classification. But there is no doubt that there has been a considerable fall in this class of occupation due to the business and trade depression, which the Census figures truly reflect. Labour of this kind includes casual and general labour which it is difficult to classify under any particular occupation. It is in fact allied to the casual labour which figures so largely in the occupational statistics of all big cities. The amount of this in Bombay City throws much light on the standard of living of a considerable section of the population. This type of labour is fluctuating in its nature and encourages the growth of a large supply of temporary workers. It is therefore a source of great instability in the labour conditions of the city. Of matters requiring special mention here the following are the most important :—

(1) *Wood-workers.*—This Census shows a fall in the number of carpenters, turners, joiners and other workers in wood from 20,034 to 5,863. Workers in wood in a city like Bombay are of course affected greatly by trade depression, particularly those who work in connection with the construction of buildings. It is doubtful however if trade depression can account entirely for the heavy fall in the number. Faulty enumeration must have been also a factor.

(2) *Metal-workers.*—The number of these has fallen from 10,807 to 3,213 and there has been a decrease under almost every item. The chief influence here must have been faulty enumeration.

(3) *Letters, Arts and Sciences.*—This class shows a rise from 4,647 in 1921 to 7,750 in 1930. The increase is not unreasonable. It is likely that the number of editors, authors and persons employed in connection with newspapers has grown and that cinema players and dramatic companies are responsible for some increase in the population. Bombay City is a local centre for the production of Indian films.

(4) In most cases otherwise where there is a considerable difference between the 1921 and the 1931 figures and where faulty enumeration is not the cause the reason must be ascribed to the business and trade depression.

Four statements have been prepared to demonstrate clearly (1) the relative importance of each sub-class of occupation in Bombay; (2) the chief items which contribute to the occupation of Industry in the City; (3) the chief items which contribute to the occupation of Trade in the City; and (4) the employments which employ individually more than 10,000 workers each. These four statements together give in brief compass a better idea of the occupational character of Bombay's population than many pages of the ordinary statistics. The statements are numbered below as 54, 55, 56 and 57.

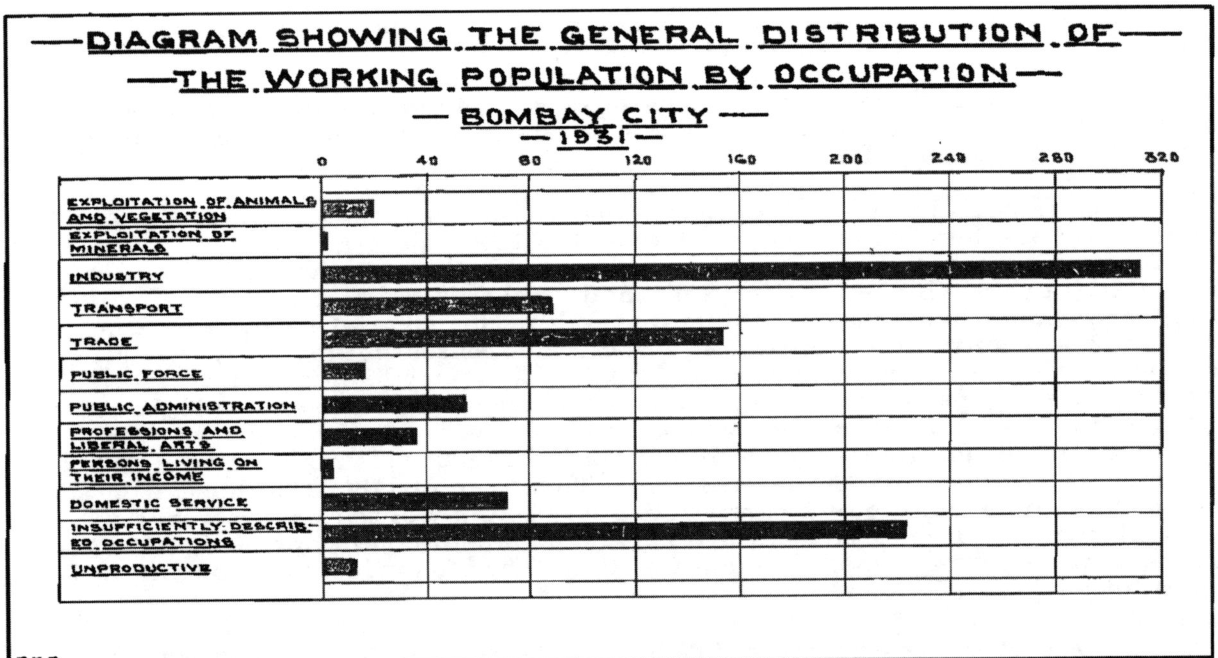

R.K.P. G.P.Z.O. Poona, 1932.

STATEMENT No. 54.

Sub-Class.	Percentage distribution.	Figures in thousands.				
		Total.	Principal earners.		Working dependents.	
			Males.	Females.	Males.	Females.
1	2	3	4	5	6	7
Total	100	563	508	52	1	2
I	2	11	10	1	..	..
II	..	1	1	..	..	..
III	31	176	154	22	..	..
IV	9	51	50	1	..	..
V	16	87	79	6	..	2
VI	2	9	9	..	..	..
VII	6	32	31	1	..	..
VIII	4	20	18	2	..	..
IX	..	2	2	..	..	..
X	7	40	34	6	..	..
XI	22	126	116	10	..	..
XII	1	7	4	2	1	..

The chief sources of occupation are seen to be (1) industry which employs 31 per cent. of the workers, (2) trade which employs 16 per cent., (3) unspecified occupations (which are mostly general undefined labour) which employ 22 per cent., and (4) transport which employs 9 per cent. About one in every three of Bombay's workers is employed in industrial occupation of one kind or another.

STATEMENT No. 55.

Industry.

Occupation.	Percentage to total earners and working *dependents.*	Workers of all kinds in hundreds			Chief contributory items—figures in hundreds.
		Persons.	Males.	Females.	
1	2	3	4	5	6
Textiles	66	1,165	997	168	Cotton ginning, cleaning and pressing (19); cotton spinning, sizing and weaving (1,131).
Hides, skins etc. ..	1	14	13	1	Working in leather (8); furriers and persons occupied with feathers (5).
Wood	4	64	62	2	Carpenters, turners and joiners (59); basket-makers etc. (5).
Metals	2	32	31	1	Blacksmiths (14); workers in other metals (13); workers in brass (3).
Ceramics	....	7	6	1	Potters and makers of earthenware (5): brick and tile-makers (1).
Chemical products ..	....	4	4	....	Other than manufacture of matches, aerated waters, vegetable oils and mineral oils (2).
Food	2	31	29	2	Butchers (10); sweetmeat and condiment-makers (5): toddy drawers (4); tobacco (3).
Dress and the toilet ..	14	248	227	21	Tailors (117); working and clearing (56); barbers (31), boot and shoe makers (37).
Furniture	1	12	12	....	Cabinet makers (10).
Building	2	34	34	....	Lime-burners, cement-workers etc. (34).
Construction of means of transport.	....	8	7	1	Persons engaged on motor vehicles and cycles (6): ship-builders (2).
Production and transmission of physical Force.	1	12	12	....	Heat, light, electricity etc.
Miscellaneous and undefined.	7	133	113	20	Printers, engravers, book-binders etc. (22); makers of jewellery (23); scavenging (60).

It will be seen from the above that textile manufacture is the only important large-scale industry in the city. This employs about two out of every three persons engaged in industry. Most of the other industries are unorganised, individual and cottage industries, though a few factories of one kind or another exist. The second most important contributor to the industrial total is industry connected with dress and the toilet. But this means in general little more than the work of tailors, washers and cleaners, barbers, boot and shoe-makers. It is not industry in any modern large-scale sense. Save for its textile manufacture Bombay has really little claim to be called an industrial city. It is textile manufacture alone that puts it into the industrial class. In this respect it resembles Sholapur where concentration on one form of industry has been carried to an even greater extent than has happened in Bombay.

STATEMENT NO. 56.

Trade.

Occupation.	Percentage to total earners and working dependents.	Workers of all kinds in hundreds			Chief contributory items—figures in hundreds.
		Persons.	Males.	Females.	
1	2	3	4	5	6
Banks, establishments of credit etc.	4·0	37	36	1	Bank managers, money-lenders, exchange and insurance agents, money changers, brokers and their employees (37).
Brokerage, commission and export.	6·0	52	48	4	Group No. 116—Brokers, commission agents, warehouse owners etc. (52).
Trade in textiles ..	1·0	10	10	....	Group No. 117—Trade in piece-goods, wool, cotton, silk, hair and other textiles (10).
Trade in skins, leather and furs.	....	1	1	....	Group No. 118—Trade in skins, leather and furs, feathers, horns etc. (1).
Trade in wood ..	0·3	3	3	....	Group No. 119—Trade in wood (1). Group No. 122—Trade in thatches etc. (1).
Trade in metals ..	0·4	4	4	....	Group No. 123—Trade in metals, machinery, knives, tools etc. (4).
Trade in pottery, bricks and tiles.	....	1	1	....	Group No. 124—Trade in pottery, bricks and tiles (1).
Trade in chemical products.	1·0	6	6	....	Group No. 125—Drugs, dyes, paints, petroleum, explosives etc. (6).
Hotels, cafés and restaurants.	12·0	102	94	8	Group No. 126—Vendors of wine, liquors etc. (7); owners and managers of hotels, cookships, serais etc. (91).
Trade in foodstuffs ..	14·5	126	99	27	Group No. 129—Grain and pulse dealers (8). Group No. 130—Dealers in sweetmeats (19). Group No. 135—Dealers in tobacco (37). Group No. 134—Dealers in foodstuffs (28).
Trade in clothing and toilet articles.	2·0	21	17	4	Group No. 138—Trade in ready-made clothing and other articles of dress and the toilet (21).
Trade in furniture ..	0·4	4	4	....	Group No. 139—Trade in furniture, carpets, curtains and bedding (2).
Trade in building materials.					
Trade in means of transport.	0·4	4	4	....	Group No. 142—Dealers and hirers of mechanical transport, motors, cycles etc. (2). Group No. 143—Dealers in carriages, carts, boats, etc. (2).
Trade in fuel ..	0·5	5	5	....	Group No. 145—Dealers in firewood, charcoal, coal etc. (5).

Occupation.	Percentage to total earners and working dependents.	Workers of all kinds in hundreds			Chief contributory items—figures in hundreds.
		Persons.	Males.	Females.	
1	2	3	4	5	6
Trade in articles of luxury etc.	1·0	10	9	1	Group No. 146—Dealers in precious stones, jewellery etc. (4). Group No. 147—Dealers in common bangles, beads, necklaces etc. (3). Group No. 148—Publishers, book-sellers, stationers etc. (2).
Trade, other sorts ..	55·5	483	456	27	Group No. 150—General store-keepers, shopkeepers otherwise unspecified (389). Group No. 151—Itinerant traders, pedlars and hawkers etc. (76).

The above statement shows the chief items in the trade occupation of the City. It will be noted that trade in foodstuffs, and hotels, cafés, restaurants and eating houses are the most important single items, employing between them about one in four of the total population employed in trade. Trade, "other sorts", is a composite miscellaneous group in which more than half the traders in the city are classified. The chief contributors to the total are general store and shopkeepers not otherwise defined and itinerant traders, pedlars and hawkers, the numbers of whom will probably surprise most readers.

STATEMENT No. 57.

Occupations employing more than 10,000 workers of all kinds.

Group No.	Occupation.	Workers following occupation.	Proportion per mille to total following occupations of all classes.
1	2	3	4
43	Cotton spinning, sizing and weaving	113,085	201
191	Labourers and workmen otherwise unspecified	61,956	110
189	Cashiers, accountants, book-keepers, clerks and other employees in unspecified offices and warehouses and shops	54,428	93
187	Other domestic service	38,893	69
150	General store-keepers, shopkeepers otherwise unspecified	38,851	69
161	Municipal and other local (not village) service	26,848	48
102	Ship-owners, boat-owners, and their employees ; officers, mariners etc., ship-brokers, boatmen and tow-men.	14,254	25
83	Tailors, milliners, dress-makers and darners	11,666	21
112	Railway employees of all kinds, other than coolies	10,152	18

The above statement shows the occupations employing more than 10,000 persons each.

Only group 43 has any claim to be called organized large-scale production by factory methods. Groups 102 and 112 are of course dependent on the organisation by modern methods of great systems of sea and land transport. But Bombay is far from being a city of the type that London is, with a vast variety of organised industry. It is a city which combines the textile specialisation of Manchester (without its imposing array of diverse modern industry) with the commercial and shipping characteristics of Liverpool. The prosperity of Bombay therefore rests upon two foundations (1) the power of its cotton mills to supply the cloth that India wants and to withstand competition from rivals in India and outside it and (2) the maintenance of the import and export trade. The last ten years have shown that in both respects Bombay is more than vulnerable.

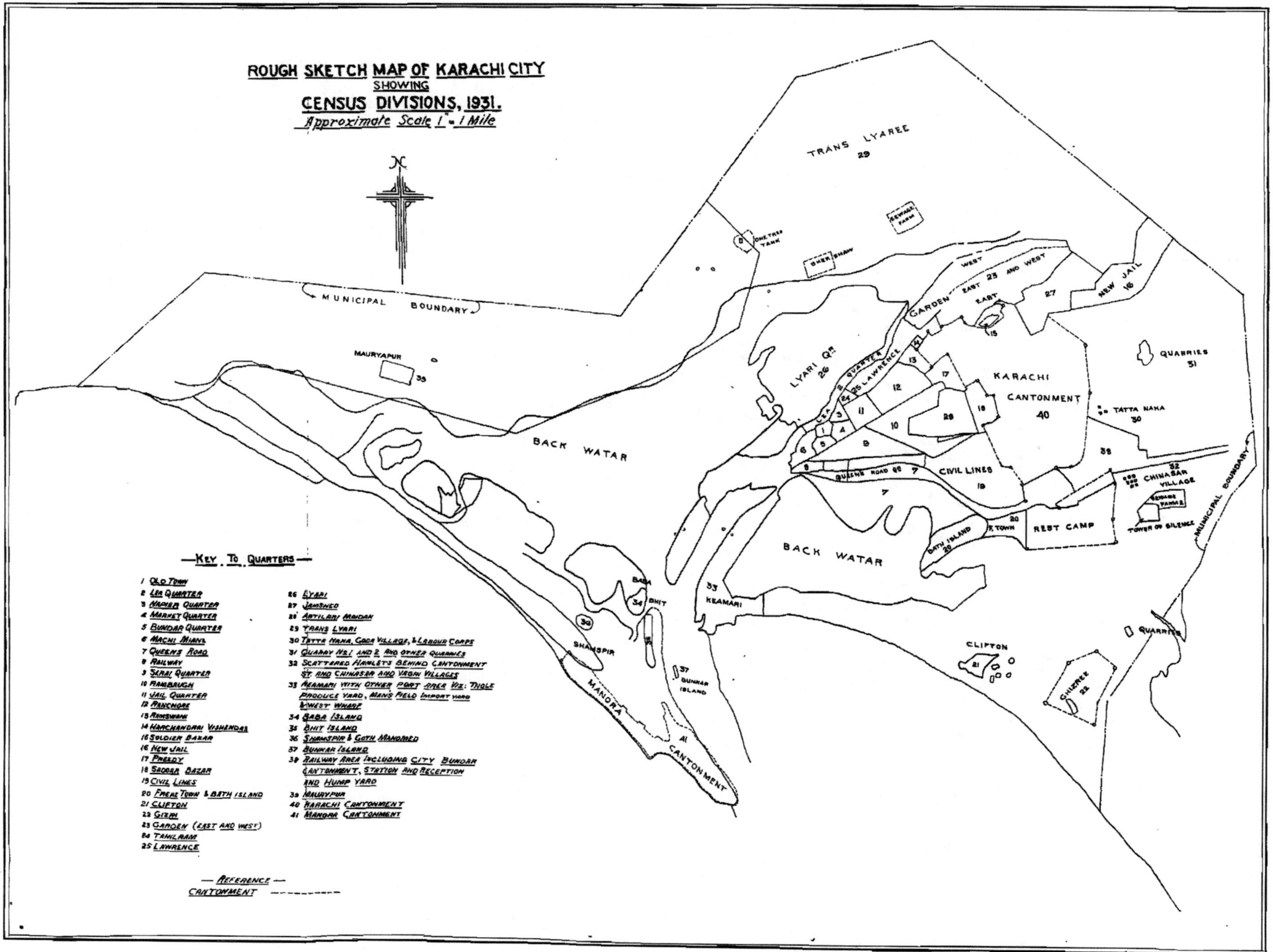

G.P.Z.O. POONA, 1952.

CHAPTER III—KARACHI CITY.

1. Introductory.

This is the second occasion on which any attempt has been made to give special Census statistics for Karachi. In the 1921 Census volume of the Cities of the Bombay Presidency Karachi received special attention for the first time. The lines followed in the present report are largely those laid down by Mr. Sedgwick in 1921. Karachi is a most irregularly shaped city which appears to be continually undergoing changes of area. No adequate map of the entire Census area is available. The map which appears in the present volume may be considered, however, to be reasonably accurate in essentials, though from a cartographical point of view it is little more than a sketch. In Bombay City wards and sections have been permanently fixed. But in Karachi a similar practice does not seem to have been adopted. Very possibly the expanding nature of the city and its form of development may make it troublesome at this stage to fix wards and sections as Bombay has done. From a Census point of view, however, the indeterminateness is unsatisfactory. Karachi is an area where there is much more space for development and much more partially-occupied land immediately surrounding developed areas than is the case with any of the other cities of the Presidency. Mr. Sedgwick said in 1921 " Karachi is a mushroom city, ever expanding over a tract of sand, its edges submerged for extensive distances to different depths at different states of the tide. There is a complicated cantonment boundary in the heart of the municipal area, a second smaller cantonment at Manora, several outlying places like Baba and Bhit, of undefined extent and only partially under municipal control, and numerous distant patches of irregular shape and size, like the municipal quarries." This description has still a good deal of truth though it is hardly true to say any longer that Karachi is a mushroom city. It is now well on the way to permanent settlement as a large and well-laid-out city containing within its limits very extensive areas of sparsely populated land. As Karachi develops it is likely to fill up these sparsely populated areas with an increasing population. But the present character of the city produces differences in the density of population in its various parts which finds no counterpart in any of the other cities of the Presidency. There have been very considerable changes in various sections of the city since 1921 and these changes, which are important for Census purposes, will be commented upon in a later section of this chapter.

2. The Enumeration and its Results.

In the following areas, though within municipal limits, the population was enumerated under the supervision of the officers shown below.

Statement No. 1.

Name of area.	Enumerated by
1	2
The Railway area and platform enumeration ..	By the Divisional Superintendent, N.-W. Railway.
	Chief Engineer, Karachi Port Trust.
Maurypur and boats leaving Maurypur ..	Superintendent of Salt Revenue.
Islands within Municipal area and portions of floating population.	Collector of Customs.
Portion of floating population	Deputy Conservator, Karachi Port Trust.
Portion of floating population	Principal Officer, Mercantile Marine Department.

Note.—The rest of the Municipal area was enumerated by the Municipality.

The enumeration of the population in cantonment areas was carried out by the cantonment authorities. At this Census the arrangements made for Census enumeration were quite satisfactory and showed a great improvement over the arrangements made in 1921. The results which might have been expected to follow from this increase in Census efficiency were however off-set to some extent by the civil disobedience movement, which affected chiefly the quarters named Old Town, Runchore, Ramaswami and portions of the quarters called Jail, Market and Sadar Bazaar. About 1,500 persons evaded enumeration and Census books pertaining to three blocks were lost. (*Vide* the Chief Officer's Report printed as Appendix B to this Volume.)

The statement below shows the result of the Census of the Karachi Municipal area and of Karachi City as a whole in 1931 and at five previous Censuses.

STATEMENT No. 2.

Year.	Karachi City.	Per cent. rise.	Karachi Municipal area.	Per cent. rise.
1	2	3	4	5
1931	265,565	22·4	247,791	22·4
1921	216,883	42·8	201,691	43·5
1911	151,903	30·2	140,511	38·5
1901	116,683	10·9	108,641	10·6
1891	105,199	43·0	98,195	45·0
1881	73,560	..	68,332	..

The rise in population from 1881 to 1931 has been 261 per cent. for the Municipal area and 262·6 per cent. for Karachi City as a whole. These are very remarkable figures and the increase in the size of Karachi in fifty years must be characterised as one of the most striking features of the Census history of the Bombay Presidency. In the Municipal area's population in 1931, 54 persons from extra-municipal limits have been included. But the enumeration has been allowed to stand as the difference is trivial.

3. UNITS FOR WHICH THE FIGURES ARE PRESENTED.

Much of what Mr. Sedgwick said in 1921 on this subject is still true. Those interested are referred to section 2 on page 69 of the Census of India, Volume IX, Part I, 1921. At this Census however an attempt has been made to ascertain and record the area of the various quarters of the city. Changes which have occurred in quarters since the 1921 Census are shown in the remarks which follow.

> "'Lea' is a new quarter altogether and comprises a portion of Lyari, Riverbed and developed since the last Census. Queen's Road East and West—two separate quarters at the last Census stood this time divided into three quarters—(1) Queen's Road, (2) Railway and (3) Railway area including City Bunder, Cantonment Stations, Reception and Pump Yard and Platform population. Bunker Island is altogether a new quarter. Harachandrai Vishandas is a new quarter coming into existence out of the area of the Police lines transferred to the Municipality. The quarters Frere Town, Bath Island, Clifton and Ghizri are parts of Old Frere Town. Jamshed is a name given to a quarter newly formed of the area transferred to the Municipality from Cantonment, so also is the Artillery Maidan. Trans-Lyari is a portion of the area of the quarter 'Scattered Hamlets' which has since developed into a new quarter; so also are Tatta Naka, Goda Village and 'Labour Corps'. The quarter known as 'Bigarikhata' has disappeared this time altogether."

In the Karachi City Table I in the 1921 Census the area of Karachi was shown as 6,434·69 acres. The area now shown is 25,150·07 acres. In 1921 no area was shown for Maurypur and Shamspir. At this Census the area of these has been furnished and there has been a further increase in area caused by development.

4. BIRTHPLACE.

The Karachi City population shows a marked degree of cosmopolitanism but it differs very considerably in this respect from Bombay. In Bombay a minority of the population is home-born. In Karachi the majority of the population is home-born. This makes it in character a city of a different kind from Bombay. Bombay is essentially a place populated by strangers who remain for the working period of their lives there and then return to their native places. Karachi is a city built up round a solid core of home-born and Sind-born population who make their permanent home in the City. Karachi, unlike Bombay, cannot be described as an industrial city and the main stimulus to the immigration of strangers from distant parts is absent. Karachi is essentially a trading town with an important entrepot trade. Towns of such a type tend to show characteristics differing considerably from those of towns of the accentuated industrial type. The large cosmopolitan population of Karachi is concerned mostly in business connected with the receipt and forwarding of goods and with the handling of merchandise at docks and emporia. There are thus two main types of Karachi's cosmopolitan immigrants ; the first is concerned with the administrative side of trade and the second consists of a general labouring class, differing in essentials very little from general labouring classes in other large cities. All cities offer many opportunities for general and casual labour and Karachi is no exception. A trading town also tends to attract dealers and merchants from many different localities. It will thus be apparent that, despite its cosmopolitanism, Karachi is not to be compared in this respect with Bombay. While the great development which Karachi has witnessed in the last half century is to be ascribed to the expansion of trade, and largely export trade, the home-born population has taken its fair share of this and has not been swamped, as in Bombay it has been, by an immigrant population coming from many parts of India in great numbers. Karachi in fact at present occupies a position midway between a city of the Bombay type and a town of the kind that Poona (City Municipality) is to-day. It is not likely to change to the Bombay type unless it develops organised large-scale industry requiring the immediate influx of able-bodied workers from areas that are able to supply them.

The statement No. 3, which follows, shows the composition of the population of Karachi City according to the Census returns of birthplace.

STATEMENT NO. 3.

Region of Birth.	Proportion per 1,000 of the whole population.	Number of females per 1,000 males in the persons born in each region.
1	2	3
Karachi district	480	753
All other Sind districts	145	637
Punjab and Delhi	84	621
United Provinces	43	662
Central Division	33	679
Northern Division	28	718
Ratnagiri	13	491
N.-W. F. Province	8	346
Bengal	5	464
Western India States Agency	3	928
Europe	3	858
Baluchistan	1	824
French and Portuguese Settlements in India	1	83
Rajputana	..	667
Other Asiatic Countries	..	1,178
Elsewhere	153	626

It will be noted how high a proportion of the Karachi population is supplied by Karachi district and by Sind generally. The ratio of females to males in the Karachi population differs remarkably from the Bombay City ratio and tends to confirm the view that much of the migration to Karachi is of the permanent type, which is what one would expect when the essentially non-industrial character of the city is borne in mind. In Karachi City nearly 60 per cent. of the population is "home-born," meaning by that Sind-born and only 40 per cent. of the population comes from outside Sind. The 1931 Census figures offer marked contrast with the 1921 Census figures. There is little doubt that the 1931 Census enumeration has been better and more efficient than the 1921 figures and that it provides a much truer picture of the composition of Karachi's population. In 1921 there must have been much inefficient enumeration and wilful omission in returning correct places of birth.

5. RELIGION.

The religious composition of Karachi follows the conditions prevalent in the Sind towns and is markedly different from those prevailing in the small villages and hamlets. In the Sind towns the Hindu population is usually at least equal to the Muslim, whereas in the villages the Muslims usually outnumber the Hindus by three to one. In Sind the Hindu is essentially a town-dweller and the Muslim primarily an agriculturist living outside towns in hamlets, "tandas", and the fields. This point has been made very clear in the Bombay Presidency Census Report, 1931, to which those interested in the subject may be referred. In Karachi the Hindu and Muslim populations are nearly evenly balanced though this Census the balance has shifted slightly in favour of Muslims, a result that may however have been contributed to by civil disobedience amongst sections of the Hindu population of Karachi. The statement (No. 4) below shows the religious composition of Karachi's population at the last two Censuses :—

STATEMENT NO. 4.

Religion.	Number per 1,000 of the whole population of the City.	
	1931	1921
Hindu	457	464
Muslim	466	463
Jain	3	5
Zoroastrian	13	13
Christian	49	44
Sikh	8	7
Jew	3	3
Other Religions	1	1

This statement shows an improvement in the Muslim and Christian ratios and a fall in the Hindu ratio. None of the other religions are numerically of sufficient importance to warrant remarks on the changes in ratio. Mr. Sedgwick remarked in 1921 : "The regional distribution of religions within the city is very irregular. The outlying portions are predominantly Muslim, the inner (Old Town) region predominantly Hindu and the Cantonment and Sadar Bazaar region cosmopolitan." This is still true ; but Karachi is lucky in not exhibiting in so acute a form the localisation of religion which prevails in Bombay in respect of Hindus and Muslims, a condition of things that has been commented upon in this report with reference to the risk of disturbances to law and order. In the statement

(No. 5) given below the religious composition of quarters and other Census units is shown for the 1931 Census.

STATEMENT No. 5.

Quarter or other Census Units.	Total population for reference.	Number per 1,000 who are		
		Hindu.	Muslim.	Other Religions.
1	2	3	4	5
Old Town	8,830	930	68	2
Lea	934	928	43	29
Napier	10,103	710	285	5
Market	6,745	807	188	5
Bunder	3,353	882	108	10
Queen's Road	153	641	111	248
Railway	358	662	263	75
Serai	13,087	795	180	25
Rambaugh	11,883	774	171	55
Jail	7,708	751	217	32
Runchore	24,924	726	226	48
Ramswami	7,038	780	122	98
Preedy	1,798	374	157	469
Civil Lines	4,432	539	219	242
Frere Town and Bath Island	2,256	518	187	295
Clifton	422	555	372	73
Lawrence	10,277	600	351	49
Jamshed	2,170	792	48	160
Artillery Maidan	554	412	213	375
Bunker Island	4	750	250	....
Drigh Road	22	682	318	....
Karachi Cantonment	6,240	362	160	478
Manora	2,018	552	348	100

6. AGE, SEX AND CIVIL CONDITION.

The age distribution of Karachi is distinctly of the City type but it is not in this respect so abnormal as the age distribution of Bombay. The reason why this should be so has been explained above in section 4. The ratio of males in the active working periods is not so high as in Bombay, and the ratio of females is higher than in Bombay. This is in consonance with the view that more of the inhabitants of Karachi are permanently resident in it. The real city character of the age and sex distribution is however apparent from the low female ratios in the 25 to 45 years age-groups. A point of interest is that the female ratio is higher than the male for the four lowest age-groups. This was so in 1921 for the three lowest age-groups. But whereas the female ratio in 1921 for the 10 to 15 years age-group was 97 per mille, it has risen to 107 in 1931. It is difficult to form conclusions from the improvement in the female ratio in the four lowest age-groups. In the absence of vital statistics it would be unsafe to conclude that there has been a definite improvement in female mortality up to the age of 20. It may be so, but the Census figures require checking against the vital statistics, which cannot be done in the present report. As far as the 1931 Census figures go, they would seem to suggest an improvement in both male and female ratios up to the age of 20 years.

STATEMENT No. 6.

Age-period	Number per 1,000. Persons.	Males.	Females.	Number of females per 100 males.
1	2	3	4	5
0—5	139	117	169	121
5—10	114	104	127	86
10—15	100	96	107	79
15—20	101	99	103	73
20—25	117	119	114	68
25—30	108	118	94	56
30—35	95	108	78	51
35—40	69	78	57	51
40—45	53	59	45	55
45—50	36	37	33	63
50—55	26	27	26	69
55—60	16	15	17	84
60—65	13	12	14	67
65—70	5	4	5	86
70 and over	8	7	11	113
Total (whole population)	..	..	..	71

As remarked in the 1921 Census report Karachi marries late. This is due partly to early marriage in Sind not being so common as it is in the rest of the Presidency and partly to the effect of city life, with its keen struggle to raise the standard of living among city workers, in postponing marriage till a satisfactory economic condition has been reached. The statement (No. 7) below shows the position in respect of early marriage in Karachi in 1931. The corresponding figures for Poona Municipality are added for comparison.

STATEMENT No. 7.

Total number of females.	Age-group.	Population.	Married or widowed.		Percentage of column 4 to column 3.
1	2	3	4		5
102,739	0—5	17,348	Married	30	0·17
			Widowed	9	0·05
	5—10	13,032	Married	640	4·9
			Widowed	16	0·12
	10—15	11,005	Married	2,045	18·6
			Widowed	44	0·39
			Poona Municipality.		
76,117	0—5	10,534	Married	87	0·8
			Widowed	8	0·08
	5—10	8,535	Married	850	10·0
			Widowed	28	0·3
	10—15	8,025	Married	2,072	25·8
			Widowed	55	0·7

The following statement (No. 8) shows in thousands the numbers of persons unmarried, married and widowed in Karachi for the various age-groups.

STATEMENT No. 8.

Age-group. 1	Unmarried. 2	Married. 3	Widowed. 4
All Ages	113	115	19
0—5	34	..	..
5—10	27	1	..
10—15	22	3	..
15—20	12	12	1
20—25	9	19	1
25—30	4	22	1
30—35	2	20	2
35—40	1	14	2
40—45	1	10	2
45—50	..	6	2
50 and over	1	9	8

7. LITERACY.

Literacy in Karachi as revealed by the 1931 Census is shown in the following statement (No. 9).

STATEMENT No. 9.

Unit and community.	Number per mille who are			
	Literate.		Literate in English.	
	Males.	Females.	Males.	Females.
1	2	3	4	5
Whole city	287	115	137	35
Hindu	365	137	159	19
Muslim	146	32	49	4
Christian	671	599	591	448

Literacy in a trading city like Karachi would be expected to be high. It would be much higher than it is if the Muslim population did not form so large a proportion of the city's population. Education amongst Muslims is still very much behind that amongst Hindus. The standard of literacy in English amongst Hindus is high. This is not surprising. Karachi attracts large numbers of the student class. Muslims in Karachi in general are drawn mostly from the labouring, artisan and small-trading class, which so far in Sind shows considerable resistance to education. The standard of literacy amongst females remains regrettably low, except in the case of Christians. The 1931 Census figures show considerable improvement over the 1921 figures as the statement given below shows.

Males only.	1921	1931
Whole city	268	287
Hindu	335	365
Muslim	131	146
Christian	639	671
The comparative figures for English literacy are :—		
Whole city	106	137
Hindu	110	159
Muslim	34	49
Christian	567	591

8. OCCUPATION AND INDUSTRIES.

The distribution of every 1,000 of the population into workers and dependents is as follows :—

Workers.		Dependents (both sexes).
Males	Females	
281	35	684

The difference between Karachi and Bombay in this respect is striking. In Bombay a much larger proportion of the population consists of workers. (See page 46 of the present Report.) Nothing could show more clearly the non-industrial character of Karachi. Comparison with the 1921 figures is not easy on account of the changes in Census classification of workers. The small proportion of female workers in Karachi is noteworthy. This is due largely to the fact that in Sind women do not normally "work" in the Census sense of the word. The large numbers of Muslims of course contribute to this result. But the Hindu population is mostly connected with trade, in which women do not usually work. The Census results are therefore largely what would be expected in the circumstances. But it is interesting comparing Karachi conditions in this respect with conditions in Gujarat, of which statistics are given in the Bombay Presidency Report.

The following statement (No. 10) shows the distribution of every 1,000 workers (principal earners and working dependents) by sub-classes for the last two Censuses :—

STATEMENT NO. 10.

Sub-Class.	Occupation.	1931	1921
I	Exploitation of animals and vegetation	47	54
II	Exploitation of minerals	3	1
III	Industry	189	175
IV	Transport	122	87
V	Trade	172	207
VI	Public Force	67	64
VII	Public Administration	42	46
VIII	Profession and Liberal Arts	68	45
IX	Persons living on their Income	8	6
X	Domestic Service	40	93
XI	Insufficiently Described Occupations	208	200
XII	Unproductive	34	22

It will be noted that the ratio of workers under trade is nearly as high as the ratio of workers under industry. This is in marked contrast to Bombay. The general decline in the ratios shown in the 1931 Census (where these are not due partly to changes in Census classification) may be held to reflect faithfully the decline in business caused by the trade slump. An exporting city like Karachi would naturally be greatly affected by a decline in the volume of business and trade transactions. One result of such a phenomenon is of course to decrease the proportion of workers to non-workers. During a slump there are fewer persons actually earning a living but the same numbers of mouths have to be fed.

The two statements which follow show the main features of Karachi's industry and trade.

STATEMENT No. 11.

Industry.—(*Total following occupation in hundreds*).

Industry	**159**	
Textiles	14	(mostly handloom and small-scale).
Hides, skins, etc.	11	
Wood	23	(of these, 21 carpenters).
Metals	8	(of these, 7 blacksmiths).
Ceramics	1	
Food industries	14	(various small-scale, butchers, sweetmeat makers).
Dress and toilet	31	(of these, 11 tailors, etc., and 13 washers).
Furniture	2	
Building	11	
Production and transmission of physical force	1	
Miscellaneous and undefined industries.	35	(of these, 25 scavengers).

It is obvious from the above that organised industry is of practically no importance in Karachi. In fact in respect of industry Karachi does not differ in essentials from the typical small Indian town.

STATEMENT No. 12.

Trade.

Item.	Number in hundreds.	Chief contributory items (figures in hundreds).
1	2	3
Trade	**148**	
Banking, establishments of credit, exchange and insurance.	21	Group No. 115. Bank managers, money-lenders, exchange and insurance agents, etc. (21).
Brokerage, commission and export	8	Group No. 116. Brokers, commission agents, commercial travellers, etc. (8).
Textiles	1	Group No. 117. Piece-goods, wool, etc. (1).
Skins, leather and furs	6	Group No. 118. Skins, etc. (6).
Pottery, bricks and tiles	5	Group No. 124. Pottery, bricks and tiles (5).
Hotels, cafés and restaurants, etc.	26	Group No. 127. Managers and owners of hotels, cafés, etc. (23).
Foodstuffs	37	Group No. 133. Fodder, etc. (12). Group No. 130. Sweetmeats, sugar, etc. (6). Group No. 135. Tobacco (4).
Clothing and toilet articles	1	Group No. 138. Ready-made clothing, etc., other articles of dress (1).
Furniture	1	Group No. 140. Hardware, porcelain, crockery, etc. (1).
Means of transport	6	Group No. 143. Carriages, carts, etc. (6).
Other sorts	34	Group No. 150. Store-keepers and shop-keepers, etc. (33).

CHAPTER IV—OTHER CITIES.

POONA.

1. Introductory.

Poona as a city has been dealt with in the 1931 Census exactly as in 1921 (*vide* map attached). It is unnecessary to repeat here what Mr. Sedgwick wrote in 1921. Readers who are interested may be referred to the Census of India, 1921, Volume IX, pages 74 and 75. The major unit for Census purposes taken as the City of Poona has been called " Greater Poona ". Greater Poona comprises five distinct areas of jurisdiction, namely Poona City Municipality, Poona Suburban Municipality, Poona Cantonment, Kirkee Cantonment and Poona Suburbs. The map will show the limits of these units. The 1931 Census enumeration of these units was as under :—

Greater Poona.	Population.
1. Poona City Municipality	162,901
2. Poona Suburban Municipality	16,676
3. Poona Cantonment	35,807
4. Kirkee Cantonment	16,302
5. Poona Suburbs	18,501
Total population ..	250,187

The detailed Census of the Poona Suburbs is as follows.

Statement No. 1.

Sub-unit	Population.		
	Persons.	Males.	Females.
1	2	3	4
Parwati	366	215	151
Bhamburda	1,316	766	550
(i) Agricultural College	520	376	144
(ii) Station	195	115	80
(iii) Remainder	601	275	326
Manjri	537	262	275
Vanavdi (Wanowri)	2,045	1,039	1,006
Bopodi (including Kirkee Station)	3,240	1,771	1,469
Ghorpadi (Ghorpuri) including Station	3,873	1,908	1,965
Yeravda	6,530	4,945	1,585
(i) Reformatory	303	248	55
(ii) Mental Hospital	1,611	904	707
(iii) Central Prison	4,047	3,495	552
(iv) Remainder	509	298	271
Yerandavana	279	161	118
Aundh (Government House only)	315	161	154
Total suburbs	18,501	11,228	7,273

Poona Taluka includes the abovementioned units, Aundh (excluding Government House) and Mundhwa village. The population on running trains enumerated

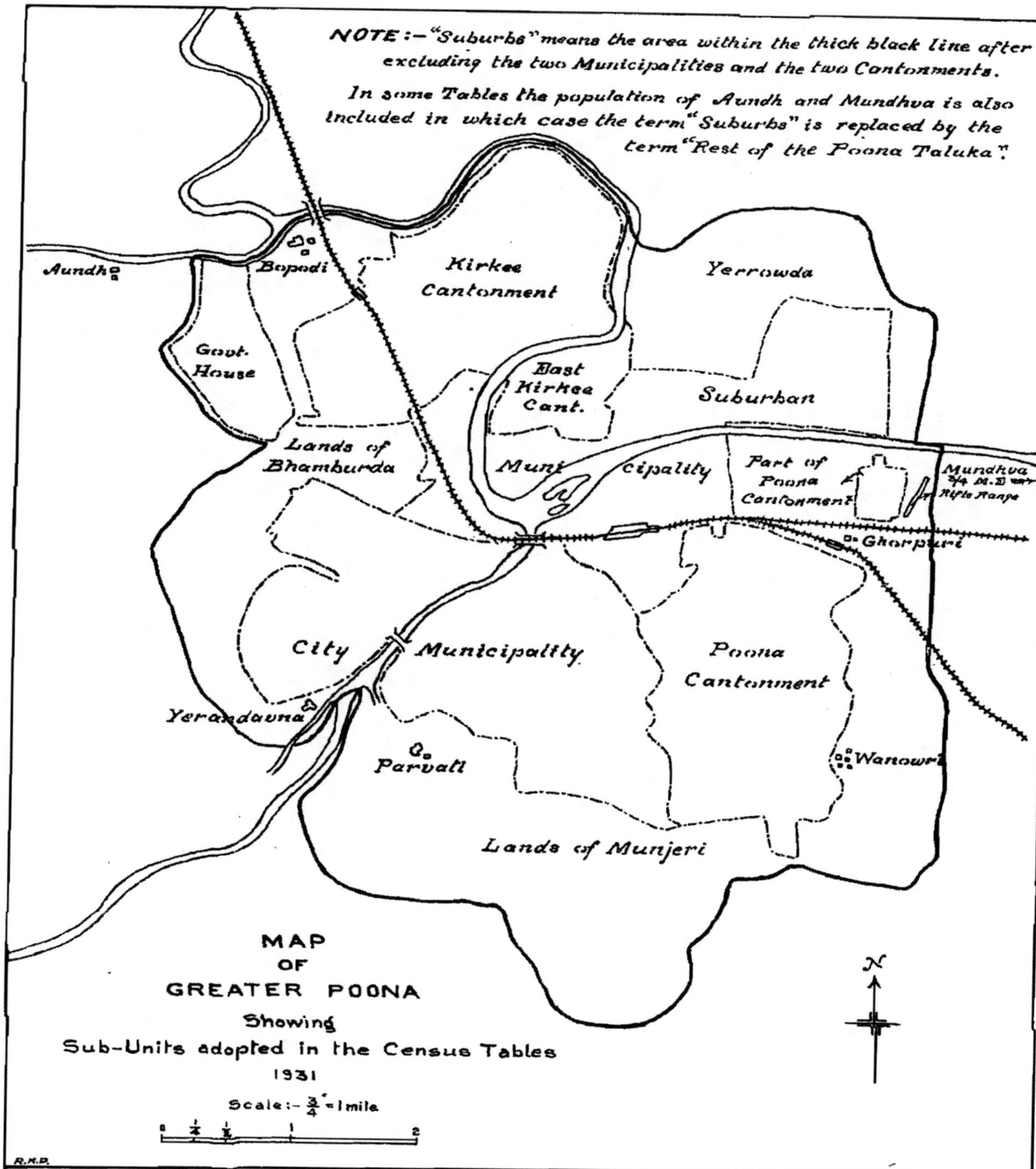

MAP OF GREATER POONA Showing Sub-Units adopted in the Census Tables 1931

G.P.Z.C. POONA, 1932.

at the railway station of Poona has been included in the population of Poona Taluka. The population of Poona Taluka is shown in the following statement.

STATEMENT No. 2.

Unit. 1	Persons. 2	Males. 3.	Females. 4
Greater Poona	250,187	138,139	12,048
Aundh, excluding Government House	1,816	978	838
Mundhwa, including Hadapsar Station	3,808	2,011	1,797
Running train population enumerated at Poona Station	192	163	29
Total, Poona Taluka	256,003	141,291	114,712

City Tables I, II and III relate to " Greater Poona ". Table VI, Part I and VII, Part I relate to Poona Taluka. Tables IV and V relate to the following units : namely (1) Poona City Municipality, (2) Poona Suburban Municipality, (3) Poona Cantonment, (4) Kirkee Cantonment, (5) The rest of Poona Taluka. The reason for this diversity of treatment of Census units is explained thus. Poona Taluka constituted a separate Census charge and the slips for the whole charge were taken out simultaneously for sorting for the various tables prepared in the Abstraction Office. It was subsequently found to be difficult weeding out slips relating to Aundh and Mundhwa and obtaining separate information for the Poona Suburbs only. Where therefore separate information had to be taken out it was taken out for " the rest of Poona Taluka ", which appellation displaced the term " Suburbs ".

2. BIRTHPLACE.

Mr. Sedgwick remarked in 1921 " In the matter of birthplace Poona is not a particularly cosmopolitan place. Poona City Municipality is essentially old fashioned and is simply the hub of Maharashtra. Very few strangers from other parts of India will be found there. In the Cantonments and Suburban Municipality, on the contrary, conditions are more mixed and the Madrasi and Pathan is a common feature. The birthplace figures were, however, tabulated for the City as a whole ; and the influence of the old fashioned City Municipal area, which alone contributes considerably more than half the total population of Greater Poona, gives an impression of homogeneity in the population which a casual visitor to the Cantonment bazaar might consider misleading." " Poona City " as a Census unit is a very heterogeneous structure. It consists of four utterly diverse elements (1) the old Maratha capital intensely conscious of Maratha history, (2) cantonment areas and a civil station with the usual mixed population found in such localities, (3) a residential suburban area of biggish houses and bungalows, mostly in the Poona Suburban Municipality, and (4) a rural fringe outside the more or less thickly populated areas and possessing characteristics of rural rather than of urban life. In applying generalisations to " Poona City ", as that term is employed in the Census, it is important to remember that the area is composed of parts of utterly different social and geographical character. What is true of the old City of Poona is not by any means true of localities having little affinity with it. The following statement (No. 3) shows the composition of Poona City according to the returns of birthplace recorded in the 1931 Census.

STATEMENT No. 3.

Region of Birth.	Proportion per 1,000 of the whole population.
Poona District	637
Bombay Presidency, including States and Agencies	251
Hyderabad State	23
Madras	16
Punjab	14

STATEMENT NO. 3—*contd.*

Region of Birth.	Proportion per 1,000 of the whole population.
India, Unspecified	9
Europe, Unspecified	9
Rajputana	6
Central Provinces and Berar	5
United Provinces	4
Ajmere-Merwara	4
Other Asiatic Countries	3
French and Portuguese Settlements in India	3
United Kingdom and Ireland	3
Asia, Unspecified	3
Elsewhere	10

It will be obvious from the above that Poona City cannot properly be called *cosmopolitan*. By far the greater part of the population in the area is home-born. The non-home-born population is to be found mostly in the Cantonment areas. In the Poona Suburban Municipal area are found most of the foreign-born population. The Poona City Municipal area is populated mostly by persons born in the City or born in various parts of Maharashtra ; it contains numbers of students who have come to colleges for study and whose native places are in various parts of the Bombay Deccan. Poona City thus differs in essentials from Bombay and Karachi. If the cosmopolitan Cantonments and suburban area be excluded from consideration, Poona will be seen to conform to the typical mofussil town with most of its population stay-at-home and home-born, and not supported by any organised industries conducted on lines of large-scale production. Poona as contrasted with Bombay, and to a smaller extent with Karachi, is essentially a residential and administrative headquarters town, on which has been superimposed an important cantonment which has altered to some extent the original character of composition of the population.

3. SEX AND AGE.

STATEMENT NO. 4.

Age-group.	Poona City Munici-pality.	Poona Suburban Munici-pality.	Poona and Kirkee Canton-ment.	Rest of the Poona Taluka.
1	*2*	*3*	*4*	*5*
0—5	129	121	124	117
5—10	111	100	105	90
10—15	108	96	102	94
15—20	111	107	114	112
20—25	118	127	129	128
25—30	97	110	110	112
30—35	89	99	91	99
35—40	68	75	63	71
40—45	53	59	50	56
45—50	38	40	36	40
50—55	29	27	27	30
55—60	19	15	19	18
60—65	15	12	15	13
65—70	6	5	7	5
70 and over	9	7	8	6

The above statement (No. 4) gives the age distribution of every 1,000 of the population in each of the units forming Poona City. The Poona and Kirkee Cantonment unit is the most abnormal. This is of course due largely to the presence of a military population, which is never typical of a natural age distribution, consisting as it does of a high concentration of males, often unmarried, in a few of the younger age-groups. The Poona City Municipality does not present any marked features of the city type of distribution. It is impossible without an elaborate analysis of the composition of the population in the various age-groups to draw any conclusions of value from disparities in the ratios at various ages in the different units. For instance, the high ratio of persons in the lowest age-group in Poona and Kirkee Cantonments is at first sight surprising. But analysis would probably disclose that the main contributors to this group must be the mixed population of servants, labourers and other kinds of miscellaneous campfollowers usually found in a cantonment. Similarly the general likeness in the ratios of the highest age-groups in all the units must be due to conditions in the case of old persons being virtually the same in all. In the case of a cantonment area it is easy to see why this should be so. The military population does not remain in a cantonment area till it dies of old age. In the case of the Poona Suburban Municipality the reason cannot be given without a detailed examination which a Census Report cannot make. But it seems probable that in the Poona Suburban Municipality there exists a fairly well-to-do and permanently settled population, which, in respect of longevity and habits, is not markedly different from that residing permanently in Poona City Municipal limits. The Census figures suggest many interesting questions which can best be considered along with a study of the vital statistics.

The following statement (No. 5) shows the proportion of females per 1,000 males.

STATEMENT No. 5.

Unit.	Females.
Poona City Municipality	877
Poona Suburban Municipality	740
Poona Cantonment	733
Kirkee Cantonment	640
Rest of Poona Taluka	697

This statement brings out more clearly the differences in the population composition of the various units. Poona City Municipality is clearly established as a typical residential area of permanent settlement. The Suburban Municipal area is less so ; and the Cantonment areas still less so. The figures of the rest of Poona Taluka are puzzling. The low ratio of females can be understood only by a close examination of the population composition. It would on examination probably be found that the area is a jumble of miscellaneous units, many of them highly uncharacteristic of a normal population distribution, and the final figures represent merely the arithmetical averaging of divergent conditions which range from typical Deccan villages to aggregations of labourers and the kinds of population groupings that are found just outside a large town.

4. RELIGION.

The following statement shows the distribution of population of Poona by religion in the 1931 Census.

STATEMENT No. 6.

Religion.	Greater Poona.	Poona City Munici-pality.	Poona Suburban Munici-pality	Both the Canton-ments.	Suburbs.
Hindu	793	872	775	541	825
Muslim	116	93	116	190	109
Jain	13	12	6	19	2
Zoroastrian	13	1	23	48	12
Christian	60	18	76	188	49
Sikh	2	..	1	11	1
Jew	3	3	3	3	1
Other religions	..	1	..	..	1

It will be noted that the Hindu predominance is greatest in the Poona City Municipal area.

5. OCCUPATION.

The following statement (No. 7) gives the distribution of every thousand workers (principal earners and working dependents) by sub-classes.

STATEMENT No. 7.

Sub-Class	I	Exploitation of animals and vegetation	88
„	II	Exploitation of minerals	....
„	III	Industry	211
„	IV	Transport	43
„	V	Trade	116
„	VI	Public Force	98
„	VII	Public Administration	87
„	VIII	Professions and liberal arts	61
„	IX	Persons living on their income	23
„	X	Domestic service	81
„	XI	Insufficiently described occupations	121
„	XII	Unproductive	71

Poona is not an industrial city. Industries show no great bias towards any one type. Textiles are unimportant and working in wood, metals, building, tailoring and other occupations of the small individual and non-factory type provide the majority of those engaged in industry with a living. In this respect Poona presents features similar to those prevailing in Karachi and quite dissimilar to those prevailing in Bombay. The Military Arsenal and Ammunition Factory at Kirkee is the only establishment employing a considerable number of workmen working under factory conditions. The number of persons shown as employed in Insufficiently Described Occupations has been returned at 9,815. Most of these must belong to the class of general labour for which there is some considerable demand in a place like Poona. The non-industrial character of Poona is proved by the fact that out of every 1,000 of the population there are only 258 male workers and 52 female workers as against 690 dependents.

2. SHOLAPUR.

1. INTRODUCTORY.

The Census city of Sholapur includes the Municipality and portions of Sholapur Revenue village lands not falling within the municipal boundary. Mr. Sedgwick remarked in 1921: "The city has gone through some vicissitudes in the way of ups and downs of population. The extraordinary drop in 1911 was due to the absence of people on account of plague. The population at the 1901 Census had been 75,288 and the 1911 Census showed a reduction to 61,345. In the 1911 Report it is mentioned that at a subsequent municipal Census taken after plague had subsided the population came out at over 89,000." The writer proceeded "It is probable that even this figure is a conservative estimate, many not having by then returned to their homes." In 1921 the population had increased to 119,581. At this Census the population has been returned at 144,654 persons, of whom 135,574 have been returned from the municipal area and 9,080 from the suburbs. The increase in population this Census is due to textile development and to the natural increase in population which has proved typical of the entire presidency during the last decade. Sholapur is a highly industrialised city in an area that sometimes suffers from drought and poor crops and it adjoins an area in the Nizam's dominions in which these conditions are more exaggerated than they are in the portion of Bombay Presidency immediately adjacent to Sholapur. The labour supply of Sholapur is drawn almost wholly from these areas and it is obvious that the two chief influences affecting the growth of the city are the prosperity or unsuccess of the cotton textile mills on which so large a proportion of the city's inhabitants are dependent for a living, and the effect of bad seasons on the city's supply of labour. These two influences will sometimes be found to be at variance with each other. In addition, epidemics must always be a source of disturbance to a city like Sholapur dependent on a single industry and situated in a portion of the country where bad times come not infrequently and render the people therefore more liable to the ravages of disease. It is the interaction of these various influences that accounts for the up and down character of Sholapur's Census record. With the development of Indian textiles, such as seems likely to come about in the near future as India endeavours to supply from its own resources more of the cloth it requires, it is probable that Sholapur will continue to grow and it may grow considerably. The extent to which it is dependent on a single industry for its well being will, however, constitute a source of danger unless the economic life of the city is put eventually on a broader basis of industry and occupation.

2. BIRTHPLACE.

In the matter of birthplace Sholapur is not at all cosmopolitan. It draws its labour from its immediate neighbourhood. As that neighbourhood includes a portion of the Hyderabad State territory it is not surprising that a large proportion of the city's population should be returned as immigrants from that area. Actually the people are socially and racially of the same type, whether they come from the Sholapur district or from the Nizam's territory adjoining it.

STATEMENT NO. 1.

Region of Birth.	Proportion per 1,000 of the whole population.
Sholapur district	687
Hyderabad State	182
Bombay Presidency (including Bombay States and Agencies)	108
Madras	11
Rajputana	5
United Provinces	1
Elsewhere	6

As compared with the 1921 Census figures the proportion of home-borns (meaning by that persons returning birthplaces in Sholapur City and the rest of Sholapur district) has risen from 636 to 687, and the proportion of persons returning the Nizam's dominions as their birthplace has fallen from 249 to 182. The only other important source of labour supply is the Bombay States and Agencies near Sholapur district and racially and socially allied to it. Sholapur is in fact a typical mofussil town that has become excessively industrialised in the one large-scale organised industry of textiles and it draws its labour supply from the area that would in any case have supplied the city with labour, though not of course in the same quantity as it does now when there is a steady demand from the cotton textile mills.

3. RELIGION.

The religious composition of Sholapur is shown in the statement (No. 2) below. Sholapur is predominantly a Hindu town. As has happened elsewhere at this Census, the proportion of Hindus has fallen this Census and the proportion of Muslims has risen. Very possibly the civil disobedience movement may have contributed to this result.

STATEMENT NO. 2.

Religion.	Number per 1,000 of the whole population of the city. 1931	1921
Hindu	770·4	786
Muslim	198·3	184
Jain	11·0	11
Zoroastrian	2·1	3
Christian	18·1	16
Other Religions	0·1	....

4. AGE, SEX AND CIVIL CONDITION.

The distribution of the population over the age-groups is as under :—

STATEMENT No. 3.

Age-group.	Number per 1,000.			Number of females per 100 males.
	Persons.	Males.	Females.	
1	2	3	4	5
0—5	143	134	153	100
5—10	117	115	119	91
10—15	110	109	112	91
15—20	108	104	114	96
20—25	116	114	118	91
25—30	95	101	89	78
30—35	81	90	73	72
35—40	63	69	55	70
40—45	50	53	46	76
45—50	36	36	36	87
50—55	27	26	28	94
55—60	20	19	21	99
60—65	17	15	18	104
65—70	7	6	7	100
70 and over	10	9	11	109
Total	1,000	1,000	1,000	

The following statement shows the number of persons married in the first four age-groups :—

0–5	396	(females 238)
5–10	1,953	(females 1,514)
10–15	4,147	(females 3,219)
15–20	9,978	(females 6,502)

It will be obvious from the above that there is a considerable amount of early marriage in Sholapur. The castes chiefly affected are Lingayats, Marathas and Kunbis, Mahars and Mangs.

5. LITERACY.

The following statement shows the extent of literacy in Sholapur in the 1931 Census.

Total population.	Literate.		Per mille.	Literate in English.		Per mille.
	Males.	Females.		Males.	Females.	
1	2	3	4	5	6	7
135,574	18,334	3,055	158	4,000	394	32

Sholapur has made much improvement in respect of literacy during the last decade. This is evident from the following :—

Comparative figures of literacy.

Religion.	Proportion per mille.			
	1921		1931	
	Literate.	Literate in English.	Literate.	Literate in English.
1	2	3	4	5
All Religions	107	21	158	32
Hindu	109	17	152	30
Muslim	112	8	123	13
Christian	551	244	540	238

The figures speak for themselves. Hindus, though behind Muslims in 1921, have made remarkable progress during the decade and have increased their number of literates from 109 to 152 per mille. English literacy also shows distinct improvement in this decade. Sholapur, unlike Bombay and Karachi, does not attract the student class and hence the figures in English literacy are not so striking. In short there is improvement in the literacy of all the communities except Christian, who have shown a slight decrease.

6. OCCUPATION AND INDUSTRY.

The total number of workers (principal earners and working dependents) returned in the 1931 Census was 54,938 and of non-working dependents 80,636 ; equivalent to 405 per mille and 595 per mille of the population respectively. It is interesting in this connection to compare Sholapur with Bombay, a large industrial town, Karachi a large commercial town, and Poona, a residential, administrative, military and educational centre. The statement below (No. 4) shows how the four cities differ in respect of the proportions of workers and non-workers. In industrial towns a larger proportion of the population is employed actively in earning a livelihood.

STATEMENT NO. 4.

Class.	Distribution of 1,000 persons into workers and dependents.			
	Sholapur.	Bombay.	Karachi.	Poona.
1	2	3	4	5
Workers, i.e. principal earners and working dependents	405	487	316	317
Non-working dependents	595	513	684	683

The distribution of every thousand workers (Principal earners and working dependents) in Sholapur by sub-classes is shown in the statement (No. 5) below :—

STATEMENT No. 5.

Sub-Class		
Sub-Class	I—Exploitation of animals and vegetation	80
,,	II—Exploitation of minerals	..—
,,	III—Industry	671
,,	IV—Transport	33
,,	V—Trade	72
,,	VI—Public Force	18
,,	VII—Public Administration	22
,,	VIII—Professions and liberal arts	19
,,	IX—Persons living on their income	5
,,	X—Domestic service	28
,,	XI—Insufficiently described occupations	41
,,	XII—Unproductive	11

The proportion of the working population employed in industry is very large. As compared with the 1921 figures the proportion of workers engaged in industry has risen from 546 per mille to 671 per mille ; while the proportion engaged in trade has fallen from 110 to 72. How far these crude proportions can be compared is difficult to say particularly as at this Census there has been a great fall in the proportion of the population engaged in insufficiently described occupations, namely from 145 per mille to 41 per mille, and it is not known how the difference has been distributed over the sub-classes. There is however every reason for thinking that in Sholapur industry has not been so adversely affected by the business slump as trade has and the rise in the ratio of industrial occupations and the fall in the ratio of trading occupations represent a real fact. An examination of the distribution of workers in the sub-class " Industry " reveals the following results. Of 37,021 persons engaged in industrial occupations in Sholapur, 31,989 or 58 per cent. of all employed persons and 24 per cent. of the total population of Sholapur are employed in textiles. Of this number 19,903 are employed in cotton ginning, cleaning and pressing and 11,589 are employed in cotton spinning, sizing and weaving. No other single order of industry in Sholapur employs over a thousand persons, except industries of dress and the toilet employing 1,566 persons. of whom 684 are tailors, etc., and 441 are barbers, etc. It will thus be obvious to what an extent Sholapur has in its industrial organisation put all its eggs into one basket, that of cotton textiles produced under modern large-scale production methods. Whether this is a healthy state of affairs must be left to sociologists to decide. It seems clear that a city dependent so largely on a single industry is open to very considerable risk, especially if the manufactured product is vulnerable by foreign competition.

CHAPTER V—HOUSING IN BOMBAY CITY.

B—HOUSING STATISTICS.

1. Introductory.

The previous history of these statistics and how and when they came to be included in the Census Cities Report for the Bombay Presidency have been explained in the Introductory section of Chapter VI of the Census of India, 1921, Volume IX, Part I. It is not therefore necessary to recapitulate these explanations here.

2. System of Enumeration and Compilation.

The block lists and family registers, the two essential schedules for the abstraction of the statistics, were received from Bombay Municipality along with the enumeration books and dealt with in the abstraction office. After a general inspection of the documents it was first contemplated to abandon any idea of preparing the statistics because of the unsatisfactory manner in which the block lists and family registers were filled up, and it was impossible abstracting the information from the block lists and family registers alone. Later, however, it was suggested that as the enumeration books (general schedules) of the Census supplied information in respect of number of houses, the number of floors and rooms, and the number of persons actually enumerated as living in houses, the statistics could be taken out from the block lists, family registers and enumeration books used together. Great difficulty was, however, experienced by the abstraction office in compiling the tables in their present form. The statistice cannot, as they stand, be regarded as absolutely correct or exhaustive. They do however represent a serious attempt to make the best of the situation and within certain limits may be considered not unreasonably inaccurate. In any case they possess great sociological value whatever their statistical worth may be.

3. Instructions.

The following special instructions were issued to the abstraction office.

" The house list and the family register from which the information required for the housing tables is to be abstracted are most carelessly written and are incomplete in many cases. It will be seen that in many block books no figures have been recorded in column 6 of the house list and in columns 6, 7, 8, 9 and 11 of the family register. Figures of preliminary census have been given in column 10 here and there. We want figures of final census for Tables II, VIA and VII and these will have to be taken as regards each room from the enumeration schedules. Again you will find that all the schedules pertaining to one building are not arranged in serial order of the floor and rooms. You will have therefore to find out this information from the enumeration books and note it separately on a piece of paper and when the information of one house is thus fully obtained post it in the family register in respective columns left blank. This means that you will have to get the family register duly completed in all the particulars before striking out the totals and completing this information in your register. If in a few cases information is forthcoming already in the family registers, the same will have to be verified in the above manner. You must therefore be careful in combing out the requisite figures from the block book and for that purpose to strain every page of the enumeration schedules assiduously."

4. Difficulties encountered.

In his report, which has been printed as Appendix A at page 109 of the present volume, the Executive Health Officer, Bombay Municipality, who conducted the census operations in Bombay City, has described the difficulties with which Census operations had to contend in 1931. It is not surprising that the housing statistics should be incomplete. Furthermore the Census abstraction office was opened at a place other than Bombay soon after the actual date of the Census and this made more troublesome the task of filling in omissions and rectifying mistakes. The abstraction office, despite these difficulties, made use of all figures obtainable directly and indirectly with the result that the tables as finally compiled do afford valuable material for statistical examination and comment.

5. Statistical Tables of Housing.

The housing statistics are contained in the following Tables printed at the end of this volume :—

Table I—General classification of buildings by uses.

Table II—Classification of rooms by number of floors.

Table III—Residential buildings classified according to the number of tenements contained in each.

Table IV—Classification of residential buildings by the number of occupants.

Table V—Distribution of persons by rooms.

Table VI-A—Tenements by rooms and population.

Table VI-B—Details of one-roomed tenements containing more than one family.

Table VII—Tenements by room and population by religion.

6. Definition of " Building " and Standards of " Overcrowding ".

The definition of " building " (and census " house ") remains what it has been since 1901 and is as follows :—" The whole of a building under one undivided roof, or under two or more roofs connected *inter se* by a subsidiary roof."

Suggestions made in 1921 by Mr. Sedgwick as regards the need for modifying the tables and reconsidering the definition of a " building " do not appear to have been considered by the Bombay Municipality. In any case, no action has been taken on Mr. Sedgwick's suggestions. The statistics presented now are therefore identical in nature with those compiled in 1921. The deficiencies have not been made good. The object of housing statistics is to explain the manner in which the population is housed and to throw light upon " overcrowding ". The statistics as they stand only partially achieve this object. In fact they are not well designed to display the facts of " overcrowding ". It is plain that " overcrowding " is a most complicated matter involving various standards of housing, which may differ among different social classes. Unless a building is adequately designated as a certain number of rooms normally available for the use of a certain number of persons on some accepted principle of housing that makes allowance for privacy, decency and the ordinary amenities of domestic life, the statistical tables of housing can be only half useful. " Overcrowding ", in fact, implies an appeal to an ethical standard for which the tables as they stand make no provision at all. It is suggested that the chief principle on which housing statistics should be compiled in future is one which definitely defines the number of rooms which should normally be available for the average family, and then examines the housing of the Bombay population according as the families composing that population are distributed over units providing, or failing to provide, accommodation of the necessary standard. Generally speaking, it can be asserted without fear of contradiction that any housing which does not provide more than one room for an average family of four persons must result in " overcrowding ". With two rooms per family of four persons the overcrowding will almost disappear, especially if cooking can be carried out in one apartment other than one of the two living rooms. In fact, to abolish overcrowding of the average family in Bombay, three rooms are necessary : one of them, a cook room, and two of them living rooms which will provide for the reasonable privacy of females and which permit one apartment to be used for sleeping purposes alone. It is recognised, however, that in India such conditions are almost everywhere at present impossible of fulfilment, from which it may be deduced that in India ideas of privacy and domestic seclusion are not to be judged by western standards at all. Social investigators, however, are unanimous in condemning the housing conditions generally prevailing in India and it is reasonable to believe that the lack of privacy and the pressure on floor space prevalent in India is something which idealists and practical social workers regard as definite evils, whether Indian public opinion generally regards them now as such or not. Apart from these ethical considerations, " overcrowding " complicates problems which are matters of deep concern to public health authorities, and to all authorities whose business it is to see that any population is well-ordered, content and physically fit. The housing tables under

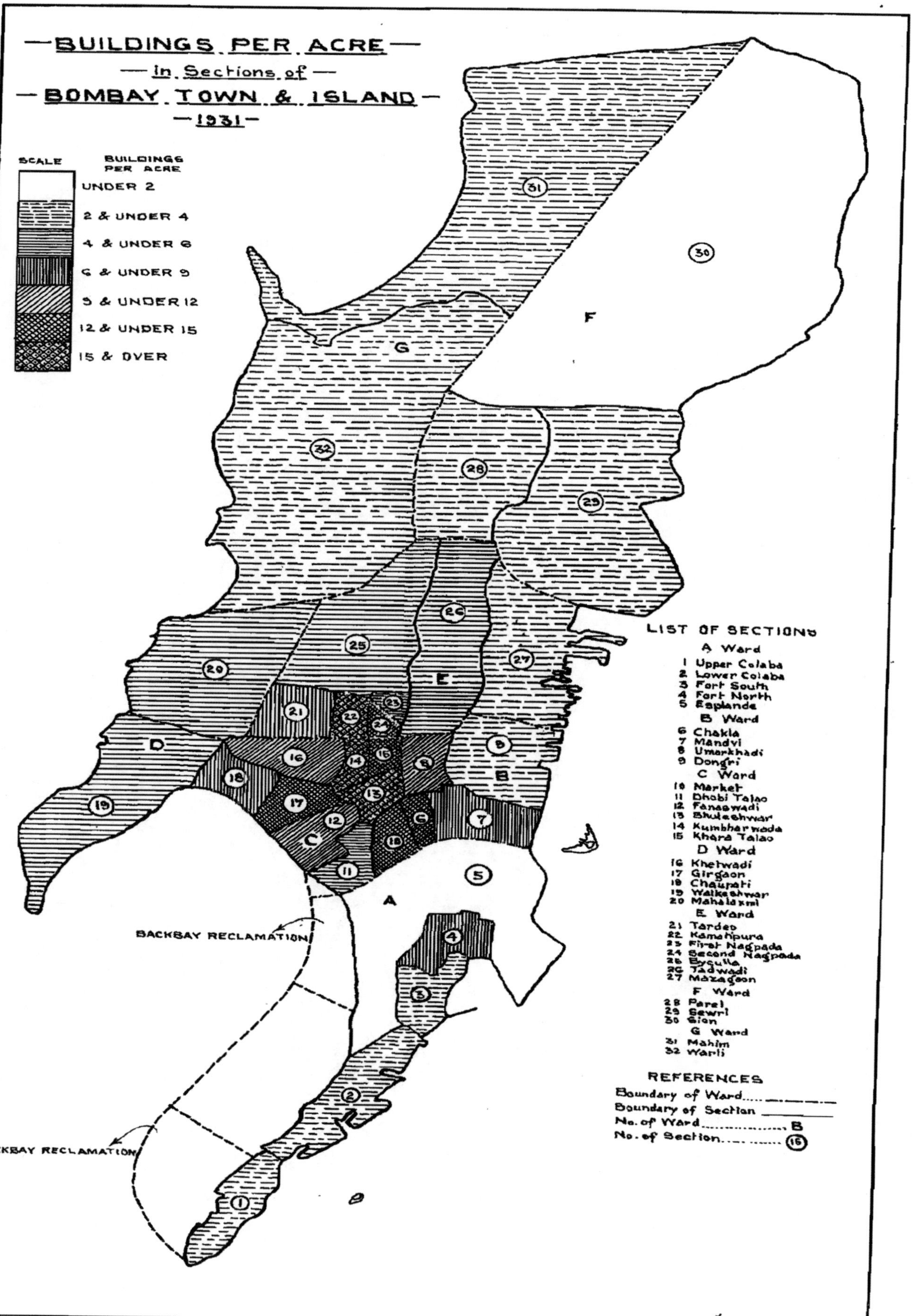
BUILDINGS PER ACRE
in Sections of
BOMBAY TOWN & ISLAND
1931
SCALE
BUILDINGS PER ACRE
UNDER 2
2 & UNDER 4
4 & UNDER 6
6 & UNDER 9
9 & UNDER 12
12 & UNDER 15
15 & OVER
LIST OF SECTIONS
A Ward
1 Upper Colaba
2 Lower Colaba
3 Fort South
4 Fort North
5 Esplanade
B Ward
6 Chakla
7 Mandvi
8 Umarkhadi
9 Dongri
C Ward
10 Market
11 Dhobi Talao
12 Fanaswadi
13 Bhuleshwar
14 Kumbharwada
15 Khara Talao
D Ward
16 Khetwadi
17 Girgaon
18 Chaupati
19 Walkeshwar
20 Mahalaxmi
E Ward
21 Tardeo
22 Kamatipura
23 First Nagpada
24 Second Nagpada
25 Byculla
26 Tadwadi
27 Mazagaon
F Ward
28 Parel
29 Sewri
30 Sion
G Ward
31 Mahim
32 Warli
REFERENCES
Boundary of Ward
Boundary of Section
No. of Ward .... B
No. of Section 15
BACKBAY RECLAMATION
BACKBAY RECLAMATION
A
B
C
D
E
F
G
G.P.Z D. POONA, 1939.

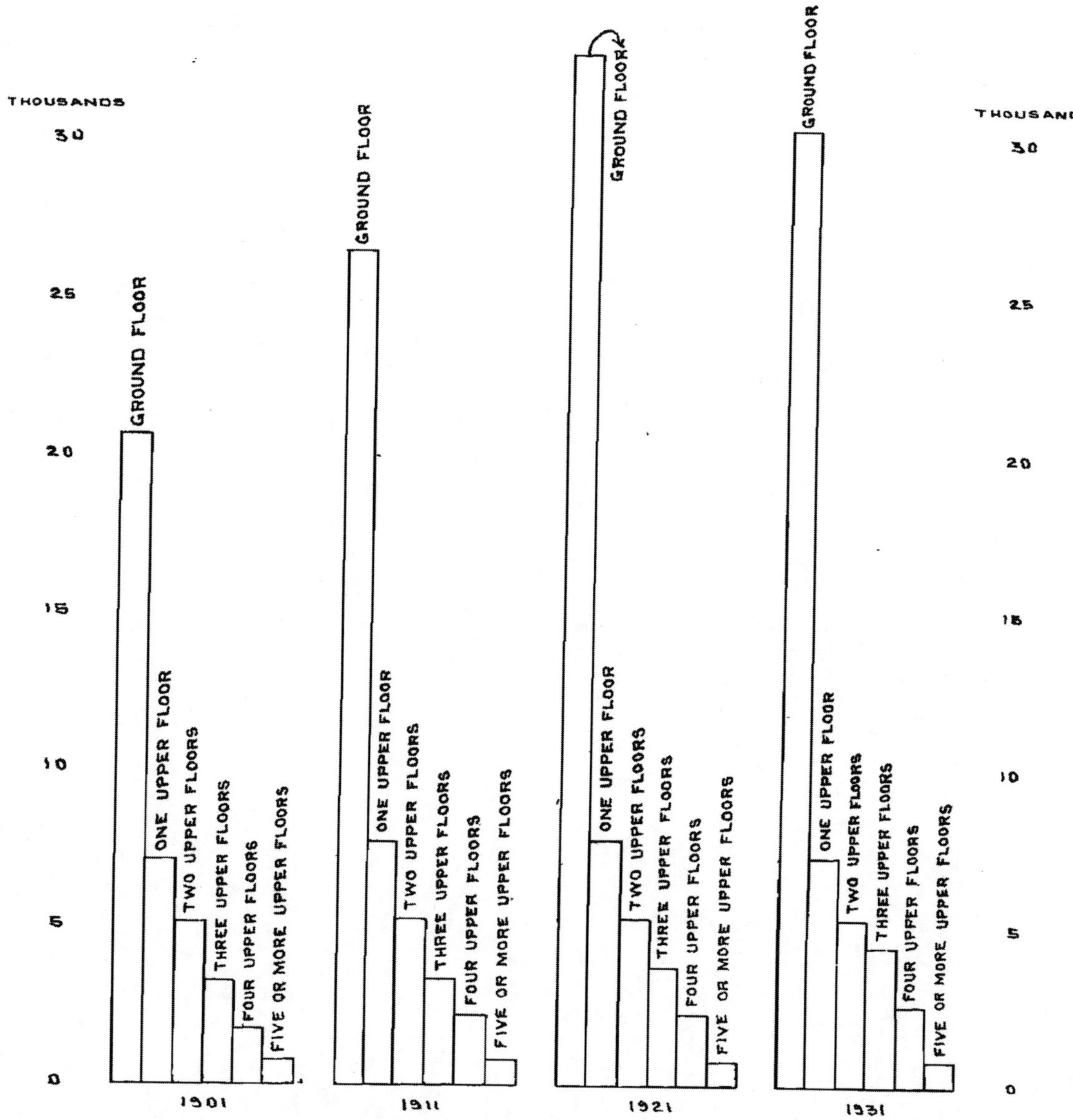

ACTUAL NUMBER OF BUILDINGS WITH DIFFERENT NUMBERS OF FLOORS IN BOMBAY CITY SINCE 1901

PERCENTAGE DISTRIBUTION OF BUILDINGS ACCORDING TO NUMBER OF FLOORS IN BOMBAY CITY SINCE 1901

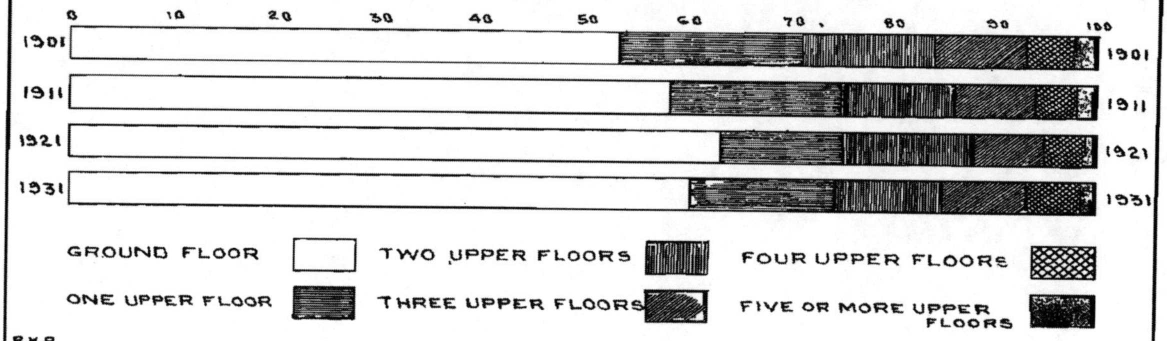

PERCENTAGE DISTRIBUTION OF TENEMENTS IN SECTIONS OF BOMBAY CITY, 1931.

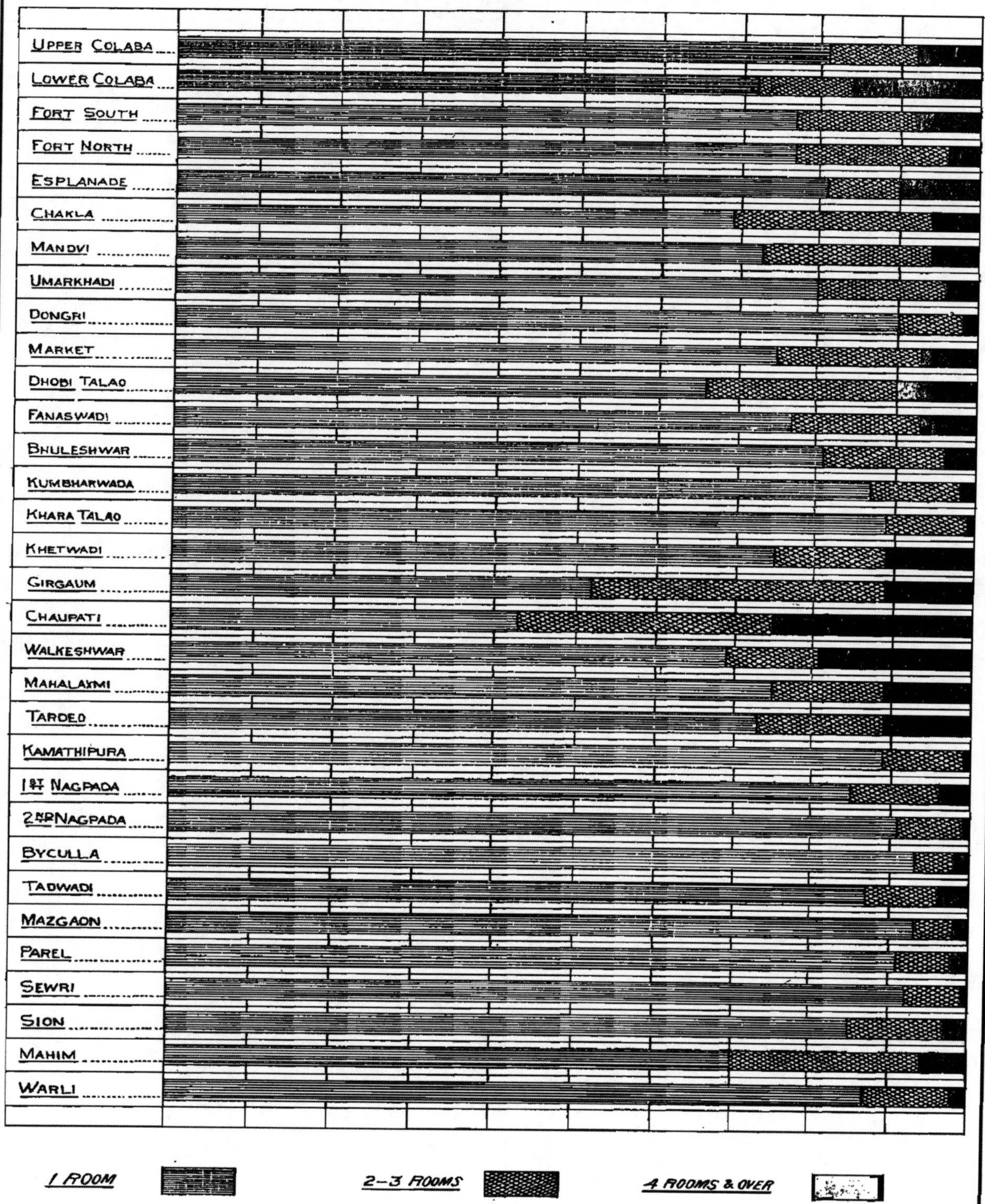

MMS

G.P.Z.O. Poona, 1933.

discussion in the present chapter, despite their inadequacy, will suggest that housing conditions generally in Bombay are of a character of which the City has no reason whatever to be proud.

7. TOTAL NUMBER OF BUILDINGS.

The total number of buildings of all classes enumerated in the last four censuses is as follows.

STATEMENT NO. 1.

Census year	Number of buildings.	Inter-census variation.
1931	50,833	—1,501
1921	52,334	+6,618
1911	45,716	+7,262
1901	38,454	....

Whether the decrease in the number of buildings this Census is real or not is hard to decide. Faulty enumeration has certainly been at work. But it is likely that there has been a change in the kind of building erected for the working classes. The practice is growing of providing large chawls containing accommodation for many families in one building instead of the smaller buildings which used to be the chief means of providing cheap housing accommodation. Thus while the total number of buildings has fallen by 1,501 the number of chawls has risen by 4,348. In order to establish the facts clearly it would be necessary to compare the number of large chawls in 1921 with the number in 1931 ; but the housing statistics are inadequate for this purpose. The number of residential buildings containing from 1 to 10 tenements was 28,155 in 1921 and is now 23,161. But the classification is statistically faulty, as Mr. Sedgwick pointed out in 1921. "The class (5 tenements and under) as it stands is heterogeneous, including all single bungalows, all semi-detached bungalows, all of the older and smaller blocks of flats, such as those in Marine Lines, and a good many moderately large ones. The sub-classes might be ....1 tenement, 2 tenements, 3 to 5 tenements and 6 to 10 tenements". No clearer instance can be given of a nearly useless statistical classification. For general purposes of comparison the figures for 1931 and 1921 for the number of buildings containing various numbers of tenements are placed side by side.

STATEMENT NO. 2.

Statement showing residential buildings by the number of tenements, 1931 and 1921.

Census year.	Number of buildings containing						Total number of buildings.
	10 tenements and under.	11 to 20 tenements.	21 to 30 tenements.	31 to 40 tenements.	41 to 50 tenements.	51 tenements and over.	
1931	23,161	4,353	4,774	986	496	973	31,743
1921	28,155	3,653	1,519	829	467	608	35,231

As observed in section 8 below this statement clearly shows a decrease in small buildings such as residential bungalows and small houses. These are being replaced by larger houses, chawls, etc.

8. BUILDINGS PER ACRE.

Kamathipura has the highest number of buildings per acre, 17·55 as against 19 in the last census ; and its density is 601·71, as against 714, whereas

Kumbharwada, with a density of 726·57 as against 736 in 1921, has only 15·54 buildings per acre. Similarly Second Nagpada with a density of 636·37 has only 15·58 buildings per acre. This is due to the fact that small buildings have been demolished and replaced by larger buildings without affecting the number of occupants per unit of surface area.

The following statement (No. 3) arranges the various wards and sections of the city in order of density according to number of buildings per acre. The general figure for Bombay City as a whole is 3·28 buildings per acre.

STATEMENT No. 3.

Ward and section.	Density of buildings per acre.
Ward C	**40·23**
Kumbharwada	15·54
Bhuleshwar	15·41
Khara-Talav	13·17
Market	12·56
Fanaswadi	10·24
Dhobitalao	5·73
Ward B	**5·66**
Chakla	14·78
Umarkhadi	10·18
Mandvi	6·47
Dongri	2·24
Ward D	**5·43**
Girgaon	12·02
Khetwadi	10·26
Chaupati	7·51
Walkeshwar	3·97
Mahalaxmi	4·16
Ward E	**4·19**
Kamathipura	17·55
Second Nagpada	15·58
Tardeo	6·95
First Nagpada	5·68
Byculla	5·01
Tarwadi	4·05
Mazagaon	2·26
Ward G	**2·88**
Mahim	3·03
Worli	2·74
Ward A	**2·42**
Fort North	7·46
Lower Colaba	3·6
Fort South	3·08
Upper Colaba	1·9
Esplanade	1·60
Ward F	**1·59**
Parel	3·68
Sewri	3·17
Sion	1·00

9. HOUSING TABLE I.

(a) *General classification of buildings by use.*—The scheme of classification adopted in 1931 is generally similar to that adopted in 1921.

The following statement shows the 1931 Bombay classification as compared with the English classification followed in 1911.

Bombay 1931.	*England and Wales 1911.*
Residential buildings.	Buildings used as dwellings.
Bungalow and dwelling houses.	Ordinary dwelling houses.
Servants' quarters.	Blocks of flats.
Chawls.	Shops.
Factories, shops, offices, etc., combined with dwellings.	Hotels, inns and public houses.
Dharmshalas.	Offices, warehouses, workshops and factories.
Institutions.	Institutions.
Huts.	Others.
Others, and unclassifiable non-residential Buildings.	Buildings not used as dwellings.
Places of worship.	Places of worship.
Institutions and places of amusement.	Government and municipal buildings.
Factories, mills and works.	Shops.
Offices and shops.	Offices.
Godowns, stables, garages, sheds and chowkis.	Warehouses, workshops, factories, theatres and other places of amusement.
Others and unclassifiable.	

The terms "Residential" and "Non-residential" refer to the ordinary uses of each building and are irrespective of whether any person was or was not enumerated in the building on the Census night.

(b) *Variation in buildings by classes.*—The statement below (No. 4) gives variations in the number of buildings of various classes for four Censuses.

STATEMENT NO. 4.

Category.	1931	1921	1911	1901	Variation.		
					1921 to 1931	1911 to 1921	1901 to 1911
Total buildings	50,833	52,334	45,716	38,454	— 1,501	+ 6,618	+ 7,262
Residential buildings	32,225	34,808	33,193	31,304	— 2,583	+ 1,615	+ 1,889
Shops and offices	3,254	2,757	1,999	2,531	+ 497	+ 758	— 532
Factories, mills and works	1,536	1,530	1,033	467	+ 6	+ 497	+ 566
Godowns, stables, garages, sheds and chowkis	12,229	11,709	8,131	3,372	+ 520	+ 3,578	+ 4,759
Other buildings	1,589	1,530	1,360	780	+ 59	+ 170	+ 580

The figures in the above table are on the whole not inconsistent, except in the case of the figures for residential buildings which show a fall of 2,583 against an increase of 6,618 in 1921 over 1911.

It will be noted that the only class showing a decrease at this Census is "Residential buildings". As previously explained part of this decrease must be due to the erection of larger buildings to take the place of older and smaller ones. This is the modern tendency of building in all large cities where pressure on ground space and the value of land are matters that architects have to consider as of primary importance. The increase in the numbers of buildings other than residential is in accordance with expectation. Comparison with figures previous to 1921 are not generally very valuable owing to differences in the detailed classification of most items. In fact permanence of definition of terms, once satisfactory definitions have been reached, is the first desideratum of all statistics and especially of housing statistics. Such satisfactoriness of definition has not yet been reached. Nor is there any real permanence of definition and interpretation, except as between 1921 and 1931, as a reference to Mr. Sedgwick's remarks in sections 16 to 20 in Chapter VI of Part B of Census of India, 1921, Volume IX, Part I will demonstrate.

(c) *Residential Buildings*—The following (statement 5) shows the numbers of each kind of residential building for the last two Censuses.

STATEMENT No. 5.

Category.	1931	1921
Bungalows and dwelling houses	9,624	12,371
Servants' quarters	1,023	2,982
Chawls	9,075	4,725
Huts	5,459	9,084
Factories, shops, etc., combined with dwellings	6,596	5,646

There is no explanation of the fall in the number of servants' quarters. It is therefore impossible to say whether faulty enumeration is responsible or a change in the nature of building, as the bungalow type with separate servants' quarters gives place to the flat. Possibly both influences are at work. The rise in the number of chawls is symptomatic of modern conditions of city life. The fall in the number of huts is a matter for congratulation if enumeration has been satisfactory in this case.

(d) *Godowns, etc.*—The statement below (No. 6) shows the number of godowns, stables and chowkis at the last two Censuses.

STATEMENT No. 6.

Category.	1901	1911	1921	1931
Godowns	1,103	3,742	11,709	12,229
Stables	1,718	3,400		
Chowkis	551	989		

The distribution by wards of this type of building is shown in the following statement (No. 7) for two Censuses.

STATEMENT No. 7.

Ward.	1931	1921	Difference
A	950	941	+ 9
B	887	1,172	— 258
C	535	594	— 59
D	2,087	1,858	+ 229
E	3,015	3,380	— 365
F	2,051	1,960	+ 91
G	2,546	1,804	+ 742
Military	158	..	+ 158
Total ..	12,229	11,709	+ 520

The control of stables and cattle-sheds in certain parts of the Municipal area is still regarded as unsatisfactory, though it is believed that serious efforts have been made to remove most of the objectionable cattle sheds to outside the chief residential areas. In the Wadala area, however, cattle sheds are still subject of complaint on the ground of insanitariness. Presumably the chief causes of variation in the number of buildings classified under godowns, etc. are the removal of dilapidated and insanitary buildings and the construction of garages for motor vehicles. Increases and decreases are distributed capriciously over the various wards.

(e) *Chawls.*—Attention is invited to the remarks made by Mr. Sedgwick in section 39, Chapter VI, of the report referred to in section 7 above. The word " chawl " is of vague meaning for Census purposes. Generally it may be described as meaning something like a " tenement house," as that phrase is understood in England. Chawls are actually cheap blocks of flats erected mostly for the accommodation of the working classes. The term " chawl ", while well understood in itself in areas where chawls exist, is from a Census point of view merely a further complication of the term " building ". It would be much better if " chawls " were enumerated under the particular types of building to which they belong with a note of the use to which they are put. The statement below (No. 8) shows the comparative number of chawls at the last two Censuses.

STATEMENT No. 8.

Number of Chawls by Wards.

Ward.	1931	1921	Difference
A	270	108	+ 162
B	334	136	+ 198
C	1,497	155	+1,342
D	1,447	852	+ 595
E	2,011	1,596	+ 415
F	1,421	895	+ 526
G	2,084	983	+1,101
Military	11	2	+ 9
Total ..	9,075	4,727	+4,348

The great increase in the number of chawls has already received comment. So far as the increase is due to the provision of a better type of building of larger size and is accompanied by the disappearance of huts and small insanitary buildings formerly in occupation, the increase marks a distinct improvement in the provision of housing. If the Bombay Municipal building rules are adequate in insisting that architects shall provide in chawl design for enough cook-rooms and privies and a satisfactory number of water-taps on each floor and if water pressure can be obtained sufficient to ensure a satisfactory supply of water to the topmost floors, the development of the modern chawl system ought in time to do much to remedy the unsatisfactory conditions in which most of the Bombay millhands live. The lower middle classes also are finding better living conditions in the modern type of chawl. The housing problem of the city is clearly capable of solution on these lines, provided most of the mistakes of earlier chawl construction are avoided. Mr. Sedgwick has described in 1921 some of these mistakes.

(*f*) *Dharmashalas and Places of Worship.*—The statement below (No. 9) shows the number of dharmashalas and places of worship by wards for two Censuses.

STATEMENT NO. 9.

Ward.	1931	1921	Difference
A	55	35	+ 20
B	85	86	— 1
C	110	106	+ 4
D	147	127	+ 20
E	140	165	— 25
F	89	103	— 14
G	128	88	+ 40
Military	1	1	*Nil.*
Total ..	755	711	+ 44

The figures show trifling variation and call for no comment.

(*g*) *Mills.*—The number of factories and mills has not been shown in the Census separately, for the same reason as prevailed in 1921, namely that the number is already well known to the departments dealing with factories and industries. It is however desirable that a record of the number should appear in a general Census report and the following statement (No. 10) prepared from the published reports of the Factories Department shows the comparative number in 1921 and 1931.

STATEMENT NO. 10.

Number of Factories and Mills.

1921	*1931*
204	381

10. HOUSING TABLE II.

Buildings are classified in Housing Table II according to the number of floors they contain. The comparative numbers of buildings of all kinds for the last two Censuses are shown in the statement below.

STATEMENT NO. 11.

Census year.	Number of buildings with						Total number of buildings.
	Ground floor only.	One upper floor.	Two upper floors.	Three upper floors.	Four upper floors.	Five upper floors.	
1921 ..	33,060	7,636	5,428	3,804	2,149	688	52,774
1931 ..	30,342	7,296	5,599	4,322	2,489	785	50,833

It will be seen that in 1931 more than three out of every five buildings have ground floors only. Of buildings with more than three upper floors there are only 3,274 in the City, or about one out of every seventeen buildings. The classification in this housing table is not satisfactory for dealing with the question of overcrowding. The buildings under enumeration are buildings of all kinds, and there is nothing standard about the size of the buildings. A truer idea of the overcrowding problem would be obtained if the statistics gave combined information (1) on the number of residential buildings by floors, (2) by number of occupants and (3) by average floor space per family. The larger chawls which have been erected in the past ten years, in replacement of smaller and less sanitary dwellings, must fall into the three, four, and five-floor classes of buildings. But the statistics in Housing Table II do not make the fact clear as they should do.

The comparative number of ground-floor buildings is shown for four Censuses in the statement below (No. 12).

STATEMENT NO. 12.

1901	20,608	....
1911	26,512	+ 5,904
1921	32,684	+ 6,172
1931	30,342	— 2,342

The fall in the number of ground-floor buildings probably represents a real fact, the disappearance of the ground-floor building in favour of the bigger chawl with several floors.

The statement below (No. 13) shows the distribution of ground-floor buildings by wards for the last two Censuses :—

STATEMENT NO. 13.

Ward.	1931	1921	Variation
A	1,987	1,905	+ 82
B	1,292	1,577	— 285
C	1,264	1,309	— 45
D	4,880	4,717	+ 163
E	6,256	7,226	— 970
F	5,730	7,529	—1,799
G	8,550	8,421	+ 129
Military	383	385	— 2
Total ..	30,342	33,069	—2,727

The decrease in the number of ground-floor buildings has been most marked in wards E and F. These wards are comparatively open and capable of development. It does not pay a modern landlord to erect ground-floor buildings for tenements and so ground-floor buildings are falling out of use. The statement below (No. 14) shows the comparative numbers for two Censuses of buildings with upper floors.

STATEMENT NO. 14.

Buildings with	1931	1921	Difference
1 upper floor	7,296	7,636	— 340
2 upper floors	5,599	5,428	+ 171
3 do.	4,322	3,804	+ 518
4 do.	2,489	2,149	+ 340
5 or more upper floors	785	688	+ 97

The tendency here is quite marked for the type of building with one or two upper floors to give place to buildings with more than two upper floors. In this respect the statistics corroborate those which show a decline in the number of buildings with ground floors only. More efficient housing service in a city can undoubtedly be rendered by large buildings than by small ones, as space is economised and water-supply, sewage disposal, electric light, gas and plumbing facilities can be arranged for on a large scale instead of by a system of comparatively expensive separate extensions.

11. Housing Table III.

The statistics in Housing Table III show buildings according to the number of tenements they contain. "Tenement" is the nearest approach to definiteness in the housing statistics and does provide some measure of the extent to which there is pressure of occupation in buildings. "Tenement" has been defined as "so much of a building as from the records is shown as occupied (or in the case of vacancies as normally occupiable) by a separate family; provided that since it is not possible to consider a single room as constituting more than one tenement, such single rooms as at the Census were occupied by more than one family are counted as one tenement each." Thus a tenement is a measure of a family's occupation and if due provision were made for unoccupied tenements in the statistics and for the floor space of tenements which are shared by more than one family, there would be a record of the housing of the city that would be fairly accurate foı the factory, labouring and lower middle classes. "Tenement" is, of course, itsell an elastic term, though it is definite in meaning. What is needed is a definitioı of "tenement" with reference to average floor space and after much greateı sub-division of the first class of buildings enumerated in Housing Table III, namely buildings containing ten tenements and under. The Table as it stands is only partially useful, as the number of tenements in a building is no adequate guide to overcrowding at all. Mr. Sedgwick said in 1921 "It has already been mentioned that this table is of rather doubtful value. But if it is retained next time it is clear that the first class must be broken up into a number of sub-classes. It is unsatisfactory to have one class that contains 80 per cent. of the total: the sub-classes might be, 1 tenement, 2 tenements, 3 to 5 tenements, and 6 to 10 tenements." With this view the present writer entirely agrees. The classification, as it now exists, is unscientific and faulty and not designed to set out the information in the manner best suited to display the facts. There is the strongest possible reason why the whole of the schedules of the Bombay Housing Statistics should be over-hauled by an expert economist with experience of housing conditions in large modern cities. The schedules could then be re-designed and the present waste of effort involved in collecting statistics of only partial value would be avoided. At present the work of any statistician dealing with Bombay housing is very difficult. Most of his work is taken up pointing out the limited way in which the statistics can be safely employed, and not in displaying unambiguously facts which should have been apparent as the result of so much time and labour in collecting statistical material.

Housing Table III deals with residential buildings only, as in 1921. It dealt with all buildings in 1911 and 1901. But the continuity was not maintained in 1921 and this time. The inclusion of non-residential buildings would raise the proportion of buildings with few tenements and thereby would not give the exact impression of actual overcrowding. This will be obvious from the following statement.

Percentage of buildings classified according to number of tenements (four Censuses)

Year.	Under 11	11–20	21–30	31–40	41–50	Over 50
1901	83	9	4	2	1	1
1911	85	8	3	2	1	1
1921	80	10	4	2	1	3
1931	73	14	5	3	2	3

The figures show a slight tendency for the type of residential accommodation to shift from the lowest to the higher classes. This fact has already been sufficiently commented upon above. Most ground-floor buildings would fall under the "under 11 tenements class".

12. HOUSING TABLE IV.

This table has been prepared for residential buildings only, precisely on the lines of the 1921 census. The table, which ought to be a guide to overcrowding, is utterly useless for the purpose because of the vagueness of the term " building ". This vagueness completely destroys any definiteness the statistics might otherwise have possessed.

The following statement (No. 15) shows the percentages, to total number of buildings, of buildings under each class according to the number of persons occupying each.

STATEMENT No. 15.

Year.	Percentage to total buildings of buildings containing persons.							
	20 and under	21–40	41–60	61–80	81–100	101–150	151–200	201 and over
1901	76	11	5	3	1	2	1	1
1911	64	17	8	4	2	3	1	1
1921	59	18	8	4	3	4	2	2
1931	52·9	20·1	9·6	5·4	3·3	4·4	2·0	2·3

Only the 1921 and 1931 figures are strictly comparable with each other. The tendency, already noticed in previous comment for population to shift from smaller buildings to larger ones, will be noted. The figures do not of course mean what they appear to mean at first sight; namely, that whereas in 1921 18 per cent. of the buildings were buildings containing 21 to 40 occupants each, and now the percentage has risen to 20·1 and that in consequence housing has definitely deteriorated. Housing conditions generally may have deteriorated, though this is doubtful. But the figures now under discussion are incapable of proving that housing has deteriorated or improved. The reason is that until the kinds and sizes of the buildings are known, the facts must remain statistically incomplete. The number of buildings treated primarily in Housing Table IV are residential buildings only, save those which were empty at the time of the Census.

Two supplements have been published to this table. Supplement No. 1 gives the number of unoccupied buildings by sections and supplement No. 2 shows the number of persons enumerated in non-residential buildings. Persons enumerated otherwise than in a building have not been taken into consideration.

13. HOUSING TABLE V.

This table has been prepared for residential buildings only on the lines followed in the 1921 census. Mr. Sedgwick remarked in 1921 : " This table is designed to show the pressure of persons upon room space. That is to say, though the rooms are not measured the number of persons per room is calculated, it being assumed that the size of a room will in the long run average out at about the same throughout the city. This is possibly not quite correct. In Esplanade the average size of a room is likely to be larger than in, say, Kamathipura. Nevertheless the difference in average space in the two sections would probably be much less than might on theory be supposed ". In fact, for " overcrowding " it is not the size of the rooms that matters but the number of rooms at the disposal of a family. Comparative differences in size of room are not likely to solve evils of overcrowding, if the number of rooms at the disposal of a family is itself inadequate. Rooms are divided into four classes according to the number of occupants, namely, 5 persons and under, 6 to 9 persons, 10 to 15 persons, and 20 persons and over. Thus the least measure by which overcrowding in Bombay is judged is one which fails to make any differentiation in cases where the number of persons per room does not exceed five. This first category alone is statistically absurd. It includes all numbers of persons from zero to 5 living together in one room, that is, it lumps sanitary and insanitary conditions of living together, and puts, into one category, conditions where there is no overcrowding and conditions where overcrowding is clear, as it must be whenever four persons live in one room. As Mr. Sedgwick remarked in 1921 : "In this case, as in Housing Table III, the first class is too large. If the table is to be maintained next time it will be desirable to split this class up ". The table remains as it was in 1921 and continues to be the despair of any scientific statistician. The following statement (No. 16) shows the percentage of the population occupying rooms according to number of persons in a room.

STATEMENT NO. 16.

Year.	5 and under	6–9	10–19	20 and over.
1911	89	20	9	3
1921	64	22	11	3
1931	67	24	8	1

Only the 1921 and the 1931 figures are comparable together. Thus by far the majority of people occupy rooms in which the number of occupants in each is five persons and under at a time. This actually means, though these statistics are unable to prove it, general overcrowding of the mass of the population. It will be shown at a later stage of this report that the average number of persons per room in one-roomed tenements, which form 81 per cent. of the total number of tenements, is 4·01, which by western standards amounts to gross overcrowding and even by Indian standards of city life must be called bad. But, as the statement given above shows, 33 per cent. of the population lives in rooms occupied by more than five persons at a time and 1 per cent. in rooms occupied by over 20 persons at a time. Such conditions must be more reminiscent of the "Black Hole" of historical memory than of any modern city pretending to sanitary living conditions. There are 15,490 persons living in rooms occupied by 20 persons or over each. The number of persons living in rooms containing from 6 to 9 persons each is 256,379 and the number of persons living in rooms occupied by 10 to 19 persons each is 80,133. Thus, even if all the persons occupying rooms containing only five persons and under were free from overcrowding, (which is the opposite of the real facts) it would still be true that 352,002 persons, or 30·3 per cent. of the total population of the city are living in conditions of the grossest overcrowding. The statement below (No. 17) shows the distribution of population by sections of the city according to the number of persons occupying single rooms.

STATEMENT NO. 17.

Section.	5 and under.	6–9.	10–19.	20 and over.
Upper Colaba	62	32	6	0
Lower Colaba	70	22	1	7
Fort South	58	27	14	1
Fort North	70	21	7	2
Esplanade	67	19	7	7
Chakla	68	18	9	5
Mandvi	65	25	9	1
Umarkhadi	74	20	5	1
Dongri	73	22	5	0
Market	64	28	6	2
Dhobitalav	74	18	6	2
Fanaswadi	70	21	8	1
Bhuleshwar	70	21	8	1
Kumbharwada	59	30	10	1
Kharatalav	58	30	11	1

STATEMENT No. 17—*contd.*

Section.	5 and under.	6–9.	10–19.	20 and over.
Khetwadi	71	19	8	2
Girgaon	78	17	4	1
Chowpati	91	8	1	0
Walkeshwar	71	17	10	2
Mahalaxmi	72	20	7	1
Tardeo	75	18	6	1
Kamathipura	65	23	10	2
First Nagpada	76	18	5	1
Second Nagpada	60	24	11	5
Byculla	62	30	7	1
Tarwadi	70	24	6	0
Mazagaon	47	34	14	5
Parel	65	27	6	2
Sewri	60	31	9	0
Sion	62	26	10	2
Mahim	75	19	5	1
Worli	66	27	7	0

The first column of figures, owing to its deficiencies of classification, is practically useless for displaying the facts of overcrowding. These facts will be displayed otherwise in a later section of this report. The second, third and fourth columns of figures show percentages of the excessive overcrowding of a minority of the population. The figures do not show the normal overcrowding of the majority of the population. The following statement by wards, to the nearest hundred persons, will show the distribution of the grossest overcrowding.

STATEMENT No. 18.

Ward.	Number living 6–9.	Number living 10–19.	Number living 20 and over	Percentages of population of wards affected by gross over-crowding.
A	125	43	15	3
B	223	72	16	27
C	482	160	22	32
D	261	91	18	24
E	690	209	50	35
F	417	123	27	36
G	365	92	7	28

Reference to Housing Table IV will show the items making up these totals in the various sections of the City. Byculla and Mazagaon are the worst parts of ward E. For the sake of comparison the 1921 figures are given below.

STATEMENT No. 19.

1921

Ward.	6 to 9 persons.	10 to 19 persons.	20 persons and over.	Percentage of the population of wards affected by gross over-crowding.
A	104	58	39	27
B	222	115	35	29
C	333	153	42	27
D	232	95	24	24
E	653	319	70	34
F	381	168	51	41
G	443	250	54	44

In ward A the population of Colaba has been considerably reduced owing to the shifting of the military from the place. Hence the percentage of overcrowding has fallen considerably. Overcrowding in wards B, C, D, E is nearly the same. There is a slight increase in ward C. Wards F and G show a decrease of overcrowding. But the chief reason is faulty enumeration in these parts and incorrect housing statistics. The chawls constructed by the Development Department for the labouring class appear to have been effective in lessening the pressure of population in G ward and especially in Worli.

14. HOUSING TABLE VI-A.

This table is specially designed to show the state of "overcrowding" in Bombay. The table displays three kinds of facts (1) the percentage of each class of tenements to the total tenements, (2) the percentage of occupants in each class of tenements to the total population, (3) the average number of persons per room in each class of tenement. The figures for 1931 are comparable with the 1921 figures but not with figures prior to 1921. The facts disclosed by Housing Table VI-A are sufficiently arresting. There are in the city 244, 121 occupied tenements. Of these 197,516 consist of one room only. One-roomed tenements form 81 per cent. of the total tenements in the city and they are occupied by 791,762 persons or 74 per cent. of the population of the city. The average number of persons per room in this class of tenement is 4·01. The facts then are, briefly, that three out of every four persons in Bombay live in single rooms and that in these rooms, with each of them, there are at least three other persons. It is perfectly impossible to view a situation like this with complacency. The minimum of accommodation required for four persons is two rooms for living and sleeping, assuming that washing and answering the calls of nature are provided for by separate domestic facilities shared in common with other persons. This of course is what happens. The provision of water taps and privies is usually made for numbers of families together. Any one familiar with Bombay is aware how the streets are used at night as sleeping places. When the overcrowding in the houses is considered, there is nothing remarkable in the fact. But the streets should not thus have to be used as a safety valve against housing inadequacies. Three-fourths of the population of Bombay live in one-roomed residences and the average floor space available for each occupant cannot be more than what could be covered by a small mat. When better housing comes and the factory, labouring, and lower middle classes can afford to pay for sanitary and properly-ventilated houses, the night population on the pavements may be expected to decrease. At present the pavement sleepers remain as a practical proof of the failure of Bombay to solve in any satisfactory way the problem of house accommodation for at least three quarters of its population, or about eight hundred thousand persons. Only 26 per cent. of the population are living in residences with more than one room each ; 11 per cent. of these live in places with two rooms each ; 3 per cent. in places with three rooms each ; 2 per cent. in places with four rooms each ; 1 per cent. in places with five rooms each ; and 2 per cent. in places with six or more rooms each. The number of persons thus provided for is as under : in two-roomed tenements, 131,872, equal to 12 per cent. of the total population and to an average of 2·51 persons per room ; in three-roomed tenements, 44,821 persons, equal to 4 per cent. of the total population and to an average of 2·01 persons per room ; in four-roomed tenements, 42,013 persons, equal to 4 per cent. of the total population and to 1·71 persons per room ; in five-roomed tenements, 22,302 persons, equal to 2 per cent. of the total population and to 1·50 persons per room ; in six-roomed tenements, 39,199 persons, equal to 4 per cent. of the total population. The general conclusions to be drawn from these striking figures are (1) that if an average of more than two and a half persons per room were taken as indicating "overcrowding" in Bombay, 86 per cent. of Bombay's population would be considered to be overcrowded and housed so inadequately that the streets have to be used universally to supplement the sleeping accommodation which the houses themselves cannot provide; (2) 96 per cent. of the individuals composing Bombay's population do not know what having a room to themselves means ; (3) only 4 per cent. of the population live in conditions which ensure reasonable privacy and domestic seclusion. In Chapter VIII of this report some examination of "overcrowding," as revealed by special enquiries made during the last decade in Bombay Presidency, will be used to supplement the conclusions drawn from the Census figures of 1931. The subject is one which is of the greatest interest to social workers, and to public authorities, who are partially at least responsible for the standards of well-being and comfort prevailing amongst the people at large. The housing problem in Bombay is not merely a problem of providing an adequate number of houses, but a problem of providing houses of the right kind. This means houses with many more facilities, especially as regards light and ventilation, cook rooms, water-supply and privies than most buildings now standing in Bombay possess.

It will be seen that the sections of the City which show overcrowding worst, as judged by the proportion of the population living in one-roomed tenements, are Byculla with 99 per cent. ; Sewri with 89 per cent. ; Mazagaon and Parel with 88 per cent. and Second Nagpada with 87 per cent. But out of the 32 sections of the City as many as 13 show percentages of 80 per cent. or more of their population living in one-roomed tenements. If the population of these thirteen sections be added together it will be found to amount to 576,858 or 50 per cent. of the City's population, and of this number 459,437 persons, or 40 per cent. of the City's population are living in one-roomed tenements in these parts of the city alone. The sections of the City which show least overcrowding are Chowpati, where only 30 per cent. of the population is housed in one-roomed tenements; Girgaum, where the proportion is 43 per cent. and Dhobi Talao where the proportion is 53 per cent. Chowpati shows also the best figures for the proportion of the population living in tenements with over two rooms, namely 52 per cent. Walkeshwar has the best figures for roomiest accommodation. In that section 22 per cent. of the population are living in tenements of 6 rooms each and over. The figures for the average number of persons per room are not so useful, but they do generally reflect the overcrowding in local areas. If the figures for one-roomed tenements only be considered, the sections showing the worst overcrowding per room are Mazagaon with 4·95; Kumbharwada with 4·52 ; Mandvi with 4·55 and Khara Talao with 4·37 per room and the sections showing the least overcrowding are First Nagpada with 3·21 ; Chowpati with 3·25 and Worli with 3·52 persons per room.

MO-III Bk Ka Cs 3—23

The comparative figures of overcrowding in Bombay for 1921 and 1931 and London 1911 are set out below.

STATEMENT NO. 20.

Number of rooms in tenement.	Percentage borne by population in each class of tenement to total population.			Average numbers of occupants per room in each class of tenement.		
	London.	Bombay.		London.	Bombay.	
	1911	1921	1931	1911	1921	1931
1 Room	6	66	74	1·92	4·03	4·01
2 Rooms	15	14	12	1·71	2·11	2·51
3 Rooms	20	8	4	1·37	1·60	2·01
4 Rooms	17	5	4	1·19	1·30	1·70
5 Rooms	11	4	2	1·03	1·06	1·50
6 Rooms and over	25	3	4	..	..	..

These figures show that Bombay is very overcrowded. The 1911 London figure for the average number of persons in one-roomed tenements is better than the 1931 Bombay figure for three-roomed tenements. Overcrowding in Bombay may be said to extend from one-roomed to three-roomed tenements, which between them comprise 95 per cent. of the housing accommodation in the City.

The following statement (No. 21) offers comparison between the 1931 and the 1921 Census figures in respect of percentages of tenements of each class, percentages of occupants to total population and average numbers of persons per room.

STATEMENT NO. 21.

Class of tenement by number of rooms.	Percentage of each class of tenement to total tenements		Percentage of occupants of each class of tenement to total population.		Average number of persons per room in each class of tenement.	
	1931	1921	1931	1921	1931	1921
1 Room	81	70	74	66	4·01	4·03
2 Rooms	11	14	12	14	2·51	2·11
3 Rooms	3	7	4	8	2·01	1·60
4 Rooms	2	4	4	5	1·70	1·30
5 Rooms	1	3	2	4	1·50	1·06
6 Rooms	2	2	4	3	..	..

The figures do not indicate general improvement in housing but they do seem to suggest that housing conditions for the working classes are better in 1931 than in 1921 since there are more tenements of the kind that meets their needs and the number of persons per room in such tenements has fallen. Thus one-roomed tenements are now 81 per cent. of the total number instead of 70 per cent. in 1921 ;

but on the other hand 74 per cent. of the City's population is living in them instead of only 66 in 1921. But, despite this fact, the average number of persons per room in one-roomed tenements has fallen from 4·03 to 4·01. Judgments on the improvement of housing are difficult but a fair conclusion on this evidence would seem to be that the improvement is due probably to a better type of one-roomed tenement being now available and attracting a larger proportion of the population. On the other hand, conditions in respect of two and three-roomed tenements seem to be worse. The proportion of two-roomed tenements has fallen from 14 to 11 per cent. in the decade and the fall in the population occupying these tenements from 14 to 12 per cent. indicates perhaps that many of the lower middle class have gone to live in one-roomed tenements. But this has led to no improvement in the two-roomed tenements where the number of persons per room has risen in the decade from 2·11 to 2·51. The comparative housing for the working classes and the lower middle classes has been discussed in Chapter VIII of this report in connection with housing conditions and economic welfare in cities. It is more than probable that the improvements in housing in the decade have benefited the working classes but not the lower middle classes.

15. HOUSING TABLE VI-B.

This table gives details by sections of one-roomed tenements containing more than one family.

The total number of one-roomed tenements returned at this census is 197,516 as against 175,001 in 1921. Of these 997 contain more than one family as against 3,126 in 1921. 65 per cent. of these tenements contain 2 families and 18 per cent. contain 3 families. Single rooms containing more than three families are not few. The occupants of these tenements are mostly millhands, labourers and persons of poor economic position. The table is an index of excessive overcrowding in one-roomed tenements. The conditions in which more than one family occupy only one room must be counted a disgrace to any civilised community. Tarwadi and Mandvi show the worst figures and the causes which make them possible are probably matters for the Health authorities of the City to consider. Insanitariness must be inevitable in the circumstances and the health of the neighbourhood imperilled.

This table is statistically most unsatisfactory because it offers no explanation of the kinds of buildings in which as many as 5, 6, 7, 8 and more families are occupying one room. It is perfectly clear that as regards 2, 3 and 4 families occupying one room, the grossest kind of overcrowding must be in existence. But when the number of families per room rises to as many as 5, 6, 7, 8 and over it is necessary to enquire what kind of building it can be that permits such conditions and whether the family unit in such cases is normal; that is, if it contains on an average about four persons. In 1921 Mr. Findlay Shirras found in his special enquiry that the average working class family in Bombay consisted of 4·2 persons, namely 1·1 men, 1·1 women and 2 children, exclusive of 0·6 dependents living outside Bombay. It must be obvious that if from twenty to forty persons are living in one room each, as shown by Housing Table VI-B for certain areas and localities in the City, something extraordinary is happening. The present writer, in the course of a visit to Bombay in 1932, endeavoured to obtain some information on the point from the Public Health authorities. No fully satisfactory explanation was available in the time at disposal. It will be seen that in Chakla there are 27 one-roomed tenements returned as occupied by 8 families and over each, and in Mazagaon there are 36 such tenements. Two possible explanations were offered. One is that some of these buildings must be godowns converted into dormitories for coolies and the like. Another is that Bhayas in Bombay, when they are single men, often club together and hire one room in order to share the expense of the rent. In both these cases the overcrowding may not be so bad as the figures suggest. But the point needs clear elucidation by the Health authorities. These facts will show that Housing Table VI-B as it exists at present must be used with the utmost caution. It shows in part of it, namely in the first three columns, the most disgraceful and indefensible overcrowding and, in another part of it, it may show still more disgraceful and indefensible overcrowding, namely in columns 4, 5, 6 and 7 or it may not, according to the actual conditions found. The table itself cannot clear the point. In Karachi similar conditions exist in respect of the statistics of Table VI-B. There too the matter should be investigated by the Health authorities.

16. HOUSING TABLE VII.

This table shows the conditions under which each community is living. The figures reveal interesting facts corroborated by every-day observation. The Zoroastrians live in more spacious and comfortable rooms than any other community. Though Jains and Zoroastrians are economically on the same level the former live in less comfortable and commodious houses than the latter. The following statement No. 22 shows the percentage of each religion occupying one-room tenements.

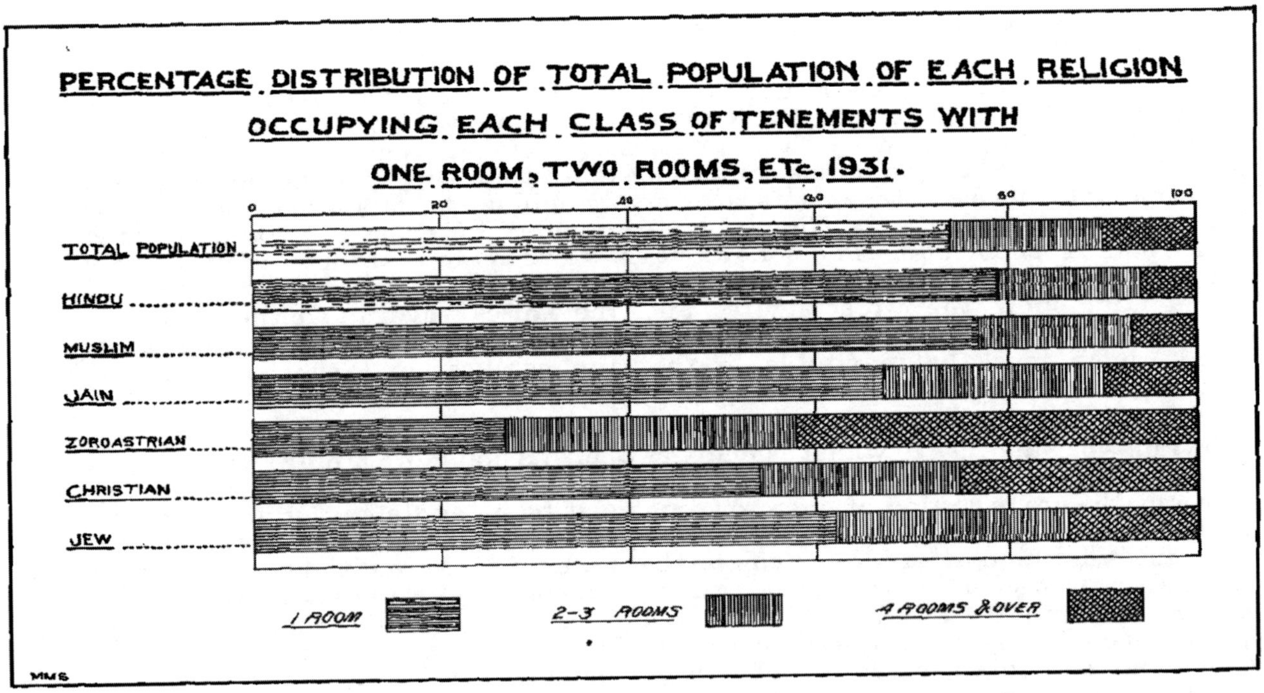

STATEMENT No. 22.

Religion.	1931	1921
Zoroastrian	27	21
Christian	54	41
Jew and others	62	50
Jains	67	66
Muhammadan	77	67
Hindus	79	71

It will be seen from the figures that the Hindus are worst off. A study of the figures throws some light on the proportion of persons in good and bad economic circumstances in each religion. As the figures in 1931 show a rise in each religion it can be safely concluded that trade depression is affecting all communities without exception.

The statistics in Housing Table VII must be read with attention to the remarks which Mr. Sedgwick offered in the 1921 Census report. The percentage distribution must in any case be checked against the number of persons enumerated. This table is more valuable as a social index than as an indication of anything concerned with religion as such.

CHAPTER VI—HOUSING IN KARACHI.

1. Introductory.

The practice of classifying buildings in Karachi City and of giving statistics of the housing accommodation there dates from 1921. At this Census, as in 1921, the tables relating to housing have been entitled "Housing Tables" (seven in all) and given a separate serial numbering.

The information required for the preparation of these tables was collected by the Municipality at the time of the preliminary and the final Census count. In Karachi a strong force of non-co-operation was directed against the Municipal efforts to achieve correct enumeration. As a result information required for the Housing Tables collected in the blocks was unsatisfactory, and in some cases many houses were omitted from the original sheets and the statistics collected for these blocks were lost. Hence, the accuracy of the statistics presented in the Housing Tables cannot be guaranteed.

2. Definition of "Building."

The definition of a "building" adopted at Karachi for this Census is identical with that adopted by the Chief Officer, Karachi City Municipality, for the Census of 1921.

"House" means premises under one undivided roof whether let off into tenements or not (one such tenement would be given a number thus—12-1, 12-2, 12-3, etc.) "provided that in the case of a terrace of dwellings or semi-detached bungalows, each such dwelling with separate access to the public street, divided off by party walls and occupied by one family from the ground upwards, shall be considered to be a separate house, although the roof of the terrace or semi-detached bungalow may be a continuous one; such cases will include dwellings of ground floor only and of two or more floors and each house is to be given a separate number."

" *Note.*—In the case of blocks of buildings forming servants' quarters to a bungalow, each of such blocks shall be classified as one house, separate tenements being numbered as above, for premises under one undivided roof according to the number of separate families occupying the same."

3. Pressure of Population on Housing.

The statement below shows the pressure of population upon housing in Bombay and Karachi according to the 1931 Census.

Unit.	Population.	Houses.	Persons per house.
Karachi	263,565	26,016	10
Bombay	1,161,383	32,930	35

This statement by itself is of little statistical value. Its meaning depends entirely on the signification attached to the word "house". As will be seen later in this chapter, Karachi possesses few large buildings of the type common in Bombay and the statement above is in consequence unduly flattering to Karachi, where housing conditions are in places very bad.

4. The Housing Tables.

The same seven tables have been prepared as in Bombay and the same general remarks apply to the statistical value to be attached to them. The tables are generally badly adapted for the purpose for which, presumably, they were designed and require drastic overhaul by an expert economist familiar with housing conditions in modern cities. By next Census perhaps some progress will have been made towards setting out the statistical material in a more logical and less unsatisfactory way. At present the preparation of the tables involves an amount of labour out of all proportion to the direct statistical value of the results.

5. HOUSING TABLE I.

As regards the grouping of buildings by classes the scheme introduced in Bombay City, modelled on the English scheme, has been followed. The buildings are mainly divided into two categories,

(1) Residential.

(2) Non-residential.

The terms "Residential" and "Non-residential" refer to the ordinary uses of each building, and are irrespective of whether any person was or was not enumerated in the building on the night of final enumeration.

The following statement shows the variation which has occurred in the number of buildings of various classes during the decade.

Residential Buildings.

Class.	1931	1921	Variation increase + decrease —
1. Bungalows and dwelling houses	15,481	13,133	+ 2,348
2. Servants' quarters	477	628	— 151
3. Chawls	135	752	— 617
4. Factories, shops, offices, etc., combined with dwellings	3,298	2,508	+ 790
5. Dharmshalas	16	11	+ 5
6. Institutions	179	68	+ 111
7. Huts	6,635	10,414	— 3,779
8. Others and unclassifiable	368	*Nil.*	+ 368
Total ..	26,589	27,514	— 925

Non-Residential Buildings.

Class.	1931	1921	Variation increase + decrease —
1. Places of worship	328	219	+ 109
2. Institutions and places of amusement	261	195	+ 66
3. Factories, mills and works	144	59	+ 85
4. Offices and shops	1,799	2,178	— 379
5. Godowns, stables, garages, sheds and chowkis	1,301	1,150	+ 151
6. Others and unclassifiable	10	..	+ 10
Total ..	3,843	3,801	+ 42

There are some puzzling features about these figures. The number of bungalows and dwelling houses has risen by 2,348 but the number of servants' quarters has fallen by 151. It is not clear whether this is due to a change in the type of residential building showing a predilection for flats in preference to the ordinary ground-floor bungalow and house. Certainly a casual inspection of Karachi does not encourage the belief that the "flats" type of building is becoming very common. The great fall in the number of chawls and the rise in the number of factories, shops, offices, etc., combined with dwellings, leads to a belief that the census classification must be responsible for the change. The fall in the number of huts is presumably a sign of progress. The number of offices and shops shows a decrease of 370. Whether bad trade is entirely responsible for this fall is doubtful. There may have been confusion in enumeration between factories, mills and works, and offices and shops. The rise in the number of godowns, stables, garages, sheds and chowkies must be due largely to the construction of motor garages and the increase might have been expected to be larger.

6. HOUSING TABLE II.

Buildings with a large number of floors are not typical of Karachi. Most buildings in Karachi have ground floors only and very few indeed have more than two upper floors. Only 9·3 per cent. of the buildings have more than one upper floor. In Bombay 25·4 per cent. of the buildings have more than one upper floor. Land is evidently much less valuable in Karachi than in Bombay. Nor is there the same need for the construction of big composite buildings with accommodation for factory people, who must reside not too far away from the mills in which they work.

The statement below (No. 1) shows the difference between Karachi and Bombay in the types of buildings.

STATEMENT No. 1.

Category.	Karachi.	Bombay.
Buildings with ground floor only	77·6	60·2
Do. one upper floor	13·1	14·4
Do. two upper floors	7·2	10·5
Do. three upper floors	2·0	8·5
Do. four upper floors	0·1	4·9
Do. five upper floors	*Nil.*	1·5
	100	100

7. HOUSING TABLES III, IV AND V.

Housing Table III shows houses classified according to the number of tenements they contain. As Karachi is not a town of large buildings by far the greatest number of the buildings are in the lowest class (one to five tenements), namely, 23,163 out of a total number of 26,396. The number of buildings containing over ten tenements apiece is only 1,334 in the whole city. The Runchore quarter contains the largest number of these.

Housing Table IV classifies buildings according to the number of occupants, a rather useless classification, when the word "building" is itself an elastic and vague term. 21,996 of the 24,397 buildings enumerated are buildings occupied by 20 persons and under each. There are no means of knowing from the table what is the number of persons under twenty in any one house or kind of house. In fact the table gives no information whatever of the distribution of the population occupying the 90 per cent. of the housing accommodation provided by the first class of buildings.

Housing Table V shows the distribution of persons by rooms in residential buildings. In this table again the lowest category (5 persons and under per room) absorbs the bulk of the population. The other categories do give some idea of gross over-crowding affecting a minority of the population but the table gives no idea of the normal over-crowding of the majority of the population. In Karachi 50,270 persons are living in rooms containing from 6 to 9 persons each. 13,026 are living in rooms containing from 10 to 19 persons each and 2,067 persons are living in rooms containing 20 persons and more each. The worst of this gross overcrowding is in the Lyari quarter, where 20,118 persons are living 6 to 9 to a room and 7,002 persons are living 10 to 19 to a room. But there is gross overcrowding of this kind in the Machi Miani, Runchore and Lawrence quarters, in all of which more than two thousand persons are living 6 to 9 to a room. There are however 12, out of the 39, quarters of the city where more than a thousand persons are living 6 to 9 to a room. The very worst overcrowding is in Lyari quarter, where 709 persons are living 20 and more to a room, and in New Jail quarter, where 672 persons are so living. Conditions like these would seem to merit examination by the Public Health authorities. It is impossible that human existence in such conditions can be anything but a source of danger and pollution to the neighbourhood. The statement below (No. 2) shows the comparative figures for the last two Censuses of the percentage of the population living in rooms classified according to number of occupants.

STATEMENT No. 2.

Persons per room.	1921	1931
5 persons and under	72·8	52·5
6 to 9 persons	20·9	32·3
10 to 19 persons	5·4	12·4
20 persons and over	0·9	2·8

The figures show such remarkable variations that constructive criticism of them is impossible. Enumeration must have been capriciously at fault. The 1931 figures are probably nearer the truth but comparison with 1921 is clearly out of the question.

The total number of persons enumerated in residential buildings falls short of the total enumerated population by 7,018. The difference is partly at least accounted for by the floating and moving port and dock population at the time of the Census.

8. HOUSING TABLES VI-A AND VI-B.

These tables are designed to show the extent of overcrowding in Karachi. A large proportion of a city population living in one-roomed tenements displays general poverty. But it proves also overcrowding, as the average number of persons living in one-roomed tenements is 3·74. In six quarters of the City, namely Ghizri, Trans-Lyari, Tatta Naka, etc., Quarries, Scattered Hamlets behind the Cantonment Station, etc., and Bunker Island, the whole of the population is living in one-roomed tenements. In none of these however are the sections of population concerned very large, being 1,024, 5,660, 860, 424, 859 and 4 persons respectively. In the case of Bunker Island there is no overcrowding ; there are only 4 persons in the island and they have three rooms between them. Bunker Island's figures are therefore merely a statistical curiosity. Overcrowding in Karachi is however bad in certain areas. Of the more thickly populated quarters of the City, Runchore has 74 per cent. of its population of 24,924 persons living in one-roomed tenements and an average of 3·81 persons per room. Lyari has 84 per cent. of its population of 58,816 persons living in one-roomed tenements with 4·55 persons per room, and Lawrence has 84 per cent. of its population of 10,167 persons living in one-roomed tenements with 3·79 persons per room. In New Jail quarter the proportion living in one-roomed tenements is 97 with 6·44 persons per room. But the population affected by these conditions is only 1,127. In Ghizri quarter already mentioned above the number of persons per room is 4·92. Kiamari is the least overcrowded quarter of Karachi, with 23 per cent. of its population living in one-roomed tenements.

The following statement (No. 3) gives the comparative figures for two censuses under the three headings dealt with in Table VI-A.

STATEMENT No. 3.

Tenements with	Percentage of each class of tenement to total tenements.		Percentage of population in each class of tenement to total population.		Average number of occupants per room in each class of tenement.	
	1931.	1921.	1931.	1921.	1931.	1921.
One room	66	69	58	58	3·74	3·46
Two rooms	22	22	24	23	2·27	2·20
Three rooms	6	4	8	7	1·85	2·24
Four rooms	3	2	5	4	1·67	1·75
Five rooms	1	1	1	2	1·56	1·81
Six rooms	2	2	4	6	..	..

The figures should be compared with the corresponding Bombay City figures in paragraphs 14, 15 and 16 of Chapter V of this Volume. It will be noted that the average number of persons per room in one and two-roomed tenements has risen and the number of persons per room in three, four, and five-roomed tenements has fallen. These two influences together suggest that the housing in Karachi has definitely deteriorated and that housing has failed to keep pace with the great increase of population witnessed during the decade. This is the general experience of the Presidency according to the 1931 Census. The grossest overcrowding is exhibited in Table VI-B, namely those cases where more than one family are occupying one room. There are in Karachi 1,490 one-roomed tenements so occupied and the Table shows that hardly one quarter of the City fails to provide examples of this gross overcrowding. It is certainly surprising that the Civil Lines should be the fourth worst offender in this respect, being surpassed by only Lyari, Railway area and Napier quarters. In the Civil Lines there are actually 78 single-roomed tenements occupied by 2 families each, 16 occupied by 3 families each, and 10 occupied by four or more families each. In Lyari quarter the number of single-roomed tenements occupied by more than one family is as high as 527. Of these 97 are occupied by three families apiece and 35 by four or more families. In one respect Karachi however is able to mitigate the rigours of room overcrowding. The Sind climate is one which compels outdoor sleeping for most days in the year and the use of string cots is almost universal. This is quite different from the conditions which make for armies of sleepers, wrapped in cloths, lining the Bombay pavements at night. The "room" in fact in Sind is less important than in Bombay. But a certain number of rooms per family is necessary for the preservation of ordinary decency and the amenities of domestic life. It is to be feared that most of the housing accommodation judged by this standard would be considered inadequate by social workers.

9. TABLE VII.

This table shows the distribution of occupied tenements by rooms and the occupants by religion. As a statement of religious distribution the table has small value, but it is useful as corroborative general evidence of the economic level of persons in the different religions. In 1921 the table was abandoned as unreliable. Jains are least overcrowded and then come Jews and Christians. The Jain community in Karachi is however numerically unimportant. Muslims with a percentage of 69 in one-roomed tenements are the worst off. It is they who probably contribute most to the overcrowding of the Lyari quarter. Sikhs have 40 per cent. of their total number in one-roomed tenements and Hindus 50 per cent. A glance at the detailed figures will however show that Karachi differs very much in respect of overcrowding in its various quarters and a general statement for the whole City has not very much value. Students are advised to study the local figures in detail instead of relying on the general averages.

CHAPTER VII—HOUSING IN SHOLAPUR.

1. Introductory.

This is the first occasion on which housing statistics for Sholapur have been incorporated in the Census Report of the Cities of the Bombay Presidency. The excessively industrialised character of Sholapur has been explained in Chapter IV of the present Volume. It was to be expected therefore that the housing conditions of the City would show some resemblance to those prevailing in Bombay. In Sholapur however land is not so valuable as in Bombay and conditions generally are not so bad in consequence. It is always where a large factory population has to be housed in cities where every square yard of land is valuable that housing conditions are usually at their worst. Sholapur is more open than Bombay and the need for constructing large chawls is not acute. A much larger proportion of the Sholapur population will therefore be found living in smaller buildings or in huts than is the case in Bombay. Living in huts need not in itself be a bad thing. But it is invariably so if the huts are erected haphazard in the midst of a settled industrial town. No sufficient information has been afforded by the Census as to the precise conditions in which so many huts exist in Sholapur. But it may be presumed that the living conditions in such huts is not inferior to the housing afforded by huts in mofussil towns similar in character to that to which Sholapur, apart from its industrialisation, approximates more than to a city like Bombay. Sholapur is really a Deccan mofussil town with a factory population super-imposed upon it. Unless therefore there is great pressure on space within the city limits, housing conditions in huts are probably not too bad ; and certainly not the menace to public health they would be in Bombay.

2. The Housing Tables.

Housing Table I shows that in Sholapur there are 20,630 buildings of all sorts and of these 14,763 are residential. Of this number 3,219 consist of huts and other small temporary buildings and most of these are in five wards only, namely ward 3 with 554, ward 4 with 431, ward 9 with 643, ward 10 with 334 and ward 11 with 1,015. Housing Table II shows that of the total number of buildings (20,630) 17,770 consist of ground floors only. There are only 2,676 buildings with one upper floor, and 2,860 with more than one upper floor in the whole city. Sholapur is thus not to be compared with Bombay at all in its kind of buildings. It is even less modern than Karachi, which is a commercial and not an industrial city. Housing Table III shows that of the total number of buildings enumerated in the table 7,551 or 37 per cent. have one room only ; 5,505 or 27 per cent. have two rooms each ; 2,110 or 10 per cent. have three rooms each ; and 1,579 or 8 per cent. have four rooms each. Houses with more than four rooms each number 3,798 or 18 per cent. of the total. In respect of the percentage of two-roomed and three-roomed houses Sholapur is superior to both Bombay and Karachi. The climatic and topographical conditions in Sholapur approximate more to those in Karachi than to those in Bombay so that overcrowding, where by mere numerical calculation it is shown to exist, is not so grave a menace to health and decency as it is in Bombay. Table IV shows that out of the 19,044 buildings enumerated in the table 14,359 or 76 per cent. are occupied by single families ; 1,892 or 10 per cent. by two families ; and 1,028 or 5 per cent. by three families. Only 1,765 buildings or 9 per cent. of the total are occupied by more than four families together. This means that the chawl and flats system is not developed in Sholapur and that most of the housing is on the individual system, which, in Sholapur, does not result in the gross overcrowding a similar system would connote in Bombay and, to a lesser degree, in Karachi. Most of the one-roomed houses are in ward 11 which has 4,854 such buildings. Ward 9 with 1,753 such buildings and ward 3 and ward 7 with 1,420 and 1,389 such buildings respectively would presumably show the greatest pressure on room space. Statistics however are not available to show what this pressure actually is, so that direct comparison between Bombay, Karachi and Sholapur in this respect is not possible.

The statistics as they stand show an abnormal rise in the number of buildings of all kinds. There is recorded a 55 per cent. increase in buildings of all kinds during the last decade : 70 per cent. in residential buildings, 52 per cent. in commercial buildings, 63 per cent. in public buildings, and 23 per cent. in huts and smaller buildings. It is hard to believe that this represents the actual state of things and that Sholapur alone in the Presidency has more than made allowance in the matter of housing for the general increase in population. Census classification and faulty enumeration must account partially for this extraordinary result. The housing statistics ought therefore to be accepted with some caution.

CHAPTER VIII—HOUSING CONDITIONS AND ECONOMIC WELFARE IN CITIES.

1. Special economic enquiries held during the decade.

Very much has been done in Bombay Presidency during the last decade towards gaining a proper understanding of the conditions under which the population of the big cities and, especially of Bombay City, lives its life. The credit for this advance in knowledge must be given to the Labour Office which has published an admirable series of monographs on housing, economic and labour conditions in the Presidency during the last ten years. Month by month too in the *Labour Gazette* articles appear of the utmost interest and value to statisticians, social workers and economists. It will be realised of course that the decennial Census of the population does not duplicate the kind of enquiry that the Labour Office has been so successful in pursuing and it is not in the present chapter intended to set up the Census figures against the figures obtained in special economic enquiries. The intention is simply to attempt to correlate some of the conclusions that can be drawn from the decennial Census with conclusions drawn by the Labour Office investigators. This correlation is from a sociological point of view of great interest and importance. It enables students to view the social conditions of workers and other persons living in cities in a manner that would not otherwise be possible without very detailed and troublesome individual research. The enquiries which are most important for correlation with the census statistics of housing are the following, published as shown in the year in brackets; (1) Report on an Enquiry into Working Class Budgets in Bombay (1923) by Mr. G. Findlay Shirras; (2) Report on an Enquiry into Middle Class Family Budgets in Bombay City (1928) by the Labour Office, Bombay; (3) Report on an Enquiry into Working Class Family Budgets in Ahmedabad (1928) by the Labour Office, Bombay; (4) Report on an Enquiry into Family Budgets of Cotton Mill workers in Sholapur City (1928) by the Labour Office, Bombay; (5) House Rents in Bombay, article in the *Labour Gazette* of October 1924, pages 159 to 168 ; (6) An enquiry into Housing Conditions among the Lower Middle Class in Bombay (South) by H. L. Kaji, M.A., B.Sc., F.S.S., in the same issue of the *Labour Gazette*, pages 169 to 181; (7) Infant Mortality among Working Classes in Bombay City (1930) by the Labour Office, Bombay; (8) Working Class House Rents in Bombay City, published in the *Labour Gazette* for May 1931 at pages 875 to 896, and written by the Labour Office, Bombay. In the sections of the chapter which follow important conclusions arrived at in these various special enquiries are discussed in relation to the Census statistics of 1931. Much that is dealt with in the present chapter must be read along with the chapters in this volume dealing with the Cities of the Bombay Presidency and in particular with the Housing Statistics compiled for the 1931 Census, which are discussed in chapters V, VI and VII above.

2. Correlation with the Census Statistics.

The Census statistics dealing with cities are not confined to the Cities volume. Many of the important tables can be studied properly only in the general statistics of the Presidency. The chief statistics that must be considered by social investigators interested in the conditions governing economic welfare in cities are found in the Imperial and City tables dealing with age, sex, occupation and civil condition. Many important general questions connected with these demographical matters have been discussed in the 1931 Census report for Bombay Presidency. The other statistics that need study at the same time are the Housing Statistics published in the present volume and the vital statistics published by the Public Health authorities.

3. The Types of City Population considered in Special Enquiries.

Two main types of population have been studied in special enquiries during the last ten years. These types are (1) the working and labouring class whose working, housing and economic conditions have been investigated in Bombay City,

Ahmedabad and Sholapur; and (2) the lower middle class, a sampling of which was examined between 1922 and 1924 in Bombay City. The investigation on the latter was undertaken to obtain reliable information on three main subjects (a) the size and earnings of the family; (b) the cost and consumption of food, fuel and lighting, furniture and household effects; and (c) house rents and housing conditions. The enquiry was restricted to middle class persons having fixed and ascertainable incomes and was therefore confined to families with an income of not less than Rs. 50 and of not more than Rs. 700 per month. Actually in the report published in 1928 the income classes dealt with ranged from Rs. 75 to Rs. 225 per month. The section of the population dealt with was thus in effect confined to the "blackcoated population" of a clerical type, of the kind employed in Government service or in commercial and similar offices. The population studied in this way was drawn largely from Girgaum (D ward) and from Mahim (G ward). There is however no reason to doubt that the sampling effected was typical of the lower middle class of the city. It is therefore easy to compare conditions prevailing amongst this class with conditions prevailing amongst the mill and labouring population in which the Royal Commission on Labour was chiefly interested. The Census statistics do not deal with economic classes as such. The Census has adopted, however, two main criteria which help in sorting out the population into economic classes, namely (1) the number of rooms in a tenement, which can be identified in general by the ward and section distribution shown in Housing Tables VI-A and VI-B for Bombay City and (2) the number of persons per occupied room. If the Census statistics are examined carefully and the local distribution by wards is studied at the same time, quite valuable results can be obtained in conjunction with the special Labour Office enquiries in respect of the housing conditions and especially in respect of overcrowding in the lower middle class and the mill and labouring classes in the city respectively. In the sections which follow it is proposed to examine these conditions under various specific heads which will make clear the domestic and economic conditions in which at least three out of every four persons in Bombay City are living to-day.

4. CHIEF HEADS OF EXAMINATION.

The chief heads of examination which will be dealt with below are (1) the housing available; (2) the evidence of family budgets in respect of two main items of expenditure, namely food and house rent; (3) mortality rates amongst working and non-working mothers in Bombay; (4) the chief defects in existing housing accommodation; and (5) overcrowding compared in Bombay, Ahmedabad, Sholapur, Karachi and London.

5. HOUSING AVAILABLE.

Bombay, Ahmedabad and Sholapur: kinds of tenements.—For the Census statistics on housing available reference should be made to relevant sections in Chapters V, VI or VII above. It will be seen from that portion of the Census report that in 1931 the housing available in Bombay was as under.

Tenements classified by number of rooms.	Number of tenements.	Per cent.	Number of occupants.	Per cent. of population.	Average number of persons per room.
1 room	197,516	81	791,762	74	4·01
2 rooms	26,231	11	131,872	12	2·51
3 rooms	7,416	3	44,821	3	2·01
4 rooms	6,169	2	42,013	4	1·70
5 rooms	2,953	1	22,302	2	1·50
6 rooms and over	3,836	2	39,199	4	....

The comparative figures of proportions of tenements of various kinds and proportion of population occupying them and average number of persons per room in each kind of tenement are compared for 1921 and 1931 as under :—

Tenements classified by number of rooms.	Percentage of tenements.		Percentage of population.		Number of persons per room.		State of overcrowding.
	1921	1931	1921	1931	1921	1931	
1 room	70	81	66	74	4·03	4·01	Better.
2 rooms	14	11	14	12	2·11	2·51	Worse.
3 rooms	7	3	8	4	1·60	2·01	Do.
4 rooms	4	2	5	4	1·30	1·70	Do.
5 rooms	3	1	4	2	1·06	1·50	Do.
6 rooms and over ..	2	2	3	4	..	..	

These figures show as regards one room tenements that they form in 1931 a much larger proportion of the available housing in the city and that the proportion of the population living in them has risen from 66 to 74 but that overcrowding has fallen slightly. The inference is that housing development is definitely taking the form of providing one-roomed tenements as the standard type of housing and that space per room is less crowded in them. This is in accord with the scheme of development pursued by the Bombay Development Department during the decade. The type of accommodation provided in the Worli Chawls, for instance, is definitely an improvement on the past. Indeed many two-roomed tenements of the old type have less accommodation in them than one-roomed tenements of the type erected by the Development Department. On the other hand the conditions in two, three and four-roomed tenements seem definitely to have worsened. There is more overcrowding in these than in 1921, though a smaller proportion of the population is living in them than in 1921. This would seem to show that the lower middle class have been more badly hit than the working classes and that they are, in respect of housing, worse off than they were in 1921. The lower middle class prefer two rooms to one room. There is little doubt that many who had two rooms in 1921 have now only one room, and these persons are suffering from overcrowding to a greater degree than before. It is believed that lower middle class people are in many instances found occupying accommodation meant to provide better one-roomed accommodation for the working classes. Housing in Bombay seems in fact to have affected the social classes differently. Millhands and labourers are better off and the lower middle class are worse off. It is quite certain that there is more crowding of the latter into the two-roomed tenements they have been able to retain. Improvement in housing for working classes is corroborated by the Labour Office enquiry in 1930. It is stated on page 876 of the *Labour Gazette* of May 1931, in respect of number of tenements under examination, "It will be seen that more than 73 per cent. of the tenements are one-roomed and 26 are two-roomed." These figures when compared with the results of the Family Budget Enquiry conducted by the Labour Office in 1921-22, which recorded that 97 per cent. of the working classes were living in one-roomed tenements, would appear to show that there is a certain amount of improvement in the housing conditions of industrial workers. The question, however, is not so much one of the proportion of the population living in one-roomed tenements as whether the one-roomed tenements are of a better type than they used to be. The efforts of the Development Department in this respect have been wholly good and it is probable that the standard of good one-roomed tenements having been thus set satisfactorily, the standard will rise in the future rather than fall. It is for this reason that the mere number of one-roomed tenements may be expected to become less and less in itself a true criterion of the quality of housing accommodation in Bombay City. In the Labour Office Report on an Enquiry into Middle Class Family Budgets in Bombay City (held in 1922 to 1924) it was found that, of the instances studied, 21·5 per cent. were living in one-roomed tenements and 59·6 in two-roomed tenements. The most common number of persons in one room was 3 and in two rooms 3 or 4, but there were frequent cases of 4 persons in a room and of over 6 in two rooms. The present writer has had recently, in 1932, the opportunity of seeing some typical lower middle class tenements in Girgaum for which rents from 13 to 17 rupees were being paid for two rooms. In only one case was the number of persons per room less than 3. In all other cases the number per room was over 3. In an Enquiry into Housing Conditions among the Lower Middle Class in Bombay (South) (see *Labour Gazette* October 1924, page 170) it is written "It is clear that the model (characteristic) dwelling of the lower middle class consists of two rooms, 38 per cent. of the tenements belonging to the type, though one-room and three-room tenements are also common enough. Four-room tenements are fewer and those with five or six rooms are rare. A middle class man requires for decency at least two rooms, one of which can be used as a cook-room, store-room and bathroom; while the other can be used as a living room and bedroom. More rooms than this his limited means do not admit of. One-room life so thoroughly militates against the ideas of comfort and decency that essentially constitute the middle class man that it is only through the impossibility of affording more roomy quarters that he puts up with it, though, even then, he tries to make two rooms out of one by a sort of partition, by almirahs, cupboards and cloth curtains." The present writer may add from his personal experience that in 1932 in Bombay in lower middle class two-roomed tenements it is impossible to provide more than two beds, at the very most, in the accommodation available and that the majority of the occupants have to sleep, where they can, on bedding on the floor after pulling various pieces of furniture out of the way. The cooking-place, which contains a bathing-stand, adjoins the living room and is often full of smoke. It appears to be the class occupying this kind of accommodation who are definitely worse off in 1931 than they were in 1921. This has to be put against the considerable improvement in working-class chawls. Housing conditions in Bombay are to be judged accordingly. Of the working classes in 1921-22 it was reported (see report on an Enquiry into Working Class Budgets in Bombay, pages 43 sqq.) that about 97 of the working class examined lived in single rooms. 70 per cent. of the total tenements were then reported to consist of one room only and 14 per cent. of two rooms. The average number of persons in one-roomed tenements was 4·03 and in two-roomed tenements 2·11. It was estimated then that if four occupants per tenement, including children, were taken, the Development Directorate alone by 1929 would have completed 50,000 tenements or accommodation for nearly 17 per cent. of the then population of Bombay. The extent to which improvement has taken place in the decade may be judged by comparing the 1921 and the 1931 Census figures. Of the working class occupants subjected to the enquiry in 1921-22, 49·5 per cent. were cotton mill workers, 14·8 per cent. were municipal workers, 8·9 per cent. were railway workers and 7·9 per cent. were engineering workers. The average working class family was found to be 4·2 persons, namely 1·1 men, 1·1 women and 2·0 children, exclusive of 0·6 dependents living outside Bombay. In Ahmedabad in 1924-1926 in the Labour Office Enquiry it was found (page 18, of the report) that 73 per cent. of the working class families examined lived in one-room tenements (or 75 per cent., if single-roomed huts were considered as well) and 19 per cent. lived in two-roomed tenements. In the Rent Enquiry held in 1926, it was found that 80 per cent. of the families examined lived in one-roomed tenements (See *Labour Gazette*, July 1927, page 1028). In Sholapur it was found in the Labour Office Enquiry (Page 49 of the report) that 33 per cent. of the working class lived in single rooms and 48·45 per cent. in two rooms but a closed-in verandah was counted as a room, which makes the Sholapur figures perhaps unduly flattering. There are no Census statistics for Ahmedabad in 1931. The Sholapur Census figures for 1931 have not been compiled in such a way as to permit comparison with the Labour Office figures. It is not therefore possible in the case of Ahmedabad and Sholapur to correlate the Labour Office figures with the Census figures, as has been done in the case of Bombay. There have been no special enquiries by the Labour Office in respect of Karachi, for which fairly full housing statistics have been compiled in the 1931 Census.

6. FAMILY BUDGETS: EXPENDITURE ON FOOD AND RENT.

As regards the working classes in Bombay, the 1921-22 enquiry yielded the following results. The average monthly income of the family based on the family-budgets tabulated (2473 in number) was Rs. 52-4-6. The average earnings per month for earning men in those budgets was Rs. 42-5-7 and, if single men's budgets (603) were included, the earnings were Rs. 42-9-6; for earning women Rs. 16-11-6; and for earning children Rs. 13-13-5. The income of 75 per cent. of the families tabulated ranged from Rs. 40 to Rs. 70 per month. The standard expenditure on the main groups when the budgets were collected was :—

Food	56·8 per cent.
Fuel and lighting	7·4 per cent.
Clothing	9·6 per cent.
House rent	7·7 per cent.
Miscellaneous expenditure	18·5 per cent.

More than half the expenditure of the family was on food. Rice was found to be the staple food of the working classes and entered into the diet of 99 per cent. of the family budgets. Bajri was consumed by 55·6 of the families, mutton by 65·8 per cent. and beef by only 5·5 per cent. The predominant range of monthly rent for working class tenements was from Rs. 3·8 to Rs. 5·8 for single rooms and Rs. 7 to Rs. 10 for double rooms. Recent enquiry shows that in 1930 the most common rent was Rs. 5-6-0 for old tenements and Rs. 7 to 8 for new tenements. (*Labour Gazette*, May 1931, page 879.)

In the enquiry into Lower Middle Class Budgets in 1922-24 the following was found to be the average expenditure on main items in the cases examined :—

Food	43·4 per cent.
Fuel and lighting	5·5 per cent.
Clothing	10·4 per cent.
Bedding and household necessaries ..	2·5 per cent.
House rent	14·8 per cent.
Miscellaneous	23·4 per cent.

It was remarked on (page 5 and 6 of the report) : " A noteworthy feature ....is the considerably higher percentage of expenditure on food among the working classes as compared with the middle classes. This is however only to be expected, for, the greater the earnings of a group of workers the smaller will be the percentage of those earnings spent on food. On the other hand, the middle classes have to spend a far higher percentage of their earnings on rent. It will be seen that, whereas the working class budgets show 7·7 per cent. expenditure on rent, the average for the middle class budgets is 14·8; and those earning less than Rs. 125 per month spend as much as 16·4 per cent. on rent. The average monthly expenditure on food on the 1325 families studied is nearly Rs. 60 or 43·4 per cent. of the total expenditure."

In the enquiries held in Ahmedabad and Sholapur the following were the chief conclusions reached. In Ahmedabad the largest number of budgets showed incomes of from Rs. 40 to Rs. 50 per month. In Sholapur the largest number of budgets showed incomes from Rs. 30 to 40. More than 8 per cent. of the families in Sholapur had incomes below Rs. 20. In Ahmedabad only 2 per cent. of the families had incomes below Rs. 20 per month. In Ahmedabad the average number of persons in a family was found to be 4·00 (3·87 living in the family : 0·13 away); 1·36 adult males, 1·22 adult females; 1·30 children under 14. In Sholapur the average number in the family was 4·47 and in Bombay 4·2. In Ahmedabad house rent was found to average 12 per cent. of earnings, from 16·22 per cent. in the under Rs. 20 class to 9·31 in the Rs. 70 to 80 class. This is to be compared with the 7·67 per cent. in Bombay (1921-22) and 7·72 per cent. in 1928 in Sholapur. As regards Sholapur the enquiry was restricted to cotton mill workers, ordinary, and from the Criminal Tribes, 902 and 153 cases respectively. The following were the income groups for ordinary workers : 8·3 per cent. below Rs. 20; 23 per cent. between Rs. 20 and 30; 25·6 per cent. between Rs. 30 and 40 (the largest class); 20·5 per cent. between Rs. 40 and 50. The average number of persons in a family was found to be 4·68 (4·57 at home and 0·11 away). The housing conditions were found to be " in many ways superior to those in Bombay and Ahmedabad. The town is not congested and there is room for expansion " (Page 19 of the report). All mills were found providing accommodation for the workers, covering nearly

12 per cent. of workers. The majority of workers in Sholapur were living in two or more rooms, counting a closed verandah as a room. In 4·88 per cent. of the cases families were living in huts where only rent for the site was paid. 65 per cent. of the families were paying rent of less than Rs. 3 per month, this being due to the fact that some employers let out buildings for employees at concession rates. The average rent paid by the working classes in Sholapur was nearly Rs. 2·8 per month, and for huts 11·1 annas per month as against Rs. 5-0-2 for one-roomed tenements in Bombay and Rs. 4-6-1 for one-roomed tenements in Ahmedabad. As regards the Criminal Tribes workers, the majority of the families were found to have an income under Rs. 40 per month. Only 19 per cent. had incomes of Rs. 40 or above. The average family amongst Criminal Tribes workers was 4·90 persons as against 4·68 for ordinary workers. The Criminal Tribes Settlement authorities, it was found, did not provide houses for all inhabitants of the settlement. There were a few chawls but the majority of the workers lived in huts and the rent varied from 7 annas to 10 annas per plot of land. Rents above Rs. 1-8-0 were for rooms in chawls. Only 3 families out of the 153 examined paid rent from Rs. 1-8-0 to Rs. 2-4-0 per month. The Criminal Tribes Settlement authorities insisted upon cleanliness.

7. MORTALITY RATES AMONGST WORKING AND NON-WORKING MOTHERS IN BOMBAY.

A special enquiry was made into this matter in Bombay in 1930. The results are of some demographic and sociological importance. The enquiry covered 2,053 cases. Of these 39·2 per cent. were working mothers and 60·8 per cent. non-working mothers ; 91·48 per cent. were Hindus ; 3·80 Muslims and 4·72 Indian Christians ; and 75 per cent. of the workers were textile workers. The average number of live births per working mother in all areas was 2·85 and per non-working mother was 2·75. In Naigaum, a sanitary area, the figures were 2·91 and 2·78 respectively. As regards still births in proportion to live births the figures were, for all areas, working mothers 34 per cent. and for non-working mothers 33 per cent. ; and for Naigaum the figures were 31 per cent. and 27 per cent. respectively. It will be obvious that the working class mothers have more children and more still births than non-working mothers, and that the Naigaum figures are better than the general figures. The statistics are curious. The greater prolificness of working class mothers seems to be due to their better economic conditions, which leads to their having more and better food than the non-working mothers. But the unfavourable figures for still births amongst working mothers seem to suggest that industrial labour, while not interfering with the conception of children, has had an effect on child-bearing itself. It is by no means unlikely that working mothers work too soon before and too soon after child-birth and so are liable to certain influences which do not affect non-working mothers. The table below shows the infant mortality by age-groups.

Age at death.	Rate of infant mortality per 1,000 live births.		
	Working mothers.	Non-working mothers.	All mothers.
Under 1 day	8	8	8
1 day or under 7 days	26	38	33
7 days or under 1 month	26	23	24
1 month and under 3 months	21	22	21
3 months and under 6 months	22	27	25
6 months to 1 year	99	85	91
Total under 1 year	202	203	202

The rate of mortality among infants under six months is greater in the case of non-working mothers than of working mothers, the actual figures being 118 as against 103. The rates for the age-group " under one day " are the same for both. The rates are higher in the case of working mothers in the age-groups " seven days and under one month" and "six months to one year." Bidimakers show as high a mortality rate as 240 and the Municipality of Bombay have recently arranged to license bidiworks in order to control the conditions under which the women employed therein are required to work. In connection with this similarity in the infant mortality rates for working and non-working mothers it may be of interest to observe that Dr. Hugh T. Ashby in his book on Infant Mortality states "that Dr. Greenwood, formerly medical officer of health for Blackburn, found very little difference in the infant mortality rates among mothers industrially employed and those not so occupied" (page 6 of the report). The facts simply seem to be that the mortality rates of infants are the result of many complex influences acting together. Some of these are favourable to working mothers and some are adverse. The figure of infant mortality which results therefore is somewhat capricious and not readily capable of statistical examination unless particulars of cases can be classified over a large number of instances. The figures, as they stand at present, do not show that industrial occupation is doing any particular harm to working mothers except in regard to the number of still births.

8. CHIEF DEFECTS IN EXISTING HOUSING.

The chief defects in the existing housing accommodation provided for the working class (and in effect for the lower middle class as well) in Bombay have been summed up in these words : "The surroundings of many tenements, especially those on the ground floor, are reported to be dirty and windows are reported as being kept closed on account of the close proximity of filthy gutters, privies, buffalo stables, etc. The closing of the windows prevents the smoke of the chula from going out of the room thereby causing great inconvenience to the occupants. Nhanis are not always provided in tenements and, even where they are, they are so small that they are found to be useless for bathing purposes. The state of repair of privately-owned tenements is not satisfactory and broken railings etc., make living on the upper floors fraught with danger. Cases are also reported in which the floor becomes damp even in the hot season. There are also cases of dirty water from the gutters overflowing into the rooms during the monsoon, thus making it impossible for the occupants to sit or sleep on the floor" (see page 895, Bombay *Labour Gazette*, May 1931). In the tenements visited in 1932 by the present writer what impressed him most unfavourably was the lack of light and proper ventilation in many of the cheaper tenements, the end-to-end building of the two rooms in two-roomed tenements and, in the older chawls, the back-to-back construction of many blocks of rooms preventing anything like proper circulation of the air. The bathing places were small and in the cooking-rooms the smell of smoke was all pervading. The greatest evil is however the cramped nature of the floor-space which will be dealt with in the section below in connection with overcrowding. One general statement can however be made here, that the main reason why the pavements are littered with sleepers in the fair weather is that there is not room for them to sleep in their houses. Bombay has a very low ratio of females to males. Any one who has seen the conditions in which most women have to live in Bombay will not have to ask the reason why. There is simply no room for women to live in comfortably. There is next to no privacy and in case of illness conditions must be very bad indeed. A great many of the chief inconveniences caused by inadequate water supply noticed by Mr. Kazi in 1922 (see page 170, Bombay *Labour Gazette*, October 1924) have now disappeared. The pressure is now generally adequate to supply water at all hours even in most top floors and the number of taps seems to have been increased considerably. Privies also seem generally to be adequate though there are still not enough of them in many of the older buildings. The interior of most of the tenements are wonderfully clean considering all the circumstances, the women in this respect rendering very great service to the community. But a general impression given by an inspection of chawls in Bombay is that too many people are housed in much too little floor-space and buildings are too crowded together. Improvement in this respect can come only gradually as old buildings are dismantled, areas cleared and large modern up-to-date buildings are erected in their place. The working population of Bombay and the middle class population also have very few open spaces to which they can resort in their leisure hours and have at present only their cramped, badly-ventilated and badly-lighted houses in which to rest when they do not want to wander about in the streets.

9. OVERCROWDING IN CITIES.

The most common area of one-roomed tenements was found in 1930 to be between 100 and 125 square feet for old tenements and 150 and 175 square feet for new tenements. In the case of two-roomed tenements the most common area is between 125 and 150 square feet for old tenements and between 150 and 175 square feet for new tenements (see *Labour Gazette,* May 1931, page 886). Now 74 per cent. of the population is living in one-roomed tenements with an average of 4·01 persons per room. This means that for the vast majority of Bombay's population only about 30 to 40 square feet are available per person, or an area of about six feet by six feet of floor-space, making no allowance for cooking-rooms and bathing places. It is obvious in such circumstance that beds must be a luxury. There is simply no room for beds in the average room and before people can sleep they must at night clear spaces on the floor and spread bedding there, sleeping in the cook-room and wherever they can find space. In the monsoon the verandahs, stairways and alleyways have all to be pressed into service as dormitories since the weather prevents the use of the pavements for the purpose. Most of the men must perforce sleep outside and leave the rooms for the women and children. What constitutes overcrowding is perhaps a matter of opinion and social custom. But if over two and a half persons may be held to be more than enough for the average room, 86 out of every 100 persons in Bombay are overcrowded according to the 1931 Census statistics given in Housing Table VI-A. In Bombay overcrowding is more serious in its effects than in any other city in the Presidency for two reasons (1) there are so few open spaces available; (2) the "room" is relatively more important in a big congested city with a rainy season of several months than it is in places like Ahmedabad, Karachi and Sholapur, where space is not so valuable and where sleeping out is easier for most of the year. Comparative figures of floor space for the various cities have to be studied with this consideration in mind. Even where, numerically, in other cities the number of persons per room is as large as in Bombay the evil is not nearly so great as in Bombay because in Bombay there is so little substitute for the room. The Royal Commission on Labour has commented unfavourably on the housing conditions in Bombay chawls and the 1931 Census proves the justice of the Commission's criticism. In Ahmedabad the Labour Office enquiry (page 19 of the report on an Enquiry into Working Class Family Budgets in Ahmedabad) showed that the average floor space per person is 47·36 square feet (38·29 in one-roomed tenements and 30·13 square feet in huts). 45·6 per cent. of the working class tenements examined had no windows at all. 29·5 per cent. had one window. Municipal privies were used by 28 per cent. of the population examined. 23·3 per cent. of the private water taps served more than 16 tenements each. In Sholapur the average floor space per room was found to be 92 square feet and the average floor space per person 36 square feet. Overcrowding was found not to be rare. In the cases examined there were 57 one-roomed tenements occupied by from six to eleven persons each (page 22 of the report on an Enquiry into Family Budgets of Cotton Millworkers in Sholapur City). Floor space per person in Karachi is not available from the Census figures but some idea of the pressure of persons on buildings will be gained from a study of Housing Tables VI-A and VII published in the present volume. In Karachi, however, the almost universal use of string cots inside and outside the houses has been commented upon and this circumstance, which is not true of Bombay city and Sholapur, does much to mitigate the overcrowding revealed by the statistics in certain quarters of the city. In a previous section of this report, overcrowding in London has been compared with overcrowding in Bombay and it has been pointed out that in Bombay there is greater pressure on the floor space of three-roomed tenements than there is on the floor space of one-roomed tenements in London. Yet Housing Table VI-A will show that very few people in Bombay can afford to live in tenements containing as many as three rooms each. From this some idea will be obtained of the severity of overcrowding in Bombay and, to a lesser degree, in Ahmedabad, Sholapur and Karachi also. It is a subject that deserves the closest attention of all social workers.

No. C. 777 of 1931-32.

From

THE EXECUTIVE HEALTH OFFICER,
Bombay Municipality;

To

THE PROVINCIAL SUPERINTENDENT OF CENSUS,
Poona.

Bombay Municipality,
31st October 1931.

Re: Census, 1931.

Sir,

I have the honour to submit my report on the Census Operations in the Town and Island of Bombay.

On the 16th June 1930 the Public Health Committee of the Corporation passed the following resolution.

Considered letter from the Municipal Commissioner No. MC.-5-B of 19th May 1930.

I have the honour to state that I received a letter from the Provincial Superintendent of Census Operations intimating that the next Census falls due in 1931 and that the 26th February 1931 has been fixed provisionally as the final date for taking the Census. The Superintendent wishes to know the name of the Officer to be appointed for the Town and Island of Bombay. It is the practice to appoint the Health Officer to be the Census Officer for Bombay and in accordance with that practice I have informed the Census Superintendent that Dr. J. S. Nerurker, the Health Officer, will be the Census Officer within the limits of Bombay Municipality. Detailed proposals regarding the conduct of the Census and the remuneration to be paid to the staff will be submitted later.

No. 39

"*Resolved*.—That it be recommended to the Corporation that the Commissioner's proposal be approved."

On the 10th October 1930 at an ordinary monthly meeting of the Corporation the following resolution was passed.

"That as recommended by the Standing Committee in their resolution No. 4260 of 3rd September 1930 sanction be given to Dr. J. S. Nerurker, Executive Health Officer, being granted a special allowance of Rs. 300 per mensem for working as Census Officer within the limits of the Bombay Municipality for the ensuing Census from September 1930 till immediately after the Census, the cost being met as proposed in Commissioner's further letter No. H.-68-B dated the 26th August 1930, received with the aforesaid resolution of the Standing Committee."

No. 5217

In accordance with the sanction contained in the resolutions quoted above I assumed charge of the Census Operations in the Town and Island of Bombay on the 1st September 1930. On the same date the services of Mr. V. G. Gokhale, Office Superintendent, Health Department, were placed at my disposal for Census work in addition to the duties of his office. Mr. D. S. Samant, Senior Superintendent, Assessment Department, who had worked in the decennial Censuses of 1911 and 1921, was appointed as a full-time Assistant and placed in charge of the Census Operations under my directions.

Charge Superintendents.

As in 1921, the City was divided into 32 main charges corresponding to the 32 sections adopted for registration and other administrative purposes.

Each Section or Charge was for Census purposes placed under one of the Municipal Inspectors, who carried out the Census work in addition to his ordinary duties and received for census purposes the title of Charge Superintendent. Owing to the retrenchment in staff since 1921 sufficient number of capable Inspectors could not be found and hence two small sections had to be placed in charge of one Superintendent. Thus (1) Upper Colaba and Lower Colaba, (2) Dhobitalao and Fanaswadi and (3) Sewri and Sion formed three charges instead of six as in 1921. On the other hand on account of the large extensions in Worli and Mahim Sections two sub-charges had to be created and placed under two separate Charge Superintendents.

Ward.	Sections.	Names of Charge Superintendents.	Office Address.
A	Upper Colaba Middle and Lower Colaba	Mr. A. Y. Raut	Health Department Stables, Palton Road.
	Fort South	Dr. G. S. Vazker	No. 294, Frere Road, No. I District Dispensary.
	Fort North	Mr. Huseinsha Makansha	Health Department Stables, Palton Road.
	Esplanade	Dr. G. D. Khandeker	Do.
B	Mandvi	Mr. S. B. Kondker Mr. S. Adams	Health Department Stables, Jail Road, North Umerkhady.
	Chakla	Dr. Jamshed B. Doctor	No. 20, Kolsa Moholla, Pydhoni.
	Umarkhady	Mr. B. A. Contractor	Health Department Stables, Jail Road, Umerkhady.
	Dongri	Dr. D. C. Chaterji	No. 569, Sandhurst Road, No. III District Dispensary.
C	Market	Dr. P. S. Pascal	No. 75, Cathedral Street, Bhuleshwar, No. IV District Dispensary.
	Dhobitalao Fanaswadi	Mr. S. M. Cooper	Do.
	Bhuleshwar	Dr. B. R. Master	Health Department Stables, opposite Northbrook Gardens, No. V District Office.
	Kharatalao	Mr. J. F. Taraporewalla Mr. D. R. Daru	Do.
	Kumbharwada	Dr. B. D. E. Kothawalla	Do.
D	Khetwadi	Mr. J. Moniz	Junction of Souter Street and Ripon Road.
	Girgaum	Dr. V. T. Vagh	Nos. 92—95, Girgaum Road, No. VI District Office.
	Chowpatty	Dr. R. V. Gokhale	Health Department Stables, Annesley Road.
	Walkeshwar	Dr. M. C. Langrana	Nos. 92—95, Girgaum Road, No. VI District Office.
	Mahaluxmi	Mr. V. K. Khote	Health Department Stables, Annesley Road.
E	Mazgaon	Mr. A. B. Malandker	Health Department Stables, Junction of Souter Street and Ripon Road.
	Tarwadi	Mr. C. K. Phatak	Souter Street, Byculla, No. VII District Office.
	Second Nagapada	Dr. F. Lobo	Do.
	Kamathipura	Mr. M. R. Aderbad	Health Department Stables, Kamathipura 10th Street.
	Tardeo	Mr. R. R. Tavergiri	No. 143, Foras Road.
	Byculla	Mr. R. C. Buch	No. 1 Souter Street, No. VII District Dispensary.
	First Nagapada	Mr. R. P. Vedak	Health Department, Bullock Hospital, Sankli Street.
F	Parel	Mr. G. M. Dandeker	Health Department Stables, Dadar Main Road.
	Sewri Sion	Mr. A. Hasan	Do.
G	Mahim	Dr. G. G. Limaye Mr. Jehangir Pestonji	No. 11, Elphinstone Road. Library Buildings, Dadar Road.
	Worli	Dr. V. M. Vatve Dr. G. G. Limaye	Do. No. 11, Elphinstone Road.

The work of circle, block and house numbering was commenced on 22nd September 1930. In some sections house numbering was not taken in hand until the blocking of the whole section had been completed; in others blocking and house numbering proceeded simultaneously; the latter method saves much time. The numbering work was finished in some sections before 1st November 1930 and was completed in all the remaining sections on 15th November 1930.

For painting circle, block and house numbers chocolate paint was used as was done in all the previous Censuses. To ensure uniformity, neatness and economy of paint and time stencil plates were supplied. Tin plates bearing the "house" number were attached to temporary structures and kutcha huts. Five sets of section maps were kindly given by the Health Department and from these Census maps had to be prepared according to the boundaries of sections and circles shown in a set of survey sheets specially prepared in 1921 and preserved for use in the Census of 1931. To assist him in the accurate circling and blocking of his section each Charge Superintendent was supplied with such a map of his section.

One set of such Census maps was cut into circles and distributed among the Government and Municipal volunteers for their use while on Census duty for checking the preliminary and final work.

One additional set of Census maps showing the revised and altered boundaries of sections, circles and blocks as in 1931, has been filed for use in the next census.

The total cost of the paint, oil, brushes, stencil plates and tin plates is as under:—

		Rs.	a.	p.
20	sets of 11 stencil plates at Rs. 3 per set	60	0	0
4,500	tin plates 6" × 6" at Rs. 2 per 100	90	0	0
5	Cwts. chocolate paint at Rs. 11 per cwt.	55	0	0
6	Drums boiled oil at Rs. 11-8-0 per drum	69	0	0
5	Gallons turpentine at Rs. 2 per gallon	10	0	0
18	Dozen brushes at Rs. 3 per dozen	54	0	0
4	Brushes at 4 annas each	1	0	0
1	Brush at annas 3	0	3	0
3	Maunds and 12 seers chalk	6	0	0
3	Seers nails	0	12	0
3	Empty gunny bags for carrying brushes etc.	0	9	0
		346	8	0

Thus the total cost of painting numbers in 1931 is Rs. 346-8-0 as against Rs. 1,468 in 1921.

Extensive changes have, since 1921, been effected in the City by the operations of various development schemes of the Municipality and the Improvement Trust; especially in the sections of Fort North, Chakla, Umerkhady, Dongri, Byculla, Parel, Sewri, Sion and Mahim. Boundaries of circles in sections were kept as before for comparison purposes except in Umerkhady and Chakla in which many buildings have been demolished and the land thus rendered vacant is utilized for new roads and foot-paths. The northern boundary of the first circle in the Tarwadi section has been extended up to Connaught road. In Fort North many buildings were acquired and demolished by the Municipality in connection with their Hornby Ballard Scheme. Similarly a number of buildings were demolished in Circle No. 4 of the Byculla section. Each of the 32 sections was divided into circles and each circle subdivided into blocks. The boundaries of each of the circles were the same as in 1921, but those of blocks had to be changed to meet the alterations due to the demolition and erection of buildings since 1921. While the house numbering was in progress House/Block lists of completed circles were prepared by the respective Charge Superintendents and submitted to the Census head office. These lists were checked by inspection by Checkers appointed for the purpose.

The total numbers of circles, blocks and buildings in different sections excluding Railway, Military, Customs and Government House buildings were as follows:—

Census, 1931.

Ward.	Name of Section.	Number of Circles.	Number of Blocks.	Number of Buildings.
A	Upper Colaba	1	3	95
	Lower Colaba	8	41	944
	Fort South	5	17	281
	Fort North	8	64	1,125
	Esplanade	4	40	893
	Total of A Ward ..	26	165	3,338

Ward.	Name of Section.	Number of Circles.	Number of Blocks.	Number of Buildings.
B	Mandvi	12	81	1,124
	Chakla	7	49	693
	Umerkhady	9	81	1,029
	Dongri	4	20	411
	Total of B Ward ..	32	231	3,257
C	Market	8	92	1,062
	Dhobitalao	7	65	1,186
	Fanaswadi	3	47	1,006
	Bhuleshwar	6	81	1,119
	Kharatalao	5	52	543
	Kumbharwada	4	48	682
	Total of C Ward ..	33	385	5,598
D	Khetwadi	8	58	1,567
	Girgaum	7	69	1,342
	Chowpati	6	34	806
	Walkeshwar	7	63	2,262
	Mahaluxmi	9	55	2,627
	Total of D Ward ..	37	279	8,604
E	Mazgaon	5	46	2,129
	Tarwadi	3	45	1,936
	2nd Nagpada	4	29	514
	Kamatipura	3	55	1,093
	Tardeo	4	56	1,046
	Byculla	8	108	2,664
	1st Nagpada	2	16	167
	Total of E Ward ..	29	355	9,549
F	Parel	9	117	1,920
	Sewri	5	55	1,458
	Sion	11	137	3,056
	Total of F Ward ..	25	309	6,434
G	Mahim	8	76	4,302
	Worli	8	154	5,963
	Total of G Ward ..	16	230	10,265
	Grand Total ..	198	1,954	47,045

The number of circles, blocks and buildings stands as under as compared with that of the two previous censuses :—

Year of Census.		Number of Circles.	Number of Blocks.	Number of Buildings.
1911	..	200	2,263	44,939
1921	..	201	2,282	48,753
1931	..	198	1,954	47,045

The average number of buildings per section, circle and block works out as under :—

Average number of buildings.

Per		1911	1921	1931
Section	..	1,404·3	1,523·5	1,470·2
Circle	..	224·7	242·5	237·6
Block	..	19·9	21·4	24

From the tables above it will be noticed that there are three circles less than in 1921. This is due to the fact that Sydenham Road Scheme which included properties on both sides of Sydenham road (now called Mahomedally Road) expunged all the buildings of two circles of Chakla and one of the Umerkhadi sections. The difference in the number of blocks is due to the particular care taken at the beginning to equalise work to be entrusted to one person in charge of a block irrespective of the area therein.

" The whole structure of a building under one undivided roof or under two or more roofs, connected *inter se* by subsidiary roofs " is, for census purposes, the definition of a building in Bombay. The same was followed this time also except in cases of buildings with the block system, that is, buildings which have blocks accessible by different staircases independent of each other, have been grouped as one building unlike that in 1921. This has tended to reduce the number of buildings. The classification of buildings has been made according to the description and use thereof, such as Chawl with shops, Bungalow with motor garage etc. The main distinction that is observed is to differentiate them into residential or non-residential or combined. Buildings with blocks or flats have been so shown separately.

Railway Premises.

As in 1921 the Census Officer for the City was made directly responsible for the enumeration of the occupants of all premises in the Island including Railway, Military, Docks and Customs premises.

Government and Railway orders were issued requiring railway officials to render every assistance in the work of enumeration of their premises.

The arrangement agreed upon was that all areas within railway boundaries should be treated as separate railway circles, that no railway circle should be so drawn as to be intersected by the boundary of a section and that with a view to co-ordinating railway with Municipal returns the numbering of railway premises, blocks and circles would be carried out by the Municipal Charge Superintendents. This plan was correctly followed and the numbering of the premises having been completed the enumeration of the occupants was carried out by railway officials under the guidance, when required, of the Charge Superintendent of the section concerned.

The Port Trust Railway, the G.I.P. Railway and the B.B. & C.I. Railway each appointed an officer to cooperate with, and advise the Census Officer for the City, and to depute railway officials for appointment by the Census Officer as Supervisors and Enumerators to count the railway personnel and passengers in their respective areas.

The enumeration of passengers and others found on railway platforms on Census night was carried out under the direction of the census officer.

The enumeration of passengers on running trains was carried out under the direction of the Provincial Superintendent.

" Military Areas."

The Station Staff Officer, Bombay, appointed Captain C. Moore as Census Officer for the military area under the direction of the Census Officer for the enumeration of the military buildings which were classified under different areas as given below :—

(1) Upper Colaba 1 to 6 areas ;
(2) Fort South Castle area as No. 7 ;
(3) Esplanade (*a*) A. F. I. buildings,
(*b*) A. F. I. buildings,
(*c*) A. F. I. buildings,
(*d*) Pavilion Section ;
(4) Mahaluxmi Battery compound ;
(5) Four Islands (*a*) Cross Island (*b*) Oyster Rock (*c*) Butcher Island (*d*) Middle Ground Island.

The work of numbering premises in the Military areas was taken up after the civil area was completed. It was agreed that tin plates bearing Census numbers should be nailed to each building by the Municipal Charge Superintendent concerned without damaging the property in any way and in consultation with the Military Census Officer by previous appointment.

Government House at Walkeshwar which hitherto formed a part of the military area was excluded by them from their areas this time. On communication with the Military Secretary to His Excellency the Governor the area known as Government House was divided into different areas under the following officers :—

(1) Director, His Excellency the Governor's Band for the Band quarters.

(2) The Indian A. D. C. for Government house, the staff bungalows, clerical quarters and servants' lines.

(3) The Commandant, His Excellency the Governor's Body Guard, the guard lines at Tardeo flats.

Each of these officers had therefore to be approached and arrangements had to be made for the supply of census forms and stationery through the respective Charge Superintendents.

MO-I Bk Ra Cs 3—29

Dockyards.

I put myself in communication with Mr. Singleton, Assistant Collector of Customs in charge Preventive Service, and he appointed his divisional Inspectors as persons responsible for Census work in their respective areas within the Dock limits. The Municipal Charge Superintendents were instructed to see the divisional Inspectors for arrangements regarding the numbering of circles, blocks and buildings within the Dockyard limits as in the case of Railways. This was done by the Municipal Charge Superintendents and after the numbering of the buildings these were identified to the divisional Inspectors. House/Block lists of premises within the Dock area were also prepared by the Municipal Charge Superintendents.

The total number of circles, blocks and buildings within Railway, Military and Customs or Dockyard limits were as follows.

Ward	Section and Agency	Number of circles	Number of blocks	Number of buildings
A	Upper Colaba Military	1	3	69
	Lower Colaba Military	1	6	291
	Fort South R. I. M.	1	2	99
	Military Castle area	1	....	30
	Fort North B. P. T.	1	2	56
	Esplanade—			
A	B. B. C. I. Churchgate Station	1	2	75
	Customs	1	1	161
	G. I. P. Railway Victoria Terminus	1	1	55
	Military, Marine Lines	....	....	3
	Pavilion	....	....	73
		8	17	912
	Mandvi—			
B	G. I. P. Masjid Station	1	1	4
	Customs	1	1	91
	Dongri—			
	Customs	1	1	124
	G. I. P. Sandhurst Road Station	1	1	6
	G. I. P. Wari Bunder Goods Yard	1	3	68
		5	7	293
	Dhobitalao—			
C	B. B. C. I. Marine Lines Station	1	1	5
		1	1	5
	Khetwady—			
D	B. B. C. I. (Cabin)	1	1	3
	Girgaum—			
	B. B. C. I. Charni Road Station	1	1	1
	Chowpaty—			
	B. B. C. I. (cabin)	1	1	2
	Walkeshwar—			
	Government House area Military	....	4	75
	Mahaluxmi—			
	B. B. C. I. Railway	2	2	44
	Military area, Body Guard Lines	....	....	26
	Military Battery area	....	....	8
		5	9	159

Ward	Section and Agency	Number of circles	Number of blocks	Number of buildings
	Mazgaon—			
E	Dockyard	1	2	7
	Reay Road	1	2	8
	Cotton Green	1	2	7
	B. P. T. Railway	1	2	76
	Customs	1	7	217
	Tarwadi—			
	G. I. P. Railway	1	1	80
	Tardeo—			
	B. B. C. I. Grant Road Station	1	1	26
	Byculla—			
	G. I. P. Railway Byculla Station	1	1	30
	G. I. P. Hospital	1	4	95
	B. B. & C. I. Central Station	1	1	23
		10	23	569
	Parel—			
F	G. I. P. Chinchpokli Station	1	1	4
	G. I. P. Curry Road Station	1	1	5
	G. I. P. Workshops	1	4	131
	Sewri—			
	Station yard	1	1	16
	B. P. T. Area	1	7	357
	Sion—			
	G. I. P. Parel Station	1	2	16
	G. I. P. Dadar Station	1	1	42
	G. I. P. Matunga Station	1	1	33
	G. I. P. Sion Station	1	1	31
	G. I. P. Gowari Station	1	1	15
	G. I. P. Koliwada Station	1	2	7
	B. P. T. Area	1	8	298
		12	30	955
G	Mahim—			
	B. B. C. I. Dadar Station	1	1	18
	B. B. C. I. Matunga Station	1	2	18
	B. B. C. I. Mahim Station	1	3	24
	G. I. P. Railway Mahim Avenue	1	1	2
	G. I. P. Railway Matunga Workshop	1	2	106
G	Worli—			
	B. B. C. I. Stores yard	1	3	50
	B. B. C. I. Carriage and Waggon shop	1	3	68
	Do. do.	1	5	98
	G. I. P. Railway Stores Lower Level DeLisle Road ..	1	1	42
		9	21	426

The area with all the buildings thereon from Churchgate Station to Colaba was handed over by the B.B. & C.I. Railway to Government on 1st January 1931, since Churchgate Station became the terminus instead of Colaba. The arrangement in respect of these buildings with the B.B.& C.I. Railway was therefore abandoned. In the absence of any other agency willing to accept the area for enumeration the Municipal Charge Superintendent was instructed to include it in his charge.

Police Enumeration.

The following Police Stations were treated as separate blocks and were enumerated by the Police Inspectors in charge under the instructions of the Commissioner of Police :—

Name of Section	Number of circles	Number of blocks	Census Nos. From	Census Nos. To	Number of buildings
Lower Colaba	6	6	141	154	15 Colaba.
Fort North	8	6	96	102	8 Goa Street.
Esplanade	3	2	19	29	13 Esplanade Police Court Compound.
		7	102	113A	15 Police Office Compound.
		11	182	188	7 Palton Road Police Station.
Umerkhady	1	8	60	64	5 Sandhurst Road.
Dongri	3	3	31	35	5 Dongri Police Station.
	4	5	116	122	7 Richur Street and Frere Road Police Station.
Market	1	4	44	45	8 Princess Street.
Khetwady	1	4	165	171	7 Lamington Road.
Girgaon	7	5	83	85	3 Mahar Bowdi Police Station.
Walkeshwar	1	8	187	190	4 Harvey Road.
Mazgaon	3	3	132	138	7 Gun Powder Road Police Quarters.
	5	16	597	603	7 Sewri Road Police Quarters.
Tarwadi	2	6	284	297A	17 Love Lane Police Station.
	3	7	383	386	4 Police Quarters at Sussex Road.
1st Nagapada	1	2	4	25	22 Armed Police Quarters.
		4	44	53	10 Police Hospital.
		12	106	113	8 Nagpada Police Station.
Sion	3	7	143	158	16 Naigaum Police Station.
	8	9	135	145	11 B. B. C. I. & G. I. P. Railway Police.
	9	11	189	194	6 Sion Road Police Station.
Mahim	4	10	352	359	8 Cadell Road Police Station.

The enumeration of the homeless and of persons in the Police lockups on Census night was also undertaken by the Commissioner of Police. The enumeration of persons in the Police lockups attached to single premises was, however, done by the Municipal Charge Superintendents along with the occupants of that building having the police lockup. The Superintendents of the various Police divisions were instructed to organize parties to search all streets, lanes, arches of bridges, maidans, station surroundings and other places where homeless persons pass the night and to take such persons found to the undermentioned enumeration stations appointed by the Commissioner of Police for enumeration on the Census night of 26th February 1931.

Statement showing the centres selected for the collection and enumeration on the night of the 26th February 1931 of homeless persons of the City and the Police Officers responsible for the work with their addresses.

Serial No.	Enumeration Centre.	Police Officer and his address.
1	Esplanade Police Court ..	Superintendent of Police, Old Bazargate Police Station.
2	Head Police Office Compound, Hornby Road.	Superintendent of Police, B Division, Princess Street Police Station.
3	Mazagaon Police Court Compound, Nesbit Road.	Superintendent of Police, D Division, Jacob Circle Police Chowkey.
4	Northbrook Gardens, Grant Road ..	Superintendent of Police, C Division, Lamington Road Police Station.
5	Kalachowky Police Station ..	Superintendent of Police, E Division, Police Head quarters, Naigaum.
6	Bhoiwada Police Station ..	
7	Kingsway Police Station ..	

Distinction had to be made between the homeless (in the real sense) to be enumerated by the Police and those who really are not homeless but on the Census night may be passing the night at the place of their work or in the open spaces or plots attached to houses, such as coolies, labourers, hawkers, etc. These were to be enumerated by the Charge Superintendents concerned against the houses where they were found. To avoid double enumeration those enumerated by the Charge Superintendents were given travellers' tickets to be shown to the Police for their exclusion by them.

The enumeration of passengers and others found on railway platforms on Census night was carried out through the Station Masters and their staff at every station of each Railway. Necessary forms, instructions and stationery was supplied by Census Office to each Station Master. Lady enumerators were applied for by the Station Master in charge of the Bombay Central Station for the enumeration of the lady passengers on Census night and a nurse of the Health Department was deputed for the work. Platform enumeration in Bombay must always be done at the latest hour of the evening in order to give time to the purely local traffic to clear. By local traffic is meant the return home of those who work in the City but reside outside, they being enumerated at the place of their residence.

Dockyards and Shipping.

As in 1921 the enumeration of all ships and launches of the Royal Navy was undertaken by the Naval Officer in command.

The Director of the Royal Indian Marine undertook all R. I. M. ships and premises and persons in the R. I. M. Dockyard. The Assistant Collector in charge Preventive Service organised the enumeration by the Customs and Port Trust authorities of the ships, bunders and dockyards shown in the sub-joined list.

The arrangement and numbering of the circles blocks and houses within Customs and Dockyard limits was, as in the case of railways, undertaken by the Municipal Charge Superintendents to prevent the intersection of circles and blocks by the boundaries of the municipal sections and wards.

The distribution of enumeration work was arranged as under :—

The Naval Officer.—All ships and launches of the Royal Navy.

The Director, Royal Indian Marine.—All R. I. M. ships and launches and the R. I. M. Dockyard.

Customs Department.—Coasting passenger steamers in harbour and alongside Princess and Victoria Dock walls. All B. I. S. N. Coy.'s steamers, country craft, all bunders, all customs launches and boats. All floating population at the bunders on cargo boats and country-craft and all floating population at Mahim, Worli and Chowpatty.

The Customs authorities enumerated the Bunders noted below :—

(1) Gun Carriage Bunder.

(2) Jamshed Bunder.

(3) Arthur Bunder.

(4) Government Dockyard compound and residential quarters therein.
(5) Bonded ware-house and opium ware-house.
(6) Town Bunder.
(7) Ballard Bunder.
(8) Alexandra Dock including the Mole.
(9) Modi Bunder.
(10) Carnac Bunder.
(11) Princess and Victoria Docks including the Dry Dock and residential quarters within the dock limits.
(12) Malet Bunder.
(13) Mazgaon Bunder.
(14) Sewri Bunder including timber ponds.
(15) Chowpati Bunder.
(16) Worli Bunder.
(17) Mahim Bunder at the Mahim Causeway.
(18) Sassoon Dock.
(19) Apollo Bunder.
(20) Old Town Custom House and adjoining stables.

Port Trust.—Steamers in Princess and Victoria Docks except B. S. N. Coy.'s.

Port Trust.—Cargo boats.
Barges.
Launches.
Dredgers.
Tugs.
Licensed passenger boats.
} In P. and V. Docks or alongside of the outside of the Dock wall.

All deep sea steamers in harbour (except R. I. M. and coasting passenger steamers).
Pilot schooners.
Light-ships.
Steam launches.
Anchor " Hoy " and water boat " Princess ".
Launches, tugs and dredgers other than the launches belonging to the R. N. and R. I. M. and Customs.

Light Houses.
Yachts.
Dubash boats, steam launches.
} Off Apollo Bunder.

All licensed passenger boats at the Bunder.

The number of census forms, stationery, etc., was supplied to the authorities concerned by the Census Office.

The Provincial Superintendent of Census Operations arranged with the managers of the coasting steamers of the following companies and supplied them with the necessary forms, etc., for the enumeration of the passengers on board their several steamers :—

(1) The British India Steam Navigation Coy. Ltd., Ballard Estate, Bombay.
(2) The Bombay Steam Navigation Coy. Ltd., 120, Frere Road, Bombay.
(3) The Scindia Steam Navigation Coy. Ltd., Sudama House, Ballard Estate, Bombay.
(4) The Merchants Steam Navigation Company, Dongri Street, Bombay.
(5) The New Bombay Steam Ships, No. 78, Frere Road, Bombay.
(6) The Malabar Steam Ship Company, Vadgadi, Bombay.
(7) The Indian Co-operative Navigation and Trading Company Limited, Ballard Estate, Bombay.
(8) The Eastern Steam Navigation Company Limited, No. 24, Mangalore Street, Bombay.
(9) Messrs. R. Assaria & Co., Katha Bazar, Mandvi, Bombay.
(10) Messrs. Lalji Naranji & Co., Tamarind Lane, Fort, Bombay.

Enumeration of Public Institutions.

Census schedule forms with a covering letter requesting the authority in charge of the hospitals and hotels, etc., in the City were issued for enumeration of the inmates in them on the census night; and these schedules were collected by the Charge Superintendents on the next day.

	Name of Institution.	Number of Schedule forms sent.	Number of specimen Schedules.
1	Ahiliabai Free Maternity Home, Koliwada, Mandvi	5	1
2	Ajinkya Hospital, Benam Hall Lane, Girgaon	5	1
3	Anand Maternity Home	5	1
4	Bhatia Maternity Home	5	1
5	Cama and Albless Hospital, Cruikshank Road	100	1
6	Dholkawala's Maternity Home	10	1
7	Dr. C. M. Mehta's Hospital, Sandhurst Road, Girgaum	5	1
8	Dr. D'Sa's Hospital, Chowpati	10	1
9	Dr. Karande's Maternity Home, Sandhurst Road	5	1
10	Dr. Pagnis' Maternity Home, Vasumal Building, Grant Road	5	1
11	Dr. Kerawala's Hospital, Tardeo Road	10	1
12	Dr. Parekh's Hospital, Khetwadi	10	1
13	Dr. Purandare's Hospital, Sandhurst Road	10	1
14	Dr. Mrs. Saldanha Fernandez's Popular Maternity Hospital, Bhendi Bazar Road	5	1
15	Drs. Kaikini and Tilak Hospital, Lamington Road	5	1
16	Dr. Sequira's Eugenic Maternity Home	5	1
17	Gordhandas Ranchoddas Bhagat Hindu Maternity Home, Kalbadevi Road	5	1
18	Haji Karim Mahomed Suleman Maternity Home, 184, Kambekar Street	5	1
19	Haji Sabu Sidik Maternity Home, Bellasis Road	5	1
20	Haji Sabu Sidik Maternity Home, Imamwada	5	1
21	Jasmine Lodge Nursing Home, Kenkoo Buildings, Outram Road	5	1
22	Kamar Khanam Maternity Home, Victoria Road	5	1
23	Kanchangawri Maternity Home, Khetwadi	5	1
24	Laxmi Maternity Home, Bhawanishankar Road	5	1
25	Dr. Masina's Hospital, Victoria Road	25	1
26	Motlibai Petit Hospital	25	1
27	Municipal Maternity Home, Worli	5	1
28	Nowroji Wadia Maternity Hospital	20	1
29	Parsee General Hospital	20	1
30	Parsee Lying-in Hospital, Outram Road	10	1
31	Poly Clinic, No. 20, New Queens Road	5	1
32	Rachel Maternity Home, Khatar Galli	5	1
33	Rukshamani Hospital, Chowpati	10	1
34	Sakinabai Musabhoy Jafferbhoy Maternity Home Nos. 20-30, Nishanpada Cross Lane	5	1
35	Shree Laxmi Maternity Home	5	1
36	Sir Harkisondas Narottamdas Hospital	25	1
37	St. George's Hospital	50	1
38	Surgical Nursing Home, Grant Road	5	1
39	Swastika Maternity Home, Lamington Road	5	1
40	Vaidya Maternity Home, New Queen's Road	5	1
41	Wadi Bunder Port Trust Maternity Home	5	1
42	Yamunabai Nair Hospital, Lamington Road	25	1
43	J. J. Hospital } J. J. Hospital Compound, Byculla	30	1
44	Sir C. J. Opthalmic Hospital } J. J. Hospital Compound, Byculla	25	1
45	B. J. Hospital for Children } J. J. Hospital Compound, Byculla	25	1
46	Arthur Road Hospital	25	1
47	Maratha Hospital	25	1
48	Turner Sanitarium for Tuberculosis, Bhoiwada Road	10	1
49	Adams Wylie Hospital, Wylie Road	25	1
50	Acworth Leper Asylum, Matunga	50	1
51	K. E. M. Hospital, Parel	50	1
52	Gokuldas Tejpal Hospital	50	1
53	Alexandra Hotel	25	1
54	All India Hotel	5	1
55	Apollo Hotel, Colaba Causeway	10	1

	Name of Institution.	Number of Schedule forms sent.	Number of specimens Schedule.
56	Carlton Hotel, Outram Road	5	1
57	Grand Hotel	10	1
58	Great Punjab Hotel, Kalbadevi Road	10	1
59	Great Western Hotel, Apollo Street	10	1
60	Green's Hotel, Apollo Bunder	25	1
61	Hotel Majestic, Wodehouse Road	25	1
62	Shahajan Palace Hotel, Sitaram Building	10	1
63	Sardar Griha, Carnac Road	10	1
64	Taj Mahal Hotel, Apollo Bunder	50	1
65	Victoria Hotel, Princess Dock	25	1
66	Victoria Hotel Annexe, opposite Princess Dock	25	1

Preliminary Enumeration.

As 26th February 1931 was fixed as the Census night and 17th to 19th February and 25th and 26th February 1931 as the preliminary period, the preliminary Enumeration of the Town and Island of Bombay had to be started on 20th January 1931. Enumerators were therefore appointed to begin work from 20th January 1931. These were not advertised for as in 1921 but were appointed only out of the large number of applicants registered in the Census Office. As the General Schedules for Bombay were printed in English, English-knowing Enumerators only were appointed and their pay fixed at Rs. 60 per mensem, the minimum pay in all local offices in Bombay.

Had it been possible to secure steady and intelligent workers 300 enumerators would have been adequate for the preliminary enumeration. Much difficulty was experienced in finding 300 really good workers, unemployed and ready to take up temporary work. The number of enumerators that had actually to be appointed in the first instance was therefore 333. Many did not join on the 20th January and others resigned after a few days experience of the difficulties of the work. Of those finally retained a certain number were irregular and careless in work.

The plan of the operations was as follows :—

Before the end of the previous year the Charge Superintendents with the assistance of a few Municipal servants in the lower grades had divided their Sections into Circles and Blocks and affixed a census number to every house. In affixing these numbers each building under a separate roof was regarded as a separate house. The servants' quarters in the compound of bungalows were treated as separate houses. Large blocks of flats or of one-room tenements for the labouring class were each counted as one house only. A building in a row of houses and attached on either side was counted as a separate house provided it was separately owned and self-contained in that it could only be entered from its own street door.

In the three weeks and a half from 20th January to 16th February 1931 when the Enumerators were appointed schedules were prepared by them showing the names and particulars of the occupants of all premises in the City. In almost all cases these particulars were entered by the Enumerators themselves in the General Schedules.

For the final stage which extended over the period 17th to 19th February and 25th and 26th February 1931 the staff of the paid Enumerators was augmented by unpaid volunteers, Government servants and Municipal servants as shown below :—

	1921	*1931*
Government Employees	878	928
Government Peons	*Nil.*	157
Municipal Employees	649	762
Municipal Peons	277	205
Volunteers from private schools	330	60
Volunteers from the Salvation Army	*Nil.*	5
Volunteers from Mr. Mohomed Umer, Honorary Secretary of the Jamitol Momin, Sadi Bazar, Madanpura	*Nil.*	8

Mr. C. S. Pagnis, Chief Clerk, Municipal Commissioner's Office, voluntarily enumerated three whole blocks of Worli Section (Blocks Nos. 34 to 36 of Circle No. 8) from its preliminary stage to the final.

There were thus available for the work of enumeration on the last five days 2,112 workers.

Out of the persons told off for Census duty, Government and Municipal Employees drawing salaries of over Rs. 150 per mensem were appointed Supervisors and others enumerators. Each Supervisor was placed in charge of one Circle and over as many Enumerators as there were blocks in the Circle. In large Circles an additional Supervisor was appointed. The total number of Enumerators which remained available for the final Census was 1,933 and was distributed at the rate of one for each block among the 1,930 blocks exclusive of the 24 Police blocks (exclusively in their charge) making in all 1,954 blocks into which the City was divided. Similarly the number of Supervisors available was 179 distributed according to necessity among 198 circles. The suggestion made in 1921 of sparing as many menials and peons to serve as messengers was greatly carried out in 1931. The Municipality spared 205 and Government Offices 157 peons for Census duty.

Quite a number of exemptions from Census duty were applied for by Government and Municipal servants under various excuses subsequent to the submission of their names by the heads of their offices. The real motive in applying for exemption was only to avoid facing all kinds of difficulties in the ensuing Census. To dispel any suspicion and to create confidence these exemptions were freely granted.

At this Census the conspicuous absence of the volunteer agency was prominently noticeable. In 1921 even when the non-cooperation movement was afoot 64 educational institutions offered volunteers for enumeration work; nine schools undertook the enumeration of certain areas of their choice and nine private firms and offices spared their 22 employees for Census work. Twenty-eight leading citizens with additional twelve volunteers offered their services in the cause of Census, whereas in 1931 only three schools, when approached personally, consented to render services for the final enumeration. With a view to avoiding any organised resistance public advertisement was dispensed with altogether and the shortage of volunteers and workers was not allowed to have any adverse effect on carrying through the Census Operations.

From the commencement of the Preliminary Enumeration daily reports of progress from each section were called for and these reports were very keenly watched by the Census Office. Charge Superintendents, who happened to be in arrears on account of circumstances beyond their control, had to be given help in various ways. Charge Superintendents whose sections were free from the infection of resistance to the Census and who were expected to finish their work in advance were instructed to render help to their neighbouring sections. In some cases the outdoor staff of the Health Department, consisting of Junior Overseers in the Malaria and Conservancy branches, Milk Sub-Inspectors and Disinfecting Sub-Inspectors had to be placed at the disposal of the Charge Superintendent concerned. Through the kindness and co-operation of the Assessor and Collector of the Municipality the help of the outdoor staff of the Assessment Department was also obtained in some sections for securing the names of the tenants through their landlords. To dispel misunderstanding among the ignorant, public leaflets in Marathi and Gujarati describing the necessity of co-operating with the Census were freely broadcast through the Charge Superintendents and Enumerators.

The Preliminary Enumeration, in spite of all such odds against it, was completed in all the Civil area on the 16th February 1931. The Customs, the Railways and the Military Officers had also finished their preliminary enumeration before the 16th February 1931 but the enumeration of the Police Stations was deferred till the first three days of the final enumeration, i.e. from 17th to 19th February 1931 since the Police Quarters were under sole Police control.

The final enumeration was fixed for 17th to 19th February 1931 and for 26th February night and morning of 27th February 1931. The gap of nearly six days caused by public holidays following 19th February 1931 entailed the retention of the paid enumerators at an extra cost of Rs. 3,000.

Employees from Government Offices spared for Census work.

	Name.	Supervisors.	Enumerators.	Peons.
1	Assistant Secretary to Government, Separate Department	..	1	1
2	Principal, Bombay Veterinary College	3	8	..
3	Rev. G. E. Dodd, M.A., J.P.	..	1	..
4	Consulting Architect to Government, P. W. D. ..	2	3	..
5	Director of Information, Record Office	1	4	..

MO-I Bk Ra Cs 3—31

	Name.	Supervisors.	Enumerators.	Peons.
6	Under Secretary to Government, Revenue Department ..		16	3
7	Principal Officer, Mercantile Marine Department ..	..	5	..
8	Secretary to Government, Political Department ..	6	9	3
9	Assistant Secretary to Government, Finance Department ..	2	16	2
10	Director, Haffkine Institute ..	5	5	7
11	Mint Master ..	..	2	..
12	C. M. Amin, Esq., B.A. ..	1	1	..
13	Assistant Registrar, Bombay ..	1	3	..
14	Superintending Engineer, N. C. ..	5	32	6
15	Registrar, High Court ..	..	15	..
16	Educational Inspector, Bombay Division ..	2	9	..
17	Chief Judge, Small Causes Court ..	..	40	..
18	Administrator General ..	..	4	3
19	Secretary to Government, Legal Department ..	2	10	..
20	Registrar of Companies ..	..	4	3
21	Under Secretary to Government, Home Department ..	5	11	..
22	Collector of Bombay ..	2	36	14
23	Deputy Educational Inspector for Mohomedan Education ..	..	1	..
24	Director of Industries ..	..	7	2
25	Principal, Elphinstone High School ..	9	32	..
26	Superintendent of Stamps ..	..	6	..
27	Government Pleader, High Court ..	..	1	..
28	Under Secretary to Government, General Department	4	16	4
29	Prothonotary and Senior Master, High Court ..	1	23	2
30	Commissioner of Workmen's Compensation ..	..	2	..
31	Chief Presidency Magistrate and Revenue Judge ..	5	37	34
32	Deputy Secretary to Government, Public Works Department ..	8	22	3
33	Director of Information, Labour Office ..	1	9	..
34	Superintendent, Government Printing and Stationery	..	26	10
35	Sub-Registrar of Bombay ..	..	11	..
36	Oriental Translator to Government ..	2	6	..
37	Commissioner of Excise ..	2	57	31
38	Manager, D. L. O. ..	..	10	..
39	Commissioner of Income Tax ..	34	170	..
40	Secretary, Accountancy Diploma Board ..	..	1	..
41	Superintendent of Police, B. B. & C. I. ..	..	1	..
42	Chemical Analyser to Government, Byculla ..	..	2	..
43	Meteorologist, Bombay ..	..	5	2
44	Land Acquisition Officer, City of Bombay ..	..	8	5
45	Dean, Grant Medical College ..	..	2	..
46	Post Master General ..	..	20	4
47	Principal, Sydenham College ..	..	1	..
48	Chief Superintendent, Central Telegraph Office ..	..	4	..
49	Chief Accountant, Bombay Improvement Trust ..	..	18	..
50	Accountant General, Record Section ..	1	27	..
51	Indian Post and Telegraph Office ..	..	7	..
52	Registrar, Small Causes Court ..	..	10	5
53	Deputy Controller of Currency ..	1	4	..
54	Manager, Development Department Chawls ..	..	2	..
55	Currency Office ..	..	20	..
56	Health Officer of the Port of Bombay ..	..	1	..
57	Presidency Post Master ..	2	8	10
58	Sheriff of Bombay ..	..	2	2
59	Presidency Surgeon ..	..	..	1
	Total ..	114	814	157

Employees from Municipal Offices spared for Census Work.

	Name.	Supervisors.	Enumerators.	Peons.
1	Curator	..	1	..
2	Chief of Fire Brigade	..	3	..
3	Municipal Secretary	1	6	4
4	Municipal Commissioner	1	10	7
5	Superintendent of Vaccination	..	7	2
6	Mechanical Engineer	5	23	5
7	Assistant Health Officer, F and G Wards ..	..	15	9
8	Executive Health Officer	1	22	8
9	Municipal Analyst	..	3	1
10	Superintendent, Municipal Gardens	..	2	1
11	Head Supervisor	..	36	5
12	Superintendent of Licenses	2	23	11
13	Assistant Health Officer, A and B Wards ..	..	19	9
14	Superintendent of Markets	..	15	18
15	Assistant Health Officer, Malaria	2	79	4
16	Assessor and Collector	..	100	18
17	City Engineer	3	63	30
18	Works Engineer	..	50	25
19	Secretary, Schools Committee	17	49	11
20	Store Keeper	..	24	3
21	Assistant Health Officer, E Ward	1	12	3
22	Town Duty Officer	..	18	2
23	Hydraulic Engineer	18	54	4
24	Chief Accountant	6	48	14
25	Assistant Health Officer, C and D Wards ..	1	21	10
26	Chairman, Research Bureau	..	1	1
	Total ..	58	704	205

Statement of forms issued by the Census Office.

Authority.	Enumeration Books.	General Schedules.	Household Schedules.	Enumeration covers.	Specimen Schedules.	Family Register.	Travellers' Tickets.
Assistant Collector of Customs, Preventive Service ..	50	3,000	500	50	500	..	5,000
Director, Royal Indian Marine ..	2	100	10	10	100	..	500
Naval Officer	1	50	5	2	5	..	500
Deputy Conservator, Bombay Port Trust	5	2,100	..	100	250	..	1,500
B. B. and C. I. Railway Platforms	22	1,700	1,300	60	1,300	..	15,000
Stations and Quarters ..	30	1,000	500	30	50	100	1,000
G. I. P. Railway Platforms ..	73	3,100	2,200	138	2,050	100	21,000
Military	16	1,000	..	10	50	250	..
Government House	5	100	..	10	20	100	..
Police	32	3,500	..	100	700	800	15,000

Statement of forms issued by the Census Office—contd.

Authority.	Port Block List.	Port Enumeration passes.	Notices to Masters of sea-going vessels.	Circle Register.	Circle Summary.	Authority Forms.
Assistant Collector of Customs, Preventive Service ..	200	150	60	10	..	
Director, Royal Indian Marine ..	40	2	..	2	..	
Naval Officer	..	..	..	2	..	
Deputy Conservator, Bombay Port Trust	150	3	100	..	150	50 16 Appendix IV to VI.
B. B. and C. I. Railway Platforms	..	..	..	24	..	
Stations and Quarters ..	..	..	..	30	..	50 2 Appendix.
G. I. P. Railway Platforms ..	..	..	..	62	..	250 10 Appendix 1.
Military	..	..	..	1 Charge Summary	10	Bombay Census Code V. C. Appendix II.
Government House	..	..	..	..	..	
Police	..	..	..	..	..	

Review of the Operations.

Bombay ranks amongst the large cities in the world and is one of the two largest cities in India. Since 1921 the area of the City has been increased by reclamation as under :—

Ward	Section	Area in Acres in 1931
A	Upper Colaba	409·51
	Middle and Lower Colaba	279·74
	Fort, South	133·11
	Fort, North	158·68
	Esplanade	787·45
		1,768·49
B	Mandvi	187·33
	Chukla	47·02
	Umarkhadi	100·64
	Dongri	302·66
		637·65
C	Market	85·21
	Dhobi Talao	208·27
	Fanaswadi	98·44
	Bhuleshwar	73·46
	Khara Talao	41·14
	Kumbharwada	44·08
		550·60
D	Khetwadi	155·00
	Girgaum	112·40
	Chowpati	108·72
	Walkeshwar	589·90
	Mahalakshmi	658·51
		1,624·53

Ward	Section	Area in Acres in 1931
E	Mazgaon	1,075·48
	Tarwadi	498·81
	Second Nagpada	33·05
	Kamathipura	62·44
	Tardeo	149·86
	Byculla	567·57
	First Nagpada	29·38
		2,416·59
F	Parel	561·25
	Sewri	577·70
	Sion	3,559·10
		4,698·05
G	Mahim	1,511·00
	Worli	2,273·38
		3,784·38
		15,480·29

To carry out the Census of such a large City with a varied and mostly ignorant population is not an easy task. To the usual indifference and apathy of the public generally seen in such matters was added the studied opposition due to the non-cooperation with the Census work declared by prominent members of the Congress. The Census of 1931 of the City thus carried out will perhaps be declared unsatisfactory. That it has been carried out at all under such adversely altered conditions reflects much credit on the well-trained organisation of the Health Department.

Having regard to the extensions and developments made in the city and to the increased activities and development in traffic since 1921 the population that was expected to be in the City was between 13 and 13½ lakhs. For statistical purposes the population for the successive years was obtained by adding 1/10 of the difference between the population figure of 1921 and 1911 to the estimated population of the previous year. Thus for the

Year 1922	the estimated population would be	12,00,473
Year 1923	Do.	12,20,120
Year 1924	Do.	12,39,767
Year 1925	Do.	12,59,414
Year 1926	Do.	12,79,061
Year 1927	Do.	12,98,708

There was, however, a reason to believe that the increase which occurred in the years 1911 to 1920 did not continue at a uniform rate and hence the estimated population for 1927 was retained unaltered for the subsequent years. Thus the population that was expected in the City was somewhere above 13,00,000.

In 1931 the final count of the population of the Bombay City that was declared was 11,57,851. This was at a time when there was trade depression all over necessitating the exodus of the unemployed to their native villages. This exodus is estimated at nearly two lakhs. In respect of the mill industry alone it was officially ascertained from the Millowners' Association that five mills were closed between April and August 1930 throwing thereby out of employment 12,669 persons who could not have been absorbed in any other industry and must have therefore left the City for their villages with their families which if calculated at four members in a family would disclose the figure of 50,000 as exodus for the mill industry alone. Although there are no data for estimating the exodus due to other industries the figure of 1,50,000 would not be an exaggeration. Owing to the movement of non-cooperation it can roughly be estimated that about 10,000 persons must have escaped enumeration altogether. This figure of exodus when added to the actual figure obtained after enumeration would give the population figure over 13,00,000 that was expected and under normal conditions this expectation would perhaps have proved true.

The establishment of the Abstraction Office for Bombay at Ahmednagar proved an added disadvantage for the Census Operations in Bombay. All the enumeration books had to be

MO-I Bk Ra Cs 3—32

despatched immediately after the Census night. There was very little time at the disposal of the Census office in Bombay to examine the enumeration books to see whether entries were complete or not. The enumeration books of the Taj Mahal Hotel and Hotel Majestic had many schedules not completely filled in. Similarly the enumeration books for the passengers and crew of two important steamers, s.s. "Multan" and s.s. "Naldera" were incomplete as regards particulars. Much correspondence ensued and time was spent in securing the particulars from the Agents of the companies and still there was very little progress. Thus incomplete books had to be sent to Ahmednagar with a suggestion that the word "unspecified" may be used for incomplete entries in the tables concerned. Many references from the Abstraction Office had to be answered and explained in respect of abbreviations common in Bombay but unknown to outsiders. Had the Abstraction Office been in Bombay all these defects could have been rectified side by side with the work of Abstraction as in 1921.

Non-cooperation or boycott of the Census was perhaps the greatest hindrance this year in carrying out the Census operations to a successful finish. Non-cooperation is an ugly word and the idea of its use in such a useful work is uglier still. The first step in connection with the Census Operations is painting Census numbers on every building and painting circle and block numbers at the beginning, end and at corners in each block and circle. While the painting was in progress and even till its completion there was no opposition. Perhaps the Congress ban on the Census was being hatched during this time. Soon after the numbering work was over organised efforts were made for removing, tarring by dammer, disfiguring, obliterating and scratching the Census numbers throughout the City in defiance of Government orders. Under the Criminal Code actions were taken by the Police for disfiguring and removing Census numbers independently of the Census Office and of the Census Act and some persons were convicted but the movement did not stop. The Census Office did not take any notice of such persons beyond issuing instructions to the Charge Superintendents to repaint the numbers. After some time repainting also was found impossible and it was then devised to have in the $\frac{\text{House}}{\text{Block}}$ lists Municipal Street numbers corresponding to the Census numbers marked to enable the Enumerator to identify the buildings at the time of enumeration. As the time of preliminary enumeration was approaching, meetings were held to instigate the public not to give any information in connection with the Census and not to cooperate with any one connected with the Census. Leaflets in different languages were published and freely distributed with a view to keep the agitation fresh.

To create self-confidence among the Charge Superintendents and their Assistants I called them to a meeting just a few days before the start of the preliminary enumeration and gave them clear instructions pointing out the situation and suggesting different ways of securing the information and the necessity of arriving at accurate figures as far as possible. To dispel any misunderstanding of the public I issued leaflets in Gujarati and Marathi, already referred to before, and gave them to the Charge Superintendents for free distribution through their enumerators. If, in spite of this, the information was refused the enumerators were instructed to note down the places and report them to the Charge Superintendents without any delay. The Charge Superintendents were in turn instructed to try personally for such information and on their failure they should approach the Assistant Health Officer of the Ward who would obtain the information as if for a Municipal purpose. All the resources of the Health Department were put into execution for securing correct information. In some cases enumeration was made through Birth Karkoons, Mill Sub-Inspectors and Malaria Junior Overseers. In some cases the help of the outdoor staff of the Assessment Department was also taken. Letters were addressed to the Chief Officer of the City Improvement Trust and the Director of the Development Department requesting them to issue orders to the Rent Collectors and caretakers of their chawls to cooperate with the enumerators in recording the particulars of the tenants as accurately as possible.

Opposition to the Census had to be faced in many ways. Sometimes the enumerator was hooted out by the Congress Volunteers. Sometimes the door was shut against the enumerator and sometimes wrong information was given by the public.

While the preliminary enumeration was in progress rumours were afloat of holding open air meetings on the Census night in order that they may be attended by the public in large numbers after locking up their houses. It was also rumoured that all the 32 Census Offices temporarily opened for the Census would be picketed, thus preventing the Government or Municipal Volunteers from taking the enumeration books for verification from the Census Offices. It was also apprehended that the enumerators would be deprived of their books in the streets while on duty on the Census night. A confidential circular was issued by me calling upon all the Charge Superintendents to deliver all their books into my office a day before the final Census. New enumeration books with $\frac{\text{House}}{\text{Block}}$ lists and family registers were made and given to the enumerators on the Census night with instruction to record only the additions or omissions against the house so that changes could be made in the original enumeration book. In two or three sections some enumerators were roughly handled by the mob and deprived of their cutcha enumeration books but these were subsequently restored by the Police.

The period of three weeks allowed for the preliminary enumeration was barely sufficient. Four weeks at least should be devoted to preliminary enumeration. The first week would be profitably utilised in training the enumerators and dismissing those who would be found incompetent and careless workers.

For the preparation of statistical evidence of overcrowding, records were made on a separate schedule of the number of rooms occupied by each family and of the number of persons occupying each room or set of rooms in the houses enumerated. On a third schedule the number of floors in each house was shown and for the Abstraction Office it accordingly became unnecessary to include any indication as to rooms or floors in the General Schedule which gives the details as to age, sex, etc., of each person enumerated.

The General Census Schedule adopted for the Presidency is not suitable for Bombay. This form has no provision for the column for floor numbers and for room numbers on each floor. For the preparation of the special City Tables these two columns are absolutely necessary. This deficiency in the General Schedule had to be overcome by devising the use of a fraction showing the floor number as the numerator and the room number as the denominator against the Census house numbers in the column provided for the serial Census house number. No great difficulty was experienced in explaining the meaning and use of this fraction to the paid enumerators but for the final enumerators, coming new to work from Government or Municipal Offices, this proved to be an added source of confusion. The columns in the General Schedule (consecutive number of floors and rooms) which were abandoned in 1921 should be restored.

On the present occasion there was only the General Schedule and the enumerators were instructed to obtain particulars themselves on the General Schedule in all cases. This led to a great waste of enumerator's time. Persons, who could write their own information in a private schedule, would not suit the convenience of the enumerator as to the hour at which they would supply the information he required and time after time directed him to call again. The result of this was that in many cases the enumerators obtained the necessary particulars from servants instead of from heads of families. The use of private schedules with printed instructions on the back should be restored with strict injunctions that such schedules should be left only with persons who are competent to fill them up correctly.

Owing to the non-cooperation the unemployment schedules were not filled up though offered to persons literate in English but unemployed. Similarly the schedules showing the fertility of Indian women could not be filled up.

In conclusion I should like to point out that the above notes are made solely to fulfil the duty of every Census Officer to his successor indicating the directions in which experience suggests that improvement may be effected.

The Charge Superintendents performed their Census duties in addition to the duties required from them by the Municipality. All worked long hours of overtime and the majority of them completed their work with conspicuous zeal.

To the Assistant Health Officers and particularly to Dr. R. K. Mhatre, Assistant Health Officer, Malaria, the fullest recognition is due for the voluntary services which they rendered during the last days of the operation.

I have the honour to be,
Sir,
Your most obedient servant,

(Signed) J. S. NERURKAR,
Executive Health Officer.

KARACHI MUNICIPALITY.
Reference No. Census 1400.

From

Municipal Office, Karachi :
4th/5th March 1931.

THE CHIEF OFFICER AND CHARGE SUPERINTENDENT,
Census Operations, Karachi ;

To

THE COLLECTOR OF KARACHI,
Karachi.

Decennial Census, 1931.

Sir,

I have the honour to submit the following summary of the figures of population in the Karachi Municipal District including the various sub-Charges which were separately enumerated by the respective authorities, as ascertained by the Census which took place on the 26th February 1931 :—

Males.	Females.	Total.
144,184	102,874	247,058

2. The original schedules and other papers will be forwarded in due course to the Provincial Superintendent's Abstraction Office at Hyderabad (Sind).

3. In view of the general opposition anticipated in certain quarters of the City, which had manifested itself by obliteration of house numbers on a large scale (reported in the President's letters to the Commissioner-in-Sind, Nos. 5B/75 and G-A/Census dated 16th December 1930, 10th January 1931, 26th January 1931 and 30th January 1931 respectively), the preliminary enumeration had been postponed to a later date than usual, but it was definitely started on 10th February 1931, no instructions for postponing the work having been received from Government by that date. Government's final orders on the subject were received on 13th February 1931. By that time however the preliminary enumeration was already in full swing. In several places where the numbers on plates had been defaced, chalk numbers were marked on the houses and the circle and block boundaries were demarcated at site in a conspicuous manner to facilitate the taking of the final census. The Supervisors were shown round their circle and block beats by Municipal Surveyors and they were instructed to take each enumerator round the boundaries of his block in like manner. The areas affected were Old Town, Runchore, Ramswami and portions of Jail, Market, Napier and Sadar Bazar Quarters. The commencement of the preliminary enumeration had been preceded by two meetings, one of supervisors only and the other of supervisors and enumerators, at which the general instructions laid down for guidance were carefully and clearly explained and in particular, it was impressed on all the workers that much depended on the courtesy and tact which they were expected to show on this occasion in obtaining information. By the time the preliminary enumeration started, the opposition, in its strong form, had greatly subsided and the enumerators were mostly able to get out full particulars even in the affected areas. In a few cases only where the parties had declined to give information particulars had to be gathered from the neighbours.

4. Another meeting of all the census workers was held in the Khalikdina Hall on the morning of the day of the census, and they were again addressed and all the necessary supplementary instructions given and stationery and writing materials, lamps etc. distributed. Additional enumerators and assistant supervisors were assigned according to necessity and the distribution of servants for carrying the lamps etc. also made. All the Supervisors and enumerators were ordered to begin work at 7-0 p.m. sharp according to programme.

5. On touring round the City in the afternoon of the day, particularly in Runchore Quarter, where preliminary enumeration had not been done in a few houses, it was found that a report had been spread that the Congress was against the taking of the Census and had advised the people to remain indoors and to withhold information when enumerators passed round in the night. A small crowd of young boys quickly gathered where I had proceeded with the Deputy Chief Officer, and the supervisor and enumerators concerned, and they were shouting. Enquiries showed that a notice recommending boycott had been published that morning in the name of the local Congress Authority. It was understood however that Census Officials would not be harassed in their work. The crowd of boys who had gathered at Runchore Quarter was dispersed by some one who appeared to have some influence over them, for the time being any way. In fact, even while I was there with the supervisors and enumerators taking preliminary observations, the crowd of boys proceeded to disperse, leaving the census workers in peace. It was hoped, in view of the above, that there would be no positive obstruction at night in Runchore Quarter or in the other near affected areas and that the census staff would be allowed to get through their work of collecting the required information from those who were not averse to giving the same. The supervisors had been informed at the meeting that they could communicate with the Chief Officer by telephoning to Fire Brigade Head Quarters. The superior officers of the Municipality had also been required to move about

and superintend the work of supervisors in specified areas that were assigned to them for the purpose that night.

6. The Undersigned with the Deputy Chief Officer went round various quarters and, in particular, the affected areas. It was soon found that there was active obstruction and serious difficulty at Runchore Lines, and orders were quickly sent to the supervisors and enumerators in Runchore and Ramswami Quarters to cease work and go away. The instructions were conveyed by two clerks who were sent round in a Municipal motor car. Demonstrations were also seen in Ramswami Old Town, Market and Jail Quarters. At all the places, the demonstrations were by crowds of boys with whom there were a few older youths. The supervisors and enumerators were advised to put out their candles (which were conspicuous) and to go away *taking particular care of their books*.

7. In three places, the workers who were being molested by boys who were attempting to snatch away the census books, were rescued and either put into a ghari or carried in a motor car near their homes, the books being retained by the undersigned. It was reported that in one place a census book had been taken away and destroyed. At 12 mid-night a report was received from an enumerator of Lyari, who was returning home after the work, that he had been set upon near the City Magistrate's Court and his book had been taken away and he himself roughly handled by a crowd of boys.

8. At the meeting of the census staff held on the following day at the Khalikdina Hall for the preparation and submission of the Circle Summaries and Schedules, the undersigned went round to every Circle Supervisor ascertaining from him and his enumerators the exact position on the previous night. A bad case of an enumerator who had been almost suffocated and robbed of his books, but had been rescued by a stalwart scout and rescued in time, was reported. He had also lost his fountain pen and muffler. Another had been rescued by a Municipal Councillor who had been kindly going round in the area to help in the census. Three or four enumerators had been assaulted but in almost all the cases, the supervisors and enumerators had managed to save their books and there were no serious consequences. In all six books had been lost, but in regard to three of them, the rough lists were available from which copies could be (and have been) made. In Machi Meani, Old Town, Market, Runchore, Ramswami and Jail Quarters, the final check was only partially done (where it was done) or not done at all. In all the other quarters, there was no difficulty whatsoever and the final check was reported to have been got through completely, the supervisors checking the percentage as required.

9. The preliminary enumeration had shown a total population of 2,34,626 (including 1,11,035 Hindus and 1,10,689 Mahomedans). The figures already reported to you were a total population of 2,31,096, of whom 1,09,008 were Hindus and 1,09,304 Mahomedans. The returns subsequently received from Circle Supervisors 12, 34, 42, 49 and 76A (all of which accompany) show a total of 3,530, with 2,027 Hindus and 1,385 Mahomedans. The total population shown by the final enumeration is 2,47,058 persons. The latter includes, *inter alia*, persons enumerated on the final night at Railway platforms (347) and on boats in the harbour (1,357) as well as pilgrims and homeless persons all of whom were necessarily newly enumerated. In Circle 42 (Runchore), the Supervisor reported that 176 houses could not be enumerated at all even by the final night. The Supervisor of Circle No. 44 (Runchore) reported that 11 houses similarly remained unenumerated. The final check could not be done properly in the affected areas and in several of them could not be done at all as already explained. The irreparable loss of the Enumeration books of three blocks (Blocks Nos. 3 and 4, Circle No. 7, and Block No. 7, Circle No. 44) has already been stated. These included 226 houses with a population of 528, as per provisional totals. No other details (excepting the total population by communities) are now available. The final figures now reported have necessarily to be taken subject to the limitations herein stated.

10. Before concluding this report, I have to refer to the excellent work done by the several Supervisors and Enumerators on this occasion. All of them worked with great zeal and this was particularly marked on the census night. The Enumerators who had to do the enumeration in the disturbed areas and their supervisors all showed a proper spirit and quietly managed to save their books (with the exceptions mentioned), despite serious difficulties and they all deserve the warmest thanks for the tact and coolness displayed. The celerity with which the preliminary enumeration was carried out (in addition to other office duties) was commendable. A few personal articles (of any value) that were reported to have been lost on the night of the census, of which a list was made on the following morning are being arranged to be paid for. The amount involved is insignificant.

11. The following documents accompany*. The favour of an acknowledgment is requested.

(1) Charge Summary .. 1 } Not printed.
(2) Circle Summaries .. 127 }

* Forwarded already.

I have the honour to be,
Sir,
Your most obedient servant,
(Signed) K. N. RAMASUBBA AIYAR,
Chief Officer and Charge Superintendent,
Census Operations, Karachi.

APPENDIX C—PART I.

Part I gives the number of children of the individual ages 4 to 15 in the Bombay City by wards in each religion and in all religions.

Part II shows the general distribution of children by main languages in each ward.

This information has been abstracted this time at the special request of the Municipality.

The number of children shown in the City Table IV—Bombay, will not agree with the number given in this Appendix as the former sets of figures have been arrived at by smoothing the crude age group figures and the latter represent the number as actually returned in the General Schedules.

CHILDREN AGED 4 TO 15

BOMBAY

All

Ward.	Total.		4		5		6		7		8	
	Males.	Females.	Males.	Females.	Males.	Females.	Males.	Females.	Males.	Females.	Males.	Females.
1	2	3	4	5	6	7	8	9	10	11	12	13
A ..	7,155	5,454	852	749	967	811	1,166	1,004	364	328	502	400
B ..	15,611	11,510	1,465	1,124	1,480	1,385	2,292	1,838	1,081	734	1,544	1,130
C ..	24,258	16,623	1,471	1,107	1,542	1,341	2,303	1,961	1,983	6,983	2,719	1,836
D ..	18,631	13,197	1,870	1,504	1,853	1,507	1,660	1,425	1,325	1,107	1,795	1,277
E ..	27,716	20,458	2,457	2,119	2,316	2,024	1,912	2,676	2,220	1,948	3,031	1,972
F ..	16,782	12,511	1,987	1,634	1,857	1,606	1,439	1,091	1,662	1,830	1,913	1,450
G ..	15,805	12,115	945	788	1,403	1,241	1,489	1,260	1,541	1,324	1,746	1,414
Railway Floating, etc.	1,255	392	36	24	35	30	47	30	69	41	47	44
Total ..	127,213	92,260	11,083	9,049	11,453	9,945	13,308	11,285	10,245	8,420	13,297	9,523

Hindu.

Ward.	Total Males	Total Females	4 Males	4 Females	5 Males	5 Females	6 Males	6 Females	7 Males	7 Females	8 Males	8 Females
A ..	4,992	3,624	733	610	839	675	986	780	213	168	329	246
B ..	8,245	5,917	933	745	1,053	899	1,330	1,065	572	335	784	556
C ..	16,352	11,009	835	665	939	770	1,515	1,226	1,329	1,116	1,927	1,322
D ..	14,505	10,240	1,640	1,313	1,643	1,335	1,180	944	1,028	873	1,438	1,026
E ..	16,179	11,654	1,494	1,291	1,343	1,187	1,521	1,280	1,450	1,208	1,915	1,261
F ..	13,143	9,661	1,707	1,373	1,610	1,331	1,076	804	1,332	1,022	1,538	1,165
G ..	12,705	9,749	746	600	1,192	1,049	1,159	935	1,336	1,116	1,448	1,170
Railway Floating, etc.	801	226	18	9	16	15	19	19	42	26	20	24
Total ..	86,922	62,080	8,106	6,606	8,635	7,261	8,786	7,103	7,302	5,864	9,399	6,770

Muslim.

Ward.	Total Males	Total Females	4 Males	4 Females	5 Males	5 Females	6 Males	6 Females	7 Males	7 Females	8 Males	8 Females
A ..	617	394	22	35	25	37	48	55	40	33	51	48
B ..	6,677	5,042	468	322	364	427	872	688	468	377	701	529
C ..	4,896	3,389	333	222	306	309	486	469	434	300	494	330
D ..	917	552	62	49	65	43	133	78	58	51	93	51
E ..	6,984	4,715	534	448	553	487	906	935	443	409	727	385
F ..	1,317	739	78	69	79	74	135	79	144	99	147	107
G ..	1,453	988	82	107	83	98	119	133	88	101	146	98
Railway Floating, etc.	313	54	5	6	6	4	8	4	12	5	16	10
Total ..	23,204	15,873	1,584	1,258	1,481	1,479	2,707	2,441	1,687	1,375	2,875	1,558

Jain.

Ward.	Total Males	Total Females	4 Males	4 Females	5 Males	5 Females	6 Males	6 Females	7 Males	7 Females	8 Males	8 Females
A ..	26	1	..	1	1	..	..	..	2	..	..	..
B ..	181	99	18	16	18	19	17	23	16	1	21	6
C ..	734	377	62	46	64	54	90	95	61	25	90	42
D ..	169	123	19	22	20	13	20	22	7	3	14	17
E ..	100	47	10	7	8	7	..	7	4	6	4	..
F ..	89	108	11	10	11	10	3	6	7	13	15	18
G ..	188	65	12	6	24	11	24	18	5	6	8	5
Railway Floating, etc.	..	..	..	..	..	..	..	..	..	..	..	..
Total ..	1,487	820	132	108	146	114	154	171	102	54	152	88

BY INDIVIDUAL AGE GROUP.

CITY.

Religions.

9		10		11		12		13		14		15	
Males.	Females.	Males.	Females.	Males.	Females.	Males.	Females.	Males.	Females.	Males.	Females.	Males.	Females.
14	15	16	17	18	19	20	21	22	23	24	25	26	27
288	242	684	502	250	158	684	544	293	216	401	207	704	293
878	568	1,893	1,353	698	428	1,506	1,004	601	492	925	619	1,248	835
1,646	1,276	3,345	2,064	1,114	797	3,015	1,694	1,030	705	1,625	1,034	2,465	2,200
1,079	886	2,072	1,263	879	552	1,977	1,093	914	594	1,422	956	1,785	1,033
1,550	1,322	3,972	2,318	1,066	830	2,896	1,666	1,160	860	1,442	1,020	2,694	1,703
844	698	1,925	1,348	604	455	1,743	1,036	652	499	927	606	1,229	758
941	867	2,116	1,454	589	495	1,870	1,164	718	490	926	674	1,521	944
53	38.	162	54	42	17	228	33	63	19	105	28	368	34
7,279	5,897	16,169	10,356	5,242	3,732	13,919	8,234	5,431	3,875	7,773	5,144	12,014	6,800
163	112	413	319	126	67	410	346	141	67	215	88	424	146
374	246	1,027	613	202	137	766	465	228	209	353	245	623	402
1,164	912	2,365	1,392	743	520	2,066	1,154	682	432	1,085	680	1,702	820
815	667	1,688	1,032	531	341	1,490	836	650	411	1,087	666	1,306	746
871	700	2,405	1;400	612	449	1,722	1,040	579	402	703	490	1,564	946
647	516	1,503	1,075	414	288	1,345	777	421	306	657	434	893	570
773	705	1,693	1,200	493	417	1,486	935	507	348	694	540	1,178	734
28	14	113	31	26	11	166	23	37	9	64	17	252	28
4,835	3,872	11,207	7,062	3,147	2,230	9,460	5,576	3,245	2,184	4,858	3,160	7,942	4,392
26	18	84	49	23	15	96	36	35	22	55	16	112	30
480	296	784	676	418	229	673	495	343	258	532	343	574	402
301	208	649	460	228	173	632	338	192	140	354	220	487	220
44	35	102	59	43	24	117	43	55	39	57	41	118	36
362	304	1,036	491-	298	195	787	285	267	178	383	226	688	369
52	47	196	80	43	27	180	65	67	25	77	30	119	37
81	56	198	110	67	48	188	89	112	38	119	43	170	67
13	3	40	7	10	4	56	2	18	1	30	6	90	2-
1,859	967	3,089	1,935	1,130	715	2,729	1,358	1,089	701	1,607	928	2,367	1,163
..	..	5	..	2	..	9	..	3	..	..	..	4	..
8	2	30	6	9	8	21	9	8	5	5	4	10	..
54	19	98	27	54	25	84	16	22	17	19	5	36	6
5	4	15	11	2	2	21	13	7	4	16	10	23	2
4	1	14	1	3	5	16	1	10	7	4	1	23	4
..	3	2	13	5	13	17	8	5	11	4	3	9	..
8	..	23	3	4	3	36	1	14	5	7	1	23	6
..	..	..	..	..	..	..	..	..	..	..	..	..	..
79	29	187	61	79	56	204	48	69	49	55	24	128	18

Zoroastrian.

Ward.	Total		4		5		6		7		8	
	Males.	Females.	Males.	Females.	Males.	Females.	Males.	Females.	Males.	Females.	Males.	Females.
1	2	3	4	5	6	7	8	9	10	11	12	13
A ..	594	652	28	37	32	28	38	65	42	63	49	46
B ..	11	6	..	1	1	..	1	..	..	..	2	..
C ..	1,160	1,049	170	105	151	142	67	74	83	84	96	78
D ..	2,076	1,585	83	72	78	68	247	248	182	139	164	134
E ..	1,185	1,085	149	143	134	96	53	43	93	110	100	72
F ..	1,082	919	89	84	81	91	64	68	79	80	85	63
G ..	156	154	8	7	6	9	9	15	17	19	12	9
Railway Floating, etc.	7	10	2	..	..	2	..	..	..	1	..	..
Total ..	6,271	5,460	529	449	483	436	479	513	496	496	508	402

Christian.

Ward.	Total Males.	Total Females.	4 Males.	4 Females.	5 Males.	5 Females.	6 Males.	6 Females.	7 Males.	7 Females.	8 Males.	8 Females.
A ..	817	682	54	50	54	53	81	91	57	56	69	52
B ..	196	149	12	7	9	7	23	15	7	4	9	14
C ..	1,115	796	71	68	82	66	145	97	76	82	112	64
D ..	907	673	61	47	47	46	75	82	48	37	81	47
E ..	2,488	2,172	193	145	191	165	335	308	185	166	218	191
F ..	1,084	1,019	96	93	72	95	156	126	92	108	121	91
G ..	1,237	1,079	91	63	92	70	171	151	89	78	125	116
Railway Floating, etc.	127	99	10	9	13	8	20	7	14	9	11	10
Total ..	7,971	6,669	588	482	560	510	1,006	877	568	540	746	585

Buddhist.

Ward.	Total Males.	Total Females.	4 Males.	4 Females.	5 Males.	5 Females.	6 Males.	6 Females.	7 Males.	7 Females.	8 Males.	8 Females.
A ..	6	2	..	..	2	1	1	..	1	..	1	..
B ..	1	1	..	..	1	..	..	..	..	..	..	1
C ..	..	..	..	..	..	..	..	..	..	..	..	..
D ..	13	7	3	..	..	..	4	..	1	..	3	2
E ..	16	14	3	..	2	..	..	3	1	2	..	3
F ..	4	..	..	..	1	..	..	..	..	..	1	..
G ..	..	..	..	..	..	..	..	..	..	..	..	..
Railway Floating, etc.	..	..	..	..	..	..	..	..	..	..	..	..
Total ..	40	24	6	..	6	1	5	3	3	2	5	6

Sikh.

Ward.	Total Males.	Total Females.	4 Males.	4 Females.	5 Males.	5 Females.	6 Males.	6 Females.	7 Males.	7 Females.	8 Males.	8 Females.
A ..	4	2	..	..	1	..	..	..	..	..	1	1
B ..	1	..	..	..	..	..	..	..	..	..	1	..
C ..	..	..	..	..	..	..	..	..	..	..	..	..
D ..	5	1	1	..	..	..	1	..	..	1	2	..
E ..	11	5	1	..	1	..	2	2	1	1	..	..
F ..	8	9	2	..	..	..	..	3	2	..	..	2
G ..	3	2	1	..	..	..	..	..	..	..	1	2
Railway Floating, etc.	3	1	1	..	..	..	..	1	1	..	..	..
Total ..	35	20	6	..	2	..	3	5	4	2	5	5

Jew.

Ward.	Total Males.	Total Females.	4 Males.	4 Females.	5 Males.	5 Females.	6 Males.	6 Females.	7 Males.	7 Females.	8 Males.	8 Females.
A ..	99	97	15	16	13	17	12	13	9	8	2	7
B ..	299	296	34	33	34	33	49	47	18	17	26	24
C ..	1	3	..	1	..	..	..	..	..	1	..	..
D ..	9	16	1	1	..	2	..	1	1	1	..	..
E ..	753	766	73	85	84	82	95	98	43	48	67	60
F ..	55	56	4	5	3	5	5	5	6	8	6	4
G ..	63	78	5	5	6	4	7	8	6	4	6	14
Railway Floating, etc.	4	2	..	..	..	1	..	..	..	..	..	..
Total ..	1,283	1,314	132	146	140	144	168	172	83	87	107	109

9		10		11		12		13		14		15	
Males.	Females.	Males.	Females.	Males.	Females.	Males.	Females.	Males.	Females.	Males.	Females.	Males.	Females.
14	15	16	17	18	19	20	21	22	23	24	25	26	27
46	54	74	57	46	47	68	76	53	73	59	55	59	51
1	..	1	2	..	1	1	1	1	..	1	1	2	..
72	78	101	105	69	61	113	100	54	61	84	69	100	92
164	148	199	107	135	70	236	130	158	111	196	172	234	186
74	93	135	97	64	94	99	95	86	70	89	75	109	97
85	79	90	81	83	55	104	84	110	90	108	71	104	73
7	18	24	20	13	8	14	14	10	10	17	11	19	14
..	2	1	..	1	1	1	1	..	..	2	2	..	1
449	472	625	469	411	337	636	501	472	415	556	456	627	514
46	52	97	71	45	23	100	78	53	53	67	43	94	60
5	9	15	13	58	45	19	7	8	8	13	8	18	12
55	59	132	79	20	18	120	86	80	55	83	60	139	62
48	30	66	51	168	115	102	69	43	28	65	61	103	60
185	171	311	258	45	54	205	180	175	164	203	161	242	209
59	49	125	93	57	70	85	95	46	62	76	64	99	73
67	83	174	115	11	10	139	120	72	82	84	75	122	116
10	18	6	16	5	1	5	7	8	9	8	2	17	3
475	471	926	696	409	336	775	642	485	461	599	474	834	595
..	..	1	1	..	..	..	..	..	..	..	..	..	..
..	..	..	..	..	..	..	..	..	..	..	..	..	..
..	..	..	..	..	..	..	..	..	..	..	..	..	..
2	..	..	1	..	..	..	1	..	..	..	1	..	..
3	2	1	2	3	..	1	2	1	..	1	1	..	1
..	..	1	..	..	..	1	..	..	..	..	..	..	..
..	..	..	..	..	..	..	..	..	..	..	..	..	..
..	..	..	..	..	..	..	..	..	..	..	..	..	..
5	2	3	4	3	..	2	3	1	..	1	2	..	1
..	..	1	1	..	..	..	..	..	..	1	..	..	..
..	..	..	..	..	..	..	..	..	..	..	..	..	..
..	..	..	..	..	..	..	..	..	..	..	..	..	..
..	..	..	..	..	..	1	..	..	..	..	..	..	..
2	1	2	1	1	..	..	..	..	..	1	..	..	..
1	1	1	..	..	..	1	1	..	..	1	..	..	2
..	..	..	..	..	..	..	..	..	..	1	..	..	..
1	..	..	..	..	..	..	..	..	..	..	1	..	..
4	2	4	2	1	..	2	1	..	..	4	1	..	2
7	6	9	4	8	6	1	8	8	1	4	5	11	6
10	15	36	43	11	8	26	27	13	12	21	18	21	19
..	..	..	1	..	..	..	..	..	..	..	..	..	..
1	2	2	2	..	..	1	1	1	1	1	2	1	3
49	50	68	65	40	33	66	63	42	39	58	66	68	77
..	3	7	6	2	2	10	6	3	5	4	4	5	3
5	5	4	6	1	9	7	5	3	7	4	4	9	7
1	1	2	..	..	..	..	..	..	..	1	..	..	..
73	82	128	127	62	58	111	110	70	65	93	99	116	115

Distribution of children in Bombay City aged 4 to 15 by main languages and wards.

Language.	Ward A.		Ward B.		Ward C.		Ward D.		Ward E.	
	Males.	Females.	Males.	Females.	Males.	Females.	Males.	Females.	Males.	Females.
1	2	3	4	5	6	7	8	9	10	11
Total ..	**7,155**	**5,454**	**15,611**	**11,510**	**24,258**	**16,623**	**18,631**	**13,197**	**27,716**	**20,458**
Marathi ..	2,150	1,675	3,266	2,847	7,168	5,840	9,846	7,232	12,647	10,113
Gujarati ..	2,841	2,160	6,651	4,760	11,765	8,136	5,630	3,580	7,334	5,991
Western Hindi ..	944	661	2,971	2,168	2,684	1,785	1,440	598	4,056	3,037
Konkani ..	630	325	85	25	1,338	397	617	383	1,003	461
Sindhi	40	18	1,672	1,056	229	180	104	70	195	124
Telugu	32	13	2	1	64	23	23	11	784	362
Tamil	48	27	9	4	47	27	67	29	69	32
English ..	292	192	11	5	16	7	82	63	320	201
Other languages ..	178	383	944	644	947	228	822	1,231	408	137

Language.	Ward F.		Ward G.		Railway Police, Homeless, etc.		Total.	
	Males.	Females.	Males.	Females.	Males.	Females.	Males.	Females.
1	12	13	14	15	16	17	18	19
Total	**6,782**	**12,511**	**15,805**	**12,115**	**1,255**	**392**	**127,213**	**92,260**
Marathi ..	9,761	8,307	9,160	8,323	506	143	54,504	44,480
Gujarati ..	3,931	2,316	2,898	1,491	320	102	41,370	28,536
Western Hindi ..	1,640	576	1,606	1,020	261	69	16,592	9,914
Konkani ..	222	134	370	201	102	2	4,367	1,928
Sindhi ..	84	29	32	4	26	2	2,382	1,483
Telugu	192	92	480	221	1	....	1,578	723
Tamil	289	148	288	159	2	....	819	426
English ..	146	61	144	69	3	1	1,014	599
Other languages ..	517	848	737	627	34	73	4,587	4,171

APPENDIX D.

This appendix gives the number of children in the Karachi City of the individual ages 6 to 11 by religion and by quarters.

The information has been abstracted this time at the special request of the Municipality.

The number of children shown in the City Table IV—Karachi will not agree with the number given in this Appendix as the former sets of figures have been arrived at by smoothing the crude age groups figures and the latter represent the number as actually returned in the General Schedules.

MO-II Bk Ra Cs 3—35

APPENDIX D.

Population of Children aged 6 to 11 by Religion.

Karachi City.

Quarter.	Population.			HINDU.				
				Total.			Boys.	
	Persons.	Boys.	Girls.	Persons.	Boys.	Girls.	6	7
1	2	3	4	5	6	7	8	9
1. **Karachi City**	30,518	15,832	14,686	13,736	7,230	6,506	1,318	1,157
2. Old Town	1,261	632	629	1,174	588	586	114	101
3. Lea	107	53	54	93	49	44	13	7
4. Napier	1,308	686	622	958	494	464	81	85
5. Market	922	487	435	735	384	351	70	62
6. Bunder	326	186	140	286	162	124	31	21
7. Machi Meani	1,201	625	576	401	272	129	61	44
8. Queen's Road	9	3	6	6	2	4	2	..
9. Railway	23	15	8	13	9	4	2	..
10. Serai	1,451	765	686	1,208	613	595	117	107
11. Rambaugh	1,578	823	755	1,358	678	680	112	111
12. Jail	959	506	453	787	384	403	63	55
13. Ranchore	4,023	2,036	1,987	3,084	1,521	1,563	255	214
14. Ramswami	853	451	402	620	337	283	45	56
15. Herchandrai Vishendas ..	126	68	58	21	12	9	1	2
16. Soldier Bazar	290	130	160	140	64	76	9	10
17. New Jail	56	43	13	17	15	2	3	4
18. Preedy	161	94	67	45	29	16	3	5
19. Saddar Bazar	913	503	410	180	116	64	26	16
20. Civil Lines	344	189	155	163	90	73	17	14
21. Frere Town and Bath Island.	140	79	61	60	36	24	6	5
22. Clifton	23	13	10	7	5	2	..	1
23. Gizri	131	69	62	5	3	2	..	3
24. Garden (East and West) ..	893	483	410	120	90	30	18	22
25. Tahilram	571	285	286	206	105	101	23	20
26. Lawrence	993	610	383	461	332	129	68	52
27. Lyari	7,611	3,786	3,825	550	313	237	67	58
28. Jamshed	319	166	153	267	138	129	28	18
29. Artillery Maidan ..	46	24	22	25	14	11	4	4
30. *Trans-Lyari*	706	357	349	7	5	2	1	..
31. Tatta Naka and Goda village and Labour Corps ..	56	27	29	21	10	11	2	1
32. Quarry Nos. 1 and 2 and other Quarries	45	23	22	1	..	1	..	..
33. Scattered Hamlets behind Cantonment Station and Chinaser and Vagri Villages.	129	68	61	24	11	13	1	3
34. Keamari with other Port Area (viz., Thole Produce Yard, Mansfield Import Yard and West Wharf) ..	1,124	637	487	460	255	205	55	38
35. Baba Island	143	60	83	4	2	2	1	..
36. Bhit Island	95	31	64	..	..	..	..	..
37. Shamspir and Goth Mahomed	59	27	32	..	..	..	..	..
38. Bunker Island	..	..	..	..	..	..	..	..
39. Port Floating Population ..	30	22	8	5	3	2	..	1
40. Railway Area including City, Bunder and Cantonment Stations and Reception and Hump Yard and Platform population ..	1,320	671	649	218	83	130	17	15
41. Maurypur	167	96	71	9	5	4	1	2
42. Drigh Road	2	1	1	2	1	1	1	..
43. Cape Manze	4	2	2	..	..	..	..	..

Quarter.	HINDU—*contd.*							
	BOYS—*contd.*				GIRLS.			
	8	9	10	11	6	7	8	9
1	10	11	12	13	14	15	16	17
1. Karachi City	**1,410**	**938**	**1,503**	**904**	**1,179**	**1,083**	**1,323**	**989**
2. Old Town	119	72	122	60	138	75	129	60
3. Lea	11	5	13	..	15	2	8	4
4. Napier	94	56	134	42	72	79	95	49
5. Market	75	44	87	46	58	44	86	42
6. Bunder	33	18	46	13	19	25	29	16
7. Machi Meani	35	41	39	52	31	24	15	18
8. Queen's Road	..	..	..	..	1	..	..	1
9. Railway	3	2	1	1	1	1	1	1
10. Serai	117	85	116	71	129	98	120	99
11. Rambaugh	138	91	148	78	110	116	138	88
12. Jail	86	51	86	43	62	64	79	66
13. Ranchore	286	192	327	247	247	268	315	305
14. Ramswami	69	46	75	46	50	47	62	35
15. Herchandrai Vishendas ..	1	2	2	4	..	1	2	1
16. Soldier Bazar	12	14	8	11	12	14	16	10
17. New Jail	2	4	..	2	..	..	1	..
18. Preedy	4	8	3	6	3	4	2	2
19. Saddar Bazar	21	18	22	13	12	10	8	14
20. Civil Lines	19	13	17	10	15	11	17	13
21. Frere Town and Bath Island .	6	9	6	4	4	3	3	6
22. Clifton	2	..	2	..	1	..	1	..
23. Gizri	..	..	..	..	..	..	2	..
24. Garden (East and West) ..	16	13	7	14	6	5	4	7
25. Tahilram	24	6	25	7	21	12	18	15
26. Lawrence	72	29	76	35	32	31	22	14
27. Lyari	64	46	40	38	46	38	52	33
28. Jamshed	25	16	32	19	21	33	18	27
29. Artillery Maidan ..	2	..	2	2	1	3	1	..
30. Trans-Lyari	1	2	..	1	..	1	..	1
31. Tatta Naka and Goda village and Labour Corps ..	3	2	2	..	1	3	2	4
32. Quarry Nos. 1 and 2 and other Quarries	..	..	..	..	1	..	..	..
33. Scattered Hamlets behind Cantonment Station and Chinaser and Vagri Villages.	2	..	4	1	2	3	4	2
34. Keamari with other Port Area (viz., Thole Produce Yard, Mansfield Import Yard and West Wharf) ..	56	32	48	26	36	47	52	28
35. Baba Island	..	..	1	..	..	1	..	..
36. Bhit Island	..	..	..	..	..	..	..	..
37. Shamspir and Goth Mahomed	..	..	..	..	..	..	..	..
38. Bunker Island	..	..	..	..	..	..	..	..
39. Port Floating Population ..	..	1	1	..	..	..	..	2
40. Railway Area including City, Bunder and Cantonment Stations and Reception and Hump Yard and Platform population ..	12	18	9	12	32	19	21	24
41. Maurypur	..	..	2	..	..	1	..	1
42. Drigh Road	..	..	..	..	..	..	..	1
43. Cape Manze	..	..	..	..	..	..	..	..

Quarter.	HINDU—*concld.*		MUSLIM.					
	GIRLS—*contd.*		TOTAL.			BOYS.		
	10	11	Persons.	Boys.	Girls.	6	7	8
1	18	19	20	21	22	23	24	25
1. **Karachi City**	**1,190**	**742**	**14,769**	**7,504**	**7,265**	**1,444**	**1,248**	**1,557**
2. Old Town	116	68	87	44	43	9	6	11
3. Lea	14	1	..	..	..	..	..	..
4. Napier	128	41	345	188	157	44	25	41
5. Market	82	39	183	101	82	19	13	23
6. Bunder	20	15	39	23	16	5	4	4
7. Machi Meani	27	14	796	351	445	75	45	76
8. Queen's Road	1	1	..	..	..	..	..	..
9. Railway	..	..	8	6	2	1	2	..
10. Serai	95	54	211	136	75	26	23	20
11. Rambaugh	125	103	144	102	42	16	23	17
12. Jail	76	56	143	106	37	23	15	22
13. Ranchore	248	180	818	447	371	73	68	101
14. Ramswami	52	37	149	66	83	14	11	17
15. Herchandrai Vishendas ..	3	2	89	47	42	7	9	9
16. Soldier Bazar	15	9	147	64	83	12	10	13
17. New Jail	1	..	37	26	11	5	..	6
18. Preedy	4	1	33	19	14	4	3	3
19. Saddar Bazar	13	7	313	145	168	30	32	24
20. Civil Lines	11	6	71	38	33	7	8	11
21. Frere Town and Bath Island .	6	2	21	12	9	3	2	3
22. Clifton	..	..	11	6	5	3	..	1
23. Gizri	..	..	126	66	60	19	9	22
24. Garden (East and West) ..	5	3	692	349	343	85	56	61
25. Tahilram	25	10	364	179	185	27	25	45
26. Lawrence	19	11	462	239	223	50	44	53
27. Lyari	41	27	6,989	3,432	3,557	648	622	713
28. Jamshed	14	16	13	9	4	2	1	..
29. Artillery Maidan ..	5	1	8	3	5	..	1	..
30. Trans-Lyari	..	..	699	352	347	45	42	75
31. Tatta Naka and Goda village and Labour Corps ..	..	1	26	12	14	2	3	..
32. Quarry Nos. 1 and 2 and other Quarries	..	..	44	23	21	3	5	4
33. Scattered Hamlets behind Cantonment Station and Chinaser and Vagri Villages ..	2	..	105	57	48	16	11	18
34. Keamari with other Port Area (viz., Thole Produce Yard, Mansfield Import Yard and West Wharf) ..	24	18	567	324	243	76	48	55
35. Baba Island	..	1	139	58	81	10	11	9
36. Bhit Island	..	..	95	31	64	6	7	4
37. Shamspir and Goth Mahomed.	..	..	59	27	32	4	2	6
38. Bunker Island	..	..	..	..	..	..	..	..
39. Port Floating Population ..	..	..	25	19	6	2	..	6
40. Railway Area including City, Bunder and Cantonment Stations and Reception and Hump Yard and Platform population	18	16	550	305	245	56	48	66
41. Maurypur	..	2	157	90	67	16	14	17
42. Drigh Road	..	..	..	...	..	..	..	..
43. Cape Manze	..	..	4	2	2	1	..	1

Quarter.	MUSLIM—*contd.*							
	Boys—*contd.*			Girls.				
	9	10	11	6	7	8	9	10
1	26	27	28	29	30	31	32	33
1. **Karachi City**	**947**	**1,680**	**628**	**1,374**	**1,339**	**1,414**	**1,039**	**1,458**
2. Old Town	9	8	1	7	8	13	5	5
3. Loa	..	..	..	..	..	..	..	..
4. Napier	15	46	17	29	25	34	19	35
5. Market	12	22	12	12	16	10	13	22
6. Bunder	1	8	1	3	3	3	3	3
7. Machi Meani	41	85	29	89	82	85	61	91
8. Queen's Road	..	..	..	..	..	..	..	..
9. Railway	1	2	..	..	..	1	..	..
10. Serai	14	35	18	19	14	22	11	6
11. Rambaugh	13	24	9	8	10	7	6	7
12. Jail	22	17	7	10	8	6	7	4
13. Ranchore	46	121	38	61	65	92	38	87
14. Ramswami	4	13	7	26	12	14	10	13
15. Herchandrai Vishendas ..	3	17	2	4	10	6	5	14
16. Soldier Bazar	9	14	6	12	20	26	7	14
17. New Jail	7	5	3	2	1	..	4	2
18. Preedy	2	6	1	4	3	2	4	1
19. Saddar Bazar	12	29	18	30	33	27	32	33
20. Civil Lines	5	3	4	3	5	12	6	2
21. Frere Town and Bath Island	2	..	2	1	..	4	..	4
22. Clifton	..	2	..	3	1	..	1	..
23. Gizri	3	12	1	18	7	23	4	6
24. Garden (East and West) ..	37	86	24	35	81	65	46	86
25. Tahilram	17	53	12	25	36	33	25	48
26. Lawrence	24	49	19	52	37	55	18	48
27. Lyari	438	756	255	681	667	626	534	712
28. Jamshed	2	3	1	..	1	..	2	1
29. Artillery Maidan ..	1	1	..	1	..	1	..	2
30. Trans-Lyari	75	76	39	59	56	85	37	86
31. Tatta Naka and Goda village and Labour Corps ..	4	2	1	2	2	3	4	2
32. Quarry Nos. 1 and 2 and other Quarries	5	4	2	3	4	3	6	2
33. Scattered Hamlets behind Cantonment Station and Chinaser and Vagri Villages .	7	5	..	14	10	13	5	5
34. Keamari with other Port Area (viz., Thole Produce Yard, Mansfield Import Yard and West Wharf) ..	42	71	32	57	37	60	23	48
35. Baba Island	12	9	7	13	10	18	14	18
36. Bhit Island	8	3	3	12	9	10	11	10
37. Shamspir and Goth Mahomed	5	7	3	6	5	4	8	4
38. Bunker Island	..	..	..	..	..	..	..	..
39. Port Floating Population ..	4	5	2	2	1	1	..	1
40. Railway Area including City, Bunder and Cantonment Stations and Reception and Hump Yard and Platform population	32	65	38	59	48	37	60	23
41. Maurypur	13	16	14	12	11	13	10	12
42. Drigh Road	..	..	..	..	..	..	..	..
43. Cape Manze	..	..	..	..	1	..	..	1

Quarter.	MUSLIM—*concld.* Girls—*contd.*	JAIN. Total.			Boys.			
	11	Persons.	Boys.	Girls.	6	7	8	9
1	34	35	36	37	38	39	40	41
1. Karachi City	**641**	**55**	**33**	**22**	**6**	**3**	**9**	**4**
2. Old Town	5	..	..	..	..	..	..	..
3. Lea	..	..	..	..	..	..	..	..
4. Napier	15	..	..	..	..	..	..	..
5. Market	9	..	..	..	..	..	..	..
6. Bunder	1	..	..	..	..	..	..	..
7. Machi Meani	37	..	..	..	..	..	..	..
8. Queen's Road	..	..	..	..	..	..	..	..
9. Railway	1	..	..	..	..	..	..	..
10. Serai	3	..	..	..	..	..	..	..
11. Rambaugh	4	..	..	..	..	..	..	..
12. Jail	2	8	5	3	2	..	..	..
13. Ranchore	28	29	20	9	2	2	5	4
14. Ramswami	8	18	8	10	2	1	4	..
15. Herchandrai Vishendas	3	..	..	..	..	..	..	..
16. Soldier Bazar	4	..	..	..	..	..	..	..
17. New Jail	2	..	..	..	..	..	..	..
18. Preedy	..	..	..	..	..	..	..	..
19. Saddar Bazar	13	..	..	..	..	..	..	..
20. Civil Lines	5	..	..	..	..	..	..	..
21. Frere Town and Bath Island	..	..	..	..	..	..	..	..
22. Clifton	..	..	..	..	..	..	..	..
23. Gizri	2	..	..	..	..	..	..	..
24. Garden (East and West)	30	..	..	..	..	..	..	..
25. Tahilram	18	..	..	..	..	..	..	..
26. Lawrence	13	..	..	..	..	..	..	..
27. Lyari	337	..	..	..	..	..	..	..
28. Jamshed	..	..	..	..	..	..	..	..
29. Artillery Maidan	1	..	..	..	..	..	..	..
30. Trans-Lyari	24	..	..	..	..	..	..	..
31. Tatta Naka and Goda village and Labour Corps	1	..	..	..	..	..	..	..
32. Quarry Nos. 1 and 2 and other Quarries	3	..	..	..	..	..	..	..
33. Scattered Hamlets behind Cantonment Station and Chinaser and Vagri Villages	1	..	..	..	..	..	..	..
34. Keamari with other Port Area (viz., Thole Produce Yard, Mansfield Import Yard and West Wharf)	18	..	..	..	..	..	..	..
35. Baba Island	8	..	..	..	..	..	..	..
36. Bhit Island	12	..	..	..	..	..	..	..
37. Shamspir and Goth Mahomed.	5	..	..	..	..	..	..	..
38. Bunker Island	..	..	..	..	..	..	..	..
39. Port Floating Population	1	..	..	..	..	..	..	..
40. Railway Area including City, Bunder and Cantonment Stations and Reception and Hump Yard and Platform population	18	..	..	..	..	..	..	..
41. Maurypur	9	..	..	..	..	..	..	..
42. Drigh Road	..	..	..	..	..	..	..	..
43. Cape Manze	..	..	..	..	..	..	..	..

Quarter.	JAIN—*contd.*							
	Boys—*contd.*		Girls.					
	10	11	6	7	8	9	10	11
1	42	43	44	45	46	47	48	49
1. **Karachi City**	8	3	8	8	2	5	5	4
2. Old Town	..	..	..	..	..	..	..	..
3. Lea	..	..	..	..	..	..	..	..
4. Napier	..	..	..	..	..	..	..	..
5. Market	..	..	..	..	..	..	..	..
6. Bunder	..	..	..	..	..	..	..	..
7. Machi Meani	..	..	..	..	..	..	..	..
8. Queen's Road	..	..	..	..	..	..	..	..
9. Railway	..	..	..	..	..	..	..	..
10. Serai	..	..	..	..	..	..	..	..
11. Rambaugh	..	..	..	..	..	..	..	..
12. Jail	1	2	1	1	..	..	1	..
13. Ranchore	7	..	1	1	1	4	1	1
14. Ramswami	..	1	1	1	1	1	3	3
15. Herchandrai Vishendas ..	..	..	..	..	..	..	..	..
16. Soldier Bazar	..	..	..	..	..	..	..	..
17. New Jail	..	..	..	..	..	..	..	..
18. Preedy	..	..	..	..	..	..	..	..
19. Saddar Bazar	..	..	..	..	..	..	..	..
20. Civil Lines	..	..	..	..	..	..	..	..
21. Frere Town and Bath Island.	..	..	..	..	..	..	..	..
22. Clifton	..	..	..	..	..	..	..	..
23. Gizri	..	..	..	..	..	..	..	..
24. Garden (East and West) ..	..	..	..	..	..	..	..	..
25. Tahilram	..	..	..	..	..	..	..	..
26. Lawrence	..	..	..	..	..	..	..	..
27. Lyari	..	..	..	..	..	..	..	..
28. Jamshed	..	..	..	..	..	..	..	..
29. Artillery Maidan ..	..	..	..	..	..	..	..	..
30. Trans-Lyari	..	..	..	..	..	..	..	..
31. Tatta Naka and Goda village and Labour Corps ..	..	..	..	..	..	..	..	..
32. Quarry Nos. 1 and 2 and other Quarries	..	..	..	..	..	..	..	..
33. Scattered Hamlets behind Cantonment Station and Chinaser and Vagri Villages ..	..	..	..	..	..	..	..	..
34. Keamari with other Port Area (viz., Thole Produce Yard, Mansfield Import Yard and West Wharf) ..	..	..	..	..	..	..	..	..
35. Baba Island	..	..	..	..	..	..	..	..
36. Bhit Island	..	..	..	..	..	..	..	..
37. Shamspir and Goth Mahomed.	..	..	..	..	..	..	..	..
38. Bunker Island	..	..	..	..	..	..	..	..
39. Port Floating Population ..	..	..	..	..	..	..	..	..
40. Railway Area including City, Bunder and Cantonment Stations and Reception and Hump Yard and Platform population	..	..	..	..	..	..	..	..
41. Maurypur	..	..	..	..	..	..	..	..
42. Drigh Road	..	..	..	..	..	..	..	..
43. Cape Manze	..	..	..	..	..	..	..	..

Quarter.	ZOROASTRIAN.							
	TOTAL.			BOYS.				
	Persons.	Boys.	Girls.	6	7	8	9	10
1	50	51	52	53	54	55	56	57
1. **Karachi City**	**361**	**218**	**143**	**32**	**33**	**39**	**46**	**34**
2. Old Town	..	..	..	..	..	..	..	..
3. Lea	..	..	..	..	..	..	..	..
4. Napier	..	..	..	..	..	..	..	..
5. Market	..	..	..	..	..	..	..	..
6. Bunder	..	..	..	..	..	..	..	..
7. Machi Meani	..	..	..	..	..	..	..	..
8. Queen's Road	2	1	1	..	..	1	..	..
9. Railway	..	..	..	..	..	..	..	..
10. Serai	9	5	4	1	1	2	..	1
11. Rambaugh	20	14	6	3	4	2	2	1
12. Jail	..	..	..	..	..	..	..	..
13. Ranchore	23	14	9	2	2	1	6	1
14. Ramswami	..	..	..	..	..	..	..	..
15. Herchandrai Vishendas ..	..	..	..	..	..	..	..	..
16. Soldier Bazar	2	1	1	..	..	1	..	..
17. New Jail	..	..	..	..	..	..	..	..
18. Preedy	39	25	14	4	2	3	5	7
19. Saddar Bazar	80	52	28	7	8	10	11	9
20. Civil Lines	19	11	8	3	2	..	2	3
21. Frere Town and Bath Island.	12	6	6	..	..	1	3	..
22. Clifton	2	1	1	..	..	..	1	..
23. Gizri	..	..	..	..	..	..	..	..
24. Garden (East and West) ..	17	10	7	2	1	1	3	1
25. Tahilram	..	..	..	..	..	..	..	..
26. Lawrence	5	3	2	..	2	..	..	..
27. Lyari	..	..	..	..	..	..	..	..
28. Jamshed	15	9	6	1	..	3	2	2
29. Artillery Maidan ..	9	4	5	..	1	3	..	..
30. Trans-Lyari	..	..	..	..	..	..	..	..
31. Tatta Naka and Goda village and Labour Corps ..	..	..	..	..	..	..	..	..
32. Quarry Nos. 1 and 2 and other Quarries	..	..	..	..	..	..	..	..
33. Scattered Hamlets behind Cantonment Station and Chinaser and Vagri Villages.	..	..	..	..	..	..	..	..
34. Keamari with other Port Area (viz., Thole Produce Yard, Mansfield Import Yard and West Wharf) ..	3	2	1	1	1	..	..	..
35. Baba Island	..	..	..	..	..	..	..	..
36. Bhit Island	..	..	..	..	..	..	..	..
37. Shamspir and Goth Mahomed.	..	..	..	..	..	..	..	..
38. Bunker Island	..	..	..	..	..	..	..	..
39. Port Floating Population ..	..	..	..	..	..	..	..	..
40. Railway Area including City, Bunder and Cantonment Stations and Reception and Hump Yard and Platform population	104	60	44	8	9	11	11	9
41. Maurypur	..	..	..	..	..	..	..	..
42. Drigh Road	..	..	..	..	..	..	..	..
43. Cape Manze	..	..	..	..	..	..	..	..

Quarter.	ZOROASTRIAN—*contd.*							
	Boys—*contd.*	Girls.						Total.
	11	6	7	8	9	10	11	Persons.
1	58	59	60	61	62	63	64	65
1. Karachi City	**34**	**22**	**18**	**26**	**32**	**22**	**23**	**1,229**
2. Old Town	..	..	..	..	..	..	..	..
3. Lea	..	..	..	..	..	..	..	..
4. Napier	..	..	..	..	..	..	..	..
5. Market	..	..	..	..	..	..	..	..
6. Bunder	..	..	..	..	..	..	..	..
7. Machi Meani	..	..	..	..	..	..	..	..
8. Queen's Road	..	..	..	..	..	..	1	1
9. Railway	..	..	..	..	..	..	..	2
10. Serai	..	..	..	..	3	..	1	19
11. Rambaugh	2	1	1	1	..	1	2	4
12. Jail	..	..	..	..	..	..	..	15
13. Ranchore	2	1	3	1	4	..	..	20
14. Ramswami	..	..	..	..	..	..	..	13
15. Herchandrai Vishendas ..	..	..	..	..	..	..	..	16
16. Soldier Bazar	..	..	..	..	..	..	1	1
17. New Jail	..	..	..	..	..	..	..	2
18. Preedy	4	3	2	4	1	3	1	44
19. Saddar Bazar	7	4	..	6	7	6	5	327
20. Civil Lines	1	4	..	..	2	2	..	91
21. Frere Town and Bath Island.	2	..	1	..	4	..	1	47
22. Clifton	..	..	1	..	..	..	..	3
23. Gizri	..	..	..	..	..	..	..	..
24. Garden (East and West) ..	2	1	1	2	..	1	2	45
25. Tahilram	..	..	..	..	..	..	..	..
26. Lawrence	1	..	..	..	1	..	1	25
27. Lyari	..	..	..	..	..	..	..	65
28. Jamshed	1	..	1	1	1	2	1	22
29. Artillery Maidan ..	..	..	..	1	1	1	2	2
30. Trans-Lyari	..	..	..	..	..	..	..	..
31. Tatta Naka and Goda village and Labour Corps ..	..	..	..	..	..	..	..	2
32. Quarry Nos. 1 and 2 and other Quarries	..	..	..	..	..	..	..	..
33. Scattered Hamlets behind Cantonment Station and Chinaser and Vagri Villages.	..	..	..	..	..	..	..	..
34. Keamari with other Port Area (viz., Thole Produce Yard, Mansfield Import Yard and West Wharf) ..	..	..	1	..	..	..	..	69
35. Baba Island	..	..	..	..	..	..	..	..
36. Bhit Island	..	..	..	..	..	..	..	..
37. Shamspir and Goth Mahomed.	..	..	..	..	..	..	..	..
38. Bunker Island	..	..	..	..	..	..	..	..
39. Port Floating Population ..	..	..	..	..	..	..	..	..
40. Railway area including City, Bunder and Cantonment Stations and Reception and Hump Yard and Platform population	12	8	7	10	8	6	5	393
41. Maurypur	..	..	..	..	..	..	..	1
42. Drigh Road	..	..	..	..	..	..	..	..
43. Cape Manze	..	..	..	..	..	..	..	..

MO-II Bk Ra Cs 3—37

Quarter.	CHRISTIAN.							
	TOTAL—*contd.*		BOYS.					
	Boys.	Girls.	6	7	8	9	10	11
1	66	67	68	69	70	71	72	73
1. **Karachi City**	**655**	**574**	**123**	**97**	**125**	**101**	**139**	**70**
2. Old Town	..	..	..	..	..	..	..	..
3. Lea	..	..	..	..	..	..	..	..
4. Napier	..	..	..	..	..	..	..	..
5. Market	..	..	..	..	..	..	..	..
6. Bunder	..	..	..	..	..	..	..	..
7. Machi Meani	..	..	..	..	..	..	..	..
8. Queen's Road	..	1	..	..	..	..	..	..
9. Railway	..	2	..	..	..	..	..	..
10. Serai	9	10	..	3	..	1	3	2
11. Rambaugh	4	..	..	1	..	..	1	2
12. Jail	8	7	2	..	2	1	2	1
13. Ranchore	9	11	1	..	1	4	2	1
14. Ramswami	10	8	3	..	3	2	1	1
15. Herchandrai Vishendas ..	9	7	5	1	1	..	2	..
16. Soldier Bazar	1	..	1	..	..	..	..	..
17. New Jail	2	..	1	..	1	..	..	..
18. Preedy	21	23	3	4	6	2	5	1
19. Saddar Bazar	182	145	36	21	33	28	46	18
20. Civil Lines	50	41	5	11	9	9	9	7
21. Frere Town and Bath Island.	25	22	6	2	7	1	6	3
22. Clifton	1	2	1	..	..	..	..	..
23. Gizri	..	..	..	..	..	..	..	..
24. Garden (East and West) ..	25	20	4	3	..	7	8	3
25. Tahilram	..	..	..	..	..	..	..	..
26. Lawrence	19	6	2	4	6	..	2	5
27. Lyari	37	28	6	7	5	8	7	4
28. Jamshed	10	12	2	1	..	3	3	1
29. Artillery Maidan ..	1	1	..	..	1	..	..	..
30. Trans-Lyari	..	..	..	..	..	..	..	..
31. Tatta Naka and Goda village and Labour Corps ..	1	1	1	..	..	..	..	..
32. Quarry Nos. 1 and 2 and other Quarries	..	..	..	..	..	..	..	..
33. Scattered Hamlets behind Cantonment Station and Chinaser and Vagri Villages.	..	..	..	..	..	..	..	..
34. Keamari with other Port Area (viz., Thole Produce Yard, Mansfield Import Yard and West Wharf) ..	39	30	6	8	8	7	6	4
35. Baba Island	..	..	..	..	..	..	..	..
36. Bhit Island	..	..	..	..	..	..	..	..
37. Shamspir and Goth Mahomed.	..	..	..	..	..	..	..	..
38. Bunker Island	..	..	..	..	..	..	..	..
39. Port Floating Population ..	..	..	..	..	..	..	..	..
40. Railway Area including City, Bunder and Cantonment Stations and Reception and Hump Yard and Platform population	191	202	38	31	41	28	36	17
41. Maurypur	1	..	..	..	1	..	..	..
42. Drigh Road	..	..	..	..	..	..	..	..
43. Cape Manze	..	..	..	..	..	..	..	..

Quarter.	CHRISTIAN—*contd.*							
	GIRLS.						TOTAL.	
	6	7	8	9	10	11	Persons.	Boys.
1	74	75	76	77	78	79	80	81
1. Karachi City	**121**	**99**	**108**	**86**	**102**	**58**	**128**	**61**
2. Old Town	..	..	..	..	..	..	..	..
3. Lea	..	..	..	..	..	..	2	2
4. Napier	..	..	..	..	..	..	..	..
5. Market	..	..	..	..	..	..	..	..
6. Bunder	..	..	..	..	..	..	..	..
7. Machi Meani	..	..	..	..	..	..	..	..
8. Queen's Road	..	..	..	1	..	..	..	..
9. Railway	1	..	1	..	..	..	..	..
10. Serai	4	2	1	..	3	..	..	..
11. Rambaugh	..	..	..	..	..	..	17	5
12. Jail	1	..	1	2	2	1	..	..
13. Ranchore	2	..	1	3	4	1	28	12
14. Ramswami	..	..	2	..	1	..	35	23
15. Herchandrai Vishendas ..	4	..	2	1	..	..	..	..
16. Soldier Bazar	..	..	..	..	..	..	..	..
17. New Jail	..	..	..	..	..	..	..	..
18. Preedy	4	5	7	2	3	2	..	..
19. Saddar Bazar	30	32	29	16	21	17	3	2
20. Civil Lines	3	12	5	13	6	2	..	..
21. Frere Town and Bath Island.	7	..	4	3	8	..	..	..
22. Clifton	2	..	..	..	..	..	..	..
23. Gizri	..	..	..	..	..	..	..	..
24. Garden (East and West) ..	5	2	3	4	3	3	13	6
25. Tahilram	..	..	..	..	..	..	..	..
26. Lawrence	3	..	2	..	1	..	10	1
27. Lyari	5	4	4	6	7	2	..	..
28. Jamshed	4	2	2	..	1	3	1	..
29. Artillery Maidan ..	..	..	..	..	1	..	..	..
30. Trans-Lyari	..	..	..	..	..	..	..	..
31. Tatta Naka and Goda village and Labour Corps ..	..	..	1	..	..	..	..	..
32. Quarry Nos. 1 and 2 and other Quarries	..	..	..	..	..	..	..	..
33. Scattered Hamlets behind Cantonment Station and Chinaser and Vagri Villages.	..	..	..	..	..	..	..	..
34. Keamari with other Port Area (viz., Thole Produce Yard, Mansfield Import Yard and West Wharf) ..	4	2	6	7	6	5	13	7
35. Baba Island	..	..	..	..	..	..	..	..
36. Bhit Island	..	..	..	..	..	..	..	..
37. Shamspir and Goth Mahomed.	..	..	..	..	..	..	..	..
38. Bunker Island	..	..	..	..	..	..	..	..
39. Port Floating Population ..	..	..	..	..	..	..	..	..
40. Railway Area including City, Bunder and Cantonment Stations and Reception and Hump Yard and Platform population	42	38	37	28	35	22	6	3
41. Maurypur	..	..	..	..	..	..	..	..
42. Drigh Road	..	..	..	..	..	..	..	..
43. Cape Manze	..	..	..	..	..	..	..	..

Quarter.	TOTAL—*contd.*	JEW.						
		BOYS.						GIRLS.
	Girls.	6	7	8	9	10	11	6
1	82	83	84	85	86	87	88	89
1. **Karachi City**	**67**	**15**	**11**	**9**	**14**	**9**	**3**	**9**
2. Old Town	..	..	..	..	..	..	..	..
3. Lea	..	..	1	..	1	..	..	..
4. Napier	..	..	..	..	..	..	..	..
5. Market	..	..	..	..	..	..	..	..
6. Bunder	..	..	..	..	..	..	..	..
7. Machi Meani	..	..	..	..	..	..	..	..
8. Queen's Road	..	..	..	..	..	..	..	..
9. Railway	..	..	..	..	..	..	..	..
10. Serai	..	..	..	..	..	..	..	..
11. Rambaugh	12	1	..	1	1	1	1	1
12. Jail	..	..	..	..	..	..	..	..
13. Ranchore	16	2	1	3	2	4	..	4
14. Ramswami	12	6	8	3	4	2	..	..
15. Herchandrai Vishendas ..	..	..	..	..	..	..	..	..
16. Soldier Bazar	..	..	..	..	..	..	..	..
17. New Jail	..	..	..	..	..	..	..	..
18. Preedy	..	..	..	..	..	..	..	..
19. Saddar Bazar	1	1	..	..	1	..	..	1
20. Civil Lines	..	..	..	..	..	..	..	..
21. Frere Town and Bath Island.	..	..	..	..	..	..	..	..
22. Clifton	..	..	..	..	..	..	..	..
23. Gizri	..	..	..	..	..	..	..	..
24. Garden (East and West) ..	7	2	1	..	1	1	1	1
25. Tahilram	..	..	..	..	..	..	..	..
26. Lawrence	9	..	..	..	1	..	..	..
27. Lyari	..	..	..	..	..	..	..	..
28. Jamshed	1	..	..	..	..	..	..	..
29. Artillery Maidan ..	..	..	..	..	..	..	..	1
30. Trans-Lyari	..	..	..	..	..	..	..	..
31. Tatta Naka and Goda village and Labour Corps ..	..	..	..	..	..	..	..	..
32. Quarry Nos. 1 and 2 and other Quarries	..	..	..	..	..	..	..	..
33. Scattered Hamlets behind Cantonment Station and Chinaser and Vagri Villages ..	..	..	..	..	..	..	..	..
34. Keamari with other Port Area (viz., Thole Produce Yard, Mansfield Import Yard and West Wharf) ..	6	2	..	1	2	1	1	1
35. Baba Island	..	..	..	..	..	..	..	..
36. Bhit Island	..	..	..	..	..	..	..	..
37. Shamspir and Goth Mahomed.	..	..	..	..	..	..	..	..
38. Bunker Island	..	..	..	..	..	..	..	..
39. Port Floating Population ..	..	..	..	..	..	..	..	..
40. Railway Area including City, Bunder and Cantonment Stations and Reception and Hump Yard and Platform population	3	1	..	1	1	..	..	..
41. Maurypur	..	..	..	..	..	..	..	..
42. Drigh Road	..	..	..	..	..	..	..	..
43. Cape Manze	..	..	..	..	..	..	..	..

Quarter.	JEW—*contd.*					SIKH.		
	GIRLS.					TOTAL.		
	7	8	9	10	11	Persons.	Boys.	Girls.
1	90	91	92	93	94	95	96	97
1. **Karachi City**	15	14	5	13	11	219	119	100
2. Old Town	..	..	..	..	..	..	..	..
3. Lea	..	..	..	..	..	12	2	10
4. Napier	..	..	..	..	..	5	4	1
5. Market	..	..	..	..	..	4	2	2
6. Bunder	..	..	..	..	..	1	1	..
7. Machi Meani	..	..	..	..	..	4	2	2
8. Queen's Road	..	..	..	..	..	..	..	..
9. Railway	..	..	..	..	..	..	..	..
10. Serai	..	..	..	..	..	4	2	2
11. Rambaugh	3	2	1	2	3	35	20	15
12. Jail	..	..	..	..	..	6	3	3
13. Ranchore	3	5	..	3	1	21	13	8
14. Ramswami	..	5	2	3	2	18	7	11
15. Herchandrai Vishendas ..	..	..	..	..	..	..	..	..
16. Soldier Bazar	..	..	..	..	..	..	..	..
17. New Jail	..	..	..	..	..	..	..	..
18. Preedy	..	..	..	..	..	..	..	..
19. Saddar Bazar	..	..	..	..	..	5	3	2
20. Civil Lines	..	..	..	..	..	..	..	..
21. Frere Town and Bath Island.	..	..	..	..	..	..	..	..
22. Clifton	..	..	..	..	..	..	..	..
23. Gizri	..	..	..	..	..	..	..	..
24. Garden (East and West) ..	2	1	..	1	2	5	3	2
25. Tahilram	..	..	..	..	..	1	1	..
26. Lawrence	4	..	1	2	2	15	7	8
27. Lyari	..	..	..	..	..	7	4	3
28. Jamshed	..	..	..	..	..	1	..	1
29. Artillery Maidan ..	..	..	..	..	..	2	2	..
30. Trans-Lyari	..	..	..	..	..	..	..	..
31. Tatta Naka and Goda Village and Labour Corps ..	..	..	..	..	..	7	4	3
32. Quarry Nos. 1 and 2 and other Quarries	..	..	..	..	..	..	..	..
33. Scattered Hamlets behind Cantonment Station and Chinaser and Vagri Villages	..	..	..	..	..	..	..	..
34. Keamari with other Port Area (viz., Thole Produce Yard, Mansfield Import Yard and West Wharf) ..	2	1	..	1	1	12	10	2
35. Baba Island	..	..	..	..	..	..	..	..
36. Bhit Island	..	..	..	..	..	..	..	..
37. Shamspir and Goth Mahomed.	..	..	..	..	..	..	..	..
38. Bunker Island	..	..	..	..	..	..	..	..
39. Port Floating Population	..	..	..	..	..	..	..	..
40. Railway Area including City, Bunder and Cantonment Stations and Reception and Hump Yard and Platform population	1	..	1	1	..	54	29	25
41. Maurypur	..	..	..	..	..	..	..	..
42. Drigh Road	..	..	..	..	..	..	..	..
43. Cape Manze	..	..	..	..	..	..	..	..

MO-II Bk Ra Cs 3—38

Quarter.	SIKH—*contd.*							
	Boys.						Girls.	
	6	7	8	9	10	11	6	7
1	98	99	100	101	102	103	104	105
1. Karachi City	**21**	**17**	**22**	**22**	**23**	**14**	**22**	**16**
2. Old Town	..	..	..	..	..	..	..	..
3. Lea	..	..	..	..	..	..	..	..
4. Napier	..	..	..	..	1	1	..	..
5. Market	..	..	1	..	2	1	1	..
6. Bunder	..	..	..	1	..	1	1	..
7. Machi Meani	..	1	1	..	..	..	..	..
8. Queen's Road	..	..	..	..	1	..	1	..
9. Railway	..	..	..	..	..	..	..	..
10. Serai	1	..	1	..	..	..	..	..
11. Rambaugh	4	3	1	3	7	2	3	3
12. Jail	..	..	1	2	..	..	..	..
13. Ranchore	4	3	3	1	2	..	2	1
14. Ramswami	..	1	1	3	2	..	2	4
15. Herchandrai Vishendas ..	..	..	..	..	..	..	..	..
16. Soldier Bazar	..	..	..	..	..	..	..	..
17. New Jail	..	..	..	..	..	..	..	..
18. Preedy	..	..	..	..	..	..	..	..
19. Saddar Bazar	1	1	..	..	1	..	..	1
20. Civil Lines	..	..	..	..	..	..	..	..
21. Frere Town and Bath Island.	..	..	..	..	..	..	..	..
22. Clifton	..	..	..	..	..	..	..	..
23. Gizri	..	..	..	..	..	..	..	..
24. Garden (East and West) ..	1	..	1	1	..	..	1	1
25. Tahilram	..	..	..	..	..	1	..	..
26. Lawrence	1	3	..	..	2	1	2	1
27. Lyari	1	..	1	1	..	1	1	..
28. Jamshed	..	..	..	..	..	..	..	1
29. Artillery Maidan ..	..	..	1	1	..	..	..	..
30. Trans-Lyari	..	..	..	..	..	..	..	..
31. Tatta Naka and Goda Village and Labour Corps ..	1	..	2	..	1	..	1	1
32. Quarry Nos. 1 and 2 and other Quarries	..	..	..	..	..	..	..	..
33. Scattered Hamlets behind Cantonment Station and Chinaser and Vagri Villages.	..	..	..	..	..	..	..	..
34. Keamari with other Port Area (viz., Thole Produce Yard, Mansfield Import Yard and West Wharf) ..	2	1	1	3	1	2	1	..
35. Baba Island	..	..	..	..	..	..	..	..
36. Bhit Island	..	..	..	..	..	..	..	..
37. Shamspir and Goth Mahomed.	..	..	..	..	..	..	..	..
38. Bunker Island	..	..	..	..	..	..	..	..
39. Port Floating Population ..	..	..	..	..	..	..	..	..
40. Railway Area including City, Bunder and Cantonment Stations and Reception and Hump Yard and Platform population	5	4	7	6	3	4	6	3
41. Maurypur	..	..	..	..	..	..	..	..
42. Drigh Road	..	..	..	..	..	..	..	..
43. Cape Manzo	..	..	..	..	..	..	..	..

Quarter.	SIKH—*concld.*				TRIBAL AND OTHERS.			
	GIRLS.				TOTAL.			BOYS.
	8	9	10	11	Persons.	Boys.	Girls.	6
1	106	107	108	109	110	111	112	113
1. Karachi City	**18**	**16**	**22**	**6**	**21**	**12**	**9**	**2**
2. Old Town	..	..	..	..	..	..	..	..
3. Lea	..	..	10	..	..	..	..	..
4. Napier	..	..	..	..	..	..	..	..
5. Market	..	1	..	..	..	..	..	..
6. Bunder	..	..	..	..	..	..	..	..
7. Machi Meani	1	..	..	..	..	..	..	..
8. Queen's Road	..	..	..	..	..	..	..	..
9. Railway	..	..	..	..	..	..	..	..
10. Serai	..	..	1	1	..	..	..	..
11. Rambaugh	3	2	3	1	..	..	..	..
12. Jail	1	..	1	1	..	..	..	..
13. Ranchore	1	1	3	..	..	..	..	..
14. Ramswami	1	2	2	..	..	..	..	..
15. Herchandrai Vishendas ..	..	..	..	..	..	..	..	..
16. Soldier Bazar	..	..	..	..	..	..	..	..
17. New Jail	..	..	..	..	..	..	..	..
18. Preedy	..	..	..	..	..	..	..	..
19. Saddar Bazar	..	..	..	1	5	3	2	..
20. Civil Lines	..	..	..	..	..	..	..	..
21. Frere Town and Bath Island.	..	..	..	..	..	..	..	..
22. Clifton	..	..	..	..	..	..	..	..
23. Gizri	..	..	..	..	..	..	..	..
24. Garden (East and West) ..	..	..	..	..	1	..	1	..
25. Tahilram	..	..	..	..	..	..	..	..
26. Lawrence	3	2	..	..	15	9	6	2
27. Lyari	1	1	..	..	..	..	..	..
28. Jamshed	..	..	..	..	..	..	..	..
29. Artillery Maidan ..	..	..	..	..	..	..	..	..
30. Trans-Lyari	..	..	..	..	..	..	..	..
31. Tatta Naka and Goda Village and Labour Corps ..	1	..	..	..	..	..	..	..
32. Quarry Nos. 1 and 2 and other Quarries	..	..	..	..	..	..	..	..
33. Scattered Hamlets behind Cantonment Station and Chinaser and Vagri Villages.	..	..	..	..	..	..	..	..
34. Keamari with other Port Area (viz., Thole Produce Yard, Mansfield Import Yard and West Wharf) ..	1	..	..	..	..	..	..	..
35. Baba Island	..	..	..	..	..	..	..	..
36. Bhit Island	..	..	..	..	..	..	..	..
37. Shamspir and Goth Mahomed.	..	..	..	..	..	..	..	..
38. Bunker Island	..	..	..	..	..	..	..	..
39. Port Floating Population ..	..	..	..	..	..	..	..	..
40. Railway Area including City, Bunder and Cantonment Stations and Reception and Hump Yard and Platform population	5	7	2	2	..	..	..	..
41. Maurypur	..	..	..	..	..	..	..	..
42. Drigh Road	..	..	..	..	..	..	..	..
43. Cape Manze	..	..	..	..	..	..	..	..

Quarter.	TRIBAL AND OTHERS.										
	Boys.					Girls.					
	7	8	9	10	11	6	7	8	9	10	11
1	114	115	116	117	118	119	120	121	122	123	124
1. Karachi City	3	3	3	1	..	2	5	..	..	2	..
2. Old Town	..	..	..	..	..	..	..	..	..	..	..
3. Lea	..	..	..	..	..	..	..	..	..	..	..
4. Napier	..	..	..	..	..	..	..	..	..	..	..
5. Market	..	..	..	..	..	..	..	..	..	..	..
6. Bunder	..	..	..	..	..	..	..	..	..	..	..
7. Machi Meani	..	..	..	..	..	..	..	..	..	..	..
8. Queen's Road	..	..	..	..	..	..	..	..	..	..	..
9. Railway	..	..	..	..	..	..	..	..	..	..	..
10. Serai	..	..	..	..	..	..	..	..	..	..	..
11. Rambaugh	..	..	..	..	..	..	..	..	..	..	..
12. Jail	..	..	..	..	..	..	..	..	..	..	..
13. Ranchore	..	..	..	..	..	..	..	..	..	..	..
14. Ramswami	..	..	..	..	..	..	..	..	..	..	..
15. Herchandrai Vishendas ..	..	..	..	..	..	..	..	..	..	..	..
16. Soldier Bazar	..	..	..	..	..	..	..	..	..	..	..
17. New Jail	..	..	..	..	..	..	..	..	..	..	..
18. Preedy	..	..	..	..	..	..	..	..	..	..	..
19. Saddar Bazar	1	..	2	..	..	..	2	..	..	..	..
20. Civil Lines	..	..	..	..	..	..	..	..	..	..	..
21. Frere Town and Bath Island.	..	..	..	..	..	..	..	..	..	..	..
22. Clifton	..	..	..	..	..	..	..	..	..	..	..
23. Gizri	..	..	..	..	..	..	..	..	..	..	..
24. Garden (East and West) ..	..	..	..	..	..	1	..	..	..	..	..
25. Tahilram	..	..	..	..	..	..	..	..	..	..	..
26. Lawrence	2	3	1	1	..	1	3	..	..	2	..
27. Lyari	..	..	..	..	..	..	..	..	..	..	..
28. Jamshed	..	..	..	..	..	..	..	..	..	..	..
29. Artillery Maidan ..	..	..	..	..	..	..	..	..	..	..	..
30. Trans-Lyari	..	..	..	..	..	..	..	..	..	..	..
31. Tatta Naka and Goda Village and Labour Corps ..	..	..	..	..	..	..	..	..	..	..	..
32. Quarry Nos. 1 and 2 and other Quarries	..	..	..	..	..	..	..	..	..	..	..
33. Scattered Hamlets behind Cantonment Station and Chinaser and Vagri Villages.	..	..	..	..	..	..	..	..	..	..	..
34. Keamari with other Port Area (viz., Thole Produce Yard, Mansfield Import Yard and West Wharf) ..	..	..	..	..	..	..	..	..	..	..	..
35. Baba Island	..	..	..	..	..	..	..	..	..	..	..
36. Bhit Island	..	..	..	..	..	..	..	..	..	..	..
37. Shamspir and Goth Mahomed.	..	..	..	..	..	..	..	..	..	..	..
38. Bunker Island	..	..	..	..	..	..	..	..	..	..	..
39. Port Floating Population ..	..	..	..	..	..	..	..	..	..	..	..
40. Railway Area including City, Bunder and Cantonment Stations and Reception and Hump Yard and Platform population	..	..	..	..	..	..	..	..	..	..	..
41. Maurypur	..	..	..	..	..	..	..	..	..	..	..
42. Drigh Road	..	..	..	..	..	..	..	..	..	..	..
43. Cape Manze	..	..	..	..	..	..	..	..	..	..	..

Part II—Statistical Tables

VARIATION IN

(Corresponding to

City.	Persons.						Variation—Increase (+) Decrease (—).				
	1931.	1921.	1911.	1901.	1891.	1881.	1921 to 1931.	1911 to 1921.	1901 to 1911.	1891 to 1901.	1881 to 1891.
1	2	3	4	5	6	7	8	9	10	11	12
Bombay	**1,161,388**	**1,175,914**	**979,445**	**776,006**	**821,764**	**773,196**	**—14,531**	**+196,469**	**+208,439**	**—45,758**	**+48,568**
Karachi	**263,565**	**216,883**	**151,903**	**116,663**	**105,199**	**73,560**	**+46,682**	**+ 64,960**	**+ 35,240**	**+11,464**	**+31,639**
(i) Municipality	247,791	201,691	140,511	108,044	98,195	68,332	+46,100	+ 61,180	+ 31,867	+10,449	+29,863
(ii) Cantonment	15,774	15,192	11,392	8,019	7,004	5,228	+ 582	+ 3,800	+ 3,373	+ 1,015	+ 1,776
Greater Poona	**250,187**	**214,796**	**188,701**	**175,463**	**182,099**	**144,840**	**+35,391**	**+ 26,095**	**+ 13,238**	**— 6,636**	**+37,759**
(i) City Municipality ..	162,901	133,227	117,256	111,381	118,700	99,622	+29,674	+ 15,971	+ 5,875	— 7,409	+19,168
(ii) Suburban Municipality ..	16,676	14,233	9,918	9,694	7,506	..	+ 2,443	+ 4,315	+ 224	+ 2,188	..
(iii) Poona Cantonment ..	35,807	32,726	32,226	32,777	35,094	30,120	+ 3,081	+ 500	— 551	— 2,317	+ 4,965
(iv) Kirkee Cantonment ..	16,302	18,357	14,028	10,797	10,951	8,012	— 2,055	+ 4,329	+ 3,231	— 154	+ 2,939
(v) Suburbs	18,501	16,253	15,273	10,814	9,758	6,577	+ 2,248	+ 980	+ 4,459	+ 1,056	+ 3,181
Sholapur	**144,654**	**119,581**	**61,345**	**75,288**	**61,915**	**59,890**	**+25,073**	**+ 58,236**	**—13,943**	**+13,373**	**+ 2,025**
(i) Municipality	135,574	113,931	55,237	75,288	61,915	59,890	+21,643	+ 58,694	—20,051	+13,373	+ 2,025
(ii) Suburbs	9,080	5,650	6,108	..	..	..	+ 3,430	— 458	..	..	..

POPULATION SINCE 1881.

Imperial Table II.)

Net variation in period 1881 to 1931, Increase (+) Decrease (—).	Males.						Females.					
	1931.	1921.	1911.	1901.	1891.	1881.	1931.	1921.	1911.	1901.	1891.	1881.
13	14	15	16	17	18	19	20	21	22	23	24	25
+ 388,187	**747,381**	**771,332**	**640,288**	**479,788**	**518,093**	**464,763**	**414,002**	**404,582**	**339,157**	**296,220**	**303,671**	**308,488**
+ 190,005	**156,120**	**133,084**	**90,233**	**68,386**	**62,486**	**43,561**	**107,445**	**83,799**	**61,670**	**48,277**	**42,718**	**29,999**
+ 179,459	145,052	121,565	82,026	62,779	57,356	39,893	102,739	80,126	58,485	45,865	40,839	28,439
+ 10,546	11,068	11,519	8,207	5,607	5,130	3,668	4,706	3,678	3,185	2,412	1,874	1,560
+ 105,847	**188,189**	**118,473**	**102,395**	**92,250**	**93,968**	**74,832**	**112,048**	**96,328**	**86,806**	**88,218**	**88,181**	**69,508**
+ 63,279	86,784	69,695	61,504	56,597	62,520	51,383	76,117	63,532	55,752	54,784	56,261	48,239
....	9,530	8,112	5,890	5,317	4,821	..	7,146	6,121	4,028	4,377	3,185	..
+ 5,678	20,657	18,990	18,200	18,420	20,247	15,540	15,150	13,736	14,026	14,357	14,847	14,589
+ 8,290	9,940	12,241	8,772	6,231	6,741	4,451	6,362	6,116	5,256	4,566	4,210	3,561
+ 11,924	11,228	9,485	8,029	5,685	5,130	3,458	7,273	6,818	7,244	5,129	4,628	3,119
+ 84,764	**76,837**	**63,115**	**31,891**	**38,163**	**31,734**	**30,410**	**67,817**	**58,466**	**29,454**	**37,125**	**30,181**	**29,480**
+ 75,684	72,079	60,224	28,553	38,163	31,734	30,410	63,495	53,707	26,684	37,125	30,181	29,480
....	4,758	2,891	3,338	..	..	..	4,322	2,759	2,770	..	..	..

AREA, HOUSES AND POPULATION.

(Corresponding to Imperial Table I.)

Ward.	Section.	Area in acres.	Houses. Occupied.	Houses. Un-occupied.	Houses. Total.	Houses per acre.	Population. Males.	Population. Females.	Population. Total.	Persons per acre.
1	2	3	4	5	6	7	8	9	10	11
	Bombay City	**15,480·29**	**82,930**	**17,903**	**50,833**	**3·28**	**747,381**	**414,002**	**1,161,383**	**75·02**
A	Upper Colaba	162·64	252	159	411	2·53	288	148	436	2·68
A	Lower Colaba	526·61	711	307	1,018	1·93	13,628	6,326	19,954	37·89
A	Fort South	133·11	242	168	410	3·08	2,854	641	3,495	26·26
A	Fort North	158·68	883	300	1,183	7·46	16,823	9,009	25,832	162·79
A	Esplanade	787·45	625	638	1,263	1·60	9,814	4,489	14,303	18·16
B	Chakla	47·02	529	166	695	14·78	12,031	6,006	18,037	383·60
B	Mandvi	187·33	825	387	1,212	6·47	27,050	14,656	41,706	222·63
B	Umarkhadi	100·64	799	226	1,025	11·18	25,588	16,006	41,594	413·30
B	Dongri	302·66	282	396	678	2·24	8,101	4,927	13,028	43·05
C	Market	85·21	861	209	1,070	12·56	26,952	11,699	38,651	453·60
C	Dhobi Talao	208·27	965	228	1,193	5·73	27,568	16,804	44,372	213·05
C	Fanaswadi	98·44	718	290	1,008	10·24	19,722	12,355	32,077	325·85
C	Bhuleshwar	73·40	960	172	1,132	15·41	23,097	12,009	35,106	477·89
C	Kumbharwada	44·08	560	125	685	15·54	19,815	12,212	32,027	726·57
C	Kharatalao	41·14	441	101	542	13·17	14,998	8,245	23,243	564·97
D	Khetwadi	155·00	1,143	448	1,591	10·36	24,350	14,957	39,307	253·59
D	Girgaum	112·40	1,086	265	1,351	12·02	24,369	14,417	38,786	345·07
D	Chaupati	108·72	583	233	816	7·51	10,091	6,106	16,197	148·98
D	Walkeshwar	589·90	1,373	968	2,341	3·97	14,523	8,211	22,734	38·54
D	Mahalaxmi	658·51	1,522	1,217	2,739	4·16	22,948	13,621	36,569	55·53
E	Tardeo	149·86	716	326	1,042	6·95	19,200	12,548	31,748	211·85
E	Kamatipura	62·44	982	114	1,096	17·55	23,488	14,083	37,571	601·71
E	1st Nagpada	29·38	129	38	167	5·68	4,672	2,551	7,223	245·85
E	2nd Nagpada	33·05	439	76	515	15·58	13,338	7,694	21,032	636·37
E	Byculla	567·57	1,838	1,007	2,845	5·01	59,098	32,887	91,985	162·07
E	Tarwadi	498·81	1,016	1,008	2,024	4·05	24,678	15,660	40,338	80·87
E	Mazagaon	1,075·48	1,215	1,215	2,430	2·26	28,414	14,739	43,153	40·12
F	Parel	561·25	1,197	868	2,065	3·68	40,407	23,153	63,560	113·25
F	Sewri	577·70	1,075	758	1,833	3·17	17,376	9,380	26,756	46·30
F	Sion	3,559·10	2,334	1,238	3,572	1·00	43,167	26,031	69,198	19·44
G	Mahim	1,511·00	3,070	1,514	4,584	3·03	30,048	19,196	49,244	32·59
G	Worli	2,273·38	3,547	2,679	6,226	2·74	73,644	40,887	114,531	50·38
	Harbour Island	....	12	59	71	..	3,353	1,202	4,555	..
	Railway Platform	....	....	..	..	..	5,216	576	5,792	..
	Floating Population	....	....	..	..	..	13,046	400	13,446	..
	Unknown	....	....	..	..	..	3,626	171	3,797	..

CITY TABLE II—BOMBAY.

VARIATION IN POPULATION SINCE 1881.

(Corresponding to Imperial Table II.)

MO-I Bk Ra Cs 3—40

Variation in Popula

(Corresponding to

In this Table, in order to enable the comparison between this Census and past Censuses to being ordinary residents, were included in the different Sections for City Table No. I (see note Hence the wording of the last item of this Table differs

Ward.	Section.	Persons.						Variation Increase (+) Decrease (—)			
		1931	1921	1911	1901	1891	1881	1921 to 1931	1911 to 1921	1901 to 1911	1891 to 1901
1	2	3	4	5	6	7	8	9	10	11	12
	Bombay City	**1,161,383**	**1,175,914**	**979,445**	**776,006**	**821,764**	**773,196**	**—14,581**	**+196,469**	**+203,439**	**—45,758**
A	Upper Colaba	436	293	1,557	3,956	4,335	2,867	+ 143	— 1,264	— 2,399	— 379
A	Lower Colaba	19,860	19,497	10,679	13,023	13,622	14,265	+ 363	— 182	+ 6,656	— 509
A	Fort South	3,368	3,956	3,462	3,309	3,951	3,515	— 588	+ 494	+ 153	— 642
A	Fort North	24,700	30,534	25,400	22,956	32,847	33,828	— 5,834	+ 5,134	+ 2,444	— 9,891
A	Esplanade	12,228	12,165	17,761	10,398	10,064	13,080	+ 63	— 5,596	+ 7,363	+ 334
B	Chakla	17,322	22,996	24,231	24,384	32,197	37,048	— 5,674	— 1,235	— 153	— 7,813
B	Mandvi	37,719	38,517	33,202	31,402	37,295	42,351	— 798	+ 5,315	+ 1,800	— 5,893
B	Umarkhadi	40,458	47,218	45,679	48,481	52,466	54,656	— 6,760	+ 1,539	— 2,802	— 3,985
B	Dongri	11,346	19,966	27,246	25,778	30,317	33,290	— 8,620	— 7,280	+ 1,468	— 4,539
C	Market	38,145	35,080	30,172	28,415	44,751	49,130	+ 3,065	+ 4,908	+ 1,757	—16,336
C	Dhobi Talao	44,250	42,171	38,684	29,553	39,945	39,409	+ 2,079	+ 3,487	+ 9,131	—10,392
C	Fanaswadi	31,928	30,105	27,403	16,354	24,069	23,218	+ 1,823	+ 2,702	+ 11,049	— 7,715
C	Bhuleshwar	34,383	34,622	36,459	30,229	38,363	38,106	— 239	— 1,837	+ 6,230	— 8,134
C	Kumbharwada	31,743	32,481	27,703	27,544	32,209	34,990	— 738	+ 4,778	+ 159	— 4,665
C	Khara Talao	22,209	23,925	22,979	23,161	27,035	28,691	— 1,716	+ 946	— 182	— 3,874
D	Khetwadi	39,164	39,615	31,937	27,160	28,814	29,436	— 451	+ 7,678	+ 4,777	— 1,654
D	Girgaum	38,476	36,003	30,779	14,866	26,999	25,319	+ 2,473	+ 5,224	+ 15,913	—12,133
D	Chaupati	16,070	14,260	11,397	6,729	11,512	10,975	+ 1,810	+ 2,863	+ 4,668	— 4,783
D	Walkeshwar	22,734	17,188	10,640	10,563	12,990	11,303	+ 5,546	+ 6,548	+ 77	— 2,427
D	Mahalaxmi	34,880	37,108	26,302	18,092	17,014	6,232	— 2,228	+ 10,806	+ 8,210	+ 1,078
E	Tardeo	31,296	31,933	27,758	20,958	18,980	20,281	— 637	+ 4,175	+ 6,800	+ 1,978
E	Kamatipura	37,571	44,585	36,751	26,706	29,203	28,455	— 7,014	+ 7,834	+ 10,045	— 2,497
E	1st Nagpada	7,223	7,645	6,414	10,577	11,133	9,372	— 422	+ 1,231	— 4,163	— 556
E	2nd Nagpada	20,737	23,103	21,700	18,591	18,768	15,922	— 2,366	+ 1,403	+ 3,109	— 177
E	Byculla	89,835	91,285	75,348	57,646	47,403	26,842	— 1,450	+ 15,937	+ 17,702	+10,243
E	Tarwadi	39,323	39,909	28,424	18,460	21,298	14,542	— 586	+ 11,485	+ 9,964	— 2,838
E	Mazagaon	42,992	32,092	30,075	27,933	33,640	27,904	+10,900	+ 2,017	+ 2,142	— 5,707
F	Parel	61,567	59,534	45,474	33,390	28,740	18,560	+ 2,033	+ 14,060	+ 12,084	+ 4,650
F	Sewri	26,556	27,124	19,067	9,294	6,063	5,555	— 568	+ 8,057	+ 9,773	+ 3,231
F	Sion	68,119	52,913	30,680	25,443	19,601	17,237	+15,206	+ 22,233	+ 5,237	+ 5,842
G	Mahim	48,502	47,171	30,492	27,386	18,505	17,309	+ 1,331	+ 16,679	+ 3,106	+ 8,881
G	Worli	114,531	118,045	89,611	45,588	25,493	14,621	— 3,514	+ 28,434	+ 44,023	+20,095
	Persons enumerated by the Military, Customs, R.I.M. and Railway authorities and Vagrants enumerated by the Police	51,712	62,875	44,979	37,681	22,142	24,887	—11,163	+ 17,896	+ 7,298	+15,539

TION SINCE 1881.

Imperial Table II.)

be exact, all the persons enumerated by the Customs, Railways, Military and R.I.M. who, to that Table), have been excluded from the Population of the Sections, as in the past. from the wording of the last item in Table I.

	Net variation in period 1881 to 1931.	Males.						Females.					
1881 to 1891	Increase (+) Decrease (—)	1931	1921	1911	1901	1891	1881	1931	1921	1911	1901	1891	1881
13	14	15	16	17	18	19	20	21	22	23	24	25	26
+48,568	+388,187	747,881	771,332	640,288	479,786	518,093	464,763	414,002	404,582	339,157	296,220	303,671	308,433
+ 1,468	— 2,431	288	177	869	2,758	3,155	1,848	148	116	688	1,198	1,180	1,019
— 643	+ 5,595	13,543	13,421	13,514	8,109	8,759	8,855	6,317	6,070	6,165	4,914	4,863	5,410
+ 436	— 147	2,735	3,304	2,825	2,680	3,064	2,633	633	652	637	629	887	882
— 981	— 9,128	15,826	19,344	15,564	18,588	19,340	19,798	8,874	11,190	9,836	9,368	13,507	14,035
— 3,016	— 852	8,208	8,791	12,544	7,264	7,145	7,942	4,020	3,374	5,217	3,134	2,919	5,138
— 4,851	— 19,726	11,331	16,533	15,768	14,672	19,633	21,875	5,991	6,463	8,463	9,712	12,564	15,173
— 5,056	— 4,632	23,847	25,700	23,317	18,413	22,981	24,877	13,872	12,817	9,885	12,989	14,314	17,474
— 2,190	— 14,198	24,524	29,635	28,491	28,041	31,068	31,033	15,934	17,583	17,188	19,840	21,398	23,623
— 2,978	— 21,944	6,668	12,130	16,985	14,559	18,680	18,442	4,678	7,836	10,261	11,219	11,637	14,848
— 4,379	— 10,985	26,453	27,008	22,011	18,734	30,126	31,458	11,692	8,072	8,161	9,681	14,625	17,672
+ 530	+ 4,841	27,457	27,873	24,670	17,737	24,508	23,278	16,798	14,298	14,014	11,816	15,437	16,131
+ 851	+ 8,710	19,584	19,732	18,125	10,034	15,420	14,187	12,344	10,373	9,278	6,320	8,649	9,031
+ 257	— 3,723	22,385	23,744	24,713	19,135	25,101	23,734	11,998	10,878	11,746	11,094	13,262	14,372
— 2,781	— 3,247	19,535	21,726	17,908	16,384	20,142	20,071	12,208	10,755	9,795	11,160	12,067	14,919
— 1,656	— 6,482	13,979	16,038	15,052	14,164	16,660	16,453	8,230	7,887	7,927	8,997	10,375	12,238
— 622	+ 9,728	24,210	24,481	19,850	16,287	18,069	17,418	14,954	15,134	12,087	10,873	10,745	12,018
+ 1,680	+ 13,157	24,078	22,333	19,156	9,151	16,806	15,030	14,398	13,670	11,623	5,715	10,193	10,289
+ 537	+ 5,095	9,970	8,870	7,088	4,104	7,011	6,359	6,100	5,390	4,309	2,625	4,501	4,616
+ 1,687	+ 11,431	14,523	10,969	6,883	6,807	8,203	6,904	8,211	6,219	3,757	3,666	4,787	4,399
+10,782	+ 28,648	21,617	23,435	16,608	10,958	10,734	3,769	13,263	13,673	9,694	7,139	6,280	2,463
— 1,801	+ 11,015	18,808	19,616	17,241	12,213	11,403	11,932	12,488	12,317	10,517	8,745	7,577	8,349
+ 748	+ 9,116	23,488	27,369	22,523	15,275	16,742	15,453	14,083	17,216	14,228	11,431	12,461	13,002
+ 1,761	— 2,149	4,672	5,131	4,182	6,308	6,674	5,442	2,551	2,514	2,232	4,269	4,459	3,930
+ 2,846	+ 4,815	13,048	14,583	13,321	10,635	10,962	8,816	7,689	8,520	8,379	7,956	7,806	7,106
+20,561	+ 62,993	57,242	58,338	47,672	34,544	29,557	15,811	32,593	32,947	27,676	23,102	17,846	11,031
+ 6,756	+ 24,781	23,896	26,216	18,141	11,509	13,587	8,802	15,427	13,693	10,288	6,951	7,711	5,740
+ 5,736	+ 15,088	23,264	20,256	19,398	16,590	20,413	16,099	14,728	11,836	10,677	11,343	13,227	11,805
+10,180	+ 43,007	38,850	37,788	28,858	20,430	18,008	10,863	22,717	21,746	16,616	12,960	10,782	7,697
+ 508	+ 21,001	17,198	16,247	11,841	5,605	3,767	3,250	9,358	10,877	7,226	3,689	2,206	2,305
+ 2,364	+ 50,882	42,380	32,338	18,463	15,139	11,983	9,932	25,739	20,575	12,217	10,304	7,618	7,305
+ 1,196	+ 31,193	29,550	28,772	18,271	15,927	10,838	9,873	18,952	18,390	12,221	11,459	7,667	7,436
+10,872	+ 99,910	73,644	77,316	58,473	27,329	15,755	8,101	40,887	40,729	31,138	18,259	9,738	6,430
— 2,745	+ 26,825	45,580	52,118	39,963	34,018	21,799	24,340	6,132	10,757	5,016	3,663	343	547

RELI

(Corresponding to

Ward.	Section.	POPULATION.			BRAHMANIC.			ARYA.		
		Persons.	Males.	Females.	Persons.	Males.	Females.	Persons.	Males.	Females.
1	2	3	4	5	6	7	8	9	10	11
	Bombay City	**1,161,383**	**747,381**	**414,002**	**788,904**	**504,963**	**283,941**	**934**	**614**	**320**
A	Upper Colaba	436	288	148	292	193	99	..	..	..
A	Lower Colaba	19,954	13,628	6,326	11,072	7,792	3,280	3	3	..
A	Fort South	3,495	2,854	641	1,688	1,515	173	2	2	..
A	Fort North	25,832	16,823	9,009	13,990	9,290	4,700	21	16	5
A	Esplanade	14,303	9,814	4,489	7,843	5,318	2,525	6	4	2
B	Chakla	18,037	12,031	6,006	5,776	3,974	1,802	10	10	..
B	Mandvi	41,706	27,050	14,656	32,663	20,854	11,809	..	..	..
B	Umarkhadi	41,594	25,588	16,006	10,397	6,163	4,234	..	..	..
B	Dongri	13,028	8,101	4,927	8,925	5,265	3,660	..	..	..
C	Market	38,651	26,952	11,699	30,483	21,114	9,369	4	4	..
C	Dhobi Talao	44,372	27,568	16,804	26,042	15,634	10,408	..	..	..
C	Fanaswadi	32,077	19,722	12,355	28,044	17,067	10,977	42	22	20
C	Bhuleshwar	35,106	23,097	12,009	21,294	13,956	7,338	10	9	1
C	Kumbharwada.. ..	32,027	19,815	12,212	29,697	18,108	11,589	33	26	7
C	Khara Talao	23,243	14,998	8,245	5,300	3,495	1,805	..	..	..
D	Khetwadi	39,307	24,350	14,957	26,912	16,984	9,928	189	124	65
D	Girgaum	38,786	24,369	14,417	36,570	22,842	13,728	33	20	13
D	Chaupati	16,197	10,091	6,106	13,397	8,378	5,019	228	136	92
D	Walkeshwar	22,734	14,523	8,211	13,648	9,263	4,385	129	77	52
D	Mahalaxmi	36,569	22,948	13,621	23,418	15,438	7,980	32	27	5
E	Tardeo	31,748	19,200	12,548	17,756	10,716	7,040	5	3	2
E	Kamatipura	37,571	23,488	14,083	26,958	15,672	11,286	10	7	3
E	1st Nagpada	7,223	4,672	2,551	3,065	2,116	949	6	6	..
E	2nd Nagpada	21,032	13,338	7,694	5,424	3,529	1,895	5	3	2
E	Byculla	91,985	59,098	32,887	52,784	33,567	19,217	28	20	8
E	Tarwadi	40,338	24,678	15,660	27,356	16,918	10,438	..	..	..
E	Mazagaon	43,153	28,414	14,739	29,153	18,750	10,403	..	..	..
F	Parel	63,560	40,407	23,153	52,633	33,551	19,082	38	28	10
F	Sewri	26,756	17,376	9,380	23,054	14,909	8,145	..	..	..
F	Sion	69,198	43,167	26,031	52,034	32,936	19,098	24	19	5
G	Mahim	49,244	30,048	19,196	36,536	22,237	14,299	10	8	2
G	Worli	114,531	73,644	40,887	100,592	64,558	36,034	41	23	18
	Harbour Islands, Railway platforms, floating population and unknown ..	27,590	25,241	2,349	14,108	12,861	1,247	25	17	8

GION.

Imperial Table XVI.)

HINDU.						MUSLIM.					
BRAHMO.			TOTAL HINDUS.			SHIA.			SUNI.		
Persons.	Males.	Females.	Persons.	Males.	Females.	Persons.	Males.	Females.	Persons.	Males.	Females.
12	13	14	15	16	17	18	19	20	21	22	23
23	**11**	**12**	**789,861**	**505,588**	**284,273**	**26,041**	**17,038**	**9,003**	**144,097**	**100,606**	**43,491**
..	..	..	292	193	99	..	..	..	47	38	9
..	..	..	11,075	7,795	3,280	144	87	57	1,451	1,184	267
..	..	..	1,690	1,517	173	83	72	11	292	286	6
..	..	..	14,011	9,306	4,705	381	244	137	1,941	1,657	284
..	..	..	7,849	5,322	2,527	429	307	122	2,375	1,904	471
..	..	..	5,786	3,984	1,802	2,395	1,555	840	8,331	5,471	2,860
..	..	..	32,663	20,854	11,809	2,250	1,407	843	3,685	2,805	880
..	..	..	10,397	6,163	4,234	4,134	2,403	1,731	17,389	11,581	5,808
..	..	..	8,925	5,265	3,660	1,185	620	565	1,517	1,284	233
..	..	..	30,487	21,118	9,369	1,828	1,217	611	1,103	729	374
..	..	..	26,042	15,634	10,408	147	92	55	858	600	258
..	..	..	28,086	17,089	10,997	11	5	6	367	242	125
..	..	..	21,304	13,965	7,339	126	85	41	11,540	7,732	3,808
..	..	..	29,730	18,134	11,596	26	21	5	1,310	994	316
..	..	..	5,300	3,495	1,805	7,274	4,981	2,293	5,503	3,392	2,111
..	..	..	27,101	17,108	9,993	162	119	43	2,414	1,740	674
..	..	..	36,603	22,862	13,741	16	13	3	159	138	21
20	10	10	13,645	8,524	5,121	65	44	21	212	183	29
..	..	..	13,777	9,340	4,437	854	617	237	910	546	364
..	..	..	23,450	15,465	7,985	642	393	249	690	514	176
..	..	..	17,761	10,719	7,042	877	594	283	4,494	3,088	1,406
..	..	..	26,968	15,679	11 289	193	146	47	7,471	5,527	1,944
..	..	..	3,071	2,122	949	77	55	22	1,537	1,046	491
..	..	..	5,429	3,532	1,897	96	74	22	13,951	8,856	5,095
1	..	1	52,813	33,587	19,226	694	445	249	23,850	16,516	7,334
..	..	..	27,356	16,918	10,438	203	137	66	1,566	1,153	413
..	..	..	29,153	18,750	10,403	240	160	80	4,517	3,212	1,305
..	..	..	52,671	33,579	19,092	186	132	54	2,550	1,858	692
..	..	..	23,054	14,909	8,145	83	67	16	2,234	1,553	681
2	1	1	52,060	32,956	19,104	216	175	41	5,002	3,511	1,491
..	..	..	36,546	22,245	14,301	458	306	152	5,437	3,545	1,892
..	..	..	100,633	64,581	36,052	253	204	49	5,460	3,938	1,522
..	..	..	14,133	12,878	1,255	313	261	52	3,934	3,783	151

Ward.	Section.	MUSLIM—*contd.*								
		SECT UNSPECIFIED.			TOTAL MUSLIMS.			SWETAMBAR.		
		Persons.	Males.	Females.	Persons.	Males.	Females.	Persons.	Males.	Females.
1	2	24	25	26	27	28	29	30	31	32
	Bombay City	**39,108**	**26,274**	**12,834**	**209,246**	**143,918**	**65,328**	**653**	**537**	**116**
A	Upper Colaba	..	..	..	47	38	9	..	..	..
A	Lower Colaba	138	110	28	1,733	1,381	352	..	..	..
A	Fort South	71	65	6	446	423	23	..	..	..
A	Fort North	596	426	170	2,918	2,327	591	5	3	2
A	Esplanade	521	369	152	3,325	2,580	745	1	1	..
B	Chakla	1,286	891	395	12,012	7,917	4,095	..	..	..
B	Mandvi	2,439	1,545	894	8,374	5,757	2,617	13	13	..
B	Umarkhadi	7,270	4,006	3,264	28,793	17,990	10,803	17	14	3
B	Dongri	271	213	58	2,973	2,117	856	86	83	3
C	Market	642	534	108	3,573	2,480	1,093	179	163	16
C	Dhobi Talao	205	125	80	1,210	817	393	3	3	..
C	Fanaswadi	55	28	27	433	275	158	..	..	..
C	Bhuleshwar	319	217	102	11,985	8,034	3,951	..	..	..
C	Kumbharwada.. ..	538	370	168	1,874	1,385	489	..	..	..
C	Khara Talao	5,028	3,011	2,017	17,805	11,384	6,421	32	31	1
D	Khetwadi	995	755	240	3,571	2,614	957	..	..	..
D	Girgaum	160	125	35	335	276	59	..	..	..
D	Chaupati	210	156	54	487	383	104	..	..	..
D	Walkeshwar	364	215	149	2,128	1,378	750	73	37	36
D	Mahalaxmi	457	320	137	1,789	1,227	562	..	..	..
E	Tardeo	706	466	240	6,077	4,148	1,929	35	32	3
E	Kamatipura	1,358	1,025	333	9,022	6,698	2,324	..	..	..
E	1st Nagpada	166	113	53	1,780	1,214	566	..	..	..
E	2nd Nagpada	523	288	235	14,570	9,218	5,352	7	1	6
E	Byculla	2,529	1,780	749	27,073	18,741	8,332	22	17	5
E	Tarwadi	2,958	1,818	1,140	4,727	3,108	1,619	..	..	..
E	Mazagaon	1,600	1,009	591	6,357	4,381	1,976	4	3	1
F	Parel	943	612	331	3,679	2,602	1,077	12	9	3
F	Sewri	321	207	114	2,638	1,827	811	7	6	1
F	Sion	672	472	200	5,890	4,158	1,732	88	61	27
G	Mahim	814	577	237	6,709	4,428	2,281	35	27	8
G	Worli	1,506	1,081	425	7,219	5,223	1,996	20	19	1
	Harbour Islands, Railway platforms, floating population and unknown..	3,447	3,345	102	7,694	7,389	305	14	14	..

JAIN.									ZOROASTRIAN.		
DIGAMBAR.			OTHERS AND SECT UNSPECIFIED			TOTAL JAINS.					
Persons.	Males.	Females.	Persons.	Males.	Females.	Persons.	Males.	Females.	Persons.	Males.	Females.
33	34	35	36	37	38	39	40	41	42	43	44
218	146	67	11,558	8,315	3,248	12,424	8,998	3,426	57,765	30,595	27,170
..	..	..	..	..	..	..	..	..	23	14	9
..	..	..	89	87	2	89	87	2	1,196	646	550
..	..	..	..	..	..	..	..	..	54	45	9
..	..	..	101	76	25	106	79	27	5,943	3,249	2,694
..	..	..	20	14	6	21	15	6	598	310	288
..	..	..	162	91	71	162	91	71	30	20	10
9	9	..	209	157	52	231	179	52	20	16	4
..	..	..	403	336	67	420	350	70	40	25	15
64	41	23	399	242	157	549	366	183	14	14	..
54	36	18	2,788	1.959	829	3,021	2,158	863	75	51	24
..	..	..	270	206	64	273	209	64	7,066	3,740	3,326
..	..	..	55	46	9	55	46	9	1,648	817	831
..	..	..	1,578	949	629	1,578	949	629	208	123	85
10	7	3	318	231	87	328	238	90	28	13	15
..	..	..	76	72	4	108	103	5	2	1	1
..	..	..	180	122	58	180	122	58	7,343	3,865	3,478
..	..	..	336	260	76	336	260	76	398	257	141
..	..	..	192	117	75	192	117	75	1,031	560	471
..	..	..	302	177	125	375	214	161	3,290	1,699	1,591
..	..	..	149	141	8	149	141	8	8,189	4,225	3,964
..	..	..	267	158	109	302	190	112	5,726	3,003	2,723
..	..	..	416	381	35	416	381	35	48	35	13
..	..	..	68	53	15	68	53	15	11	11	..
..	..	..	102	102	..	109	103	6	46	24	22
5	2	3	876	666	210	903	685	218	903	475	428
18	18	..	114	70	44	132	88	44	2,567	1,282	1,285
..	..	..	113	97	16	117	100	17	1,138	629	509
11	6	5	425	290	135	448	305	143	2,802	1,603	1,199
15	10	5	174	109	65	196	125	71	56	35	21
10	5	5	347	301	46	445	367	78	5,341	2,679	2,662
10	6	4	309	246	63	354	279	75	400	213	187
4	3	1	602	456	146	626	478	148	1,234	681	553
3	3	..	118	103	15	135	120	15	297	235	62

Ward.	Section.	CHRISTIAN.			TRIBAL.			SIKH.		
		Persons.	Males.	Females.	Persons.	Males.	Females.	Persons.	Males.	Females.
1	2	45	46	47	48	49	50	51	52	53
	Bombay City	**80,728**	**51,466**	**29,262**	**2**	**2**	..	**985**	**752**	**233**
A	Upper Colaba	72	42	30	..	..	..	..	..	..
A	Lower Colaba	5,457	3,499	1,958	..	..	..	6	5	1
A	Fort South	1,189	804	385	..	..	..	1	1	..
A	Fort North	2,753	1,802	951	..	..	..	57	39	18
A	Esplanade	2,302	1,467	835	..	..	..	49	34	15
B	Chakla	36	13	23	..	..	..	8	4	4
B	Mandvi	177	98	79	..	..	..	17	13	4
B	Umarkhadi	667	382	285	..	..	..	..	..	..
B	Dongri	201	146	55	..	..	..	2	2	..
C	Market	1,477	1,136	341	..	..	..	3	3	..
C	Dhobi Talao	9,757	7,150	2,607	..	..	..	11	9	2
C	Fanaswadi	1,853	1,493	360	..	..	..	2	2	..
C	Bhuleshwar	25	20	5	..	..	..	6	6	..
C	Kumbharwada.. ..	51	37	14	..	..	..	1	1	..
C	Khara Talao	25	13	12	..	..	..	..	..	..
D	Khetwadi	1,083	626	457	..	..	..	7	4	3
D	Girgaum	1,104	709	395	..	..	..	3	3	..
D	Chaupati	789	475	314	..	..	..	7	6	1
D	Walkeshwar	2,980	1,793	1,187	1	1	..	27	21	6
D	Mahalaxmi	2,877	1,810	1,067	..	..	..	61	48	13
E	Tardeo	1,679	976	703	..	..	..	11	7	4
E	Kamatipura	380	146	234	..	..	..	..	..	..
E	1st Nagpada	850	499	351	..	..	..	..	..	..
E	2nd Nagpada	202	111	91	..	..	..	..	..	..
E	Byculla	8,215	4,462	3,753	..	..	..	146	115	31
E	Tarwadi	4,914	2,909	2,005	..	..	..	54	43	11
E	Mazagaon	6,120	4,360	1,760	..	..	..	9	7	2
F	Parel	3,593	2,112	1,481	..	..	..	66	51	15
F	Sewri	760	442	318	..	..	..	28	21	7
F	Sion	5,068	2,753	2,315	..	..	..	176	116	60
G	Mahim	5,158	2,837	2,321	..	..	..	34	25	9
G	Worli	4,285	2,391	1,894	1	1	..	44	36	8
	Harbour Islands, Railway platforms, floating population and unknown..	4,629	3,953	676	..	..	..	149	130	19

JEW.			BUDDHISTS.			OTHERS.		
Persons.	Males.	Females.	Persons.	Males.	Females.	Persons.	Males.	Females.
54	55	56	57	58	59	60	61	62
8,621	**4,604**	**4,017**	**1,630**	**1,359**	**271**	**121**	**99**	**22**
2	1	1	....	....	....	....	....	....
351	181	170	47	34	13	....	....	....
109	60	49	5	3	2	1	1	....
36	17	19	8	4	4	....	....	....
85	44	41	72	41	31	2	1	1
....	....	....	3	2	1	....	....	....
176	88	88	43	40	3	5	5	....
1,263	673	590	2	1	1	12	4	8
360	189	171	4	2	2	....	....	....
10	4	6	5	2	3	....	....	....
10	7	3	3	2	1	....	....	....
....	....	....	....	....	....	....	....	....
....	....	....	....	....	....	....	....	....
10	5	5	5	2	3	....	....	....
3	2	1	....	....	....	....	....	....
15	9	6	5	2	3	2	....	2
7	2	5	....	....	....	....	....	....
29	13	16	15	11	4	2	2	....
45	14	31	111	63	48	....	....	....
3	2	1	51	30	21	....	....	....
58	31	27	134	126	8	....	....	....
205	113	92	440	353	87	92	83	9
1,442	772	670	1	1	....	....	....	....
676	350	326	....	....	....	....	....	....
1,876	987	889	56	46	10	....	....	....
585	328	257	3	2	1	....	....	....
178	124	54	81	63	18	....	....	....
290	148	142	11	7	4	....	....	....
24	17	7	....	....	....	....	....	....
176	98	78	42	40	2	....	....	....
39	19	20	....	....	....	4	2	2
489	253	236	....	....	....	....	....	....
69	53	16	483	482	1	1	1	....

MC-I Bk Rs Cs 3—42

Religion.

Details of Others.

Religion.	Persons.	Males.	Females.
1	2	3	4
Total Others	**121**	**99**	**22**
Negroes and Egyptians	12	5	7
Confusionists and Linchins	10	10	....
Indefinite beliefs	99	84	15

Details of Indefinite beliefs.

Religion.	Persons.	Males.	Females.
Atheists	92	80	12
Agnostics	1	1	....
Free-thinkers	4	2	2
Non-religionists	2	1	1

Details of Christian Population.

Roman Catholics.		Romo Syrians.		Other Syrians.		Other Christians.	
Males.	Females.	Males.	Females.	Males.	Females.	Males.	Females.
42,000	23,035	3	2	10	13	9,453	6,212

AGE, SEX AND CIVIL CONDITION.

(Corresponding to Imperial Table VII.)

A—All Religions.

Age.	Population.			Unmarried.			Married.			Widowed.		
	Persons.	Males.	Females.	Persons.	Males.	Females.	Persons.	Males.	Females.	Persons.	Males.	Females.
1	2	3	4	5	6	7	8	9	10	11	12	13
0—1 ..	16,226	8,033	8,193	16,207	8,025	8,182	19	8	11	..	..	..
1—2 ..	19,322	9,848	9,474	19,282	9,824	9,458	39	24	15	1	..	1
2—3 ..	23,203	11,891	11,312	23,127	11,847	11,280	74	44	30	2	..	2
3—4 ..	22,546	11,786	10,760	22,444	11,736	10,708	98	50	48	4	..	4
4—5 ..	22,041	11,948	10,093	21,778	11,812	9,966	253	131	122	10	5	5
Total 0—5 ..	**103,338**	**53,506**	**49,832**	**102,838**	**53,244**	**49,594**	**483**	**257**	**226**	**17**	**5**	**12**
5—10 ..	93,921	53,713	40,208	91,545	52,705	38,840	2,312	992	1,320	64	16	48
10—15 ..	86,031	50,852	35,179	78,643	48,410	30,233	7,258	2,414	4,844	130	28	102
15—20 ..	115,323	67,890	47,433	57,100	45,060	12,040	57,377	22,640	34,737	846	190	656
20—25 ..	152,336	92,248	60,088	50,008	42,586	7,422	100,575	49,218	51,357	1,753	444	1,309
25—30 ..	179,784	124,579	55,205	24,156	21,457	2,699	151,614	101,984	49,630	4,014	1,138	2,876
30—35 ..	164,260	120,374	43,886	15,083	13,259	1,824	143,754	105,626	38,128	5,423	1,489	3,934
35—40 ..	100,166	75,446	24,720	5,724	4,829	895	86,630	68,643	17,987	7,812	1,974	5,838
40—45 ..	70,777	51,795	18,982	3,511	2,861	650	58,775	46,949	11,826	8,491	1,985	6,506
45—50 ..	36,825	23,913	12,912	1,459	1,087	372	26,434	20,969	5,465	8,932	1,857	7,075
50—55 ..	26,227	15,953	10,274	921	671	250	17,252	13,622	3,630	8,054	1,060	6,394
55—60 ..	14,263	7,600	6,663	455	315	140	7,711	6,021	1,690	6,097	1,264	4,833
60—65 ..	10,329	5,300	5,029	302	215	87	5,182	4,037	1,145	4,845	1,048	3,797
65—70 ..	3,612	1,911	1,701	125	88	37	1,746	1,382	364	1,741	441	1,300
70 and over ..	3,895	2,045	1,850	97	65	32	1,817	1,431	386	1,981	549	1,432
Unspecified ..	296	256	40	17	17	..	40	..	40	239	239	..
Total ..	**1,161,383**	**747,381**	**414,002**	**431,984**	**286,869**	**145,115**	**668,960**	**446,185**	**222,775**	**60,439**	**14,327**	**46,112**

B—Hindu.

0—1 ..	11,228	5,508	5,720	11,214	5,500	5,714	14	8	6	..	..	..
1—2 ..	13,720	7,014	6,706	13,692	6,995	6,697	27	19	8	1	..	1
2—3 ..	16,808	8,620	8,188	16,751	8,588	8,163	55	32	23	2	..	2
3—4 ..	16,309	8,543	7,766	16,229	8,506	7,723	76	37	39	4	..	4
4—5 ..	15,400	8,509	6,900	15,318	8,415	6,903	173	89	84	8	5	3
Total 0—5 ..	**73,564**	**38,194**	**35,370**	**73,204**	**38,004**	**35,200**	**345**	**185**	**160**	**15**	**5**	**10**
5—10 ..	64,325	37,061	27,264	62,434	36,309	26,125	1,837	738	1,099	54	14	40
10—15 ..	56,623	33,691	22,932	50,803	31,926	18,877	5,725	1,745	3,980	95	20	75
15—20 ..	78,660	44,871	33,789	33,255	27,585	5,670	44,750	17,166	27,584	655	120	535
20—25 ..	106,850	62,724	44,126	28,143	25,095	3,048	77,353	37,347	40,006	1,354	282	1,072
25—30 ..	128,240	88,535	39,705	11,893	10,981	912	113,814	76,797	36,517	3,033	757	2,276
30—35 ..	116,002	85,449	30,553	7,114	6,493	621	104,865	77,981	26,884	4,023	975	3,048
35—40 ..	66,636	50,712	15,924	2,514	2,220	294	58,580	47,245	11,335	5,542	1,247	4,295
40—45 ..	45,214	33,285	11,929	1,379	1,177	202	37,877	30,843	7,034	5,958	1,265	4,693
45—50 ..	22,023	14,012	8,011	471	372	99	15,437	12,498	2,939	6,115	1,142	4,973
50—55 ..	15,300	8,988	6,312	266	215	51	9,619	7,766	1,853	5,415	1,007	4,408
55—60 ..	7,728	3,830	3,898	109	85	24	3,784	3,021	763	3,835	724	3,111
60—65 ..	5,421	2,588	2,833	72	58	14	2,453	1,945	508	2,896	585	2,311
65—70 ..	1,590	781	809	27	19	8	699	562	137	864	200	664
70 and over ..	1,676	858	818	22	18	4	761	600	161	893	240	653
Unspecified ..	9	9	..	9	9	..	..	..	..	..	..	..
Total ..	**789,861**	**505,588**	**284,273**	**271,715**	**180,566**	**91,149**	**477,399**	**316,439**	**160,960**	**40,747**	**8,583**	**32,164**

C—Muslim.

0—1 ..	2,541	1,296	1,245	2,538	1,296	1,242	3	..	3	..	..	..
1—2 ..	3,138	1,606	1,532	3,129	1,602	1,527	9	4	5	..	..	..
2—3 ..	3,615	1,856	1,759	3,604	1,850	1,754	11	6	5	..	..	..
3—4 ..	3,572	1,852	1,720	3,557	1,843	1,714	15	9	6	..	..	..
4—5 ..	3,650	1,924	1,726	3,599	1,899	1,700	50	25	25	1	..	1
Total 0—5 ..	**16,516**	**8,534**	**7,982**	**16,427**	**8,490**	**7,937**	**88**	**44**	**44**	**1**	..	**1**
5—10 ..	16,506	9,615	6,891	16,173	9,430	6,743	326	183	143	7	2	5
10—15 ..	16,010	9,747	6,263	14,882	9,273	5,609	1,104	467	637	24	7	17
15—20 ..	20,123	13,173	6,950	11,088	9,087	2,001	8,908	4,034	4,874	127	52	75
20—25 ..	26,383	17,864	8,519	9,932	8,941	991	16,176	8,791	7,385	275	132	143
25—30 ..	31,726	23,382	8,344	5,375	5,108	267	25,720	17,974	7,746	631	300	331
30—35 ..	29,620	22,677	6,943	3,416	3,246	170	25,338	19,035	6,303	866	396	470
35—40 ..	19,637	15,520	4,117	1,313	1,240	73	16,969	13,768	3,201	1,355	512	843
40—45 ..	14,169	11,065	3,104	789	747	42	11,901	9,837	2,064	1,479	481	998
45—50 ..	7,233	5,205	2,028	286	268	18	5,393	4,506	887	1,554	431	1,123
50—55 ..	4,993	3,412	1,581	160	151	9	3,439	2,878	561	1,394	383	1,011
55—60 ..	2,760	1,651	1,109	67	57	10	1,588	1,320	268	1,105	274	831
60—65 ..	2,051	1,171	880	38	35	3	1,099	909	190	914	227	687
65—70 ..	666	401	265	17	16	1	343	294	49	306	91	215
70 and over ..	845	493	352	23	15	8	408	349	59	414	129	285
Unspecified ..	8	8	..	8	8	..	..	..	..	..	..	..
Total ..	**209,246**	**142,918**	**65,328**	**79,994**	**56,112**	**23,882**	**118,800**	**84,389**	**34,411**	**10,452**	**3,417**	**7,035**

D—Jain.

Age.	Population.			Unmarried.			Married.			Widowed.		
	Persons.	Males.	Females.	Persons.	Males.	Females.	Persons.	Males.	Females.	Persons.	Males.	Females.
1	2	3	4	5	6	7	8	9	10	11	12	13
0—1 ..	122	62	60	122	62	60	..	..	..	..	..	..
1—2 ..	164	65	99	163	65	98	1	..	1	..	..	..
2—3 ..	208	85	123	206	84	122	2	1	1	..	..	..
3—4 ..	201	96	105	200	96	104	1	..	1	..	..	..
4—5 ..	275	144	131	272	142	130	3	2	1	..	..	..
Total 0—5 ..	**970**	**452**	**518**	**963**	**449**	**514**	**7**	**3**	**4**	..	..	..
5—10 ..	1,041	652	389	1,029	645	384	12	7	5	..	..	..
10—15 ..	1,091	776	315	1,001	733	268	89	42	47	1	1	..
15—20 ..	1,436	1,066	370	830	752	78	605	313	292	1	1	..
20—25 ..	1,721	1,231	490	637	613	24	1,078	616	462	6	2	4
25—30 ..	1,693	1,223	470	192	180	12	1,493	1,039	454	8	4	4
30—35 ..	1,750	1,412	338	109	105	4	1,622	1,300	322	19	7	12
35—40 ..	1,162	988	174	52	50	2	1,056	910	146	54	28	26
40—45 ..	754	644	110	26	26	..	672	594	78	56	24	32
45—50 ..	334	268	66	14	14	..	272	232	40	48	22	26
50—55 ..	103	75	28	3	3	..	76	66	10	24	6	18
55—60 ..	182	118	64	4	4	..	112	99	13	66	15	51
60—65 ..	118	60	58	3	3	..	48	43	5	67	14	53
65—70 ..	47	23	24	2	2	..	18	15	3	27	6	21
70 and over ..	22	10	12	..	..	..	6	5	1	16	5	11
Unspecified ..	..	..	..	..	..	..	..	..	..	..	..	..
Total ..	**12,424**	**8,998**	**3,426**	**4,865**	**3,579**	**1,286**	**7,166**	**5,284**	**1,882**	**393**	**135**	**258**

E—Zoroastrian.

Age.	Population. Persons.	Population. Males.	Population. Females.	Unmarried. Persons.	Unmarried. Males.	Unmarried. Females.	Married. Persons.	Married. Males.	Married. Females.	Widowed. Persons.	Widowed. Males.	Widowed. Females.
0—1 ..	734	378	356	734	378	356	..	..	..	..	..	..
1—2 ..	750	384	366	750	384	366	..	..	..	..	..	..
2—3 ..	883	446	437	881	444	437	2	2	..	..	..	..
3—4 ..	906	461	445	904	460	444	2	1	1	..	..	..
4—5 ..	963	497	466	955	491	464	8	6	2	..	..	..
Total 0—5 ..	**4,236**	**2,166**	**2,070**	**4,224**	**2,157**	**2,067**	**12**	**9**	**3**	..	..	..
5—10 ..	4,839	2,544	2,295	4,816	2,530	2,286	23	14	9	..	..	..
10—15 ..	5,105	2,720	2,385	5,030	2,682	2,348	74	38	36	1	..	1
15—20 ..	5,207	2,771	2,436	4,623	2,612	2,011	569	158	411	15	1	14
20—25 ..	5,341	2,808	2,533	4,124	2,451	1,673	1,195	351	844	22	6	16
25—30 ..	5,540	2,879	2,661	2,568	1,685	883	2,894	1,175	1,719	78	19	59
30—35 ..	5,526	2,896	2,630	1,906	1,255	651	3,487	1,610	1,877	133	31	102
35—40 ..	4,855	2,062	2,193	936	592	344	3,629	2,003	1,626	290	67	223
40—45 ..	4,411	2,435	1,976	695	427	268	3,347	1,930	1,417	369	78	291
45—50 ..	3,553	1,915	1,638	406	228	178	2,578	1,578	1,000	569	109	460
50—55 ..	3,147	1,711	1,436	316	188	128	2,194	1,385	809	637	138	499
55—60 ..	2,232	1,170	1,062	188	117	71	1,387	901	486	657	152	505
60—65 ..	1,824	935	889	133	84	49	1,070	713	357	621	138	483
65—70 ..	947	492	455	49	30	19	503	359	144	395	103	292
70 and over ..	1,000	491	509	31	17	14	465	335	130	504	139	365
Unspecified ..	2	..	2	..	..	..	2	..	2	..	..	..
Total ..	**57,765**	**30,595**	**27,170**	**30,045**	**17,055**	**12,990**	**23,429**	**12,559**	**10,870**	**4,291**	**981**	**3,310**

F—Christian.

Age.	Population. Persons.	Population. Males.	Population. Females.	Unmarried. Persons.	Unmarried. Males.	Unmarried. Females.	Married. Persons.	Married. Males.	Married. Females.	Widowed. Persons.	Widowed. Males.	Widowed. Females.
0—1 ..	1,355	671	684	1,354	671	683	1	..	1	..	..	..
1—2 ..	1,320	664	656	1,318	663	655	2	1	1	..	..	..
2—3 ..	1,434	740	694	1,431	787	694	3	3	..	..	..	..
3—4 ..	1,324	702	622	1,320	699	621	4	3	1	..	..	..
4—5 ..	1,341	718	623	1,323	711	612	17	7	10	1	..	1
Total 0—5 ..	**6,774**	**3,495**	**3,279**	**6,746**	**3,481**	**3,265**	**27**	**14**	**13**	**1**	..	**1**
5—10 ..	6,069	3,269	2,800	5,973	3,228	2,745	94	41	53	2	..	2
10—15 ..	6,107	3,354	2,753	5,897	3,264	2,633	201	90	111	9	..	9
15—20 ..	8,746	5,347	3,399	6,480	4,471	2,009	2,226	863	1,363	40	13	27
20—25 ..	10,734	6,829	3,905	6,453	4,932	1,521	4,201	1,879	2,322	80	18	62
25—30 ..	11,176	7,631	3,545	3,706	3,154	552	7,239	4,429	2,810	231	48	183
30—35 ..	10,043	7,027	3,016	2,284	1,939	345	7,415	5,016	2,399	344	72	272
35—40 ..	6,951	4,919	2,032	838	664	174	5,608	4,151	1,457	505	104	401
40—45 ..	5,548	3,907	1,641	584	455	129	4,404	3,328	1,076	560	124	436
45—50 ..	3,279	2,250	1,029	260	190	70	2,444	1,922	522	575	138	437
50—55 ..	2,438	1,622	816	173	112	61	1,746	1,393	353	519	117	402
55—60 ..	1,194	743	451	82	49	33	740	603	137	372	91	281
60—65 ..	795	486	309	54	33	21	447	372	75	294	81	213
65—70 ..	301	179	122	29	20	9	146	125	21	126	34	92
70 and over ..	296	169	127	21	15	6	147	121	26	128	33	95
Unspecified ..	277	239	38	..	..	..	38	..	38	239	239	..
Total ..	**80,728**	**51,466**	**29,262**	**39,580**	**26,007**	**13,573**	**37,123**	**24,847**	**12,776**	**4,025**	**1,112**	**2,913**

G—Tribal.

Age.	Population.			Unmarried.			Married.			Widowed.		
	Persons.	Males.	Females.	Persons.	Males.	Females.	Persons.	Males.	Females.	Persons.	Males.	Females.
1	2	3	4	5	6	7	8	9	10	11	12	13
0—1 ..	..	..	..	..	..	..	..	..	..	..	..	..
1—2 ..	..	..	..	..	..	..	..	..	..	..	..	..
2—3 ..	..	..	..	..	..	..	..	..	..	..	..	..
3—4 ..	..	..	..	..	..	..	..	..	..	..	..	..
4—5 ..	..	..	..	..	..	..	..	..	..	..	..	..
Total 0—5 ..	..	..	..	..	..	..	..	..	..	..	..	..
5—10 ..	..	..	..	..	..	..	..	..	..	..	..	..
10—15 ..	..	..	..	..	..	..	..	..	..	..	..	..
15—20 ..	..	..	..	..	..	..	..	..	..	..	..	..
20—25 ..	2	2	..	1	1	..	..	..	..	..	..	..
25—30 ..	..	..	..	..	..	..	1	1	..	..	..	..
30—35 ..	..	..	..	..	..	..	..	..	..	..	..	..
35—40 ..	..	..	..	..	..	..	..	..	..	..	..	..
40—45 ..	..	..	..	..	..	..	..	..	..	..	..	..
45—50 ..	..	..	..	..	..	..	..	..	..	..	..	..
50—55 ..	..	..	..	..	..	..	..	..	..	..	..	..
55—60 ..	..	..	..	..	..	..	..	..	..	..	..	..
60—65 ..	..	..	..	..	..	..	..	..	..	..	..	..
65—70 ..	..	..	..	..	..	..	..	..	..	..	..	..
70 and over ..	..	..	..	..	..	..	..	..	..	..	..	..
Unspecified ..	..	..	..	..	..	..	..	..	..	..	..	..
Total ..	2	2	..	1	1	..	1	1	..	..	..	..

H—Other Religions.

Age.	Population.			Unmarried.			Married.			Widowed.		
	Persons.	Males.	Females.	Persons.	Males.	Females.	Persons.	Males.	Females.	Persons.	Males.	Females.
0—1 ..	246	118	128	245	118	127	1	..	1	..	..	..
1—2 ..	230	115	115	230	115	115	..	..	..	..	..	..
2—3 ..	255	144	111	254	144	110	1	..	1	..	..	..
3—4 ..	234	132	102	234	132	102	..	..	..	..	..	..
4—5 ..	313	156	157	311	154	157	2	2	..	..	..	..
Total 0—5 ..	1,278	665	613	1,274	663	611	4	2	2	..	..	..
5—10 ..	1,141	572	569	1,120	563	557	20	9	11	1	..	1
10—15 ..	1,095	564	531	1,030	532	498	65	32	33	..	..	..
15—20 ..	1,151	662	489	824	553	271	319	106	213	8	3	5
20—25 ..	1,305	790	515	718	553	165	571	233	338	16	4	12
25—30 ..	1,409	929	480	422	349	73	954	570	384	33	10	23
30—35 ..	1,319	913	406	254	221	33	1,027	684	343	38	8	30
35—40 ..	925	645	280	71	63	8	788	566	222	66	16	50
40—45 ..	681	459	222	38	29	9	574	417	157	69	13	56
45—50 ..	403	263	140	22	15	7	310	233	77	71	15	56
50—55 ..	246	145	101	3	2	1	178	134	44	65	9	56
55—60 ..	167	88	79	5	3	2	100	77	23	62	8	54
60—65 ..	120	60	60	2	2	..	65	55	10	53	3	50
65—70 ..	61	35	26	1	1	..	37	27	10	23	7	16
70 and over ..	56	24	32	..	..	..	30	21	9	26	3	23
Unspecified ..	..	..	..	..	..	..	..	..	..	..	..	..
Total ..	11,357	6,814	4,543	5,784	3,549	2,235	5,042	3,166	1,876	581	99	432

CITY TABLE V—PART I—BOMBAY.

Literacy by Religion and Age.

(Corresponding to Imperial Table XIII.)

Age.	Population. Total. Persons.	Total. Males.	Total. Females.	Literate. Persons.	Literate. Males.	Literate. Females.	Illiterate. Persons.	Illiterate. Males.	Illiterate. Females.	Literate in English. Persons.	Literate in English. Males.	Literate in English. Females.
1	2	3	4	5	6	7	8	9	10	11	12	13
A—All Religions .. Total ..	**1,161,383**	**747,381**	**414.002**	**280,923**	**217,770**	**63,153**	**880,164**	**529,355**	**350,809**	**134,916**	**106,240**	**28,676**
0—5 ..	103,338	53,506	49,832	..	..	..	103,338	53,506	49,832	..	..	..
5—10 ..	93,921	53,713	40,208	11,792	7,418	4,374	82,129	46,295	35,834	4,172	2,516	1,656
10—15 ..	86,031	50,852	35,179	18,081	11,773	6,308	67,950	39,079	28,871	7,341	4,749	2,592
15—20 ..	115,323	67,890	47,433	31,137	22,050	9,087	84,186	45,840	38,346	15,696	11,256	4,440
20 and over ..	762,474	521,164	241,310	219,018	176,529	43,384	542,561	344,635	197,026	107,707	87,719	19,988
Unspecified ..	296	256	40	..	..	..	..	..	..	..	..	..
B—Hindu .. Total ..	**789,861**	**505,588**	**284,273**	**148,129**	**123,338**	**24,791**	**641,723**	**382,241**	**259,482**	**55,692**	**50,539**	**5,153**
0—5 ..	73,564	38,194	35,370	..	..	..	73,564	38,194	35,370	..	..	..
5—10 ..	64,325	37,061	27,264	5,465	3,682	1,783	58,860	33,379	25,481	847	613	234
10—15 ..	56,623	33,691	22,932	8,814	6,067	2,747	47,809	27,624	20,185	2,157	1,608	549
15—20 ..	78,060	44,871	33,789	16,554	12,338	4,216	62,106	32,533	29,573	6,368	5,278	1,090
20 and over ..	516,680	351,762	164,918	117,296	101,251	16,045	399,384	250,511	148,873	46,320	43,040	3,280
Unspecified ..	9	9	..	..	..	..	..	..	..	..	..	..
C—Muslim .. Total ..	**209,246**	**143,918**	**65,328**	**40,374**	**35,493**	**4,881**	**168,864**	**108,417**	**60,447**	**10,201**	**9,385**	**816**
0—5 ..	16,516	8,534	7,982	..	..	..	16,516	8,534	7,982	..	..	..
5—10 ..	16,506	9,615	6,891	1,542	1,087	455	14,964	8,528	6,436	273	183	90
10—15 ..	16,010	9,747	6,263	2,460	1,814	646	13,550	7,933	5,617	450	442	8
15—20 ..	20,123	13,173	6,950	4,141	3,356	785	15,982	9,817	6,165	1,214	997	217
20 and over ..	140,083	102,841	37,242	32,231	29,236	2,995	107,852	73,605	34,247	8,264	7,763	501
Unspecified ..	8	8	..	..	..	..	..	..	..	..	..	..
D—Jain .. Total ..	**12,424**	**8,998**	**3,426**	**3,159**	**2,824**	**335**	**9,265**	**6,174**	**3,091**	**755**	**697**	**58**
0—5 ..	970	452	518	..	..	..	970	452	518	..	..	..
5—10 ..	1,041	652	389	106	79	27	935	573	362	20	15	5
10—15 ..	1,091	776	315	211	168	43	880	608	272	59	47	12
15—20 ..	1,436	1,066	370	419	373	46	1,017	693	324	123	112	11
20 and over ..	7,886	6,052	1,834	2,423	2,204	219	5,463	3,848	1,615	553	523	30
E—Zoroastrian .. Total ..	**57,765**	**30,595**	**27,170**	**42,834**	**24,234**	**18,600**	**14,929**	**6,361**	**8,568**	**30,641**	**20,082**	**10,559**
0—5 ..	4,236	2,166	2,070	..	..	..	4,236	2,166	2,070	..	..	..
5—10 ..	4,839	2,544	2,295	2,111	1,178	933	2,728	1,366	1,362	966	558	408
10—15 ..	5,105	2,720	2,385	3,214	1,790	1,424	1,891	930	961	1,818	1,049	769
15—20 ..	5,207	2,771	2,436	4,372	2,397	1,975	835	374	461	3,847	1,960	1,887
20 and over ..	38,376	20,394	17,982	33,137	18,869	14,268	5,239	1,525	3,714	24,510	16,515	7,995
Unspecified ..	2	..	2	..	..	..	..	..	..	..	..	..
F—Christian .. Total ..	**80,728**	**51,466**	**29,262**	**41,200**	**28,324**	**12,876**	**39,251**	**22,903**	**16,348**	**34,272**	**23,183**	**11,089**
0—5 ..	6,774	3,495	3,279	..	..	..	6,774	3,495	3,279	..	..	..
5—10 ..	6,069	3,269	2,800	2,241	1,219	1,022	3,828	2,050	1,778	1,881	1,041	840
10—15 ..	6,107	3,354	2,753	2,904	1,681	1,223	3,203	1,673	1,530	2,555	1,432	1,123
15—20 ..	8,746	5,347	3,399	5,050	3,204	1,846	3,696	2,143	1,553	4,230	2,642	1,588
20 and over ..	52,755	35,762	16,993	31,005	22,220	8,785	21,750	13,542	8,208	25,606	18,068	7,538
Unspecified ..	277	239	38	..	..	..	..	..	..	..	..	..
G—Jew .. Total ..	**8,621**	**4,604**	**4,017**	**3,929**	**2,409**	**1,520**	**4,692**	**2,195**	**2,497**	**2,723**	**1,799**	**924**
0—5 ..	1,087	558	529	..	..	..	1,087	558	529	..	..	..
5—10 ..	1,040	521	510	315	166	149	725	355	370	179	104	75
10—15 ..	1,021	530	491	452	238	214	569	292	277	292	165	127
15—20 ..	924	496	428	499	297	202	425	199	226	374	234	140
20 and over ..	4,549	2,499	2,050	2,663	1,708	955	1,886	791	1,095	1,878	1,296	582
H—Other Religions . Total ..	**2,738**	**2,212**	**526**	**1,298**	**1,148**	**150**	**1,440**	**1,064**	**376**	**632**	**555**	**77**
0—5 ..	191	107	84	..	..	..	191	107	84	..	..	..
5—10 ..	101	51	50	12	7	5	89	44	45	6	2	4
10—15 ..	74	34	40	26	15	11	48	19	29	10	6	4
15—20 ..	227	166	61	102	85	17	125	81	44	40	33	7
20 and over ..	2,145	1,854	291	1,158	1,041	117	987	813	174	576	514	62

CITY TABLE V—PART II—BOMBAY.

Literacy by Religion and Age.

(Corresponding to Imperial Table XIII.)

District and age.	POPULATION.									Literate in English.		
	Total.			Literate.			Illiterate.					
	Persons.	Males.	Females.	Persons.	Males.	Females.	Persons.	Males.	Females.	Persons.	Males.	Females.
1	2	3	4	5	6	7	8	9	10	11	12	13
1. Upper Colaba—												
Hindu .. Total ..	**292**	**193**	**99**	**39**	**37**	**2**	**253**	**156**	**97**	**22**	**20**	**2**
0—5	23	11	12	..	..	..	23	11	12	..	..	..
5—10	10	6	4	..	..	..	10	6	4	..	..	..
10—15	16	11	5	1	1	..	15	10	5	1	1	..
15—20 ..	45	27	18	6	5	1	39	22	17	5	4	1
20 and over ..	198	138	60	32	31	1	166	107	59	16	15	1
Muslim .. Total ..	**47**	**38**	**9**	**12**	**12**	..	**35**	**26**	**9**	**2**	**2**	..
0—5 ..	2	1	1	..	..	..	2	1	1	..	..	..
5—10 ..	3	1	2	..	..	..	3	1	2	..	..	..
10—15 ..	5	4	1	..	..	..	5	4	1	..	..	..
15—20 ..	5	5	..	1	1	..	4	4	..	..	..	..
20 and over ..	32	27	5	11	11	..	21	16	5	2	2	..
2. Lower Colaba—												
Hindu .. Total ..	**11,075**	**7,795**	**3,280**	**1,529**	**1,452**	**77**	**9,546**	**6,343**	**3,203**	**352**	**339**	**13**
0—5 ..	746	378	368	..	..	..	746	378	368	..	..	..
5—10 ..	677	395	282	38	33	5	639	362	277	2	2	..
10—15 ..	675	431	244	75	70	5	600	361	239	17	16	1
15—20 ..	1,200	855	345	187	176	11	1,013	679	334	65	64	1
20 and over ..	7,777	5,736	2,041	1,229	1,173	56	6,548	4,563	1,985	268	257	11
Muslim .. Total ..	**1,733**	**1,381**	**352**	**413**	**363**	**50**	**1,820**	**1,018**	**302**	**171**	**141**	**30**
0—5 ..	89	49	40	..	..	..	89	49	40	..	..	..
5—10 ..	82	47	35	13	8	5	69	39	30	7	4	3
10—15 ..	90	57	33	21	16	5	69	41	28	11	11	..
15—20 ..	189	144	45	49	43	6	140	101	39	25	20	5
20 and over ..	1,283	1,084	199	330	296	34	953	788	165	128	106	22
3. Fort South—												
Hindu .. Total ..	**1,690**	**1,517**	**173**	**277**	**268**	**9**	**1,413**	**1,249**	**164**	**88**	**83**	**5**
0—5 ..	35	17	18	..	..	..	35	17	18	..	..	..
5—10 ..	34	26	8	5	5	..	29	21	8	2	2	..
10—15 ..	60	53	7	11	10	1	49	43	6	3	3	..
15—20 ..	258	235	23	42	40	2	216	195	21	9	7	2
20 and over ..	1,303	1,186	117	219	213	6	1,084	973	111	74	71	3
Muslim .. Total ..	**446**	**423**	**23**	**107**	**106**	**1**	**339**	**317**	**22**	**53**	**53**	..
0—5 ..	5	3	2	..	..	..	5	3	2	..	..	..
5—10 ..	10	7	3	1	1	..	9	6	3	1	1	..
10—15 ..	21	16	5	3	3	..	18	13	5	2	2	..
15—20 ..	56	53	3	10	9	1	46	44	2	6	6	..
20 and over ..	354	344	10	93	93	..	261	251	10	44	44	..
4. Fort North—												
Hindu .. Total ..	**14,011**	**9,306**	**4,705**	**3,796**	**3,360**	**436**	**10,215**	**5,946**	**4,269**	**1,385**	**1,317**	**68**
0—5 ..	1,277	697	580	..	..	..	1,277	697	580	..	..	..
5—10 ..	979	583	396	119	98	21	860	485	375	13	10	3
10—15 ..	965	621	344	203	167	36	762	454	308	35	30	5
15—20 ..	1,508	898	610	393	306	87	1,115	592	523	134	118	16
20 and over ..	9,282	6,507	2,775	3,081	2,789	292	6,201	3,718	2,483	1,203	1,159	44
Muslim .. Total ..	**2,918**	**2,327**	**591**	**860**	**770**	**90**	**2,058**	**1,557**	**501**	**219**	**214**	**5**
0—5 ..	138	76	62	..	..	..	138	76	62	..	..	..
5—10 ..	132	78	54	20	13	7	112	65	47	3	3	..
10—15 ..	159	109	50	33	23	10	126	86	40	7	7	..
15—20 ..	304	238	66	75	62	13	229	176	53	20	20	..
20 and over ..	2,185	1,826	359	732	672	60	1,453	1,154	299	189	184	5
5. Esplanade—												
Hindu .. Total ..	**7,849**	**5,322**	**2,527**	**1,534**	**1,372**	**162**	**6,315**	**3,950**	**2,365**	**500**	**426**	**74**
0—5 ..	708	356	352	..	..	..	708	356	352	..	..	..
5—10 ..	504	288	216	62	44	18	442	244	198	7	6	1
10—15 ..	477	282	195	91	69	22	386	213	178	20	15	5
15—20 ..	834	500	334	190	166	24	644	334	310	111	100	11
20 and over ..	5,326	3,896	1,430	1,191	1,093	98	4,135	2,803	1,332	332	305	57

District and age.	POPULATION.									Literate in English.		
	Total.			Literate.			Illiterate.					
	Persons.	Males.	Females.	Persons.	Males.	Females.	Persons.	Males.	Females.	Persons.	Males.	Females.
1	2	3	4	5	6	7	8	9	10	11	12	13
5. Esplanade—*contd.*												
Muslim .. Total ..	**3,325**	**2,580**	**745**	**767**	**692**	**75**	**2,558**	**1,888**	**670**	**233**	**230**	**3**
0—5 ..	146	77	69	..	..	..	146	77	69	..	..	..
5—10 ..	175	97	78	21	13	8	154	84	70	1	1	..
10—15 ..	189	126	63	52	41	11	137	85	52	20	20	..
15—20 ..	314	253	61	108	99	9	206	154	52	54	53	1
20 and over ..	2,501	2,027	474	586	539	47	1,915	1,488	427	158	156	2
6. Chakla—												
Hindu .. Total ..	**5,786**	**3,984**	**1,802**	**1,338**	**1,139**	**199**	**4,448**	**2,845**	**1,603**	**371**	**350**	**21**
0—5 ..	460	246	214	..	..	..	460	246	214	..	..	..
5—10 ..	555	327	228	38	23	15	517	304	213	3	2	1
10—15 ..	494	300	194	55	36	19	439	264	175	7	4	3
15—20 ..	602	388	214	127	92	35	475	296	179	30	25	5
20 and over ..	3,675	2,723	952	1,118	988	130	2,557	1,735	822	331	319	12
Muslim .. Total ..	**12,012**	**7,917**	**4,095**	**3,142**	**2,553**	**589**	**8,870**	**5,364**	**3,506**	**1,164**	**1,005**	**159**
0—5 ..	990	504	486	..	..	..	990	504	486	..	..	..
5—10 ..	1,164	668	496	139	90	49	1,025	578	447	32	23	9
10—15 ..	1,210	725	485	237	159	78	973	566	407	49	48	1
15—20 ..	1,342	879	463	374	285	89	968	594	374	164	114	50
20 and over ..	7,306	5,141	2,165	2,392	2,019	373	4,914	3,122	1,792	919	820	99
7. Mandvi—												
Hindu .. Total ..	**32,663**	**20,854**	**11,809**	**7,280**	**5,908**	**1,372**	**25,383**	**14,946**	**10,437**	**1,805**	**1,650**	**155**
0—5 ..	2,829	1,544	1,285	..	..	..	2,829	1,544	1,285	..	..	..
5—10 ..	2,923	1,770	1,153	170	103	67	2,753	1,667	1,086	17	11	6
10—15 ..	2,646	1,579	1,067	390	244	146	2,256	1,335	921	63	44	19
15—20 ..	2,911	1,708	1,203	806	564	242	2,105	1,144	961	200	170	30
20 and over ..	21,354	14,253	7,101	5,914	4,997	917	15,440	9,256	6,184	1,525	1,425	100
Muslim .. Total ..	**8,374**	**5,757**	**2,617**	**1,807**	**1,532**	**275**	**6,567**	**4,225**	**2,342**	**490**	**474**	**16**
0—5 ..	626	337	289	..	..	..	626	337	289	..	..	..
5—10 ..	683	390	293	55	33	22	628	357	271	7	6	1
10—15 ..	703	405	298	102	63	39	601	342	259	16	16	..
15—20 ..	808	556	252	172	120	52	636	436	200	57	50	7
20 and over ..	5,554	4,069	1,485	1,478	1,316	162	4,076	2,753	1,323	410	402	8
8. Umerkhadi—												
Hindu .. Total ..	**10,397**	**6,163**	**4,234**	**1,113**	**1,047**	**66**	**9,284**	**5,116**	**4,168**	**183**	**179**	**4**
0—5 ..	1,089	534	555	..	..	..	1,089	534	555	..	..	..
5—10 ..	883	504	379	19	17	2	864	487	377	..	..	..
10—15 ..	697	423	274	36	32	4	661	391	270	2	2	..
15—20 ..	967	499	468	96	90	6	871	409	462	18	18	..
20 and over ..	6,761	4,203	2,558	962	908	54	5,799	3,295	2,504	163	159	4
Muslim .. Total ..	**28,793**	**17,990**	**10,803**	**5,505**	**4,739**	**766**	**23,288**	**13,243**	**10,037**	**2,101**	**1,968**	**133**
0—5 ..	2,585	1,353	1,232	..	..	..	2,585	1,353	1,232	..	..	..
5—10 ..	2,728	1,518	1,210	221	162	59	2,507	1,356	1,151	28	23	5
10—15 ..	2,600	1,464	1,136	390	288	102	2,210	1,176	1,034	85	84	1
15—20 ..	2,676	1,559	1,117	599	443	156	2,077	1,116	961	200	176	24
20 and over ..	18,196	12,088	6,108	4,295	3,846	449	13,901	8,242	5,659	1,788	1,685	103
Unspecified ..	8	8	..	..	..	..	..	..	..	..	..	..
9. Dongri—												
Hindu .. Total ..	**8,925**	**5,265**	**3,660**	**1,490**	**1,363**	**127**	**7,435**	**3,902**	**3,533**	**261**	**248**	**13**
0—5 ..	974	479	495	..	..	..	974	479	495	..	..	..
5—10 ..	774	400	374	60	44	16	714	356	358	7	5	2
10—15 ..	674	372	302	85	65	20	589	307	282	10	8	2
15—20 ..	855	454	401	143	122	21	712	332	380	25	22	3
20 and over ..	5,648	3,560	2,088	1,202	1,132	70	4,446	2,428	2,018	219	213	6
Muslim .. Total ..	**2,973**	**2,117**	**856**	**993**	**743**	**250**	**1,980**	**1,374**	**606**	**291**	**271**	**20**
0—5 ..	228	109	119	..	..	..	228	109	119	..	..	..
5—10 ..	225	124	101	88	34	54	137	90	47	15	5	10
10—15 ..	238	142	96	105	50	55	133	92	41	9	9	..
15—20 ..	366	267	99	105	87	18	261	180	81	31	29	2
20 and over ..	1,916	1,475	441	695	572	123	1,221	903	318	236	228	8

District and age.	POPULATION.									LITERATE IN ENGLISH.		
	TOTAL.			LITERATE.			ILLITERATE.					
	Persons.	Males.	Females.	Persons.	Males.	Females.	Persons.	Males.	Females.	Persons.	Males.	Females.
1	2	3	4	5	6	7	8	9	10	11	12	13
10. Market—												
Hindu .. Total	**30,487**	**21,118**	**9,369**	**8,978**	**7,890**	**1,088**	**21,509**	**13,228**	**8,281**	**2,489**	**2,378**	**111**
0—5	2,480	1,308	1,122	..	..	..	2,430	1,308	1,122	..	..	..
5—10	2,499	1,570	929	195	134	61	2,304	1,436	868	26	20	6
10—15	2,230	1,477	753	315	239	76	1,915	1,238	677	67	55	12
15—20	2,695	1,676	1,019	632	495	137	2,063	1,181	882	194	174	20
20 and over	20,633	15,087	5,546	7,836	7,022	814	12,797	8,065	4,732	2,202	2,129	73
Muslim .. Total	**3,573**	**2,480**	**1,093**	**892**	**814**	**78**	**2,681**	**1,666**	**1,015**	**174**	**173**	**1**
0—5	298	161	137	..	..	..	298	161	137	..	..	..
5—10	358	227	131	30	25	5	328	202	126	4	4	..
10—15	369	250	119	51	41	10	318	209	109	7	7	..
15—20	391	264	127	83	72	11	308	192	116	16	15	1
20 and over	2,157	1,578	579	728	676	52	1,429	902	527	147	147	..
11. Dhobi Talao—												
Hindu .. Total	**26,042**	**15,634**	**10,408**	**5,232**	**4,392**	**840**	**20,810**	**11,242**	**9,568**	**1,936**	**1,770**	**166**
0—5	2,386	1,270	1,116	..	..	..	2,386	1,270	1,116	..	..	..
5—10	2,635	1,483	1,152	225	148	77	2,410	1,335	1,075	40	29	11
10—15	2,387	1,396	991	311	213	98	2,076	1,183	893	78	61	17
15—20	2,570	1,381	1,189	470	358	112	2,100	1,023	1,077	201	175	26
20 and over	16,064	10,104	5,960	4,226	3,673	553	11,838	6,431	5,407	1,617	1,505	112
Muslim .. Total	**1,210**	**817**	**393**	**207**	**192**	**15**	**1,003**	**625**	**378**	**55**	**54**	**1**
0—5	105	60	45	..	..	..	105	60	45	..	..	..
5—10	88	54	34	3	2	1	85	52	33	..	..	..
10—15	87	52	35	7	5	2	80	47	33	..	..	..
15—20	129	80	49	24	23	1	105	57	48	5	5	..
20 and over	801	571	230	173	162	11	628	409	219	50	49	1
13. Fanaswadi—												
Hindu .. Total	**28,086**	**17,089**	**10,997**	**7,015**	**5,310**	**1,705**	**21,071**	**11,779**	**9,292**	**3,546**	**3,141**	**405**
0—5	2,604	1,327	1,277	..	..	..	2,604	1,327	1,277	..	..	..
5—10	2,707	1,511	1,196	317	200	117	2,390	1,311	1,079	49	37	12
10—15	2,536	1,474	1,062	480	306	174	2,056	1,168	888	139	106	33
15—20	2,844	1,475	1,369	777	516	261	2,067	959	1,108	384	320	64
20 and over	17,395	11,302	6,093	5,441	4,288	1,153	11,954	7,014	4,940	2,974	2,678	296
Muslim .. Total	**433**	**275**	**158**	**27**	**22**	**5**	**406**	**253**	**153**	**13**	**11**	**2**
0—5	44	27	17	..	..	..	44	27	17	..	..	..
5—10	32	16	16	..	..	..	32	16	16	..	..	..
10—15	32	16	16	..	..	..	32	16	16	..	..	..
15—20	38	23	15	1	..	1	37	23	14	..	..	..
20 and over	287	193	94	26	22	4	261	171	90	13	11	2
13. Bhuleshwar—												
Hindu .. Total	**21,304**	**13,965**	**7,339**	**7,431**	**6,478**	**953**	**13,873**	**7;487**	**6,386**	**1,714**	**1,657**	**57**
0—5	1,861	898	963	..	..	..	1,861	898	963	..	..	..
5—10	2,140	1,198	942	215	149	66	1,925	1,049	876	16	13	3
10—15	1,924	1,191	733	350	254	96	1,574	937	637	44	36	8
15—20	1,880	1,248	632	560	431	129	1,320	817	503	102	93	9
20 and over	13,499	9,430	4,069	6,306	5,644	662	7,193	3,786	3,407	1,552	1,515	37
Muslim .. Total	**11,985**	**8,034**	**3,951**	**3,512**	**3,076**	**436**	**8,473**	**4,958**	**3,515**	**407**	**398**	**9**
0—5	1,007	544	463	..	..	..	1,007	544	463	..	..	..
5—10	1,112	628	484	139	102	37	973	526	447	10	10	..
10—15	1,086	638	448	228	175	53	858	463	395	26	26	..
15—20	1,194	741	453	385	311	74	809	430	379	61	58	3
20 and over	7,586	5,483	2,103	2,760	2,488	272	4,826	2,995	1,831	310	304	6
14. Kumbharwada—												
Hindu .. Total	**29,730**	**18,134**	**11,596**	**5,169**	**4,465**	**704**	**24,561**	**13,669**	**10,892**	**1,359**	**1,261**	**98**
0—5	3,319	1,607	1,712	..	..	..	3,319	1,607	1,712	..	..	..
5—10	2,980	1,736	1,244	176	124	52	2,804	1,612	1;192	14	12	2
10—15	2,355	1,442	913	283	204	79	2,072	1,238	834	41	33	8
15—20	2,364	1,629	735	530	398	132	1,834	1,231	603	137	117	20
20 and over	18,712	11,720	6,992	4,180	3,739	441	14,532	7,981	6,551	1,167	1,099	68
Muslim .. Total	**1,874**	**1,385**	**489**	**387**	**347**	**40**	**1,487**	**1,038**	**449**	**85**	**81**	**4**
0—5	142	72	70	..	..	..	142	72	70	..	..	..
5—10	141	91	50	10	9	1	131	82	49	..	..	..
10—15	139	97	42	19	16	3	120	81	39	2	2	..
15—20	223	159	64	33	28	5	190	131	59	7	7	..
20 and over	1,229	966	263	325	294	31	904	672	232	76	72	4

District and age.	POPULATION. Total. Persons.	Total. Males.	Total. Females.	Literate. Persons.	Literate. Males.	Literate. Females.	Illiterate. Persons.	Illiterate. Males.	Illiterate. Females.	Literate in English. Persons.	Literate in English. Males.	Literate in English. Females.
1	2	3	4	5	6	7	8	9	10	11	12	13
15. Khara Talao—												
Hindu .. Total	**5,300**	**3,495**	**1,805**	**1,169**	**1,113**	**56**	**4,131**	**2,382**	**1,749**	**102**	**100**	**2**
0—5	479	277	202	..	..	..	479	277	202	..	..	..
5—10	417	264	153	32	23	9	385	241	144	1	1	..
10—15	397	238	159	50	40	10	347	198	149	2	2	..
15—20	623	355	268	126	118	8	497	237	260	6	6	..
20 and over	3,384	2,361	1,023	961	932	29	2,423	1,429	994	93	91	2
Muslim .. Total	**17,805**	**11,384**	**6,421**	**4,713**	**4,410**	**303**	**13,092**	**6,974**	**6,118**	**645**	**617**	**28**
0—5	1,681	869	812	..	..	..	1,681	869	812	..	..	..
5—10	1,777	1,014	763	173	146	27	1,604	868	736	8	5	3
10—15	1,657	988	669	258	216	42	1,399	772	627	18	18	..
15—20	1,613	1,001	612	406	355	51	1,207	646	561	27	23	4
20 and over	11,077	7,512	3,565	3,876	3,693	183	7,201	3,819	3,382	592	571	21
16. Khetwadi—												
Hindu .. Total	**27,101**	**17,108**	**9,993**	**10,860**	**8,033**	**2,827**	**16,241**	**9,075**	**7,166**	**5,315**	**4,703**	**612**
0—5	2,424	1,290	1,134	..	..	..	2,424	1,290	1,134	..	..	..
5—10	2,303	1,291	1,012	507	292	215	1,796	999	797	94	66	28
10—15	2,254	1,321	933	778	481	297	1,476	840	636	237	173	64
15—20	3,068	1,805	1,263	1,284	829	455	1,784	976	808	617	474	143
20 and over	17,052	11,401	5,651	8,291	6,431	1,860	8,761	4,970	3,791	4,367	3,990	377
Muslim .. Total	**3,571**	**2,614**	**957**	**787**	**696**	**91**	**2,784**	**1,918**	**866**	**150**	**147**	**3**
0—5	248	125	123	..	..	..	248	125	123	..	..	..
5—10	249	168	81	29	27	2	220	141	79	1	1	..
10—15	241	179	62	56	51	5	185	128	57	12	12	..
15—20	322	237	85	72	63	9	250	174	76	21	20	1
20 and over	2,511	1,905	606	630	555	75	1,881	1,350	531	116	114	2
17. Girgaum—												
Hindu .. Total	**36,603**	**22,862**	**13,741**	**15,971**	**12,273**	**3,698**	**20,632**	**10,589**	**10,043**	**8,167**	**7,660**	**507**
0—5	3,662	1,927	1,735	..	..	..	3,662	1,927	1,735	..	..	..
5—10	3,445	2,037	1,408	747	501	246	2,698	1,536	1,162	84	67	17
10—15	3,278	1,939	1,339	1,240	818	422	2,038	1,121	917	293	229	64
15—20	4,284	2,464	1,820	1,943	1,352	591	2,341	1,112	1,229	804	693	111
20 and over	21,934	14,495	7,439	12,041	9,602	2,439	9,893	4,893	5,000	6,986	6,671	315
Muslim .. Total	**335**	**276**	**59**	**75**	**73**	**2**	**260**	**203**	**57**	**11**	**11**	..
0—5	14	7	7	..	..	..	14	7	7	..	..	..
5—10	15	10	5	..	..	..	15	10	5	..	..	..
10—15	12	9	3	1	1	..	11	8	3	..	..	..
15—20	25	21	4	9	9	..	16	12	4	2	2	..
20 and over	269	229	40	65	63	2	204	166	38	9	9	..
18. Chaupati—												
Hindu .. Total	**13,645**	**8,524**	**5,121**	**6,628**	**4,591**	**2,037**	**7,017**	**3,933**	**3,084**	**4,136**	**3,460**	**676**
0—5	1,341	695	646	..	..	..	1,341	695	646	..	..	..
5—10	1,166	659	507	371	207	164	795	452	343	99	64	35
10—15	1,167	673	494	570	323	247	597	350	247	243	158	85
15—20	1,611	978	633	916	575	341	695	403	292	584	439	145
20 and over	8,360	5,519	2,841	4,771	3,486	1,285	3,589	2,033	1,556	3,210	2,799	411
Muslim .. Total	**487**	**383**	**104**	**196**	**148**	**48**	**291**	**235**	**56**	**91**	**77**	**14**
0—5	21	13	8	..	..	..	21	13	8	..	..	..
5—10	34	18	16	12	7	5	22	11	11	3	2	1
10—15	41	27	14	17	11	6	24	16	8	5	5	..
15—20	56	43	13	27	19	8	29	24	5	15	12	3
20 and over	335	282	53	140	111	29	195	171	24	68	58	10
19. Walkeshwar—												
Hindu .. Total	**13,777**	**9,340**	**4,437**	**4,375**	**3,359**	**1,016**	**9,402**	**5,981**	**3,421**	**2,037**	**1,553**	**484**
0—5	1,203	573	630	..	..	..	1,203	573	630	..	..	..
5—10	1,175	686	489	222	166	56	953	520	433	75	47	28
10—15	1,095	696	399	365	250	115	730	446	284	149	96	53
15—20	1,467	960	507	590	434	156	877	526	351	333	239	94
20 and over	8,837	6,425	2,412	3,198	2,509	689	5,639	3,916	1,723	1,480	1,171	309
Muslim .. Total	**2,128**	**1,378**	**750**	**982**	**652**	**330**	**1,146**	**726**	**420**	**482**	**366**	**116**
0—5	203	107	96	..	..	..	203	107	96	..	..	..
5—10	198	107	91	78	44	34	120	63	57	42	22	20
10—15	204	111	93	108	56	52	96	55	41	36	34	2
15—20	257	169	88	132	83	49	125	86	39	78	49	29
20 and over	1,266	884	382	664	469	195	602	415	187	326	261	65

District and age.	POPULATION.									LITERATE IN ENGLISH.		
	TOTAL.			LITERATE.			ILLITERATE.					
	Persons.	Males.	Females.	Persons.	Males.	Females.	Persons.	Males.	Females.	Persons.	Males.	Females.
1	2	3	4	5	6	7	8	9	10	11	12	13
20. Mahalaxmi—												
Hindu .. Total ..	**23,450**	**15,465**	**7,985**	**5,387**	**4,455**	**912**	**18,083**	**11,010**	**7,073**	**1,870**	**1,622**	**248**
0—5 ..	2,089	1,115	974	..	..	..	2,089	1,115	974	..	..	..
5—10 ..	1,828	1,103	725	207	134	73	1,621	969	652	34	24	10
10—15 ..	1,641	1,032	609	321	210	111	1,320	822	498	81	55	26
15—20 ..	2,485	1,437	1,048	585	436	149	1,900	1,001	899	218	162	56
20 and over ..	15,407	10,778	4,629	4,254	3,675	579	11,153	7,103	4,050	1,537	1,381	156
Muslim .. Total ..	**1,789**	**1,227**	**562**	**589**	**455**	**134**	**1,200**	**772**	**428**	**215**	**153**	**62**
0—5 ..	161	70	91	..	..	..	161	70	91	..	..	..
5—10 ..	112	64	48	36	21	15	76	43	33	14	7	7
10—15 ..	114	70	44	42	25	17	72	45	27	8	8	..
15—20 ..	188	117	71	62	41	21	126	76	50	37	14	23
20 and over ..	1,214	906	308	449	368	81	765	538	227	156	124	32
21. Tardeo—												
Hindu .. Total ..	**17,761**	**10,719**	**7,042**	**2,209**	**1,921**	**288**	**15,552**	**8,798**	**6,754**	**914**	**817**	**97**
0—5 ..	1,670	894	776	..	..	..	1,670	894	776	..	..	..
5—10 ..	1,363	750	613	71	50	21	1,292	700	592	16	8	8
10—15 ..	1,235	670	565	106	76	30	1,129	594	535	30	19	11
15—20 ..	1,732	867	865	233	178	55	1,499	689	810	99	79	20
20 and over ..	11,761	7,538	4,223	1,799	1,617	182	9,962	5,921	4,041	769	711	58
Muslim .. Total ..	**6,077**	**4,148**	**1,929**	**1,003**	**904**	**99**	**5,074**	**3,244**	**1,830**	**142**	**121**	**21**
0—5 ..	494	273	221	..	..	..	494	273	221	..	..	..
5—10 ..	442	264	178	31	27	7	408	237	171	5	4	1
10—15 ..	405	261	144	47	40	7	358	221	137	5	5	..
15—20 ..	544	346	198	80	64	16	464	282	182	17	12	5
20 and over ..	4,192	3,004	1,188	842	773	69	3,350	2,231	1,119	115	100	15
22. Kamathipura—												
Hindu .. Total ..	**26,968**	**15,679**	**11,289**	**1,915**	**1,775**	**140**	**25,053**	**13,904**	**11,149**	**347**	**340**	**7**
0—5 ..	2,340	1,240	1,100	..	..	..	2,340	1,240	1,100	..	..	..
5—10 ..	2,082	1,175	907	96	80	16	1,986	1,095	891	5	5	..
10—15 ..	1,855	1,084	771	136	115	21	1,719	969	750	16	15	1
15—20 ..	2,492	1,358	1,134	204	185	19	2,288	1,173	1,115	47	46	1
20 and over ..	18,199	10,822	7,377	1,479	1,395	84	16,720	9,427	7,293	279	274	5
Muslim .. Total ..	**9,022**	**6,698**	**2,324**	**876**	**821**	**55**	**8,146**	**5,877**	**2,269**	**133**	**127**	**6**
0—5 ..	487	267	220	..	..	..	487	267	220	..	..	..
5—10 ..	491	292	199	48	37	11	443	255	188	7	7	..
10—15 ..	471	317	154	62	58	4	409	259	150	8	8	..
15—20 ..	717	531	186	58	54	4	659	477	182	2	2	..
20 and over ..	6,856	5,291	1,565	708	672	36	6,148	4,619	1,529	116	110	6
23. First Nagpada—												
Hindu .. Total ..	**3,071**	**2,122**	**949**	**1,056**	**914**	**142**	**2,015**	**1,208**	**807**	**474**	**455**	**19**
0—5 ..	225	118	107	..	..	..	225	118	107	..	..	..
5—10 ..	178	99	79	32	22	10	146	77	69	6	6	..
10—15 ..	174	107	67	44	31	13	130	76	54	13	12	1
15—20 ..	324	203	121	124	99	25	200	104	96	56	54	2
20 and over ..	2,170	1,595	575	856	762	94	1,314	833	481	399	383	16
Muslim .. Total ..	**1,780**	**1,214**	**566**	**561**	**482**	**79**	**1,219**	**732**	**487**	**216**	**200**	**16**
0—5 ..	94	50	44	..	..	..	94	50	44	..	..	..
5—10 ..	85	75	10	28	18	10	57	57	..	8	5	3
10—15 ..	151	86	65	31	21	10	120	65	55	5	5	..
15—20 ..	185	117	68	48	41	7	137	76	61	20	17	3
20 and over ..	1,265	886	379	454	402	52	811	484	327	183	173	10
24. Second Nagpada—												
Hindu .. Total ..	**5,429**	**3,532**	**1,897**	**250**	**227**	**23**	**5,179**	**3,305**	**1,874**	**25**	**23**	**2**
0—5 ..	473	229	244	..	..	..	473	229	244	...	..	..
5—10 ..	401	216	185	13	11	2	388	205	183	..	..	..
10—15 ..	369	200	169	15	14	1	354	186	168	1	1	..
15—20 ..	549	332	217	30	24	6	519	308	211	3	3	..
20 and over ..	3,637	2,555	1,082	192	178	14	3,445	2,377	1,068	21	19	2
Muslim .. Total ..	**14,570**	**9,218**	**5,352**	**1,396**	**1,262**	**134**	**13,174**	**7,956**	**5,218**	**430**	**418**	**12**
0—5 ..	1,282	625	657	..	..	..	1,282	625	657	..	..	..
5—10 ..	1,269	677	592	41	26	15	1,228	651	577	8	6	2
10—15 ..	1,184	655	529	67	45	22	1,117	610	507	13	13	..
15—20 ..	1,496	884	612	157	128	29	1,339	756	583	53	47	6
20 and over ..	9,339	6,377	2,962	1,131	1,063	68	8,208	5,314	2,894	356	352	4

District and age.	POPULATION.									LITERATE IN ENGLISH.		
	TOTAL.			LITERATE.			ILLITERATE.					
	Persons.	Males.	Females.	Persons.	Males.	Females.	Persons.	Males.	Females.	Persons.	Males.	Females.
1	2	3	4	5	6	7	8	9	10	11	12	13
25. Byculla—												
Hindu .. Total ..	**52,813**	**33,587**	**19,226**	**5,265**	**4,831**	**434**	**47,548**	**28,756**	**18,792**	**956**	**885**	**71**
0—5 ..	5,360	2,698	2,662	..	..	..	5,360	2,698	2,662	..	..	..
5—10 ..	4,342	2,495	1,847	178	138	40	4,164	2,357	1,807	6	4	2
10—15 ..	3,436	2,059	1,377	289	232	57	3,147	1,827	1,320	26	20	6
15—20 ..	4,888	2,586	2,302	609	516	93	4,279	2,070	2,209	123	102	21
20 and over ..	34,787	23,749	11,038	4,189	3,945	244	30,598	19,804	10,794	801	759	42
Muslim .. Total ..	**27,073**	**18,741**	**8,332**	**3,749**	**3,318**	**431**	**23,324**	**15,423**	**7,901**	**725**	**654**	**71**
0—5 ..	2,216	1,122	1,094	..	..	..	2,216	1,122	1,094	..	..	..
5—10 ..	2,087	1,191	896	162	120	42	1,925	1,071	854	40	28	12
10—15 ..	1,782	1,075	707	217	165	52	1,565	910	655	40	38	2
15—20 ..	2,282	1,375	907	318	251	67	1,964	1,124	840	85	64	21
20 and over ..	18,706	13,978	4,728	3,052	2,782	270	15,654	11,196	4,458	560	524	36
26. Tarwadi—												
Hindu .. Total ..	**27,356**	**16,918**	**10,438**	**1,269**	**1,070**	**199**	**26,087**	**15,848**	**10,239**	**410**	**349**	**61**
0—5 ..	2,649	1,438	1,211	..	..	..	2,649	1,438	1,211	..	..	..
5—10 ..	1,936	1,157	779	44	32	12	1,892	1,125	767	7	5	2
10—15 ..	1,661	997	664	69	51	18	1,592	946	646	12	9	3
15—20 ..	2,725	1,252	1,473	136	97	39	2,589	1,155	1,434	46	34	12
20 and over ..	18,385	12,074	6,311	1,020	890	130	17,365	11,184	6,181	345	301	44
Muslim .. Total ..	**4,727**	**3,108**	**1,619**	**703**	**514**	**189**	**4,024**	**2,594**	**1,430**	**217**	**202**	**15**
0—5 ..	377	199	178	..	..	..	377	199	178	..	..	..
5—10 ..	321	189	132	32	15	17	289	174	115	..	..	..
10—15 ..	311	183	128	57	36	21	254	147	107	4	..	4
15—20 ..	440	263	177	78	51	27	362	212	150	18	17	1
20 and over ..	3,278	2,274	1,004	536	412	124	2,742	1,862	880	106	164	2
27. Mazagaon—												
Hindu .. Total ..	**29,153**	**18,750**	**10,403**	**1,628**	**1,456**	**172**	**27,525**	**17,294**	**10,231**	**351**	**313**	**38**
0—5 ..	3,278	1,785	1,493	..	..	..	3,278	1,785	1,493	..	..	..
5—10 ..	2,642	1,621	1,021	55	37	18	2,587	1,584	1,003	9	7	2
10—15 ..	2,094	1,279	815	76	55	21	2,018	1,224	794	15	12	3
15—20 ..	2,628	1,499	1,129	166	143	23	2,462	1,356	1,106	37	31	6
20 and over ..	18,511	12,566	5,945	1,331	1,221	110	17,180	11,345	5,835	290	263	27
Muslim .. Total ..	**6,357**	**4,381**	**1,976**	**444**	**385**	**59**	**5,913**	**3,996**	**1,917**	**128**	**111**	**17**
0—5 ..	603	299	304	..	..	..	603	299	304	..	..	..
5—10 ..	489	291	198	16	10	6	473	281	192	5	2	3
10—15 ..	420	257	163	31	23	8	389	234	155	11	10	1
15—20 ..	564	368	196	49	36	13	515	332	183	22	16	6
20 and over ..	4,281	3,166	1,115	348	316	32	3,933	2,850	1,083	90	83	7
28. Parel—												
Hindu .. Total ..	**52,671**	**33,579**	**19,092**	**8,666**	**8,165**	**501**	**44,005**	**25,414**	**18,591**	**3,073**	**2,839**	**234**
0—5 ..	4,643	2,366	2,277	..	..	..	4,643	2,366	2,277	..	..	..
5—10 ..	3,674	2,064	1,610	178	145	33	3,498	1,910	1,577	37	25	12
10—15 ..	3,172	1,840	1,332	309	258	51	2,863	1,582	1,281	86	63	23
15—20 ..	5,791	3,063	2,728	915	815	100	4,876	2,248	2,628	365	311	54
20 and over ..	35,391	24,246	11,145	7,264	6,947	317	28,127	17,299	10,828	2,585	2,440	145
Muslim .. Total ..	**3,679**	**2,602**	**1,077**	**705**	**662**	**43**	**2,974**	**1,940**	**1,034**	**156**	**148**	**8**
0—5 ..	239	121	118	..	..	..	239	121	118	..	..	..
5—10 ..	269	166	103	17	15	2	252	151	101	3	3	..
10—15 ..	246	160	86	29	24	5	217	136	81	4	4	..
15—20 ..	354	224	130	74	63	11	280	161	119	23	20	3
20 and over ..	2,571	1,931	640	585	560	25	1,986	1,371	615	126	121	5
29. Sewri—												
Hindu .. Total ..	**23,054**	**14,909**	**8,145**	**954**	**913**	**41**	**22,100**	**13,996**	**8,104**	**201**	**197**	**4**
0—5 ..	2,418	1,270	1,148	..	..	..	2,418	1,270	1,148	..	..	..
5—10 ..	1,782	1,081	701	34	28	6	1,748	1,053	695	4	4	..
10—15 ..	1,375	884	491	56	49	7	1,319	835	484	8	8	..
15—20 ..	2,140	1,211	929	82	74	8	2,058	1,137	921	21	20	1
20 and over ..	15,339	10,463	4,876	782	762	20	14,557	9,701	4,856	168	165	3

District and age.	POPULATION.									LITERATE IN ENGLISH.		
	TOTAL.			LITERATE.			ILLITERATE.					
	Persons.	Males.	Females.	Persons.	Males.	Females.	Persons.	Males.	Females.	Persons.	Males.	Females.
1	2	3	4	5	6	7	8	9	10	11	12	13
29. Sewri—contd.												
Muslim .. Total	**2,638**	**1,827**	**811**	**208**	**199**	**9**	**2,430**	**1,628**	**802**	**24**	**24**	..
0—5	278	177	101	..	..	..	278	177	101	..	..	..
5—10	204	128	76	7	6	1	197	122	75	1	1	..
10—15	175	120	55	9	9	..	166	111	55	2	2	..
15—20	228	146	82	19	16	3	209	130	79	3	3	..
20 and over	1,753	1,256	497	173	168	5	1,580	1,088	492	18	18	..
30. Sion—												
Hindu .. Total	**52,060**	**32,956**	**19,104**	**7,168**	**5,964**	**1,204**	**44,892**	**26,992**	**17,900**	**3,716**	**3,373**	**343**
0—5	5,753	3,058	2,695	..	..	..	5,753	3,058	2,695	..	..	..
5—10	4,506	2,551	1,955	241	165	76	4,265	2,386	1,879	50	37	13
10—15	3,822	2,174	1,648	390	261	129	3,432	1,913	1,519	106	76	30
15—20	5,494	3,035	2,459	951	696	255	4,543	2,339	2,204	489	411	78
20 and over	32,485	22,138	10,347	5,586	4,842	744	26,899	17,296	9,603	3,071	2,849	222
Muslim .. Total	**5,890**	**4,158**	**1,732**	**902**	**826**	**76**	**4,988**	**3,332**	**1,656**	**226**	**206**	**20**
0—5	451	239	212	..	..	..	451	239	212	..	..	..
5—10	456	291	165	25	21	4	431	270	161	4	2	2
10—15	436	292	144	49	38	11	387	254	133	8	8	..
15—20	618	413	205	104	92	12	514	321	193	28	22	6
20 and over	3,929	2,923	1,006	724	675	49	3,205	2,248	957	186	174	12
31. Mahim—												
Hindu .. Total	**36,546**	**22,245**	**14,301**	**8,432**	**6,553**	**1,879**	**28,114**	**15,692**	**12,422**	**3,686**	**3,381**	**305**
0—5	4,298	2,202	2,096	..	..	..	4,298	2,202	2,096	..	..	..
5—10	3,503	1,911	1,592	356	220	136	3,147	1,691	1,456	56	43	13
10—15	3,034	1,747	1,287	620	388	232	2,414	1,359	1,055	147	113	34
15—20	3,744	2,046	1,698	1,215	778	437	2,529	1,268	1,261	442	359	83
20 and over	21,967	14,339	7,628	6,241	5,167	1,074	15,726	9,172	6,554	3,041	2,866	175
Muslim .. Total	**6,709**	**4,428**	**2,281**	**908**	**889**	**19**	**5,801**	**3,539**	**2,262**	**292**	**280**	**12**
0—5	709	303	406	..	..	..	709	303	406	..	..	..
5—10	498	357	141	27	25	2	471	332	139	8	5	3
10—15	611	399	212	48	45	3	563	354	209	12	12	..
15—20	714	469	245	111	107	4	603	362	241	40	38	2
20 and over	4,177	2,900	1,277	722	712	10	3,455	2,188	1,267	232	225	7
32. Worli—												
Hindu .. Total	**100,633**	**64,581**	**36,052**	**9,811**	**8,530**	**1,281**	**90,813**	**56,042**	**34,771**	**2,921**	**2,699**	**222**
0—5	8,205	4,176	4,029	..	..	..	8,205	4,176	4,029	..	..	..
5—10	6,908	3,828	3,080	406	282	124	6,502	3,546	2,956	64	48	16
10—15	5,816	3,197	2,619	615	441	174	5,201	2,756	2,445	149	119	30
15—20	9,424	4,952	4,472	1,120	902	218	8,304	4,050	4,254	349	304	45
20 and over	70,271	48,419	21,852	7,670	6,905	765	62,601	41,514	21,087	2,359	2,228	131
Unspecified	9	9	..	..	..	..	..	..	..	..	..	..
Muslim .. Total	**7,219**	**5,223**	**1,996**	**846**	**782**	**64**	**6,373**	**4,441**	**1,932**	**116**	**111**	**5**
0—5	472	254	218	..	..	..	472	254	218	..	..	..
5—10	455	273	182	24	19	5	431	254	177	3	2	1
10—15	396	254	142	35	26	9	361	228	133	3	3	..
15—20	632	413	219	69	57	12	563	356	207	13	10	3
20 and over	5,264	4,029	1,235	718	680	38	4,546	3,349	1,197	97	96	1
33. Harbour Islands, Railways Platforms, Police Homeless and unknown, etc.—												
Hindu .. Total	**14,133**	**12,878**	**1,255**	**2,915**	**2,714**	**201**	**11,218**	**10,164**	**1,054**	**980**	**951**	**29**
0—5	313	171	142	..	..	..	313	171	142	..	..	..
5—10	374	276	98	36	27	9	338	249	89	4	3	1
10—15	612	502	110	79	64	15	533	438	95	16	14	2
15—20	1,658	1,495	163	366	328	38	1,292	1,167	125	114	104	10
20 and over	11,176	10,434	742	2,434	2,295	139	8,742	8,139	603	846	830	16
Muslim .. Total	**7,694**	**7,389**	**305**	**2,100**	**2,054**	**46**	**5,594**	**5,335**	**259**	**344**	**337**	**7**
0—5	81	41	40	..	..	..	81	41	40	..	..	..
5—10	122	94	28	13	11	2	109	83	26	1	1	..
10—15	225	203	22	48	44	4	177	159	18	8	8	..
15—20	853	815	38	249	243	6	604	572	32	53	52	1
20 and over	6,413	6,236	177	1,790	1,756	34	4,623	4,480	143	282	276	6

BIRTH-

(Corresponding to

District or State where born.	Enumerated in whole City.			A Ward.		B Ward.		C Ward.	
	Persons.	Males.	Females.	Males.	Females.	Males.	Females.	Males.	Females.
1	2	3	4	5	6	7	8	9	10
Total Population	**1,161,383**	**747,381**	**414,002**	**39,774**	**19,381**	**73,846**	**38,950**	**129,649**	**71,636**
A—India excluding Aden ..	**1,146,038**	**735,644**	**410,394**	**38,198**	**18,118**	**73,013**	**38,719**	**128,225**	**71,390**
A-I—Bombay Presidency including Bombay States and Agencies	**856,689**	**527,968**	**328,726**	**27,590**	**14,857**	**49,005**	**24,966**	**92,121**	**55,459**
(a) British Districts ..	**833,683**	**512,778**	**320,910**	**26,674**	**14,454**	**48,151**	**24,657**	**90,081**	**54,094**
(1) Bombay City ..	285,585	165,233	120,352	7,936	6,018	23,642	13,321	33,879	21,426
(2) Northern Division ..	**99,525**	**63,098**	**36,427**	**5,391**	**2,003**	**6,007**	**3,702**	**22,212**	**14,740**
(3) Ahmedabad ..	20,470	13,209	7,261	513	334	1,906	1,207	5,175	2,814
(4) Broach	4,497	2,924	1,573	449	90	312	185	725	560
(5) Kaira	4,017	2,820	1,197	214	79	249	184	841	315
(6) Panch Mahals ..	401	309	92	51	4	38	5	81	48
(7) Surat	58,275	36,532	21,743	3,781	1,336	3,176	1,936	14,691	10,547
(8) Thana	11,865	7,304	4,561	383	160	326	185	699	461
(9) Central Division ..	**165,037**	**101,490**	**63,547**	**3,771**	**2,408**	**8,562**	**3,397**	**12,826**	**7,121**
(10) Ahmednagar ..	17,467	10,049	7,418	351	214	369	242	807	564
(11) Khandesh East ..	1,707	1,094	613	39	24	46	24	215	125
(12) Khandesh West ..	449	298	151	18	1	14	15	57	32
(13) Nasik	17,347	10,331	7,016	349	276	499	181	931	634
(14) Poona	66,999	40,327	26,672	2,017	1,284	3,728	1,816	4,356	2,668
(15) Satara	53,211	34,445	18,766	877	553	3,513	972	5,782	2,731
(16) Sholapur	7,367	4,592	2,775	118	56	390	147	675	367
(17) Bombay Suburban District	490	354	136	2	..	3	..	3	..
(18) Southern Division ..	**280,437**	**181,050**	**99,387**	**9,445**	**3,971**	**9,892**	**4,010**	**20,912**	**10,642**
(19) Belgaum	3,171	2,061	1,110	173	56	93	14	236	93
(20) Bijapur	1,165	748	417	51	27	16	7	111	74
(21) Dharwar	1,307	790	517	57	10	47	26	81	21
(22) Kanara	4,872	3,290	1,582	451	191	219	30	351	104
(23) Kolaba ..	32,666	20,180	12,486	1,577	968	1,166	735	2,723	1,674
(24) Ratnagiri	237,256	153,981	83,275	7,136	2,719	7,851	3,198	17,110	8,676
(25) Sind	**3,099**	**1,902**	**1,197**	**131**	**59**	**548**	**227**	**252**	**165**
(26) Hyderabad ..	1,422	852	570	59	8	280	69	55	71
(27) Karachi	1,469	903	566	70	49	169	123	186	85
(28) Larkana	24	11	13	1	..	..	..	..	..
(29) Nawabshah	3	3	..	..	..	2	..	..	..
(30) Sukkur	172	124	48	..	2	97	35	11	9
(31) Thar and Parkar ..	1	1	..	1	..	..	..	..	..
(32) Upper Sind Frontier ..	8	8	..	..	..	..	..	..	..
(b) Bombay States and Agencies ..	**20,631**	**14,002**	**6,629**	**805**	**258**	**824**	**298**	**1,500**	**858**
(1) Bhor	536	384	152	4	12	4	2	11	16
(2) Cambay	1,002	560	442	31	20	68	40	285	215
(3) Idar	284	230	54	1	1	6	1	165	32
(4) Janjira	448	307	141	..	..	..	..	63	37
(5) Khairpur	285	193	92	3	1	10	10	..	..
(6) Kolhapur	5,391	2,761	2,630	99	32	158	57	333	190
(7) Rajpipla	48	31	17	2	2	2	..	..	..
(8) Sangli	1,124	765	359	13	19	18	..	20	15
(9) Savantwadi ..	4,273	2,790	1,483	134	65	114	56	253	132
(10) S. M. C. Other States ..	7,007	5,900	1,107	478	100	426	132	368	221
(11) Surat Agency ..	233	81	152	40	6	18	..	2	..
(c) Bombay Unspecified ..	**2,375**	**1,188**	**1,187**	**111**	**145**	**30**	**11**	**540**	**507**
A-II—Provinces and States in India beyond Bombay	**289,349**	**207,681**	**81,668**	**10,603**	**3,256**	**24,008**	**13,753**	**36,104**	**15,931**
(a) Provinces and States adjacent to Bombay ..	**72,609**	**51,921**	**20,688**	**5,166**	**1,294**	**3,809**	**1,164**	**5,960**	**3,017**
(1) Baroda	6,027	3,900	2,127	266	82	652	216	702	862
(2) Baluchistan ..	1,266	848	418	26	56	28	7	73	143
(3) Central India Agency ..	3,330	2,063	1,267	154	65	205	128	493	90
(4) Central Provinces and Berar	4,814	3,470	1,344	188	60	179	57	488	217
(5) Hyderabad Deccan ..	15,914	11,031	4,883	434	163	400	177	516	325
(6) Madras	21,415	14,876	6,539	2,813	667	1,021	272	627	443
(7) Mysore	2,937	2,036	901	208	75	87	27	206	90
(8) Punjab	8,517	6,863	1,654	828	57	725	154	953	216
(9) Rajputana ..	8,389	6,834	1,555	299	69	512	126	1,813	631

PLACE.

Imperial Table VI.)

D Ward.		E Ward.		F Ward.		G Ward.		Harbour Islands, Railway and Floating population and unknown	
Males.	Females.	Males.	Females.	Males.	Females.	Males.	Females.	Males.	Females.
11	12	13	14	15	16	17	18	19	20
94,672	**56,807**	**177,504**	**106,928**	**101,156**	**58,565**	**105,030**	**59,370**	**25,750**	**2,465**
93,611	**56,371**	**174,705**	**106,031**	**100,516**	**58,399**	**104,704**	**59,269**	**22,677**	**2,102**
77,673	**49,336**	**117,727**	**82,422**	**76,110**	**50,164**	**74,149**	**50,148**	**13,588**	**1,379**
75,657	**48,177**	**115,196**	**80,588**	**74,258**	**48,821**	**69,652**	**48,912**	**13,109**	**1,207**
25,630	21,537	38,094	29,968	13,919	11,314	20,734	16,393	1,399	380
11,260	**6,116**	**6,322**	**3,571**	**3,829**	**2,378**	**5,517**	**3,797**	**2,560**	**120**
1,507	737	1,779	949	600	293	1,375	903	354	24
530	304	606	282	140	70	86	70	67	3
479	207	455	222	73	32	468	152	41	6
28	26	76	4	25	2	5	8	5	..
6,750	3,644	2,653	1,622	2,198	1,368	1,702	1,230	1,581	60
1,966	1,198	758	492	784	613	1,881	1,425	512	27
8,622	**5,521**	**31,393**	**22,367**	**18,573**	**12,890**	**15,328**	**9,378**	**2,415**	**465**
507	364	3,562	2,821	3,015	2,355	1,071	786	367	72
134	44	272	169	168	90	161	132	59	5
55	28	73	24	28	10	29	41	24	..
929	598	2,736	1,733	3,515	2,794	1,132	747	240	53
3,568	2,442	15,306	11,556	5,529	3,940	4,768	2,708	1,055	258
3,170	1,842	8,358	5,299	5,148	2,950	7,060	4,353	537	66
255	201	1,085	765	1,151	727	785	501	133	11
4	2	1	....	19	24	322	110	..	..
29,933	**14,870**	**39,199**	**24,400**	**37,818**	**22,163**	**27,733**	**19,145**	**8,618**	**186**
364	208	336	249	213	124	585	348	61	18
70	36	140	118	107	78	225	75	28	2
147	113	129	92	109	57	195	196	25	2
859	731	658	319	270	140	69	65	113	2
2,771	1,617	3,799	2,669	3,734	2,229	3,532	2,569	878	25
25,722	12,165	34,137	20,953	33,385	19,535	23,127	15,802	5,513	137
212	**133**	**188**	**282**	**114**	**76**	**340**	**199**	**117**	**56**
112	38	16	178	20	16	299	183	11	12
99	90	157	107	93	60	32	14	97	38
..	.5	3	2	....	....	..	..	7	6
..	..	....	....	....	....	..	..	1	..
1	..	12	....	1	....	1	2	1	..
..	..	....	....	....	....	..	..	..	..
..	..	....	....	....	....	8	..	..	..
1,954	**1,115**	**2,294**	**1,405**	**1,728**	**1,380**	**4,452**	**1,193**	**445**	**172**
37	28	176	60	37	8	105	26	10	..
72	51	67	43	8	9	2	1	27	63
36	9	11	8	3	4	4	4	4	..
..	..	58	6	59	1	66	67	61	30
53	..	26	33	98	48	..	..	8	..
642	319	857	559	169	745	362	681	141	47
..	4	11	....	10	1	1	1	5	9
20	4	31	52	614	254	29	15	20	..
777	502	636	330	158	194	660	183	58	21
314	173	421	319	565	66	3,212	94	116	2
3	25	....	....	7	....	11	121	..	..
62	**44**	**237**	**429**	**129**	**18**	**45**	**38**	**34**	..
15,938	**7,035**	**56,978**	**23,609**	**24,406**	**8,235**	**30,555**	**9,126**	**9,089**	**723**
4,621	**2,017**	**12,881**	**5,027**	**7,062**	**3,587**	**8,891**	**4,181**	**3,531**	**401**
786	367	403	236	390	172	315	178	296	14
20	26	452	62	101	20	98	92	50	12
162	97	420	539	147	111	377	228	105	9
347	253	1,115	331	431	246	561	150	211	30
370	182	4,959	1,522	1,232	807	2,874	1,678	247	34
1,334	588	2,252	1,367	3,025	1,664	3,004	1.400	800	138
194	85	733	277	425	220	50	102	133	25
596	147	1,064	475	642	242	567	252	1,488	111
812	272	1,483	218	669	105	1,046	106	201	28

District or State where born.	Enumerated in whole City.			A Ward.		B Ward.		C Ward.	
	Persons.	Males.	Females.	Males.	Females.	Males.	Females.	Males.	Females.
1	2	3	4	5	6	7	8	9	10
(10) Western India States Agency	**73,317**	**45,640**	**27,677**	**1,586**	**857**	**14,520**	**11,055**	**15,993**	**8,593**
(i) Bhavnagar	4,728	2,709	1,929	32	41	1,062	962	1,212	780
(ii) Cutch	20,029	12,205	7,824	276	177	6,387	5,165	1,161	426
(iii) Gondal	210	184	26	..	..	27	1	139	19
(iv) Jamnagar	926	662	264	29	10	132	69	319	83
(v) Junagadh	990	635	355	13	26	100	100	300	168
(vi) Khatiawar Unspecified ..	42,401	27,117	15,284	1,055	557	6,785	4,703	12,361	6,399
(vii) Limbdi	4	3	1	..	..	..	..	..	..
(viii) Morvi	366	239	127	..	..	..	..	44	117
(ix) Nawanagar	105	41	64	4	..	4	1	5	7
(x) Palanpur	1,964	1,051	913	7	1	6	..	110	303
(xi) Porbandar	209	73	136	18	28	..	46	50	..
(xii) Rajkot	1,385	631	754	152	17	17	8	286	291
(b) Other Provinces and States in India	**102,214**	**81,934**	**20,280**	**2,439**	**440**	**5,308**	**1,354**	**5,595**	**1,842**
(1) Ajmer and Merwara ..	8,588	8,036	552	17	19	186	32	1,739	324
(2) Andamans	69	57	12	..	3	..	..	..	..
(3) Assam	221	207	14	10	3	20	2	6	2
(4) Bengal	2,476	1,902	574	164	104	211	35	274	74
(5) Bihar and Orissa ..	544	362	182	3	1	25	11	19	19
(6) Burma	258	183	75	13	11	30	8	4	7
(7) Cochin	2,946	642	2,304	13	7	8	5	5	4
(8) Coorg	124	104	20	3	..	5	..	4	1
(9) Delhi	3,320	2,496	824	84	30	417	108	362	138
(10) Gwalior	606	402	204	17	10	66	14	73	76
(11) Kashmir	376	311	65	16	..	90	10	27	13
(12) Nikobar	8	7	1	..	..	..	..	..	..
(13) North West Frontier ..	3,091	2,697	394	117	34	783	69	81	7
(14) Sikkim	724	283	441	190	25	6	416	1	..
(15) Travancore	540	422	118	61	13	159	5	4	..
(16) United Provinces ..	83,323	68,823	14,500	1,731	180	3,302	639	2,996	1,177
A-III—French and Portuguese Settlements	**38,702**	**25,915**	**12,787**	**1,849**	**661**	**305**	**137**	**8,536**	**2,469**
A-IV—India Unspecified	**2,507**	**2,271**	**236**	**63**	**4**	**66**	**43**	**20**	**10**
Aden	**80**	**35**	**45**	..	..	**5**	**18**	**11**	..
B—Other Asiatic Countries ..	**7,832**	**6,485**	**1,367**	**813**	**200**	**790**	**159**	**447**	**80**
(a) Within British Dominions ..	**341**	**325**	**16**	**25**	**9**	**60**	**2**	**41**	**1**
(1) Ceylon	183	176	7	21	5	..	..	3	1
(2) Straits Settlements Malaya ..	17	14	3	3	..	..	..	..	..
(3) Elsewhere	141	135	6	1	4	60	2	38	..
(b) Outside British Dominions ..	**6,397**	**5,151**	**1,246**	**668**	**157**	**730**	**157**	**383**	**76**
(1) Afganistan	1,000	913	87	83	5	270	23	209	7
(2) China	525	481	44	20	4	57	..	1	5
(3) Nepal	561	492	69	9	..	..	3	..	..
(4) Elsewhere	4,311	3,265	1,046	556	148	394	131	173	64
(c) Asia Unspecified	**1,094**	**989**	**105**	**120**	**34**	..	..	**23**	**3**
C—Europe	**6,665**	**4,736**	**1,929**	**620**	**885**	**16**	**12**	**948**	**150**
(a) Within British Dominions ..	**6,222**	**4,493**	**1,729**	**552**	**866**	**15**	**12**	**947**	**148**
(1) United Kingdom and Ireland	5,288	3,907	1,381	522	805	14	8	931	78
(2) Other British Possessions in Europe	984	586	348	30	61	1	4	16	70
(b) Europe Unspecified	**443**	**243**	**200**	**68**	**19**	**1**	..	**1**	**2**
D—Africa	**373**	**205**	**168**	**17**	**22**	**22**	**42**	**10**	**11**
(a) Within British Dominions ..	**80**	**40**	**40**	**6**	**7**	**3**	..	**7**	**2**
(1) Cape Colony	32	15	17	..	2	..	..	7	2
(2) Natal	1	1	..	1	..	..	..	..	..
(3) Unganda	4	..	4	..	..	..	..	..	..
(4) Zanzibar	9	5	4	1	2	..	..	..	..
(5) Elsewhere	34	19	15	4	3	3	..	..	..
(b) Africa Unspecified	**293**	**165**	**128**	**11**	**15**	**19**	**42**	**3**	**9**
E—America	**210**	**142**	**68**	**18**	**43**	..	..	**6**	**4**
(a) Canada and other British Possessions	**45**	**20**	**25**	**4**	**16**	..	..	**4**	..
(b) Outside British Possessions ..	**144**	**111**	**33**	**5**	**17**	..	..	..	**4**
(1) United States of America	144	111	33	5	17	..	..	..	4
(c) America Unspecified ..	**21**	**11**	**10**	**9**	**10**	..	..	**2**	..
F—Australasia	**185**	**154**	**31**	**113**	**18**	..	..	**2**	**1**
(1) Fizi Islands	10	10	..	..	..	..	..	..	..
(2) Newzealand	6	4	2	2	..	..	..	..	1
(3) Tasmania	155	127	28	100	18	..	..	2	..
(4) Other British Possessions in Australasia ..	14	13	1	11	..	..	..	..	..

D Ward.		E Ward.		F Ward.		G Ward.		Harbour Islands, Railway and Floating population and unknown.	
Males.	Females.	Males.	Females.	Males.	Females.	Males.	Females.	Males.	Females.
11	12	13	14	15	16	17	18	19	20
2,326	1,332	5,455	3,069	1,909	1,288	2,616	1,379	1,235	64
64	19	117	106	66	15	124	..	122	6
632	244	1,569	929	1,002	587	995	278	183	18
2	..	....	8	....	....	16	3	..	..
1	10	64	3	10	13	97	74	10	2
4	8	75	42	63	3	5	5	75	3
1,425	806	2,626	1,378	660	400	1,372	987	883	54
..	..	....	....	....	....	..	..	3	1
..	3	198	....	....	....	..	7	2	..
..	2	14	13	9	30	..	2	5	..
179	65	723	539	11	5	7	..	2	..
3	5	2	37	....	....	..	20	..	..
16	170	72	39	88	226	..	3	..	..
4,170	794	30,583	11,539	14,134	2,273	16,636	1,860	3,069	178
339	15	179	58	101	59	400	39	75	6
..	..	....	8	49	1	..	..	8	..
6	..	65	4	6	....	2	..	92	3
96	54	263	186	332	90	60	21	502	10
31	3	183	11	32	133	11	3	58	1
4	7	106	31	17	7	4	2	5	2
16	3	523	2,232	32	88	36	14	9	1
7	4	32	8	8	7	3	..	42	..
199	44	811	364	345	59	192	71	36	10
69	13	69	30	24	17	30	31	54	13
39	1	39	15	17	23	5	1	78	2
..	..	....	....	6	1	1	..	..	..
74	10	934	141	452	104	176	12	80	17
4	..	78	....	....	....	1	..	3	..
89	11	5	52	55	14	29	15	20	8
3,197	629	27,296	8,399	12,658	1,720	15,686	1,651	1,957	105
4,790	2,690	6,180	3,909	1,188	1,008	2,331	1,670	1,236	43
31	2	1,879	45	113	79	81	36	13	17
1	4	5	23	....	....	..	..	13	..
669	149	2,233	683	503	60	223	27	787	9
6	..	143	3	12	1	..	..	33	..
2	..	143	....	6	1	..	..	1	..
4	..	....	3	6	....		..	1	..
..	..	....	....	....	....	..	..	36	..
572	104	1,433	660	491	59	125	24	749	9
6	..	165	27	77	3	77	22	17	..
30	..	215	30	131	....	3	2	24	3
..	..	418	62	21	8	43	..	1	1
536	104	635	541	262	53	2	..	707	5
91	45	657	20	....	....	98	8	..	..
331	256	438	139	111	90	89	57	2,183	340
320	127	282	93	107	86	88	57	2,182	340
9	52	256	29	107	85	85	55	1,983	269
311	75	26	64	....	1	3	2	199	71
11	129	156	46	4	4	1	..	1	..
30	11	65	45	23	14	13	14	25	9
9	4	4	18	9	5	1	2	1	2
8	4	....	9	....	....	..	..	..	..
..	..	....	....	....	....	..	..	..	..
..	..	....	....	....	4	..	..	..	..
1	..	....	....	1	1	1	1	1	..
..	..	4	9	8	....	..	1	..	2
21	7	61	27	14	9	12	12	24	7
23	12	34	2	3	2	..	1	58	4
..	8	7	1	....	2	..	..	5	..
23	6	27	1	3	....	..	1	53	4
23	6	27	1	3	....	..	1	53	4
..	..	....	....	....	....	..	..	..	..
7	4	24	5	....	....	1	2	7	1
..	..	7	....	....	....	..	..	3	..
..	..	....	....	....	....	..	..	2	1
7	4	15	4	....	....	1	2	2	..
..	..	2	1	....	....	..	..	..	..

MO-I Bk Ra Cs 3—46

CITY TABLE VI—PART II—BOMBAY.

Special statistics regarding Birth-place combined with Age, Caste and Occupation.

This Table is partly complete and partly selective. The districts of Birth and Castes in column 1 are selected, and represent those from which the bulk of Bombay immigrants is known to come. A district having once been selected, the totals shown in columns 2 to 14 are complete and are the figures of all persons born in that district. But the castes shown in column 1 and the occupations in columns 15 to 30 are selective only. Only those castes who usually immigrate to Bombay are selected ; in certain cases in making the selection their number is taken into account. The selection of occupations has been made according to the economic importance. As this year, there are no data to separate mill-operatives from persons of other ranks employed in Textile industries, all these persons are shown together. The figures in columns 15 and 16, therefore, do not represent the total number of millhands of all kinds in textile industries or mills. Reference has to be made to columns 29 and 30. The persons shown under " insufficiently described occupations " are mainly persons whose occupation was described as simply " Labour " And in many cases these labourers are either regular or occasional millhands.

CITY TABLE VI—PART II—BOMBAY.

SPECIAL STATISTICS REGARDING BIRTH-PLACE COMBINED WITH AGE, CASTE AND OCCUPATION.

SPECIAL STATISTICS REGARDING BIRTH-PLACE

Birth-place and Caste.	Total Number of Immigrants.			Age. 0–15.		Age. 15–40.		Age. 40 and over.		Workers.		Dependents.	
	Persons.	Males.	Females.	Males.	Females.	Males.	Females.	Males.	Females.	Males.	Females.	Males.	Females.
1	2	3	4	5	6	7	8	9	10	11	12	13	14
Ahmedabad .. Total ..	**20,470**	**13,209**	**7,261**	**1,500**	**700**	**9,317**	**4,659**	**2,392**	**1,902**	**11,504**	**1,248**	**1,705**	**6,018**
Bhangi ..	1,010	945	65	260	15	530	27	155	23	654	7	291	58
Brahman Audich ..	272	175	97	40	55	93	10	42	32	145	1	30	96
„ Others ..	1,205	900	305	125	100	628	187	147	18	730	51	170	254
Darji, Shimpi ..	340	275	65	19	7	230	43	26	15	251	11	24	54
Dhed, Mahar ..	222	90	132	15	35	54	60	21	37	71	21	19	111
Kunbi, Kanbi ..	178	130	48	12	6	90	25	28	17	112	9	18	39
Lohana ..	200	150	50	12	20	120	13	18	17	114	2	36	48
Lohar ..	1,820	1,400	420	150	65	1,102	303	148	52	1,250	18	250	402
Sutar ..	200	150	50	25	15	120	30	5	5	132	7	18	43
Vani ..	4,000	2,500	1,500	450	120	2,001	1,111	49	209	1,603	108	897	1,392
Bohra ..	505	380	215	130	120	232	85	18	10	271	11	109	204
Memon ..	525	350	175	25	23	278	120	47	32	227	34	123	141
Broach .. Total ..	**4,497**	**2,924**	**1,573**	**490**	**243**	**1,830**	**870**	**604**	**460**	**2,390**	**140**	**534**	**1,438**
Brahman ..	102	112	50	14	9	75	34	23	7	90	15	22	35
Vani ..	630	461	169	150	88	261	60	50	21	280	50	81	119
Zoroastrian ..	1,607	890	717	68	120	573	313	249	284	506	30		687
Kaira .. Total ..	**4,017**	**2,820**	**1,197**	**620**	**375**	**2,050**	**625**	**150**	**197**	**2,062**	**445**		
Brahman ..	210	150	60	27	21	110	28	13	11	120	3		
Dhed, Mahar ..	400	230	170	55	58	150	102	25	10	178	98		72
Kunbi, Kanbi, Patidar ..	118	90	28	17	12	64	14	9	2	63	2	7	26
Vani ..	600	422	178	80	40	300	85	42	53	309	8	113	170
Bohra ..	330	165	165	32	36	110	81	23	48	121	11	44	154
Surat .. Total ..	**58,275**	**36,532**	**21,743**	**12,337**	**7,339**	**18,592**	**9,743**	**5,603**	**4,661**	**27,992**	**9,632**	**8,540**	**12,111**
Bhandari ..	982	603	279	190	60	302	182	111	37	382	99	221	180
Bhatia ..	754	264	490	90	122	85	165	89	203	165	45	99	445
Brahman ..	2,519	1,903	616	126	198	1,098	329	679	89	1,565	79	338	537
Chambhar ..	1,090	888	202	198	42	467	108	223	52	656	42	232	160
Darji, Shimpi ..	740	480	260	99	86	298	116	83	58	362	56	118	204
Dhed, Mahar ..	4,540	2,998	1,542	479	145	1,897	909	622	488	2,685	676	313	866
Kasar ..	316	253	63	29	18	147	30	77	15	212	5	41	58
Kayastha Prabhu ..	360	178	182	17	25	119	89	42	68	148	12	30	170
Kharva ..	4,005	2,973	1,032	357	269	2,018	629	598	134	2,658	683	315	349
Koli ..	1,013	1,503	410	201	68	988	265	314	77	1,167	52	336	358
Kunbi ..	3,983	2,502	1,481	583	285	1,328	794	591	402	2,172	517	330	964
Lohana ..	1,803	990	813	37	43	560	480	393	390	878	179	112	634
Lohar ..	1,009	648	361	80	76	449	197	119	88	566	63	82	298
Panchal ..	333	257	76	47	18	162	48	48	10	205	6	52	70
Rajput ..	507	302	205	65	40	169	106	68	50	236	58	66	147
Sonar ..	840	523	317	49	36	351	208	123	73	472	92	51	225
Sutar ..	820	483	337	101	128	290	144	92	65	385	35	98	302
Bohra ..	2,302	1,509	793	247	161	823	388	439	244	1,086	37	428	756
Memon ..	390	210	180	38	22	117	109	55	49	164	..	46	180
Sheikh ..	2,076	1,042	1,036	129	143	708	698	205	195	735	234	307	802
Sayyad ..	190	121	69	30	21	71	35	20	13	75	10	46	59
Zoroastrian ..	2,803	1,844	959	297	170	913	625	631	158	1,415	154	429	805
Thana .. Total ..	**11,865**	**7,304**	**4,561**	**1,228**	**952**	**4,249**	**2,561**	**1,827**	**948**	**4,500**	**2,155**	**2,304**	**2,406**
Agri ..	285	240	45	18	11	150	12	72	22	160	32	80	13
Bhandari ..	620	300	320	90	21	205	220	5	70	225	212	75	108
Brahman Chitpavan ..	135	120	15	10	5	110	2	..	8	115	3	5	12
„ Deshasth ..	302	180	122	25	35	145	75	10	12	155	60	25	62
„ Others ..	591	418	173	30	38	240	72	148	68	230	21	188	152
Dhed, Mahar ..	400	301	99	58	33	203	41	40	25	218	43	88	56
Kayastha Prabhu ..	732	422	310	110	89	234	132	78	89	244	137	178	173
Kunbi, Kanbi and Mahratta ..	998	624	374	132	90	380	165	112	119	385	175	239	199
Sonar ..	250	140	110	30	31	85	75	25	4	90	70	50	40
Sutar ..	111	78	33	11	9	55	12	12	12	60	17	18	16
Vani ..	240	101	139	30	45	65	85	6	9	78	38	23	101
Zoroastrian ..	454	350	104	12	11	202	82	136	11	210	35	140	69
Caste unspecified (Muslims) ..	2,125	1,832	293	101	90	1,373	146	358	57	1,401	150	431	143
Ahmednagar .. Total ..	**17,467**	**10,049**	**7,418**	**2,340**	**2,832**	**4,873**	**3,210**	**2,336**	**1,376**	**7,420**	**4,560**	**2,629**	**2,858**
Brahman Deshasth ..	80	50	30	5	4	35	15	10	11	40	15	10	15
„ Others ..	200	131	69	16	25	81	41	34	3	90	25	41	44
Chambhar ..	1,002	509	493	120	150	302	201	87	142	350	405	159	88
Dhed, Mahar ..	6,100	3,505	2,604	830	720	2,300	1,585	375	299	2,511	1,600	994	1,004
Kunbi, Mahratta ..	4,800	2,905	1,805	201	180	2,102	1,303	602	412	2,206	1,409	699	486
Mali ..	201	109	92	13	12	78	60	18	20	82	68	27	29
Nhavi ..	155	130	25	8	3	111	22	11	..	120	23	10	2
Vanjari ..	160	70	90	11	9	50	60	9	21	55	65	15	25
Vani ..	90	80	10	8	1	62	6	10	3	70	3	10	7
Pathan ..	52	30	22	..	..	25	15	5	7	30	6	..	16
Sheikh ..	1,201	705	496	22	12	502	401	181	88	515	40	190	456

COMBINED WITH AGE, CASTE AND OCCUPATION.

Textile Industries.		Persons of all ranks occupied in industries other than textile.		Transport.		Trade.		Public force and Administration.		Professions and liberal arts (excluding religious Mendicants).		Domestic service.		Insufficiently described occupation.	
Males.	Females.	Males.	Females.	Males.	Females.	Males.	Females.	Males.	Females.	Males.	Females.	Males.	Females.	Males.	Females.
15	16	17	18	19	20	21	22	23	24	25	26	27	28	29	30
431	**31**	**2,805**	**414**	**547**	**3**	**1,572**	**92**	**68**	**42**	**251**	**14**	**604**	**51**	**2,804**	**177**
22	..	471	5	57	..	6	..	4	..	1	..	1	..	25	..
2	..	4	..	21	..	30	..	..	..	14	..	18	..	36	..
17	..	16	4	9	..	107	8	4	5	61	3	99	..	257	18
..	1	201	3	..	..	3	..	..	..	..	..	..	2	12	..
4	..	16	1	3	..	..	2	2	..	..	..	14	..	18	9
12	2	19	..	5	..	9	1	..	..	1	..	9	2	40	2
..	..	..	..	..	..	24	..	..	..	1	..	1	..	48	1
1	..	927	10	28	..	8	..	..	..	4	..	..	..	29	4
1	..	75	2	3	..	7	2	1	..	1	..	..	..	18	1
22	2	29	8	44	..	477	16	4	4	29	..	14	12	437	36
..	..	13	1	1	..	97	3	..	..	..	..	6	..	127	4
5	1	21	3	42	3	37	4	..	..	2	..	36	2	20	13
287	**5**	**345**	**3**	**89**	..	**217**	**23**	**79**	**5**	**86**	**12**	**234**	**31**	**478**	**23**
..	..	4	..	..	..	5	..	7	..	8	1	17	5	11	3
..	..	4	..	7	..	95	13	..	..	..	..	48	12	39	6
47	..	86	..	23	..	46	4	27	2	34	5	55	5	107	7
315	**77**	**268**	**56**	**45**	**11**	**272**	**25**	**57**	**7**	**27**	**5**	**257**	**87**	**328**	**57**
8	..	11	..	5	..	12	..	10	..	11	..	17	1	23	1
24	15	28	17	7	3	..	..	9	..	..	..	19	12	25	18
15	..	13	..	6	..	8	..	..	..	..	..	8	4	2	2
7	..	6	..	8	..	87	5	5	..	3	..	47	..	49	..
4	..	18	..	7	..	42	..	..	..	..	..	5	..	19	..
734	**388**	**5,328**	**586**	**2,476**	**105**	**3,526**	**137**	**482**	**16**	**516**	**66**	**5,352**	**2,933**	**4,932**	**2,078**
18	48	65	..	8	..	10	2	..	..	..	..	103	15	133	17
7	..	6	..	2	..	72	8	5	..	6	..	27	15	18	13
18	..	7	..	55	..	366	5	108	..	78	8	363	35	368	21
6	7	376	15	28	..	45	..	9	..	..	..	65	12	72	3
..	..	238	18	..	..	..	..	10	..	6	..	42	21	18	10
118	42	543	72	87	12	68	..	57	..	15	..	872	317	483	218
..	..	133	..	..	..	32	..	..	..	..	..	12	4	15	1
..	..	5	..	8	..	32	..	26	..	11	2	25	6	22	2
126	35	687	42	82	6	123	12	37	..	..	..	736	267	586	222
55	..	242	10	28	..	85	2	..	..	..	..	437	23	215	12
88	25	372	62	78	12	55	8	47	..	15	..	073	235	464	225
26	11	237	35	15	..	122	12	15	..	..	..	127	62	247	33
..	..	377	8	..	..	32	..	..	..	..	..	47	32	56	12
10	..	47	..	8	..	22	..	8	..	..	..	54	3	32	2
5	12	77	..	28	..	35	..	12	..	..	..	10	35	31	8
..	..	246	18	8	..	72	4	13	..	5	..	24	41	38	20
..	..	235	5	12	..	25	..	..	..	..	..	25	18	38	7
15	..	218	..	28	..	328	15	15	..	8	..	112	10	243	7
3	..	52	..	5	..	32	..	..	..	..	..	12	..	32	..
48	25	125	67	27	7	138	23	22	..	14	4	147	57	113	22
..	..	18	..	5	..	10	2	4	..	2	1	11	4	12	2
68	..	386	6	92	8	248	12	57	4	45	8	123	67	262	27
429	**251**	**550**	**380**	**768**	**42**	**205**	**150**	**44**	**38**	**108**	**54**	**357**	**310**	**1,030**	**455**
30	7	6	..	77	..	3	..	..	..	2	..	4	4	20	12
30	28	41	18	53	15	22	7	..	..	..	..	15	28	37	41
1	..	..	..	8	..	..	1	1	..	4	..	5	1	66	..
..	..	..	..	16	..	15	..	12	2	20	5	30	7	50	15
11	..	5	3	40	..	21	..	6	..	47	..	12	9	51	7
51	17	16	..	12	..	7	1	4	6	..	..	53	3	47	..
3	..	9	..	24	23	6	6	7	3	5	5	4	18	129	61
48	41	20	13	38	1	16	12	1	4	1	1	5	17	90	32
5	..	24	25	1	..	3	..	..	..	3	..	..	..	19	25
..	..	23	..	16	..	..	..	..	..	..	..	1	4	17	8
1	..	1	3	5	..	15	6	1	..	3	..	2	..	25	15
7	..	22	2	17	..	35	..	1	..	15	..	18	..	30	17
201	5	37	1	..	..	58	3	..	..	..	..	171	17	303	67
1,484	**858**	**1,931**	**710**	**179**	**77**	**216**	**65**	**188**	..	**78**	**19**	**1,492**	**1,576**	**1,087**	**688**
..	..	..	..	3	..	3	..	6	..	10	2	4	8	8	3
..	..	3	..	4	..	10	..	12	..	18	5	15	12	17	4
17	6	315	127	..	..	..	..	..	..	..	..	..	237	16	22
616	273	663	234	37	13	..	..	49	..	8	4	536	526	415	273
626	347	517	178	47	17	58	25	58	..	15	5	524	544	313	172
..	..	..	..	..	..	15	27	..	..	..	..	42	28	16	2
..	..	105	5	..	..	..	..	..	..	..	..	..	9	5	5
..	..	9	2	27	32	11	4	..	..	..	..	..	12	..	6
..	..	..	..	..	..	32	3	..	..	..	..	15	..	14	..
6	..	10	..	..	..	..	..	..	..	..	..	9	4	..	..
87	7	148	4	12	..	37	..	18	..	12	..	94	18	78	7

Birth-place and Caste.	Total Number of Immigrants.			Age. 0–15		15–40		40 and over.		Workers.		Dependents.	
	Persons.	Males.	Females.	Males.	Females.	Males.	Females.	Males.	Females.	Males.	Females.	Males.	Females.
1	2	3	4	5	6	7	8	9	10	11	12	13	14
Nasik .. Total ..	**17,347**	**10,331**	**7,016**	**1,316**	**1,528**	**6,943**	**4,290**	**2,072**	**1,198**	**7,988**	**2,028**	**2,343**	**4,988**
Brahman ..	880	535	345	103	97	343	185	89	63	323	37	212	308
Chambhar, Mochi ..	424	302	122	46	88	212	68	44	16	240	31	53	91
Dhed, Mahar ..	6,349	4,307	2,012	656	508	2,943	1,142	708	362	3,717	1,203	590	809
Mahratta ..	6,092	3,698	2,394	220	694	2,640	1,396	838	304	2,961	609	737	1,785
Vanjari ..	511	257	254	40	68	182	146	35	40	201	63	56	191
Sheikh ..	463	339	124	51	29	178	68	110	27	251	27	88	97
Poona .. Total ..	**66,999**	**40,327**	**26,672**	**10,897**	**8,392**	**22,102**	**12,407**	**7,328**	**5,873**	**29,309**	**10,927**	**11,018**	**15,745**
Bhandari ..	127	99	28	17	9	69	15	13	4	78	16	21	12
Brahman Chitpavan ..	990	687	203	201	81	398	98	88	24	420	21	267	182
,, Deshasth ..	728	549	179	102	60	390	82	57	37	337	8	212	171
,, Karhada ..	201	178	23	36	6	89	12	53	5	103	2	75	21
,, Kudal Deshkar ..	108	88	20	28	4	50	11	10	5	45	..	43	20
,, Others ..	901	625	276	101	68	428	176	96	82	469	11	156	265
Chambhar ..	2,890	1,929	961	501	311	1,128	398	300	252	1,229	369	700	592
Darji Shimpi ..	588	398	190	101	42	198	101	99	47	263	60	135	130
Dhangar ..	290	195	95	48	17	108	52	39	26	108	59	92	36
Dhed, Mahar ..	7,829	4,290	3,539	621	998	2,939	1,928	730	613	3,192	2,137	1,098	1,402
Dhobi ..	495	280	215	60	47	163	126	57	42	159	90	121	125
Gavli ..	210	95	115	17	29	62	76	16	10	56	48	39	67
Kayastha Prabhu ..	215	109	106	17	19	68	71	24	16	79	2	30	104
Koli ..	300	185	115	17	11	108	83	60	21	121	67	64	48
Kumbhar ..	202	110	92	8	9	89	67	13	16	66	35	44	57
Kunbi, Mahratta ..	29,845	16,729	13,116	1,895	3,009	11,282	7,728	3,552	2,379	11,102	5,320	5,627	7,796
Lohar ..	184	137	47	12	16	109	18	16	13	88	21	49	26
Mali ..	687	341	346	88	90	146	190	107	66	226	119	115	227
Nhavi ..	800	519	281	105	87	348	146	66	48	383	103	136	178
Sonar ..	467	268	199	58	51	167	121	43	27	209	1	59	198
Sutar ..	230	147	83	21	17	83	36	43	30	86	6	61	77
Teli ..	637	302	335	60	82	166	173	76	80	246	63	56	272
Vani others (Hindu) ..	334	185	149	37	26	97	91	51	32	118	24	67	125
Bohra ..	203	157	46	12	19	110	28	35	4	103	..	54	40
Memon ..	123	93	30	22	5	46	17	25	8	60	9	33	21
Pathan ..	325	219	106	32	32	141	49	46	25	167	12	52	94
Sheikh ..	1,082	840	242	140	67	555	115	145	60	433	41	407	201
Sayyad ..	206	117	91	16	22	72	36	29	33	58	14	59	77
Zoroastrian ..	446	209	237	22	34	114	101	73	102	136	6	73	231
Satara .. Total ..	**53,211**	**34,445**	**18,766**	**6,840**	**3,892**	**18,901**	**9,926**	**8,704**	**4,948**	**27,583**	**6,254**	**6,862**	**12,512**
Brahman, Deshasth ..	319	201	118	29	21	146	78	26	19	138	3	63	115
,, Karhada ..	442	227	215	68	54	136	127	23	34	106	2	121	213
,, Others ..	1,197	634	563	137	197	399	293	98	73	478	62	156	501
Chambhar ..	3,550	1,859	1,691	516	433	1,026	965	317	293	1,315	594	544	1,097
Dhangar ..	223	134	89	42	30	64	52	28	7	107	28	27	61
Dhed, Mahar ..	11,816	6,269	5,547	899	607	3,982	3,490	1,388	1,450	5,211	2,163	1,058	3,374
Dhobi ..	204	136	68	18	6	21	40	97	22	112	31	24	37
Koli ..	480	360	120	30	27	243	61	87	32	333	72	27	48
Kunbi, Mahratta ..	20,817	13,921	6,896	2,688	1,420	8,328	3,629	2,905	1,847	11,909	2,458	2,012	4,438
Mali ..	327	196	131	27	19	131	69	38	43	139	24	57	107
Nhavi ..	792	599	193	105	41	383	109	111	43	531	31	68	162
Darji ..	397	276	121	96	48	106	57	74	16	207	12	69	109
Sonar ..	228	137	91	25	23	86	59	26	9	97	13	40	78
Sutar ..	224	142	82	12	24	103	40	27	18	124	16	18	66
Vani (Hindu) ..	389	221	168	57	43	137	100	27	25	176	8	45	160
Sheikh ..	619	395	224	54	84	274	94	67	46	296	34	99	190
Sayyad ..	130	95	35	11	6	71	19	13	10	81	3	14	32
Sholapur .. Total ..	**7,367**	**4,592**	**2,775**	**1,448**	**968**	**2,404**	**1,487**	**740**	**320**	**3,521**	**930**	**1,071**	**1,845**
Brahman ..	260	167	93	31	20	109	39	27	34	118	11	49	82
Chambhar ..	1,249	494	755	30	181	276	426	188	148	399	267	95	488
Dhed, Mahar ..	2,229	1,227	1,002	237	228	505	496	485	279	997	421	230	581
Mahratta ..	2,998	1,529	1,469	237	317	1,025	923	267	229	1,176	497	353	972
Sheikh ..	480	251	229	80	67	108	102	63	60	159	31	92	198
Belgaum .. Total ..	**3,171**	**2,061**	**1,110**	**332**	**301**	**1,493**	**540**	**236**	**269**	**1,608**	**440**	**453**	**670**
Brahman, Gaud Saraswat ..	110	75	35	15	7	53	25	7	3	60	2	15	33
,, Others ..	302	243	59	46	12	135	23	62	24	132	5	111	54
Dhed, Mahar ..	403	210	193	22	35	120	92	68	66	187	101	23	92
Lingayat ..	122	91	31	14	3	61	17	16	11	78	3	13	28
Mahratta ..	1,090	702	388	102	107	492	112	108	169	530	116	172	272
Sheikh ..	130	75	55	23	15	40	18	12	22	40	14	35	41
Bijapur .. Total ..	**1,165**	**748**	**417**	**135**	**98**	**539**	**220**	**74**	**99**	**610**	**120**	**138**	**297**
Brahman ..	120	85	35	14	13	60	17	11	5	70	3	15	32
Mahratta ..	137	69	68	9	7	53	38	7	28	64	13	5	55
Sheikh ..	160	97	63	21	11	63	32	13	20	70	8	27	55
Dharwar .. Total ..	**1,307**	**790**	**517**	**188**	**118**	**432**	**224**	**220**	**175**	**501**	**102**	**289**	**415**
Brahman ..	172	118	54	26	14	66	25	26	15	76	7	42	47

Textile Industries.		Persons of all ranks occupied in industries other than Textile.		Transport.		Trade.		Public Force and Administration.		Professions and Liberal Arts (excluding religious Mendicants).		Domestic service.		Insufficiently described occupation.	
Males.	Females.	Males.	Females.	Males.	Females.	Males.	Females.	Males.	Females.	Males.	Females.	Males.	Females.	Males.	Females.
15	16	17	18	19	20	21	22	23	24	25	26	27	28	29	30
592	**282**	**391**	**92**	**1,032**	**68**	**280**	**77**	**167**	**82**	**23**	**21**	**268**	**88**	**2,391**	**710**
25	1	16	4	44	..	22	1	11	..	15	..	18	6	70	12
18	16	50	5	8	..	3	..	2	..	..	..	..	1	97	5
110	35	70	31	504	34	18	9	203	71	9	1	30	7	1,509	478
281	141	75	21	278	9	112	29	6	1	7	24	118	40	998	271
14	6	3	6	30	..	17	4	2	..	..	..	44	3	75	38
35	5	50	1	22	..	40	3	1	..	..	..	8	1	51	11
4,167	**2,500**	**2,537**	**896**	**3,081**	**178**	**273**	**999**	**471**	**129**	**411**	**78**	**2,361**	**307**	**6,061**	**3,105**
9	2	7	..	3	1	9	..	..	..	1	..	3	1	31	9
4	..	62	1	35	..	60	..	14	..	26	1	14	1	158	13
6	..	7	..	47	..	45	..	6	..	28	1	2	1	117	3
..	..	7	..	17	..	22	..	2	..	11	1	..	..	29	..
2	..	6	..	1	..	7	..	..	..	4	..	..	..	11	..
41	1	32	..	..	..	22	1	12	..	33	1	12	..	175	5
244	89	567	104	37	2	30	4	..	..	1	..	6	2	147	18
3	..	153	28	14	..	27	1	..	1	..	..	1	1	24	8
14	7	9	11	5	2	7	6	7	..	16	..	..	..	31	23
151	150	161	140	268	90	47	12	32	64	5	..	171	108	1,984	904
14	18	61	39	6	..	19	..	1	..	..	..	6	6	18	15
4	3	1	5	2	..	20	8	..	3	1	..	2	..	9	9
3	..	2	..	7	..	8	..	4	..	3	..	7	1	20	1
21	16	14	..	7	12	16	2	2	..	..	..	5	4	27	18
13	15	16	14	5	..	6	..	..	..	..	..	2	..	15	1
2,015	989	427	239	1,457	37	889	507	333	17	237	9	1,201	127	3,302	1,118
3	..	46	12	..	..	..	..	1	..	..	..	..	..	12	1
65	44	16	3	22	2	19	24	1	..	1	..	4	1	27	25
17	11	196	17	9	..	3	4	1	6	1	..	1	..	15	43
7	..	125	..	10	..	5	..	1	..	21	..	4	..	17	1
4	1	55	1	2	..	1	..	..	..	..	..	..	..	8	3
30	13	20	3	27	..	62	29	..	..	..	..	..	1	32	12
4	..	15	..	3	..	22	8	2	..	6	..	2	..	25	6
..	..	15	..	6	..	18	..	..	..	3	..	9	..	42	..
11	..	..	..	4	..	13	4	..	..	1	..	8	..	20	2
6	..	11	2	16	2	10	2	48	..	1	..	4	..	25	2
42	2	46	5	31	1	59	2	11	..	5	8	112	1	75	20
4	..	9	..	6	..	9	2	2	..	2	3	3	1	11	4
1	..	5	..	12	..	30	2	3	..	15	1	2	1	40	1
4,705	**1,293**	**3,105**	**451**	**1,533**	**81**	**1,269**	**248**	**351**	**14**	**167**	**11**	**723**	**178**	**6,151**	**1,529**
1	..	2	..	23	..	21	..	5	..	17	..	2	..	22	..
..	..	5	..	12	..	11	..	1	1	16	..	..	..	35	..
15	9	59	..	70	..	36	..	4	..	8	..	7	1	119	38
50	44	715	151	26	..	74	12	16	..	..	1	28	3	70	158
14	4	19	1	11	2	7	1	1	..	2	..	2	3	17	4
1,341	763	239	79	208	15	88	21	124	12	13	2	268	39	1,504	527
24	5	48	15	3	..	3	..	1	..	..	..	2	2	12	2
2	..	14	..	155	..	9	..	24	..	..	..	8	..	43	61
2,209	818	635	187	743	61	807	189	57	1	48	3	326	89	4,358	804
21	4	19	1	10	..	11	6	1	..	..	..	3	2	41	7
15	17	399	..	1	..	2	..	3	..	..	..	..	2	19	5
6	1	107	1	3	..	22	1	4	..	..	1	1	..	18	5
3	7	39	..	5	..	11	..	1	..	10	..	..	..	12	2
..	6	58	..	..	..	2	..	4	..	1	..	..	..	23	4
1	..	16	..	..	..	20	3	37	..	2	..	1	..	40	2
50	3	58	5	49	1	67	4	5	..	4	..	19	2	12	6
15	..	6	1	8	..	13	..	2	..	1	..	1	..	20	1
658	**152**	**347**	**132**	**239**	**5**	**251**	**48**	**53**	**5**	**44**	**4**	**71**	**36**	**1,118**	**380**
9	..	3	6	7	..	16	..	..	..	7	1	3	..	31	..
123	50	84	87	1	..	3	..	..	..	..	..	2	1	35	36
99	29	47	30	89	5	37	4	22	2	1	..	21	30	490	215
209	80	68	14	68	..	62	31	2	..	20	..	18	23	337	214
13	2	8	2	9	1	23	1	3	..	2	1	10	2	30	2
215	**114**	**217**	**58**	**70**	**2**	**185**	**12**	**77**	**..**	**58**	**10**	**127**	**55**	**423**	**46**
..	..	7	..	..	..	8	..	6	..	5	2	12	..	2	..
..	..	15	..	3	..	7	..	12	..	13	3	15	1	17	..
22	22	20	12	5	..	..	..	5	..	..	..	20	12	52	21
16	..	8	..	..	..	18	2	5	..	2		6	..	7	..
77	26	158	4	27	..	..	6	4	..	4	..	22	14	118	7
8	..	5	..	4	..	2	..	2	..	..	..	3	4	2	2
47	**36**	**93**	**17**	**15**	**2**	**52**	**5**	**15**	**..**	**15**	**..**	**32**	**26**	**216**	**35**
..	..	3	..	2	..	5	..	2	..	5	..	12	2	17	..
6	2	8	..	3	1	4	..	..	..	..	..	3	1	23	3
4	1	13	..	8	..	12	..	1	..	..	..	7	2	13	2
42	**31**	**59**	**13**	**11**	**..**	**66**	**14**	**12**	**..**	**11**	**2**	**55**	**37**	**169**	**28**
..	..	8	..	5	..	8	..	2	..	3	1	14	..	18	2

Birth-place and Caste.	Total Number of Immigrants.			Age. 0–15.		15–40.		40 and over.		Workers.		Dependents.	
	Persons.	Males.	Females.	Males.	Females.	Males.	Females.	Males.	Females.	Males.	Females.	Males.	Females.
1	2	3	4	5	6	7	8	9	10	11	12	13	14
Kanara .. Total ..	**4,872**	**3,290**	**1,582**	**520**	**401**	**2,235**	**736**	**535**	**445**	**2,118**	**210**	**1,172**	**1,372**
Brahman Gaud Saraswat ..	1,010	568	442	88	76	307	280	173	86	389	30	179	412
,, Others ..	507	329	178	38	63	257	96	34	19	260	9	69	169
Mahratta ..	529	240	289	45	53	147	172	48	64	160	129	80	160
Sheikh ..	107	86	21	10	5	66	11	10	5	55	3	31	18
Kolaba .. Total ..	**32,666**	**20,180**	**12,486**	**2,242**	**3,603**	**14,582**	**6,301**	**3,356**	**2,582**	**16,164**	**3,174**	**4,016**	**9,312**
Agri ..	1,320	742	578	236	263	403	202	103	113	567	129	175	449
Bhandari ..	1,206	622	584	173	101	340	394	109	89	490	137	132	447
Brahman Chitpavan ..	1,020	698	322	113	118	498	109	87	95	489	21	209	301
,, Deshasth ..	389	221	168	57	43	137	100	27	25	140	14	81	154
,, Gaud Saraswat ..	587	361	226	96	88	149	89	116	49	241	16	120	210
,, Others ..	976	601	375	142	107	385	248	74	20	432	29	169	346
Chambhar, Mochigar, Mochi ..	2,201	1,183	1,018	270	256	664	483	249	279	897	370	286	639
Darji ..	274	186	88	35	23	123	47	28	18	149	8	37	80
Dhed, Mahar ..	3,940	2,545	1,395	510	343	1,390	785	645	267	2,117	489	428	906
Dhobi ..	196	139	57	23	14	90	33	26	10	114	26	25	31
Gavli ..	13	9	4	..	..	6	3	3	1	7	1	2	3
Kayastha Prabhu ..	1,203	737	466	172	204	447	120	118	142	490	31	247	435
Koli ..	1,124	1,002	122	188	13	699	68	165	41	814	55	188	67
Kunbi, Mahratta ..	14,993	8,542	6,451	1,229	1,393	6,007	3,801	1,306	1,257	6,425	2,014	2,117	4,437
Sonar ..	382	203	179	33	47	136	89	34	43	153	6	50	173
Vani others (Hindu) ..	348	212	136	40	53	134	70	38	13	150	6	62	130
Sheikh ..	555	487	68	86	16	242	36	159	16	391	9	96	59
Ratnagiri .. Total ..	**237,256**	**153,981**	**83,275**	**29,029**	**21,258**	**99,466**	**49,184**	**25,486**	**12,833**	**121,937**	**28,380**	**32,044**	**54,895**
Agri ..	617	365	252	82	27	232	190	51	35	327	55	38	197
Brahman Chitpavan ..	2,218	1,767	451	273	142	1,233	272	261	37	1,251	28	516	423
,, Deshastha ..	955	838	117	53	22	587	68	198	27	623	11	215	106
,, Devrukha ..	117	93	24	24	10	56	11	13	3	69	3	24	21
,, Gaud Saraswat ..	1,644	969	675	209	188	533	348	227	139	739	46	230	629
,, Karhada ..	296	219	77	32	30	148	40	39	7	157	9	62	68
,, Kudal Deshkar ..	173	99	74	27	24	53	35	19	15	82	12	17	62
,, Saraswat ..	2,283	1,521	762	340	255	885	363	296	144	827	54	694	708
,, Others ..	3,360	2,448	912	260	203	1,697	563	491	146	1,872	62	576	830
Bhandari ..	14,797	9,648	5,149	1,920	1,525	5,934	2,624	1,794	1,000	7,230	1,143	2,418	4,006
Bhoi ..	211	168	43	43	6	100	29	25	8	143	18	25	25
Chambhar, Mochi ..	6,349	4,307	2,042	539	319	2,833	1,239	935	484	3,551	701	756	1,341
Darji, Shimpi ..	614	438	176	80	43	265	121	93	12	335	18	103	158
Dhangar ..	189	80	109	7	9	60	76	4	24	73	14	7	95
Dhed, Mahar ..	17,845	10,805	7,040	1,560	1,201	7,235	3,496	2,010	2,343	8,421	1,958	2,384	5,082
Dhobi ..	1,120	795	325	91	82	518	201	186	42	602	89	193	236
Gavli ..	1,307	891	416	128	34	612	296	151	86	784	173	107	243
Gurav ..	221	198	23	19	7	98	10	81	6	171	6	27	17
Kamathi ..	432	379	53	65	17	197	26	117	10	325	11	54	42
Kasar ..	410	361	49	70	8	159	30	132	11	276	13	85	36
Kayastha Prabhu ..	708	312	396	34	87	189	218	89	91	228	37	84	359
Kharva ..	628	599	29	87	8	393	16	119	5	502	7	97	22
Koli ..	789	608	181	69	72	432	99	107	10	525	30	83	142
Koshti ..	380	180	200	23	59	112	103	45	38	157	51	23	149
Kumbhar ..	1,027	798	229	132	88	561	108	105	33	589	95	209	134
Kunbi, Mahratta ..	135,899	89,464	46,435	18,520	10,323	51,221	25,892	19,723	10,220	69,788	18,972	19,676	27,463
Lohar ..	518	392	126	15	50	165	44	212	32	324	21	68	105
Mali ..	735	428	207	46	39	310	130	60	38	367	22	61	185
Nhavi ..	1,720	1,429	291	196	106	928	147	305	48	1,228	41	201	250
Panchal ..	219	150	69	18	10	110	43	22	16	118	1	32	68
Sonar ..	4,721	2,974	1,747	669	620	1 642	898	663	229	1,747	198	1,227	1,519
Sutar ..	2,789	1,926	863	187	102	1,408	660	331	101	1,753	89	173	774
Teli ..	1,937	1,280	657	323	218	809	320	148	110	858	177	422	480
Vani (Hindu) ..	5,985	3,603	2,382	560	387	1,980	1,249	1,063	746	2,939	95	664	2,287
Pathan ..	400	292	108	29	17	217	69	46	22	248	16	44	92
Sheikh ..	6,945	5,603	1,342	690	367	4,125	598	788	377	3,987	176	1,616	1,166
Sayyad ..	319	197	122	51	27	118	70	28	25	156	13	41	109
Hyderabad .. Total ..	**1,422**	**852**	**570**	**182**	**163**	**523**	**229**	**147**	**178**	**608**	**210**	**249**	**360**
Brahman Audich ..	123	96	27	23	12	60	11	13	4	80	3	16	24
Dhed, Mahar ..	137	88	49	23	5	42	31	23	13	63	21	25	28
Lohana ..	180	135	45	6	4	99	32	30	9	89	7	46	38
Mahratta ..	214	108	106	19	32	75	54	14	20	80	47	28	59
Sheikh ..	230	167	63	45	21	64	20	58	22	103	13	64	50
Karachi .. Total ..	**1,469**	**903**	**566**	**155**	**175**	**570**	**290**	**178**	**101**	**682**	**71**	**221**	**495**
Khoja ..	139	89	50	19	12	55	31	15	7	57	6	32	44
Sheikh ..	147	107	40	14	10	76	26	17	4	76	6	31	34
Sukkur .. Total ..	**172**	**124**	**48**	**16**	**12**	**86**	**27**	**22**	**9**	**100**	**14**	**24**	**34**
Lohana ..	130	102	28	10	7	80	16	12	5	88	1	14	27
Bhor .. Total ..	**536**	**384**	**152**	**52**	**54**	**293**	**73**	**39**	**25**	**301**	**47**	**83**	**105**
Mahratta ..	209	107	102	12	10	78	70	17	22	83	30	24	72

TEXTILE INDUSTRIES.		Persons of all ranks occupied in industries other than textile.		Transport.		Trade.		Public force and Administration.		Professions and liberal arts (excluding religious Mendicants).		Domestic service.		Insufficiently described occupation.	
Males.	Females.	Males.	Females.	Males.	Females.	Males.	Females.	Males.	Females.	Males.	Females.	Males.	Females.	Males.	Females.
15	16	17	18	19	20	21	22	23	24	25	26	27	28	29	30
114	**39**	**145**	**17**	**127**	**6**	**138**	**9**	**62**	..	**47**	**3**	**223**	**37**	**546**	**51**
..	..	11	..	5	..	37	..	16	..	11	2	25	6	67	7
..	..	19	..	6	..	15	..	13	..	9	1	23	2	26	4
17	13	7	5	3	3	6	3	3	..	..	..	30	11	35	23
3	..	5	..	8	..	7	..	2	..	1	..	7	1	16	1
2,561	**981**	**1,915**	**208**	**1,301**	**74**	**791**	**118**	**264**	**91**	**197**	**6**	**307**	**65**	**2,740**	**617**
88	32	150	1	93	11	23	2	12	..	6	..	5	3	78	54
31	84	58	5	66	1	42	3	10	..	3	1	5	1	96	10
12	..	17	..	71	..	30	..	47	..	38	..	32	5	148	5
..	..	74	..	17	..	45	..	21	..	24	2	8	2	49	3
25	..	17	..	51	..	15	..	6	..	13	..	2	4	79	5
19	..	32	4	52	..	28	6	9	..	41	3	15	..	96	6
105	61	181	77	50	2	9	7	14	1	28	..	11	..	167	104
7	1	60	1	3	..	17	..	..	..	..	..	..	..	16	1
351	71	170	17	249	6	36	4	129	71	..	..	45	18	777	139
21	5	37	6	14	3	12	..	1	..	..	..	..	..	22	3
8	..	..	..	..	..	2	1	..	..	..	..	..	..	1	..
29	9	151	3	23	..	9	..	18	..	23	..	3	..	115	2
37	..	99	1	189	..	43	28	10	..	..	..	5	..	89	7
987	417	405	47	304	4	217	27	97	1	48	..	177	31	1,103	308
6	..	75	..	6	..	17	..	1	..	5	..	..	2	21	1
6	..	10	..	7	..	75	..	1	..	2	..	..	1	12	3
89	..	37	3	17	..	26	1	1	..	3	..	7	..	189	1
20,262	**9,304**	**6,308**	**592**	**8,156**	**307**	**5,352**	**709**	**2,603**	**209**	**728**	**101**	**2,304**	**656**	**11,807**	**2,115**
22	3	63	..	18	3	8	1	3	..	2	..	3	..	39	18
13	1	27	3	97	..	122	..	40	..	81	..	19	15	271	15
2	..	47	2	24	..	50	..	14	..	23	1	9	1	59	1
1	..	6	1	1	..	7	..	..	..	6	..	2	..	7	1
..	..	127	..	..	..	40	5	15	..	1	..	2	2	107	..
3	1	2	..	15	..	22	..	2	..	18	..	3	2	30	4
1	..	8	..	4	..	4	1	8	..	1	..	1	..	10	2
15	1	10	..	28	..	32	..	12	..	14	..	1	1	108	1
112	5	60	..	80	..	84	3	22	1	81	..	31	12	302	13
905	205	903	25	340	9	340	47	88	1	22	1	60	9	818	167
..	..	3	..	54	..	..	..	1	..	..	..	12	5	13	1
718	125	208	40	60	6	12	17	1	..	8	..	12	14	210	19
10	..	100	5	5	..	12	1	1	..	2	..	..	..	45	3
17	1	3	..	3	..	5	..	2	..	..	..	1	..	10	5
1,102	364	351	140	556	55	93	3	279	80	17	2	90	70	1,317	260
80	18	158	32	6	..	35	..	1	..	4	..	7	2	60	15
232	70	22	1	24	7	48	3	4	1	3	1	12	1	98	29
28	..	18	..	17	..	15	..	3	1	..	..	5	3	51	..
88	1	11	..	37	..	22	1	..	..	..	..	5	2	30	1
18	..	97	1	..	..	21	..	5	..	7	1	2	1	12	3
48	2	23	..	..	..	7	..	4	..	7	1	10	2	37	8
6	1	4	..	301	..	17	..	5	..	2	..	18	..	16	2
17	3	37	1	132	..	10	1	12	..	..	..	16	1	97	7
40	8	19	..	5	..	3	5	..	..	5	..	..	..	40	8
203	38	47	1	18	4	23	2	5	..	1	..	3	3	127	7
12,307	9,470	3,713	91	3,325	40	1,405	379	2,318	39	271	105	1,320	712	13,872	2,812
17	..	79	..	18	..	52	..	..	..	..	..	..	2	18	12
37	..	21	2	18	..	22	1	5	..	..	..	17	5	57	4
87	7	330	2	56	1	9	..	7	..	3	..	6	3	160	7
5	..	67	..	..	..	..	..	..	..	1	..	2	..	21	..
60	45	1,187	50	42	12	135	22	11	..	60	..	12	10	230	25
08	12	901	16	38	2	40	12	..	2	11	1	10	2	92	12
135	125	143	..	30	..	60	3	24	4	3	..	9	4	113	7
751	41	141	8	88	..	790	24	28	..	33	..	22	1	392	13
30	2	35	2	60	..	22	..	9	..	2	..	4	..	35	10
07	14	301	48	1,115	2	227	6	128	2	70	7	75	8	540	18
5	2	9	..	41	..	14	..	3	..	3	..	8	5	21	4
146	**29**	**58**	**33**	**17**	**3**	**57**	**9**	**17**	**6**	**5**	**2**	**46**	**29**	**83**	**27**
..	..	7	..	3	..	12	..	14	..	2	..	4	..	9	1
12	..	3	4	4	2	..	..	..	5	..	..	8	4	7	1
13	..	7	..	..	..	7	1	4	..	..	..	8	..	15	3
19	6	8	7	5	..	..	2	2	..	..	..	12	11	14	3
21	2	16	3	..	..	15	2	2	..	..	..	3	1	18	2
112	**10**	**50**	**5**	**5**	**1**	**100**	**2**	**5**	**1**	**10**	**2**	**13**	**12**	**45**	**2**
10	..	4	..	1	..	7	..	..	..	2	..	2	3	2	..
12	..	5	..	1	..	7	..	1	..	3	..	5	3	4	..
15	**2**	**5**	**1**	..	..	..	..	**2**	..	**5**	..	**6**	**4**	**5**	..
12	..	4	..	..	..	..	..	1	..	4	..	5	1	4	..
75	**5**	**10**	**2**	**15**	**5**	**2**	**1**	**1**	..	..	..	**15**	**7**	**7**	**1**
12	3	5	1	10	1	1	..	..	..	3	1	9	9	1	..

Birth-place and caste.	Total Number of Immigrants.			Age. 0–15.		15–40.		40 and over.		Workers.		Dependents.	
	Persons.	Males.	Females.	Males.	Females.	Males.	Females.	Males.	Females.	Males.	Females.	Males.	Females.
1	2	3	4	5	6	7	8	9	10	11	12	13	14
Sawantwadi .. Total ..	**4,273**	**2,790**	**1,483**	**428**	**405**	**1,884**	**842**	**478**	**236**	**2,092**	**247**	**698**	**1,236**
Bhandari ..	299	267	32	40	2	189	23	38	7	230	4	37	28
Brahman Gaud Saraswat ..	203	178	25	24	1	126	19	28	5	140	1	38	24
Mahratta ..	1,205	999	206	201	36	507	101	291	69	660	30	339	176
Sheikh ..	304	227	77	29	8	186	52	112	17	155	5	72	72
***Kolhapur* .. Total ..**	**5,391**	**2,761**	**2,630**	**620**	**397**	**1,526**	**1,409**	**615**	**824**	**2,200**	**800**	**561**	**1,830**
Brahman ..	59	38	21	4	2	22	12	12	7	31	1	7	20
Dhed or Mahar ..	640	439	201	101	37	268	109	75	65	366	115	78	86
Mahratta ..	1,249	797	452	197	120	438	243	162	89	636	91	161	361
Sheikh ..	293	169	124	20	29	88	65	61	30	107	28	62	96
Cutch .. Total ..	**20,029**	**12,205**	**7,824**	**2,897**	**2,840**	**6,742**	**3,921**	**2,566**	**1,063**	**8,745**	**3,163**	**3,460**	**4,661**
Bhatia ..	2,752	1,604	1,148	325	357	997	648	282	143	1,036	254	568	894
Brahman Gaud Saraswat ..	309	198	111	35	29	128	66	35	16	105	28	93	83
,, Others ..	957	490	467	75	100	350	295	65	72	347	142	143	325
Lohana ..	4,433	2,387	2,046	618	785	1,320	1,059	449	202	1,578	1,056	809	990
Vani (Hindu) ..	2,010	1,408	602	310	201	801	303	297	98	967	151	441	451
Khoja ..	1,827	1,302	525	243	98	681	320	378	107	846	162	456	363
Memon ..	1,507	1,067	440	197	150	784	228	86	62	695	53	372	387
Sheikh ..	1,560	898	662	207	198	449	357	242	107	556	142	342	520
Sayyad ..	160	90	70	25	14	48	40	17	16	52	18	38	57
Vani Oswal (Jain) ..	182	126	56	17	18	92	34	17	4	83	12	43	44
,, Others (Jain) ..	1,529	1,229	300	329	81	720	137	180	82	767	75	462	225
Palanpur .. Total ..	**1,964**	**1,051**	**913**	**128**	**148**	**585**	**605**	**338**	**160**	**929**	**145**	**122**	**768**
Vani (Hindu) ..	98	87	11	6	2	76	6	5	3	79	..	8	11
Bohra ..	225	215	10	21	2	175	0	19	2	195	1	20	9
Sheikh ..	219	185	34	41	9	127	20	17	5	137	2	48	32
Vani (Jain) ..	175	150	25	22	8	109	12	19	5	129	1	21	24
Rest of the Western *India States Agency* .. Total ..	**51,324**	**32,384**	**18,940**	**5,290**	**4,389**	**17,845**	**9,982**	**9,249**	**4,569**	**27,213**	**3,557**	**5,171**	**15,383**
Bhangi ..	805	492	313	68	58	270	188	154	67	431	73	61	240
Bhatia ..	607	475	132	170	39	267	71	38	22	352	5	123	127
Brahman ..	2,128	1,901	227	90	29	1,298	107	513	91	1,795	13	106	214
Chambhar ..	1,295	710	585	91	198	380	285	239	102	639	131	71	454
Darji ..	2,821	1,925	896	282	163	1,302	467	341	266	1,709	108	216	793
Dhed ..	2,804	1,267	1,537	458	233	624	1,018	185	286	906	355	361	1,182
Dhobi ..	428	234	194	47	71	165	99	22	24	190	107	44	87
Kharva ..	1,165	810	355	121	87	559	204	130	64	687	74	123	281
Koli ..	351	284	67	15	12	218	42	51	13	253	37	31	30
Kumbhar ..	525	465	60	30	7	361	41	74	12	430	28	35	32
Mahratta ..	1,329	797	532	304	287	189	101	304	144	587	217	210	315
Lohana ..	161	103	58	47	5	43	40	13	13	72	9	31	49
Lohar ..	845	482	363	132	43	256	238	94	82	366	86	116	277
Rajput ..	328	209	119	39	36	126	61	44	22	169	21	40	98
Sonar ..	1,801	1,319	482	186	114	923	290	210	78	1,138	19	181	463
Sutar ..	504	366	138	44	35	261	83	61	20	324	7	42	131
Vani Modh ..	123	58	65	8	10	38	41	12	14	48	2	10	63
,, Kapol ..	329	181	148	17	12	109	98	55	38	165	7	16	141
,, Others ..	5,954	3,029	2,925	921	797	1,511	1,719	597	409	2,449	21	580	2,904
Bohra ..	2,697	2,370	327	604	134	1,354	145	412	48	1,790	40	580	287
Khoja ..	2,220	1,340	880	95	89	943	636	302	155	1,248	137	92	743
Memon ..	1,524	1,191	333	107	98	889	177	195	58	1,074	67	117	266
Pathan ..	355	261	94	41	16	129	49	91	29	224	19	37	75
Sheikh ..	403	227	176	27	57	150	82	50	37	198	27	29	149
Vani others (Jain) ..	443	353	90	68	23	207	46	78	21	289	3	64	87
Ajmer Merwara .. Total ..	**3,588**	**3,036**	**552**	**438**	**121**	**1,729**	**350**	**869**	**81**	**2,265**	**74**	**771**	**478**
Brahman ..	278	197	81	41	6	87	59	69	16	135	10	62	71
Vani Oswal (Hindu) ..	301	202	99	34	18	128	61	40	20	152	14	50	85
Sheikh ..	597	404	193	80	23	203	89	121	81	213	9	191	184
Bengal .. Total ..	**2,476**	**1,902**	**574**	**430**	**110**	**1,004**	**395**	**468**	**69**	**1,360**	**98**	**542**	**476**
Brahman ..	120	92	28	10	5	73	12	9	11	78	9	14	19
Sheikh ..	230	190	40	14	9	119	22	57	9	152	10	38	30
C. P. & Berar .. Total ..	**4,814**	**3,470**	**1,344**	**812**	**310**	**2,125**	**901**	**533**	**133**	**2,726**	**311**	**744**	**1,033**
Brahman ..	248	178	70	27	24	125	35	26	11	150	5	28	65
Mahratta ..	625	421	204	91	58	230	100	100	46	280	41	141	163
Sheikh ..	421	293	128	65	17	180	89	48	22	252	12	41	116
Delhi .. Total ..	**3,320**	**2,496**	**824**	**614**	**165**	**259**	**554**	**623**	**105**	**1,800**	**224**	**696**	**600**
Kharva ..	260	148	112	30	32	80	60	38	20	120	28	28	84
Vani (Hindu) ..	235	210	25	30	8	153	12	27	5	160	1	60	24
Sheikh ..	223	172	51	20	8	124	32	28	11	150	10	22	41

Textile Industries.		Persons of all ranks occupied in industries other than textile.		Transport.		Trade.		Public force and Administration.		Professions and liberal arts (excluding religious Mendicants).		Domestic Service.		Insufficiently described occupation.	
Males.	Females.	Males.	Females.	Males.	Females.	Males.	Females.	Males.	Females.	Males.	Females.	Males.	Females.	Males.	Females.
15	16	17	18	19	20	21	22	23	24	25	26	27	28	29	30
605	**61**	**137**	**9**	**9**	..	**43**	..	**17**	..	**21**	..	**58**	**40**	**202**	**10**
51	..	6	..	..	..	37	..	2	..	1	..	..	..	28	..
33	..	7	..	..	..	3	..	1	..	2	..	5	..	19	..
203	2	31	..	1	..	..	..	1	..	1	..	33	11	60	2
6	..	3	..	6	..	3	..	..	..	4	..	20	2	30	..
567	**31**	**301**	**24**	**4**	..	**6**	..	**30**	..	**8**	..	**87**	**125**	**199**	**217**
..	..	..	..	..	..	..	..	3	..	1	..	..	..	11	..
20	9	11	2	..	..	..	..	7	..	..	..	40	7	105	39
167	7	43	2	1	..	1	..	4	..	4	..	37	18	61	18
6	..	3	..	3	..	4	..	7	..	3	..	5	14	22	..
543	**134**	**1,432**	**215**	**120**	**22**	**2,414**	**124**	**144**	..	**112**	**26**	**1,574**	**1,477**	**1,612**	**654**
90	..	29	3	17	4	563	22	5	..	16	5	13	95	135	69
3	..	3	..	..	..	35	5	..	..	7	1	5	15	38	3
..	..	15	..	9	..	45	..	42	..	22	7	115	85	56	23
30	17	468	143	15	..	142	66	..	..	..	..	353	446	292	233
..	..	48	..	16	5	377	29	7	..	11	..	165	63	218	28
25	..	212	..	32	7	192	43	8	..	9	..	134	62	142	25
15	..	127	..	18	..	263	..	12	..	8	..	35	29	117	12
25	12	145	18	12	..	136	..	23	..	6	..	64	72	78	18
2	..	7	..	..	..	12	..	4	..	7	2	5	7	8	3
..	..	..	..	..	..	43	1	..	..	..	..	12	8	15	2
..	..	56	..	..	..	335	10	10	..	8	..	114	36	154	20
37	**1**	**25**	**1**	**40**	..	**197**	..	**5**	..	**9**	..	**48**	**32**	**103**	**40**
1	..	3	..	7	..	17	..	..	..	..	..	5	..	6	..
..	..	..	..	2	..	81	..	..	..	..	..	..	..	14	..
3	..	4	..	10	..	28	..	..	..	..	..	5	1	18	..
..	..	..	..	3	..	57	..	..	..	..	..	..	..	4	..
766	**104**	**1,350**	**417**	**500**	**75**	**4,480**	**160**	**580**	**130**	**415**	**14**	**808**	**371**	**4,707**	**468**
1	1	4	2	2	..	..	..	20	3	..	..	9	2	179	28
..	..	1	..	..	..	157	..	5	..	3	..	..	2	10	..
..	..	..	..	17	..	8	..	150	1	7	..	128	4	686	1
17	..	28	..	1	..	37	..	7	..	3	..	104	3	610	3
37	..	17	..	5	..	304	27	8	..	9	..	174	16	300	8
106	23	218	27	..	..	..	..	6	..	..	..	5	77	148	50
3	1	7	2	1	..	30	..	..	..	..	..	45	43	9	7
18	3	17	2	25	..	243	..	..	..	..	..	13	28	27	4
3	1	7	..	..	..	100	10	..	..	..	..	7	2	9	..
17	..	40	..	6	..	109	9	..	..	..	..	13	9	30	..
140	17	98	25	5	..	6	..	..	..	..	..	5	36	39	30
2	..	5	..	3	..	17	..	..	..	..	..	4	3	5	1
18	2	21	7	13	1	97	5	3	..	5	..	6	22	20	6
2	..	3	..	1	..	35	..	4	..	7	..	18	8	14	2
7	..	212	..	21	..	108	..	19	..	12	..	17	7	173	2
21	..	53	..	5	..	61	..	2	..	7	..	4	3	9	..
..	..	..	..	..	..	18	..	..	..	..	..	1	1	5	..
..	..	..	..	..	..	47	..	..	..	..	..	5	2	30	1
30	..	41	..	17	..	508	..	9	..	17	..	12	7	590	3
1	..	2	..	5	..	725	..	1	..	7	..	100	7	144	13
53	..	37	..	15	..	304	..	23	..	10	..	53	20	129	48
104	1	57	1	29	..	207	..	3	..	7	..	43	27	87	4
27	..	23	..	17	..	38	..	6	..	..	..	..	9	1	..
18	1	7	2	8	..	62	..	..	..	..	..	..	7	3	3
3	..	1	..	1	..	92	..	1	..	7	..	12	1	27	..
305	**1**	**99**	**1**	**3**	..	**249**	**3**	**22**	..	**12**	..	**235**	**30**	**232**	**8**
..	..	2	..	1	..	1	..	12	..	3	..	5	5	42	..
..	..	3	..	..	..	62	3	1	..	3	..	..	4	10	..
21	..	4	..	2	..	7	..	9	..	6	..	7	1	50	3
312	**17**	**48**	**5**	**25**	..	**7**	**3**	**12**	..	**51**	**3**	**12**	**12**	**28**	**3**
..	..	2	..	2	..	1	..	7	..	9	..	3	4	10	..
30	..	5	..	7	..	5	..	1	..	..	..	6	5	6	..
308	**13**	**199**	..	**201**	..	**60**	..	**29**	..	**18**	**10**	**201**	**20**	**342**	**112**
2	..	3	..	6	..	1	..	17	..	5	..	6	2	35	..
41	2	37	..	15	..	..	..	1	..	1	..	18	11	27	7
17	..	5	..	..	..	47	..	1	..	3	6	13	..	40	..
477	**77**	**68**	**8**	**51**	**2**	**70**	**2**	**3**	..	**6**	**3**	**80**	**15**	**25**	**1**
36	9	9	1	1	1	..	..	..	..	3	..	11	3	..	..
2	..	6	..	1	..	63	..	1	..	2	..	2	1	3	..
20	1	5	..	12	..	3	..	1	..	1	..	6	4	2	..

Birth-place and Caste.		Total Number of Immigrants.		Age.						Workers.		Dependents.	
				0–15.		15–40.		40 and over.					
	Persons.	Males.	Females.	Males.	Females.	Males.	Females.	Males.	Females.	Males.	Females.	Males.	Females.
1	2	3	4	5	6	7	8	9	10	11	12	13	14
N. W. F. Province .. Total ..	**724**	**283**	**441**	**51**	**49**	**142**	**258**	**90**	**134**	**200**	**60**	**83**	**381**
Brahman ..	87	81	6	6	..	70	5	5	1	64	..	17	6
Pathan ..	119	87	32	19	17	57	10	11	5	65	..	22	32
Sheikh ..	92	89	3	9	1	77	2	3	..	80	..	9	3
Punjab .. Total ..	**8,517**	**6,863**	**1,654**	**962**	**357**	**4,054**	**1,189**	**1,847**	**108**	**6,015**	**220**	**848**	**1,434**
Brahman ..	320	253	67	25	18	177	31	51	18	202	1	51	66
Memon ..	210	184	26	14	2	143	19	27	5	158	2	26	24
Pathan ..	1,009	858	151	53	22	608	115	197	14	807	12	51	139
Sheikh ..	1,890	1,436	454	163	63	1,002	365	271	26	957	51	479	403
Sikh ..	298	288	5	23	1	172	3	93	1	231	..	57	5
United Provinces ..	**83,328**	**68,828**	**14,500**	**6,304**	**3,002**	**50,102**	**8,377**	**12,417**	**3,121**	**56,320**	**2,892**	**12,503**	**11,608**
Ahir ..	1,140	1,017	123	43	4	766	89	208	30	904	24	113	99
Brahman ..	4,550	3,904	646	200	75	3,001	428	703	143	3,643	97	261	549
Chambhar	760	685	75	93	26	483	30	109	19	587	40	98	35
Dhobi ..	1,240	1,090	150	85	27	836	109	169	14	694	60	396	90
Maratha ..	4,003	3,742	261	197	62	2,942	127	603	72	1,871	65	1,871	196
Rajput ..	1,320	1,024	296	103	23	792	187	129	86	745	59	279	237
Teli ..	645	638	7	27	1	541	4	70	2	532	1	106	6
Thakur ..	2,103	2,002	101	197	13	1,703	67	102	21	1,913	34	89	67
Vani (Hindu) ..	1,002	943	59	76	8	742	37	125	14	804	12	139	47
Memon ..	1,320	1,140	180	222	13	643	117	275	50	814	27	326	153
Pathan ..	2,472	1,993	749	140	102	1,243	607	610	140	1,708	151	285	598
Sheikh ..	13,302	11,147	2,155	1,803	702	8,043	1,023	1,301	430	9,289	359	1,858	1,796
Sayyad ..	1,063	943	120	103	23	567	82	273	15	825	12	118	108
Madras .. Total ..	**21,415**	**14,876**	**6,539**	**1,920**	**1,192**	**10,547**	**3,640**	**2,409**	**1,707**	**10,612**	**2,635**	**4,264**	**3,904**
Bhandari ..	260	248	12	29	3	198	6	21	3	187	6	61	6
Brahman Saraswat ..	915	600	315	103	84	424	171	73	60	456	52	144	263
„ Others ..	1,821	1,229	592	125	129	901	357	203	106	1,021	98	208	494
Maratha ..	1,229	968	261	102	38	760	142	106	81	795	112	173	149
Naidu ..	295	225	70	39	27	156	32	30	11	168	10	57	60
Vani (Hindu) ..	195	151	44	27	12	95	21	29	11	110	7	41	37
Sheikh ..	1,025	894	131	140	18	598	72	156	41	682	12	212	119
Baroda .. Total ..	**6,027**	**3,900**	**2,127**	**647**	**309**	**2,029**	**1,197**	**1,224**	**621**	**3,412**	**382**	**488**	**1,745**
Bhangi ..	171	70	101	15	59	48	28	7	14	50	21	20	80
Bhatia ..	98	77	21	8	2	58	15	11	4	61	1	16	20
Brahman ..	521	389	132	82	17	186	77	121	38	312	9	77	123
Dhed ..	305	185	120	19	21	103	67	63	32	156	24	29	96
Koli ..	224	169	55	10	7	88	34	71	14	131	1	38	54
Lohana ..	170	129	41	57	3	49	29	23	9	104	2	25	39
Mahratta ..	501	323	178	40	58	230	96	44	24	209	41	54	137
Vani (Hindu) ..	521	340	181	44	24	182	96	114	61	260	5	80	176
Bohra ..	249	197	52	50	10	103	29	44	13	121	5	76	50
Sheikh ..	271	198	73	40	11	120	39	38	23	146	10	52	63
Zoroastrian ..	1,529	903	626	201	98	305	388	397	140	404	23	409	603
Central India Agency Total ..	**3,330**	**2,063**	**1,267**	**225**	**199**	**1,292**	**803**	**546**	**265**	**1,708**	**127**	**355**	**1,140**
Brahman ..	320	303	17	21	2	175	9	107	6	238	3	65	14
Mahratta ..	193	164	29	15	3	110	18	39	8	148	8	16	21
Bohra ..	167	132	35	22	9	80	20	30	6	94	2	38	33
Sheikh ..	240	207	33	28	4	147	17	32	12	164	9	43	24
Hyderabad .. Total ..	**15,914**	**11,031**	**4,883**	**2,027**	**1,503**	**7,342**	**2,823**	**1,662**	**557**	**7,817**	**2,115**	**3,214**	**2,768**
Brahman ..	360	190	170	60	34	83	57	47	79	105	55	85	115
Dhobi ..	163	114	49	24	7	65	14	25	23	75	36	39	13
Koli ..	1,897	1,501	396	203	91	1,121	229	177	76	1,172	147	329	249
Mahratta ..	3,201	2,580	621	390	150	1,567	396	623	75	2,115	328	465	293
Lohana ..	283	263	20	40	2	201	14	22	4	202	8	61	12
Vani (Hindu) ..	164	129	35	10	9	85	15	34	11	95	6	34	29
Pathan ..	283	209	74	44	18	123	38	42	18	150	12	59	62
Sheikh ..	864	369	495	63	33	207	321	99	141	258	146	111	349
Mysore .. Total ..	**2,937**	**2,036**	**901**	**429**	**207**	**1,120**	**450**	**487**	**244**	**1,309**	**198**	**727**	**703**
Brahman ..	498	328	170	71	49	210	88	47	33	182	9	146	161
Dhed ..	397	298	99	101	40	133	44	64	15	213	26	85	73
Mahratta ..	221	158	63	31	14	85	30	42	19	103	23	55	40
Rajputana .. Total ..	**8,389**	**6,834**	**1,555**	**1,890**	**307**	**4,201**	**789**	**743**	**459**	**5,228**	**311**	**1,611**	**1,244**
Brahman ..	425	318	107	20	15	259	79	39	13	290	13	28	94
Mahratta ..	410	357	53	28	11	249	32	80	10	324	18	33	35
Rajput ..	550	492	58	19	4	351	43	122	11	467	6	25	52
Vani (Hindu) ..	894	749	145	84	21	527	89	138	35	611	14	138	131
Sheikh ..	1,426	1,141	285	118	46	899	187	124	52	1,064	41	77	244
Vani Oswal (Jain) ..	876	813	63	211	19	484	36	118	8	739	3	74	60
Vani Others (Jain) ..	899	847	52	213	18	490	29	144	5	462	2	385	56
French and Portuguese Settlement in India Total ..	**38,702**	**25,915**	**12,787**	**3,343**	**2,540**	**18,858**	**7,682**	**3,714**	**2,565**	**21,363**	**4,262**	**[illegible],552**	**8,525**
Bhandari ..	363	247	116	48	30	129	64	70	22	189	29	58	87
Brahman Gaud Saraswat ..	710	543	167	100	23	360	87	83	57	362	8	181	159
Dhed ..	200	163	37	26	7	113	24	24	6	102	28	61	9
Mahratta ..	1,500	880	620	118	110	648	401	114	109	625	310	255	310
Sonar ..	128	78	40	19	6	43	29	16	5	75	2	3	38
Sutar ..	124	67	57	9	8	46	38	12	11	48	2	19	55
Sheikh ..	157	98	59	8	6	53	39	37	14	88	2	10	57
Goanese Christian ..	18,975	14,027	4,948	1,769	488	8,190	2,824	4,068	1,636	11,689	1,979	2,338	2,969

Textile Industries.		Persons of all ranks occupied in industries other than textile.		Transport.		Trade.		Public force and Administration.		Professions and liberal arts (excluding religious Mendicants).		Domestic service.		Insufficiently described occupation.	
Males.	Females.	Males.	Females.	Males.	Females.	Males.	Females.	Males.	Females.	Males.	Females.	Males.	Females.	Males.	Females.
15	16	17	18	19	20	21	22	23	24	25	26	27	28	29	30
27	1	19	1	31	..	17	..	8	..	2	1	12	17	20	..
3	..	1	..	3	..	1	..	1	..	1	..	2	..	13	..
10	..	7	..	5	..	6	..	..	..	..	..	2	..	..	..
13	..	9	..	1	..	3	..	1	..	1	..	..	..	4	..
1,339	2	732	1	301	..	93	..	21	..	27	2	112	67	148	3
3	..	1	..	9	..	4	..	7	..	9	..	31	1	31	..
37	..	1	..	17	..	10	..	1	..	3	..	6	2	4	..
167	..	34	..	109	..	27	..	1	..	2	1	37	9	3	..
170	..	47	..	112	..	29	..	..	..	2	..	30	23	93	..
1	..	1	..	47	..	16	..	7	..	6	..	1	..	11	..
13,267	507	362	167	1,927	39	2,140	..	800	9	205	..	3,302	326	6,157	411
167	4	10	..	63	..	97	..	13	..	..	..	54	5	132	3
420	..	201	..	43	..	67	..	83	3	87	..	17	30	904	15
193	7	40	1	3	3	8	..	1	..	..	..	13	6	40	6
53	2	31	5	..	..	..	..	..	..	7	..	87	6	167	17
403	7	186	3	156	7	5	..	2	..	1	..	73	14	127	8
103	2	7	1	9	..	17	..	5	..	1	..	27	20	205	6
71	..	49	..	1	..	50	..	1	..	..	..	7	..	86	..
467	7	304	6	..	9	..	..	..	..	..	..	71	30	114	27
2	..	1	..	..	..	257	..	..	..	73	..	30	6	40	..
17	..	13	..	5	..	105	..	2	..	3	..	69	2	201	11
117	1	167	..	17	..	28	..	2	..	1	..	149	57	461	12
2,904	25	1,746	12	4	..	8	..	4	..	1	..	56	79	504	63
202	..	68	..	..	..	3	..	..	..	..	..	37	6	100	..
557	127	1,076	238	178	15	745	47	365	..	148	45	2,592	788	2,682	652
18	..	30	..	..	..	7	..	5	..	..	..	37	6	35	..
12	..	47	..	8	..	85	..	27	..	15	7	74	18	88	8
25	..	176	..	11	..	38	..	59	..	28	15	216	28	223	17
63	8	178	12	12	..	..	..	16	..	6	..	178	45	165	18
4	..	12	..	3	..	26	..	16	..	7	2	25	5	32	..
..	..	..	..	2	..	62	4	..	..	..	..	17	2	5	..
23	..	75	..	10	..	112	..	37	..	6	..	137	5	135	4
357	7	205	8	167	8	380	2	61	4	17	1	136	81	467	89
9	3	5	4	2	2	..	..	9	1	..	..	..	..	..	..
2	..	5	..	3	..	17	..	..	..	..	..	..	..	3	..
1	..	3	..	7	..	1	..	8	..	2	..	47	4	87	..
2	1	1	1	1	..	..	..	..	..	..	..	40	3	34	7
3	..	7	..	15	..	27	..	..	..	..	..	..	..	14	..
..	..	..	..	..	..	30	..	..	..	..	..	2	..	20	..
30	1	17	..	20	..	8	..	..	..	..	..	15	7	41	12
..	..	..	..	..	..	53	..	..	..	..	..	9	2	68	..
..	..	..	..	..	..	51	..	..	..	..	..	..	..	9	..
7	..	3	..	8	..	45	..	..	..	..	..	..	5	10	..
1	..	1	..	2	..	137	..	27	2	5	..	..	8	29	..
347	..	71	..	..	..	203	..	47	..	7	..	83	36	125	17
..	..	4	..	..	..	..	..	30	..	1	..	1	1	53	..
30	..	5	..	..	..	1	..	3	..	1	..	5	1	29	3
..	..	..	..	..	..	41	..	1	..	2	..	..	1	3	..
7	..	3	..	..	..	37	..	5	..	2	..	..	2	28	2
257	87	1,786	142	89	15	235	83	137	..	38	16	1,378	845	1,025	378
..	..	4	..	5	..	12	..	10	..	12	7	23	28	18	10
..	..	65	23	..	..	..	..	..	..	..	..	..	5	5	3
18	..	419	12	8	..	17	..	8	..	..	..	323	58	145	39
125	16	547	27	87	8	27	5	38	..	7	..	557	134	468	55
..	..	67	..	3	..	28	..	..	..	..	..	13	3	55	2
..	..	4	..	..	..	47	3	..	..	..	..	7	2	18	..
1	..	12	..	..	..	5	..	12	..	..	..	52	6	32	..
7	4	32	12	5	..	25	12	27	..	4	2	52	42	47	28
197	27	83	11	20	..	12	..	6	..	9	..	123	43	207	22
1	..	2	..	1	..	..	..	..	..	2	..	7	4	77	..
47	8	13	2	..	..	..	..	..	..	..	..	13	..	33	3
14	5	..	..	..	..	4	..	3	..	7	..	..	4	13	2
293	13	360	17	240	5	467	..	15	..	13	..	361	105	862	15
1	..	2	..	7	..	2	..	1	..	7	..	21	5	104	1
31	1	47	..	20	..	..	..	..	..	..	..	22	7	42	1
5	..	7	..	32	..	60	..	..	..	..	..	31	3	98	..
1	..	1	..	5	..	117	..	7	..	..	..	65	7	109	..
140	..	99	..	37	..	51	..	1	..	..	..	64	13	136	7
1	..	1	..	3	..	150	..	..	..	..	..	27	..	187	..
..	..	..	..	..	..	128	..	1	..	..	..	31	..	86	..
667	100	2,225	309	1,504	15	597	35	150	5	225	30	1,550	1,045	2,073	591
40	5	37	3	..	..	..	..	..	..	..	..	7	2	10	4
11	..	40	..	17	..	5	..	41	..	10	..	8	4	47	..
27	..	14	..	2	..	..	..	..	..	..	..	2	3	6	11
112	52	99	36	9	..	..	..	1	..	1	..	17	28	87	36
..	..	2	..	..	..	..	..	..	..	9	..	5	1	21	..
9	..	7	..	5	..	1	..	2	..	..	..	..	1	..	..
3	..	4	..	..	..	17	..	..	..	..	..	..	1	5	..
85	1	1,417	36	1,322	12	328	31	27	..	166	29	1,125	716	1,103	164

MO-I Bk Ra Cs 3—49

Occupation or Means of Livelihood.

(Corresponding to Imperial Table X—Part I.)

—	Persons.	Males.	Females.
Total Earners	563,042	507,599 *2,521	52,327 *595
Total Working Dependents	2,861	1,096	1,765
Total Non-working Dependents	595,480	236,165	359,315
Total Population ..	1,161,383	747,381	414,002

*Earners who refused to return their occupations.

Occupation or Means of Livelihood.

(Corresponding to Imperial Table X—Part I.)

Group No.	Occupation.	Total following occupation.	As principal occupation.		As working dependents.		As subsidiary to other occupation.	
			Males.	Females.	Males.	Females.	Males.	Females.
1	2	3	4	5	6	7	8	9
	Total All Classes	562,871	507,599	52,327	1,096	1,765	84	..
	Earners who refused to return their occupations	..	2,521	595	..	..	..	..
	Total Class A—Production of Raw Materials	11,943	10,491	1,276	89	65	22	..
	Total Sub-Class I—Exploitation of Animals and Vegetation	10,866	9,530	1,160	89	65	22	..
	Total Order 1—Pasture and Agriculture	8,394	7,699	538	89	65	3	..
	Total Sub-Order 1 (a)—Cultivation	2,734	2,219	358	89	65	3	..
1	Non-cultivating proprietors taking rent in money or kind	1,626	1,172	300	89	65	..	..
2	Estate Agents and Managers of owners	68	66	2	..	..	..	..
3	Estate Agents and Managers of Government	11	4	7	..	..	..	..
4	Rent collectors, clerks, etc.	13	13	..	..	..	..	..
5	Cultivating owners	414	386	25	..	..	3	..
6	Tenant cultivators	94	82	12	..	..	..	..
7	Agricultural labourers	508	496	12	..	..	..	..
	Total Sub-Order 1 (b)—Cultivation of special crops, fruits, etc. (Planters, Managers, Clerks and Labourers)	2,118	2,015	103	..	..	..	..
9	Cinchona	75	75	..	..	..	..	..
10	Coconut	2	1	1	..	..	..	..
11	Coffee	6	6	..	..	..	..	..
13	Pan-Vine	21	21	..	..	..	..	..
14	Rubber	13	13	..	..	..	..	..
15	Tea	30	28	2	..	..	..	..
16	Market gardeners, flower and fruit growers	1,971	1,871	100	..	..	..	..
	Total Sub-Order 1 (c)—Forestry	319	297	22	..	..	..	..
17	Forest officers, rangers, guards, etc.	15	12	3	..	..	..	..
18	Wood cutters and charcoal burners	218	218	..	..	..	..	..
19	Collectors of forest produce	80	61	19	..	..	..	..
20	Collectors of lac	6	6	..	..	..	..	..
	Total Sub-Order 1 (d)—Stock-raising	3,176	3,123	53	..	..	..	..
21	Cattle and buffalo breeders and keepers	3,156	3,103	53	..	..	..	..
22	Breeders of transport animals	12	12	..	..	..	..	..
23	Herdsmen, shepherds and breeders of other animals	8	8	..	..	..	..	..
	Total Sub-Order 1 (e)—Raising of Small Animals and Insects	47	45	2	..	..	..	..
24	Birds, bees, etc.	1	1	..	..	..	..	..
26	Lac cultivation	46	44	2	..	..	..	..
	Total Order 2—Fishing and Hunting	2,472	1,831	622	..	..	19	..
27	Fishing and pearling	2,470	1,829	622	..	..	19	..
28	Hunting	2	2	..	..	..	..	..
	Total Sub-Class II—Exploitation of Minerals	1,077	961	116	..	..	..	..
	Total Order 3—Metallic Minerals	86	85	1	..	..	..	..
30	Iron	1	1	..	..	..	..	..
33	Tin and wolfram	43	43	..	..	..	..	..
34	Other metallic minerals	42	41	1	..	..	..	..
	Total Order 4—Non-Metallic Minerals	991	876	115	..	..	..	..
35	Coal	22	16	6	..	..	..	..
37	Building materials (including stone, materials for cement-manufacture and clays)	302	267	35	..	..	..	..
40	Salt, saltpetre and other saline substances	666	592	74	..	..	..	..
41	Other non-metallic minerals	1	1	..	..	..	..	..
	Total Class B—Preparation and Supply of Material Substances	313,961	283,914	28,100	231	1,656	60	..
	Total Sub-Class III—Industry	176,338	154,446	21,866	20	1	5	..
	Total Order 5—Textiles	116,534	99,708	16,825	1	..	..	..
42	Cotton ginning, cleaning and pressing	1,875	1,641	234	..	..	..	..
43	Cotton spinning, sizing and weaving	113,085	96,614	16,470	1	..	..	..
44	Jute pressing, spinning and weaving	77	52	25	..	..	..	..
45	Rope, twine, string and other fibres	82	54	28	..	..	..	..
46	Wool carding, spinning and weaving	24	12	12	..	..	..	..
47	Silk spinning and weaving	11	6	5	..	..	..	..
48	Hair (horse-hair), etc.	1	1	..	..	..	..	..
49	Dyeing, bleaching, printing, preparation and sponging of textiles	934	900	34	..	..	..	..
50	Lace, crepe, embroideries, fringes, etc., and insufficiently described textile industries	445	428	17	..	..	..	..

Group No.	Occupation.	Total following occupation.	As principal occupation.		As working dependents.		As subsidiary to other occupation.	
			Males.	Females.	Males.	Females.	Males.	Females.
1	2	3	4	5	6	7	8	9
	Total Order 6—Hides, Skins and Hard Materials from the animal kingdom	**1,354**	**1,266**	**88**	..	..	..	..
51	Working in leather	772	746	26	..	..	..	..
52	Furriers and persons occupied with feathers and bristles ; brush makers	517	460	57	..	..	..	..
53	Bone, ivory, horn, shell, etc., workers (except buttons)	65	60	5	..	..	..	..
	Total Order 7—Wood	**6,418**	**6,172**	**246**	..	..	..	..
54	Sawyers	72	72	..	..	..	..	..
55	Carpenters, turners and joiners, etc.	5,863	5,804	59	..	..	..	..
56	Basket makers and other industries of woody materials, including leaves and thatchers and builders working with bamboo, reeds or similar materials	483	296	187	..	..	..	..
	Total Order 8—Metals	**3,213**	**3,125**	**88**	..	..	..	..
57	Smelting, forging and rolling of iron and other metals	76	74	2	..	..	..	..
58	Makers of arms, guns, etc.	65	64	1	..	..	..	..
59	Blacksmiths, other workers in iron, makers of implements	1,409	1,365	44	..	..	..	..
60	Workers in brass, copper and bell metal	282	279	3	..	..	..	..
61	Workers in other metals (except precious metals)	1,330	1,293	37	..	..	..	..
62	Workers in mints, diesinkers, etc.	51	50	1	..	..	..	..
	Total Order 9—Ceramics	**667**	**576**	**91**	..	..	..	..
63	Potters and makers of earthen-ware	486	417	69	..	..	..	..
64	Brick and tile makers	116	116	..	..	..	..	..
65	Other workers in ceramics	65	43	22	..	..	..	..
	Total Order 10—*Chemical Products properly so-called and Analogous*	**439**	**399**	**40**	..	..	..	..
66	Manufacture of matches, fire works and other explosives	96	86	10	..	..	..	..
67	Manufacture of aerated and mineral waters and ice	71	71	..	..	..	..	..
68	Manufacture and refining of vegetable oils	16	13	3	..	..	..	..
69	Manufacture and refining of mineral oils	16	16	..	..	..	..	..
70	Others	240	213	27	..	..	..	..
	Total Order 11—Food Industries	**3,109**	**2,889**	**209**	**11**	..	..	..
71	Rice pounders and huskers and flour grinders	52	51	1	..	..	..	..
72	Grain parchers, etc.	286	277	9	..	..	..	..
73	Butchers	977	953	14	10	..	..	..
74	Makers of sugar, molasses and gur	17	17	..	..	..	..	..
75	Sweet-meat and condiment makers	533	528	5	..	..	..	..
76	Toddy drawers	420	404	16	..	..	..	..
77	Brewers and distillers	2	2	..	..	..	..	..
78	Manufacturers of tobacco	324	182	141	1	..	..	..
80	Manufacturers of ganja	54	54	..	..	..	..	..
81	Others	444	421	23	..	..	..	..
	Total Order 12—Industries of Dress and the Toilet	**24,784**	**22,730**	**2,048**	..	**1**	**5**	..
82	Boot, shoe, sandal and clog makers	3,672	3,372	299	..	1	..	..
83	Tailors, milliners, dress makers and darners	11,666	10,516	1,145	..	..	5	..
84	Embroiderers, hat makers and makers of other articles of wear	185	157	28	..	..	..	..
85	Washing and cleaning	5,588	5,053	535	..	..	..	..
86	Barbers, hair dressers and wig makers	3,068	3,034	34	..	..	..	..
87	Other industries connected with the toilet	605	598	7	..	..	..	..
	Total Order 13—Furniture Industries	**1,179**	**1,177**	**2**	..	..	..	..
88	Cabinet-makers, carriage painters, etc.	1,038	1,036	2	..	..	..	..
89	Upholsterers, tent makers, etc.	141	141	..	..	..	..	..
	Total Order 14—Building Industries	**3,371**	**3,336**	**35**	..	..	..	..
90	Lime burners, cement workers, excavators and well sinkers ; Stone cutters and dressers ; Brick-layers and masons ; Builders (other than buildings made of bamboo or similar materials), painters, decorators of houses, tilers, plumbers, etc.	3,371	3,336	35	..	..	..	..
	Total Order 15—Construction of Means of Transport	**771**	**643**	**128**	..	..	..	..
91	Persons engaged in making, assembling or repairing motor vehicles or cycles	583	484	99	..	..	..	..
92	Carriage, cart, palki, etc., makers and wheel-wrights	26	7	19	..	..	..	..
93	Ship, boat, aeroplane builders	162	152	10	..	..	..	..
	Total Order 16—Production and Transmission of Physical Force	**1,205**	**1,184**	**21**	..	..	..	..
94	Heat, light, electricity, motive power, etc., gas works and electric light and power	1,205	1,184	21	..	..	..	..
	Total Order 17—Miscellaneous and Undefined Industries	**13,294**	**11,241**	**2,045**	**8**	..	..	..
95	Printers, engravers, book-binders, etc.	2,171	2,096	75	..	..	..	..
96	Makers of musical instruments	614	585	29	..	..	..	..
97	Makers of clocks and surgical or scientific instruments, etc.	300	297	3	..	..	..	..
98	Makers of jewellery and ornaments	2,316	2,288	28	..	..	..	..
99	Other miscellaneous and undefined industries (toy making, taxi dermy, etc).	1,889	1,508	381	..	..	..	..
100	Scavenging	6,004	4,467	1,529	8	..	..	..

Group No.	Occupation.	Total following occupation.	As principal occupation.		As working dependents.		As subsidiary to other occupation.	
			Males.	Females.	Males.	Females.	Males.	Females.
1	2	3	4	5	6	7	8	9
	Total Sub-Class IV—Transport	**50,783**	**50,148**	**580**	..	..	**55**	..
	Total Order 18—Transport by Air	**45**	**39**	**6**	..	..	..	..
101	Persons concerned with aerodromes and aeroplanes	45	39	6	..	..	..	..
	Total Order 19—Transport by Water	**21,051**	**20,773**	**223**	..	..	**55**	..
102	Ship-owners, boat-owners and their employees, officers, mariners, etc. Ships' brokers, boatmen and tow men	14,254	14,166	33	..	..	55	..
103	Persons (other than labourers) employed in harbours, docks, rivers and canals, including pilots	1,531	1,502	29	..	..	..	..
104	Labourers employed on harbours, docks, rivers and canals	5,266	5,105	161	..	..	..	..
	Total Order 20—Transport by Road	**14,977**	**14,803**	**174**		..	..	..
105	Persons (other than labourers) employed on the construction and maintenance of roads and bridges	522	520	2	..	..	..	..
106	Labourers employed on roads and bridges	700	598	102	..	..	..	..
107	Owners, managers and employees (excluding personal servants) connected with mechanically driven vehicles (including trams)	5,302	5,276	26	..	..	..	..
108	Owners, managers and employees (excluding personal servants) connected with other vehicles	3,465	3,441	24	..	..	..	..
109	Palki, etc., bearers and owners	21	20	1	..	..	..	..
110	Pack elephant, camel, mule, ass and bullock owners and drivers	14	13	1	..	..	..	..
111	Porters and messengers	4,953	4,935	18	..	..	..	..
	Total Order 21—Transport by Rail	**13,344**	**13,196**	**148**	..	..	..	..
112	Railway employees of all kinds other than coolies	10,152	10,080	72	..	..	..	..
113	Labourers employed on railway construction and maintenance and coolies and porters employed on railway premises	3,192	3,116	76	..	..	..	..
	Total Order 22—Post Office, Telegraph and Telephone Services	**1,366**	**1,337**	**29**	..	..	..	..
114	Post office, telegraph and telephone services	1,366	1,337	29	..	..	..	..
	Total Sub-Class V—Trade	**86,840**	**79,320**	**5,654**	**211**	**1,655**	..	..
	Total Order 23—Banks, Establishments of Credit, Exchange and Insurance	**3,672**	**3,618**	**54**	..	..	..	..
115	Bank managers, money-lenders, exchange and insurance agents, money changers and brokers and their employees	3,672	3,618	54	..	..	..	..
	Total Order 24—Brokerage Commission and Export	**5,199**	**4,815**	**36**	**5**	**343**	..	..
116	Brokers, commission agents, commercial travellers, wear-house owners and employees	5,199	4,815	36	5	343	..	..
	Total Order 25—Trade in Textiles	**992**	**963**	**29**	..	..	..	..
117	Trade in piece-goods, wool, cotton, silk, hair and other textiles	992	963	29	..	..	..	..
	Total Order 26—Trade in Skins, Leather and Furs	**91**	**81**	**10**	..	..	..	..
118	Trade in skins, leather, furs, feathers, horn, etc., and the articles made from these	91	81	10	..	..	..	..
	Total Order 27—Trade in Wood	**346**	**309**	**37**	..	..	..	..
119	Trade in wood (not fire-wood)	146	114	32	..	..	..	..
120	Trade in barks	38	38	..	..	..	..	..
121	Trade in bamboos and canes	29	24	5	..	..	..	..
122	Trade in thatches and other forest produce	133	133	..	..	..	..	..
	Total Order 28—Trade in Metals	**385**	**375**	**10**	..	..	..	..
123	Trade in metals, machinery, knives, tools, etc.	385	375	10	..	..	..	..
	Total Order 29—Trade in Pottery, Bricks and Tiles	**73**	**70**	**3**	..	..	..	..
124	Trade in pottery, bricks and tiles	73	70	3	..	..	..	..
	Total Order 30—Trade in Chemical Products	**629**	**586**	**43**	..	..	..	..
125	Drugs, dyes, paints, petroleum, explosives, etc.	629	586	43	..	..	..	..
	Total Order 31—Hotels, Cafes, Restaurants, etc.	**10,184**	**9,407**	**776**	**1**	..	..	..
126	Vendors of wine, liquors, aerated waters and ice	664	643	21	..	..	..	..
127	Owners and managers of hotels, cookshops, sarais, etc. (and employees)	9,081	8,325	755	1	..	..	..
128	Hawkers of drink and food stuffs	439	439	..	..	..	..	..
	Total Order 32—Other Trade in Food Stuffs	**12,555**	**9,897**	**2,652**	**5**	**1**	..	..
129	Grain and pulse dealers	820	799	21	..	..	..	..
130	Dealers in sweet-meats, sugar and spices	1,809	1,516	383	..	..	..	..
131	Dealers in dairy products, eggs and poultry	3,049	2,969	80	..	..	..	..
132	Dealers in animals for food	22	19	3	..	..	..	..
133	Dealers in fodder for animals	51	50	1	..	..	..	..
134	Dealers in other food stuffs	2,773	2,430	338	5	..	..	..
135	Dealers in tobacco	3,749	1,929	1,820	..	..	..	..
136	Dealers in opium	27	27	..	..	..	..	..
137	Dealers in Ganja	165	158	6	..	1	..	..

Group No.	Occupation.	Total following occupation.	As principal occupation.		As working dependents.		As subsidiary to other occupation.	
			Males.	Females.	Males.	Females.	Males.	Females.
1	2	3	4	5	6	7	8	9
	Total Order 33—Trade in Clothing and Toilet Articles	**2,147**	**1,770**	**5**	**12**	**360**	..	..
138	Trade in ready-made clothing and other articles of dress and the toilet (hats, umbrellas, socks, ready-made shoes, perfumes, etc.)	2,147	1,770	5	12	360	..	..
	Total Order 34—Trade in Furniture	**373**	**359**	**14**	..	..	..	..
139	Trade in furniture, carpets, curtain and beddings	225	215	10	..	..	..	..
140	Hardware, cooking utensils, porcelain, crockery, glassware bottles, articles for gardening, etc.	148	144	4	..	..	..	..
	Total Order 35—Trade in Building Materials	**12**	**12**	..	..	..	..	..
141	Trade in building materials (other than bricks, tiles and woody materials)	12	12	..	..	..	..	..
	Total Order 36—Trade in Means of Transport	**384**	**362**	**22**	..	..	..	..
142	Dealers and hirers and mechanical transport, motors, cycles, etc.	151	150	1	..	..	..	..
143	Dealers and hirers and other carriages, carts, boats, etc.	184	170	14	..	..	..	..
144	Dealers and hirers of elephants, camels, horses, cattle, asses, mules, etc.	49	42	7	..	..	..	..
	Total Order 37—Trade in Fuel	**540**	**479**	**53**	**8**	..	..	..
145	Dealers in fire-wood, charcoal, coal, cowdung, etc.	540	479	53	8	..	..	..
	Total Order 38—Trade in Articles of Luxury and those pertaining to Letters and the Arts and Sciences	**970**	**841**	**129**	..	..	..	..
146	Dealers in precious stones, jewellery (real and imitation), clocks, optical instruments, etc.	394	393	1	..	..	..	..
147	Dealers in common bangles, bead necklaces, fans, small articles, toys, hunting and fishing tackle, flowers, etc.	334	227	107	..	..	..	..
148	Publishers, booksellers, stationers, dealers in music, pictures, musical instruments and curiosities	242	221	21	..	..	..	..
	Total Order 39—Trade of Other Sorts	**48,288**	**45,376**	**1,781**	**180**	**951**	..	..
149	Dealers in rags, stable refuse, etc.	15	9	6	..	..	..	..
150	General store-keepers, shop-keepers, otherwise unspecified	38,851	36,706	1,016	180	949	..	..
151	Itinerant traders, pedlars and hawkers (of other than food, etc.)	7,603	6,842	759	..	2	..	..
152	Other trades (including farmers of pounds, tools and markets)	1,819	1,819	..	..	..	..	..
	Total Class C—Public Administration and Liberal Arts	**61,317**	**57,224**	**4,078**	**12**	**1**	**2**	..
	Total Sub-Class VI—Public Force	**9,042**	**8,872**	**170**	..	..	..	..
	Total Order 40—Army	**3,053**	**2,919**	**134**	..	..	..	..
153	Army (Imperial)	2,991	2,864	127	..	..	..	..
154	Army (Indian States)	62	55	7	..	..	..	..
	Total Order 41—Navy	**674**	**672**	**2**	..	..	..	..
155	Navy	674	672	2	..	..	..	..
	Total Order 42—Air Force	**16**	**14**	**2**	..	..	..	..
156	Air force	16	14	2	..	..	..	..
	Total Order 43—Police	**5,299**	**5,267**	**32**	..	..	..	..
157	Police	4,166	4,139	27	..	..	..	..
158	Village watchmen	1,133	1,128	5	..	..	..	..
	Total Sub-Class VII—Public Administration	**32,286**	**30,832**	**1,452**	**2**	..	..	..
	Total Order 44—Public Administration	**32,286**	**30,832**	**1,452**	**2**	..	..	..
159	Service of the State	5,054	4,783	270	1	..	..	..
160	Service of Indian and Foreign States	164	157	7	..	..	..	..
161	Municipal and other local (not village) service	26,848	25,672	1,175	1	..	..	..
162	Village officials and servants other than watchmen	220	220	..	..	..	..	..
	Total Sub-Class VIII—Professions and Liberal Arts	**19,989**	**17,520**	**2,456**	**10**	**1**	**2**	..
	Total Order 45—Religion	**2,800**	**2,710**	**85**	**5**	..	..	..
163	Priests, ministers, etc.	1,155	1,119	36	..	..	..	..
164	Monks, nuns, religious mendicants	841	821	15	5	..	..	..
165	Other religious workers	165	159	6	..	..	..	..
166	Servants in religious edifices, burial and burning ground, pilgrim conductors and circumcisers, etc.	639	611	28	..	..	..	..
	Total Order 46—Law	**1,732**	**1,715**	**16**	..	**1**	..	..
167	Lawyers of all kinds, including Quazis, law agents and Mukhtiars	1,620	1,605	14	..	1	..	..
168	Lawyers, clerks, petition writers, etc.	112	110	2	..	..	..	..
	Total Order 47—Medicine	**3,768**	**2,585**	**1,179**	**4**	..	..	..
169	Registered medical practitioners including oculists	1,755	1,687	68	..	..	..	..
170	Other persons practising the healing arts without being registered	208	198	10	..	..	..	..
171	Dentists	77	30	43	4	..	..	..
172	Midwives, vaccinators, compounders, nurses, masseurs, etc.	1,684	646	1,038	..	..	..	..
173	Veterinary surgeons	44	24	20	..	..	..	..

Group No.	Occupation.	Total following occupation	As principal occupation.		As working dependents.		As subsidiary to other occupation.	
			Males.	Females.	Males.	Females.	Males.	Females.
1	2	3	4	5	6	7	8	9
	Total Order 48—Instruction	**3,939**	**3,258**	**679**	..	..	**2**	..
174	Professors and teachers of all kinds	2,996	2,329	665	..	..	2	..
175	Clerks and servants connected with education	943	929	14	..	..	..	..
	Total Order 49—Letters Arts and Sciences (other than 44)	**7,750**	**7,252**	**497**	**1**	..	..	..
176	Public scribes, stenographers, etc.	287	182	105	..	..	..	..
177	Architects, surveyors, engineers and their employees (not being State servants)	195	188	7	..	..	..	..
178	Authors, editors, journalists and photographers	393	380	13	..	..	..	..
179	Artists, sculptors and image makers	533	520	13	..	..	..	..
180	Scientists (astronomers, botanists, etc.)	82	70	12	..	..	..	..
181	Horoscope casters, astrologers, fortune-tellers, wizards, witches and medium	623	619	4	..	..	..	..
182	Musicians (composers and performers other than military), actors, dancers, etc.	1,142	953	189	..	..	..	..
183	Managers and employees of places of public entertainments, race courses, societies clubs	4,348	4,197	150	1	..	..	..
184	Conjurors, acrobats, recitors, exhibitors of curiosities and wild animals, etc.	147	143	4	..	..	..	..
	Total Class D—Miscellaneous	**175,650**	**155,970**	**18,873**	**784**	**43**	..	..
	Total Sub-Class IX—Persons living on their Income	**1,855**	**1,666**	**188**	..	**1**	..	..
	Total Order 50—Persons living principally on their Income	**1,855**	**1,666**	**188**	..	**1**	..	..
185	Proprietors (other than of agricultural land), fund and scholarships holders and pensioners	1,855	1,666	188	..	1	..	..
	Total Sub-Class X—Domestic Service	**40,297**	**34,110**	**6,149**	**7**	**31**	..	..
	Total Order 51—Domestic Service	**40,297**	**34,110**	**6,149**	**7**	**31**	..	..
186	Private motor-drivers and cleaners	1,404	1,387	17	..	..	..	..
187	Other domestic service	38,893	32,723	6,132	7	31	..	..
	Total Sub-Class XI—Insufficiently described Occupations	**126,000**	**115,812**	**10,183**	**2**	**3**	..	..
	Total Order 52—General terms which do not indicate a definite Occupation ..	**126,000**	**115,812**	**10,183**	**2**	**3**	..	..
188	Manufacturers, business men and contractors otherwise unspecified ..	6,631	6,287	343	1	..	..	..
189	Cashiers, accountants, book-keepers, clerks and other employees in unspecified offices and ware-houses and shops	52,428	50,016	2,408	1	3	..	..
190	Mechanics, otherwise unspecified	4,985	4,941	44	..	..	..	..
191	Labourers and workmen otherwise unspecified	61,956	54,568	7,388	..	..	..	..
	Total Sub-Class XII—Unproductive	**7,498**	**4,382**	**2,353**	**755**	**8**	..	..
	Total Order 53—Inmates of Jails, Asylums and Alms Houses	**960**	**206**	**2**	**750**	**2**	..	..
192	Inmates of jails, asylums and alms houses	960	206	2	750	2	..	..
	Total Order 54—Beggars, Vagrants and Prostitutes	**6,175**	**3,835**	**2,329**	**5**	**6**	..	..
193	Beggars and vagrants	5,025	3,821	1,193	5	6	..	..
194	Procurers and prostitutes	1,150	14	1,136	..	..	..	..
	Total Order 55—Other unclassified non-productive Industries	**363**	**341**	**22**	..	..	..	..
195	Other unclassified non-productive industries	363	341	22	..	..	..	..

OCCUPATIONS OR MEANS OF LIVELIHOOD—BY RELIGION.

(Corresponding to Imperial Table X, Part I.)

Details showing total earners, working dependants, non-working dependants and total population of each religion.

	HINDU.			MUSLIM.			JAIN.		
	Persons.	Males.	Females.	Persons.	Males.	Females.	Persons.	Males.	Females.
1	2	3	4	5	6	7	8	9	10
Total earners	389,054	345,995	41,205	103,904	99,118	4,089	6,334	5,964	61
		*1,312	*542		*683	*14		*309	*..
Total working dependants ..	2,396	751	1,645	336	232	104	8	..	8
Total non-working dependants ..	398,411	157,530	240,881	105,006	43,885	61,121	6,082	2,725	3,357
Total population	789,861	505,588	284,273	209,246	143,918	65,328	12,424	8,998	3,426

	ZOROASTRIAN.			CHRISTIAN.			JEW.			OTHER RELIGIONS.		
	Persons.	Males.	Females.	Persons.	Males.	Females.	Persons.	Males.	Females.	Persons.	Males.	Females.
1	11	12	13	14	15	16	17	18	19	20	21	22
Total earners	17,030	16,029	934	42,424	36,528	5,725	2,485	2,264	220	1,811	1,701	93
		*59	*8		*143	*28		*..	*1		*15	*2
Total working dependants ..	94	94	..	10	10	..	4	4	..	13	5	8
Total non-working dependants ..	40,641	14,413	26,228	38,294	14,785	23,509	6,132	2,336	3,796	914	491	423
Total population	57,765	30,595	27,170	80,728	51,466	29,262	8,621	4,604	4,017	2,738	2,212	526

* Who refused to return their occupation.

CITY TABLE VII—PART II—BOMBAY CITY.

MO-III Bk Ra Cs 3—51

Occupations or Means of

(Corresponding to Imperial

Group No.	Occupation.	Hindu.							
		As principal occupation.		As working dependants.		As subsidiary to other occupation.		As principal occupation.	
		Males.	Females.	Males.	Females.	Males.	Females.	Males.	Females.
1	2	3	4	5	6	7	8	9	10
	Total All Classes	345,995	41,205	751	1,645	84	..	99,118	4,089
	Earners who refused to return their occupation	1,312	542	..	..	..	..	683	14
	Total Class A—Production of Raw Materials	8,943	970	..	..	22	..	855	86
	Total Sub-Class I—Exploitation of Animals and Vegetation	8,028	859	..	..	22	..	820	83
	Total Order I—Pasture and Agriculture	6,420	328	..	..	3	..	802	90
	Total Sub-order 1—(a) Cultivation	1,262	187	..	..	3	..	612	75
1	Non-cultivating proprietors taking rent in money or kind	585	124	..	..	..	..	392	70
2	Estate Agents and Managers of owners	40	..	..	..	..	..	4	..
3	Estate Agents and Managers of Government	..	6	..	..	..	..	..	..
4	Rent *Collectors, Clerks, etc.*	3	..	..	..	..	..	8	..
5	Cultivating owners	280	18	..	..	3	..	58	4
6	Tenant cultivators	72	12	..	..	..	..	10	..
7	Agricultural labourers	282	7	..	..	..	..	140	1
	Total Sub-order 1—(b) Cultivation of special crops, fruit, etc. (Planters, Managers, Clerks and Labourers)	1,830	97	..	..	..	..	63	2
9	Cinchona	..	..	..	..	..	..	..	..
10	Cocoanut	1	1	..	..	..	..	..	..
11	Coffee	1	..	..	..	..	..	5	..
13	Pan-Vine	21	..	..	..	..	..	..	..
14	Rubber	..	..	..	..	..	..	..	..
15	Tea	18	..	..	..	..	..	6	..
16	Market gardeners, flower and fruit growers	1,789	96	..	..	..	..	52	2
	Total Sub-order 1—(c) *Forestry*	266	22	..	..	..	..	25	..
17	Forest Officers, Rangers, Guards, etc.	12	3	..	..	..	..	..	..
18	Wood cutters and char-coal burners	194	..	..	..	..	..	24	..
19	Collectors of Forest produce	60	19	..	..	..	..	1	..
20	Collectors of lac	..	..	..	..	..	..	..	..
	Total *Sub-order* 1—(d) Stock Raising	3,023	40	..	..	..	..	96	13
21	Cattle and buffalo breeders and keepers	3,010	40	..	..	..	..	90	13
22	Breeders of transport animals	11	..	..	..	..	..	1	..
23	Herdsmen, shepherds and breeders of other animals	2	..	..	..	..	..	5	..
	Total Sub-order 1—(e) Raising of small Animals and Insects	39	2	..	..	..	..	6	..
24	Birds, bees, etc.	..	..	..	..	..	..	1	..
26	Lac cultivation	39	2	..	..	..	..	5	..
	Total Order 2—Fishing and Hunting	1,608	531	..	..	19	..	18	3
27	Fishing and Pearling	1,607	531	..	..	19	..	17	3
28	Hunting	1	..	..	..	..	..	1	..
	Total Sub-Class II—Exploitation of Minerals	915	111	..	..	..	..	35	3
	Total Order 3—Metallic Minerals	83	1	..	..	..	..	2	..
30	Iron	..	..	..	..	..	..	1	..
33	Tin and wolfram	43	..	..	..	..	..	..	..
34	Other metallic minerals	40	1	..	..	..	..	1	..
	Total Order 4—Non-Metallic Minerals	832	110	..	..	..	..	33	3
35	Coal	..	3	..	..	..	..	13	3
37	Building materials (including stone, materials for cement manufacture and clays)	248	35	..	..	..	..	10	..
40	Salt, saltpetre and other saline substances	583	72	..	..	..	..	1	..
41	Other non-metallic minerals	1	..	..	..	..	..	..	..

Livelihood—by Religion.

Table X, Part I.)

Muslim.				Jain.						Zoroastrian.			
As working dependants.		As subsidiary to other occupation.		As principal occupation.		As working dependants.		As subsidiary to other occupation.		As principal occupation.		As working dependants.	
Males.	Females.	Males.	Females.	Males.	Females.	Males.	Females.	Males.	Females.	Males.	Females.	Males.	Females.
11	12	13	14	15	16	17	18	19	20	21	22	23	24
282	104	..	..	5,964	61	..	8	..	..	16,029	934	94	..
..	....	..	..	309	..	..	..	..	..	59	8	..	..
..	65	..	..	158	1	..	..	..	..	145	95	89	..
..	65	..	..	158	1	..	..	..	..	142	95	89	..
..	65	..	..	158	1	..	..	..	..	142	95	89	..
..	65	..	..	68	1	..	..	..	..	138	95	89	..
..	65	..	..	14	1	..	..	..	..	112	89	89	..
..	....	..	..	13	..	..	..	..	..	9	2	..	..
..	....	..	..	4	..	..	..	..	..	..	1	..	..
..	....	..	..	..	..	..	..	..	..	..	..	..	..
..	....	..	..	37	..	..	..	..	..	7	1	..	..
..	....	..	..	..	..	..	..	..	..	..	..	..	..
..	....	..	..	..	..	..	..	..	..	10	2	..	..
..	....	..	..	88	..	..	..	..	..	4	..	..	..
..	....	..	..	75	..	..	..	..	..	..	..	..	..
..	....	..	..	..	..	..	..	..	..	..	..	..	..
..	....	..	..	..	..	..	..	..	..	..	..	..	..
..	....	..	..	..	..	..	..	..	..	..	..	..	..
..	....	..	..	13	..	..	..	..	..	..	..	..	..
..	....	..	..	..	..	..	..	..	..	3	..	..	..
..	....	..	..	..	..	..	..	..	..	1	..	..	..
..	....	..	..	..	..	..	..	..	..	..	..	..	..
..	....	..	..	..	..	..	..	..	..	..	..	..	..
..	....	..	..	..	..	..	..	..	..	..	..	..	..
..	....	..	..	..	..	..	..	..	..	..	..	..	..
..	....	..	..	..	..	..	..	..	..	..	..	..	..
..	....	..	..	2	..	..	..	..	..	..	..	..	..
..	....	..	..	2	..	..	..	..	..	..	..	..	..
..	....	..	..	..	..	..	..	..	..	..	..	..	..
..	....	..	..	..	..	..	..	..	..	..	..	..	..
..	....	..	..	..	..	..	..	..	..	..	..	..	..
..	....	..	..	..	..	..	..	..	..	..	..	..	..
..	....	..	..	..	..	..	..	..	..	..	..	..	..
..	....	..	..	..	..	..	..	..	..	..	..	..	..
..	....	..	..	..	..	..	..	..	..	..	..	..	..
..	....	..	..	..	..	..	..	..	..	..	..	..	..
..	....	..	..	..	..	..	..	..	..	3	..	..	..
..	....	..	..	..	..	..	..	..	..	..	..	..	..
..	....	..	..	..	..	..	..	..	..	..	..	..	..
..	....	..	..	..	..	..	..	..	..	..	..	..	..
..	....	..	..	..	..	..	..	..	..	..	..	..	..
..	....	..	..	..	..	..	..	..	..	3	..	..	..
..	....	..	..	..	..	..	..	..	..	1	..	..	..
..	....	..	..	..	..	..	..	..	..	..	..	..	..
..	....	..	..	..	..	..	..	..	..	2	..	..	..
..	....	..	..	..	..	..	..	..	..	..	..	..	..

OCCUPATIONS OR MEANS OF

(Corresponding to Imperial

Group No.	Occupation.	ZOROASTRIAN—*contd.* As subsidiary to other occupation. Males.	ZOROASTRIAN—*contd.* As subsidiary to other occupation. Females.	CHRISTIAN. As principal occupation. Males.	CHRISTIAN. As principal occupation. Females.	CHRISTIAN. As working dependants. Males.	CHRISTIAN. As working dependants. Females.	CHRISTIAN. As subsidiary to other occupation. Males.	CHRISTIAN. As subsidiary to other occupation. Females.
1	2	25	26	27	28	29	30	31	32
	Total All Classes	..	..	36,528	5,725	10	..	..	..
	Earners who refused to return their occupation	..	..	143	28	..	..	..	..
	Total Class A—Production of Raw Materials	..	..	321	113	..	..	..	..
	Total Sub-Class I—Exploitation of Animals and Vegetation	..	..	313	111	..	..	..	..
	Total Order I—Pasture and Agriculture	..	..	108	23	..	..	..	..
	Total Sub-order 1—(a) Cultivation	..	..	71	19	..	..	..	..
1	Non-cultivating proprietors taking rent in money or kind	..	..	62	16	..	..	..	..
2	Estate Agents and Managers of owners	..	..	..	..	..	..	..	..
3	Estate Agents and Managers of Government	..	..	..	..	..	..	..	..
4	Rent Collectors, Clerks, etc.	..	..	2	..	..	..	..	..
5	Cultivating owners	..	..	4	1	..	..	..	..
6	Tenant cultivators	..	..	..	..	..	..	..	..
7	Agricultural labourers	..	..	3	2	..	..	..	..
	Total Sub-order 1—(b) Cultivation of special crops, fruit, etc. (Planters, Managers, Clerks and Labourers)	..	..	29	4	..	..	..	..
9	Cinchona	..	..	..	..	..	..	..	..
10	Cocoanut	..	..	..	..	..	..	..	..
11	Coffee	..	..	..	..	..	..	..	..
13	Pan-Vine	..	..	..	..	..	..	..	..
14	Rubber	..	..	..	..	..	..	..	..
15	Tea	..	..	1	2	..	..	..	..
16	Market gardeners, flower and fruit growers	..	..	28	2	..	..	..	..
	Total Sub-order 1—(c) Forestry	..	..	6	..	..	..	..	..
17	Forest Officers, Rangers, Guards, etc.	..	..	..	..	..	..	..	..
18	Wood cutters and char-coal burners	..	..	..	..	..	..	..	..
19	Collectors of Forest produce	..	..	..	..	..	..	..	..
20	Collectors of lac	..	..	6	..	..	..	..	..
	Total Sub-order 1—(d) Stock Raising	..	..	2	..	..	..	..	..
21	Cattle and buffalo breeders and keepers	..	..	1	..	..	..	..	..
22	Breeders of transport animals	..	..	..	..	..	..	..	..
23	Herdsmen, shepherds and breeders of other animals	..	..	1	..	..	..	..	..
	Total Sub-order 1—(e) Raising of small Animals and Insects	..	..	..	..	..	..	..	..
24	Birds, bees, etc.	..	..	..	..	..	..	..	..
26	Lac cultivation	..	..	..	..	..	..	..	..
	Total Order 2—Fishing and Hunting	..	..	205	88	..	..	..	..
27	Fishing and Pearling	..	..	205	88	..	..	..	..
28	Hunting	..	..	..	..	..	..	..	..
	Total Sub-Class II—Exploitation of Minerals	..	..	8	2	..	..	..	..
	Total Order 3—Metallic Minerals	..	..	..	..	..	..	..	..
30	Iron	..	..	..	..	..	..	..	..
33	Tin and wolfram	..	..	..	..	..	..	..	..
34	Other metallic minerals	..	..	..	..	..	..	..	..
	Total Order 4—Non-Metallic Minerals	..	..	8	2	..	..	..	..
35	Coal	..	..	2	..	..	..	..	..
37	Building materials (including stone, materials for cement manufacture and clays)	..	..	..	..	..	..	..	..
40	Salt, saltpetre and other saline substances	..	..	6	2	..	..	..	..
41	Other non-metallic minerals	..	..	..	..	..	..	..	..

LIVELIHOOD—BY RELIGION—*contd.*

Table X, Part I)—contd.

Jew.						Other Religions.					
As principal occupation.		As working dependants.		As subsidiary to other occupation.		As principal occupation.		As working dependants.		As subsidiary to other occupation.	
Males.	Females.	Males.	Females.	Males.	Females.	Males.	Females.	Males.	Females.	Males.	Females.
33	34	35	36	37	38	39	40	41	42	43	44
2,264	220	4	..	..	..	1,701	93	5	8	..	..
....	1	..	..	..	..	15	2	..	..	..	..
5	1	..	..	..	..	64	..	..	..	..	..
5	1	..	..	..	..	64	..	..	..	..	..
5	1	..	..	..	..	64	..	..	..	..	..
4	1	..	..	..	..	64	..	..	..	..	..
4	....	..	..	..	..	3	..	..	..	..	..
....	....	..	..	..	..	..	..	..	..	..	..
....	....	..	..	..	..	..	..	..	..	..	..
....	....	..	..	..	..	..	..	..	..	..	..
....	1	..	..	..	..	..	..	..	..	..	..
....	....	..	..	..	..	..	..	..	..	..	..
....	....	..	..	..	..	61	..	..	..	..	..
1	....	..	..	..	..	..	..	..	..	..	..
....	....	..	..	..	..	..	..	..	..	..	..
....	....	..	..	..	..	..	..	..	..	..	..
....	....	..	..	..	..	..	..	..	..	..	..
....	....	..	..	..	..	..	..	..	..	..	..
....	....	..	..	..	..	..	..	..	..	..	..
....	....	..	..	..	..	..	..	..	..	..	..
1	....	..	..	..	..	..	..	..	..	..	..
....	....	..	..	..	..	..	..	..	..	..	..
....	....	..	..	..	..	..	..	..	..	..	..
....	....	..	..	..	..	..	..	..	..	..	..
....	....	..	..	..	..	..	..	..	..	..	..
....	....	..	..	..	..	..	..	..	..	..	..
....	....	..	..	..	..	..	..	..	..	..	..
....	....	..	..	..	..	..	..	..	..	..	..
....	....	..	..	..	..	..	..	..	..	..	..
....	....	..	..	..	..	..	..	..	..	..	..
....	....	..	..	..	..	..	..	..	..	..	..
....	....	..	..	..	..	..	..	..	..	..	..
....	....	..	..	..	..	..	..	..	..	..	..
....	....	..	..	..	..	..	..	..	..	..	..
....	....	..	..	..	..	..	..	..	..	..	..
....	....	..	..	..	..	..	..	..	..	..	..
....	....	..	..	..	..	..	..	..	..	..	..
....	....	..	..	..	..	..	..	..	..	..	..
....	....	..	..	..	..	..	..	..	..	..	..
....	....	..	..	..	..	..	..	..	..	..	..
....	....	..	..	..	..	..	..	..	..	..	..
....	....	..	..	..	..	..	..	..	..	..	..
....	....	..	..	..	..	..	..	..	..	..	..
....	....	..	..	..	..	..	..	..	..	..	..
....	....	..	..	..	..	..	..	..	..	..	..
....	....	..	..	..	..	..	..	..	..		
....	....	..	..	..	..	..	..	..	..		
....	....	..	..	..	..	..	..	..	..		
....	....	..	..	..	..	..	..	..	..		
....	....	..	..	..	..	..	..	..	..		

Group No.	Occupation.	Hindu.							
		As principal occupation.		As working dependants.		As subsidiary to other occupation.		As principal occupation.	
		Males.	Females.	Males.	Females.	Males.	Females.	Males.	Females.
1	2	3	4	5	6	7	8	9	10
	Total Class B—Preparation and supply of Material Substances	**196,728**	**25,185**	**210**	**1,643**	**60**	..	**61,941**	**1,806**
	Total Sub-Class III—Industry	**123,206**	**20,377**	**9**	..	**5**	..	**22,676**	**1,156**
	Total Order 5—Textiles	**85,049**	**15,850**	..	..	..	..	**12,224**	**885**
42	Cotton ginning, cleaning and pressing	1,522	226	..	..	..	..	114	7
43	Cotton spinning, sizing and weaving	83,220	15,546	..	..	..	..	11,187	841
44	Jute pressing, spinning and weaving	22	25	..	..	..	..	2	..
45	Rope, twine, string and other fibres	31	15	..	..	..	..	18	13
46	Wool carding, spinning and weaving	5	12	..	..	..	..	3	..
47	Silk spinning and weaving	5	..	..	..	..	..	..	..
48	Hair (horse-hair) etc.	..	..	..	..	..	..	..	..
49	Dyeing, bleaching, printing, preparation and sponging of textiles	186	17	..	..	..	..	572	16
50	Lace, crope, embroideries, fringes, etc. and insufficiently described textile industries	58	9	..	..	..	..	328	8
	Total Order 6—Hides Skins and Hard Materials from the Animal Kingdom	**1,053**	**83**	..	..	..	..	**190**	**4**
51	Working in leather	582	23	..	..	..	..	144	2
52	Furriers and persons occupied with feathers, and bristles; brush makers	449	57	..	..	..	..	9	..
53	Bone, ivory, horn, shell etc., workers (except buttons)	22	3	..	..	..	..	37	2
	Total Order 7—Wood	**3,946**	**224**	..	..	..	..	**786**	**11**
54	Sawyers	72	..	..	..	..	..	..	..
55	Carpenters, turners and joiners, etc.	3,661	40	..	..	..	..	707	10
56	Basket makers, and other industries of woody materials, including leaves and thatchers and builders working with bamboo, reeds or similar materials	213	184	..	..	..	..	79	1
	Total Order 8—Metals	**1,730**	**53**	..	..	..	..	**1,015**	**12**
57	Smelting, forgoing and rolling of iron and other metals	51	1	..	..	..	..	16	1
58	Makers of arms, guns, etc.	4	1	..	..	..	..	59	..
59	Blacksmiths, other workers in iron, makers of implements	878	42	..	..	..	..	400	1
60	Workers in brass-copper and bell metal	179	3	..	..	..	..	47	..
61	Workers in other metals (except precious metals)	580	6	..	..	..	..	484	9
62	Workers in mints, diesinkers, etc.	38	..	..	..	..	..	9	1
	Total Order 9—Ceramics	**481**	**83**	..	..	..	..	**49**	**4**
63	Potters and makers of earthern-ware	370	63	..	..	..	..	27	2
64	Brick and tile makers	72	..	..	..	..	..	18	..
65	Other workers in ceramics	39	20	..	..	..	..	4	2
	Total Order 10—Chemical Products Properly so-called and Analogous	**116**	**17**	..	..	..	..	**238**	**23**
66	Manufacture of matches, fire-works and other explosives	32	..	..	..	..	..	52	10
67	Manufacture of aerated and mineral waters and ice	20	..	..	..	..	..	37	..
68	Manufacture and refining of vegetable oils	5	3	..	..	..	..	8	..
69	Manufacture and refinding of mineral oils	14	..	..	..	..	..	..	..
70	Others	45	14	..	..	..	..	141	13
	Total Order 11—Food Industries	**1,186**	**143**	**1**	..	..	..	**1,266**	**52**
71	Rice pounders and huskers and flour grinders	42	..	..	..	..	..	6	..
72	Grain parchers, etc.	208	9	..	..	..	..	10	..
73	Butchers	82	1	..	..	..	..	853	13
74	Makers of sugar, molasses and gur	15	..	..	..	..	..	2	..
75	Sweetmeat and condiment makers	359	2	..	..	..	..	100	3
76	Toddy drawers	235	8	..	..	..	..	15	..
77	Brewers and distillers	2	..	..	..	..	..	..	..
78	Manufacturers of Tobacco	149	119	1	..	..	..	10	21
80	Manufacturers of Ganja	13	..	..	..	..	..	22	..
81	Others	81	4	..	..	..	..	248	15
	Total Order 12—Industries of Dress and the Toilet	**17,542**	**1,818**	..	..	**5**	..	**3,672**	**89**
82	Boot, shoe, sandal and clog makers	3,174	297	..	..	..	..	87	1
83	Tailors, milliners, dressmakers and darners	7,892	1,006	..	..	5	..	1,409	27
84	Embroiderers, hatmakers and makers of other articles of wear	28	1	..	..	..	..	89	6
85	Washing and cleaning	4,203	485	..	..	..	..	781	49
86	Barbers, hairdressers and wig-makers	1,830	27	..	..	..	..	1,176	2
87	Other industries connected with the toilet	415	2	..	..	..	..	130	4

Muslim.				Jain.						Zoroastrian.			
As working dependants.		As subsidiary to other occupation.		As principal occupation.		As working dependants.		As subsidiary to other occupation.		As principal occupation.		As working dependants.	
Males.	Females.	Males.	Females.	Males.	Females.	Males.	Females.	Males.	Females.	Males.	Females.	Males.	Females.
11	12	13	14	15	16	17	18	19	20	21	22	23	24
6	1	..	..	4,281	41	..	5	..	..	5,633	195	..	..
1	1	..	..	1,255	..	..	..	..	..	1,026	81	..	..
1	..	..	..	133	..	..	..	..	..	417	5	..	..
..	..	..	..	..	..	..	..	..	..	..	..	..	..
1	..	..	..	78	..	..	..	..	..	403	4	..	..
..	..	..	..	..	..	..	..	..	..	4	..	..	..
..	..	..	..	..	..	..	..	..	..	4	..	..	..
..	..	..	..	..	..	..	..	..	..	3	..	..	..
..	..	..	..	..	..	..	..	..	..	..	..	..	..
..	..	..	..	..	..	..	..	..	..	..	..	..	..
..	..	..	..	13	..	..	..	..	..	3	1	..	..
..	..	..	..	42	..	..	..	..	..	..	..	..	..
..	..	..	..	..	..	..	..	..	..	5	..	..	..
..	..	..	..	..	..	..	..	..	..	2	..	..	..
..	..	..	..	..	..	..	..	..	..	2	..	..	..
..	..	..	..	..	..	..	..	..	..	1	..	..	..
..	..	..	..	108	..	..	..	..	..	89	1	..	..
..	..	..	..	..	..	..	..	..	..	..	..	..	..
..	..	..	..	103	..	..	..	..	..	89	1	..	..
..	..	..	..	..	..	..	..	..	..	..	..	..	..
..	..	..	..	259	..	..	..	..	..	39	1	..	..
..	..	..	..	..	..	..	..	..	..	1	..	..	..
..	..	..	..	..	..	..	..	..	..	..	..	..	..
..	..	..	..	..	..	..	..	..	..	36	..	..	..
..	..	..	..	52	..	..	..	..	..	..	..	..	..
..	..	..	..	207	..	..	..	..	..	2	1	..	..
..	..	..	..	..	..	..	..	..	..	..	..	..	..
..	..	..	..	..	..	..	..	..	..	20	4	..	..
..	..	..	..	..	..	..	..	..	..	20	4	..	..
..	..	..	..	..	..	..	..	..	..	..	..	..	..
..	..	..	..	..	..	..	..	..	..	..	..	..	..
..	..	..	..	..	..	..	..	..	..	37	..	..	..
..	..	..	..	..	..	..	..	..	..	..	..	..	..
..	..	..	..	..	..	..	..	..	..	13	..	..	..
..	..	..	..	..	..	..	..	..	..	..	..	..	..
..	..	..	..	..	..	..	..	..	..	..	..	..	..
..	..	..	..	..	..	..	..	..	..	24	..	..	..
..	..	..	..	157	..	..	..	..	..	12	3	..	..
..	..	..	..	..	..	..	..	..	..	2	..	..	..
..	..	..	..	59	..	..	..	..	..	..	..	..	..
..	..	..	..	..	..	..	..	..	..	..	..	..	..
..	..	..	..	..	..	..	..	..	..	..	..	..	..
..	..	..	..	66	..	..	..	..	..	2	..	..	..
..	..	..	..	..	..	..	..	..	..	4	1	..	..
..	..	..	..	..	..	..	..	..	..	..	..	..	..
..	..	..	..	13	..	..	..	..	..	..	..	..	..
..	..	..	..	19	..	..	..	..	..	..	..	..	..
..	..	..	..	..	..	..	..	..	..	4	2	..	..
..	1	..	..	240	..	..	..	..	..	46	58	..	..
..	1	..	..	69	..	..	..	..	..	1	..	..	..
..	..	..	..	107	..	..	..	..	..	34	57	..	..
..	..	..	..	18	..	..	..	..	..	2	1	..	..
..	..	..	..	..	..	..	..	..	..	9	..	..	..
..	..	..	..	..	..	..	..	..	..	..	..	..	..
..	..	..	..	46	..	..	..	..	..	..	..	..	..

Group No.	Occupation.	ZOROASTRIAN—*contd.*		CHRISTIAN.					
		As subsidiary to other occupation.		As principal occupation.		As working dependants.		As subsidiary to other occupation.	
		Males.	Females.	Males.	Females.	Males.	Females.	Males.	Females.
1	2	25	26	27	28	29	30	31	32
	Total Class B—Preparation and supply of Material Substances	..	..	**12,967**	**807**	**10**	..	..	..
	Total Sub-Class III—Industry	..	..	**5,228**	**220**	**10**	..	..	..
	Total Order 5—Textiles	..	..	**1,680**	**72**	..	..	..	..
42	Cotton ginning, cleaning and pressing	..	..	5	..	..	..	..	..
43	Cotton spinning, sizing and weaving	..	..	1,523	67	..	..	..	..
44	Jute pressing, spinning and weaving	..	..	22	..	..	..	..	..
45	Rope, twine, string and other fibres	..	..	1	..	..	..	..	..
46	Wool carding, spinning and weaving	..	..	1	..	..	..	..	..
47	Silk spinning and weaving	..	..	1	5	..	..	..	..
48	Hair (horse-hair) etc.	..	..	1	..	..	..	..	..
49	Dyeing, bleaching, printing, preparation and sponging of textiles	..	..	126	..	..	..	..	..
50	Lace, crepe, embroideries, fringes, etc., and insufficiently described textile industries	..	..	..	..	..	..	..	..
	Total Order 6—Hides Skins and Hard Materials from the Animal Kingdom	..	..	**5**	**1**	..	..	..	..
51	Working in leather	..	..	5	1	..	..	..	..
52	Furriers and persons occupied with feathers, and bristles: brush makers	..	..	..	..	..	..	..	..
53	Bone, ivory, horn, shell, etc., workers (except buttons)	..	..	..	..	..	..	..	..
	Total Order 7—Wood	..	..	**617**	**4**	..	..	..	..
54	Sawyers	..	..	..	..	..	..	..	..
55	Carpenters, turners and joiners, etc.	..	..	615	4	..	..	..	..
56	Basket makers, and other industries of woody materials including leaves and thatchers and builders working with bamboo, reeds or similar materials	..	..	2	..	..	..	..	..
	Total Order 8—Metals	..	..	**57**	**22**	..	..	..	..
57	Smelting, forgoing and rolling of iron and other metals	..	..	2	..	..	..	..	..
58	Makers of arms, guns, etc.	..	..	..	..	..	..	..	..
59	Blacksmiths, other workers in iron, makers of implements	..	..	35	1	..	..	..	..
60	Workers in brass-copper and bell metal	..	..	1	..	..	..	..	..
61	Workers in other metals (except precious metals)	..	..	16	21	..	..	..	..
62	Workers in mints, diesinkers, etc.	..	..	3	..	..	..	..	..
	Total Order 9—Ceramics	..	..	**26**	..	..	..	..	..
63	Potters and makers of earthern-ware	..	..	..	..	..	..	..	..
64	Brick and tile makers	..	..	26	..	..	..	..	..
65	Other workers in ceramics	..	..	..	..	..	..	..	..
	Total Order 10—Chemical Products Properly so-called and Analogous	..	..	**7**	..	..	..	..	..
66	Manufacture of matches, fire-works and other explosives	..	..	2	..	..	..	..	..
67	Manufacture of ærated and mineral waters and ice	..	..	1	..	..	..	..	..
68	Manufacture and refining of vegetable oils	..	..	..	..	..	..	..	..
69	Manufacture and refinding of mineral oils	..	..	2	..	..	..	..	..
70	Others	..	..	2	..	..	..	..	..
	Total Order 11—Food Industries	..	..	**259**	**9**	**10**	..	..	..
71	Rice pounders and huskers and flour grinders	..	..	1	1	..	..	..	..
72	Grain parchers, etc.	..	..	..	..	..	..	..	..
73	Butchers	..	..	10	..	10	..	..	..
74	Makers of sugar, molasses and gur	..	..	..	..	..	..	..	..
75	Sweetmeat and condiment makers	..	..	1	..	..	..	..	..
76	Toddy drawers	..	..	150	7	..	..	..	..
77	Brewers and distillers	..	..	..	..	..	..	..	..
78	Manufacturers of Tobacco	..	..	10	1	..	..	..	..
80	Manufacturers of Ganja	..	..	..	..	..	..	..	..
81	Others	..	..	87	..	..	..	..	..
	Total Order 12—Industries of Dress and the Toilet	..	..	**1,150**	**73**	..	..	..	..
82	Boot, shoe, sandal and clog makers	..	..	33	1	..	..	..	..
83	Tailors, milliners, dressmakers and darners	..	..	1,053	49	..	..	..	..
84	Embroiderers, hatmakers and makers of other articles of wear	..	..	16	20	..	..	..	..
85	Washing and cleaning	..	..	22	1	..	..	..	..
86	Barbers, hairdressers and wig-makers	..	..	19	1	..	..	..	..
87	Other industries connected with the toilet	..	..	7	1	..	..	..	..

Jew.						Other Religions.					
As principal occupation.		As working dependants.		As subsidiary to other occupation.		As principal occupation.		As working dependants.		As subsidiary to to other occupation.	
Males.	Females.	Males.	Females.	Males.	Females.	Males.	Females.	Males.	Females.	Males.	Females.
33	34	35	36	37	38	39	40	41	42	43	44
1,159	41	..	..	..	..	1,205	25	5	7	..	..
623	24	..	..	..	..	437	8	..	..	..	..
151	13	..	..	..	..	54	..	..	..	..	..
....	1	..	..	..	..	..	..	..	..	..	..
149	12	..	..	..	..	54	..	..	..	..	..
2	....	..	..	..	..	..	..	..	..	..	..
....	....	..	..	..	..	..	..	..	..	..	..
....	....	..	..	..	..	..	..	..	..	..	..
....	....	..	..	..	..	..	..	..	..	..	..
....	....	..	..	..	..	..	..	..	..	..	..
....	....	..	..	..	..	..	..	..	..	..	..
....	....	..	..	..	..	..	..	..	..	...	..
....	....	..	..	..	..	13	..	..	..	..	..
....	....	..	..	..	..	13	..	..	..	..	..
....	....	..	..	..	..	..	..	..	..	..	..
....	....	..	..	..	..	..	..	..	..	..	..
370	2	..	..	..	..	261	4	..	..	..	..
....	....	..	..	..	..	..	..	..	..	..	..
370	2	..	..	..	..	259	2	..	..	..	..
....	....	..	..	..	..	2	2	..	..	..	..
11	....	..	..	..	..	14	..	..	..	..	..
4	....	..	..	..	..	..	..	..	..	..	..
1	....	..	..	..	..	..	..	..	..	..	..
2	....	..	..	..	..	14	..	..	..	..	..
....	....	..	..	..	..	..	..	..	..	..	..
4	....	..	..	..	..	..	..	..	..	..	..
....	....	..	..	..	..	..	..	..	..	..	..
....	....	..	..	..	..	..	..	..	..	..	..
....	....	..	..	..	..	..	..	..	..	..	..
....	....	..	..	..	..	..	..	..	..	..	..
....	....	..	..	..	..	..	..	..	..	..	..
1	....	..	..	..	..	..	..	..	..	..	..
....	....	..	..	..	..	..	..	..	..	..	..
....	....	..	..	..	..	..	..	..	..	..	..
....	....	..	..	..	..	..	..	..	..	..	..
....	....	..	..	..	..	..	..	..	..	..	..
1	....	..	..	..	..	..	..	..	..	..	..
9	2	..	..	..	..	..	..	..	..	..	..
....	....	..	..	..	..	..	..	..	..	..	..
....	....	..	..	..	..	..	..	..	..	..	..
8	....	..	..	..	..	..	..	..	..	..	..
....	....	..	..	..	..	..	..	..	..	..	..
....	....	..	..	..	..	..	..	..	..	..	..
....	....	..	..	..	..	..	..	..	..	..	..
....	....	..	..	..	..	..	..	..	..	..	..
....	....	..	..	..	..	..	..	..	..	..	..
....	....	..	..	..	..	..	..	..	..	..	..
1	2	..	..	..	..	..	..	..	..	..	..
18	6	..	..	..	..	62	4	..	..	..	..
....	....	..	..	..	..	8	..	..	..	..	..
12	6	..	..	..	..	9	..	..	..	..	..
4	....	..	..	..	..	..	..	..	..	..	..
2	....	..	..	..	..	36	..	..	..	..	..
....	....	..	..	..	..	9	4	..	..	..	..
....	....	..	..	..	..	..	..	..	..	..	..

MO III Bk Ra Cs 3—53

Group No.	Occupation.	Hindu.							
		As principal occupation.		As working dependants.		As subsidiary to other occupation.		As principal occupation.	
		Males.	Females.	Males.	Females.	Males.	Females.	Males.	Females.
1	2	3	4	5	6	7	8	9	10
	Total Order 13—Furniture Industries	201	2	..	..	..	..	114	..
88	Cabinet makers, carriage painters, etc.	171	2	..	..	..	..	33	..
89	Upholsterers, tent makers, etc.	30	..	..	..	..	..	81	..
	Total Order 14—Building Industries }	1,565	22	..	..	..	..	1,583	8
90	Lime burners, cement workers: Excavators and well sinkers; Stone cutters and dressers; Brick layers and masons: Builders (other than buildings made of bamboo or similar materials), painters, decorators of houses, tilers, plumbers, etc. }								
	Total Order 15—Construction of Means of Transport	278	100	..	..	..	..	235	28
91	Persons engaged in making, assembling or repairing motor vehicles or cycle	169	98	..	..	..	..	208	1
92	Carriage, cart, palki, etc., makers and wheel-wrights	3	2	..	..	..	..	1	17
93	Ship, boat, aeroplane builders	106	..	..	..	..	..	26	10
	Total Order 16—Production and Transmission of Physical Force }	638	14	..	..	..	..	190	1
94	Heat, light, electricity, motive power, etc., Gas works and electric light and power }								
	Total Order 17—Miscellaneous and undefined Industries	9,421	1,968	8	..	..	..	1,114	39
95	Printers, engravers, bookbinders, etc.	1,433	68	..	..	..	..	349	2
96	Makers of musical instruments	535	23	..	..	..	..	18	3
97	Makers of clocks and surgical or scientific instruments, etc.	111	..	..	..	..	..	122	1
98	Makers of jewellery and ornaments	2,180	28	..	..	..	..	50	..
99	Other miscellaneous and undefined industries (toymaking, taxidermy, etc.)	854	366	..	..	..	..	463	6
100	Scavenging	4,308	1,483	8	..	..	..	112	27
	Total Sub-Class IV—Transport	29,707	408	..	..	55	..	13,291	60
	Total Order 18—Transport by Air }	13	..	..	..	..	..	25	6
101	Persons concerned with aerodromes and aeroplanes }								
	Total Order 19—Transport by Water	10,582	152	..	..	55	..	7,202	15
102	Ship-owners, boat-owners and their employees, officers, mariners, Ships' brokers, boatmen and tow men	6,051	6	..	..	55	..	5,506	..
103	Persons (other than labourers) employed in harbours, docks, rivers and canals, including pilots	1,000	1	..	..	..	..	289	..
104	Labourers employed on harbours, docks, rivers and canals	3,531	145	..	..	..	..	1,407	15
	Total Order 20—Transport by Road	9,395	146	..	..	..	..	4,270	19
105	Persons (other than labourers) employed on the construction and maintenance of roads and bridges	74	1	..	..	..	..	32	..
106	Labourers employed on roads and bridges	587	102	..	..	..	..	11	..
107	Owners, managers and employees (excluding personal servants) connected with mechanically driven vehicles (including trams)	2,330	15	..	..	..	..	2,290	7
108	Owners, managers and employees (excluding personal servants) connected with other vehicles	2,299	15	..	..	..	..	1,092	8
109	Palki, etc., bearers and owners	6	..	..	..	..	..	7	..
110	Pack elephant, camel, mule, ass and bullock, owners and drivers	7	1	..	..	..	..	6	..
111	Porters and messengers	4,092	14	..	..	..	..	882	4
	Total Order 21—Transport by Rail	8,889	104	..	..	..	..	1,649	20
112	Railway employees of all kinds other than coolies	6,150	46	..	..	..	..	1,358	3
113	Labourers employed on railway construction and maintenance and coolies and porters employed on railway premises	2,739	58	..	..	..	..	291	17
	Total Order 22—Post Office, Telegraph and Telephone Services }	828	4	..	..	..	..	145	..
114	Post Office, Telegraph and Telephone services }								

Muslim.				Jain.						Zoroastrian.			
As working dependents.		As subsidiary to other occupation.		As principal occupation.		As working dependants.		As subsidiary to other occupation.		As principal occupation.		As working dependants.	
Males.	Females.	Males.	Females.	Males.	Females.	Males.	Females.	Males.	Females.	Males.	Females.	Males.	Females.
11	12	13	14	15	16	17	18	19	20	21	22	23	24
..	..	..	..	17	..	..	..	..	..	17	..	..	..
..	..	..	..	..	..	..	..	..	..	5	..	..	..
..	..	..	..	17	..	..	..	..	..	12	..	..	..
..	..	..	..	9	..	..	..	..	..	43	3	..	..
..	..	..	..	68	..	..	..	..	..	18	..	..	..
..	..	..	..	68	..	..	..	..	..	15	..	..	..
..	..	..	..	..	..	..	..	..	..	3	..	..	..
..	..	..	..	..	..	..	..	..	..	..	..	..	..
..	..	..	..	..	..	..	..	..	..	137	..	..	..
..	..	..	..	269	..	..	..	..	..	146	6	..	..
..	..	..	..	89	..	..	..	..	..	73	2	..	..
..	..	..	..	23	..	..	..	..	..	..	..	..	..
..	..	..	..	..	..	..	..	..	..	36	2	..	..
..	..	..	..	34	..	..	..	..	..	9	..	..	..
..	..	..	..	123	..	..	..	..	..	28	2	..	..
..	..	..	..	..	..	..	..	..	..	..	..	..	..
..	..	..	..	108	..	..	..	..	..	1,107	4	..	..
..	..	..	..	..	..	..	..	..	..	..	..	..	
..	..	..	..	15	..	..	..	..	..	103	1	..	..
..	..	..	..	15	..	..	..	..	..	22	..	..	..
..	..	..	..	..	..	..	..	..	..	56	1	..	..
..	..	..	..	..	..	..	..	..	..	25	..	..	..
..	..	..	..	..	..	..	..	..	..	264	1	..	..
..	..	..	..	..	..	..	..	..	..	87	..	..	..
..	..	..	..	..	..	..	..	..	..	..	..	..	..
..	..	..	..	..	..	..	..	..	..	161	1	..	..
..	..	..	..	..	..	..	..	..	..	11	..	..	..
..	..	..	..	..	..	..	..	..	..	3	..	..	..
..	..	..	..	..	..	..	..	..	..	..	..	..	..
..	..	..	..	..	..	..	..	..	..	2	..	..	..
..	..	..	..	29	..	..	..	..	..	708	2	..	..
..	..	..	..	29	..	..	..	..	..	701	2	..	..
..	..	..	..	..	..	..	..	..	..	7	..	..	..
..	..	..	..	64	..	..	..	..	..	32	..	..	..

Group No.	Occupation.	Zoroastrian—contd. As subsidiary to other occupation. Males.	Females.	Christian. As principal occupation. Males.	Females.	As working dependants. Males.	Females.	As subsidiary to other occupation. Males.	Females.
1	2	25	26	27	28	29	30	31	32
	Total Order 13—Furniture Industries	..	..	826	..	..	..	..	..
88	Cabinet makers, carriage painters, etc.	..	..	826	..	..	..	..	..
89	Upholsterers, tent makers, etc.	..	..	..	..	..	..	..	..
	Total Order 14—Building Industries								
90	Lime burners, cement workers: Excavators and well sinkers; Stone cutters and dressers; Brick layers and masons: Builders (other than buildings made of bamboo or similar materials), painters, decorators of houses, tilers, plumbers, etc.	..	..	125	1	..	..	..	..
	Total Order 15—Construction of Means of Transport	..	..	44	..	..	..	..	..
91	Persons engaged in making, assembling or repairing motor vehicles or cycle	..	..	24	..	..	..	..	..
92	Carriage, cart, palki, etc., makers and wheel-wrights	..	..	..	..	..	..	..	..
93	Ship, boat, aeroplane builders	..	..	20	..	..	..	..	..
	Total Order 16—Production and Transmission of Physical Force	..	..	205	6	..	..	..	..
94	Heat, light, electricity, motive power, etc., Gas works and electric light and power								
	Total Order 17—Miscellaneous and undefined Industries	..	..	222	32	..	..	..	..
95	Printers, engravers, bookbinders, etc.	..	..	117	3	..	..	..	..
96	Makers of musical instruments	..	..	6	3	..	..	..	..
97	Makers of clocks and surgical or scientific instruments, etc.	..	..	21	..	..	..	..	..
98	Makers of jewellery and ornaments	..	..	15	..	..	..	..	..
99	Other miscellaneous and undefined industries (toy-making, taxidermy, etc.)	..	..	17	7	..	..	..	..
100	Scavenging	..	..	46	19	..	..	..	..
	Total Sub-Class IV—Transport	..	..	5,190	106	..	..	..	..
	Total Order 18—Transport by Air	..	..	1	..	..	..	..	..
101	Persons concerned with aerodromes and aeroplanes								
	Total Order 19—Transport by Water	..	..	2,417	54	..	..	..	..
102	Ship-owners, boat-owners and their employees, officers, mariners, Ships' brokers, boatmen and tow men	..	..	2,154	27	..	..	..	..
103	Persons (other than labourers) employed in harbours, docks, rivers and canals, including pilots	..	..	122	26	..	..	..	..
104	Labourers employed on harbours, docks, rivers and canals	..	..	141	1	..	..	..	..
	Total Order 20—Transport by Road	..	..	786	6	..	..	..	..
105	Persons (other than labourers) employed on the construction and maintenance of roads and bridges	..	..	321	1	..	..	..	..
106	Labourers employed on roads and bridges	..	..	..	..	..	..	..	..
107	Owners, managers and employees (excluding personal servants) connected with mechanically driven vehicles (including trams)	..	..	421	3	..	..	..	..
108	Owners, managers and employees (excluding personal servants) connected with other vehicles	..	..	36	1	..	..	..	..
109	Palki, etc., bearers and owners	..	..	3	1	..	..	..	..
110	Pack elephant, camel, mule, ass and bullock, owners and drivers	..	..	..	..	..	..	..	..
111	Porters and messengers	..	..	5	..	..	..	..	..
	Total Order 21—Transport by Rail	..	..	1,734	22	..	..	..	..
112	Railway employees of all kinds other than coolies	..	..	1,660	21	..	..	..	..
113	Labourers employed on railway construction and maintenance and coolies and porters employed on railway premises	..	..	74	1	..	..	..	..
	Total Order 22—Post Office, Telegraph and Telephone Services	..	..	252	24	..	..	..	..
114	Post Office, Telegraph and Telephone services								

Jew.						Other Religions.					
As principal occupation.		As working dependants.		As subsidiary to other occupation.		As principal occupation.		As working dependants.		As subsidiary to other occupation.	
Males.	Females.	Males.	Females.	Males.	Females.	Males.	Females.	Males.	Females.	Males.	Females.
33	34	35	36	37	38	39	40	41	42	43	44
2	....	..	..	..	..	..	..	..	..	..	..
1	....	..	..	..	..	..	..	..	..	..	..
1	....	..	..	..	..	..	..	..	..	..	..
4	1	..	..	..	..	7	..	..	..	..	..
....	....	..	..	..	..	..	..	..	..	..	..
....	....	..	..	..	..	..	..	..	..	..	..
....	....	..	..	..	..	..	..	..	..	..	..
....	....	..	..	..	..	..	..	..	..	..	..
14	....	..	..	..	..	..	..	..	..	..	..
43	....	..	..	..	..	26	..	..	..	..	..
35	....	..	..	..	..	..	..	..	..	..	..
....	....	..	..	..	..	3	..	..	..	..	..
7	....	..	..	..	..	..	..	..	..	..	..
....	....	..	..	..	..	..	..	..	..	..	..
....	....	..	..	..	..	23	..	..	..	..	..
1	....	..	..	..	..	..	..	..	..	..	..
260	2	..	..	..	..	485	..	..	..	..	..
....	....	..	..	..	..	..	..	..	..	..	..
16	1	..	..	..	..	438	..	..	..	..	..
3	....	..	..	..	..	415	..	..	..	..	..
12	1	..	..	..	..	23	..	..	..	..	..
1	....	..	..	..	..	..	..	..	..	..	..
83	....	..	..	..	..	5	..	..	..	..	..
6	....	..	..	..	..	..	..	..	..	..	..
....	....	..	..	..	..	..	..	..	..	..	..
71	....	..	..	..	..	3	..	..	..	..	..
2	....	..	..	..	..	1	..	..	..	..	..
....	....	..	..	..	..	1	..	..	..	..	..
....	....	..	..	..	..	..	..	..	..	..	..
4	....	..	..	..	..	..	..	..	..	..	..
145	....	..	..	..	..	42	..	..	..	..	..
140	....	..	..	..	..	42	..	..	..	..	..
5	....	..	..	..	..	..	..	..	..	..	..
16	1	..	..	..	..	..	..	..	..	..	..

MO-III Bk Ra Cs 3—54

Group No.	Occupation.	Hindu. As principal occupation. Males.	Females.	As working dependants. Males.	Females.	As subsidiary to other occupation. Males.	Females.	As principal occupation. Males.	Females.
1	2	3	4	5	6	7	8	9	10
	Total Sub-Class V—Trade	**43,815**	**4,400**	**201**	**1,643**	..	..	**25,974**	**590**
	Total Order 23—Banks, Establishments of Credit, Exchange and Insurance	**2,261**	**18**	..	..	..	..	**763**	**3**
115	Bank managers, money lenders, exchange and insurance agents, money changers and brokers and their employees								
	Total Order 24—Brokerage Commission and Export	**3,326**	**14**	**4**	**343**	..	..	**668**	**4**
116	Brokers, commission agents commercial travellers, warehouse owners and employees								
	Total Order 25—Trade in Textiles	**357**	**24**	..	..	..	..	**287**	**4**
117	Trade in piece-goods, wool, cotton, silk hair and other textiles								
	Total Order 26—Trade in Skins, Leather and Furs	**65**	**7**	..	..	..	..	**6**	..
118	Trade in skins, leather, furs, feathers, horn, etc. and the articles made from these								
	Total Order 27—Trade in Wood	**87**	**33**	..	..	..	..	**205**	**3**
119	Trade in wood (not firewood)	27	30	..	..	..	..	78	2
120	Trade in barks	36	..	..	..	..	..	..	..
121	Trade in bamboos and canes	13	3	..	..	..	..	5	1
122	Trade in thatches and other forest produce	11	..	..	..	..	..	122	..
	Total Order 28—Trade in Metals	**151**	**6**	..	..	..	..	**156**	**3**
123	Trade in metals, machinery, knives, tools, etc.								
	Total Order 29—Trade in Pottery, Bricks and Tiles	**18**	**3**	..	..	..	..	**52**	..
124	Trade in pottery, bricks and tiles								
	Total Order 30—Trade in Chemical Products	**326**	**25**	..	..	..	..	**154**	**14**
125	Drugs, dyes, paints, petroleum, explosives, etc.								
	Total Order 31—Hotels, Cafes, Restaurants, etc.	**4,301**	**354**	..	..	..	..	**2,642**	**56**
126	Vendors of wine, liquors, aerated waters and ice	453	10	..	..	..	..	38	..
127	Owners and Managers of hotels, cook shops, *sarais*, etc. (and employees)	3,656	344	..	..	..	..	2,603	56
128	Hawkers of drink and food stuffs	102	..	..	..	..	..	1	..
	Total Order 32—Other Trade in Food Stuffs	**7,215**	**2,472**	**5**	..	..	..	**2,069**	**311**
129	Grain and pulse dealers	536	16	..	..	..	..	39	3
130	Dealers in sweetmeats, sugar and spices	1,173	362	..	..	..	..	166	14
131	Dealers in dairy product, eggs and poultry	2,297	61	..	..	..	..	662	16
132	Dealers in animals for food	4	1	..	..	..	..	14	2
133	Dealers in fodder for animals	35	..	..	..	..	..	14	1
134	Dealers in other food stuffs	1,501	265	5	..	..	..	754	44
135	Dealers in tobacco	1,501	1,763	..	..	..	..	405	51
136	Dealers in opium	26	..	..	..	..	..	1	..
137	Dealers in ganja	142	4	..	..	..	..	14	..
	Total Order 33—Trade in Clothing and Toilet Articles	**1,508**	**1**	**12**	**360**	..	..	**188**	**3**
138	Trade in ready-made clothing and other articles of dress and the toilet (hats, umbrellas, socks, ready-made shoes, perfumes, etc.								
	Total Order 34—Trade in Furniture	**185**	**9**	..	..	..	..	**158**	**5**
139	Trade in furniture, carpets, curtain, and beddings	163	9	..	..	..	..	48	1
140	Hardware, cooking utensils, porcelain, crockery, glassware, bottles, articles for gardening, etc.	22	..	..	..	..	..	110	4
	Total Order 35—Trade in Building Materials	**5**	..	..	..	..	..	**6**	..
141	Trade in building materials (other than bricks, tiles and woody materials)								

Muslim.				Jain.						Zoroastrian.			
As working dependants.		As subsidiary to other occupation.		As principal occupation.		As working dependants.		As subsidiary to other occupation.		As principal occupation.		As working dependants.	
Males.	Females.	Males.	Females.	Males.	Females.	Males.	Females.	Males.	Females.	Males.	Females.	Males.	Females.
11	12	13	14	15	16	17	18	19	20	21	22	23	24
5	..	..	..	2,918	41	..	5	..	..	3,500	110	..	..
..	..	..	..	21	..	..	..	..	..	450	26	..	..
1	..	..	..	469	8	..	..	..	..	169	1	..	..
..	..	..	..	203	..	..	..	..	..	20	..	..	..
..	..	..	..	..	..	..	..	..	..	9	3	..	..
..	..	..	..	..	..	..	..	..	..	11	..	..	..
..	..	..	..	..	..	..	..	..	..	4	..	..	..
..	..	..	..	..	..	..	..	..	..	2	..	..	..
..	..	..	..	..	..	..	..	..	..	5	..	..	..
..	..	..	..	..	..	..	..	..	..	..	..	..	..
..	..	..	..	54	..	..	..	..	..	4	1	..	..
..	..	..	..	..	..	..	..	..	..	..	..	..	..
..	..	..	..	59	..	..	..	..	..	14	2	..	..
1	..	..	..	421	..	..	..	..	..	740	19	..	..
..	..	..	..	..	..	..	..	..	..	133	8	..	..
1	..	..	..	176	..	..	..	..	..	607	11	..	..
..	..	..	..	245	..	..	..	..	..	..	..	..	..
..	..	..	..	517	7	..	1	..	..	21	2	..	..
..	..	..	..	219	2	..	..	..	..	..	..	..	..
..	..	..	..	136	..	..	..	..	..	9	..	..	..
..	..	..	..	3	..	..	..	..	..	2	2	..	..
..	..	..	..	..	..	..	..	..	..	..	..	..	..
..	..	..	..	..	..	..	..	..	..	..	..	..	..
..	..	..	..	159	3	..	..	..	..	5	..	..	..
..	..	..	..	..	..	..	..	..	..	3	..	..	..
..	..	..	..	..	..	..	..	..	..	..	..	..	..
..	..	..	..	..	2	..	1	..	..	2	..	..	..
..	..	..	..	56	..	..	..	..	..	3	1	..	..
..	..	..	..	9	..	..	..	..	..	4	..	..	..
..	..	..	..	..	..	..	..	..	..	3	..	..	..
..	..	..	..	9	..	..	..	..	..	1	..	..	..
..	..	..	..	..	..	..	..	..	..	..	..	..	..

Group No.	Occupation.	ZOROASTRIAN—*contd.* As subsidiary to other occupation. Males.	Females.	CHRISTIAN. As principal occupation. Males.	Females.	As working dependants. Males.	Females.	As subsidiary to other occupation. Males.	Females.
1	2	25	26	27	28	29	30	31	32
	Total Sub-Class V—Trade	..	..	2,554	481	..	..	..	..
	Total Order 23—Banks, Establishments of Credit, Exchange and Insurance	..	..	115	6	..	..	..	..
115	Bank managers, money lenders, exchange and insurance agents, money changers and brokers and their employees								
	Total Order 24—Brokerage Commission and Export	..	..	148	7	..	..	..	..
116	Brokers, commission agents commercial travellers, warehouse owners and employees								
	Total Order 25—Trade in Textiles	..	..	73	..	..	..	..	..
117	Trade in piece-goods, wool, cotton, silk hair and other textiles								
	Total Order 26—Trade in Skins, Leather and Furs	..	..	1	..	..	..	..	..
118	Trade in skins, leather, furs, feathers, horn, etc. and the articles made from these								
	Total Order 27—Trade in Wood	..	..	6	1	..	..	..	..
119	Trade in wood (not firewood)	..	..	5	..	..	..	..	..
120	Trade in barks	..	..	..	..	..	..	..	..
121	Trade in bamboos and canes	..	..	1	1	..	..	..	..
122	Trade in thatches and other forest produce	..	..	..	..	..	..	..	..
	Total Order 28—Trade in Metals	..	..	2	..	..	..	..	..
123	Trade in metals, machinery, knives, tools, etc.								
	Total Order 29—Trade in Pottery, Bricks and Tiles	..	..	..	..	..	..	..	..
124	Trade in pottery, bricks and tiles								
	Total Order 30—Trade in Chemical Products	..	..	32	2	..	..	..	..
125	Drugs, dyes, paints, petroleum, explosives, etc.								
	Total Order 31—Hotels, Cafes, Restaurants, etc.	..	..	1,283	339	..	..	..	..
126	Vendors of wine, liquors, aerated waters and ice	..	..	19	3	..	..	..	..
127	Owners and Managers of hotels, cook shops, sarais, etc. (and employees)	..	..	1,264	336	..	..	..	..
128	Hawkers of drink and food stuffs	..	..	..	..	..	..	..	..
	Total Order 32—Other Trade in Food Stuffs	..	..	65	38	..	..	..	..
129	Grain and pulse dealers	..	..	5	..	..	..	..	..
130	Dealers in sweetmeats, sugar and spices	..	..	25	6	..	..	..	..
131	Dealers in dairy product, eggs and poultry	..	..	5	1	..	..	..	..
132	Dealers in animals for food	..	..	1	..	..	..	..	..
133	Dealers in fodder for animals	..	..	..	..	..	..	..	..
134	Dealers in other food stuffs	..	..	9	26	..	..	..	..
135	Dealers in tobacco	..	..	20	5	..	..	..	..
136	Dealers in opium	..	..	..	..	..	..	..	..
137	Dealers in ganja	..	..	..	..	..	..	..	..
	Total Order 33—Trade in Clothing and Toilet Articles	..	..	5	..	..	..	..	..
138	Trade in ready-made clothing and other articles of dress and the toilet (hats, umbrellas, socks, ready-made shoes, perfumes, etc.								
	Total Order 34—Trade in Furniture	..	..	3	..	..	..	..	..
139	Trade in furniture, carpets, curtain, and beddings	..	..	1	..	..	..	..	..
140	Hardware, cooking utensils, porcelain, crockery, glassware, bottles, articles for gardening, etc.	..	..	2	..	..	..	..	..
	Total Order 35—Trade in Building Materials	..	..	1	..	..	..	..	..
141	Trade in building materials (other than bricks, tiles and woody materials)								

Jew.						Other Religions.					
As principal occupation.		As working dependants.		As subsidiary to other occupation.		As principal occupation.		As working dependants.		As subsidiary to other occupation.	
Males.	Females.	Males.	Females.	Males.	Females.	Males.	Females.	Males.	Females.	Males.	Females.
33	34	35	36	37	38	39	40	41	42	43	44
276	15	..	..	..	..	283	17	5	7	..	..
8	1	..	..	..	..	..	..	..	..	..	..
35	2	..	..	..	..	..	..	..	..	..	..
5	1	..	..	..	..	18	..	..	..	..	..
....	....	..	..	..	..	..	..	..	..	..	..
....	....	..	..	..	..	..	..	..	..	..	..
....	....	..	..	..	..	..	..	..	..	..	..
....	....	..	..	..	..	..	..	..	..	..	..
....	....	..	..	..	..	..	..	..	..	..	..
....	....	..	..	..	..	..	..	..	..	..	..
....	....	..	..	..	..	8	..	..	..	..	..
....	....	..	..	..	..	..	..	..	..	..	..
1	....	..	..	..	..	..	..	..	..	..	.
8	1	..	..	..	..	12	7	.		..	..
....	....	..	..	..	..	..	..	..	..	..	..
7	1	..	..	..	..	12	7	..	..	..	..
1	....	..	..	..	..	..	..	..	..	..	..
10	2	..	..	..	..	..	..	..	..	..	..
....	....	..	..	..	..	..	..	..	..	..	..
7	1	..	..	..	..	..	..	..	..	..	..
....	....	..	..	..	..	..	..	..	..	..	..
....	....	..	..	..	..	..	..	..	..	..	..
1	....	..	..	..	..	..	..	..	..	..	..
2	....	..	..	..	..	..	..	..	..	..	..
....	1	..	..	..	..	..	..	..	..	..	..
....	....	..	..	..	..	..	..	..	..	..	..
....	....	..	..	..	..	..	..	..	..	..	..
10	....	..	..	..	..	..	..	..	..	..	..
....	....	..	..	..	..	..	..	..	..	..	..
....	....	..	..	..	..	..	..	..	..		
....	....	..	..	..	..	..	..	..	..		
....	....	..	..	..	..	..	..	..	..		

MO-III Bk Ra Cs 3—55

Group No.	Occupation.	Hindu.							
		As principal occupation.		As working dependants.		As subsidiary to other occupation.		As principal occupation.	
		Males.	Females.	Males.	Females.	Males.	Females.	Males.	Females.
1	2	3	4	5	6	7	8	9	10
	Total Order 36—Trade in Means of Transport	47	14	..	..	..	..	208	1
142	Dealers and hirers in mechanical transport motors, cycles, etc.	14	1	..	..	..	..	51	..
143	Dealers and hirers in other carriages, carts, boats, etc.	33	13	..	..	..	..	131	..
144	Dealers and hirers of elephants, camels, horses, cattle, asses, mules, etc.	..	..	..	..	..	..	26	1
	Total Order 37—Trade in Fuel	240	45	8	..	..	..	202	8
145	Dealers in firewood, charcoal, coal, cowdung, etc.								
	Total Order 38—Trade in Articles of Luxury and those Pertaining to Letters and the Arts and Sciences	417	93	..	..	..	..	184	7
146	Dealers in precious stones, jewellery (real and imitation), clocks, optical instruments, etc.	249	..	..	..	..	..	74	1
147	Dealers in common bangles, bead necklaces, fans, small articles, toys, hunting and fishing tackle, flowers, etc.	107	79	..	..	..	..	81	4
148	Publishers, book-sellers, stationers, dealers in music, pictures, musical instruments and curiosities	61	14	..	..	..	..	29	2
	Total Order 39—Trade of other Sorts	23,306	1,282	172	940	..	..	18,026	348
149	Dealers in rags, stable refuse, etc.	9	..	..	..	..	..	..	3
150	General store-keepers and shop-keepers otherwise unspecified	20,489	617	172	940	..	..	12,497	258
151	Itinerant traders, pedlars, and hawkers (of other than food, etc.)	2,524	665	..	..	..	..	4,078	87
152	Other trades (including farmers of pounds, tolls and markets)	284	..	..	..	..	..	1,451	..
	Total Class C—Public Administration and Liberal Arts	37,406	1,672	..	..	2	..	10,173	399
	Total Sub-Class VI—Public Force	4,777	100	..	..	..	..	1,991	14
	Total Order 40—Army	1,222	87	..	..	..	..	542	11
153	Army (Imperial)	1,171	87	..	..	..	..	539	4
154	Army (Indian States)	51	..	..	..	..	..	3	7
	Total Order 41—Navy	16	..	..	..	..	..	44	1
155	Navy								
	Total Order 42—Air Force	13	2	..	..	..	..	..	..
156	Air Force								
	Total Order 43—Police	3,526	11	..	..	..	..	1,405	2
157	Police	3,016	6	..	..	..	..	800	2
158	Village watchmen	510	5	..	..	..	..	605	..
	Total Sub-Class VII—Public Administration	23,867	984	..	..	..	..	3,792	191
	Total Order 44—Public Administration	23,867	984	..	..	..	..	3,792	191
159	Service of the State	3,188	173	..	..	..	..	323	44
160	Service of Indian and Foreign States	96	6	..	..	..	..	5	1
161	Municipal and other local (not village) service	20,414	805	..	..	..	..	3,419	146
162	Village officials and servants other than watchmen	174	..	..	..	..	..	45	..
	Total Sub-Class VIII—Professions and Liberal Arts	8,762	588	..	..	2	..	4,390	194
	Total Order 45—Religion	1,130	24	..	..	..	..	924	17
163	Priests, ministers, etc.	416	8	..	..	..	..	138	4
164	Monks, nuns, religious mendicants	151	4	..	..	..	..	669	11
165	Other religious workers	99	..	..	..	..	..	23	1
166	Servants in religious edifices, burial and burning grounds, pilgrim conductors, circumcisers, etc.	464	12	..	..	..	..	94	1
	Total Order 46—Law	1,324	6	..	..	..	..	80	1
167	Lawyers of all kinds, including Qazis, Law Agents and Mukhtiars	1,311	6	..	..	..	..	59	..
168	Lawyers' clerks, petition writers, etc.	13	..	..	..	..	..	21	1

Muslim — As working dependants. Males.	Muslim — As working dependants. Females.	Muslim — As subsidiary to other occupation. Males.	Muslim — As subsidiary to other occupation. Females.	Jain — As principal occupation. Males.	Jain — As principal occupation. Females.	Jain — As working dependants. Males.	Jain — As working dependants. Females.	Jain — As subsidiary to other occupation. Males.	Jain — As subsidiary to other occupation. Females.	Zoroastrian — As principal occupation. Males.	Zoroastrian — As principal occupation. Females.	Zoroastrian — As working dependants. Males.	Zoroastrian — As working dependants. Females.
11	12	13	14	15	16	17	18	19	20	21	22	23	24
..	..	..	..	21	..	..	..	..	..	32	2	..	..
..	..	..	..	21	..	..	..	..	..	25	..	..	..
..	..	..	..	..	..	..	..	..	..	5	1	..	..
..	..	..	..	..	..	..	..	..	..	1	1	..	..
..	..	..	..	36	..	..	..	..	..	1	..	..	..
..	..	..	..	137	..	..	..	..	..	41	1	..	..
..	..	..	..	59	..	..	..	..	..	4	..	..	..
..	..	..	..	..	..	..	..	..	..	1	..	..	..
..	..	..	..	78	..	..	..	..	..	36	1	..	..
3	..	..	..	915	26	..	4	..	..	1,981	52	..	..
..	..	..	..	..	..	..	..	..	..	..	3	..	..
3	..	..	..	826	20	..	4	..	..	1,968	49	..	..
..	..	..	..	10	..	..	..	..	..	9	..	..	..
..	..	..	..	79	..	..	..	..	..	4	..	..	..
10	..	..	..	588	6	..	..	..	..	2,690	250	2	..
..	..	..	..	5	..	..	..	..	..	19	..	..	..
..	..	..	..	..	..	..	..	..	..	6	..	..	..
..	..	..	..	..	..	..	..	..	..	6	..	..	..
..	..	..	..	..	..	..	..	..	..	..	..	..	..
..	..	..	..	..	..	..	..	..	..	6	..	..	..
..	..	..	..	..	..	..	..	..	..	..	..	..	..
..	..	..	..	5	..	..	..	..	..	7	..	..	..
..	..	..	..	5	..	..	..	..	..	6	..	..	..
..	..	..	..	..	..	..	..	..	..	1	..	..	..
1	..	..	..	122	..	..	..	..	..	972	33	1	..
1	..	..	..	122	..	..	..	..	..	972	33	1	..
1	..	..	..	10	..	..	..	..	..	468	18	..	..
..	..	..	..	..	..	..	..	..	..	..	..	..	..
..	..	..	..	112	..	..	..	..	..	509	15	1	..
..	..	..	..	..	..	..	..	..	..	..	..	..	..
9	..	..	..	461	6	..	..	..	..	1,699	217	1	..
5	..	..	..	45	2	..	..	..	..	478	13	..	..
..	..	..	..	15	2	..	..	..	..	464	11	..	..
5	..	..	..	..	..	..	..	..	..	..	..	..	..
..	..	..	..	..	..	..	..	..	..	2	..	..	..
..	..	..	..	30	..	..	..	..	..	12	2	..	..
..	..	..	..	49	..	..	..	..	..	167	4	..	..
..	..	..	..	..	..	..	..	..	..	149	4	..	..
..	..	..	..	49	..	..	..	..	..	18	..	..	..
											3		

Group No.	Occupation.	Zoroastrian—contd. As subsidiary to other occupation. Males.	Zoroastrian—contd. As subsidiary to other occupation. Females.	Christian. As principal occupation. Males.	Christian. As principal occupation. Females.	Christian. As working dependants. Males.	Christian. As working dependants. Females.	Christian. As subsidiary to other occupation. Males.	Christian. As subsidiary to other occupation. Females
1	2	25	26	27	28	29	30	31	32
	Total Order 36—Trade in Means of Transport	..	..	51	5	..	..	..	..
142	Dealers and hirers in mechanical transport motors, cycles, etc.	..	..	35	..	..	..	..	..
143	Dealers and hirers in other carriages, carts, boats, etc.	..	..	1	..	..	..	..	..
144	Dealers and hirers of elephants, camels, horses, cattle, asses, mules, etc.	..	..	15	5	..	..	..	..
	Total Order 37—Trade in Fuel	..	..	..	..	..	..	..	..
145	Dealers in firewood, charcoal, coal, cowdung, etc.								
	Total Order 38—Trade in Articles of Luxury and those Pertaining to Letters and the Arts and Sciences	..	..	54	28	..	..	..	..
146	Dealers in precious stones, jewellery (real and imitation), clocks, optical instruments, etc.	..	..	..	..	..	..	..	..
147	Dealers in common bangles, bead necklaces, fans, small articles, toys, hunting and fishing tackle, flowers, etc.	..	..	37	24	..	..	..	..
148	Publishers, book-sellers, stationers, dealers in music, pictures, musical instruments and curiosities	..	..	17	4	..	..	..	..
	Total Order 39—Trade of other Sorts	..	..	715	55	..	..	..	..
149	Dealers in rags, stable refuse, etc.	..	..	..	..	..	..	..	..
150	General store-keepers and shop-keepers otherwise unspecified	..	..	696	54	..	..	..	..
151	Itinerant traders, pedlars, and hawkers (of other than food, etc.)	..	..	18	1	..	..	..	..
152	Other trades (including farmers of pounds, tools and markets)	..	..	1	..	..	..	..	..
	Total Class C—Public Administration and Liberal Arts	..	..	5,920	1,649	..	..	..	..
	Total Sub-Class VI—Public Force	..	..	2,040	55	..	..	..	..
	Total Order 40—Army	..	..	1,127	35	..	..	..	..
153	Army (Imperial)	..	..	1,126	35	..	..	..	..
154	Army (Indian States)	..	..	1	..	..	..	..	..
	Total Order 41—Navy	..	..	594	1	..	..	..	..
155	Navy								
	Total Order 42—Air Force	..	..	1	..	..	..	..	..
156	Air Force								
	Total Order 43—Police	..	..	318	19	..	..	..	..
157	Police	..	..	307	19	..	..	..	..
158	Village watchmen	..	..	11	..	..	..	..	..
	Total Sub-Class VII—Public Administration	..	..	1,932	239	..	..	..	..
	Total Order 44—Public Administration	..	..	1,932	239	..	..	..	..
159	Service of the State	..	..	754	35	..	..	..	..
160	Service of Indian and Foreign States	..	..	56	..	..	..	..	..
161	Municipal and other local (not village) service	..	..	1,121	204	..	..	..	..
162	Village officials and servants other than watchmen	..	..	1	..	..	..	..	..
	Total Sub-Class VIII—Professions and Liberal Arts	..	..	1,948	1,355	..	..	..	..
	Total Order 45—Religion	..	..	113	29	..	..	..	..
163	Priests, ministers, etc.	..	..	80	11	..	..	..	..
164	Monks, nuns, religious mendicants	..	..	..	..	..	..	..	..
165	Other religious workers	..	..	24	5	..	..	..	..
166	Servants in religious edifices, burial and burning grounds, pilgrim conductors, circumcisers, etc.	..	..	9	13	..	..	..	..
	Total Order 46—Law	..	..	73	2	..	..	..	..
167	Lawyers of all kinds, including Qazis, Law Agents and Mukhtiars	..	..	70	1	..	..	..	..
168	Lawyers' clerks, petition writers, etc.	..	..	3	1	..	..	..	..

Jew.						Other Religions.					
As principal occupation.		As working dependants.		As subsidiary to other occupation.		As principal occupation.		As working dependants.		As subsidiary to other occupation.	
Males.	Females.	Males.	Females.	Males.	Females.	Males.	Females.	Males.	Females.	Males.	Females.
33	34	35	36	37	38	39	40	41	42	43	44
3	....	..	..	..	..	..	..	..	..	..	..
3	....	..	..	..	..	..	..	..	..	..	..
....	....	..	..	..	..	..	..	..	..	..	..
....	....	..	..	..	..	..	..	..	..	..	..
....	....	..	..	..	..	..	..	..	..	..	..
1	....	..	..	..	..	7	..	..	..	..	..
....	....	..	..	..	..	7	..	..	..	..	..
1	....	..	..	..	..	..	..	..	..	..	..
....	....	..	..	..	..	..	..	..	..	..	..
195	8	..	..	..	..	238	10	5	7	..	..
....	....	..	..	..	..	..	..	..	..	..	..
151	6	..	..	..	..	79	6	5	5	..	..
44	2	..	..	..	..	159	4	..	2	..	..
....	....	..	..	..	..	..	..	..	..	..	..
324	88	..	..	..	..	123	14	..	1	..	..
12	1	..	..	..	..	28	..	..	..	..	..
5	1	..	..	..	..	17	..	..	..	..	..
5	1	..	..	..	..	17	..	..	..	..	..
....	....	..	..	..	..	..	..	..	..	..	..
1	....	..	..	..	..	11	..	..	..	..	..
....	....	..	..	..	..	..	..	..	..	..	..
6	....	..	..	..	..	..	..	..	..	..	..
5	....	..	..	..	..	..	..	..	..	..	..
1	....	..	..	..	..	..	..	..	..	..	..
91	5	..	..	..	..	56	..	..	..	..	..
91	5	..	..	..	..	56	..	..	..	..	..
81	....	..	..	..	..	19	..	..	..	..	..
....	....	..	..	..	..	..	..	..	..	..	..
60	5	..	..	..	..	37	..	..	..	..	..
....	....	..	..	..	..	..	..	..	..	..	..
221	82	..	..	..	..	39	14	..	1	..	..
20	....	..	..	..	..	..	..	..	..	..	..
6	....	..	..	..	..	..	..	..	..	..	..
1	....	..	..	..	..	..	..	..	..	..	..
11	....	..	..	..	..	..	..	..	..	..	..
2	....	..	..	..	..	..	..	..	..	..	..
22	....	..	..	..	..	..	3	..	1	..	..
16	....	..	..	..	..	..	3	..	1	..	..
6	....	..	..	..	..	..	..	..	..	..	..

Group No.	Occupation.	Hindu. As principal occupation. Males.	Hindu. As principal occupation. Females.	Hindu. As working dependants. Males.	Hindu. As working dependants. Females.	Hindu. As subsidiary to other occupation. Males.	Hindu. As subsidiary to other occupation. Females.	As principal occupation. Males.	As principal occupation. Females.
1	2	3	4	5	6	7	8	9	10
•	**Total Order 47—Medicine**	1,194	290	..	..	..	..	302	34
169	Registered medical practitioners including oculists	776	14	..	..	..	..	151	1
170	Other persons practising the healing arts without being registered	70	5	..	..	..	..	108	2
171	Dentists	3	42	..	..	..	..	4	..
172	Midwives, Vaccinators, compounders, nurses, masseurs, etc.	327	213	..	..	..	..	35	30
173	Veterinary surgeons	18	16	..	..	..	..	4	1
	Total Order 48—Instruction	2,030	130	..	..	2	..	549	36
174	Professors and teachers of all kinds	1,189	128	..	..	2	..	548	36
175	Clerks and servants connected with education	841	2	..	..	..	..	1	..
	Total Order 49—Letters, Arts and Sciences (other than 44)	3,084	138	..	..	..	..	2,535	106
176	Public scribes, stenographers, etc.	125	4	..	..	..	..	2	..
177	Architects, surveyors, engineers, and their employees (not being State Servants)	98	1	..	..	..	..	9	2
178	Authors, editors, journalists and photographers	188	2	..	..	..	..	49	..
179	Artists, sculptors and image-makers	370	4	..	..	..	..	52	1
180	Scientists (astronomers, botanists, etc.)	49	..	..	..	..	..	20	12
181	Horoscope casters, astrologers, fortune-tellers, wizards, witches and medium	277	2	..	..	..	..	268	..
182	Musicians (composers and performers other than military) actors, dancers, etc.	469	62	..	..	..	..	218	38
183	Managers and employees of places of public entertainments, race courses, societies, clubs	1,455	63	..	..	..	..	1,897	53
184	Conjurors, acrobats, reciters, exhibitors of curiosities and wild animals, etc.	58	..	..	..	..	..	20	..
	Total Class D—Miscellaneous	102,918	13,878	541	2	..	..	26,149	1,788
	Total Sub-Class IX—Persons living on their Income	695	34	..	..	..	..	149	8
	Total Order 50—Persons living Principally on their Income	695	34	..	..	..	..	149	8
185	Proprietors (other than of agricultural land), fund and scholarships holders and pensioners								
	Total Sub-Class X—Domestic Service	18,793	2,912	7	..	..	..	5,572	619
	Total Order 51—Domestic Service	18,793	2,912	7	..	..	..	5,572	619
186	Private motor drivers and cleaners	618	8	..	..	..	..	409	..
187	Other domestic service	18,175	2,904	7	..	..	..	5,163	619
	Total Sub-Class XI—Insufficiently described occupations	81,096	8,609	..	..	..	..	18,447	779
	Total Order 52—General terms which do not indicate a Definite occupation	81,096	8,609	..	..	..	..	18,447	779
188	Manufacturers, businessmen and contractors otherwise unspecified	4,275	278	..	..	..	..	778	25
189	Cashiers, accountants, book-keepers, clerks and other employees in unspecified offices and warehouses and shops	29,084	1,416	..	..	..	..	9,225	406
190	Mechanics otherwise unspecified	1,605	7	..	..	..	..	1,196	8
191	Labourers and workmen otherwise unspecified	46,182	6,908	..	..	..	..	7,248	340
	Total Sub-Class XII—Unproductive	2,334	1,823	584	2	..	..	1,981	382
	Total Order 53—Inmates of Jails, Asylums and Alms Houses	169	1	584	2	..	..	36	1
192	Inmates of jails, asylums and alms houses								
	Total Order 54—Beggars, Vagrants, Prostitutes	2,086	1,816	..	..	..	..	1,695	380
193	Beggars and vagrants	2,077	1,002	..	..	..	..	1,691	172
194	Procurers and prostitutes	9	814	..	..	..	..	4	208
	Total Order 55—Other unclassified Non-Productive Industries	79	6	..	..	..	..	250	1
195	Other unclassified non-productive industries								

Muslim.				Jain.						Zoroastrian.			
As working dependants.		As subsidiary to other occupation.		As principal occupation.		As working dependants.		As subsidiary to other occupation.		As principal occupation.		As working dependants.	
Males.	Females.	Males.	Females.	Males.	Females.	Males.	Females.	Males.	Females.	Males.	Females.	Males.	Females.
11	12	13	14	15	16	17	18	19	20	21	22	23	24
4	..	..	..	78	2	..	..	..	..	375	48	..	..
..	..	..	..	29	2	..	..	..	..	350	20	..	..
..	..	..	..	..	..	..	..	..	..	2	..	..	..
4	..	..	..	..	..	..	..	..	..	14	..	..	..
..	..	..	..	49	..	..	..	..	..	9	28	..	..
..	..	..	..	..	..	..	..	..	..	..	..	..	..
..	..	..	..	179	2	..	..	..	..	235	126	..	..
..	..	..	..	97	2	..	..	..	..	235	114	..	..
..	..	..	..	82	..	..	..	..	..	..	12	..	..
..	..	..	..	110	..	..	..	..	..	444	26	1	..
..	..	..	..	22	..	..	..	..	..	10	4	..	..
..	..	..	..	..	..	..	..	..	..	17	1	..	..
..	..	..	..	12	..	..	..	..	..	63	8	..	..
..	..	..	..	..	..	..	..	..	..	7	..	..	..
..	..	..	..	..	..	..	..	..	..	..	..	..	..
..	..	..	..	67	..	..	..	..	..	2	1	..	..
..	..	..	..	6	..	..	..	..	..	45	2	..	..
..	..	..	..	3	..	..	..	..	..	238	9	1	..
..	..	..	..	..	..	..	..	..	..	62	1	..	..
216	33	..	..	937	18	..	3	..	..	7,581	394	3	..
..	1	..	..	..	..	..	..	..	.	584	100	..	..
..	1	..	..	..	..	..	..	..	...	584	100	..	..
..	28	..	..	258	12	..	3	..	..	487	123	..	..
..	28	..	..	258	12	..	3	..	..	487	123	..	..
..	..	..	..	40	..	..	..		..	78	2	..	..
..	28	..	..	218	12	..	3		..	409	121	..	..
1	3	..	..	676	1	..	..	..	..	6,483	141	1	..
1	3	..	..	676	1	..	..	..	..	6,483	141	1	..
..	..	..	..	232	..	..	..	..	..	495	26	1	..
1	3	..	..	264	1	..	..	..	..	5,415	107	..	..
..	..	..	..	58	..	..	..	..	..	298	1	..	..
..	..	..	..	122	..	..	..	..	..	275	7	..	..
215	6	..	..	3	..	..	..	..	..	7	30	2	..
210	..	..	..	..	..	..	..	..	..	...	..	2	..
5	6	..	..	3	..	..	..	..	..	7	18	..	..
5	6	..	..	3	..	..	..	..	..	7	14	..	..
..	..	..	..	..	..	..	..	..	..	..	4	..	..
..	..	..	..	..	..	..	..	..	..	..	12	..	..
											9		

Group No.	Occupation.	ZOROASTRIAN—*contd.* As subsidiary to other occupation. Males.	ZOROASTRIAN—*contd.* As subsidiary to other occupation. Females.	CHRISTIAN. As principal occupation. Males.	CHRISTIAN. As principal occupation. Females.	CHRISTIAN. As working dependants. Males.	CHRISTIAN. As working dependants. Females.	CHRISTIAN. As subsidiary to other occupation. Males.	CHRISTIAN. As subsidiary to other occupation. Females.
1		25	26	27	28	29	30	31	32
	Total Order 47—Medicine	..	..	590	767	..	..	..	..
169	Registered medical practitioners including oculists	..	..	361	25	..	..	..	..
170	Other persons practising the healing arts without being registered	..	..	2	2	..	..	..	..
171	Dentists	..	..	5	1	..	..	..	..
172	Midwives, Vaccinators, compounders, nurses, masseurs, etc.	..	..	222	739	..	..	..	..
173	Veterinary surgeons	..	..	..	..	..	..	..	..
	Total Order 48—Instruction	..	..	221	340	..	..	..	..
174	Professors and teachers of all kinds	..	..	218	340	..	..	..	..
175	Clerks and servants connected with education	..	..	3	..	..	..	..	..
	Total Order 49—Letters, Arts and Sciences (other than 44)	..	..	951	217	..	..	..	..
176	Public scribes, stenographers, etc.	..	..	14	89	..	..	..	..
177	Architects, surveyors, engineers, and their employees (not being State Servants)	..	..	43	2	..	..	..	..
178	Authors, editors, journalists and photographers	..	..	47	2	..	..	..	..
179	Artists, sculptors and image-makers	..	..	85	8	..	..	..	..
180	Scientists (astronomers, botanists, etc.)	..	..	1	..	..	..	..	..
181	Horoscope casters, astrologers, fortune-tellers, wizards, witches and medium	..	..	5	1	..	..	..	..
182	Musicians (composers and performers other than military), actors, dancers, etc.	..	..	211	87	..	..	..	..
183	Managers and employees of places of public entertainments, race courses, societies, clubs	..	..	537	25	..	..	..	..
184	Conjurors, acrobats, recitors, exhibitors of curiosities and wild animals, etc.	..	..	8	3	..	..	..	..
	Total Class D—Miscellaneous	..	..	17,320	3,156	..	..	..	..
	Total Sub-Class IX—Persons living on their Income	..	..	205	43	..	..	..	..
	Total Order 50—Persons living Principally on their Income								
185	Proprietors (other than of agricultural land), fund and scholarships holders and pensioners	..	..	205	43	..	..	..	..
	Total Sub-Class X—Domestic Service	..	..	8,904	2,434	..	..	..	..
	Total Order 51—Domestic Service	..	..	8,904	2,434	..	..	..	..
186	Private motor drivers and cleaners	..	..	230	7	..	..	..	..
187	Other domestic service	..	..	8,674	2,427	..	..	..	..
	Total Sub-Class XI—Insufficiently described occupations	..	..	8,155	609	..	..	..	..
	Total Order 52—General terms which do not indicate a Definite occupation	..	..	8,155	609	..	..	..	..
188	Manufacturers, businessmen and contractors otherwise unspecified	..	..	426	12	..	..	..	..
189	Cashiers, accountants, book-keepers, clerks and other employees in unspecified offices and warehouses and shops	..	..	5,357	440	..	..	..	..
190	Mechanics otherwise unspecified	..	..	1,639	26	..	..	..	..
191	Labourers and workmen otherwise unspecified	..	..	733	131	..	..	..	..
	Total Sub-Class XII—Unproductive	..	..	56	70	..	..	..	..
	Total Order 53—Inmates of Jails, Asylums and Alms Houses								
192	Inmates of jails, asylums and alms houses	..	..	1	..	..	..	..	..
	Total Order 54—Beggars, Vagrants, Prostitutes	..	..	43	67	..	..	..	..
193	Beggars and vagrants	..	..	42	5	..	..	..	..
194	Procurers and prostitutes	..	..	1	62	..	..	..	..
	Total Order 55—Other unclassified Non-Productive Industries								
195	Other unclassified non-productive industries	..	..	12	3	..	..	..	..

Jew.						Other Religions.					
As principal occupation.		As working dependants.		As subsidiary to other occupation.		As principal occupation.		As working dependants.		As subsidiary to other occupation.	
Males.	Females.	Males.	Females.	Males.	Females.	Males.	Females.	Males.	Females.	Males.	Females.
33	34	35	36	37	38	39	40	41	42	43	44
33	31	..	..	..	..	13	7	..	..	..	..
11	1	..	..	..	..	9	5	..	..	..	..
16	1	..	..	..	..	..	..	..	..	..	..
....	....	..	..	..	..	4	..	..	..	..	..
4	26	..	..	..	..	..	2	..	..	..	..
2	3	..	..	..	..	..	..	..	..	..	..
39	41	..	..	..	..	5	4	..	..	..	..
37	41	..	..	..	..	5	4	..	..	..	..
2	....	..	..	..	..	..	..	..	..	..	..
107	10	..	..	..	..	21	..	..	..	..	..
4	8	..	..	..	..	5	..	..	..	..	..
21	1	..	..	..	..	..	..	..	..	..	..
14	1	..	..	..	..	7	..	..	..	..	..
8	....	..	..	..	..	3	..	..	..	..	..
....	....	..	..	..	..	..	..	..	..	..	..
....	....	..	..	..	..	..	..	..	..	..	..
4	....	..	..	..	..	..	..	..	..	..	..
61	....	..	..	..	..	6	..	..	..	..	..
....	....	..	..	..	..	..	..	..	..	..	..
776	90	4	..	..	..	309	54	..	..	..	..
29	8	..	..	..	..	4	..	..	..	..	..
29	8	..	..	..	..	4	..	..	..	..	
28	36	..	..	..	..	68	13	..	..	..	..
28	36	..	..	..	..	68	13	..	..	..	..
3	....	..	..	..	..	9	..	..	..	..	..
25	36	..	..	..	..	59	13	..	..	..	..
718	41	..	..	..	..	237	3	..	..	..	..
718	41	..	..	..	..	237	3	..	..	..	..
45	2	..	..	..	..	36	..	..	..	..	..
522	35	..	..	..	..	149	3	..	..	..	..
129	2	..	..	..	..	16	..	..	..	..	..
22	2	..	..	..	..	36	..	..	..	..	..
1	10	4	..	..	..	..	38	..	..	..	..
....	....	4	..	..	..	..	..	..	..	..	..
1	10	..	..	..	..	..	38	..	..	..	..
1	....	..	..	..	..	..	..	..	..	..	..
....	10	..	..	..	..	..	38	..	..	..	..
....	....	..	..	..	..	..	..	..	..	..	..

EUROPEAN AND ALLIED RACES AND ANGLO-INDIANS BY RACE AND AGE.

(Corresponding to Imperial Table XIX.)

NOTE.—This table has nothing to do with Sects of Christians. It consists of two main parts—(*a*) Europeans and Allied Races including Armenians, and (*b*) Anglo-Indians. "Allied Races" is loosely used to cover Americans, and any other foreigners of the Christian Religion. Part (*a*) is divided into British Subjects and Others. Part (*b*) is not so divided, it being assumed that all Anglo-Indians are British Subjects. Actually, the classification of any person or persons into British Subjects and Others is a matter of inference only, the Census schedules having contained information as to *Race* and not Political Nationality. But the errors, if any, would balance out.

(A) European and Allied Races (including Armenians).

City.	Total.			British Subjects.																	
				All Ages.			0–13		14–16		17–23		24–33		34–43		44–53		54 and over.	
	Total.	Males.	Females.	Total.	Males.	Females.	Males.	Females.	Males.	Females.	Males.	Females.	Males.	Females.	Males.	Females.	Males.	Females.	Males.	Females.
	2	3	4	5	6	7	8	9	10	11	12	13	14	15	16	17	18	19	20	21
Bombay City ..	**9,409**	**6,071**	**3,338**	**8,400**	**5,394**	**3,006**	**623**	**573**	**127**	**96**	**789**	**377**	**1,688**	**776**	**1,180**	**659**	**719**	**303**	**373**	**222**
A Ward ..	2,861	1,843	1,018	2,495	1,596	899	170	158	32	27	109	84	431	249	469	213	287	104	98	64
B ,, ..	470	104	366	431	87	344	21	35	4	8	7	72	16	93	19	79	15	35	5	22
C ,, ..	22	18	4	18	16	2	5	1	1	..	4	..	2	..	3	..	1	1	..	..
D ,, ..	1,087	632	455	983	570	413	51	45	7	4	25	43	154	143	184	104	115	45	34	29
E ,, ..	1,595	888	707	1,412	811	601	228	144	44	35	92	100	181	105	124	103	117	58	75	56
F ,, ..	493	234	259	461	225	236	46	64	2	15	17	21	62	49	52	38	28	18	18	31
G ,, ..	215	127	88	215	127	88	15	14	5	3	18	13	30	23	29	15	23	11	7	9
Harbour, Islands, Railway Platforms, Floating population and unknown ..	2,666	2,225	441	2,385	1,962	423	87	112	32	4	517	44	857	114	300	107	133	31	36	11

City.	Others (including Armenians).																
	All Ages.			0–13		14–16		17–23		24–33		34–43		44–53		54 and over.	
	Total.	Males.	Females.	Males.	Females.	Males.	Females.	Males.	Females.	Males.	Females.	Males.	Females.	Males.	Females.	Males.	Females.
1	22	23	24	25	26	27	28	29	30	31	32	33	34	35	36	37	38
Bombay City ..	**1,009**	**677**	**332**	**44**	**61**	**10**	**9**	**96**	**43**	**236**	**93**	**143**	**70**	**97**	**38**	**51**	**18**
A Ward ..	366	247	119	23	29	4	2	20	15	82	36	57	20	45	10	16	7
B ,, ..	39	17	22	3	3	..	..	3	3	..	2	6	9	5	5	..	..
C ,, ..	4	2	2	..	..	..	..	..	1	1	..	..	..	1	1	..	..
D ,, ..	104	62	42	6	3	2	1	4	3	22	13	17	17	4	5	7	..
E ,, ..	183	77	106	8	21	2	6	5	14	20	26	17	20	15	13	10	6
F ,, ..	32	9	23	1	2	1	..	..	7	1	9	5	1	..	2	1	2
G ,, ..	..	..	..	..	..	..	..	..	..	..	..	..	..	..	..	..	..
Harbour, Islands, Railway Platforms, Floating population and unknown ..	281	263	18	3	3	1	..	64	..	110	7	41	3	27	2	17	3

(B) Anglo-Indians.

City.	All Ages.			0–3		4–6		7–13		14–16		17–19	
	Total.	Males.	Females.	Males.	Females.	Males.	Females.	Males.	Females.	Males.	Females.	Males.	Females.
1	2	3	4	5	6	7	8	9	10	11	12	13	14
Bombay City	**7,039**	**3,905**	**3,134**	**227**	**230**	**200**	**189**	**611**	**450**	**239**	**157**	**325**	**295**
A Ward	901	468	433	24	24	15	20	56	38	15	23	40	42
B ,, ...	159	96	63	3	7	3	3	9	11	8	3	7	5
C ,, ...	74	40	34	3	3	1	1	3	1	2	..	2	2
D ,, ...	210	90	120	6	5	6	3	7	10	9	5	8	11
E ,, ...	3,686	1,989	1,697	97	111	109	102	393	279	153	81	145	166
F ,, ...	1,408	849	559	70	54	53	42	96	77	31	28	84	49
G ,, ...	435	241	194	23	21	11	17	43	32	19	13	21	17
Harbour, Islands, Railway Platforms, Floating population and unknown.	166	132	34	1	5	2	1	4	2	2	4	18	3

City.	20–29		30–39		40–49		50–59		60–69		70 and over.	
	Males.	Females.	Males.	Females.	Males.	Females.	Males.	Females.	Males.	Females.	Males.	Females.
1	15	16	17	18	19	20	21	22	23	24	25	26
Bombay City	**819**	**750**	**772**	**567**	**441**	**266**	**169**	**131**	**85**	**71**	**17**	**28**
A Ward	110	117	100	84	62	48	32	16	13	16	1	5
B ,, ...	25	11	18	17	10	4	10	1	3	1	..	..
C ,, ...	4	7	14	8	6	5	1	2	1	5	3	..
D ,, ...	19	31	14	31	12	14	6	8	3	1	..	1
E ,, ...	366	402	378	297	226	135	70	78	42	30	10	16
F ,, ...	195	134	190	98	84	41	30	19	13	13	3	4
G ,, ...	49	35	30	29	22	16	15	7	8	5	..	2
Harbour, Islands, Railway Platforms, Floating population and unknown.	51	13	28	3	19	3	5	..	2	..	..	..

CITY TABLE I—KARACHI.

Area, Houses and Population.

(Corresponding to Imperial Table I.)

Quarter.	Area in acres.	Houses. Occupied.	Houses. Unoccupied.	Houses. Total.	Houses per acre.	Population. Persons.	Population. Males.	Population. Females.	Persons per acre.
1	2	3	4	5	6	7	8	9	10
Karachi City	**25,150·07**	**26,016**	**6,035**	**32,051**	**1·27**	**263,565**	**156,120**	**107,445**	**10·48**
Old Town	29·90	804	348	1,152	38·53	8,830	4,651	4,179	295·32
Lea	62·03	37	20	57	0·92	934	502	432	15·06
Napier	39·52	562	569	1,131	28·62	10,103	5,555	4,548	255·64
Market	32·90	450	154	604	18·36	6,745	3,805	2,940	205·02
Bunder	24·63	114	61	175	7·11	3,363	2,484	869	136·13
Machi Meani	57·70	279	150	429	7·44	8,886	4,914	3,972	154·00
Queens Road	156·60	22	2	24	0·15	153	105	48	0·98
Railway	73·95	62	99	161	2·18	358	263	95	4·81
Serai	162·01	555	301	856	5·28	13,087	8,414	4,673	80·78
Rambaugh	190·91	423	98	521	2·73	11,883	6,826	5,057	62·24
Jail	91·37	294	127	421	4·61	7,708	4,210	3,498	84·36
Ranchore	209·17	1,269	157	1,426	6·82	24,924	14,597	10,327	119·16
Ramswami	40·49	314	38	352	8·69	7,038	3,982	3,056	173·82
Harchandrai Vishendas	76·68	437	134	571	7·45	2,266	1,412	854	29·55
Soldier Bazar	15·98	196	97	293	18·34	1,592	906	686	99·63
New Jail	284·70	95	38	133	0·47	1,159	968	191	4·07
Preedy	71·40	177	89	266	3·73	1,798	1,064	734	25·18
Saddar Bazar	87·92	656	206	862	9·80	10,516	6,191	4,325	119·61
Civil Lines	201·85	429	143	572	2·83	4,432	2,936	1,496	21·96
Frere Town and Bath Island	149·39	256	82	288	1·93	2,256	1,434	822	15·10
Clifton	119·94	96	44	140	1·17	422	253	169	3·52
Gizri	27·95	208	17	225	8·05	1,029	574	455	36·82
Garden (East and West)	1,107·30	1,248	399	1,647	1·49	8,091	4,537	3,554	7·31
Tahilram	29·96	213	52	265	8·85	4,643	2,642	2,001	154·97
Lawrence	105·49	695	152	847	8·03	10,277	6,238	4,039	97·42
Lyari	1,322·72	9,206	1,492	10,698	8·09	60,017	32,773	27,244	45·37
Jamshed	252·00	285	73	358	1·42	2,170	1,276	894	8·61
Artillery Maidan	214·04	49	69	118	0·55	554	378	176	2·59
Trans Lyari	4,078·27	1,385	177	1,562	0·38	5,763	3,142	2,621	1·41
Tatta Naka and Goda Village and Labour Corps	45·09	101	10	111	2·46	860	534	326	19·07
Quarry No. 1 and 2 and other Quarries ..	67·90	102	11	113	1·66	424	240	184	6·24
Scattered Hamlets behind Cantonment Station and Chinasar and Vagri Villages ..	193·15	187	23	210	1·09	870	448	422	4·50
Keamari with other Port viz., Thole Produce Yard, Mansfield Import Yard and West Wharf	737·36	465	258	723	0·98	11,553	7,683	3,870	15·67
Baba Island	13·39	283	38	321	23·97	1,202	614	588	89·77
Bhit Island	9·00	159	22	181	20·11	796	414	382	88·44
Shampir and Goth Mahomed	103·00	106	21	127	1·23	464	225	239	4·50
Bunker Island	4·34	2	6	8	1·84	4	4	....	0·92
Port Floating population	....	..	..	..	..	2,709	2,633	76	..
Railway Area, including City Bunder and Cantonment Stations and Receiption and Hump Yard and Platform population ..	694·10	1,786	281	2,067	2·98	6,468	4,374	2,094	9·32
Maurypur	6,876·00	390	27	417	0·06	1,400	817	583	0·20
Drigh Road	5,263·50	13		13	..	22	17	5	..
Cape Manze	....	11		11	..	32	17	15	..
Karachi Cantonment	1,637·36	1,154	Not available.	1,154	0·70	6,240	3,707	2,533	3·81
Manora	189·11	441		441	2·33	2,018	1,255	763	10·67
Karachi Military Area	....	..		..	..	7,516	6,106	1,410	..

RELIGION.

(Corresponding to Imperial Table XVI.)

The Head " Others " Persons 10, Males 7, Females 3 is composed of Theosophists (Males 2, Females 3) Dadupanthi (5 Males.)

Quarter.	Population.			Hindu.			Muslim.		
	Persons.	Males.	Females.	Persons.	Males.	Females.	Persons.	Males.	Females.
1	2	3	4	5	6	7	8	9	10
Old Town	8,830	4,651	4,179	8,216	4,307	3,909	603	336	267
Lea	934	502	432	867	469	398	40	15	25
Napier	10,103	5,555	4,548	7,169	3,864	3,305	2,880	1,654	1,226
Market	6,745	3,805	2,940	5,446	3,066	2,380	1,271	719	552
Bunder	3,353	2,484	869	2,957	2,223	734	363	230	133
Machi Meani	8,886	4,914	3,972	3,932	2,362	1,570	4,916	2,534	2,382
Queens Road	153	105	48	98	72	26	17	10	7
Railway	358	263	95	237	180	57	94	70	24
Serai	13,087	8,414	4,673	10,405	6,738	3,667	2,350	1,475	875
Rambaugh	11,883	6,826	5,057	9,193	5,331	3,862	2,035	1,134	901
Jail	7,708	4,210	3,498	5,788	3,147	2,641	1,673	923	750
Runchore	24,924	14,597	10,327	18,098	10,677	7,421	5,622	3,242	2,380
Ramswami	7,038	3,982	3,056	5,490	3,136	2,354	857	474	383
Herchandrai Vishendas	2,266	1,412	854	918	545	373	1,216	800	416
Soldier Bazar	1,592	906	686	786	453	333	784	438	346
New Jail	1,159	968	191	362	317	45	772	631	141
Preedy	1,798	1,064	734	672	429	243	283	210	73
Saddar Bazar	10,516	6,191	4,325	2,798	1,707	1,091	4,140	2,450	1,690
Civil Lines	4,432	2,936	1,496	2,389	1,585	804	969	707	262
Frere Town and Bath Island	2,256	1,434	822	1,168	758	410	422	300	122
Clifton	422	253	169	234	145	89	157	91	66
Gizri	1,029	574	455	105	65	40	924	509	415
Garden (East and West)	8,091	4,537	3,554	2,105	1,371	734	5,268	2,773	2,495
Tahilram	4,643	2,642	2,001	1,749	1,054	695	2,868	1,571	1,297
Lawrence	10,277	6,238	4,039	6,162	3,862	2,300	3,603	2,051	1,552
Lyari	60,017	32,773	27,244	6,175	3,545	2,630	53,164	28,812	24,352
Jamshed	2,170	1,276	894	1,719	1,020	699	105	74	31
Artillary Maidân	554	378	176	288	206	82	118	84	34
Trans Lyari	5,763	3,142	2,621	188	128	60	5,569	3,008	2,561
Tatta Naka and Goda Village and Labour Corps	860	534	326	283	187	96	500	293	207
Quarry Nos. 1 and 2 and other quarries	424	240	184	13	9	4	411	231	180
Scattered Hamlets, behind Cantonment Station and Chinaser and Vagri Villages	870	448	422	203	109	94	667	339	328
Keamari with other Port area (viz. Thole Produce Yard Man's field, Import Yard and West Wharf)	11,553	7,683	3,870	5,320	3,673	1,647	5,424	3,519	1,905
Baba Islands	1,202	614	588	46	25	21	1,156	589	567
Bhit Islands	796	414	382	9	6	3	787	408	379
Shamespir and Goth Mahomed	464	225	239	3	3	..	461	222	239
Bunker Island	4	4	..	3	3	..	1	1	..
Port Floating Population	2,709	2,633	76	498	473	25	1,919	1,885	34
Railway Area including City Bunder and Cantonment Stations and Receiption and Hump Yard and Platform Population	6,468	4,374	2,094	3,158	2,201	957	2,772	1,843	920
Maurypur	1,400	817	583	194	138	56	1,193	672	521
Drigh Road	22	17	5	15	11	4	7	6	1
Cape Mouze	32	17	15	1	1	..	31	16	15
Karachi Cantonment	6,240	3,707	2,533	2,256	1,453	803	997	721	276
Manora	2,018	1,255	763	1,114	715	399	703	422	281
Karachi Military Area	7,516	6,106	1,410	1,765	1,328	437	2,735	2,239	496
Total	263,965	156,120	107,445	120,595	73,097	47,498	122,847	70,731	52,116

Quarter.	Jains.			Zoroastrians.			Christian.			Sikhs.		
	Persons.	Males.	Females.	Persons.	Males.	Females.	Persons.	Males.	Females.	Persons.	Males.	Females.
1	11	12	13	14	15	16	17	18	19	20	21	22
Old Town	..	..	..	..	..	..	..	..	..	10	7	3
Loa	..	..	..	..	..	..	4	3	1	12	8	4
Napier	..	..	..	2	2	..	..	..	..	51	34	17
Market	1	1	..	1	1	..	1	1	..	25	17	8
Bunder	..	..	..	..	..	..	..	..	..	33	31	2
Machi Meani	..	..	..	1	1	..	..	..	..	37	17	20
Queens Road	..	..	..	14	6	8	24	17	7	..	..	..
Railway	..	..	..	..	..	..	14	5	9	7	4	3
Serai	19	12	7	78	37	41	117	64	53	79	60	19
Rambaugh	..	..	..	206	110	96	52	28	24	273	171	102
Jail	45	26	19	8	1	7	133	66	67	53	43	10
Runchore	416	244	172	284	163	121	203	89	114	170	103	67
Ramswami	121	64	57	..	..	..	63	38	25	186	102	84
Herchandrai Vishendas	..	..	..	..	..	..	60	28	32	19	10	9
Soldier Bazar	..	..	..	12	7	5	10	8	2	..	..	..
New Jail	2	2	..	2	2	..	13	9	4	8	7	1
Preedy	..	..	..	403	201	202	435	221	214	..	..	..
Saddar Bazar	9	6	3	813	420	393	2,616	1,518	1,098	56	38	18
Civil Lines	2	1	1	120	66	54	897	542	355	19	14	5
Frere Town and Bath Island	..	..	..	73	39	34	576	328	248	15	7	8
Clifton	..	..	..	12	5	7	18	11	7	1	1	..
Gizri	..	..	..	..	..	..	..	..	..	..	..	..
Garden (East and West)	2	2	..	109	57	52	488	269	219	36	21	15
Tahilram	..	..	..	..	..	..	..	..	..	23	16	7
Lawrence	2	1	1	25	14	11	165	102	63	229	164	65
Lyari	..	..	..	3	..	3	622	381	241	42	28	14
Jamshed	..	..	..	97	53	44	229	120	109	11	5	6
Artillary Maidan	..	..	..	78	43	35	32	18	14	38	27	11
Trans Lyari	..	..	..	..	..	..	..	..	..	6	6	..
Tatta Naka and Goda Village and Labour Corps	..	..	..	..	..	..	15	9	6	62	45	17
Quarry Nos. 1 and 2 and other quarries	..	..	..	..	..	..	..	..	..	..	..	..
Scattered Hamlets, behind Cantonment Station and Chinaser and Vagri Villages	..	..	..	..	..	..	..	..	..	..	..	..
Keamari with other Port area (viz. Thole Produce Yard Man's field, Import Yard and West Wharf)	..	..	..	39	23	16	536	315	221	154	112	42
Baba Islands	..	..	..	..	..	..	..	..	..	..	..	..
Bhit Islands	..	..	..	..	..	..	..	..	..	..	..	..
Shamespir and Goth Mahomed	..	..	..	..	..	..	..	..	..	..	..	..
Bunker Island	..	..	..	..	..	..	..	..	..	..	..	..
Port Floating Population	1	1	..	22	14	8	262	253	9	4	4	..
Railway Area including City Bunder and Cantonment Stations and Receiption and Hump Yard and Platform Population	..	..	..	6	6	..	259	152	107	252	161	91
Maurypur	..	..	..	..	..	..	8	4	4	5	3	2
Drigh Road	..	..	..	..	..	..	..	..	..	..	..	..
Cape Mouze	..	..	..	..	..	..	..	..	..	..	..	..
Karachi Cantonment	..	..	..	926	473	453	2,043	1,052	991	2	2	..
Manora	..	..	..	..	..	..	159	91	68	40	26	14
Karachi Military Area	9	6	3	..	..	..	2,711	2,338	373	296	195	101
Total	629	366	263	3,334	1,744	1,590	12,765	8,080	4,685	2,254	1,489	765

Quarter.	Jews.			Buddhists.			Tribal.			Others.		
	Persons.	Males.	Females.	Persons.	Males.	Females.	Persons.	Males.	Females.	Persons.	Males.	Females.
1	23	24	25	26	27	28	29	30	31	32	33	34
Old Town	1	1	..	..	..	..	..	..	..	..	..	..
Lea	11	7	4	..	..	..	..	..	..	..	..	..
Napier	1	1	..	..	..	..	..	..	..	..	..	..
Market	..	..	..	..	..	..	..	..	..	..	..	..
Bunder	..	..	..	..	..	..	..	..	..	..	..	..
Machi Moani	..	..	..	..	..	..	..	..	..	..	..	..
Queens Road	..	..	..	..	..	..	..	..	..	..	..	..
Railway	6	4	2	..	..	..	..	..	..	..	..	..
Serai	12	7	5	..	..	..	27	21	6	..	..	..
Rambaugh	124	52	72	..	..	..	..	..	..	..	..	..
Jail	8	4	4	..	..	..	..	..	..	..	..	..
Runchore	130	78	52	..	..	..	1	1	..	..	..	..
Ramswami	321	168	153	..	..	..	..	..	..	..	..	..
Herchandrai Vishendas	53	29	24	..	..	..	..	..	..	..	..	..
Soldier Bazar	..	..	..	..	..	..	..	..	..	..	..	..
New Jail	..	..	..	..	..	..	..	..	..	..	..	..
Preedy	5	3	2	..	..	..	..	..	..	..	..	..
Saddar Bazar	17	10	7	53	28	25	14	14	..	..	..	..
Civil Lines	13	6	7	..	..	..	23	15	8	..	..	..
Frere Town and Bath Island ..	..	..	..	..	..	..	2	2	..	..	..	..
Clifton	..	..	..	..	..	..	..	..	..	..	..	..
Gizri	..	..	..	..	..	..	..	..	..	..	..	..
Garden (East and West)	75	39	36	..	..	..	3	3	..	5	2	3
Tahilram	3	1	2	..	..	..	..	..	..	..	..	..
Lawrence	30	13	17	..	..	..	61	31	30	..	..	..
Lyari	5	1	4	..	..	..	1	1	..	5	5	..
Jamshed	9	4	5	..	..	..	..	..	..	..	..	..
Artillary Maidan	..	..	..	..	..	..	..	..	..	..	..	..
Trans Lyari	..	..	..	..	..	..	..	..	..	..	..	..
Tatta Naka and Goda Village and Labour Corps	..	..	..	..	..	..	..	..	..	..	..	..
Quarry Nos. 1 and 2 and other quarries	..	..	..	..	..	..	..	..	..	..	..	..
Scattered Hamlets, behind Cantonment Station and Chinaser and Vagri Villages	..	..	..	..	..	..	..	..	..	..	..	..
Keamari with other Port area (viz. Thole Produce Yard Man's field, Import Yard and West Wharf) ..	80	41	39	..	..	..	..	..	..	..	..	..
Baba Islands	..	..	..	..	..	..	..	..	..	..	..	..
Bhit Islands	..	..	..	..	..	..	..	..	..	..	..	..
Shamespir and Goth Mahomed ..	..	..	..	..	..	..	..	..	..	..	..	..
Bunker Island	..	..	..	..	..	..	..	..	..	..	..	..
Port Floating Population	..	..	..	..	..	..	3	3	..	..	..	..
Railway Area including City Bunder and Cantonment Stations and Reception and Hump Yard and Platform Population	21	11	10	..	..	..	..	..	..	..	..	..
Maurypur	..	..	..	..	..	..	..	..	..	..	..	..
Drigh Road	..	..	..	..	..	..	..	..	..	..	..	..
Cape Mouze	..	..	..	..	..	..	..	..	..	..	..	..
Karachi Cantonment	16	6	10	..	..	..	..	..	..	..	..	..
Mapora	2	1	1	..	..	..	..	..	..	..	..	..
Karachi Military Area	..	..	..	..	..	..	..	..	..	..	..	..
Total ..	943	487	456	53	28	25	135	91	44	10	7	3

CITY TABLE IV—KARACHI MUNICIPALITY.

Age, Sex and Civil Condition.

(Corresponding to Imperial Table VII.)

A. All Religions.

Age.	Population.			Unmarried.			Married.			Widowed.		
	Persons.	Males.	Females.	Persons.	Males.	Females.	Persons.	Males.	Females.	Persons.	Males.	Females.
1	2	3	4	5	6	7	8	9	10	11	12	13
0—1	6,718	3,369	3,349	6,717	3,368	3,349	..	..	..	1	1	..
1—2	6,604	3,236	3,368	6,600	3,234	3,366	1	..	1	3	2	1
2—3	7,335	3,565	3,770	7,325	3,558	3,767	9	6	3	1	1	..
3—4	7,058	3,467	3,501	7,028	3,452	3,576	25	14	11	5	1	4
4—5	6,630	3,360	3,270	6,589	3,338	3,251	36	21	15	5	1	4
Total 0—5 ..	34,345	16,997	17,348	34,259	16,950	17,309	71	41	30	15	6	9
5—10	28,171	15,139	13,032	27,231	14,855	12,376	911	271	640	29	13	16
10—15	24,918	13,913	11,005	22,119	13,203	8,916	2,727	682	2,045	72	28	44
15—20	24,961	14,412	10,549	11,850	9,453	2,397	12,489	4,555	7,934	622	404	218
20—25	29,102	17,299	11,803	9,169	8,004	1,165	18,982	8,736	10,246	951	559	392
25—30	26,807	17,159	9,648	3,948	3,614	334	21,560	12,932	8,628	1,299	613	686
30—35	23,552	15,575	7,977	2,436	2,224	212	19,505	12,628	6,877	1,611	723	888
35—40	17,119	11,308	5,811	1,041	925	116	13,870	9,620	4,250	2,208	763	1,445
40—45	13,150	8,475	4,675	626	545	81	10,202	7,224	2,978	2,322	706	1,616
45—50	8,819	5,400	3,419	318	269	49	6,014	4,450	1,564	2,487	681	1,806
50—55	6,556	3,894	2,662	204	168	36	4,149	3,131	1,018	2,203	595	1,608
55—60	3,939	2,190	1,749	102	82	20	2,041	1,643	398	1,796	465	1,331
60—65	3,141	1,709	1,432	93	75	18	1,508	1,239	269	1,540	395	1,145
65—70	1,138	609	529	32	24	8	494	406	88	612	179	433
70 and over ..	2,073	973	1,100	50	41	9	769	547	222	1,254	385	869
Total ..	247,791	145,052	102,739	113,478	70,432	43,046	115,292	68,105	47,187	19,021	6,515	12,506

B. Hindu.

Age.	Population.			Unmarried.			Married.			Widowed.		
	Persons.	Males.	Females.	Persons.	Males.	Females.	Persons.	Males.	Females.	Persons.	Males.	Females.
0—1	3,195	1,624	1,571	3,195	1,624	1,571	..	..	..	..	..	..
1—2	3,057	1,527	1,530	3,057	1,527	1,530	..	..	..	..	..	..
2—3	3,376	1,660	1,716	3,376	1,660	1,716	..	..	..	..	..	..
3—4	3,157	1,564	1,593	3,149	1,559	1,590	8	5	3	..	..	..
4—5	2,896	1,459	1,437	2,881	1,450	1,431	15	9	6	..	..	..
Total 0—5 ..	15,681	7,834	7,847	15,658	7,820	7,838	23	14	9	..	..	..
5—10	12,476	6,650	5,826	12,161	6,554	5,607	308	95	213	7	1	6
10—15	11,110	6,230	4,880	9,825	5,886	3,939	1,261	330	931	24	14	10
15—20	12,142	7,237	4,905	5,153	4,400	753	6,563	2,500	4,063	426	337	89
20—25	14,557	8,923	5,634	4,014	3,696	318	9,944	4,816	5,128	599	411	188
25—30	13,244	8,855	4,389	1,595	1,497	98	11,034	7,064	3,970	615	294	321
30—35	11,433	7,974	3,459	954	889	65	9,705	6,726	2,979	774	359	415
35—40	8,041	5,585	2,456	391	364	27	6,507	4,825	1,742	1,083	396	687
40—45	6,044	4,051	1,993	242	227	15	4,674	3,457	1,217	1,128	367	761
45—50	3,876	2,425	1,451	121	112	9	2,557	1,963	594	1,198	350	848
50—55	2,890	1,733	1,157	78	71	7	1,735	1,360	375	1,077	302	775
55—60	1,614	887	727	32	28	4	779	646	133	803	213	590
60—65	1,225	649	576	24	21	3	543	454	89	658	174	484
65—70	445	236	209	10	9	1	167	141	26	268	86	182
70 and over ..	682	332	350	14	14	..	192	159	33	476	159	317
Total ..	115,460	69,601	45,859	50,272	31,588	18,684	56,052	34,550	21,502	9,136	3,463	5,673

C. Muslim.

Age.	Population.			Unmarried.			Married.			Widowed.		
	Persons.	Males.	Females.	Persons.	Males.	Females.	Persons.	Males.	Females.	Persons.	Males.	Females.
0—1	3,214	1,610	1,604	3,213	1,609	1,604	..	..	..	1	1	..
1—2	3,230	1,564	1,666	3,226	1,562	1,664	1	..	1	3	2	1
2—3	3,616	1,734	1,882	3,607	1,728	1,879	8	5	3	1	1	..
3—4 ..	3,557	1,728	1,829	3,537	1,718	1,810	16	9	7	4	1	3
4—5	3,408	1,734	1,674	3,383	1,722	1,661	20	11	9	5	1	4
Total 0—5 ..	17,025	8,370	8,655	16,966	8,339	8,627	45	25	20	14	6	8
5—10	14,192	7,663	6,529	13,593	7,491	6,102	577	160	417	22	12	10
10—15	12,394	6,877	5,517	10,938	6,543	4,395	1,409	320	1,089	47	14	33
15—20	11,416	6,391	5,025	5,670	4,400	1,270	5,553	1,925	3,628	193	66	127
20—25	13,008	7,506	5,502	4,291	3,717	574	8,376	3,644	4,732	341	145	196
25—30	12,147	7,440	4,707	1,957	1,798	159	9,563	5,346	4,217	627	296	331
30—35	10,814	6,791	4,023	1,212	1,110	102	8,836	5,344	3,492	766	337	429
35—40	8,041	5,062	2,979	521	464	57	6,481	4,267	2,214	1,039	331	708
40—45	6,232	3,856	2,376	294	258	36	4,838	3,297	1,541	1,100	301	799
45—50	4,347	2,576	1,771	145	123	22	3,016	2,165	851	1,186	288	898
50—55	3,198	1,863	1,335	87	73	14	2,087	1,537	550	1,024	253	771
55—60	2,052	1,141	911	45	38	7	1,099	880	219	908	223	685
60—65	1,709	930	779	49	41	8	855	699	156	805	190	615
65—70	596	323	273	15	12	3	283	232	51	298	79	219
70 and over ..	1,241	560	681	28	23	5	527	348	179	686	189	497
Total ..	118,412	67,349	51,063	55,811	34,430	21,381	53,545	30,189	23,356	9,056	2,730	6,326

D. Jain.

Age.	Population.			Unmarried.			Married.			Widowed.		
	Persons.	Males.	Females.	Persons.	Males.	Females.	Persons.	Males.	Females.	Persons.	Males.	Females.
1	2	3	4	5	6	7	8	9	10	11	12	13
0—1	20	10	10	20	10	10	..	..	..	..	..	..
1—2	20	9	11	20	9	11	..	..	..	..	..	..
2—3	17	8	9	17	8	9	..	..	..	..	..	..
3—4	19	9	10	19	9	10	..	..	..	..	..	..
4—5	20	10	10	20	10	10	..	..	..	..	..	..
Total 0—5 ..	96	46	50	96	46	50	..	..	..	..	..	..
5—10	75	38	37	75	38	37	..	..	..	..	..	..
10—15	60	34	26	57	34	23	3	..	3	..	..	..
15—20	67	38	29	26	24	2	41	14	27	..	..	..
20—25	79	44	35	17	16	1	62	28	34	..	..	..
25—30	65	39	26	6	5	1	57	33	24	2	1	1
30—35	60	39	21	5	5	..	51	33	18	4	1	3
35—40	46	33	13	2	2	..	39	29	10	5	2	3
40—45	30	21	9	1	1	..	25	19	6	4	1	3
45—50	15	9	6	..	..	..	10	7	3	5	2	3
50—55	12	8	4	..	..	..	9	6	3	3	2	1
55—60	8	6	2	..	..	..	6	5	1	2	1	1
60—65	4	4	..	..	..	..	3	3	..	1	1	..
65—70	1	..	1	..	..	..	..	..	..	1	..	1
70 and over ..	2	1	1	..	..	..	..	..	..	2	1	1
Total ..	620	360	260	285	171	114	306	177	129	29	12	17

E. Zoroastrian.

Age.	Persons.	Males.	Females.	Persons.	Males.	Females.	Persons.	Males.	Females.	Persons.	Males.	Females.
0—1	35	14	21	35	14	21	..	..	..	..	..	..
1—2	43	17	26	43	17	26	..	..	..	..	..	..
2—3	49	26	23	48	25	23	1	1	..	..	..	..
3—4	48	28	20	48	28	20	..	..	..	..	..	..
4—5	45	23	22	45	23	22	..	..	..	..	..	..
Total 0—5 ..	220	108	112	219	107	112	1	1	..	..	..	..
5—10	253	140	113	248	136	112	5	4	1	..	..	..
10—15	254	142	112	246	137	109	8	5	3	..	..	..
15—20	218	115	103	185	100	85	33	15	18	..	..	..
20—25	219	112	107	162	89	73	54	22	32	3	1	2
25—30	214	107	107	90	60	30	118	45	73	6	2	4
30—35	220	112	108	65	46	19	145	65	80	10	1	9
35—40	179	98	81	34	20	14	129	74	55	16	4	12
40—45	167	96	71	26	14	12	127	78	49	14	4	10
45—50	133	73	60	14	7	7	101	63	38	18	3	15
50—55	110	56	54	10	6	4	77	45	32	23	5	18
55—60	72	39	33	10	7	3	41	25	16	21	7	14
60—65	63	34	29	7	5	2	31	21	10	25	8	17
65—70	34	15	19	..	..	..	17	11	6	17	4	13
70 and over ..	52	24	28	2	1	1	13	9	4	37	14	23
Total ..	2,408	1,271	1,137	1,318	735	583	900	483	417	190	53	137

F. Christian.

Age.	Persons.	Males.	Females.	Persons.	Males.	Females.	Persons.	Males.	Females.	Persons.	Males.	Females.
0—1	181	84	97	181	84	97	..	..	..	..	..	..
1—2	173	85	88	173	85	88	..	..	..	..	..	..
2—3	199	101	98	199	101	98	..	..	..	..	..	..
3—4	199	98	101	197	98	99	1	..	1	1	..	1
4—5	185	93	92	184	92	92	1	1	..	..	..	..
Total 0—5 ..	937	461	476	934	460	474	2	1	1	1	..	1
5—10	845	470	375	826	460	366	19	10	9	..	..	..
10—15	768	443	325	738	429	309	29	14	15	1	..	1
15—20	754	412	342	605	373	232	149	39	110	..	..	..
20—25	827	456	371	533	357	176	292	99	193	2	..	2
25—30	787	466	321	244	203	41	511	253	258	32	10	22
30—35	749	456	293	170	146	24	537	295	242	42	15	27
35—40	618	398	220	83	65	18	487	311	176	48	22	26
40—45	525	347	178	55	38	17	411	282	129	59	27	32
45—50	361	252	109	33	22	11	269	202	67	59	28	31
50—55	286	193	93	26	15	11	207	154	53	53	24	29
55—60	154	95	59	14	8	0	98	73	25	42	14	28
60—65	109	74	35	12	7	5	64	53	11	33	14	19
65—70	53	30	23	7	3	4	24	19	5	22	8	14
70 and over ..	79	46	33	6	3	3	31	26	5	42	17	25
Total ..	7,852	4,599	3,253	4,286	2,589	1,697	3,130	1,831	1,299	436	179	257

G. Tribal.

Age.	Population.			Unmarried.			Married.			Widowed.		
	Persons.	Males.	Females.	Persons.	Males.	Females.	Persons.	Males.	Females.	Persons.	Males.	Females.
1	2	3	4	5	6	7	8	9	10	11	12	13
0—1	..	..	..	..	..	..	..	..	..	..	..	..
1—2	..	..	..	..	..	..	..	..	..	..	..	..
2—3	1	1	..	1	1	..	..	..	..	..	..	..
3—4	4	2	2	4	2	2	..	..	..	..	..	..
4—5	4	2	2	4	2	2	..	..	..	..	..	..
Total 0—5 ..	9	5	4	9	5	4	..	..	..	..	..	..
5—10	17	9	8	17	9	8	..	..	..	..	..	..
10—15	15	8	7	15	8	7	..	..	..	..	..	..
15—20	8	5	3	2	2	..	6	3	3	..	..	..
20—25	18	13	5	3	3	..	15	10	5	..	..	..
25—30	24	18	6	3	3	..	21	15	6	..	..	..
30—35	16	13	3	3	3	..	13	10	3	..	..	..
35—40	10	8	2	3	3	..	7	5	2	..	..	..
40—45	6	5	1	1	1	..	4	3	1	1	1	..
45—50	..	..	..	..	..	..	..	..	..	..	..	..
50—55	2	2	..	1	1	..	1	1	..	..	..	..
55—60	4	2	2	..	..	..	..	..	..	4	2	2
60—65	6	3	3	..	..	..	..	..	..	6	3	3
65—70	..	..	..	..	..	..	..	..	..	..	..	..
70 and over ..	..	..	..	..	..	..	..	..	..	..	..	..
Total ..	135	91	44	57	38	19	67	47	20	11	6	5

H. Sikh.

Age.	Population.			Unmarried.			Married.			Widowed.		
	Persons.	Males.	Females.	Persons.	Males.	Females.	Persons.	Males.	Females.	Persons.	Males.	Females.
0—1	48	15	33	48	15	33	..	..	..	..	..	..
1—2	56	22	34	56	22	34	..	..	..	..	..	..
2—3	52	22	30	52	22	30	..	..	..	..	..	..
3—4	46	23	23	46	23	23	..	..	..	..	..	..
4—5	40	22	18	40	22	18	..	..	..	..	..	..
Total 0—5 ..	242	104	138	242	104	138	..	..	..	..	..	..
5—10	172	100	72	170	98	72	2	2	..	..	..	..
10—15	178	118	60	161	105	56	17	13	4	..	..	..
15—20	247	158	89	109	99	10	136	58	78	2	1	1
20—25	294	189	105	81	79	2	208	108	100	5	2	3
25—30	245	186	59	32	31	1	200	147	53	13	8	5
30—35	192	147	45	15	15	..	164	123	41	13	9	4
35—40	124	93	31	4	4	..	108	82	26	12	7	5
40—45	94	73	21	5	5	..	79	64	15	10	4	6
45—50	57	48	9	4	4	..	40	35	5	13	9	4
50—55	31	26	5	1	1	..	18	17	1	12	8	4
55—60	14	7	7	1	1	..	8	5	3	5	1	4
60—65	11	7	4	1	1	..	6	4	2	4	2	2
65—70	6	4	2	..	..	..	2	2	..	4	2	2
70 and over ..	9	6	3	..	..	..	3	2	1	6	4	2
Total ..	1,916	1,266	650	826	547	279	991	662	329	99	57	42

I. Jew.

Age.	Population.			Unmarried.			Married.			Widowed.		
	Persons.	Males.	Females.	Persons.	Males.	Females.	Persons.	Males.	Females.	Persons.	Males.	Females.
0—1	24	12	12	24	12	12	..	..	..	..	..	..
1—2	24	12	12	24	12	12	..	..	..	..	..	..
2—3	22	11	11	22	11	11	..	..	..	..	..	..
3—4	25	13	12	25	13	12	..	..	..	..	..	..
4—5 ..	28	15	13	28	15	13	..	..	..	..	..	..
Total 0—5 ..	123	63	60	123	63	60	..	..	..	..	..	..
5—10	133	64	69	133	64	69	..	..	..	..	..	..
10—15	136	60	76	136	60	76	..	..	..	..	..	..
15—20	108	56	52	99	55	44	8	1	7	1	..	1
20—25	93	54	39	67	47	20	25	7	18	1	..	1
25—30	66	40	26	19	15	4	43	23	20	4	2	2
30—35	58	35	23	10	8	2	46	26	20	2	1	1
35—40	56	28	28	2	2	..	49	25	24	5	1	4
40—45	50	25	25	2	1	1	42	23	19	6	1	5
45—50	29	16	13	1	1	..	20	14	6	8	1	7
50—55	27	13	14	1	1	..	15	11	4	11	1	10
55—60	21	13	8	..	..	..	10	9	1	11	4	7
60—65	14	8	6	..	..	..	6	5	1	8	3	5
65—70	3	1	2	..	..	..	1	1	..	2	..	2
70 and over ..	8	4	4	..	..	..	3	3	..	5	1	4
Total ..	925	480	445	593	317	276	268	148	120	64	15	49

J. Buddhist.

Age.	Population.			Unmarried.			Married.			Widowed.		
	Persons.	Males.	Females.	Persons.	Males.	Females.	Persons.	Males.	Females.	Persons.	Males.	Females.
1	2	3	4	5	6	7	8	9	10	11	12	13
0—1	1	..	1	1	..	1	..	..	..	..	..	..
1—2	1	..	1	1	..	1	..	..	..	..	..	..
2—3	3	2	1	3	2	1	..	..	..	..	..	..
3—4	3	2	1	3	2	1	..	..	..	..	..	..
4—5	2	1	1	2	1	1	..	..	..	..	..	..
Total 0—5 ..	10	5	5	10	5	5	..	..	..	..	..	..
5—10	5	3	2	5	3	2	..	..	..	..	..	..
10—15	3	1	2	3	1	2	..	..	..	..	..	..
15—20	1	..	1	1	..	1	..	..	..	..	..	..
20—25	5	..	5	1	..	1	4	..	4	..	..	..
25—30	13	7	6	2	2	..	11	5	6	..	..	..
30—35	9	7	2	1	1	..	8	6	2	..	..	..
35—40	4	3	1	1	1	..	3	2	1	..	..	..
40—45	2	1	1	..	..	..	2	1	1	..	..	..
45—50	1	1	..	..	..	..	1	1	..	..	..	..
50—55	..	..	..	..	..	..	..	..	..	..	..	..
55—60	..	..	..	..	..	..	..	..	..	..	..	..
60—65	..	..	..	..	..	..	..	..	..	..	..	..
65—70	..	..	..	..	..	..	..	..	..	..	..	..
70 and over ..	..	..	..	..	..	..	..	..	..	..	..	..
Total ..	53	28	25	24	13	11	29	15	14	..	..	..

K. Other Religions.

Age.	Population.			Unmarried.			Married.			Widowed.		
	Persons.	Males.	Females.	Persons.	Males.	Females.	Persons.	Males.	Females.	Persons.	Males.	Females.
0—1	..	..	..	..	..	..	..	..	..	..	..	..
1—2	..	..	..	..	..	..	..	..	..	..	..	..
2—3	..	..	..	..	..	..	..	..	..	..	..	..
3—4	..	..	..	..	..	..	..	..	..	..	..	..
4—5	2	1	1	2	1	1	..	..	..	..	..	..
Total 0—5 ..	2	1	1	2	1	1	..	..	..	..	..	..
5—10	3	2	1	3	2	1	..	..	..	..	..	..
10—15	..	..	..	..	..	..	..	..	..	..	..	..
15—20	..	..	..	..	..	..	..	..	..	..	..	..
20—25	2	2	..	..	..	..	2	2	..	..	..	..
25—30	2	1	1	..	..	..	2	1	1	..	..	..
30—35	1	1	..	1	1	..	..	..	..	..	..	..
35—40	..	..	..	..	..	..	..	..	..	..	..	..
40—45	..	..	..	..	..	..	..	..	..	..	..	..
45—50	..	..	..	..	..	..	..	..	..	..	..	..
50—55	..	..	..	..	..	..	..	..	..	..	..	..
55—60	..	..	..	..	..	..	..	..	..	..	..	..
60—65	..	..	..	..	..	..	..	..	..	..	..	..
65—70	..	..	..	..	..	..	..	..	..	..	..	..
70 and over ..	..	..	..	..	..	..	..	..	..	..	..	..
Total ..	10	7	3	6	4	2	4	3	1	..	..	..

CITY TABLE IV—KARACHI CANTONMENT.

Age, Sex and Civil Conditions.

(Corresponding to Imperial Table VII.)

A. All Religions.

Age.	Population.			Unmarried.			Married.			Widowed.		
	Persons.	Males.	Females.	Persons.	Males.	Females.	Persons.	Males.	Females.	Persons.	Males.	Females.
1	2	3	4	5	6	7	8	9	10	11	12	13
0—1	363	197	166	363	197	166	..	..	..	..	..	..
1—2	319	171	148	319	171	148	..	..	..	..	..	..
2—3	349	185	164	349	185	164	..	..	..	..	..	..
3—4	326	162	164	326	162	164	..	..	..	..	..	..
4—5	294	149	145	294	149	145	..	..	..	..	..	..
Total 0—5 ..	1,651	864	787	1,651	864	787	..	..	..	..	..	..
5—10	1,197	626	571	1,192	623	569	5	3	2	..	..	..
10—15	1,042	568	474	974	546	428	67	22	45	1	..	1
15—20	2,050	1,540	510	1,304	1,143	161	729	382	347	17	15	2
20—25	2,833	2,243	590	1,630	1,527	103	1,167	683	484	36	33	3
25—30	2,325	1,838	487	850	811	39	1,423	986	437	52	41	11
30—35	1,764	1,364	400	379	349	30	1,315	969	346	70	46	24
35—40	1,014	763	251	115	99	16	828	629	199	71	35	36
40—45	711	508	203	69	53	16	570	423	147	72	32	40
45—50	421	287	134	28	25	3	307	228	79	86	34	52
50—55	309	202	107	17	15	2	210	158	52	82	29	53
55—60	162	97	65	6	4	2	88	68	20	68	25	43
60—65	133	78	55	8	5	3	70	51	19	55	22	33
65—70	58	31	27	3	1	2	24	20	4	31	10	21
70 and over ..	104	59	45	3	2	1	34	30	4	67	27	40
Total ..	15,774	11,068	4,706	8,229	6,067	2,162	6,837	4,652	2,185	708	349	359

B. Hindu.

Age.	Population: Persons.	Males.	Females.	Unmarried: Persons.	Males.	Females.	Married: Persons.	Males.	Females.	Widowed: Persons.	Males.	Females.
0—1	155	84	71	155	84	71	..	..	..	..	..	..
1—2	125	65	60	125	65	60	..	..	..	..	..	..
2—3	140	83	57	140	83	57	..	..	..	..	..	..
3—4	131	72	59	131	72	59	..	..	..	..	..	..
4—5	109	55	54	109	55	54	..	..	..	..	..	..
Total 0—5 ..	660	359	301	660	359	301	..	..	..	..	..	..
5—10	426	228	198	424	228	196	2	..	2	..	..	..
10—15	367	208	159	329	196	133	37	12	25	1	..	1
15—20	610	420	190	259	241	18	345	174	171	6	5	1
20—25	808	579	229	254	249	5	538	316	222	16	14	2
25—30	677	516	161	93	90	3	557	406	151	27	20	7
30—35	570	446	124	47	45	2	484	376	108	39	25	14
35—40	364	283	81	15	15	..	313	249	64	36	19	17
40—45	248	189	59	11	11	..	207	163	44	30	15	15
45—50	154	109	45	6	6	..	113	88	25	35	15	20
50—55	100	67	33	3	3	..	71	55	16	26	9	17
55—60	61	38	23	..	..	..	31	26	5	30	12	18
60—65	46	31	15	1	1	..	22	18	4	23	12	11
65—70	15	10	5	1	1	..	6	6	..	8	3	5
70 and over ..	29	13	16	..	..	..	9	8	1	20	5	15
Total ..	5,135	3,496	1,639	2,103	1,445	658	2,735	1,897	838	297	154	143

C. Muslim.

Age.	Population: Persons.	Males.	Females.	Unmarried: Persons.	Males.	Females.	Married: Persons.	Males.	Females.	Widowed: Persons.	Males.	Females.
0—1	84	48	36	84	48	36	..	..	..	..	..	..
1—2	76	43	33	76	43	33	..	..	..	..	..	..
2—3	89	44	45	89	44	45	..	..	..	..	..	..
3—4	85	40	45	85	40	45	..	..	..	..	..	..
4—5	74	36	38	74	36	38	..	..	..	..	..	..
Total 0—5 ..	408	211	197	408	211	197	..	..	..	..	..	..
5—10	285	156	129	282	153	129	3	3	..	..	..	..
10—15	241	142	99	214	133	81	27	9	18	..	..	..
15—20	724	585	139	429	411	18	284	164	120	11	10	1
20—25	906	739	167	465	456	9	423	266	157	18	17	1
25—30	633	522	111	144	143	1	470	361	109	19	18	1
30—35	543	464	79	80	78	2	442	369	73	21	17	4
35—40	282	243	39	22	22	..	243	209	34	17	12	5
40—45	168	142	26	11	9	2	140	122	18	17	11	6
45—50	91	73	18	5	5	..	68	60	8	18	8	10
50—55	65	49	16	4	4	..	44	38	6	17	7	10
55—60	28	18	10	1	1	..	15	12	3	12	5	7
60—65	25	14	11	1	1	..	13	10	3	11	3	8
65—70	8	6	2	..	..	..	5	5	..	3	1	2
70 and over ..	28	18	10	2	2	..	12	10	2	14	6	8
Total ..	4,435	3,382	1,053	2,068	1,629	439	2,189	1,638	551	178	115	63

D. Jain.

Age.	Population.			Unmarried.			Married.			Widowed.		
	Persons.	Males.	Females.	Persons.	Males.	Females.	Persons.	Males.	Females.	Persons.	Males.	Females.
1	2	3	4	5	6	7	8	9	10	11	12	13
0—1	1	1	..	1	1	..	..	..	..	..	..	..
1—2	..	..	..	..	..	..	..	..	..	..	..	..
2—3	..	..	..	..	..	..	..	..	..	..	..	..
3—4	1	1	..	1	1	..	..	..	..	..	..	..
4—5	..	..	..	..	..	..	..	..	..	..	..	..
Total 0—5 ..	2	2	..	2	2	..	..	..	..	..	..	..
5—10	..	..	..	..	..	..	..	..	..	..	..	..
10—15	2	1	1	2	1	1	..	..	..	..	..	..
15—20	..	..	..	..	..	..	..	..	..	..	..	..
20—25	1	..	1	..	..	..	1	..	1	..	..	..
25—30	3	2	1	..	..	..	3	2	1	..	..	..
30—35	1	1	..	..	..	..	1	1	..	..	..	..
35—40	..	..	..	..	..	..	..	..	..	..	..	..
40—45	..	..	..	..	..	..	..	..	..	..	..	..
45—50	..	..	..	..	..	..	..	..	..	..	..	..
50—55	..	..	..	..	..	..	..	..	..	..	..	..
55—60	..	..	..	..	..	..	..	..	..	..	..	..
60—65	..	..	..	..	..	..	..	..	..	..	..	..
65—70	..	..	..	..	..	..	..	..	..	..	..	..
70 and over ..	..	..	..	..	..	..	..	..	..	..	..	..
Total ..	9	6	3	4	3	1	5	3	2	..	..	..

E. Zoroastrian.

Age.	Persons.	Males.	Females.	Persons.	Males.	Females.	Persons.	Males.	Females.	Persons.	Males.	Females.
0—1	12	4	8	12	4	8	..	..	..	..	..	..
1—2	17	8	9	17	8	9	..	..	..	..	..	..
2—3 ..	21	8	13	21	8	13	..	..	..	..	..	..
3—4	20	9	11	20	9	11	..	..	..	..	..	..
4—5	20	13	7	20	13	7	..	..	..	..	..	..
Total 0—5 ..	90	42	48	90	42	48	..	..	..	..	..	..
5—10	99	57	42	99	57	42	..	..	..	..	..	..
10—15	101	55	46	101	55	46	..	..	..	..	..	..
15—20	89	48	41	89	48	41	..	..	..	..	..	..
20—25	78	40	38	72	40	32	6	..	6	..	..	..
25—30	65	28	37	27	19	8	37	9	28	1	..	1
30—35	73	35	38	18	14	4	52	21	31	3	..	3
35—40	78	39	30	8	6	2	65	33	32	5	..	5
40—45	70	32	38	8	5	3	55	27	28	7	..	7
45—50	49	25	24	1	1	..	38	22	16	10	2	8
50—55	49	27	22	..	..	..	38	23	15	11	4	7
55—60	30	16	14	..	..	..	21	14	7	9	2	7
60—65	21	12	9	..	..	..	13	10	3	8	2	6
65—70	14	7	7	..	..	..	5	5	..	9	2	7
70 and over ..	20	10	10	..	..	..	6	6	..	14	4	10
Total ..	926	473	453	513	287	226	336	170	166	77	16	61

F. Christian.

Age.	Persons.	Males.	Females.	Persons.	Males.	Females.	Persons.	Males.	Females.	Persons.	Males.	Females.
0—1	95	52	43	95	52	43	..	..	..	..	..	..
1—2	89	50	39	89	50	39	..	..	..	..	..	..
2—3	88	45	43	88	45	43	..	..	..	..	..	..
3—4	80	37	43	80	37	43	..	..	..	..	..	..
4—5	81	41	40	81	41	40	..	..	..	..	..	..
Total 0—5 ..	433	225	208	433	225	208	..	..	..	..	..	..
5—10	354	169	185	354	169	185	..	..	..	..	..	..
10—15	305	148	157	305	148	157	..	..	..	..	..	..
15—20	591	467	124	513	431	82	78	36	42	..	..	..
20—25	984	849	135	822	765	57	161	88	78	1	1	..
25—30	892	727	165	579	552	27	308	172	136	5	3	2
30—35	537	384	153	232	210	22	298	170	128	7	4	3
35—40	273	183	90	68	55	13	192	124	68	13	4	9
40—45	211	135	76	39	28	11	155	101	54	17	6	11
45—50	119	74	45	15	12	3	81	58	28	23	9	14
50—55	88	53	35	9	7	2	53	38	15	26	8	18
55—60	42	24	18	5	3	2	20	15	5	17	6	11
60—65	39	20	19	6	3	3	20	12	8	13	5	8
65—70	20	7	13	2	..	2	7	3	4	11	4	7
70 and over ..	25	16	9	1	..	1	6	5	1	18	11	7
Total ..	4,913	3,481	1,432	3,383	2,608	775	1,379	812	567	151	61	90

G. Sikh.

Age.	Population.			Unmarried.			Married.			Widowed.		
	Persons.	Males.	Females.	Persons.	Males.	Females.	Persons.	Males.	Females.	Persons.	Males.	Females.
1	2	3	4	5	6	7	8	9	10	11	12	13
0—1	15	8	7	15	8	7	..	..	..	..	..	..
1—2	11	5	6	11	5	6	..	..	..	..	..	..
2—3	10	5	5	10	5	5	..	..	..	..	..	..
3—4	9	3	6	9	3	6	..	..	..	..	..	..
4—5	10	4	6	10	4	6	..	..	..	..	..	..
Total 0—5 ..	55	25	30	55	25	30	..	..	..	..	..	..
5—10	30	15	15	30	15	15	..	..	..	..	..	..
10—15	24	14	10	21	13	8	3	1	2	..	..	..
15—20	35	19	16	18	11	2	22	8	14	..	..	..
20—25	55	35	20	16	16	..	38	18	20	1	1	..
25—30	54	43	11	7	7	..	47	36	11	..	..	..
30—35	39	34	5	2	2	..	37	32	5	..	..	..
35—40	15	13	2	1	..	1	14	13	1	..	..	..
40—45	13	10	3	..	..	..	12	10	2	1	..	1
45—50	7	6	1	1	1	..	6	5	1	..	..	..
50—55	5	4	1	..	..	..	3	3	..	2	1	1
55—60	1	1	..	..	..	..	1	1	..	..	..	..
60—65	2	1	1	..	..	..	2	1	1	..	..	..
65—70	1	1	..	..	..	..	1	1	..	..	..	..
70 and over ..	2	2	..	..	..	..	1	1	..	1	1	..
Total ..	338	223	115	146	90	56	187	130	57	5	3	2

H. Jew.

Age.	Population.			Unmarried.			Married.			Widowed.		
	Persons.	Males.	Females.	Persons.	Males.	Females.	Persons.	Males.	Females.	Persons.	Males.	Females.
0—1	1	..	1	1	..	1	..	..	..	..	..	..
1—2	1	..	1	1	..	1	..	..	..	..	..	..
2—3	1	..	1	1	..	1	..	..	..	..	..	..
3—4	..	..	..	..	..	..	..	..	..	..	..	..
4—5	..	..	..	..	..	..	..	..	..	..	..	..
Total 0—5 ..	3	..	3	3	..	3	..	..	..	..	..	..
5—10	3	1	2	3	1	2	..	..	..	..	..	..
10—15	2	..	2	2	..	2	..	..	..	..	..	..
15—20	1	1	..	1	1	..	..	..	..	..	..	..
20—25	1	1	..	1	1	..	..	..	..	..	..	..
25—30	1	..	1	..	..	..	1	..	1	..	..	..
30—35	1	..	1	..	..	..	1	..	1	..	..	..
35—40	2	2	..	1	1	..	1	1	..	..	..	..
40—45	1	..	1	..	..	..	1	..	1	..	..	..
45—50	1	..	1	..	..	..	1	..	1	..	..	..
50—55	2	2	..	1	1	..	1	1	..	..	..	..
55—60	..	..	..	..	..	..	..	..	..	..	..	..
60—65	..	..	..	..	..	..	..	..	..	..	..	..
65—70	..	..	..	..	..	..	..	..	..	..	..	..
70 and over ..	..	..	..	..	..	..	..	..	..	..	..	..
Total ..	18	7	11	12	5	7	6	2	4	..	..	..

CITY TABLE V—PART I—KARACHI CITY.

Literacy by Religion and Age.

(Corresponding to Imperial Table XIII.)

Religion and Age.	Population.									Literate in English.		
	Total.			Literate.			Illiterate.					
	Persons.	Males.	Females.	Persons.	Males.	Females.	Persons.	Males.	Females.	Persons.	Males.	Females.
1	2	3	4	5	6	7	8	9	10	11	12	13
(A)—All Religions Total ..	**263,565**	**156,120**	**107,445**	**56,880**	**44,651**	**12,229**	**206,686**	**111,469**	**95,216**	**25,139**	**21,365**	**3,774**
0—10	65,364	33,626	31,738	3,652	2,296	1,356	61,712	31,330	30,382	785	535	250
10—15	25,960	14,481	11,479	4,984	3,290	1,694	20,976	11,191	9,785	1,535	1,101	434
15—20	27,011	15,952	11,059	8,169	6,151	2,018	18,842	9,801	9,041	4,042	3,373	669
20 and over ..	145,230	92,061	53,169	40,075	32,914	7,161	105,155	59,147	46,008	18,777	16,356	2,421
(B)—Hindu .. Total ..	**120,595**	**73,097**	**47,498**	**33,052**	**26,589**	**6,463**	**87,543**	**46,508**	**41,035**	**12,499**	**11,612**	**887**
0—10	29,243	15,071	14,172	2,251	1,371	880	26,992	13,700	13,292	288	210	78
10—15	11,477	6,438	5,039	3,091	2,029	1,062	8,386	4,409	3,977	744	577	167
15—20	12,752	7,657	5,095	4,801	3,645	1,156	7,951	4,012	3,939	2,131	1,895	236
20 and over ..	67,123	43,931	23,192	22,909	19,544	3,365	44,214	24,387	19,827	9,336	8,930	406
(C)—Muslim .. Total ..	**122,847**	**70,731**	**52,116**	**11,986**	**10,323**	**1,663**	**110,851**	**60,408**	**50,453**	**3,673**	**3,469**	**204**
0—10	31,910	16,400	15,510	697	511	186	31,213	15,889	15,324	59	49	10
10—15	12,635	7,019	5,616	1,062	800	262	11,573	6,219	5,354	190	165	25
15—20	12,140	6,976	5,164	1,833	1,519	314	10,307	5,457	4,850	696	652	44
20 and over ..	66,162	40,336	25,826	8,394	7,493	901	57,768	32,843	24,925	2,728	2,603	125
(D)—Jain .. Total ..	**629**	**366**	**263**	**276**	**222**	**54**	**353**	**144**	**209**	**109**	**108**	**1**
0—10	173	86	87	18	11	7	155	75	80	1	1	..
10—15	62	35	27	26	18	8	36	17	19	6	6	..
15—20	67	38	29	37	28	9	30	10	20	19	19	..
20 and over ..	327	207	120	195	165	30	132	42	90	83	82	1
(E)—Zoroastrian Total ..	**3,334**	**1,744**	**1,590**	**2,012**	**1,276**	**736**	**1,322**	**468**	**854**	**1,255**	**844**	**411**
0—10	662	347	315	84	63	21	578	284	294	32	26	6
10—15	355	197	158	112	46	66	243	151	92	97	55	42
15—20	307	163	144	223	137	86	84	26	58	179	107	72
20 and over ..	2,010	1,037	973	1,593	1,030	563	417	7	410	947	656	291
(F)—Christian .. Total ..	**12,765**	**8,080**	**4,685**	**8,228**	**5,424**	**2,804**	**4,537**	**2,656**	**1,881**	**6,875**	**4,778**	**2,097**
0—10	2,569	1,325	1,244	503	288	215	2,066	1,037	1,029	366	231	135
10—15	1,073	591	482	545	312	233	528	279	249	436	258	178
15—20	1,345	879	466	1,068	687	381	277	192	85	911	617	294
20 and over ..	7,778	5,285	2,493	6,112	4,137	1,975	1,666	1,148	518	5,162	3,672	1,490
(G)—Jew .. Total ..	**943**	**487**	**456**	**524**	**295**	**229**	**419**	**192**	**227**	**382**	**245**	**137**
0—10	262	128	134	50	21	29	212	107	105	30	14	16
10—15	138	60	78	69	32	37	69	28	41	43	23	20
15—20	109	57	52	74	40	34	35	17	18	51	31	20
20 and over ..	434	242	192	331	202	129	103	40	63	258	177	81
(H)—Sikh .. Total ..	**2,254**	**1,489**	**765**	**732**	**473**	**259**	**1,522**	**1,016**	**506**	**305**	**280**	**25**
0—10	499	244	255	43	29	14	456	215	241	6	4	2
10—15	202	132	70	74	50	24	128	82	46	17	15	2
15—20	282	177	105	130	93	37	152	84	68	55	52	3
20 and over ..	1,271	936	335	485	301	184	786	635	151	227	209	18
(I) Other Religions Total ..	**198**	**126**	**72**	**70**	**49**	**21**	**128**	**77**	**51**	**41**	**29**	**12**
0—10	46	25	21	6	2	4	40	23	17	3	..	3
10—15	18	9	9	5	3	2	13	6	7	2	2	..
15—20	9	5	4	3	2	1	6	3	3	..	..	..
20 and over ..	125	87	38	56	42	14	69	45	24	36	27	9

CITY TABLE V—PART II—KARACHI MUNICIPALITY.

LITERACY BY RELIGION AND AGE BY QUARTERS.

(Corresponding to Imperial Table XIII.)

Quarter, Religion and Age.	POPULATION.									LITERATE IN ENGLISH.		
	TOTAL.			LITERATE.			ILLITERATE.					
	Persons.	Males.	Females.	Persons.	Males.	Females.	Persons.	Males.	Females.	Persons.	Males.	Females.
1	2	3	4	5	6	7	8	9	10	11	12	13
Karachi City.												
Hindu Total ..	**115;460**	**69,601**	**45,859**	**31,166**	**25,047**	**6,119**	**84,294**	**44,554**	**39,740**	**11,965**	**11,090**	**875**
0—10	28,157	14,484	13,673	2,108	1,306	802	26,049	13,178	12,871	280	205	75
10—15	11,110	6,230	4,880	2,955	1,948	1,007	8,155	4,282	3,873	708	547	161
15—20	12,142	7,237	4,905	4,508	3,421	1,087	7,634	3,816	3,816	2,010	1,782	228
20 and over ..	64,051	41,650	22,401	21,595	18,372	3,223	42,456	23,278	19,178	8,967	8,556	411
Muslim Total ..	**118,412**	**67,349**	**51,063**	**10,980**	**9,400**	**1,580**	**107,432**	**57,949**	**49,483**	**3,485**	**3,300**	**185**
0—10	31,217	16,033	15,184	664	495	169	30,553	15,538	15,015	57	48	9
10—15	12,394	6,877	5,517	1,026	776	250	11,368	6,101	5,267	183	161	22
15—20	11,416	6,391	5,025	1,671	1,378	293	9,745	5,013	4,732	666	623	43
20 and over ..	63,385	38,048	25,337	7,619	6,751	868	55,766	31,297	24,469	2,579	2,468	111
Old Town—												
Hindu Total ..	**8,216**	**4,307**	**3,909**	**3,026**	**2,398**	**628**	**5,190**	**1,'909**	**3,281**	**784**	**697**	**87**
0—10	1,920	879	1,041	288	210	78	1,632	669	963	24	18	6
10—15	839	458	381	343	217	126	496	241	255	86	63	23
15—20	1,166	645	521	505	401	104	661	244	417	227	201	26
20 and over ..	4,291	2,325	1,966	1,890	1,570	320	2,401	755	1,646	447	415	32
Muslim Total ..	**603**	**336**	**267**	**294**	**263**	**31**	**309**	**73**	**236**	**122**	**118**	**4**
0—10	133	55	78	19	16	3	114	30	75	6	6	..
10—15	57	28	29	24	19	5	33	9	24	5	4	1
15—20	40	22	18	23	18	5	17	4	13	14	12	2
20 and over ..	373	231	142	228	210	18	145	21	124	97	96	1
Lea—												
Hindu Total ..	**867**	**469**	**398**	**243**	**195**	**48**	**624**	**274**	**350**	**47**	**34**	**13**
0—10	283	150	133	8	6	2	275	144	131	2	2	..
10—15	140	70	70	28	24	4	112	46	66	5	4	1
15—20	192	101	91	36	24	12	156	77	79	10	4	6
20 and over ..	252	148	104	171	141	30	81	7	74	30	24	6
Muslim Total ..	**40**	**15**	**25**	**8**	**7**	**1**	**32**	**8**	**24**	**2**	**2**	..
0—10	6	2	4	..	..	..	6	2	4	..	..	..
10—15	3	1	2	1	1	..	2	2	2	..	..	..
15—20	1	..	1	..	..	..	1	..	1	..	..	..
20 and over ..	30	12	18	7	6	1	23	6	17	2	2	..
Napier—												
Hindu Total ..	**7,169**	**3,864**	**3,305**	**1,435**	**1,108**	**327**	**5,734**	**2,756**	**2,978**	**537**	**503**	**34**
0—10	1,914	1,001	913	105	70	35	1,809	931	878	6	6	..
10—15	746	413	333	162	102	60	584	311	273	40	27	13
15—20	778	468	310	309	256	53	469	212	257	189	184	5
20 and over ..	3,731	1,982	1,749	859	680	179	2,872	1,302	1,570	302	286	16
Muslim Total ..	**2,880**	**1,654**	**1,226**	**268**	**239**	**29**	**2,612**	**1,415**	**1,197**	**94**	**90**	**4**
0—10	671	333	338	6	3	3	665	330	335	..	..	..
10—15	285	158	127	13	10	3	272	148	124	2	2	..
15—20	225	140	85	54	49	5	171	91	80	18	16	2
20 and over ..	1,699	1,023	676	195	177	18	1,504	846	658	74	72	2
Market—												
Hindu Total ..	**5,446**	**3,066**	**2,380**	**1,716**	**1,624**	**92**	**3,730**	**1,442**	**2,288**	**485**	**478**	**7**
0—10	1,234	618	616	70	52	18	1,164	566	598	..	..	..
10—15	387	207	180	66	52	14	321	155	166	14	13	1
15—20	613	354	259	300	280	20	313	74	239	177	175	2
20 and over ..	3,212	1,887	1,325	1,280	1,240	40	1,932	647	1,285	294	290	4
Muslim Total ..	**1,271**	**719**	**552**	**274**	**222**	**52**	**997**	**497**	**500**	**122**	**117**	**5**
0—10	329	177	152	26	16	10	303	161	142	3	3	..
10—15	165	106	59	48	35	13	117	71	46	12	10	2
15—20	114	69	45	60	54	6	54	15	39	41	40	1
20 and over ..	663	367	296	140	117	23	523	250	270	66	64	2

Quarter, Religion and Age.	POPULATION.									LITERATE IN ENGLISH.		
	TOTAL.			LITERATE.			ILLITERATE.					
	Persons.	Males.	Females.	Persons.	Males.	Females.	Persons.	Males.	Females.	Persons.	Males.	Females.
1	2	3	4	5	6	7	8	9	10	11	12	13
Bunder—												
Hindu Total ..	**2,957**	**2,223**	**734**	**1,470**	**1,318**	**152**	**1,487**	**905**	**582**	**440**	**407**	**33**
0—10	608	363	245	86	50	36	522	313	209	..	..	..
10—15	281	197	84	84	66	18	197	131	66	21	21	..
15—20	427	220	198	175	151	24	252	78	174	88	79	9
20 and over ..	1,641	1,434	207	1,125	1,051	74	516	383	133	331	307	24
Muslim Total ..	**363**	**230**	**133**	**236**	**179**	**59**	**125**	**51**	**74**	**112**	**104**	**8**
0—10	86	49	37	22	17	5	64	32	32	1	1	..
10—15	49	33	16	38	29	9	11	4	7	12	10	2
15—20	35	23	12	25	21	4	10	2	8	21	19	2
20 and over ..	193	125	68	153	112	41	40	13	27	78	74	4
Machi Meani—												
Hindu Total ..	**3,932**	**2,362**	**1,570**	**1,146**	**1,038**	**108**	**2,786**	**1,324**	**1,462**	**272**	**261**	**11**
0—10	1,181	609	572	68	51	17	1,113	558	555	20	14	6
10—15	324	204	120	102	78	24	222	126	96	9	6	3
15—20	566	358	208	144	128	16	422	230	192	45	43	2
20 and over ..	1,861	1,101	670	832	781	51	1,029	410	610	198	198	..
Muslim Total ..	**4,916**	**2,534**	**2,382**	**785**	**642**	**93**	**4,131**	**1,892**	**2,239**	**179**	**172**	**7**
0—10	1,326	657	669	69	52	17	1,257	605	652	4	3	1
10—15	608	341	267	102	78	24	506	263	243	16	14	2
15—20	419	202	217	105	96	9	314	106	208	54	52	2
20 and over ..	2,563	1,334	1,229	459	416	43	2,104	918	1,186	105	103	2
Queen's Road—												
Hindu Total ..	**98**	**72**	**26**	**72**	**55**	**17**	**26**	**17**	**9**	**39**	**29**	**10**
0—10	14	11	3	7	6	1	7	5	2	..	..	..
10—15	19	15	4	16	14	2	3	1	2	10	9	1
15—20	18	12	6	14	10	4	4	2	2	9	7	2
20 and over ..	47	34	13	35	25	10	12	9	3	20	13	7
Muslim Total ..	**17**	**10**	**7**	**7**	**6**	**1**	**10**	**4**	**6**	**4**	**4**	..
0—10	3	2	1	..	..	..	3	2	1	..	..	..
10—15	3	2	1	1	1	..	2	1	1	1	1	..
15—20	4	2	2	2	2	..	2	..	2	2	2	..
20 and over ..	7	4	3	4	3	1	3	1	2	1	1	..
Railway—												
Hindu Total ..	**237**	**180**	**57**	**127**	**106**	**21**	**110**	**74**	**36**	**60**	**49**	**11**
0—10	29	22	7	18	16	2	11	6	5	2	2	..
10—15	44	36	8	28	24	4	16	12	4	14	13	1
15—20	42	29	13	23	20	3	19	9	10	12	10	2
20 and over ..	122	93	29	58	46	12	64	47	17	32	24	8
Muslim Total ..	**94**	**70**	**24**	**40**	**34**	**6**	**54**	**36**	**18**	**16**	**14**	**2**
0—10	18	14	4	2	2	..	16	12	4	..	..	..
10—15	9	7	2	5	5	..	4	2	2	3	3	..
15—20	12	8	4	8	6	2	4	2	2	5	4	1
20 and over ..	55	41	14	25	21	4	30	20	10	8	7	1
Serai—												
Hindu Total ..	**10,405**	**6,738**	**3,667**	**4,441**	**3,363**	**1,078**	**5,964**	**3,375**	**2,589**	**2,376**	**2,232**	**144**
0—10	2,777	1,451	1,326	357	201	156	2,420	1,250	1,170	28	16	12
10—15	1,256	690	566	517	319	198	739	371	368	81	56	25
15—20	1,166	686	480	500	306	194	666	380	286	206	240	56
20 and over ..	5,206	3,911	1,295	3,067	2,537	530	2,139	1,374	765	1,971	1,920	51
Muslim Total ..	**2,350**	**1,475**	**875**	**750**	**594**	**156**	**1,600**	**881**	**719**	**201**	**188**	**13**
0—10	361	244	117	61	38	23	300	206	94	8	8	..
10—15	288	221	67	85	50	35	203	171	32	13	12	1
15—20	267	178	89	154	121	33	113	57	56	72	63	4
20 and over ..	1,434	832	602	450	385	65	984	447	537	108	100	8

Quarter, Religion and Age.	POPULATION.									LITERATE IN ENGLISH.		
	TOTAL.			LITERATE.			ILLITERATE.					
	Persons.	Males.	Females.	Persons.	Males.	Females.	Persons.	Males.	Females.	Persons.	Males.	Females.
1	2	3	4	5	6	7	8	9	10	11	12	13
Rambaugh—												
Hindu Total ..	**9,193**	**5,331**	**3,862**	**3,278**	**2,483**	**795**	**5,915**	**2,848**	**3,067**	**1,272**	**1,176**	**96**
0—10	2,971	1,380	1,591	270	151	119	2,701	1,229	1,472	26	20	6
10—15	805	416	389	286	179	107	519	237	282	74	50	24
15—20	858	480	378	398	242	156	460	238	222	229	204	25
20 and over ..	4,559	3,055	1,504	2,324	1,911	413	2,235	1,144	1,091	943	902	41
Muslim Total ..	**2,035**	**1,134**	**901**	**653**	**537**	**116**	**1,382**	**597**	**785**	**255**	**240**	**15**
0—10	308	239	69	47	32	15	261	207	54	0	6	..
10—15	198	131	67	71	49	22	127	82	45	9	8	1
15—20	226	157	69	144	109	35	82	48	34	84	80	4
20 and over ..	1,303	607	696	391	347	44	912	260	652	156	146	10
Jail—												
Hindu Total ..	**5,788**	**3,147**	**2,641**	**2,405**	**1,701**	**704**	**3,383**	**1,446**	**1,937**	**987**	**885**	**102**
0—10	2,166	1,060	1,106	216	115	101	1,950	945	1,005	35	30	5
10—15	536	301	235	285	181	104	251	120	131	85	55	30
15—20	653	359	294	279	154	125	374	205	169	132	101	31
20 and over ..	2,433	1,427	1,006	1,625	1,251	374	808	176	632	735	699	36
Muslim Total ..	**1,673**	**923**	**750**	**613**	**477**	**136**	**1,060**	**446**	**614**	**195**	**179**	**16**
0—10	262	201	61	44	29	15	218	172	46	7	6	1
10—15	133	84	49	72	55	17	61	29	32	6	5	1
15—20	120	85	35	93	64	29	27	21	6	49	45	4
20 and over ..	1,158	553	605	404	329	75	754	224	530	133	123	10
Ranchore—												
Hindu Total ..	**18,098**	**10,677**	**7,421**	**3,578**	**2,882**	**696**	**14,520**	**7,795**	**6,725**	**1,577**	**1,483**	**94**
0—10	5,103	2,457	2,646	145	79	66	4,958	2,378	2,580	25	16	9
10—15	2,091	966	1,125	304	167	137	1,787	799	988	70	62	8
15—20	1,735	1,078	657	724	588	136	1,011	490	521	251	222	29
20 and over ..	9,169	6,176	2,993	2,405	2,048	357	6,764	4,128	2,636	1,231	1,183	48
Muslim Total ..	**5,622**	**3,242**	**2,380**	**577**	**481**	**96**	**5,045**	**2,761**	**2,284**	**180**	**167**	**13**
0—10	1,386	697	689	25	13	12	1,361	684	677	4	2	2
10—15	672	411	261	54	43	11	618	368	250	20	18	2
15—20	510	291	219	64	46	18	446	245	201	18	16	2
20 and over ..	3,054	1,843	1,211	434	379	55	2,620	1,464	1,156	138	131	7
Ramswami—												
Hindu Total ..	**5,490**	**3,136**	**2,354**	**1,530**	**1,175**	**355**	**3,960**	**1,961**	**1,999**	**512**	**485**	**27**
0—10	1,705	835	870	99	54	45	1,606	781	825	29	20	9
10—15	491	293	198	141	93	48	350	200	150	33	30	3
15—20	857	464	393	185	125	60	672	339	333	43	40	3
20 and over ..	2,437	1,544	893	1,105	903	202	1,332	641	691	407	395	12
Muslim Total ..	**857**	**474**	**383**	**227**	**190**	**37**	**630**	**284**	**346**	**55**	**50**	**5**
0—10	215	104	111	8	6	2	207	98	109	..	..	..
10—15	133	72	61	17	14	3	116	58	58	6	6	..
15—20	84	51	33	26	24	2	58	27	31	7	6	1
20 and over ..	425	247	178	176	146	30	249	101	148	42	38	4
Herchandrai Vishendas—												
Hindu Total ..	**918**	**545**	**373**	**316**	**205**	**111**	**602**	**340**	**262**	**85**	**71**	**14**
0—10	235	140	95	22	13	9	213	127	86	4	2	2
10—15	118	70	48	63	45	18	55	25	30	9	9	..
15—20	188	136	52	75	54	21	113	82	31	18	15	3
20 and over ..	377	199	178	156	93	63	221	106	115	54	45	9
Muslim Total ..	**1,216**	**800**	**416**	**231**	**185**	**46**	**985**	**615**	**370**	**105**	**100**	**5**
0—10	203	89	114	16	10	6	187	79	108	1	1	..
10—15	156	78	78	35	26	9	121	52	69	7	6	1
15—20	135	69	66	60	48	12	75	21	54	10	8	2
20 and over	722*	564	158	120	101	19	602	463	139	57	85	2

Quarter, Religion and Age.	POPULATION.									LITERATE IN ENGLISH.		
	TOTAL.			LITERATE.			ILLITERATE.					
	Persons.	Males.	Females.	Persons.	Males.	Females.	Persons.	Males.	Females.	Persons.	Males.	Females.
1	2	3	4	5	6	7	8	9	10	11	12	13
Soldier Bazar—												
Hindu Total ..	**786**	**453**	**333**	**234**	**147**	**87**	**552**	**306**	**246**	**72**	**63**	**9**
0—10	194	97	97	21	15	6	173	82	91	5	4	1
10—15	120	72	57	36	27	9	93	45	48	7	6	1
15—20	115	67	48	66	42	24	49	25	24	17	16	1
20 and over ..	348	217	131	111	63	48	237	154	83	43	37	6
Muslim Total ..	**784**	**438**	**346**	**174**	**146**	**28**	**610**	**292**	**318**	**65**	**59**	**6**
0—10	195	98	97	12	9	3	183	89	94	..	..	..
10—15	132	73	60	18	13	5	114	60	54	5	4	1
15—20	109	62	47	24	20	4	85	42	43	8	7	1
20 and over ..	348	205	143	120	104	16	228	101	127	52	48	4
New Jail—												
Hindu Total ..	**362**	**317**	**45**	**143**	**137**	**6**	**219**	**180**	**39**	**95**	**93**	**2**
0—10	94	78	16	2	2	..	92	76	16	..	..	..
10—15	65	61	4	25	24	1	40	37	3	7	7	..
15—20	38	35	3	17	16	1	21	19	2	11	11	..
20 and over ..	165	143	22	99	95	4	66	48	18	77	75	2
Muslim Total ..	**772**	**631**	**141**	**206**	**191**	**15**	**566**	**440**	**126**	**136**	**133**	**3**
0—10	80	48	32	6	4	2	74	44	30	..	..	..
10—15	45	28	17	14	11	3	31	17	14	2	2	..
15—20	51	32	19	15	13	2	36	19	17	6	5	1
20 and over ..	596	523	73	171	163	8	425	360	65	128	126	2
Preedy—												
Hindu Total ..	**672**	**429**	**243**	**257**	**196**	**61**	**415**	**233**	**182**	**137**	**124**	**13**
0—10	136	78	58	4	3	1	132	75	57	..	..	..
10—15	88	61	27	35	25	10	53	36	17	13	12	1
15—20	50	35	15	30	24	6	20	11	9	20	18	2
20 and over ..	398	255	143	188	144	44	210	111	99	104	94	10
Muslim Total ..	**283**	**210**	**73**	**78**	**63**	**15**	**205**	**147**	**58**	**17**	**14**	**3**
0—10	64	41	23	15	13	2	49	28	21	..	..	..
10—15	64	43	21	17	14	3	47	29	18	5	4	1
15—20	49	33	16	24	18	6	25	15	10	4	3	1
20 and over ..	106	93	13	22	18	4	84	75	9	8	7	1
Saddar Bazar—												
Hindu Total ..	**2,798**	**1,707**	**1,091**	**583**	**468**	**115**	**2,215**	**1,239**	**976**	**235**	**212**	**23**
0—10	634	335	299	54	33	21	580	302	278	11	6	5
10—15	274	176	98	48	29	19	226	147	79	25	22	3
15—20	210	134	76	98	81	17	112	53	59	34	31	3
20 and over ..	1,680	1,062	618	383	325	58	1,297	737	560	165	153	12
Muslim Total ..	**4,140**	**2,450**	**1,690**	**889**	**784**	**155**	**3,251**	**1,716**	**1,585**	**357**	**333**	**24**
0—10	895	456	439	31	25	6	864	431	433	3	2	1
10—15	421	242	179	86	65	21	335	177	158	9	8	1
15—20	343	197	146	160	123	37	183	74	109	70	68	2
20 and over ..	2,481	1,555	926	612	521	91	1,869	1,034	835	275	255	20
Civil Lines—												
Hindu Total ..	**2,389**	**1,585**	**804**	**432**	**875**	**57**	**1,957**	**1,210**	**747**	**178**	**159**	**19**
0—10	706	437	269	26	20	6	680	417	263	5	4	1
10—15	217	155	62	28	25	3	189	130	59	6	5	1
15—20	190	142	48	48	42	6	142	100	42	14	12	2
20 and over ..	1,276	851	425	330	288	42	946	563	383	153	138	15
Muslim Total ..	**969**	**707**	**262**	**208**	**191**	**17**	**761**	**516**	**245**	**93**	**89**	**4**
0—10	268	195	73	17	15	2	251	180	71	2	2	..
10—15	92	71	21	9	7	2	83	64	19	5	4	1
15—20	76	62	14	37	34	3	39	28	11	19	18	1
20 and over ..	533	379	154	145	135	10	388	244	144	67	65	2

Quarter, Religion and Age.	POPULATION.									LITERATE IN ENGLISH.		
	TOTAL.			LITERATE.			ILLITERATE.					
	Persons.	Males.	Females.	Persons.	Males.	Females.	Persons.	Males.	Females.	Persons.	Males.	Females.
1	2	3	4	5	6	7	8	9	10	11	12	13
Frere Town and Bath Island—												
Hindu Total ..	**1,168**	**758**	**410**	**138**	**118**	**20**	**1,030**	**640**	**390**	**74**	**70**	**4**
0—10	262	176	86	10	7	3	252	169	83	1	1	..
10—15	190	123	67	24	22	2	166	101	65	3	3	..
15—20	170	113	57	30	27	3	140	86	54	8	7	1
20 and over ..	546	346	200	74	62	12	472	284	188	62	59	3
Muslim Total ..	**422**	**300**	**122**	**56**	**50**	**6**	**366**	**250**	**116**	**15**	**14**	**1**
0—10	91	60	31	4	3	1	87	57	30	..	..	..
10—15	51	35	16	5	5	..	46	30	16	1	1	..
15—20	41	31	10	7	6	1	34	25	9	1	1	..
20 and over ..	239	174	65	40	36	4	199	138	61	13	12	1
Clifton—												
Hindu Total ..	**234**	**145**	**89**	**96**	**74**	**22**	**188**	**71**	**67**	**49**	**41**	**8**
0—10	33	21	12	7	5	2	26	16	10	1	1	..
10—15	48	35	13	24	19	5	24	16	8	13	11	2
15—20	46	27	19	19	15	4	27	12	15	9	8	1
20 and over ..	107	62	45	46	35	11	61	27	34	26	21	5
Muslim Total ..	**157**	**91**	**66**	**40**	**31**	**9**	**117**	**60**	**57**	**6**	**5**	**1**
0—10	31	17	14	6	6	..	25	11	14	..	..	..
10—15	22	17	5	12	10	2	10	7	3	2	2	..
15—20	23	14	9	12	8	4	11	6	5	3	2	1
20 and over ..	81	43	38	10	7	3	71	36	35	1	1	..
Gizri—												
Hindu Total ..	**105**	**65**	**40**	**31**	**21**	**10**	**74**	**44**	**30**	**5**	**4**	**1**
0—10	20	13	13	5	4	1	21	9	12	..	..	..
10—15	26	12	14	9	7	2	17	5	12	2	2	..
15—20	19	10	9	9	5	4	10	5	5	2	1	1
20 and over ..	34	30	4	8	5	3	26	25	1	1	1	..
Muslim Total ..	**924**	**509**	**415**	**259**	**236**	**23**	**665**	**273**	**392**	**40**	**38**	**2**
0—10	208	111	97	20	18	2	188	93	95	..	..	..
10—15	144	79	65	13	11	2	131	68	63	2	2	..
15—20	108	54	54	32	29	3	76	25	51	8	7	1
20 and over ..	464	265	199	194	178	16	270	87	183	30	29	1
Garden (East and West)—												
Hindu Total ..	**2,105**	**1,371**	**734**	**272**	**249**	**23**	**1,833**	**1,122**	**711**	**99**	**93**	**6**
0—10	241	171	70	11	9	2	230	162	68	2	2	..
10—15	110	72	38	12	9	3	98	63	35	3	2	1
15—20	102	68	34	17	13	4	85	55	30	6	5	1
20 and over ..	1,652	1,060	592	232	218	14	1,420	842	578	88	84	4
Muslim Total ..	**5,268**	**2,773**	**2,495**	**211**	**172**	**39**	**5,057**	**2,601**	**2,456**	**86**	**83**	**3**
0—10	1,157	546	611	15	12	3	1,142	534	608	..	..	..
10—15	670	360	310	24	19	5	646	341	305	2	2	..
15—20	602	331	271	15	11	4	587	320	267	7	6	1
20 and over ..	2,839	1,536	1,303	157	130	27	2,682	1,406	1,276	77	75	2
Tahilram—												
Hindu Total ..	**1,749**	**1,054**	**695**	**297**	**269**	**28**	**1,452**	**785**	**667**	**70**	**64**	**6**
0—10	458	288	170	9	7	2	449	281	168	2	2	..
10—15	238	142	96	19	15	4	219	127	92	8	7	1
15—20	264	160	104	30	26	4	234	134	100	8	7	1
20 and over ..	789	464	325	239	221	18	550	243	307	52	48	4
Muslim Total ..	**2,868**	**1,571**	**1,297**	**251**	**220**	**31**	**2,617**	**1,351**	**1,266**	**73**	**70**	**3**
0—10	560	261	299	20	15	5	540	246	294	..	..	..
10—15	352	191	161	16	15	1	336	176	160	5	5	..
15—20	319	173	146	35	30	5	284	143	141	5	5	..
20 and over ..	1,637	946	691	180	160	20	1,457	786	671	63	60	3

Quarter, Religion and Age.*	POPULATION.									LITERATE IN ENGLISH.		
	TOTAL.			LITERATE.			ILLITERATE.					
	Persons.	Males.	Females.	Persons.	Males.	Females.	Persons.	Males.	Females.	Persons.	Males.	Females.
1	2	3	4	5	6	7	8	9	10	11	12	13
Lawrence—												
Hindu Total ..	**6,162**	**3,862**	**2,300**	**911**	**845**	**66**	**5,251**	**3,017**	**2,284**	**392**	**370**	**22**
0—10	690	449	241	22	18	4	668	431	237	7	6	1
10—15	386	221	165	23	15	8	363	206	157	9	6	3
15—20	347	196	151	70	58	12	277	138	139	23	20	3
20 and over ..	4,730	2,996	1,743	796	754	42	3,943	2,242	1,701	353	338	15
Muslim Total ..	**3,603**	**2,051**	**1,552**	**297**	**255**	**42**	**3,306**	**1,796**	**1,510**	**100**	**96**	**4**
0—10	677	363	314	25	18	7	652	345	307	..	..	..
10—15	454	260	104	24	21	3	430	239	191	7	6	1
15—20	402	227	175	44	37	7	358	190	168	21	19	2
20 and over ..	2,070	1,201	869	204	179	25	1,866	1,022	844	72	71	1
Lyari—												
Hindu Total ..	**6,175**	**3,545**	**2,630**	**851**	**784**	**67**	**5,324**	**2,761**	**2,563**	**129**	**113**	**16**
0—10	651	406	245	20	14	6	631	302	239	6	4	2
10—15	330	211	119	30	20	10	300	191	109	5	4	1
15—20	247	178	69	69	59	10	178	119	59	9	6	3
20 and over ..	4,947	2,750	2,197	732	691	41	4,215	2,059	2,156	109	99	10
Muslim Total ..	**53,164**	**28,812**	**24,352**	**1,681**	**1,470**	**211**	**51,483**	**27,342**	**24,141**	**370**	**356**	**14**
0—10	17,365	8,723	8,642	90	72	18	17,275	8,651	8,624	5	3	2
10—15 ..	5,502	2,861	2,641	129	101	28	5,373	2,760	2,613	12	10	2
15—20	5,381	2,787	2,594	233	203	30	5,148	2,584	2,564	47	45	2
20 and over ..	24,916	14,441	10,475	1,229	1,094	135	23,687	13,347	10,340	306	298	8
Jamshed—												
Hindu Total ..	**1,719**	**1,020**	**699**	**767**	**515**	**252**	**952**	**505**	**447**	**431**	**387**	**44**
0—10	493	223	270	89	49	40	404	174	230	28	20	8
10—15	169	91	78	100	55	45	69	36	33	33	21	12
15—20	191	106	85	103	66	37	88	40	48	26	20	6
20 and over ..	866	600	266	475	345	130	391	255	136	344	326	18
Muslim Total ..	**105**	**74**	**31**	**23**	**18**	**5**	**82**	**56**	**26**	**7**	**6**	**1**
0—10	18	12	6	..	..	..	18	12	6	..	..	..
10—15	20	14	6	4	3	1	16	11	5	1	1	..
15—20	23	15	8	6	4	2	17	11	6	1	1	..
20 and over ..	44	33	11	13	11	2	31	22	9	5	4	1
Artillary Maidan—												
Hindu Total ..	**288**	**206**	**82**	**68**	**60**	**8**	**220**	**146**	**74**	**14**	**13**	**1**
0—10	72	51	21	6	4	2	66	47	19	1	1	..
10—15	51	36	15	5	5	..	46	31	15	1	1	..
15—20	43	31	12	8	6	2	35	25	10	2	2	..
20 and over ..	122	88	34	49	45	4	73	43	30	10	9	1
Muslim Total ..	**118**	**84**	**34**	**17**	**14**	**3**	**101**	**70**	**31**	**4**	**4**	..
0—10	22	13	9	..	..	..	22	13	9	..	..	..
10—15	17	10	7	3	2	1	14	8	6	..	..	..
15—20	13	9	4	6	5	1	7	4	3	1	1	..
20 and over ..	66	52	14	8	7	1	58	45	13	3	3	..
Trans Lyari—												
Hindu Total ..	**188**	**128**	**60**	**56**	**46**	**10**	**132**	**82**	**50**	**22**	**20**	**2**
0—10	36	24	12	3	3	..	33	21	12	..	..	..
10—15	30	21	9	10	9	1	20	12	8	2	2	..
15—20	31	22	9	17	13	4	14	9	5	7	6	1
20 and over ..	91	61	30	26	21	5	65	40	25	13	12	1
Muslim Total ..	**5,569**	**3,008**	**2,561**	**251**	**226**	**25**	**5,318**	**2,782**	**2,536**	**91**	**87**	**4**
0—10	1,525	811	714	12	9	3	1,513	802	711	..	..	..
10—15	502	231	271	19	15	4	483	216	267	3	2	1
15—20	238	125	113	17	13	4	221	112	109	5	4	1
20 and over ..	3,304	1,841	1,463	203	189	14	3,101	1,652	1,449	83	81	2

Quarter, Religion and Age.	POPULATION.									LITERATE IN ENGLISH.		
	TOTAL.			LITERATE.			ILLITERATE.					
	Persons.	Males.	Females.	Persons.	Males.	Females.	Persons.	Males.	Females.	Persons.	Males.	Females.
1	2	3	4	5	6	7	8	9	10	11	12	13
Tatta Naka and Goda Village and Labour Corps—												
Hindu Total ..	**283**	**187**	**96**	**59**	**46**	**13**	**224**	**141**	**83**	**16**	**15**	**1**
0—10	52	36	16	2	2	..	50	34	16	..	..	..
10—15	46	32	14	11	9	2	35	23	12	2	2	..
15—20	50	34	16	16	14	2	34	20	14	4	4	..
20 and over ..	135	85	50	30	21	9	105	64	41	10	9	1
Muslim Total ..	**500**	**293**	**207**	**35**	**24**	**11**	**465**	**269**	**196**	**7**	**5**	**2**
0—10	124	71	53	4	3	1	120	68	52	..	..	..
10—15	68	39	29	5	3	2	63	36	27	1	1	..
15—20	41	24	17	7	4	3	34	20	14	2	1	1
20 and over ..	267	159	108	19	14	5	248	145	103	4	3	1
Quarry No. 1 and 2 and other Quarries—												
Hindu Total ..	**13**	**9**	**4**	**3**	**3**	..	**10**	**6**	**4**	..	..	..
0—10	2	..	2	..	..	..	2	..	2	..	..	..
10—15	2	1	1	..	..	..	2	1	1	..	..	..
15—20	1	1	..	1	1	..	..	..	..	..	..	..
20 and over ..	8	7	1	2	2	..	6	5	1	..	..	..
Muslim Total ..	**411**	**231**	**180**	**23**	**17**	**6**	**388**	**214**	**174**	**2**	**2**	..
0—10	176	90	86	..	..	..	176	90	86	..	..	..
10—15	48	27	21	3	2	1	45	25	20	..	..	..
15—20	21	9	12	5	3	2	16	6	10	1	1	..
20 and over ..	166	105	61	15	12	3	151	93	58	1	1	..
Scattered Hamlets, behind Cantonment Station and Chinaser and Vagri Villages—												
Hindu Total ..	**203**	**109**	**94**	**16**	**13**	**3**	**187**	**96**	**91**	..	..	..
0—10	44	21	23	..	..	..	44	21	23	..	..	..
10—15	31	19	12	4	3	1	27	16	11	..	..	..
15—20	36	18	18	2	2	..	34	16	18	..	..	..
20 and over ..	92	51	41	10	8	2	82	43	39	..	..	..
Muslim Total ..	**667**	**339**	**328**	**38**	**32**	**6**	**629**	**307**	**322**	**5**	**4**	**1**
0—10	151	60	91	..	..	..	151	60	91	..	..	..
10—15	57	25	32	3	2	1	54	23	31	..	..	..
15—20	44	22	22	7	5	2	37	17	20	1	1	..
20 and over ..	415	232	183	28	25	3	387	207	180	4	3	1
Keamari with other Port Area (via Thola Produce Yard, Mansfield Import Yard and West Wharf)—												
Hindu Total ..	**5,320**	**3,673**	**1,647**	**585**	**538**	**47**	**4,735**	**3,135**	**1,600**	**284**	**272**	**12**
0—10	742	405	337	28	20	8	714	385	329	8	6	2
10—15	424	253	171	49	39	10	375	214	161	12	10	2
15—20	467	284	183	93	88	5	374	196	178	45	44	1
20 and over ..	3,687	2,731	956	415	391	24	3,272	2,340	932	219	212	7
Muslim Total ..	**5,424**	**3,519**	**1,905**	**523**	**474**	**49**	**4,901**	**3,045**	**1,856**	**174**	**162**	**12**
0—10	723	398	325	30	28	2	693	370	323	7	5	2
10—15	374	243	131	32	22	10	342	221	121	8	7	1
15—20	453	284	169	67	59	8	386	225	161	26	25	1
20 and over ..	3,874	2,594	1,280	394	365	29	3,480	2,229	1,251	133	125	8
Baba Islands—												
Hindu Total ..	**46**	**25**	**21**	**14**	**14**	..	**32**	**11**	**21**	**2**	**2**	..
0—10	9	3	6	..	..	..	9	3	6	..	..	..
10—15	5	4	1	..	..	..	5	4	1	..	..	..
15—20	5	3	2	1	1	..	4	2	2	1	1	..
20 and over ..	27	15	12	13	13	..	14	2	12	1	1	..
Muslim Total ..	**1,156**	**589**	**567**	**37**	**30**	**7**	**1,119**	**559**	**560**	**1**	**1**	..
0—10	232	81	151	3	2	1	229	79	150	..	..	..
10—15	91	49	42	4	3	1	87	46	41	..	..	..
15—20	123	72	51	4	2	2	119	70	49	..	..	..
20 and over ..	710	387	323	26	23	3	684	364	320	1	1	..

Quarter, Religion and Age.	POPULATION.									LITERATE IN ENGLISH.		
	TOTAL.			LITERATE.			ILLITERATE.					
	Persons.	Males.	Females.	Persons.	Males.	Females.	Persons.	Males.	Females.	Persons.	Males.	Females.
1	2	3	4	5	6	7	8	9	10	11	12	13
Bhit Islands—												
Hindu Total ..	9	6	3	2	2	..	7	4	3	..	..	..
0—10	3	2	1	..	..	..	3	2	1	..	..	..
10—15	1	1	..	..	..	..	1	1	..	..	..	..
15—20	..	..	..	..	..	..	..	..	..	..	..	..
20 and over ..	5	3	2	2	2	..	3	1	2	..	..	..
Muslim Total ..	787	408	379	20	18	2	767	390	377	..	..	..
0—10	152	51	101	1	1	..	151	50	101	..	..	..
10—15	64	31	33	2	1	1	62	30	32	..	..	..
15—20	99	64	35	1	1	..	98	63	35	..	..	..
20 and over ..	472	262	210	16	15	1	456	247	209	..	..	..
Shamespir and Goth Mahomed—												
Hindu Total ..	3	3	..	..	..	..	3	3	..	..	..	..
0—10	..	..	..	..	..	..	..	..	..	..	..	..
10—15	..	..	..	..	..	..	..	..	..	..	..	..
15—20	..	..	..	..	..	..	..	..	..	..	..	..
20 and over ..	3	3	..	..	..	..	3	3	..	..	..	..
Muslim Total ..	461	222	239	10	10	..	451	212	239	..	..	..
0—10	154	88	66	1	1	..	153	87	66	..	..	..
10—15	48	27	21	1	1	..	47	26	21	..	..	..
15—20	23	11	12	..	..	..	23	11	12	..	..	..
20 and over ..	236	96	140	8	8	..	228	88	140	..	..	..
Bunker Island—												
Hindu Total ..	3	3	..	..	..	..	3	3	..	..	..	..
0—10	..	..	..	..	..	..	..	..	..	..	..	..
10—15	..	..	..	..	..	..	..	..	..	..	..	..
15—20	..	..	..	..	..	..	..	..	..	..	..	..
20 and over ..	3	3	..	..	..	..	3	3	..	..	..	..
Muslim Total ..	1	1	..	..	..	..	1	1	..	..	..	..
0—10	..	..	..	..	..	..	..	..	..	..	..	..
10—15	..	..	..	..	..	..	..	..	..	..	..	..
15—20	..	..	..	..	..	..	..	..	..	..	..	..
20 and over ..	1	1	..	..	..	..	1	1	..	..	..	..
Port Floating Population—												
Hindu Total ...	498	473	25	120	120	..	378	353	25	14	14	..
0—10	8	5	3	..	..	..	8	5	3	..	..	..
10—15	14	10	4	2	2	..	12	8	4	..	..	..
15—20	25	23	2	13	13	..	12	10	2	1	1	..
20 and over ..	451	435	16	105	105	..	346	330	16	13	13	..
Muslim Total ..	1,919	1,885	34	315	313	2	1,604	1,572	32	40	40	..
0—10	29	23	6	..	..	..	29	23	6	..	..	..
10—15	54	49	5	..	..	..	54	49	5	..	..	..
15—20	237	231	6	34	34	..	203	197	6	4	4	..
20 and over ..	1,599	1,582	17	281	279	2	1,318	1,303	15	36	36	..
Railway Area including City Bunder and Cantonment Stations and Reception and Hump Yard and Platform Population—												
Hindu Total ..	3,158	2,201	957	409	321	88	2,749	1,880	869	153	150	3
0—10	410	181	229	30	17	13	380	164	216	2	2	..
10—15	135	67	68	36	28	8	99	39	60	6	6	..
15—20	206	128	78	76	64	12	130	64	66	34	34	..
20 and over ..	2,407	1,825	582	267	212	55	2,140	1,613	527	111	108	3
Muslim Total ..	2,772	1,843	929	351	337	14	2,421	1,506	915	146	146	..
0—10	615	336	279	2	2	..	613	334	279	..	..	..
10—15	216	126	90	9	7	2	207	119	88	1	1	..
15—20	291	168	123	53	50	3	238	118	120	31	31	..
20 and over ..	1,650	1,213	437	287	278	9	1,363	935	428	114	114	..

Quarter, Religion and Age.	POPULATION.									LITERATE IN ENGLISH.		
	TOTAL.			LITERATE.			ILLITERATE.					
	Persons.	Males.	Females.	Persons.	Males.	Females.	Persons.	Males.	Females.	Persons.	Males.	Females.
1	2	3	4	5	6	7	8	9	10	11	12	13
Maurypur—												
Hindu Total ..	**194**	**138**	**56**	**34**	**30**	**4**	**160**	**108**	**52**	**17**	**17**	..
0—10	17	5	12	..	..	..	17	5	12	..	..	..
10—15	22	16	6	..	..	..	22	16	6	..	..	..
15—20	27	21	6	7	5	2	20	16	4	3	3	..
20 and over ..	128	96	32	27	25	2	101	71	30	14	14	..
Muslim Total ..	**1,193**	**672**	**521**	**64**	**64**	..	**1,129**	**608**	**521**	**4**	**4**	..
0—10	385	211	174	5	5	..	380	206	174	..	..	..
10—15	124	71	53	8	8	..	116	63	53	..	..	..
15—20	113	56	57	8	8	..	105	48	57	..	..	..
20 and over ..	571	334	237	43	43	..	528	291	237	4	4	..
Drigh Road—												
Hindu Total ..	**15**	**11**	**4**	**5**	**5**	..	**10**	**6**	**4**	**4**	**4**	..
0—10	4	3	1	..	..	..	4	3	1	..	..	..
10—15	2	2	..	..	..	..	2	2	..	..	..	..
15—20	3	2	1	1	1	..	2	1	1	..	..	..
20 and over ..	6	4	2	4	4	..	2	..	2	4	4	..
Muslim Total ..	**7**	**6**	**1**	**4**	**4**	..	**3**	**2**	**1**	**2**	**2**	..
0—10	1	1	..	..	..	..	1	1	..	..	..	..
10—15	..	..	..	..	..	..	..	..	..	..	..	..
15—20	1	1	..	..	..	..	1	1	..	..	..	..
20 and over ..	5	4	1	4	4	..	1	..	1	2	2	..
Cape Mouze—												
Hindu Total ..	**1**	**1**	..	..	..	..	**1**	**1**	..	..	..	..
0—10	..	..	..	..	..	..	..	..	..	..	..	..
10—15	..	..	..	..	..	..	..	..	..	..	..	..
15—20	..	..	..	..	..	..	..	..	..	..	..	..
20 and over ..	1	1	..	..	..	..	1	1	..	..	..	..
Muslim Total ..	**31**	**16**	**15**	**4**	**4**	..	**27**	**12**	**15**	**2**	**2**	..
0—10	12	5	7	..	..	..	12	5	7	..	..	..
10—15	3	2	1	..	..	..	3	2	1	..	..	..
15—20	..	..	..	..	..	..	..	..	..	..	..	..
20 and over ..	16	9	7	4	4	..	12	5	7	2	2	..

CITY TABLE VI—PART I—KARACHI.

BIRTH-PLACE.

(Corresponding to Imperial Table VI.)

District or State where born.	Persons.	Males.	Females.
Total Population	**263,565**	**156,120**	**107,445**
A. India excluding Aden	**262,409**	**155,501**	**106,908**
A.–I. Bombay Presidency including Bombay—States and Agencies	**211,032**	**120,779**	**90,253**
British Districts	**202,143**	**117,439**	**84,704**
Bombay	15,344	8,473	6,871
Northern Division	**7,505**	**4,368**	**3,137**
Ahmedabad	2,897	1,757	1,140
Broach	600	358	242
Kaira	625	353	272
Panch-Mahals	211	123	88
Surat	2,629	1,483	1,146
Thana	543	294	249
Central Division	**8,607**	**5,126**	**3,481**
Ahmednagar	1,855	698	1,157
Khandesh-East	371	238	133
Khandesh-West	816	658	158
Nasik	1,120	779	341
Poona	2,456	1,488	968
Satara	1,669	1,048	621
Sholapur	320	217	103
Southern Division	**5,962**	**3,934**	**2,028**
Belgaum	750	497	253
Bijapur	369	238	131
Dharwar	486	292	194
Kanara	481	273	208
Kolaba	406	306	100
Ratnagiri	3,470	2,328	1,142
Sind	**164,725**	**95,538**	**69,187**
Hyderabad	13,544	7,923	5,621
Karachi	126,412	72,132	54,280
Larkana	4,908	2,868	2,040
Nawabshah	5,522	3,433	2,089
Sukkur	12,271	7,742	4,529
Thar and Parkar	1,175	803	372
Upper Sind Frontier	893	637	256
Bombay States and Agencies	**1,817**	**1,310**	**507**
Kolhapur	9	9	....
Khairpur	1,808	1,301	507
Bombay Presidency including Bombay States and Agencies Unspecified	**7,072**	**2,030**	**5,042**
A.–II. Provinces and States in India beyond Bombay	**51,377**	**34,722**	**16,655**
(a) Provinces and States adjacent to Bombay Presidency	**36,519**	**25,331**	**11,188**
(1) British Provinces	**35,607**	**24,853**	**10,754**
(i) Madras	1,582	1,141	441
(ii) Central Provinces and Berar	11,455	9,817	1,638
(iii) Punjab	22,218	13,702	8,516
(iv) Baluchistan	352	193	159

District or State where born.	Persons.	Males.	Females.
(2) States	**912**	**478**	**434**
(i) Western India States Agencies	887	460	427
(ii) Mysore	7	4	3
(iii) Hyderabad	2	2	....
(iv) Rajputana	10	6	4
(v) Baroda	6	6	....
(b) Other Provinces and States	**14,663**	**9,211**	**5,452**
(i) Ajmer-Merwara	16	9	7
(ii) Bengal	1,190	813	377
(iii) Delhi	11	11	....
(iv) Kashmir	1	1	....
(v) N. W. F. Provinces	2,045	1,519	526
(vi) United Provinces	11,400	6,858	4,542
(c) French and Portuguese Settlements in India	**195**	**180**	**15**
B. Other Asiatic Countries	**98**	**45**	**53**
(i) Outside British Dominions	**82**	**45**	**37**
Afghanistan	46	24	22
China	7	5	2
Nepal	2	2	....
Elsewhere	27	14	13
(ii) Asia Unspecified	**16**	....	**16**
C. Europe	**823**	**443**	**380**
(i) United Kingdom and Irish Free State	689	400	289
(ii) Continental Europe	134	43	91
D. Africa	**10**	**9**	**1**
(i) Africa Unspecified	**10**	**9**	**1**
E. America	**225**	**122**	**103**
(i) America Unspecified	**225**	**122**	**103**

CITY TABLE VI—PART II—KARACHI.

Selected Birth-places combined with Age and Selected Occupations.

(Excluding Cantonment Military Area and the Floating Population of the Port.)

Birth-place.	Total number of Immigrants.			Age Distribution.						Workers.	
				0—15		15—40		40 and over.			
	Males.	Females.	Total.	Males.	Females.	Males.	Females.	Males.	Females.	Males.	Females.
1	2	3	4	5	6	7	8	9	10	11	12
Other Districts of Sind ..	13,751	7,684	21,435	3,178	2,052	8,640	4,601	1,933	1,031	8,805	275
Ratnagiri	2,105	1,109	3,214	313	235	1,515	770	277	104	1,652	35
Ahmedabad	674	411	1,085	84	77	445	254	145	80	571	44
Surat	508	326	834	76	35	287	204	145	87	381	16
Western India States Agency	433	394	827	47	39	317	303	69	52	270	55
Baluchistan	163	141	304	20	19	103	84	40	38	115	20
Punjab and N.-W. F. Provinces	11,994	4,515	16,509	2,061	1,045	8,253	2,848	1,680	627	9,577	325
United Provinces ..	4,392	1,424	5,816	407	186	3,501	1,078	484	160	3,854	56
Rajputana	5	3	8	..	..	3	2	2	1	4	..
Afghanistan	19	18	37	3	5	15	11	1	2	11	..

Birth-place.	Dependants.		Selected Occupation.									
			Shopkeepers and money-lenders.		Artisans of all kinds.		Clerks of all kinds.		Sweepers.		Porters, messengers and labourers unspecified.	
	Males.	Females.	Males.	Females.	Males.	Females.	Males.	Females.	Males.	Females.	Males.	Females.
1	13	14	15	16	17	18	19	20	21	22	23	24
Other Districts of Sind ..	4,946	7,409	3,044	19	799	27	1,750	4	11	17	764	53
Ratnagiri	453	1,074	112	2	226	5	298	1	49	1	453	3
Ahmedabad	103	367	131	5	175	8	91	1	62	11	33	9
Surat	127	310	103	1	54	2	111	2	..	..	25	5
Western India States Agency	163	339	44	3	64	4	20	..	7	4	99	34
Baluchistan	48	121	2	1	1	..	4	..	..	..	97	16
Punjab and N.-W. F. Provinces	2,417	4,190	1,540	15	1,985	27	821	2	402	153	1,936	45
United Provinces ..	538	1,368	390	5	438	11	246	..	24	..	1,609	22
Rajputana	1	3	2	..	..	..	2	..	..	..	..	..
Afghanistan	8	18	4	..	..	..	2	..	..	..	5	..

CITY TABLE VII—PART I—KARACHI CITY.

OCCUPATION OR MEANS OF LIVELIHOOD.

(Corresponding to Imperial Table X—Part I.)

—	Persons.	Males.	Females.
Total Earners	75,918	68,664	7,254
Total working dependants	7,364	5,437	1,927
Total non-working dependants	180,283	82,019	98,264
Total Population ..	263,565	156,120	107,445

CITY TABLE VII—PART I—KARACHI CITY.

Occupation or Means of Livelihood.

(Corresponding to Imperial Table X—Part I.)

Group No.	Occupation.	Total following occupation.	As principal occupation.		As working dependants.		As subsidiary to other occupation.	
			Males.	Females.	Males.	Females.	Males.	Females.
1	2	3	4	5	6	7	8	9
	Total All Classes	**85,340**	**68,664**	**7,254**	**5,437**	**1,927**	**2,043**	**15**
	Total Class A—Production of Raw Materials	**4,908**	**3,528**	**266**	**287**	**137**	**685**	**5**
	Total Sub-Class I—Exploitation of Animals and Vegetation	**4,610**	**3,235**	**265**	**287**	**137**	**681**	**5**
	Total Order 1—Pasture and Agriculture	**4,142**	**2,776**	**264**	**279**	**137**	**681**	**5**
	Total Sub-Order 1 (a)—Cultivation	**3,432**	**2,108**	**222**	**279**	**137**	**681**	**5**
1	Non-cultivating proprietors taking rent in money or kind	2,600	1,506	181	258	..	664	
2	Estate Agents and Managers of owners	45	45	..	..	..	..	..
4	Rent collectors, clerks, etc.	222	28	41	8	137	3	5
5	Cultivating owners	355	329	..	13	..	13	..
7	Agricultural labourers	111	110	..	..	..	1	..
	Total Sub-Order 1 (b)—Cultivation of Special Crops, Fruit, etc. (Planters, Managers, Clerks and Labourers)	**568**	**532**	**36**	..	..	..	..
16	Market gardeners, flower and fruit growers	568	532	36	..	..	..	..
	Total Sub-Order 1 (d)—Stock Raising	**142**	**136**	**6**	..	..	..	..
21	Cattle and buffalo breeders and keepers	80	74	6	..	..	..	..
22	Breeders of transport animals	58	58	..	..	..	..	..
23	Herdsmen, shepherds and breeders of other animals	4	4	..	..	..	..	..
	Total Order 2—Fishing and Hunting	**468**	**459**	**1**	**8**	..	..	..
27	Fishing and pearling	410	410	1	8	..	..	..
28	Hunting	49	49	..	..	..	..	..
	Total Sub-Class II—Exploitation of Minerals	**298**	**293**	**1**	..	..	**4**	..
	Total Order 4—Non-Metallic Minerals	**298**	**293**	**1**	..	..	**4**	..
40	Salt, saltpetre and other saline substances	298	293	1	..	..	4	..
	Total Class B—Preparation and Supply of Material Substances	**41,099**	**33,515**	**2,531**	**3,406**	**692**	**948**	**7**
	Total Sub-Class III—Industry	**15,887**	**12,137**	**1,795**	**1,164**	**619**	**172**	..
	Total Order 5—Textiles	**1,350**	**971**	**267**	**96**	..	**16**	..
42	Cotton ginning, cleaning and pressing	311	247	..	58	..	6	..
43	Cotton spinning, sizing and weaving	392	376	2	14	..	..	..
49	Dyeing, bleaching, printing, preparation and sponging of textiles.	173	153	..	10	..	10	..
50	Lace, crepe, embroideries, fringes, etc., and insufficiently described textile industries	474	105	265	14	..	..	..
	Total Order 6—Hides, Skins and Hard Materials from the Animal Kingdom	**1,007**	**862**	**40**	**68**	..	**37**	..
51	Working in leather	928	819	4	68	..	37	..
52	Furries and persons occupied with feathers, and bristles; brush makers	79	43	36	..	..	..	..
	Total Order 7—Wood	**2,298**	**1,894**	**8**	**228**	**167**	**1**	..
55	Carpenters, turners and joiners, etc.	2,298	1,894	8	228	167	1	..
	Total Order 8—Metals	**781**	**781**	..	..	..	..	..
58	Makers of arms, guns, etc.	56	56	..	..	..	..	..
59	Blacksmiths, other workers in iron, makers of implements	725	725	..	..	..	..	..
	Total Order 9—Ceramics	**90**	**90**	..	..	..	..	..
63	Potters and makers of earthen-ware	4	4	..	..	..	..	..
64	Brick and tile makers	86	86	..	..	..	..	..

Group No.	Occupation.	Total following occupation.	As principal occupation.		As working dependants.		As subsidiary to other occupation.	
			Males.	Females.	Males.	Females.	Males.	Females.
1	2	3	4	5	6	7	8	9
	Total Order 10—Chemical Products Properly so-called and Analogous	**953**	**871**	**32**	**7**	..	**43**	..
67	Manufacture of aerated and mineral waters and ice	766	684	32	7	..	43	..
68	Manufacture and refining of vegetable oils	50	50	..	..	..	..	..
69	Manufacture and refining of mineral oils	17	17	..	..	..	..	..
70	Others	120	120	..	..	..	..	..
	Total Order 11—Food Industries	**1,368**	**1,166**	**118**	**59**	..	**25**	..
73	Butchers	263	256	..	4	..	3	..
74	Makers of sugar, molasses and gur	80	56	..	2	..	22	..
75	Sweetmeat and condiment makers	231	231	..	..	..	..	..
77	Brewers and distillers	8	8	..	..	..	..	..
78	Manufacturers of Tobacco	365	312	..	53	..	..	..
81	Others	421	303	118	..	..	..	..
	Total Order 12—Industries of Dress and the Toilet ..	**3,181**	**2,174**	**525**	**367**	**115**	..	..
82	Boot, shoe, sandal and clog makers	104	63	..	41	..	..	..
83	Tailors, milliners, dressmakers and darners	1,119	848	143	128	..	..	..
84	Embroiderers, hat makers and makers of other articles of wear ..	19	19	..	..	..	..	..
85	Washing and cleaning	1,294	678	380	121	115	..	..
86	Barbers, hairdressers and wig makers	645	566	2	77	..	..	..
	Total Order 13—Furniture Industries	**152**	**140**	..	**8**	..	**4**	..
88	Cabinet-makers, carriage painters, etc.	152	140	..	8	..	4	..
	Total Order 14—Building Industries	**1,081**	**944**	**14**	**103**	..	**20**	..
90	Lime burners, cement workers; Excavators and well sinkers; Stone cutters and dressers, Bricklayers and masons; Builders (other than buildings made of bamboo or similar materials), painters, decorators of houses, tillers, plumbers, etc. ..	1,081	944	14	103	..	20	..
	Total Order 16—Production and Transmission of Physical Force ..	**74**	**74**	..	..	..	..	..
94	Heat, light, electricity, motive power, etc., Gas works and electric light and power	74	74	..	..	..	..	..
	Total Order 17—Miscellaneous and Undefined Industries ..	**3,552**	**2,170**	**791**	**228**	**337**	**26**	..
95	Printers, engravers, bookbinders, etc.	425	421	..	4	..	..	..
97	Makers of clocks and surgical or scientific instruments, etc. ..	13	13	..	..	..	..	..
98	Makers of jewellery and ornaments	466	354	..	86	..	26	..
99	Other miscellaneous and undefined industries (toy-making, taxidermy etc.)	68	68	..	..	..	..	..
100	Scavenging	2,580	1,314	791	138	337	..	..
	Total Sub-Class IV—Transport	**10,394**	**9,736**	**49**	**355**	..	**254**	..
	Total Order 19—Transport by Water	**4,412**	**4,069**	**5**	**145**	..	**193**	..
102	Ship-owners, boat-owners and their employees, officers, mariners, etc., Ships brokers, boatmen and tow men	2,932	2,698	5	41	..	193	..
103	Persons (other than labourers) employed in harbours, docks, rivers and canals, including pilots	828	778	..	50	..	..	..
104	Labourers employed on harbours, docks, rivers and canals ..	652	598	..	54	..	..	..
	Total Order 20—Transport by Road	**2,123**	**2,057**	**1**	**65**	..	..	..
105	*Persons (other than labourers) employed on the construction and* maintenance of roads and bridges	197	197	..	..	..	..	..
107	Owners, managers and employees (excluding personal servants) connected with mechanically driven vehicles (including trams) ..	413	412	1	..	..	..	..
108	Owners, managers and employees (excluding personal servants) connected with other vehicles	1,319	1,254	..	65	..	..	..
111	Portors and messengers	194	194	..	..	..	..	..
	Total Order 21—Transport by Rail	**3,091**	**2,995**	**16**	**19**	..	**61**	..
112	Railway employees of all kinds other than coolies	2,374	2,374	..	..	..	..	..
113	Labourers employed on railway construction and maintenance and coolies and porters employed on railway premises	717	621	16	19	..	61	..
	Total Order 22—Post Office, Telegraph and Telephone Services ..	**768**	**615**	**27**	**126**	..	..	..
114	Post Office, Telegraph and Telephone services	768	615	27	126	..	..	..

Group No.	Occupation.	Total following occupation.	As principal occupation.		As working dependants.		As subsidiary to other occupation.	
			Males.	Females.	Males.	Females.	Males.	Females.
1	2	3	4	5	6	7	8	9
	Total Sub-Class V—Trade	**14,818**	**11,642**	**687**	**1,887**	**73**	**522**	**7**
	Total Order 23—Banks, Establishments of Credit, Exchange and Insurance	**2,148**	**1,943**	**86**	**12**	**12**	**88**	**7**
115	Bank managers, money lenders, exchange and insurance agents, money changers and brokers and their employees	2,148	1,943	86	12	12	88	7
	Total Order 24—Brokerage Commission and Export	**793**	**752**	**9**	**17**	..	**15**	..
116	Brokers, commission agents, commercial travellers, ware-house owners and employees	793	752	9	17	..	15	..
	Total Order 25—Trade in Textiles	**49**	**45**	..	**4**	..	..	..
117	Trade in piece-goods, wool, cotton, silk, hair and other textiles	49	45	..	4	..	..	..
	Total Order 26—Trade in Skins, Leather and Furs	**623**	**606**	..	**6**	..	**11**	..
118	Trade in skins, leathers, furs, feathers, horn etc., and the articles made from these	623	606	..	6	..	11	..
	Total Order 27—Trade in Wood	**87**	**6**	**17**	**8**	**56**	..	..
121	Trade in bamboos and canes	87	6	17	8	56	..	..
	Total Order 28—Trade in Metals	**14**	**14**	..	..	..	..	..
123	Trade in metals, machinery, knives tools etc.	14	14	..	..	..	..	..
	Total Order 29—Trade in Pottery, Bricks and Tiles	**285**	**262**	**23**	..	..	..	..
124	Trade in pottery, bricks and tiles	285	262	23	..	..	..	..
	Total Order 31—Hotels, Cafes, Restaurants, etc.	**2,515**	**2,151**	**51**	**288**	**5**	**20**	..
126	Vendors of wine, liquors, aerated waters and ice	273	273	..	..	..	..	..
127	Owners and Managers of hotels, cook shops, sarais etc. (and employees)	2,239	1,878	48	288	5	20	..
128	Hawkers of drink and food stuffs	3	..	3	..	..	..	..
	Total Order 32—Other Trade in Food Stuffs	**3,860**	**3,179**	**269**	**342**	..	**70**	..
129	Grain and pulse dealers	22	22	..	..	..	..	..
130	Dealers in sweetmeats, sugar and spices	628	624	2	2	..	..	..
131	Dealers in dairy product, eggs and poultry	520	459	..	12	..	49	..
133	Dealers in fodder for animals	1,209	914	263	32	..	..	..
134	Dealers in other food stuffs	761	589	4	147	..	21	..
135	Dealers in tobacco	495	346	..	149	..	..	..
136	Dealers in opium	206	206	..	..	..	..	..
137	Dealers in ganja	19	19	..	..	..	..	..
	Total Order 33—Trade in Clothing and Toilet Articles	**146**	**146**	..	..	..	..	..
138	Trade in ready-made clothing and other articles of dress and the toilet (hats, umbrellas, socks, ready-made shoes, perfumes, etc.).	146	146	..	..	..	..	..
	Total Order 34—Trade in Furniture	**85**	**68**	..	**3**	..	**14**	..
140	Hardware, cooking utensils, porcelain, crockery, glassware, bottles, articles for gardening, etc.	85	68	..	3	..	14	..
	Total Order 36—Trade in Means of Transport	**642**	**510**	**19**	**87**	..	**26**	..
142	Dealers and hirers in mechanical transport motors, cycles, etc.	398	392	..	6	..	..	..
143	Dealers and hirers in other carriages, carts, boats, etc.	244	118	19	81	..	26	..
	Total Order 38—Trade in Articles of Luxury and those Pertaining to Letters and the Arts and Sciences	**19**	**19**	..	..	..	..	..
147	Dealers in common bangles, bead necklaces, fans, small articles, toys, hunting and fishing tackle, flowers, etc.	19	19	..	..	..	..	..
	Total Order 39—Trade of other Sorts	**3,552**	**1,941**	**213**	**1,120**	..	**278**	..
150	General store-keepers and shop-keepers otherwise unspecified	3,439	1,837	213	1,118	..	271	..
151	Itinerant traders, pedlars and hawkers (of other than food, etc.)	113	104	..	2	..	7	..

Group No.	Occupation.	Total following occupation.	As principal occupation.		As working dependants.		As subsidiary to other occupation.	
			Males.	Females.	Males.	Females.	Males.	Females.
1	2	3	4	5	6	7	8	9
	Total Class C—Public Administration and Liberal Arts ..	**14,801**	**13,649**	**774**	**147**	**122**	**109**	..
	Total Sub-Class VI—Public Force	**5,486**	**5,448**	**4**	**34**	..	..	..
	Total Order 40—Army	**4,349**	**4,311**	**4**	**34**	..	..	..
153	Army (Imperial)	4,231	4,193	4	34	..	..	..
154	Army (Indian States)	118	118	..	..	..	..	..
	Total Order 42—Air Force	**720**	**720**	..	..	..	..	..
156	Air Force	720	720	..	..	..	..	..
	Total Order 43—Police	**417**	**417**	..	..	..	..	..
157	Police	417	417	..	..	..	..	..
	Total Sub-Class VII—Public Administration	**3,495**	**3,445**	**34**	**1**	..	**15**	..
	Total Order 44—Public Administration	**3,495**	**3,445**	**34**	**1**	..	**15**	..
159	Service of the State	3,135	3,117	3	..	..	15	..
161	Municipal and other local (not village) service	360	328	31	1	..	..	..
	Total Sub-Class VIII—Professions and Liberal Arts	**5,820**	**4,756**	**736**	**112**	**122**	**94**	..
	Total Order 45—Religion	**950**	**694**	**186**	..	**70**	..	..
163	Priests, ministers, etc.	347	347	..	..	..	..	..
164	Monks, nuns, religious mendicants	587	335	182	..	70	..	..
166	Servants in religious edifices, burial and burning grounds, pilgrim conductors, circumcisers, etc.	16	12	4	..	..	..	..
	Total Order 46—Law	**982**	**920**	..	**3**	..	**59**	..
167	Lawyers of all kinds, including Qazis, Law Agents and Mukhtiars.	218	218	..	..	..	..	..
168	Lawyers' clerks, petition writers, etc.	764	702	..	3	..	59	..
	Total Order 47—Medicine	**1,921**	**1,492**	**337**	**22**	**39**	**31**	..
169	Registered medical practitioners including oculists	1,713	1,427	237	13	5	31	..
170	Other persons practising the healing arts without being registered.	46	37	..	9	..	..	..
171	Dentists	26	26	..	..	..	..	..
172	Midwives, Vaccinators, compounders, nurses, masseurs, etc. ..	136	2	100	..	34	..	..
	Total Order 48—Instruction	**831**	**542**	**210**	**65**	**13**	**1**	..
174	Professors and Teachers of all kinds	772	542	151	65	13	1	..
175	Clerks and servants connected with education	59	..	59	..	..	..	..
	Total Order 49—Letters Arts and Sciences (other than 44) ..	**1,136**	**1,108**	**3**	**22**	..	**3**	..
177	Architects, surveyors, engineers, and their employees (not being State servants)	137	137	..	..	..	..	..
178	Authors, editors, journalists, and photographers	192	192	..	..	..	..	..
179	Artists, sculptors and image-makers	261	261	..	..	..	..	..
180	Scientists (astronomers, botanists, etc.)	7	7	..	..	..	..	..
181	Horoscope casters, astrologers, fortune-tellers, wizards, witches and medium	10	10	..	..	..	..	..
182	Musicians (composers and performers other than military) actors dancers, etc.	481	455	1	22	..	3	..
184	Conjurors, acrobats, recitors, exhibitors of curiosities and wild animals	48	46	2	..	..	..	..
	Total Class D—Miscellaneous	**24,532**	**17,972**	**3,683**	**1,597**	**976**	**301**	**3**
	Total Sub-Class IX—Persons Living on their Income	**867**	**649**	**61**	**5**	..	**152**	..
	Total Order 50—Persons Living Principally on their income ..	**867**	**649**	**61**	**5**	..	**152**	..
185	Proprietors (other than of agricultural land) fund and scholarships holders and pensioners	867	649	61	5	..	152	..

Group No.	Occupation.	Total following occupation.	As principal occupation.		As working dependants.		As subsidiary to other occupation.	
			Males.	Females.	Males.	Females.	Males.	Females.
1		3	4	5	6	7	8	9
	Total Sub-Class X—Domestic Service	3,366	2,874	385	74	..	33	..
	Total Order 51—Domestic Service	3,366	2,874	385	74	..	33	..
186	Private motor-drivers and cleaners	3	3	..	..	..	..	..
187	Other domestic service	3,363	2,871	385	74	..	33	..
	Total Sub-Class XI—Insufficiently Described Occupations	17,474	12,916	2,566	1,516	360	116	..
	Total Order 52—General Terms which do not indicate a definite occupation	17,474	12,916	2,566	1,516	360	116	..
188	Manufacturers, businessmen and contractors otherwise unspecified	1,176	991	26	64	..	95	..
189	Cashiers, accountant, book-keepers, clerks and other employees in unspecified offices ware-houses and shops	464	431	13	7	..	13	..
190	Mechanics otherwise unspecified	84	84	..	..	..	..	..
191	Labourers and workmen otherwise unspecified	15,750	11,410	2,527	1,445	360	8	..
	Total Sub-Class XII—Unproductive	2,825	1,533	671	2	616	..	3
	Total Order 53—Inmates of Jails, Asylums and Alms Houses	727	699	26	2	..	..	..
192	Inmates of jails, asylums and alms houses	727	699	26	2	..	..	..
	Total Order 54—Beggars, Vagrants, Prostitutes	1,482	834	645	..	..	..	3
193	Beggars and vagrants	741	741	..	..	..	..	..
194	Procurers and prostitutes	741	93	645	..	..	..	3
	Total Order 55—Others Unclassified Non-Productive Industries	616	..	..	..	616	..	..
195	Other unclassified non-productive industries	616	..	..	..	616	..	..

CITY TABLE I—GREATER POONA.

Area, Houses, and Population.

(Corresponding to Imperial Table I.)

City.	Area in acres.	Houses.			Houses per acre.	Population.			Persons per acre.
		Occupied.	Unoccupied.	Total.		Males.	Females.	Total.	
1	2	3	4*	5*	6	7	8	9	10
Greater Poona	25,423	57,460	..	..	2·26	138,139	112,048	250,187	9·84
City Municipality	4,083	38,490	..	..	9·43	86,784	76,117	162,901	39·90
Suburban Municipality	3,206	4,196	..	..	1·31	9,530	7,146	16,676	5·20
Poona Cantonment	2,938·58	8,292	..	..	2·83	20,657	15,150	35,807	12·21
Kirkee Cantonment	3,399·86	2,803	..	..	0·82	9,940	6,362	16,302	4·79
Suburbs	11,800·56	3,679	..	..	0·31	11,228	7,273	18,501	1·57

* *Note.*—Figures not available.

RELIGION.

(Corresponding to Imperial Table XVI.)

City.	POPULATION.			HINDU.								
				BRAHMANIC.			ARYA.			BRAHMO.		
	Persons.	Males.	Females.	Persons.	Males.	Females.	Persons.	Males.	Females.	Persons.	Males.	Females.
1	2	3	4	5	6	7	8	9	10	11	12	13
GREATER POONA ..	**250,187**	**138,139**	**112,048**	**198,372**	**107,754**	**90,618**	**27**	**11**	**16**	..	..	..
City Municipality ..	162,901	86,784	76,117	141,997	75,289	66,708	15	6	9	..	..	.
Suburban Municipality ..	16,676	9,530	7,146	12,923	7,417	5,506	12	5	7	..	..	..
Poona Cantonment ..	35,807	20,657	15,150	17,852	10,110	7,742	..	..	..	..	..	..
Kirkee Cantonment ..	16,302	9,940	6,362	10,333	5,818	4,515	..	..	..	..	..	..
Suburbs	18,501	11,228	7,273	15,267	9,120	6,147	..	..	..	..	..	..

City.	HINDU—*concld.*			MUSLIM.								
	TOTAL—HINDUS.			SHIA.			SUNNI.			OTHERS AND SECT UNSPECIFIED.		
	Persons.	Males.	Females.	Persons.	Males.	Females.	Persons.	Males.	Females.	Persons.	Males.	Females.
1	14	15	16	17	18	19	20	21	22	23	24	25
GREATER POONA ..	**198,399**	**107,765**	**90,634**	**2,406**	**1,711**	**695**	**26,206**	**15,320**	**10,886**	**313**	**268**	**45**
City Municipality ..	142,012	75,295	66,717	1,154	860	294	13,925	7,551	6,374	19	10	9
Suburban Municipality ..	12,935	7,422	5,513	91	44	47	1,787	1,085	702	52	25	27
Poona Cantonment ..	17,852	10,110	7,742	710	418	292	6,153	3,752	2,401	18	9	9
Kirkee Cantonment ..	10,333	5,818	4,515	92	53	39	2,907	2,112	795	4	4	..
Suburbs	15,267	9,120	6,147	359	336	23	1,434	820	614	220	220	..

City.	MUSLIM—*concld.*			JAIN.								
	TOTAL—MUSLIMS.			SWETAMBAR.			DIGAMBAR.			OTHERS AND SECT UNSPECIFIED.		
	Persons.	Males.	Females.	Persons.	Males.	Females.	Persons.	Males.	Females.	Persons.	Males.	Females.
1	26	27	28	29	30	31	32	33	34	35	36	37
GREATER POONA ..	**28,925**	**17,299**	**11,626**	**1,114**	**667**	**447**	**133**	**77**	**56**	**1,875**	**1,288**	**587**
City Municipality ..	15,098	8,421	6,677	285	114	171	101	60	41	1,618	1,103	515
Suburban Municipality ..	1,930	1,154	776	53	30	23	3	3	..	40	31	9
Poona Cantonment ..	6,881	4,179	2,702	690	469	221	26	12	14	145	102	43
Kirkee Cantonment ..	3,003	2,169	834	85	53	32	3	2	1	43	27	16
Suburbs	2,013	1,376	637	1	1	..	..	..	..	29	25	4

City.	JAIN—*concld.* TOTAL—JAINS.			ZOROASTRIAN.			CHRISTIAN. ROMAN-CATHOLIC.			CHRISTIAN. ROMO-SYRIAN.		
	Persons.	Males.	Females.	Persons.	Males.	Females.	Persons.	Males.	Females.	Persons.	Males.	Females.
1	38	39	40	41	42	43	44	45	46	47	48	49
GREATER POONA ..	3,122	2,032	1,090	3,267	1,627	1,640	3,987	2,242	1,745	25	11	14
City Municipality ..	2,004	1,277	727	181	107	74	239	123	116	14	6	8
Suburban Municipality ..	96	64	32	380	195	185	500	300	200	5	3	2
Poona Cantonment ..	861	583	278	2,394	1,134	1,260	1,855	1,079	776	2	1	1
Kirkee Cantonment ..	131	82	49	87	53	34	1,074	548	526	..	..	..
Suburbs	30	26	4	225	138	87	319	192	127	4	1	3

City.	CHRISTIAN—*contd.* OTHER SYRIAN.			CHRISTIAN—*contd.* OTHER CHRISTIANS.			CHRISTIAN—*contd.* TOTAL—CHRISTIANS.			TRIBAL.		
	Persons.	Males.	Females.	Persons.	Males.	Females.	Persons.	Males.	Females.	Persons.	Males.	Females.
1	50	51	52	53	54	55	56	57	58	59	60	61
GREATER POONA ..	..	..	..	10,939	6,191	4,748	14,951	8,444	6,507	45	30	15
City Municipality ..	..	..	..	2,711	1,248	1,463	2,964	1,377	1,587	45	30	15
Suburban Municipality ..	..	..	..	768	355	413	1,273	658	615	..	..	..
Poona Cantonment ..	..	..	..	5,743	3,449	2,294	7,600	4,529	3,071	..	..	..
Kirkee Cantonment ..	..	..	..	1,124	792	332	2,198	1,340	858	..	..	..
Suburbs	..	..	..	593	347	246	916	540	376	..	..	..

City.	SIKH.			JEW.			BUDDHIST.			OTHERS.		
	Persons.	Males.	Females.	Persons.	Males.	Females.	Persons.	Males.	Females.	Persons.	Males.	Females.
1	62	63	64	65	66	67	68	69	70	71	72	73
GREATER POONA ..	660	562	98	787	361	426	21	13	8	10	6	4
City Municipality ..	54	37	17	532	233	299	11	7	4	..	..	..
Suburban Municipality ..	17	13	4	45	24	21	..	..	..	..	..	..
Poona Cantonment ..	43	35	8	171	83	88	5	4	1	..	..	..
Kirkee Cantonment ..	534	469	65	11	7	4	..	..	..	5	2	3
Suburbs	12	8	4	28	14	14	5	2	3	5	4	1

AGE, SEX AND CIVIL CONDITION.

(Corresponding to Imperial Table VII.)

A—All Religions.

Age.	Total Population.			Unmarried.			Married.			Widowed.		
	Persons.	Males.	Females.	Persons.	Males.	Females.	Persons.	Males.	Females.	Persons.	Males.	Females.
1	2	3	4	5	6	7	8	9	10	11	12	13
0—1	4,385	2,264	2,121	4,378	2,262	2,116	7	2	5	..	..	..
1—2	4,342	2,202	2,140	4,327	2,100	2,128	13	3	10	2	..	2
2—3	4,286	2,079	2,207	4,268	2,075	2,193	17	4	13	1	..	1
3—4	4,059	1,958	2,101	4,028	1,951	2,077	29	6	23	2	1	1
4—5	3,894	1,929	1,965	3,840	1,915	1,925	48	12	36	6	2	4
Total 0—5 ..	**20,966**	**10,432**	**10,534**	**20,841**	**10,402**	**10,439**	**114**	**27**	**87**	**11**	**3**	**8**
5—10	18,129	9,594	8,535	16,840	9,183	7,657	1,255	405	850	34	6	28
10—15	17,544	9,519	8,025	14,699	8,801	5,898	2,780	708	2,072	65	10	55
15—20	18,015	9,682	8,333	9,477	6,968	2,509	8,227	2,664	5,563	311	50	261
20—25	19,224	10,290	8,934	7,363	5,439	1,924	11,239	4,716	6,523	622	135	487
25—30	15,890	8,765	7,125	2,830	1,612	1,218	11,834	6,880	4,954	1,226	273	953
30—35	14,517	8,318	6,199	1,535	821	714	11,303	7,159	4,144	1,679	338	1,341
35—40	11,021	6,213	4,808	380	307	73	8,332	5,496	2,836	2,309	410	1,899
40—45	8,571	4,577	3,994	230	181	49	5,930	3,986	1,944	2,411	410	2,001
45—50	6,226	3,118	3,108	142	115	27	3,674	2,577	1,097	2,410	426	1,984
50—55	4,754	2,393	2,361	100	80	20	2,615	1,904	711	2,039	409	1,630
55—60	3,120	1,545	1,575	35	27	8	1,487	1,150	337	1,598	368	1,230
60—65	2,467	1,178	1,289	26	19	7	1,067	848	219	1,374	311	1,063
65—70	1,023	513	510	12	8	4	403	336	67	608	169	439
70 and over	1,434	647	787	27	16	11	508	373	135	899	258	641
Total ..	**162,901**	**86,784**	**76,117**	**74,537**	**43,979**	**30,558**	**70,768**	**39,229**	**31,539**	**17,596**	**3,576**	**14,020**

B—Hindu.

Age.	Total Population.			Unmarried.			Married.			Widowed.		
	Persons.	Males.	Females.	Persons.	Males.	Females.	Persons.	Males.	Females.	Persons.	Males.	Females.
0—1	3,871	1,997	1,874	3,869	1,997	1,872	2	..	2	..	..	..
1—2	3,828	1,935	1,893	3,816	1,933	1,883	10	2	8	2	..	2
2—3	3,748	1,807	1,941	3,732	1,805	1,927	15	2	13	1	..	1
3—4	3,547	1,706	1,841	3,520	1,700	1,820	25	5	20	2	1	1
4—5	3,388	1,676	1,712	3,342	1,665	1,677	41	9	32	5	2	3
Total 0—5 ..	**18,382**	**9,121**	**9,261**	**18,279**	**9,100**	**9,179**	**93**	**18**	**75**	**10**	**3**	**7**
5—10	15,753	8,326	7,427	14,557	7,940	6,617	1,166	381	785	30	5	25
10—15	15,279	8,306	6,973	12,709	7,637	5,072	2,509	659	1,850	61	10	51
15—20	15,705	8,493	7,212	8,283	6,084	2,199	7,138	2,364	4,774	284	45	239
20—25	16,705	8,950	7,755	6,448	4,701	1,747	9,701	4,138	5,563	556	111	445
25—30	13,819	7,580	6,239	2,512	1,338	1,174	10,202	6,019	4,183	1,105	223	882
30—35	12,654	7,195	5,459	1,350	666	684	9,787	6,251	3,536	1,517	278	1,239
35—40	9,637	5,368	4,269	301	246	55	7,273	4,773	2,500	2,063	349	1,714
40—45	7,454	3,910	3,544	181	145	36	5,134	3,423	1,711	2,139	342	1,797
45—50	5,427	2,660	2,767	113	94	19	3,161	2,206	955	2,153	360	1,793
50—55	4,181	2,076	2,105	71	59	12	2,282	1,661	621	1,828	356	1,472
55—60	2,716	1,319	1,397	29	23	6	1,277	983	294	1,410	313	1,097
60—65	2,141	997	1,144	18	12	6	910	717	193	1,213	268	945
65—70	898	442	456	8	5	3	344	285	59	546	152	394
70 and over	1,261	552	709	23	14	9	430	303	127	808	235	573
Total ..	**142,012**	**75,295**	**66,717**	**64,882**	**38,064**	**26,818**	**61,407**	**34,181**	**27,226**	**15,723**	**3,050**	**12,673**

C—Muslim.

Age.	Total Population.			Unmarried.			Married.			Widowed.		
	Persons.	Males.	Females.	Persons.	Males.	Females.	Persons.	Males.	Females.	Persons.	Males.	Females.
0—1	383	200	183	378	198	180	5	2	3	..	..	..
1—2	376	198	178	373	197	176	3	1	2	..	..	..
2—3	394	205	189	392	203	189	2	2	..	..	..	..
3—4	381	192	189	378	191	187	3	1	2	..	..	..
4—5	376	187	189	370	186	184	5	1	4	1	..	1
Total 0—5 ..	**1,910**	**982**	**928**	**1,891**	**975**	**916**	**18**	**7**	**11**	**1**	**..**	**1**
5—10	1,711	925	786	1,634	907	727	74	17	57	3	1	2
10—15	1,563	847	716	1,336	809	527	223	38	185	4	..	4
15—20	1,547	796	751	697	578	119	831	214	617	19	4	15
20—25	1,765	946	819	555	504	51	1,161	424	737	49	18	31
25—30	1,534	888	646	210	196	14	1,234	653	581	90	39	51
30—35	1,393	855	538	123	112	11	1,150	696	454	120	47	73
35—40	1,043	647	396	55	48	7	792	546	246	196	53	143
40—45	824	497	327	33	29	4	578	413	165	213	55	158
45—50	594	347	247	15	14	1	377	280	97	202	53	149
50—55	427	240	187	14	12	2	248	184	64	165	44	121
55—60	299	173	126	2	2	..	156	128	28	141	43	98
60—65	244	140	104	1	1	..	120	103	17	123	36	87
65—70	97	57	40	..	..	..	47	42	5	50	15	35
70 and over	147	81	66	..	..	..	67	61	6	80	20	60
Total ..	**15,098**	**8,421**	**6,677**	**6,566**	**4,187**	**2,379**	**7,076**	**3,806**	**3,270**	**1,456**	**438**	**1,028**

MO-II Bk Ra Cs 3—66

AGE, SEX AND CIVIL CONDITION.

(Corresponding to Imperial Table VII.)

A—All Religions.

Age.	Total Population.			Unmarried.			Married.			Widowed.		
	Persons.	Males.	Females.	Persons.	Males.	Females.	Persons.	Males.	Females.	Persons.	Males.	Females.
1	2	3	4	5	6	7	8	9	10	11	12	13
0—1	462	234	228	461	233	228	1	1	..	..	..	..
1—2	405	205	200	405	205	200	..	..	..	..	..	..
2—3	420	206	214	420	206	214	..	..	..	..	..	..
3—4	391	197	194	388	196	192	3	1	2	..	..	..
4—5	367	186	181	358	182	176	9	4	5	..	..	..
Total 0—5 ..	2,045	1,028	1,017	2,032	1,022	1,010	13	6	7	..	..	..
5—10	1,692	871	821	1,488	812	676	199	58	141	5	1	4
10—15	1,612	840	772	1,258	772	486	346	66	280	8	2	6
15—20	1,805	1,000	805	787	644	143	982	345	637	36	11	25
20—25	2,147	1,243	904	613	522	91	1,469	697	772	65	24	41
25—30	1,862	1,169	693	221	191	30	1,527	929	598	114	49	65
30—35	1,666	1,084	582	118	102	16	1,401	929	472	147	53	94
35—40	1,264	819	445	50	39	11	1,024	730	294	190	50	140
40—45	987	639	348	37	27	10	742	550	192	208	62	146
45—50	683	426	257	20	14	6	466	359	107	197	53	144
50—55	452	256	196	13	7	6	293	223	70	146	26	120
55—60	255	127	128	8	6	2	132	106	26	115	15	100
60—65	196	93	103	4	2	2	91	77	14	101	14	87
65—70	83	42	41	1	1	..	40	31	9	42	10	32
70 and over	119	56	63	2	..	2	36	28	8	81	28	53
Total ..	16,868	9,693	7,175	6,652	4,161	2,491	8,761	5,134	3,627	1,455	398	1,057

B—Hindu.

Age.	Total Population.			Unmarried.			Married.			Widowed.		
	Persons.	Males.	Females.	Persons.	Males.	Females.	Persons.	Males.	Females.	Persons.	Males.	Females.
0—1	377	190	187	377	190	187	..	..	..	..	..	..
1—2	331	168	163	331	168	163	..	..	..	..	..	..
2—3	343	168	175	343	168	175	..	..	..	..	..	..
3—4	320	162	158	317	161	156	3	1	2	..	..	..
4—5	289	152	137	280	148	132	9	4	5	..	..	..
Total 0—5 ..	1,660	840	820	1,648	835	813	12	5	7	..	..	..
5—10	1,304	685	619	1,144	663	481	155	21	134	5	1	4
10—15	1,204	635	569	916	612	304	281	22	259	7	1	6
15—20	1,368	756	612	491	452	39	849	296	553	28	8	20
20—25	1,672	967	705	372	347	25	1,247	601	646	53	19	34
25—30	1,473	926	547	121	113	8	1,258	774	484	94	39	55
30—35	1,335	868	467	59	58	1	1,150	765	385	126	45	81
35—40	992	647	345	19	19	..	812	588	224	161	40	121
40—45	750	495	255	14	14	..	562	429	133	174	52	122
45—50	508	321	187	6	5	1	350	273	77	152	43	109
50—55	327	179	148	1	..	1	215	160	55	111	19	92
55—60	180	80	100	1	..	1	87	68	19	92	12	80
60—65	137	60	77	1	..	1	60	51	9	76	9	67
65—70	54	24	30	..	..	..	23	19	4	31	5	26
70 and over	81	37	44	..	..	..	30	23	7	51	14	37
Total ..	13,045	7,520	5,525	4,793	3,118	1,675	7,091	4,095	2,996	1,161	307	854

C—Muslim.

Age.	Total Population.			Unmarried.			Married.			Widowed.		
	Persons.	Males.	Females.	Persons.	Males.	Females.	Persons.	Males.	Females.	Persons.	Males.	Females.
0—1	41	22	19	40	21	19	1	1	..	..	..	..
1—2	32	17	15	32	17	15	..	..	..	..	..	..
2—3	38	19	19	38	19	19	..	..	..	..	..	..
3—4	38	17	21	38	17	21	..	..	..	..	..	..
4—5	39	17	22	39	17	22	..	..	..	..	..	..
Total 0—5 ..	188	92	96	187	91	96	1	1	..	..	..	..
5—10	213	105	108	207	105	102	6	..	6	..	..	..
10—15	222	119	103	204	118	86	18	1	17	..	..	..
15—20	223	140	83	133	108	25	85	30	55	5	2	3
20—25	250	158	92	100	90	10	142	64	78	8	4	4
25—30	207	138	69	38	35	3	157	95	62	12	8	4
30—35	175	125	50	21	20	1	141	98	43	13	7	6
35—40	136	93	43	9	9	..	110	78	32	17	6	11
40—45	107	71	36	5	5	..	82	59	23	20	7	13
45—50	80	49	31	2	2	..	52	39	13	26	8	18
50—55	61	37	24	2	1	1	39	31	8	20	5	15
55—60	39	24	15	1	1	..	23	21	2	15	2	13
60—65	30	16	14	..	..	..	14	13	1	16	3	13
65—70	11	6	5	..	..	..	4	3	1	7	3	4
70 and over	19	9	10	..	..	..	3	2	1	16	7	9
Total ..	1,961	1,182	779	909	585	324	877	535	342	175	62	113

Age, Sex and Civil Condition.

(Corresponding to Imperial Table VII.)

A—All Religions.

Age.	Total Population.			Unmarried.			Married.			Widowed.		
	Persons.	Males.	Females.	Persons.	Males.	Females.	Persons.	Males.	Females.	Persons.	Males.	Females.
1	2	3	4	5	6	7	8	9	10	11	12	13
0—1	842	443	399	839	441	398	3	2	1	..	..	..
1—2	859	433	426	850	428	422	9	5	4	..	..	..
2—3	933	465	468	924	463	461	8	2	6	..	..	..
3—4	854	419	435	845	415	430	9	4	5	1	..	1
4—5	880	389	491	789	377	412	89	12	77	2	..	2
Total 0—5 ..	4,368	2,149	2,219	4,247	2,124	2,123	118	25	93	3	..	3
5—10 ..	3,792	1,882	1,910	3,479	1,826	1,653	306	54	252	7	2	5
10—15	3,806	1,844	1,962	3,032	1,754	1,278	768	89	679	6	1	5
15—20	4,019	2,376	1,643	2,201	1,734	467	1,768	627	1,141	50	15	35
20—25	4,459	2,915	1,544	2,030	1,753	277	2,333	1,133	1,200	96	29	67
25—30	3,833	2,544	1,289	941	843	98	2,714	1,642	1,072	178	59	119
30—35	3,137	2,103	1,034	469	394	75	2,428	1,630	798	240	79	161
35—40	2,258	1,392	866	175	119	56	1,748	1,185	563	335	88	247
40—45	1,811	1,068	743	126	74	52	1,320	916	404	365	78	287
45—50	1,337	758	579	75	43	32	868	634	234	394	81	313
50—55	1,040	594	446	51	33	18	632	479	153	357	82	275
55—60	762	418	344	33	19	14	405	317	88	324	82	242
60—65	580	318	262	20	9	11	286	235	51	274	74	200
65—70	262	129	133	14	7	7	119	85	34	129	37	92
70 and over	343	167	176	21	16	5	125	104	21	197	47	150
Total ..	35,807	20,657	15,150	16,914	10,748	6,166	15,938	9,155	6,783	2,955	754	2,201

B—Hindu.

Age.	Persons.	Males.	Females.	Persons.	Males.	Females.	Persons.	Males.	Females.	Persons.	Males.	Females.
0—1	450	239	211	448	238	210	2	1	1	..	..	..
1—2	463	239	224	458	238	220	5	1	4	..	..	..
2—3	517	266	251	512	266	246	4	..	4	1	..	1
3—4	477	239	238	474	238	236	3	1	2	..	..	..
4—5	504	206	298	423	200	223	79	6	73	2	..	2
Total 0—5 ..	2,411	1,189	1,222	2,315	1,180	1,135	93	9	84	3	..	3
5—10	1,981	953	1,028	1,721	921	800	256	31	225	4	1	3
10—15	2,024	914	1,110	1,356	855	501	663	58	605	5	1	4
15—20	1,975	1,118	857	704	646	58	1,237	464	773	34	8	26
20—25	2,088	1,348	740	547	517	30	1,479	811	668	62	20	42
25—30	1,864	1,234	630	201	185	16	1,553	1,013	540	110	36	74
30—35	1,554	1,071	483	114	101	13	1,293	929	364	147	41	106
35—40	1,114	701	413	37	30	7	868	624	244	209	47	162
40—45	860	523	337	21	14	7	618	473	145	221	36	185
45—50	644	353	291	15	8	7	404	311	93	225	34	191
50—55	477	267	210	9	7	2	269	219	50	199	41	158
55—60	350	181	169	6	5	1	170	135	35	174	41	133
60—65	257	132	125	1	..	1	113	97	16	143	35	108
65—70	115	55	60	2	1	1	54	37	17	59	17	42
70 and over	138	71	67	10	9	1	51	50	1	77	12	65
Total ..	17,852	10,110	7,742	7,059	4,479	2,580	9,121	5,261	3,860	1,672	370	1,302

C—Muslim.

Age.	Persons.	Males.	Females.	Persons.	Males.	Females.	Persons.	Males.	Females.	Persons.	Males.	Females.
0—1	169	86	83	169	86	83	..	..	..	..	..	..
1—2	169	79	90	167	77	90	2	2	..	..	..	..
2—3	180	83	97	177	81	96	3	2	1	..	..	..
3—4	158	75	83	154	73	81	4	2	2	..	..	..
4—5	153	74	79	149	72	77	4	2	2	..	..	..
Total 0—5 ..	829	397	432	816	389	427	13	8	5	..	..	..
5 10	716	394	322	691	385	306	24	9	15	1	..	1
10—15	670	388	282	603	372	231	66	16	50	1	..	1
15—20	709	422	287	382	314	68	318	103	215	9	5	4
20—25	846	516	330	337	303	34	487	206	281	22	7	15
25—30	776	524	252	165	158	7	564	346	218	47	20	27
30—35	672	480	192	97	93	4	518	358	160	57	29	28
35—40	464	312	152	43	40	3	351	247	104	70	25	45
40—45	362	227	135	30	25	5	249	174	75	83	28	55
45—50	262	169	93	13	11	2	160	125	35	80	33	56
50—55	207	130	77	7	6	1	124	98	26	76	26	50
55—60	151	92	59	5	3	2	80	67	13	66	22	44
60—65	116	74	42	2	2	..	59	52	7	55	20	35
65—70	45	26	19	2	1	1	18	14	4	25	11	14
70 and over	56	28	28	1	..	1	13	13	..	42	15	27
Total ..	6,881	4,179	2,702	3,194	2,102	1,092	3,044	1,836	1,208	643	241	402

AGE, SEX AND CIVIL CONDITION.

(Corresponding to Imperial Table VII.)

A—All Religions.

Age.	Total Population.			Unmarried.			Married.			Widowed.		
	Persons.	Males.	Females.	Persons.	Males.	Females.	Persons.	Males.	Females.	Persons.	Males.	Females.
1	2	3	4	5	6	7	8	9	10	11	12	13
0—1	440	224	216	440	224	216	..	..	..	..	..	..
1—2	440	220	220	440	220	220	..	..	..	..	..	..
2—3	432	220	212	420	218	211	3	2	1	..	..	..
3—4	402	202	200	396	201	195	6	1	5	..	..	..
4—5	404	185	219	373	182	191	29	3	26	2	..	2
Total 0—5 ..	2,118	1,051	1,067	2,078	1,045	1,033	38	6	32	2	..	2
5—10	1,670	804	866	1,481	787	694	186	15	171	3	2	1
10—15	1,518	741	777	1,157	704	453	358	37	321	3	..	3
15—20	1,900	1,240	660	881	801	80	992	432	560	27	7	20
20—25	2,254	1,549	705	848	801	47	1,352	731	621	54	17	37
25—30	1,883	1,346	537	316	303	13	1,476	1,004	472	91	39	52
30—35	1,617	1,170	447	164	149	15	1,336	974	362	117	47	70
35—40	1,027	674	353	48	42	6	823	586	237	156	46	110
40—45	771	486	285	21	18	3	588	424	164	162	44	118
45—50	535	340	195	13	12	1	372	285	87	150	43	107
50—55	377	231	146	8	8	..	241	188	53	128	35	93
55—60	257	130	127	4	3	1	129	102	27	124	25	99
60—65	206	100	106	2	1	1	93	78	15	111	21	90
65—70	84	41	43	..	..	..	34	30	4	50	11	39
70 and over	85	37	48	..	..	..	23	23	..	62	14	48
Total ..	16,302	9,940	6,362	7,021	4,674	2,347	8,041	4,915	3,126	1,240	351	889

B—Hindu.

Age.	Total Population.			Unmarried.			Married.			Widowed.		
	Persons.	Males.	Females.	Persons.	Males.	Females.	Persons.	Males.	Females.	Persons.	Males.	Females.
0—1	309	158	151	309	158	151	..	..	..	..	..	..
1—2	309	157	152	309	157	152	..	..	..	..	..	..
2—3	296	150	146	296	150	146	..	..	..	..	..	..
3—4	281	142	139	281	142	139	..	..	..	..	..	..
4—5	268	134	134	262	131	131	4	3	1	2	..	2
Total 0—5 ..	1,463	741	722	1,457	738	719	4	3	1	2	..	2
5—10	1,132	586	546	1,054	575	479	76	10	66	2	1	1
10—15	1,032	531	501	806	502	304	223	29	194	3	..	3
15—20	1,141	657	484	425	387	38	695	266	429	21	4	17
20—25	1,294	762	532	334	315	19	919	436	483	41	11	30
25—30	1,063	652	411	94	92	2	899	533	366	70	27	43
30—35	937	600	337	57	54	3	792	516	276	88	30	58
35—40	660	394	266	23	20	3	520	345	175	117	29	88
40—45	519	304	215	11	10	1	382	263	119	126	31	95
45—50	381	230	151	5	5	..	258	194	64	118	31	87
50—55	270	160	110	5	5	..	166	129	37	99	26	73
55—60	183	86	97	1	1	..	87	67	20	95	18	77
60—65	147	66	81	1	..	1	63	52	11	83	14	69
65—70	57	28	29	..	..	..	24	21	3	33	7	26
70 and over	54	21	33	..	..	..	16	16	..	38	5	33
Total ..	10,333	5,818	4,515	4,273	2,704	1,569	5,124	2,880	2,244	936	234	702

C—Muslim.

Age.	Total Population.			Unmarried.			Married.			Widowed.		
	Persons.	Males.	Females.	Persons.	Males.	Females.	Persons.	Males.	Females.	Persons.	Males.	Females.
0—1	60	23	37	60	23	37	..	..	..	..	..	..
1—2	58	25	33	58	25	33	..	..	..	..	..	..
2—3	61	31	30	58	29	29	3	2	1	..	..	..
3—4	58	28	30	52	27	25	6	1	5	..	..	..
4—5	70	23	47	45	23	22	25	..	25	..	..	..
Total 0—5 ..	307	130	177	273	127	146	34	3	31	..	..	..
5—10	289	96	193	181	93	88	108	3	105	..	..	..
10—15	267	91	176	143	84	59	124	7	117	..	..	..
15—20	393	321	72	210	201	9	177	117	60	6	3	3
20—25	483	430	53	227	219	8	247	207	40	9	4	5
25—30	421	381	40	82	72	10	326	302	24	13	7	6
30—35	369	337	32	46	36	10	304	290	14	19	11	8
35—40	179	159	20	9	9	..	147	138	9	23	12	11
40—45	105	88	17	2	2	..	85	79	6	18	7	11
45—50	65	55	10	2	2	..	48	47	1	15	6	9
50—55	44	36	8	1	1	..	29	29	..	14	6	8
55—60	33	20	13	2	1	1	15	15	..	16	4	12
60—65	26	15	11	..	..	..	11	11	..	15	4	11
65—70	9	4	5	..	..	..	2	2	..	7	2	5
70 and over	13	6	7	..	..	..	2	2	..	11	4	7
Total ..	3,003	3,169	834	1,178	847	331	1,659	1,252	407	166	70	96

AGE, SEX AND CIVIL CONDITION.

(Corresponding to Imperial Table VII.)

A—All Religions.

Age.	Total Population.			Unmarried.			Married.			Widowed.		
	Persons.	Males.	Females.	Persons.	Males.	Females.	Persons.	Males.	Females.	Persons.	Males.	Females.
1	2	3	4	5	6	7	8	9	10	11	12	13
0—1	592	289	303	572	278	294	20	11	9	..	..	..
1—2	551	272	279	543	268	275	7	4	3	1	..	1
2—3	591	281	310	582	277	305	8	3	5	1	1	..
3—4	553	256	297	539	251	288	11	3	8	3	2	1
4—5	540	264	276	519	257	262	17	4	13	4	3	1
Total 0—5 ..	**2,827**	**1,362**	**1,465**	**2,755**	**1,331**	**1,424**	**63**	**25**	**38**	**9**	**6**	**3**
5—10	2,388	1,218	1,170	2,081	1,152	920	293	57	236	14	9	5
10—15	2,261	1,192	1,069	1,667	1,045	622	562	125	437	32	22	10
15—20	2,695	1,659	1,036	1,143	1,005	138	1,471	604	867	81	50	31
20—25	3,117	1,985	1,132	1,000	938	62	2,000	988	1,012	117	59	58
25—30	2,698	1,746	952	434	412	22	2,086	1,262	824	178	72	106
30—35	2,398	1,578	820	255	245	10	1,917	1,253	664	226	80	146
35—40	1,718	1,111	607	109	102	7	1,335	936	399	274	73	201
40—45	1,357	854	503	87	79	8	987	713	274	283	62	221
45—50	970	584	386	50	46	4	647	487	160	273	51	222
50—55	719	431	288	30	29	1	453	356	97	236	46	190
55—60	421	216	205	10	9	1	231	187	44	180	20	160
60—65	301	155	146	6	6	...	151	127	24	144	22	122
65—70	116	60	56	5	4	1	62	54	8	49	2	47
70 and over	139	66	73	9	7	2	61	56	5	69	3	66
Total ..	**24,125**	**14,217**	**9,908**	**9,641**	**6,410**	**3,231**	**12,319**	**7,230**	**5,089**	**2,165**	**577**	**1,588**

B—Hindu.

Age.	Total Population.			Unmarried.			Married.			Widowed.		
	Persons.	Males.	Females.	Persons.	Males.	Females.	Persons.	Males.	Females.	Persons.	Males.	Females.
0—1	525	254	271	508	246	262	17	8	9	..	..	..
1—2	485	238	247	477	234	243	7	4	3	1	..	1
2—3	524	249	275	514	245	269	8	3	5	2	1	1
3—4	492	231	261	479	226	253	11	3	8	2	2	..
4—5	479	234	245	459	227	232	16	4	12	4	3	1
Total 0—5 ..	**2,505**	**1,206**	**1,299**	**2,437**	**1,178**	**1,259**	**59**	**22**	**37**	**9**	**6**	**3**
5—10	2,113	1,075	1,038	1,821	1,014	807	279	52	227	13	9	4
10—15	1,965	1,042	923	1,413	905	508	523	116	407	29	21	8
15—20	2,297	1,436	861	908	828	80	1,313	561	752	76	47	29
20—25	2,663	1,698	965	775	738	37	1,780	904	876	108	56	52
25—30	2,266	1,429	837	271	259	12	1,842	1,111	731	153	59	94
30—35	2,028	1,292	736	151	143	8	1,681	1,087	594	196	62	134
35—40	1,447	908	539	56	49	7	1,144	800	344	247	59	188
40—45	1,141	689	452	42	35	7	840	605	235	259	49	210
45—50	817	464	353	26	23	3	546	405	141	245	36	209
50—55	596	335	261	16	15	1	375	288	87	205	32	173
55—60	357	179	178	6	5	1	197	159	38	154	15	139
60—65	260	132	128	3	3	..	132	110	22	125	19	106
65—70	96	48	48	3	2	1	54	46	8	39	..	39
70 and over	118	51	67	7	5	2	51	46	5	60	..	60
Total ..	**20,669**	**11,984**	**8,685**	**7,935**	**5,202**	**2,733**	**10,816**	**6,312**	**4,504**	**1,918**	**470**	**1,448**

C—Muslim.

Age.	Total Population.			Unmarried.			Married.			Widowed.		
	Persons.	Males.	Females.	Persons.	Males.	Females.	Persons.	Males.	Females.	Persons.	Males.	Females.
0—1	37	19	18	36	18	18	1	1	..	..	..	..
1—2	37	19	18	37	19	18	..	..	..	..	..	..
2—3	41	19	22	41	19	22	..	..	..	..	..	..
3—4	40	18	22	40	18	22	..	..	..	..	..	..
4—5	38	17	21	37	17	20	1	..	1	..	..	..
Total 0—5 ..	**193**	**92**	**101**	**191**	**91**	**100**	**2**	**1**	**1**	..	..	..
5—10	181	92	89	108	88	80	12	4	8	1	..	1
10—15	191	106	85	158	99	59	30	6	24	3	1	2
15—20	220	145	75	123	113	10	95	31	64	2	1	1
20—25	272	192	80	130	126	4	134	64	70	8	2	6
25—30	293	226	67	100	96	4	172	119	53	21	11	10
30—35	256	201	55	58	56	2	175	130	45	23	15	8
35—40	170	131	39	17	17	..	184	102	32	19	12	7
40—45	133	102	31	15	14	1	101	78	23	17	10	7
45—50	96	76	20	9	9	..	62	53	9	25	14	11
50—55	75	55	20	4	4	..	46	40	6	25	11	14
55—60	43	23	20	2	2	..	21	18	3	20	3	17
60—65	30	14	16	..	..	..	13	11	2	17	3	14
65—70	12	5	7	..	..	..	3	3	..	9	2	7
70 and over	15	9	6	..	..	..	6	6	..	9	3	6
Total ..	**2,180**	**1,469**	**711**	**975**	**715**	**260**	**1,006**	**666**	**340**	**199**	**88**	**111**

CITY TABLE V—PART I—GREATER POONA.

LITERACY BY RELIGION AND AGE.

(Corresponding to Imperial Table XIII.)

City Municipality.

Religion and Age.	POPULATION.											
	TOTAL.			LITERATE.			ILLITERATE.			LITERATE IN ENGLISH.		
	Persons.	Males.	Females.	Persons.	Males.	Females.	Persons.	Males.	Females.	Persons.	Males.	Females.
1	2	3	4	5	6	7	8	9	10	11	12	13
(A)—All Religions Total	**162,901**	**86,784**	**76,117**	**51,826**	**39,609**	**12,217**	**111,075**	**47,175**	**63,900**	**19,507**	**16,844**	**2,663**
0—10	39,095	20,026	19,069	3,701	2,703	1,000	35,392	17,323	18,069	649	472	177
10—15	17,544	9,519	8,025	6,709	4,340	2,369	10,835	5,179	5,656	1,821	1,372	449
15—20	18,015	9,682	8,333	8,705	6,221	2,484	9,310	3,461	5,849	4,212	3,532	680
20 and over	88,247	47,557	40,690	32,709	26,345	6,364	55,538	21,212	34,326	12,825	11,468	1,357
(B)—Hindu Total	**142,012**	**75,295**	**66,717**	**46,184**	**34,957**	**11,227**	**95,828**	**40,338**	**55,490**	**17,562**	**15,395**	**2,187**
0—10	34,135	17,447	16,688	3,397	2,411	986	30,738	15,036	15,702	564	432	132
10—15	15,279	8,306	6,973	5,961	3,856	2,105	9,318	4,450	4,868	1,646	1,256	390
15—20	15,705	8,493	7,212	7,840	5,665	2,175	7,865	2,828	5,037	3,907	3,309	598
20 and over	76,893	41,049	35,844	28,986	23,025	5,961	47,907	18,024	29,883	11,465	10,398	1,067
(C)—Muslim Total	**15,098**	**8,421**	**6,677**	**3,238**	**2,878**	**360**	**11,860**	**5,543**	**6,317**	**704**	**661**	**43**
0—10	3,621	1,907	1,714	236	191	45	3,385	1,716	1,669	27	13	14
10—15	1,563	847	716	311	253	58	1,252	594	658	43	36	7
15—20	1,547	796	751	324	267	57	1,223	529	694	89	78	11
20 and over	8,367	4,871	3,496	2,367	2,167	200	6,000	2,704	3,296	545	534	11
(D)—Jain Total	**2,004**	**1,277**	**727**	**1,055**	**942**	**113**	**949**	**335**	**614**	**195**	**192**	**3**
0—10	372	217	155	62	47	15	310	170	140	7	6	1
10—15	202	125	77	138	114	24	64	11	53	44	43	1
15—20	284	183	101	170	144	26	114	39	75	56	56	..
20 and over	1,146	752	394	685	637	48	461	115	346	88	87	1
(E)—Christian Total	**2,964**	**1,377**	**1,587**	**905**	**569**	**336**	**2,059**	**808**	**1,251**	**681**	**396**	**285**
0—10	777	375	402	40	28	12	737	347	390	29	10	19
10—15	398	192	206	126	84	142	272	108	164	48	17	31
15—20	389	158	231	296	102	194	93	56	37	103	55	48
20 and over	1,400	652	748	443	355	88	957	297	600	501	314	187
(F)—Zoroastrian Total	**181**	**107**	**74**	**151**	**91**	**60**	**30**	**16**	**14**	**123**	**78**	**45**
0—10	23	9	14	9	3	6	14	6	8	3	1	2
10—15	12	7	5	9	5	4	3	2	1	7	4	3
15—20	24	16	8	22	15	7	2	1	1	19	14	5
20 and over	122	75	47	111	68	43	11	7	4	94	59	35
(G) Tribals Total	**45**	**30**	**15**	..	..	..	**45**	**30**	**15**	..	..	..
0—10	9	5	4	..	..	..	9	5	4	..	..	..
10—15	6	3	3	..	..	..	6	3	3	..	..	..
15—20	7	6	1	..	..	..	7	6	1	..	..	..
20 and over	23	16	7	..	..	..	23	16	7	..	..	..
(H)—Other Religions Total	**597**	**277**	**320**	**293**	**172**	**121**	**304**	**105**	**199**	**222**	**122**	**100**
0—10	158	6	92	59	23	36	99	43	56	19	10	9
10—15	84	39	45	64	28	36	20	11	9	33	16	17
15—20	59	30	29	53	28	25	6	2	4	38	20	18
20 and over	296	142	154	117	117	24	179	49	130	132	76	56

Suburban Municipality.

Religion and Age.	POPULATION. Total. Persons.	Total. Males.	Total. Females.	Literate. Persons.	Literate. Males.	Literate. Females.	Illiterate. Persons.	Illiterate. Males.	Illiterate. Females.	Literate in English. Persons.	Literate in English. Males.	Literate in English. Females.
1	2	3	4	5	6	7	8	9	10	11	12	13
(A)—All Religions Total ..	**16,868**	**9,693**	**7,175**	**4,035**	**3,134**	**901**	**12,833**	**6,559**	**6,274**	**1,761**	**1,223**	**538**
0—10	3,737	1,899	1,838	217	123	94	3,520	1,776	1,744	88	46	42
10—15	1,612	840	772	324	194	130	1,288	646	642	128	74	54
15—20	1,805	1,000	805	571	419	152	1,234	581	653	328	237	91
20 and over	9,714	5,954	3,760	2,923	2,398	525	6,791	3,556	3,235	1,217	866	351
(B)—Hindu Total ..	**13,045**	**7,520**	**5,525**	**2,370**	**2,143**	**227**	**10,675**	**5,377**	**5,298**	**771**	**680**	**91**
0—10	2,964	1,525	1,439	70	51	19	2,894	1,474	1,420	12	7	5
10—15	1,204	635	569	125	97	28	1,079	538	541	28	20	8
15—20	1,368	756	612	316	270	46	1,052	486	566	157	136	21
20 and over	7,509	4,604	2,905	1,859	1,725	134	5,650	2,879	2,771	574	517	57
(C)—Muslim Total ..	**1,961**	**1,182**	**779**	**566**	**424**	**142**	**1,395**	**758**	**637**	**223**	**183**	**40**
0—10	401	197	204	43	22	21	358	175	183	12	8	4
10—15	222	119	103	70	38	32	152	81	71	30	17	13
15—20	223	140	83	90	66	24	133	74	59	54	42	12
20 and over	1,115	726	389	363	298	65	752	428	324	127	116	11
(D)—Jain Total ..	**113**	**77**	**36**	**66**	**59**	**7**	**47**	**18**	**29**	**15**	**15**	..
0—10	19	9	10	4	3	1	15	6	9	..	..	..
10—15	15	11	4	6	5	1	9	6	3	1	1	..
15—20	14	11	3	8	8	..	6	3	3	4	4	..
20 and over	65	46	19	48	43	5	17	3	14	10	10	..
(E)—Christian Total ..	**1,302**	**679**	**623**	**690**	**332**	**358**	**612**	**347**	**265**	**461**	**204**	**257**
0—10	280	135	145	74	37	37	206	98	108	42	23	19
10—15	128	55	73	88	36	52	40	19	21	40	22	18
15—20	148	64	84	108	48	60	40	16	24	68	30	38
20 and over	746	425	321	420	211	209	326	214	112	311	129	182
(F)—Zoroastrian Total ..	**384**	**197**	**187**	**301**	**149**	**152**	**83**	**48**	**35**	**268**	**128**	**140**
0—10	62	28	34	23	9	14	39	19	20	20	7	13
10—15	36	16	20	30	15	15	6	1	5	26	12	14
15—20	44	25	19	43	24	19	1	1	..	40	22	18
20 and over	242	128	114	205	101	104	37	27	10	182	87	95
(G)—Other Religions Total ..	**63**	**38**	**25**	**42**	**27**	**15**	**21**	**11**	**10**	**23**	**13**	**10**
0—10	11	5	6	3	1	2	8	4	4	2	1	1
10—15	7	4	3	5	3	2	2	1	1	3	2	1
15—20	8	4	4	6	3	3	2	1	1	5	3	2
20 and over	37	25	12	28	20	8	9	5	4	13	7	6

Poona Cantonment.

Religion and Age.	Total. Persons.	Total. Males.	Total. Females.	Literate. Persons.	Literate. Males.	Literate. Females.	Illiterate. Persons.	Illiterate. Males.	Illiterate. Females.	Literate in English. Persons.	Literate in English. Males.	Literate in English. Females.
(A)—All Religions Total ..	**35,807**	**20,657**	**15,150**	**11,495**	**8,440**	**3,055**	**24,312**	**12,217**	**12,095**	**6,574**	**4,518**	**2,056**
0—10	8,160	4,031	4,129	690	381	309	7,470	3,650	3,820	363	191	172
10—15	3,806	1,844	1,962	1,044	590	454	2,762	1,254	1,508	555	297	258
15—20	4,019	2,376	1,643	1,508	1,293	215	2,511	1,083	1,428	1,051	748	303
20 and over	19,822	12,406	7,416	8,253	6,176	2,077	11,569	6,230	5,339	4,605	3,282	1,323
(B)—Hindu Total ..	**17,852**	**10,110**	**7,742**	**4,547**	**3,615**	**935**	**13,305**	**6,495**	**6,810**	**539**	**496**	**43**
0—10	4,392	2,142	2,250	130	95	35	4,262	2,047	2,215	21	18	3
10—15	2,024	914	1,110	235	163	68	1,789	747	1,042	43	37	6
15—20	1,975	1,118	857	427	408	19	1,548	710	838	97	89	8
20 and over	9,461	5,936	3,525	3,755	2,945	810	5,706	2,991	2,715	378	352	26
(C)—Muslim Total ..	**6,881**	**4,179**	**2,702**	**1,843**	**1,510**	**333**	**5,038**	**2,669**	**2,369**	**545**	**496**	**49**
0—10	1,545	791	754	110	75	35	1,435	716	719	20	15	5
10—15	670	388	282	172	121	51	498	267	231	47	38	9
15—20	709	422	287	264	203	61	445	219	226	87	77	10
20 and over	3,957	2,578	1,379	1,297	1,111	186	2,660	1,467	1,193	391	366	25

Poona Cantonment—contd.

Religion and Age.	POPULATION.											
	TOTAL.			LITERATE.			ILLITERATE.			LITERATE IN ENGLISH.		
	Persons.	Males.	Females.	Persons.	Males.	Females.	Persons.	Males.	Females.	Persons.	Males.	Females.
1	2	3	4	5	6	7	8	9	10	11	12	13
(D)—Jain Total ..	**861**	**583**	**278**	**489**	**433**	**56**	**372**	**150**	**222**	**65**	**64**	**1**
0—10	164	94	70	24	17	7	140	77	63	2	2	..
10—15	89	61	28	49	38	11	40	23	17	7	7	..
15—20	123	86	37	81	68	13	42	18	24	13	13	..
20 and over	485	342	143	335	310	25	150	32	118	43	42	1
(E)—Christian Total ..	**7,600**	**4,529**	**3,071**	**3,229**	**2,138**	**1,091**	**4,371**	**2,391**	**1,980**	**4,024**	**2,704**	**1,320**
0—10	1,499	728	771	263	102	161	1,236	626	610	227	112	115
10—15	716	341	375	380	172	208	336	169	167	310	154	156
15—20	952	628	324	597	503	94	355	125	230	659	479	180
20 and over	4,433	2,832	1,601	1,989	1,361	628	244	1,471	978	2,828	1,959	809
(F)—Zoroastrian Total ..	**2,394**	**1,134**	**1,260**	**1,231**	**644**	**587**	**1,163**	**490**	**673**	**1,299**	**698**	**601**
0—10	502	245	257	132	67	65	370	178	192	80	40	40
10—15	278	127	151	193	86	107	85	41	44	138	56	82
15—20	236	108	128	118	98	20	118	10	108	181	81	100
20 and over	1,378	654	724	788	393	395	590	261	329	894	521	373
(G)—Other Religions Total ..	**219**	**122**	**97**	**156**	**100**	**56**	**63**	**22**	**41**	**102**	**60**	**42**
0—10	58	31	27	31	25	6	27	6	21	7	4	3
10—15	29	13	16	15	6	9	14	7	7	10	5	5
15—20	24	14	10	21	13	8	3	1	2	14	9	5
20 and over	108	64	44	89	56	33	19	8	11	71	42	29

Kirkee Cantonment.

1	2	3	4	5	6	7	8	9	10	11	12	13
(A)—All Religions Total ..	**16,302**	**9,940**	**6,362**	**2,926**	**2,415**	**511**	**13,394**	**7,525**	**5,869**	**1,220**	**1,025**	**195**
0—10	3,788	1,855	1,933	66	50	16	3,722	1,805	1,917	24	17	7
10—15	1,518	741	777	121	83	38	1,397	658	739	37	25	12
15—20	1,900	1,240	660	476	407	69	1,424	833	591	167	149	18
20 and over	9,096	6,104	2,992	2,263	1,875	388	6,851	4,229	2,622	992	834	158
(B)—Hindu Total ..	**10,333**	**5,818**	**4,515**	**1,109**	**1,045**	**64**	**9,224**	**4,773**	**4,451**	**371**	**361**	**10**
0—10	2,595	1,327	1,268	31	27	4	2,564	1,300	1,264	5	5	..
10—15	1,032	531	501	55	47	8	977	484	493	9	8	1
15—20	1,141	657	484	186	171	15	955	486	469	53	51	2
20 and over	5,565	3,303	2,262	837	800	37	4,728	2,503	2,225	304	297	7
(C)—Muslim Total ..	**3,003**	**2,169**	**834**	**546**	**535**	**11**	**2,457**	**1,634**	**823**	**91**	**89**	**2**
0—10	596	226	370	4	4	..	592	222	370	..	..	..
10—15	267	91	176	11	10	1	256	81	175	1	1	..
15—20	393	321	72	104	102	2	289	219	70	13	13	..
20 and over	1,747	1,531	216	427	419	8	1,320	1,112	208	77	75	2
(D)—Jain Total ..	**131**	**82**	**49**	**36**	**34**	**2**	**95**	**48**	**47**	**4**	**4**	..
0—10	24	18	6	..	..	..	24	18	6	..	..	..
10—15	18	9	9	3	3	..	15	6	9	..	..	..
15—20	29	17	12	8	7	1	21	10	11	1	1	..
20 and over	60	38	22	25	24	1	35	14	21	3	3	..
(E)—Christian Total ..	**2,198**	**1,340**	**858**	**955**	**544**	**411**	**1,243**	**796**	**447**	**694**	**511**	**183**
0—10	516	251	265	30	18	12	486	233	253	18	11	7
10—15	182	100	82	48	20	28	134	80	54	24	13	11
15—20	240	164	76	134	84	50	106	80	26	92	76	16
20 and over	1,260	825	435	743	422	321	517	403	114	560	411	149

Kirkee Cantonment—contd.

Religion and Age.	POPULATION.											
	TOTAL.			LITERATE.			ILLITERATE.			LITERATE IN ENGLISH.		
	Persons.	Males.	Females.	Persons.	Males.	Females.	Persons.	Males.	Females.	Persons.	Males.	Females.
1	2	3	4	5	6	7	8	9	10	11	12	13
(F)—Zoroastrian Total ..	87	53	34	34	34	..	53	19	34	29	29	..
0—10	20	13	7	1	1	..	19	12	7	1	1	..
10—15	8	6	2	2	2	..	6	4	2	2	2	..
15—20	4	3	1	3	3	..	1	..	1	2	2	..
20 and over	55	31	24	28	28	..	27	3	24	24	24	..
(G)—Other Religions Total ..	550	478	72	246	223	23	304	255	49	31	31	..
0—10	37	20	17	..	..	..	37	20	17	..	..	..
10—15	11	4	7	2	1	1	9	3	4	1	1	..
15—20	93	78	15	41	40	1	52	38	14	6	6	..
20 and over	409	376	33	203	182	21	206	194	12	24	24	..

Rest of Poona City Taluka.

Religion and Age.	Persons.	Males.	Females.	Persons.	Males.	Females.	Persons.	Males.	Females.	Persons.	Males.	Females.
(A)—All Religions Total ..	24,125	14,217	9,908	4,521	4,061	460	19,604	10,156	9,448	1,671	1,528	143
0—10	5,215	2,580	2,635	165	118	47	5,050	2,462	2,588	38	29	9
10—15	2,261	1,192	1,069	293	225	68	1,968	967	1,001	62	40	22
15—20	2,695	1,659	1,036	870	768	102	1,825	891	934	327	288	39
20 and over	13,954	8,786	5,168	3,191	2,948	243	10,763	5,838	4,925	1,244	1,171	73
(B)—Hindu Total ..	20,669	11,934	8,685	3,415	3,110	305	17,254	8,874	8,380	1,052	1,003	49
0—10	4,618	2,281	2,337	126	90	36	4,492	2,191	2,301	16	13	3
10—15	1,965	1,042	923	228	184	44	1,737	858	879	35	29	6
15—20	2,297	1,436	861	696	639	57	1,601	797	804	238	226	12
20 and over	11,789	7,225	4,564	2,365	2,197	168	9,424	5,028	4,396	763	735	28
(C)—Muslim Total ..	2,180	1,469	711	424	409	15	1,756	1,060	696	92	92	..
0—10	374	184	190	14	11	3	360	173	187	2	2	..
10—15	191	106	85	28	26	2	163	80	83	3	3	..
15—20	220	145	75	76	71	5	144	74	70	18	18	..
20 and over	1,395	1,034	361	306	301	5	1,089	733	356	69	60	..
(D)—Jain Total ..	41	32	9	28	28	..	13	4	9	8	8	..
0—10	5	2	3	..	..	..	5	2	3	..	..	..
10—15	1	1	..	1	1	..	..	..	..	1	1	..
15—20	7	5	2	5	5	..	2	..	2	2	2	..
20 and over	28	24	4	22	22	..	6	2	4	5	5	..
(E) Christian Total ..	947	557	390	465	397	68	482	160	322	375	331	44
0—10	187	97	90	19	16	3	168	81	87	14	13	1
10—15	84	37	47	25	12	13	59	25	34	17	6	11
15—20	129	60	69	64	45	19	65	15	50	48	34	14
20 and over	547	363	184	357	324	33	190	39	151	296	278	18
(F)—Zoroastrian Total ..	232	141	91	164	100	64	68	41	27	128	85	43
0—10	22	11	11	6	1	5	16	10	6	6	1	5
10—15	18	5	13	11	2	9	7	3	4	6	1	5
15—20	37	9	28	28	8	20	9	1	8	20	8	12
20 and over	155	116	39	119	89	30	36	27	9	96	75	21
(G)—Other Religions Total ..	56	34	22	..	17	8	31	17	14	16	9	7
0—10	9	5	4	..	..	..	9	5	4	..	..	..
10—15	2	1	1	..	..	..	2	1	1	..	..	..
15—20	5	4	1	3	2	1	2	2	..	1	..	1
20 and over	40	24	16	22	15	7	18	9	9	15	9	6

CITY TABLE VI—PART I—POONA.

(POONA CITY TALUKA.)

BIRTH-PLACE.

(Corresponding to Imperial Table VI.)

Province or State where born.	Persons.	Males.	Females.
1	2	3	4
Total Population	**256,003**	**141,291**	**114,712**
A—India excluding Aden	**252,206**	**138,278**	**113,928**
A—I—Bombay Presidency including Bombay States and Agencies	**227,352**	**121,778**	**105,574**
Poona District	163,027	83,418	79,609
Bombay Presidency including Bombay States and Agencies	64,325	38,360	25,965
A—II—Provinces and States in India beyond Bombay Presidency	**24,854**	**16,500**	**8,354**
(a) Provinces and States adjacent to Bombay Presidency	**18,139**	**11,684**	**6,455**
(1) British Provinces	**9,452**	**6,505**	**2,947**
(i) Madras	4,229	2,471	1,758
(ii) Central Provinces and Berar	1,291	746	545
(iii) Punjab	3,763	3,160	603
(iv) Baluchistan	169	128	41
(2) States	**8,687**	**5,179**	**3,508**
(i) Western India States Agency	74	1	73
(ii) Mysore	555	330	225
(iii) Hyderabad	5,882	3,395	2,487
(iv) Central India Agency	139	63	76
(v) Rajputana	1,594	1,185	409
(vi) Baroda	443	205	238
(b) Other Provinces and States	**3,097**	**2,410**	**687**
(i) Ajmer-Merwara	1,046	835	211
(ii) Assam	54	....	54
(iii) Bengal	147	96	51
(iv) Burma	14	10	4
(v) Delhi	201	179	22
(vi) Gwalior	122	84	38
(vii) Kashmir	41	1	40
(viii) North-West Frontier Provinces	60	56	4
(ix) United Provinces	1,412	1,149	263
(c) French and Portuguese Settlements in India	**901**	**639**	**262**
(d) India unspecified	**2,717**	**1,767**	**950**
B—Other Asiatic Countries	**690**	**506**	**184**
(a) Within British Dominions	**35**	**25**	**10**
(i) Ceylon	35	25	10
(b) Outside British Dominions	**146**	**120**	**26**
(i) Afghanistan	71	68	3
(ii) China	28	21	7
(iii) Nepal	24	12	12
(iv) Elsewhere	23	19	4
(c) Asia unspecified	**509**	**361**	**148**
C—Europe	**2,962**	**2,425**	**537**
(1) United Kingdom and Ireland	686	507	179
(2) Continental Europe	9	5	4
(3) Europe Unspecified	2,267	1,913	354

Province or State where born.	Persons.	Males.	Females.
1	2	3	4
D—Africa	87	55	32
(a) Within British Dominions	1	....	1
(i) Natal	1	....	1
(b) Africa unspecified	86	55	31
E—America	....	....	....
F—Australasia	58	27	31
(a) Within British Dominions	22	11	11
(i) Australia	8	1	7
(ii) New Zealand	14	10	4
(b) Outside British Dominions	36	16	20

CITY TABLE VII—PART I—POONA.

Occupation or Means of Livelihood.

(Corresponding to Imperial Table X, Part I.)

	Persons.	Males.	Females.
Total Earners	77,195	65,103	12,092
Total Working Dependants	2,125	810	1,315
Total Non-Working Dependants	176,683	75,378	101,305
Total population ..	**256,003**	**141,291**	**114,712**

CITY TABLE VII—PART I—POONA.

Occupation or Means of Livelihood.

(Corresponding to Imperial Table X, Part I.)

Group No.	Occupation.	Total following occupation.	As principal occupation.		As working dependants.		As subsidiary to other occupation.	
			Males.	Females.	Males.	Females.	Males.	Females.
1	2	3	4	5	6	7	8	9
	Total All Classes	82,640	65,103	12,092	810	1,315	3,092	228
	Total Class A—Production of Raw Materials	8,876	5,241	1,221	169	309	1,905	31
	Total Sub-Class I—Exploitation of Animals and Vegetation	8,876	5,241	1,221	169	309	1,905	31
	Total Order 1—Pasture and Agriculture	8,709	5,104	1,204	168	308	1,895	30
	Total Sub-order 1 (a)—Cultivation	6,632	3,821	797	139	301	1,551	28
1	Non-cultivating proprietors taking rent in money or kind	729	324	90	39	5	266	5
4	Rent collectors, clerks, etc.	107	79	..	..	..	28	..
5	Cultivating owners	465	398	21	5	2	39	..
6	Tenant cultivators	37	22	11	..	..	..	4
7	Agricultural labourers	5,294	2,998	675	95	294	1,218	14
	Total Sub-Order 1 (b)—Cultivation of Special Crops, Fruits, etc. *(Planters, Managers, Clerks and Labourers)*	*1,500*	*822*	*319*	*21*	5	328	5
16	Market gardeners, flower and fruit growers	1,500	822	319	21	5	328	5
	Total Sub-Order 1 (c)—Forestry	116	94	21	..	1	..	..
17	Forest officers, rangers, guards, etc.	7	7	..	..	..	..	..
18	Wood cutters and charcoal burners	108	86	21	..	1	..	..
19	Collectors of forest produce	1	1	..	..	..	..	..
	Total Sub-Order 1 (d)—Stock Raising	461	367	67	8	1	16	2
21	Cattle and buffalo breeders and keepers	390	299	64	8	1	16	2
23	Herdsmen, shepherds and breeders of other animals	71	68	3	..	..	..	..
	Total Order 2—Fishing and Hunting	167	137	17	1	1	10	1
27	Fishing and Pearling	160	130	17	1	1	10	1
28	Hunting	7	7	..	..	..	..	..
	Total Class B—Preparation and Supply of Material Substances	30,407	24,762	3,955	404	307	903	76
	Total Sub-Class III—Industry	17,494	13,751	2,641	216	167	682	37
	Total Order 5—Textiles	1,790	1,331	222	54	78	104	1
43	Cotton spinning, sizing and weaving	822	618	43	29	43	88	1
45	Rope, twine, string and other fibres	183	82	91	..	..	10	..
46	Wool carding, spinning and weaving	51	50	1	..	..	..	..
47	Silk spinning and weaving	635	484	85	25	35	6	..
49	Dyeing, bleaching, printing, preparation and sponging of textiles	99	97	2	..	..	..	..
	Total Order 6—Hides, Skins and Hard Materials from the Animal Kingdom	57	57	..	..	..	..	..
51	Working in leather	57	57	..	..	..	..	..
	Total Order 7—Wood	1,892	1,688	127	54	4	19	..
54	Sawyers	157	154	1	..	..	2	..
55	Carpenters, turners and joiners, etc.	1,435	1,354	16	46	2	17	..
56	Basket makers and other industries of woody materials, including leaves and thatchers and builders working with bamboo, reeds or similar materials	300	180	110	8	2	..	..
	Total Order 8—Metals	661	588	36	27	2	8	..
59	Blacksmiths, other workers in iron, makers of implements	303	250	25	25	2	1	..
60	Workers in brass, copper and bell meta	170	163	5	2	..	..	..
61	Workers in other metals (except precious metals)	188	175	6	..	..	7	..
	Total Order 9—Ceramics	503	341	139	9	2	12	..
63	Potters and makers of earthern-ware	455	308	136	9	2	..	..
64	Brick and tile makers	48	33	3	..	..	12	..

Group. No.	Occupation.	Total following occupation.	As principal occupation.		As working dependants.		As subsidiary to other occupation.	
			Males.	Females.	Males.	Females.	Males.	Females.
1	2	3	4	5	6	7	8	9
	Total Order 10—Chemical Products properly so-called and Analogous	**66**	**58**	**7**	..	**1**	..	..
66	Manufacture of matches, fire-works and other explosives ..	16	10	..	..	..	..	..
67	Manufacture of ærated and mineral waters and ice	25	24	1	..	..	..	..
68	Manufacture and refining of vegetable oils	25	18	6	..	1	..	..
	Total Order 11—Food Industries	**1,698**	**1,168**	**392**	**1**	**16**	**99**	**22**
71	Rice pounders and huskers and flour grinders	24	23	..	..	..	1	..
72	Grain parchers, etc.	44	34	10	..	..	..	..
73	Butchers	319	236	82	1	..	..	..
74	Makers of sugar, molasses and gur	200	52	31	..	..	95	22
75	Sweetmeat and condiment makers	440	351	93	..	..	2	..
76	Toddy drawers	65	53	12	..	..	..	..
78	*Manufacturers of Tobacco*	197	146	40	..	10	1	..
81	Others	403	273	124	..	6	..	..
	Total Order 12—Industries of Dress and the Toilet	**4,553**	**3,524**	**549**	**42**	**26**	**398**	**14**
82	Boot, shoe, sandal and clog makers	542	716	90	16	4	116	..
83	Tailors, milliners, dress-makers and darners	1,835	1,378	180	23	2	241	11
84	Embroiderers, hat-makers and makers of other articles of wear ..	299	45	238	..	15	1	..
85	Washing and cleaning	699	645	41	1	5	4	3
86	Barbers, hair-dressers and wig-makers	778	740	..	2	..	36	..
	Total Order 13—Furniture Industries	**88**	**88**	..	..	..	..	..
88	Cabinet-makers, carriage painters, etc.	88	88	..	..	..	..	..
	Total Order 14—Building Industries	**2,166**	**1,684**	**427**	**1**	**31**	**23**	..
90	Lime burners, cement workers; Excavators and well sinkers; Stone cutters and dressers: Brick layers and masons: Builders (other than buildings made of bamboo or similar materials), painters, decorators of houses, tilers, plumbers, etc.	2,166	1,684	427	1	31	23	..
	Total Order 15—Construction of Means of Transport	**261**	**256**	**4**	..	..	**1**	..
91	Persons engaged in making, assembling or repairing motor vehicles or cycles	258	253	4	..	..	1	..
93	Ship, boat, aeroplane builders	3	3	..	..	..	..	..
	Total Order 16—Production and Transmission of Physical Force ..	**60**	**60**	..	..	..	..	..
94	Heat, light, electricity, motive power, etc., Gas works and electric light and power	60	60	..	..	..	..	..
	Total Order 17—Miscellaneous and Undefined Industries ..	**3,699**	**2,908**	**738**	**28**	**7**	**18**	..
95	Printers, engravers, book-binders, etc.	169	168	1	..	..	..	..
96	Makers of musical instruments	4	4	..	..	..	..	..
97	Makers of clocks and surgical or scientific instruments, etc. ..	87	87	..	..	..	..	..
98	Makers of jewellery and ornaments	517	479	19	15	..	4	..
99	Other miscellaneous and undefined industries (toy-making, taxidermy, etc.)	1,661	1,364	260	10	4	14	..
100	Scavenging	1,261	806	440	3	3	..	..
	Total Sub-Class IV—Transport	**3,451**	**3,375**	**72**	..	..	**4**	..
	Total Order 20—Transport by Road	**890**	**843**	**43**	..	..	**4**	..
105	Persons (other than labourers) employed on the construction and maintenance of roads and bridges	2	2	..	..	..	..	..
106	Labourers employed on roads and bridges ..	6	6	..	..	..	..	..
107	Owners, managers and employees (excluding personal servants) connected with mechanically driven vehicles (including trams)	289	278	9	..	..	2	..
108	Owners, managers and employees (excluding personal servants) connected with other vehicles	66	66	..	..	..	..	..
110	Pack elephant, camel, mule, ass and bullock, owners and drivers	502	466	34	..	..	2	..
111	Porters and messengers	25	25	..	..	..	..	..
	Total Order 21—Transport by Rail	**2,432**	**2,405**	**27**	....	..	..	..
112	Railway employees of all kinds other than coolies	1,131	1,130	1	..	..	..	..
113	Labourers employed on railway construction and maintenance and coolies and porters employed on railway premises ..	1,301	1,275	26	..	..	..	..
	Total Order 22—Post Office, Telegraph and Telephone Services ..	**129**	**127**	**2**	..	..	..	..
114	Post Office, Telegraph and Telephone services	129	127	2	..	..	..	..

Group No.	Occupation.	Total following occupation.	As principal occupation.		As working dependants.		As subsidiary to other occupation.	
			Males.	Females.	Male.	Females.	Males.	Females.
1	2	3	4	5	6	7	8	9
	Total Sub-Class V—Trade	9,462	7,636	1,242	188	140	217	39
	Total Order 23—Banks, Establishments of Credit, Exchange and Insurance	597	526	41	3	19	8	..
115	Bank managers, money lenders, exchange and insurance agents, money changers and brokers and their employees	597	526	41	3	19	8	..
	Total Order 24—Brokerage Commission and Export	151	144	1	..	..	6	..
116	Brokers, commission agents, commercial travellers, ware-house owners and employees	151	144	1	..	..	6	..
	Total Order 25—Trade in Textiles	599	577	5	..	2	15	..
117	Trade in piece-goods, wool, cotton, silk, hair and other textiles	599	577	5	..	2	15	..
	Total Order 26—Trade in Skins, Leather and Furs	78	74	4	..	..	..	..
118	Trade in skins, leather, furs, feathers, horn, etc. and the articles made from these	78	74	4	..	..	..	..
	Total Order 27—Trade in Wood	116	111	5	..	..	..	..
119	Trade in wood (not fire-wood)	76	76	..	..	..	..	..
120	Trade in barks	4	2	2	..	..	..	..
121	Trade in bamboos and canes	36	33	3	..	..	..	..
	Total Order 28—Trade in Metals	3	3	..	..	..	..	..
123	Trade in metals, machinery, knives, tools, etc.	3	3	..	..	..	..	..
	Total Order 29—Trade in Pottery, Bricks and Tiles	1	1	..	..	..	..	..
124	Trade in pottery, bricks and tiles	1	1	..	..	..	..	..
	Total Order 30—Trade in Chemical Products	64	58	6	..	..	..	..
125	Drugs, dyes, paints, petroleum, explosives, etc.	64	58	6	..	..	..	..
	Total Order 31—Hotels, Cafes, Restaurants, etc.	2,028	1,731	277	6	13	1	..
126	Vendors of wine, liquors, aerated waters and ice	83	71	1	..	11	..	..
127	Owners and Managers of hotels, cook-shops, sarais, etc. (and employees)	1,507	1,625	273	6	2	1	..
128	Hawkers of drink and food stuffs	38	35	3	..	..	..	..
	Total Order 32—Other Trade in Food Stuffs	3,282	2,480	603	32	76	72	19
129	Grain and pulse dealers	258	234	11	3	..	10	..
130	Dealers in sweetmeats, sugar and spices	81	80	1	..	..	..	..
131	Dealers in dairy product, eggs and poultry	810	552	176	..	48	25	9
132	Dealers in animals for food	9	9	..	..	..	..	..
133	Dealers in fodder for animals	29	19	5	..	..	5	..
134	Dealers in other food stuffs	1,962	1,465	398	29	28	32	10
135	Dealers in tobacco	54	43	11	..	..	..	..
136	Dealers in opium	28	28	..	..	..	..	..
137	Dealers in ganja	51	50	1	..	..	..	..
	Total Order 33—Trade in Clothing and Toilet Articles	80	80	..	..	..	..	..
138	Trade in ready-made clothing and other articles of dress and the toilet (hats, umbrellas, socks, ready-made shoes, perfumes, etc.)	80	80	..	..	..	..	..
	Total Order 34—Trade in Furniture	238	226	12	..	..	..	..
139	Trade in furniture, carpets, curtain, and beddings	49	49	..	..	..	..	..
140	Hardware, cooking utensils, porcelain, crockery, glassware bottles, articles for gardening, etc.	189	177	12	..	..	..	..
	Total Order 36—Trade in Means of Transport	523	435	18	..	..	70	..
142	Dealers and hirers, in mechanical transport motors, cycles, etc.	69	66	3	..	..	..	..
143	Dealers and hirers in other carriages, carts, boats, etc.	444	359	15	..	..	70	..
144	Dealers and hirers of elephants, camels, horses, cattle, asses, mules, etc.	10	10	..	..	..	..	..

Group No.	Occupation.	Total following occupation.	As principal occupation.		As working dependants.		As subsidiary to other occupation.	
			Males.	Females.	Males.	Females.	Males.	Females.
1	2	3	4	5	6	7	8	9
	Total Order 37—Trade in Fuel	**511**	**216**	**79**	**146**	**19**	**41**	**10**
145	Dealers in firewood, charcoal, coal, cowdung, etc.	511	216	79	146	19	41	10
	Total Order 38—Trade in Articles of Luxury and those pertaining to Letters and the Arts and Sciences	**352**	**265**	**75**	..	..	**4**	**8**
146	Dealers in precious stones, jewellery (real and imitation), clocks optical instruments, etc.)	43	38	5	..	..	..	..
147	Dealers in common bangles, bead necklaces, fans, small articles toys, hunting and fishing tackle, flowers, etc.	·245	165	68	..	..	4	8
148	Publishers, book-sellers, stationers, dealers in music pictures, musical instruments and curiosities	64	62	2	..	..	..	..
	Total Order 39—Trade of Order Sorts	**839**	**709**	**116**	**1**	**11**	..	**2**
149	Dealers in rags, stable refuse, etc.	501	439	59	..	1	..	2
150	General store-keepers and shop-keepers otherwise unspecified ..	338	270	57	1	10	..	..
	Total Class C—Public Administration and Liberal Arts ..	**19,527**	**18,154**	**1,158**	**170**	**10**	**35**	..
	Total Sub-Class VI—Public Force	**7,785**	**7,778**	**5**	..	..	**2**	..
	Total Order 40—Army	**6,293**	**6,290**	**2**	..	..	**1**	..
153	Army (Imperial)	6,293	6,290	2	..	..	1	..
	Total Order 43—Police	**1,492**	**1,488**	**3**	..	..	**1**	..
157	Police	1,232	1,230	2	..	..	..	..
158	Village watchmen	260	258	1	..	..	1	..
	Total Sub-Class VII—Public Administration	**6,924**	**6,422**	**320**	**162**	**5**	**15**	..
	Total Order 44—Public Administration	**6,924**	**6,422**	**320**	**162**	**5**	**15**	..
159	Service of the State	6,145	5,802	172	162	..	9	..
160	Service of Indian and Foreign States	7	7	..	..	..	..	..
161	Municipal and other local (not village) service	546	422	124	..	..	..	..
162	Village officials and servants other than watchmen	226	191	24	..	5	6	..
	Total Sub-Class VIII—Professions and Liberal Arts	**4,818**	**3,954**	**833**	**8**	**5**	**18**	..
	Total Order 45—Religion	**800**	**737**	**54**	**6**	..	**3**	..
163	Priests, Ministers, etc.	104	82	20	2	..	..	..
164	Monks, nuns, religious mendicants	390	365	25	3	..	3	..
165	Religious workers	254	247	7	..	..	..	..
166	Servants in religious edifices, burial and burning grounds, pilgrim conductors, circumcisers, etc.	46	43	2	1	..	..	..
	Total Order 46—Law	**318**	**317**	..	..	..	**1**	..
167	Lawyers of all kinds, including Qazis, Law Agents and Mukhtiars..	232	231	..	..	..	1	..
168	Lawyers' clerks, petition writers, etc.	86	86	..	..	..	..	..
	Total Order 47—Medicine	**495**	**164**	**327**	..	**2**	**2**	..
169	Registered medical practitioners including oculists	61	58	3	..	..	..	..
170	Other persons practising the healing arts without being registered	32	31	..	..	..	1	..
171	Dentists	9	8	1	..	..	..	..
172	Midwives, Vaccinators, compounders, nurses, masseurs, etc. ..	391	65	323	..	2	1	..
173	Veterinary surgeons	2	2	..	..	..	..	..
	Total Order 48—Instruction	**2,227**	**1,843**	**379**	**2**	**3**	..	..
174	Professors and teachers of all kinds	1,316	969	342	2	3	..	..
175	Clerks and servants connected with education	911	874	37	..	..	..	..
	Total Order 49—Letters Arts and Sciences (other than 44) ..	**978**	**893**	**73**	..	..	**12**	..
176	Public scribes, stenographers, etc.	1	..	1	..	..	..	..
177	Architects, surveyors, engineers, and their employees (not being State servants)	468	468	..	..	..	..	..
178	Authors, editors, journalists and photographers	53	50	..	..	..	3	..
179	Artists, sculptors and image-makers	4	4	..	..	..	..	..
181	Horoscope casters, astrologers, fortune-tellers, wizards witches and medium	2	2	..	..	..	..	..
182	Musicians (composers and performers other than military) actors dangers, etc.	369	294	69	..	..	6	..
183	Managers and employees of places of public entertainments, race courses, societies, clubs	68	68	..	..	..	..	..
184	Conjurors, acrobats, recitors, exhibitors of curiosities and wild animals, etc.	13	7	3	..	..	3	..

Group No.	Occupation.	Total following occupation.	As principal occupation.		As working dependants.		As subsidiary to other occupation.	
			Males.	Females.	Males.	Females.	Males.	Females.
1	2	3	4	5	6	7	8	9
	Total Class D—Miscellaneous	**23,830**	**16,946**	**5,758**	**67**	**689**	**249**	**121**
	Total Sub-Class IX—Persons Living on Their Income	**1,917**	**1,457**	**315**	**34**	**32**	**51**	**28**
	Total Order 50—Persons Living Principally on their Income ..	**1,917**	**1,457**	**315**	**34**	**32**	**51**	**28**
185	Proprietors (other than of agricultural land), fund and scholarships holders and pensioners	1,917	1,457	315	34	32	51	28
	Total Sub-Class X—Domestic Service	**6,458**	**4,698**	**1,303**	**16**	**394**	**8**	**39**
	Total Order 51—Domestic Service	**6,458**	**4,698**	**1,303**	**16**	**394**	**8**	**39**
186	Private motor-drivers and cleaners	639	616	22	1	..	..	..
187	Other domestic service	5,819	4,082	1,281	15	394	8	39
	Total Sub-Class XI—Insufficiently described occupations ..	**9,815**	**6,578**	**2,820**	**11**	**197**	**188**	**21**
	Total Order 52—General Terms which do not Indicate a Definite Occupation	**9,815**	**6,578**	**2,820**	**11**	**197**	**188**	**21**
188	Manufacturers, businessmen and contractors otherwise unspecified	62	62	..	..	..	..	..
189	Cashiers, accountants, book-keepers, clerks and other employees in unspecified offices and warehouses and shops	997	802	153	8	2	32	..
190	Mechanics otherwise unspecified	2	..	2	..	..	..	..
191	Labourers and workmen otherwise unspecified	8,754	5,714	2,665	3	195	156	21
	Total Sub-Class XII—Unproductive	**5,640**	**4,213**	**1,320**	**6**	**66**	**2**	**33**
	Total Order 54—Beggars, Vagrants, Prostitutes	**837**	**560**	**263**	**1**	**3**	**1**	**9**
193	Beggars and vagrants	830	560	256	1	3	1	9
194	Procurers and prostitutes	7	..	7	..	..	..	..
	Total Order 55—Other unclassified Non-Productive Industries ..	**4,803**	**3,653**	**1,057**	**5**	**63**	**1**	**24**
195	Other unclassified non-productive industries	4,803	3,653	1,057	5	63	1	24

CITY TABBE I—SHOLAPUR.

Area, Houses and Population.

(Corresponding to Imperial Table I.)

City.	Area in Acres.	Houses.			Houses per Acre	Population.			Persons. per Acre.
		Occupied.	Unoccu-pied.	Total.		Males.	Females.	Total.	
1	2	3	4	5	6	7	8	9	10
Sholapur	..	19,715	..	..	..	76,837	67,817	144,654	..
(1) Municipality	4,557	17,656	1,586	19,242	4·22	72,079	63,495	135,574	29·8
(ii) Suburbs	..	2,059	..	..	..	4,758	4,322	9,080	..

CITY TABLE III—SHOLAPUR.

Religion.

(Corresponding to Imperial Table XVI.)

City.	Population.			Hindu. Brahmanic.			Hindu. Arya.			Hindu. Total Hindus.		
	Persons.	Males.	Females.	Persons.	Males.	Females.	Persons.	Males.	Females.	Persons.	Males.	Females.
1	2	3	4	5	6	7	8	9	10	11	12	13
Sholapur ..	144,654	76,837	67,817	111,417	59,292	52,125	17	9	8	111,434	59,301	52,133
(i) Municipality ..	135,574	72,079	63,495	104,013	55,423	48,590	17	9	8	104,030	55,432	48,598
(ii) Suburbs ..	9,080	4,758	4,322	7,404	3,869	3,535	..	..	..	7,404	3,869	3,535

City.	Muslim. Shia.			Muslim. Sunni.			Muslim. Others and Sect Unspecified.			Muslim. Total Muslims.			Jain. Swetambar.		
	Persons.	Males.	Females.	Persons.	Males.	Females.	Persons.	Males.	Females.	Persons.	Males.	Females.	Persons.	Males.	Females.
1	14	15	16	17	18	19	20	21	22	23	24	25	26	27	28
Sholapur ..	137	97	40	21,580	11,372	10,208	6,965	3,717	3,248	28,682	15,186	13,496	250	165	85
(i) Municipality ..	126	91	35	20,630	10,847	9,783	6,488	3,484	3,004	27,244	14,422	12,822	246	163	83
(ii) Suburbs ..	11	6	5	950	525	425	477	233	244	1,438	764	674	4	2	2

City.	Jain—(contd.) Digambar.			Jain—(contd.) Others and Sect Unspecified.			Jain—(contd.) Total Jains.			Zoroastrian.			Christian. Roman-Catholic.		
	Persons.	Males.	Females.	Persons.	Males.	Females.	Persons.	Males.	Females.	Persons.	Males.	Females.	Persons.	Males.	Females.
1	29	30	31	32	33	34	35	36	37	38	39	40	41	42	43
Sholapur ..	921	471	450	422	250	172	1,593	886	707	304	164	140	697	373	324
(i) Municipality ..	917	469	448	420	248	172	1,583	880	703	304	164	140	688	368	320
(ii) Suburbs ..	4	2	2	2	2	..	10	6	4	..	..	..	9	5	4

City.	Christian—(contd.) Other Christians.			Christian—(contd.) Total Christians.			Tribal.			Sikh.			Jew.		
	Persons.	Males.	Females.	Persons.	Males.	Females.	Persons.	Males.	Females.	Persons.	Males.	Females.	Persons.	Males.	Females.
1	44	45	46	47	48	49	50	51	52	53	54	55	56	57	58
Sholapur ..	1,926	914	1,012	2,623	1,287	1,336	1	1	..	4	4	..	13	8	5
(i) Municipality ..	1,708	801	907	2,396	1,169	1,227	1	1	..	4	4	..	12	7	5
(ii) Suburbs ..	218	113	105	227	118	109	..	..	..	..	..	..	1	1	..

Age, Sex and Civil Condition.

(Corresponding to Imperial Table VII).

A—All Religions.

Age.	Population.			Unmarried.			Married.			Widowed.		
	Persons.	Males.	Females.	Persons.	Males.	Females.	Persons.	Males.	Females.	Persons.	Males.	Females.
1	2	3	4	5	6	7	8	9	10	11	12	13
0—1	4,344	2,149	2,195	4,295	2,122	2,173	49	27	22	..	..	..
1—2	4,104	2,033	2,071	4,054	2,009	2,045	50	24	26	..	..	..
2—3	3,843	1,901	1,942	3,779	1,870	1,909	64	31	33	..	..	..
3—4	3,585	1,798	1,787	3,484	1,762	1,722	98	35	63	3	1	2
4—5	3,532	1,807	1,725	3,394	1,766	1,628	135	41	94	3	..	3
Total 0—5	19,408	9,688	9,720	19,006	9,529	9,477	396	158	238	6	1	5
5—10	15,776	8,249	7,527	13,785	7,796	5,989	1,953	439	1,514	38	14	24
10—15	14,965	7,836	7,129	10,739	6,884	3,855	4,147	928	3,219	79	24	55
15—20	14,660	7,464	7,196	4,387	3,907	480	9,978	3,476	6,502	295	81	214
20—25	15,749	8,239	7,510	2,926	2,713	213	12,300	5,368	6,932	523	158	365
25—30	12,914	7,248	5,666	873	786	87	11,163	6,199	4,964	878	263	615
30—35	11,036	6,486	4,650	381	316	65	9,640	5,856	3,785	1,115	315	800
35—40	8,491	4,982	3,509	170	131	39	6,809	4,509	2,300	1,512	342	1,170
40—45	6,821	3,827	2,894	118	87	31	5,009	3,404	1,605	1,594	336	1,258
45—50	4,851	2,593	2,258	64	43	21	3,026	2,194	832	1,761	356	1,405
50—55	3,684	1,903	1,781	43	29	14	2,082	1,565	517	1,559	309	1,250
55—60	2,690	1,352	1,338	25	17	8	1,284	1,024	260	1,381	311	1,070
60—65	2,261	1,110	1,151	21	16	5	1,002	796	206	1,238	298	940
65—70	898	448	450	11	7	4	349	286	63	538	155	383
70 and over	1,370	654	716	16	12	4	463	386	77	891	256	635
Total	135,574	72,079	63,495	52,565	32,273	20,292	69,601	36,587	33,014	13,408	3,219	10,189

B—Hindu.

Age.	Persons.	Males.	Females.	Persons.	Males.	Females.	Persons.	Males.	Females.	Persons.	Males.	Females.
0—1	3,331	1,659	1,672	3,292	1,637	1,655	39	22	17	..	..	..
1—2	3,138	1,545	1,593	3,095	1,526	1,569	43	19	24	..	..	..
2—3	2,925	1,423	1,502	2,872	1,401	1,471	53	22	31	..	..	..
3—4	2,719	1,351	1,368	2,631	1,323	1,308	86	27	59	2	1	1
4—5	2,647	1,354	1,293	2,528	1,322	1,206	117	32	85	2	..	2
Total 0—5	14,760	7,332	7,428	14,418	7,209	7,209	338	122	216	4	1	3
5—10	11,855	6,223	5,632	10,105	5,827	4,278	1,718	386	1,332	32	10	22
10—15	11,308	5,048	5,260	7,728	5,100	2,628	3,513	828	2,685	67	20	47
15—20	11,275	5,768	5,507	3,018	2,784	234	8,019	2,917	5,102	238	67	171
20—25	12,216	6,434	5,782	1,906	1,805	101	9,894	4,506	5,388	416	123	293
25—30	10,110	5,722	4,388	508	455	53	8,919	5,068	3,851	683	199	484
30—35	8,701	5,112	3,589	265	226	39	7,570	4,644	2,926	866	242	624
35—40	6,619	3,908	2,711	125	95	30	5,294	3,546	1,748	1,200	267	933
40—45	5,231	2,977	2,254	89	64	25	3,859	2,645	1,214	1,283	268	1,015
45—50	3,714	1,954	1,760	47	33	14	2,285	1,048	637	1,382	273	1,109
50—55	2,802	1,414	1,388	31	22	9	1,556	1,161	395	1,215	231	984
55—60	2,062	1,019	1,043	18	13	5	972	770	202	1,072	236	836
60—65	1,722	829	893	15	11	4	758	597	161	949	221	728
65—70	661	322	339	7	6	1	248	203	45	406	113	293
70 and over	994	470	524	11	8	3	332	277	55	651	185	466
Total	104,030	55,432	48,598	38,291	23,658	14,633	55,275	29,318	25,957	10,464	2,456	8,008

C—Muslim.

Age.	Persons.	Males.	Females.	Persons.	Males.	Females.	Persons.	Males.	Females.	Persons.	Males.	Females.
0—1	911	443	468	905	441	464	6	2	4	..	..	..
1—2	854	434	420	851	431	420	3	3	..	..	..	..
2—3	801	420	381	793	413	380	8	7	1	..	..	..
3—4	758	395	363	746	387	359	11	8	3	1	..	1
4—5	764	395	369	749	387	362	14	8	6	1	..	1
Total 0—5	4,088	2,087	2,001	4,044	2,059	1,985	42	28	14	2	..	2
5—10	3,360	1,741	1,619	3,135	1,687	1,448	221	51	170	4	3	1
10—15	3,126	1,612	1,514	2,512	1,513	999	603	95	508	11	4	7
15—20	2,938	1,488	1,450	1,086	955	131	1,799	520	1,279	53	13	40
20—25	3,090	1,597	1,493	829	785	44	2,165	780	1,385	96	32	64
25—30	2,442	1,340	1,102	307	290	17	1,964	993	971	171	57	114
30—35	2,094	1,190	904	80	69	11	1,797	1,059	738	217	62	155
35—40	1,586	908	678	29	26	3	1,288	820	468	269	62	207
40—45	1,262	715	547	18	14	4	972	643	329	272	58	214
45—50	970	540	430	12	8	4	629	464	165	329	68	261
50—55	746	410	336	9	6	3	441	340	101	296	64	232
55—60	541	284	257	4	3	1	264	218	46	273	63	210
60—65	468	243	225	3	3	..	211	175	36	254	65	189
65—70	199	106	93	2	1	1	86	71	15	111	34	77
70 and over	334	161	173	4	3	1	118	97	21	212	61	151
Total	27,244	14,422	12,822	12,074	7,422	4,652	12,600	6,354	6,246	2,570	646	1,924

D—Christian.

Age.	Population.			Unmarried.			Married.			Widowed.		
	Persons.	Males.	Females.	Persons.	Males.	Females.	Persons.	Males	Females.	Persons.	Males.	Females.
1	2	3	4	5	6	7	8	9	10	11	12	13
0—1	67	31	36	63	28	35	4	3	1	..	..	..
1—2	74	34	40	71	32	39	3	2	1	..	..	..
2—3	76	36	40	75	35	40	1	1	..	..	..	..
3—4	67	31	36	67	31	36	..	..	..	..	..	..
4—5	77	36	41	74	35	39	3	1	2	..	..	..
Total 0—5	361	168	193	350	161	189	11	7	4	..	..	..
5—10	338	164	174	331	163	168	7	1	6	..	..	..
10—15	307	149	158	298	147	151	9	2	7	..	..	..
15—20	252	103	149	177	86	91	73	16	57	2	1	1
20—25	254	110	144	120	65	55	129	43	86	5	2	3
25—30	191	94	97	34	21	13	148	70	78	9	3	6
30—35	*180*	*89*	*91*	*20*	*8*	*12*	*145*	*76*	*69*	*15*	*5*	*10*
35—40	151	82	69	8	3	5	125	75	50	18	4	14
40—45	112	65	47	4	2	2	95	60	35	13	3	10
45—50	83	52	31	3	1	2	64	46	18	16	5	11
50—55	60	43	26	2	1	1	51	38	13	16	4	12
55—60	41	23	18	1	..	1	28	21	7	12	2	10
60—65	28	13	15	1	..	1	16	11	5	11	2	9
65—70	12	6	6	1	..	1	6	5	1	5	1	4
70 and over	17	8	9	..	..	..	7	6	1	10	2	8
Total ..	2,396	1,169	1,227	1,350	658	692	914	477	437	132	34	98

CITY TABLE V—PART I—SHOLAPUR.

Literacy by Religion and Age.

(Corresponding to Imperial Table XIII.)

Religion and Age.	Population.									Literate in English.		
	Total.			Literate.			Illiterate.					
	Persons.	Males.	Females.	Persons.	Males.	Females.	Persons.	Males.	Females.	Persons.	Males.	Females.
1	2	3	4	5	6	7	8	9	10	11	12	13
(A) ALL RELIGIONS.												
Total	135,574	72,079	63,495	21,389	18,334	3,055	114,185	53,745	60,440	4,394	4,000	394
0—10	65,184	17,937	17,247	1,637	1,356	281	33,547	16,581	16,966	83	68	15
10—15	14,965	7,836	7,129	2,572	2,093	479	12,393	5,743	6,650	337	273	64
15—20	14,660	7,464	7,196	3,380	2,729	651	11,280	4,735	6,545	793	697	96
20 and over	70,765	38,842	31,923	13,800	12,156	1,644	56,965	26,686	30,279	3,181	2,962	219
(B) HINDU.												
Total	104,030	55,432	48,598	15,782	13,885	1,897	88,248	41,547	46,701	3,126	3,001	125
0—10	26,615	13,555	13,060	1,220	1,039	181	25,395	12,516	12,879	53	45	8
10—15	11,308	5,948	5,360	1,903	1,610	293	9,405	4,338	5,067	208	194	14
15—20	11,275	5,768	5,507	2,537	2,103	434	8,738	3,665	5,073	575	548	27
20 and over	54,832	30,161	24,671	10,122	9,133	989	44,710	21,028	23,682	2,290	2,214	76
(C) MUSLIM.												
Total	27,244	14,422	12,822	3,344	3,073	271	23,900	11,349	12,551	358	350	8
0—10	7,448	3,828	3,620	249	213	36	7,199	3,615	3,584	3	3	..
10—15	3,126	1,612	1,514	358	308	50	2,768	1,304	1,464	20	19	1
15—20	2,938	1,488	1,450	501	454	47	2,437	1,034	1,403	67	64	3
20 and over	13,732	7,494	6,288	2,236	2,098	188	11,496	5,896	6,100	268	264	4
(D) JAIN.												
Total	1,583	880	703	715	575	140	868	305	563	159	155	4
0—10	360	189	171	60	44	16	300	145	155	8	8	..
10—15	194	110	84	92	69	23	102	41	61	20	19	1
15—20	163	91	72	97	78	19	66	13	53	31	30	1
20 and over	866	490	376	466	384	82	400	106	294	100	98	2
(E) ZOROASTRIAN.												
Total	304	164	140	241	139	102	63	25	38	175	114	61
0—10	61	32	29	19	9	10	42	23	19	11	5	6
10—15	28	15	13	24	14	10	4	1	3	15	8	7
15—20	29	13	16	24	12	12	5	1	4	20	10	10
20 and over	186	104	82	174	104	70.	12	..	12	129	91	38
(F) CHRISTIAN.												
Total	2,396	1,169	1,227	1,293	651	642	1,103	518	585	569	374	195
0—10	690	332	367	89	51	38	610	281	329	8	7	1
10—15	307	149	158	193	90	103	114	59	55	73	32	41
15—20	252	103	149	220	81	139	32	22	10	99	44	55
20 and over	1,138	585	553	791	429	362	347	156	191	389	291	98
(G) TRIBAL AND OTHERS.												
Total	17	12	5	14	11	3	3	1	2	7	6	1
0—10	1	1	..	..	..	..	1	1	..	..	..	..
10—15	2	2	..	2	2	..	..	..	..	1	1	..
15—20	3	1	2	1	1	..	2	..	2	1	1	..
20 and over	11	8	3	11	8	3	..	..	..	5	4	1

CITY TABLE VI—PART I—SHOLAPUR.

BIRTH-PLACE.

(Corresponding to Imperial Table VI.)

Province or State where born.	Persons.	Males.	Females.
1	2	3	4
Total Population	**135,574**	**72,079**	**63,495**
A—India excluding Aden	**135,485**	**72,024**	**63,461**
A I—Bombay Presidency including Bombay States and Agencies	**107,892**	**56,815**	**51,077**
Sholapur District	93,136	48,907	44,229
Rest of the Bombay Presidency including Bombay States and Agencies	14,756	7,908	6,848
A II—Provinces and States in India beyond Bombay	**27,593**	**15,209**	**12,384**
(a) Provinces and States adjacent to Bombay Presidency	**27,230**	**14,947**	**12,283**
(1) British Provinces	**1,778**	**999**	**779**
(i) Madras	1,472	783	689
(ii) Central Provinces and Berar	115	57	58
(iii) Punjab	121	89	32
(iv) Baluchistan	70	70	....
(2) States	**25,452**	**13,948**	**11,504**
(i) Western India States Agency	41	41	....
(ii) Mysore	35	16	19
(iii) Hyderabad	24,559	13,350	11,209
(iv) Central India Agency	66	63	3
(v) Rajputana	710	447	263
(vi) Baroda	41	31	10
(b) Other Provinces and States	**295**	**218**	**77**
(i) Ajmer-Merwara	43	39	4
(ii) Bengal	20	17	3
(iii) Burma	8	5	3
(iv) Delhi	14	13	1
(v) Gwalior	50	29	21
(vi) North-West Frontier Province	11	11	....
(vii) United Provinces	149	104	45
(c) French and Portuguese Settlement in India	**68**	**44**	**24**
B—Other Asiatic Countries	**28**	**26**	**2**
(a) Outside British Dominions	**28**	**26**	**2**
(1) Afghanistan	23	21	2
(2) Nepal	5	5	....
C—Europe	**51**	**25**	**26**
(a) Continental Europe	46	25	21
(b) Europe unspecified	*5*	....	*5*
D—Africa	**2**	....	**2**
(a) Africa Unspecified	**2**	....	**2**
E—America	**1**	**1**	....
(b) America unspecified	**1**	**1**	....
F—Australasia	**7**	**3**	**4**
(a) Within British Dominions	**7**	**3**	**4**
(i) New Zealand	3	3	....
(ii) Australia	4	....	4

CITY TABLE VII—PART I—SHOLAPUR.

OCCUPATION OR MEANS OF LIVELIHOOD.

(Corresponding to Imperial Table X—Part I.)

——	Persons.	Males.	Females.
Total earners	51,352	43,366	7,986
Total working dependants	3,586	287	3,299
Total non-working dependants	80,636	28,426	52,210
Total Population ..	**135,574**	**72,079**	**63,495**

CITY TABLE VII—PART I—SHOLAPUR.

OCCUPATION OR MEANS OF LIVELIHOOD.

(Corresponding to Imperial Table X—Part I.)

Group No.	Occupation.	Total following occupation.	As principal occupation.		As working dependants.		As subsidiary to other occupation.	
			Males.	Females.	Males.	Females.	Males.	Females.
1	2	3	4	5	6	7	8	9
	Total all classes	55,363	43,366	7,986	287	3,299	371	54
	Total Class A—Production of Raw Materials	4,426	3,395	916	42	30	32	9
	Total Sub-Class I—Exploitation of Animals and Vegetation	4,425	3,394	918	42	30	32	9
	Total Order 1—Pasture and Agriculture	4,392	3,362	917	42	30	32	9
	Total Sub-Order (a) Cultivation	3,197	2,451	673	29	9	28	7
1	Non-cultivating proprietors taking rent in money of kind	269	242	10	4	1	11	1
5	Cultivating owners	147	140	2	..	..	4	1
6	Tenant cultivators	72	65	1	1	..	5	..
7	Agricultural labourers	2,709	2,004	660	24	8	8	5
	Total Sub-Order 1 (b) Cultivation of special crops, fruit, etc. (Planters, managers, clerks and labourers)	586	356	211	4	10	4	1
16	Market gardeners, flower and fruit growers	586	356	211	4	10	4	1
	Total Sub-Order 1 (c) Forestry	141	116	14	2	9	..	..
18	Wood cutters and charcoal burners	141	116	14	2	9	..	..
	Total Sub-Order 1 (d) Stock raising	468	439	19	7	2	..	1
21	Cattle and buffalo breeders and keepers	342	314	18	7	2	..	1
23	Herdsmen, shepherds and breeders of other animals	126	125	1	..	..	..	..
	Total Order 2—Fishing and Hunting	33	32	1	..	..	..	..
27	Fishing and Pearling	32	32	..	..	..	..	..
28	Hunting	1	..	1	..	..	..	..
	Total Sub-Class II—Exploitation of Minerals	1	1	..	..	..	..	..
	Total Order 4—Non-Metallic Minerals	1	1	..	..	..	..	..
40	Salt, saltpetre and other saline substances	1	1	..	..	..	..	..
	Total Class B—Preparation and Supply of Material substances	42,916	33,175	6,087	193	3,201	220	40
	Total Sub-Class III—Industry	37,021	27,977	5,682	180	3,140	104	38
	Total Order 5—Textiles	31,989	23,520	5,183	137	3,102	11	36
42	Cotton ginning, cleaning and pressing	19,903	16,637	3,188	15	24	4	35
43	Cotton spinning, sizing and weaving	11,589	6,787	1,876	122	2,849	4	1
45	Rope, twine, string and other fibres	127	67	47	..	11	2	..
46	Wool carding, spinning and weaving	230	3	60	..	167	..	..
47	Silk spinning and weaving	97	39	7	..	51	..	..
49	Dyeing, bleaching, printing, preparation and sponging of textiles	32	30	2	..	..	..	..
50	Lace, crepe, embroideries, fringes, etc., and insufficiently described textile industries	11	7	3	..	..	1	..
	Total Order 6—Hides, skins and Hard Materials from the Animal Kingdom	42	38	2	..	1	1	..
51	Working in leather	42	38	2	..	1	1	..
	Total Order 7—Wood	693	654	19	2	16	2	..
54	Sawyers	5	3	2	..	..	..	..
55	Carpenters, turners and joiners, etc.	630	623	3	2	..	2	..
56	Basket-makers and other industries of woody materials, including leaves and thatchers and builders working with bamboo, reeds or similar materials	58	28	14	..	16	..	..
	Total Order 8—Metals	424	399	16	2	3	4	..
59	Blacksmiths, other workers in iron, makers of implements	146	133	9	1	3	..	..
60	Workers in brass, copper and bell metal	61	59	..	..	..	2	..
61	Workers in other metals (except precious metals)	217	207	7	1	..	2	..
	Total Order 9—Ceramics	260	231	24	..	..	5	..
63	Potters and makers of earthenware	259	230	24	..	..	5	..
64	Brick and tile-makers	1	1	..	..	..	..	..

Group No.	Occupation.	Total following occupation.	As principal occupation.		As working dependants.		As subsidiary to other occupation.	
			Males.	Females.	Males.	Females.	Males.	Females.
1	2	3	4	5	6	7	8	9
	Total Order 10—Chemical Products Properly so called and Analogous.	34	29	1	..	2	2	..
66	Manufacture of matches, fire-works and other explosives ..	7	7	..	..	..	..	..
67	Manufacture of aerated and mineral waters and ice	13	13	..	..	..	..	..
68	Manufacture and refining of vegetable oils	14	9	1	..	2	2	..
	Total Order 11—Food Industries	774	644	76	11	11	32	..
71	Rice pounders and huskers and flour-grinders	79	59	14	..	4	2	..
72	Grain parchers, etc.	96	51	32	5	..	8	..
73	Butchers	361	346	7	4	4	..	..
75	Sweetmeat and condiment makers	122	106	1	2	3	10	..
76	Toddy drawers	11	11	..	..	..	..	..
77	Brewers and distillers	1	1	..	..	..	..	..
78	Manufacturers of Tobacco	101	67	22	..	..	12	..
80	Manufacturers of Ganja	3	3	..	..	..	..	..
	Total Order 12—Industries of Dress and the Toilet	1,566	1,363	151	20	3	27	2
82	Boot, shoe, sandal and clog makers	223	168	55	..	..	..	..
83	Tailors, milliners, dressmakers and darners	684	621	44	13	1	5	..
84	Embroiderers, hat-makers and makers of other articles of wear ..	1	1	..	..	..	..	..
85	Washing and cleaning	215	146	51	7	2	7	2
86	Barbers, hair-dressers and wig-makers	441	425	1	..	..	15	..
87	Other industries connected with the toilet	2	2	..	..	..	..	..
	Total Order 13—Furniture Industries	2	..	1	..	1	..	..
88	Cabinet-makers, carriage-painters, etc.	2	..	1	..	1	..	..
	Total Order 14—Building Industries	508	456	39	3	1	9	..
90	Lime burners, cement workers, excavators and well sinkers : Stone cutters and dressers : Brick layers and masons : Builders (other than building made of bamboo or similar materials), painters, decorators of houses, tilers, plumbers	508	456	39	3	1	9	..
	Total Order 16—Production and Transmission of Physical Force ..	28	26	2	..	..	..	..
94	Heat, light, electricity, motive power, etc., Gas works and electric light and power	28	26	2	..	..	..	..
	Total Order 17—Miscellaneous and Undefined Industries ..	701	517	168	5	..	11	..
95	Printers, engravers, bookbinders, etc.	16	14	..	2	..	4	..
98	Makers of jewellery and ornaments	8	6	2	..	..	..	..
99	Other miscellaneous and undefined industries (toy-making, taxidermy, etc.)	331	247	70	3	..	11	..
100	Scavenging	346	250	96	..	..	..	..
	Total Sub-Class IV—Transport	1,816	1,717	99	..	..	..	..
	Total Order 19—Transport by Water	2	2	..	..	..	..	..
102	Ship-owners, boat-owners and their employees, officers, mariners, etc., Ships brokers, boatmen and two men	2	2	..	..	..	..	..
	Total Order 20—Transport by Road	371	348	23	..	..	..	..
105	Persons (other than labourers) employed on the construction and maintenance of roads and bridges	4	4	..	..	..	..	..
107	Owners, managers and employees (excluding personal servants) connected with mechanically driven vehicles (including trams) ..	32	9	23	..	..	..	..
110	Pack elephant, camel, mule, ass and bullock, owners and drivers ..	330	330	..	..	..	..	..
111	Porters and messengers	5	5	..	..	..	..	..
	Total Order 21—Transport by Rail	988	912	76	..	..	..	..
112	Railway employees of all kinds other than coolies	975	903	72	..	..	..	..
113	Labourers employed on railway construction and maintenance and coolies and porters employed on railway premises	13	9	4	..	..	..	..
	Total Order 22—Post Office, Telegraph and Telephone Services ..	455	455	..	..	..	..	..
114	Post Office, Telegraph and Telephone services	455	455	..	..	..	..	..
	Total Sub-Class V—Trade	4,079	3,581	306	13	61	116	2
	Total Order 23—Banks, Establishments of Credit, Exchange and Insurance	343	265	4	..	1	73	..
115	Ban managers, money-lenders, exchange and insurance agents, money-changers and brokers and their employees	343	265	4	..	1	73	..

Group No.	Occupation.	Total following occupation.	As principal occupation.		As working dependants.		As subsidiary to other occupation.	
			Males.	Females.	Males.	Females.	Males.	Females.
1	2	3	4	5	6	7	8	9
	Total Order 24—Brokerage Commission and export	8	7	..	..	..	..	1
116	Brokers, commission agents, commercial travellers, warehouse-owners and employees	8	7	..	..	..	..	1
	Total Order 25—Trade in Textiles	30	30	..	..	..	..	..
117	Trade in piece-goods, wool, cotton, silk, hair and other textiles ..	30	30	..	..	..	..	..
	Total Order 26—Trade in Skins, Leather and Furs	7	7	..	..	..	..	..
118	Trade in skins, leather, furs, feathers, horn, etc., and the articles made from these	7	7	..	..	..	..	..
	Total Order 27—Trade in Wood	7	7	..	..	..	..	..
119	Trade in wood (not firewood)	7	7	..	..	..	..	..
	Total Order 28—Trade in Metals	326	325	..	..	..	1	..
123	Trade in metals, machinery, knives, tools, etc.	326	325	..	..	..	1	..
	Total Order 29—Trade in Pottery, Bricks and Tiles	2	2	..	..	..	..	..
124	Trade in pottery, bricks and tiles	2	2	..	..	..	..	..
	Total Order 30—Trade in Chemical Products	105	90	15	..	..	..	..
125	Drugs, dyes, paints, petroleum, explosives, etc.	105	90	15	..	..	..	..
	Total Order 31—Hotels, Cafes, Restaurants, etc.	329	280	36	5	..	7	1
126	Vendors of wine, liquors, aerated waters and ice	32	29	..	1	..	1	1
127	Owners and Managers of hotels, cook-shops, sarais, etc. (and employees)	297	251	36	4	..	6	..
	Total Order 32—Other Trade in Food stuffs	1,135	939	135	1	50	10	..
129	Grain and pulse dealers	95	80	13	..	2	..	..
131	Dealers in dairy products, eggs and poultry	179	145	26	..	7	1	..
133	Dealers in fodder for animals	31	31	..	..	..	..	..
134	Dealers in other foods-stuffs	616	565	39	1	3	8	..
135	Dealers in tobacco	204	108	57	..	38	1	..
136	Dealers in opium	10	10	..	..	..	..	..
	Total Order 33—Trade in Clothing and Toilet Articles	281	270	2	4	..	5	..
138	Trade in ready-made clothing and other articles of dress and the toilet (hats, umbrellas, socks, ready-made shoes, perfumes, etc.) ..	281	270	2	4	..	5	..
	Total Order 36—Trade in Means of Transport	444	441	..	..	..	3	..
142	Dealers and hirers, in mechanical transport motors, cycles, etc. ..	55	53	..	..	..		..
143	Dealers and hirers in other carriages, carts, boats, etc. ..	389	388	..	..	..	1	..
	Total Order 37—Trade in Fuel	25	25	..	..	..	..	..
145	Dealers in firewood, charcoal, coal, cowdung, etc.	25	25	..	..	..	..	..
	Total Order 38—Trade in Articles of Luxury and those Pertaining to Letters and the Arts and Sciences	748	651	78	3	10	6	..
146	Dealers in precious stones, jewellery (real and imitation), clocks, optical instruments, etc.	447	441	1	1	..	4	..
147	Dealers in common bangles, bead necklaces, fans, small articles, toys, hunting and fishing tackle, flowers, etc.	86	48	27	..	10	1	..
148	Publishers, booksellers, stationers, dealers in music, pictures, musical instruments and curiosities	215	162	50	2	..	1	..
	Total Order 39—Trade of other Sorts	289	242	36	..	..	11	..
149	Dealers in rags, stable refuse, etc.	16	13	3	..	..	..	..
150	General store-keepers and shop-keepers otherwise unspecified ..	273	229	33	..	..	11	..
	Total Class C—Public Administration and Liberal Arts ..	3,260	2,889	334	17	1	19	..
	Total Sub-Class VI—Public Force	991	991	..	..	..	..	..
	Total Order 40—Army	1	1	..	..	..	..	..
153	Army (Imperial)	1	1	..	..	..	..	..
	Total Order 43—Police	990	990	..	..	..	..	..
157	Police	988	988	..	..	..	..	..
158	Village watchmen	2	2	..	..	..	..	..

Group No.	Occupation.	Total following occupation.	As principal occupation.		As working dependants.		As subsidiary to other occupation.	
			Males.	Females.	Males.	Females.	Males.	Females.
1	2	3	4	5	6	7	8	9
	Total Sub-Class VII—Public Administration	1,198	994	201	3	..	..	..
	Total Order 44—Public Administration	1,198	994	201	3	..	..	..
159	Service of the State	491	487	4	..	..	..	..
160	Service of Indian and Foreign States	4	..	4	..	..	..	..
161	Municipal and other local (not village) service	646	458	188	..	..	..	..
162	Village officials and servants other than watchmen	57	49	5	3	..	..	..
	Total Sub-Class VIII—Professions and Liberal Arts	1,071	904	133	14	1	19	..
	Total Order 45—Religion	277	249	15	8	1	4	..
163	Priests, ministers, etc.	25	14	11				..
164	Monks, nuns, religious mendicants	241	226	2	8	1	4	..
165	Religious workers	9	7	2	..	..	..	..
166	Servants in religious edifices, burial and burning grounds, pilgrim conductors, circumcisers, etc.	2	2	..	..	..	..	..
	Total Order 46—Law	193	182	2	6	..	3	..
167	Lawyers of all kinds, including Qazis, Law Agents and Mukhtiars.	124	120	2	..	..	2	..
168	Lawyers' clerks, petition writers, etc.	69	62	..	6	..	1	..
	Total Order 47—Medicine	187	146	37	..	..	4	..
169	Registered medical practitioners including oculists	37	36	1	..	..	..	..
170	Other persons practising the healing arts without being registered	75	72	..	..	..	3	..
172	Midwives, Vaccinators, compounders, nurses, masseurs, etc. ..	75	38	36	..	..	1	..
	Total Order 48—Instruction	190	122	68	..	..	..	..
174	Professors and teachers of all kinds	172	108	64	..	..	..	..
175	Clerks and servants connected with education	18	14	4	..	..	..	..
	Total Order 49—Letters, Arts and Sciences (other than 44) ..	224	205	11	..	..	8	..
177	Architects, surveyors, engineers, and their employees (not being State servants)	63	58	..	..	..	5	..
179	Artists, sculptors and image-makers	38	38	..	..	..	..	..
181	Horoscope casters, astrologers, fortune-tellers, wizards, witches and medium	90	77	10	..	..	3	..
182	Musicians (composers and performers other than military), actors, dancers, etc.	32	32	..	..	..	..	..
183	Managers and employees of places of public entertainments, race courses, societies, clubs	1	..	1	..	..	..	..
	Total Class D—Miscellaneous	4,761	3,907	647	35	67	100	5
	Total Sub-Class IX—Persons living on their Income	318	203	68	4	24	14	5
	Total Order 50—Persons living Principally on their Income ..	318	203	68	4	24	14	5
185	Proprietors (other than of agricultural land), fund and scholarships holders and pensioners	318	203	68	4	24	14	5
	Total Sub-Class X—Domestic Service	1,614	1,342	169	11	15	77	..
	Total Order 51—Domestic Service	1,614	1,342	169	11	15	77	..
186	Private motor-drivers and cleaners	386	374	..	..	..	12	..
187	Other domestic service	1,228	968	169	11	15	65	..
	Total Sub-Class XI—Insufficiently Described Occupations ..	2,244	2,010	216	11	3	4	..
	Total Order 52—General terms which do not indicate a definite occupation	2,244	2,010	216	11	3	4	..
188	Manufacturers, businessmen and contractors, otherwise unspecified	2	2	..	..	..	..	..
189	Cashiers, accountants, book-keepers, clerks and other employees in unspecified offices and warehouses and shops	672	607	49	11	1	4	..
191	Labourers and workmen otherwise unspecified	1,570	1,401	167	..	2	..	..
	Total Sub-Class XII—Unproductive	585	352	194	9	25	5	..
	Total Order 54—Beggars, Bagrants, Prostitutes	383	232	127	9	15	..	..
193	Beggars and vagrants	335	232	83	9	11	..	..
194	Procurers and prostitutes	48	..	44	..	4	..	..
	Total Order 55—Other Unclassified Non-Productive Industries ..	202	120	67	..	10	5	..
195	Other unclassified non-productive industries	202	120	67	..	10	5	..

CITY TABLE VIII—CITIES OTHER THAN BOMBAY AND KARACHI (POONA AND SHOLAPUR).

(Corresponding to Imperial Table XIX.)

EUROPEAN AND ALLIED RACES AND ANGLO-INDIANS BY RACE AND AGE.

(A) Europeans and Allied Races (including Armenians).

Name of City.	Total.			British Subjects.														
				All Ages.			0–13.		14–16.		17–23.		24–33.		34–43.		44–53.	
	Total.	Males.	Females.	Total.	Males.	Females.	Males.	Females.	Males.	Females.	Males.	Females.	Males.	Females.	Males.	Females.	Males.	Females.
1	2	3	4	5	6	7	8	9	10	11	12	13	14	15	16	17	18	19
Poona ..	3,503	2,619	884	3,459	2,595	864	164	178	46	26	870	114	1,055	224	229	186	121	90
Sholapur ..	57	34	23	56	33	23	10	5	2	..	..	2	5	7	8	4	7	4

Name of City.	British Subjects—concld.		Others (including Armenians).																	
	54 and over.		All Ages.			0–13.		14–16.		17–23.		24–33.		34–43.		44–53.		54 and over.	
	Males.	Females.	Total.	Males.	Females.	Males.	Females.	Males.	Females.	Males.	Females.	Males.	Females.	Males.	Females.	Males.	Females.	Males.	Females.
1	20	21	22	23	24	25	26	27	28	29	30	31	32	33	34	35	36	37	38
Poona ..	110	40	44	24	20	..	2	..	..	..	1	2	8	9	4	10	5	3	..
Sholapur ..	1	1	1	1	..	..	..	..	..	..	..	..	..	..	..	..	..	1	..

(B) Anglo-Indians.

Name of City.	All Ages.			0–3.		4–6.		7–13.		14–16.		17–19.		20–29.		30–39.		40–49.		50–59.		60–69.		70 and over.	
	Total.	Males.	Females.	Males.	Females.	Males.	Females.	Males.	Females.	Males.	Females.	Males.	Females.	Males.	Females.	Males.	Females.	Males.	Females.	Males.	Females.	Males.	Females.	Males.	Females.
1	2	3	4	5	6	7	8	9	10	11	12	13	14	15	16	17	18	19	20	21	22	23	24	25	26
Poona	1,476	621	855	32	52	44	65	83	188	39	102	39	70	119	145	82	80	63	79	43	40	15	29	62	5
Sholapur	176	52	124	17	13	12	15	14	14	1	7	2	10	2	30	2	17	..	8	..	7	2	3	..	..

MO-I Bk Ra Cs 3—73

General Classification of Buildings by uses.

The scheme of classification adopted on this occasion is generally the same as that adopted at the 1921 Census.

Building means.—" The whole building under one undivided roof, or under two or more roofs connected *inter se* by subsidiary roofs."

Bungalows and dwelling houses.—This includes blocks of flats, residential hotels, club chambers, etc.

Servant's quarters includes cases of servants' quarters attached to or over kitchens, godowns, garages, stables, etc.

Chawl means a building containing a number of separate small tenements.

Factories, shops, offices, etc., combined with dwellings.—This is used in a wide sense, and includes all cases of buildings which contain partly offices (of all kinds including public offices), or shops, or rooms used for any commercial purpose, and partly rooms used as ordinary dwellings.

Institutions includes Hospitals, Jails, Asylums, Hostels, " Lines " etc.

Huts includes tents, lean-tos, and all other temporary structures used as dwellings.

Institutions and places of amusement.—This includes Theatres, Assembly Rooms, Libraries, Gymkhanas, Club houses, Schools, Colleges and all Public buildings not combined with dwellings.

Factories, mills and works.—This includes all kinds of workshops and repair shops, and any building in which anything is manufactured, for instance a bakery.

Godowns, stables, garages, sheds and chowkies.—Here are placed all buildings in which any kind of stores are placed, or animals or conveyances are kept, or which are used for night or day watchmen to sit in, without constituting residential quarters.

The terms " Residential " and " Non-residential " refer to the *ordinary* uses of each building, and are irrespective of whether any person was or was not enumerated in the building on the Census night.

Buildings under the control of the Royal Indian Marine, Customs and Railways are shown separately at the end of each Section, and not in the Circle within which they are situated. Buildings under Military control are shown at the end of the table.

The figures in the Table include buildings under construction or demolition. These are also separately shown below for each Ward. But those under control of the Royal Indian Marine, Customs and Railways are not separated.

Number of buildings under construction or demolition.

Ward.	Under construction.	Under demolition.
A	13	29
B	4	30
C	21	16
D	15	52
E	5	67
F	5	37
G	8	48
Total	71	279

Out of these 228 are residential and 122 non-residential.

General Classification of Buildings.

Ward.	Serial No. of section.	Name of Section.	Serial No. of circle.	Residential Buildings.								Non-Residential Buildings.						Total number of buildings.
				Bungalows and dwelling houses.	Servant's quarters.	Chawls.	Factories, shops, offices, etc. combined with dwellings.	Dharmashalas.	Institutions.	Huts.	Others and unclassifiable.	Places of worship.	Institutions and places of amusements.	Factories, Mills and Works.	Offices and shops.	Godowns, stables, garages, sheds and chowkies.	Others and unclassifiable.	
		Grand total of Bombay City	..	9,624	1,023	9,075	6,596	106	307	5,459	33	755	612	1,535	3,254	12,229	222	50,833
A		Grand total for A Ward ..	..	668	214	270	898	5	47	166	14	55	71	146	372	950	10	3,886
	1	Upper Colaba—Total ..	1	25	8	7	2	..	..	32	..	13	3	3	4	19	2	118
	2	Lower Colaba—Total ..	..	306	111	74	88	1	5	82	1	13	9	20	35	271	2	1,018
			1	73	39	3	5	..	1	2	..	2	..	..	1	49	..	175
			2	37	21	16	13	..	1	4	..	..	1	10	6	66	..	175
			3	54	..	4	24	1	..	..	..	2	..	..	2	2	..	89
			4	24	..	6	5	..	..	8	..	1	1	..	2	5	1	53
			5	22	..	13	8	..	..	40	..	4	..	..	2	10	..	99
			6	31	33	18	8	..	8	6	..	3	4	4	6	63	..	179
			7	3	3	7	5	..	..	1	..	..	1	1	1	10	..	32
			8	56	12	..	10	..	..	12	1	1	..	1	9	83	1	145
			Customs	..	..	..	..	..	..	..	..	..	..	..	..	2	..	2
			B.B.C.I.	6	3	7	..	..	..	9	..	..	2	4	6	30	..	67
			B.P.T.	..	..	..	1	..	..	..	..	..	..	..	..	1	..	2
	3	Fort, South—Total ..	..	22	23	..	101	..	8	1	..	4	6	53	100	67	..	380
			1	2	1	..	28	..	..	..	..	..	..	1	22	4	..	58
			2	7	3	..	28	..	1	..	..	2	1	8	33	12	..	95
			3	2	3	..	14	..	..	..	..	2	1	4	23	5	..	54
			4	2	..	..	20	..	..	..	..	..	..	4	10	4	..	40
			5	3	5	..	9	..	..	1	..	..	2	1	4	9	..	34
			6	..	2	..	1	..	..	..	..	..	..	1	4	10	..	18
			Customs	..	..	..	1	..	..	..	..	..	1	..	1	1	..	4
			B.P.T.	..	..	..	..	..	..	..	..	..	..	..	..	6	..	6
			R. I. M.	6	9	..	..	..	2	..	..	..	1	34	3	16	..	71
	4	Fort, North—Total ..	..	197	16	9	617	..	8	15	12	16	10	51	73	156	3	1,183
			1	31	1	..	88	..	..	1	11	5	..	1	4	5	..	147
			2	16	3	..	37	..	2	4	..	..	..	..	13	7	..	82
			3	69	..	..	61	..	..	..	..	2	1	7	2	6	1	149
			4	31	..	..	59	..	1	1	..	3	3	2	5	4	..	109
			5	14	..	..	77	..	..	..	..	1	1	2	14	12	1	122
			6	11	1	1	144	..	..	..	..	4	..	5	5	7	..	178
			7	8	..	1	81	..	..	3	..	1	1	8	1	6	..	110
			8	12	9	7	67	..	3	5	1	..	4	26	19	69	1	223
			Customs	5	1	..	1	..	2	1	..	..	..	..	5	22	..	37
			B.P.T.	..	1	..	2	..	..	..	..	..	..	..	5	18	..	26
	5	Esplanade—Total ..	..	118	56	180	90	4	31	36	1	9	43	19	160	437	3	1,187
			1	53	12	53	24	..	4	12	..	1	8	1	18	55	..	241
			2	16	13	7	25	..	1	1	1	1	9	..	22	26	1	123
			3	29	21	84	16	4	18	7	..	5	19	5	27	76	..	311
			4	15	2	29	16	..	3	11	..	1	1	7	29	91	..	205
			Customs	3	4	2	..	..	..	1	..	..	2	..	17	74	2	105
			B. P. T.	..	..	..	7	..	..	..	..	..	..	..	10	56	..	73
			G. I. P.	..	4	..	1	..	4	..	..	..	..	6	16	24	..	55
			B.B.C.I.	2	..	5	1	..	1	4	..	1	4	..	21	35	..	74
B		Grand Total for B Ward	..	398	7	334	1,262	6	12	81	4	85	54	61	390	887	29	3,610
	6	Chakla—Total ..	..	24	..	5	482	1	1	4	..	15	8	13	95	47	..	695
			1	1	..	..	78	..	..	..	..	2	..	1	1	7	..	90
			2	3	..	..	97	..	..	..	..	2	..	2	35	3	..	142
			3	..	..	1	80	1	..	..	..	3	..	..	1	..	..	86
			4	8	..	2	79	..	..	..	..	2	3	..	9	5	..	108
			5	1	..	..	63	..	1	2	..	3	2	1	5	6	..	84
			6	7	..	2	48	..	..	2	..	1	2	8	31	15	..	116
			7	4	..	..	37	..	..	..	..	2	1	1	13	11	..	69
	7	Mandvi—Total ..	..	28	1	10	562	2	1	8	4	26	14	7	211	335	3	1,212
			1	8	..	1	58	..	..	..	..	1	..	1	9	8	..	86
			2	..	..	..	18	..	..	..	..	3	1	..	..	..	..	22
			3	4	..	1	25	..	..	..	..	4	5	1	12	7	..	59
			4	3	..	2	49	..	..	..	..	1	1	..	11	9	..	76
			5	..	..	..	33	..	..	..	..	2	..	..	7	2	..	44
			6	1	..	..	32	..	..	..	..	1	1	..	3	5	..	43
			7	..	..	1	41	..	..	..	..	1	..	..	22	29	..	94
			8	1	..	1	36	..	..	..	..	..	..	..	24	24	..	86
			9	3	..	..	103	1	1	..	..	5	3	1	19	25	..	161
			10	3	..	..	74	..	..	..	..	4	1	..	21	16	..	119
			11	3	..	..	46	1	..	..	..	1	1	1	14	45	..	112
			12	..	..	..	47	..	..	8	4	8	..	3	52	90	1	208
			Customs	1	1	..	..	..	..	..	..	..	..	..	3	13	..	18
			B.P.T.	1	..	4	..	..	..	..	..	..	1	..	12	60	2	80
			G. I. P.	..	..	..	..	..	..	..	..	..	..	..	2	2	..	4

Ward.	Serial No. of section.	Name of Section.	Serial No. of circle.	Residential Buildings.								Non-Residential Buildings.						Total number of buildings.
				Bungalows and dwelling houses.	Servant's quarters.	Chawls.	Factories, shops, offices, etc. combined with dwellings.	Dharmashalas.	Institutions.	Huts.	Others and unclassifiable.	Places of worship.	Institutions and places of amusements.	Factories, Mills and Works.	Offices and shops.	Godowns, stables, garages, sheds and chowkies.	Others and unclassifiable.	
	8	Umarkhadi—Total ..	..	304	3	257	186	2	7	19	..	30	26	22	41	107	21	1,025
			1	7	..	24	21	..	..	6	..	3	..	1	5	8	1	76
			2	40	..	15	20	..	..	..	..	1	1	1	2	2	..	91
			3	16	..	12	10	1	..	..	..	4	3	2	2	4	4	58
			4	43	..	2	8	..	..	..	..	3	4	..	..	5	..	65
			5	33	..	..	9	..	1	..	..	3	1	1	1	3	1	53
			6	73	..	9	25	..	1	..	..	2	1	2	4	15	..	132
			7	22	..	80	33	..	2	..	..	6	3	..	11	15	1	173
			8	19	2	42	36	..	1	13	..	5	4	13	6	28	4	173
			9	51	1	73	15	1	2	..	..	3	9	2	10	27	10	204
	9	Dongri—Total ..	..	42	3	62	32	1	3	50	..	14	6	19	43	398	5	678
			1	14	..	6	11	..	..	..	..	2	..	2	..	9	..	44
			2	4	..	16	5	..	..	12	..	5	1	2	5	24	..	74
			3	7	1	19	..	..	3	3	..	4	1	3	..	7	..	48
			4	9	2	13	11	1	..	28	..	2	4	2	10	150	1	233
			Customs	..	..	..	1	..	..	..	..	..	..	2	5	107	..	115
			B. P. T.	5	..	..	..	..	..	1	..	..	..	3	11	12	..	32
			G. I. P.	3	..	8	4	..	..	6	..	1	..	5	12	89	4	132
C		Grand Total for C Ward	..	946	17	1,497	1,846	48	11	50	2	110	65	128	354	535	21	5,630
	10	Market—Total ..	..	142	1	68	593	6	..	11	..	25	4	24	116	75	5	1,070
			1	12	..	14	61	1	..	1	..	..	..	4	5	10	..	111
			2	18	..	..	38	..	..	7	..	2	..	2	7	13	..	87
			3	25	..	..	21	..	..	..	..	2	1	1	29	7	..	86
			4	10	1	1	37	..	..	..	..	..	..	2	3	9	2	65
			5	25	..	13	116	..	..	1	..	3	..	5	21	17	..	201
			6	46	..	40	65	2	..	1	..	4	..	4	8	9	..	179
			7	4	..	..	80	3	..	1	..	10	3	5	24	7	1	138
			8	2	..	..	172	..	..	..	..	4	..	1	19	3	2	203
	11	Dhobi Talao—Total ..	..	323	12	344	268	14	3	8	1	15	16	5	55	126	3	1,193
			1	132	1	44	64	1	..	3	..	2	2	..	3	34	1	287
			2	29	..	11	21	..	..	..	..	7	4	2	6	9	2	91
			3	81	1	40	19	13	..	..	..	3	1	..	4	18	..	180
			4	27	..	7	51	..	..	..	..	1	1	..	3	9	..	99
			5	29	8	5	51	..	..	4	1	1	3	..	6	10	..	118
			6	21	..	79	40	..	2	..	..	..	3	2	17	21	..	185
			7	4	2	158	22	..	1	1	..	1	2	1	13	23	..	228
			B.B.C.I.	..	..	..	..	..	..	..	..	..	..	..	3	2	..	5
	12	Panaswadi—Total ..	..	273	3	266	165	13	3	9	..	29	20	41	55	128	3	1,008
			1	141	2	52	79	2	3	5	..	19	12	13	21	75	2	426
			2	77	1	119	51	2	..	3	..	3	1	21	21	29	1	329
			3	55	..	95	35	9	..	1	..	7	7	7	13	24	..	253
	13	Bhuleshwar—Total ..	..	139	..	385	388	6	1	16	..	23	15	15	38	102	4	1,132
			1	17	..	69	54	1	1	5	..	8	3	..	6	4	..	168
			2	7	..	65	33	..	..	6	..	3	2	2	4	7	..	129
			3	6	..	40	19	2	..	3	..	3	5	8	13	35	3	137
			4	57	..	121	78	..	..	2	..	6	3	3	6	29	..	305
			5	38	..	54	123	..	..	..	..	1	1	2	6	19	..	244
			6	14	..	36	81	3	..	..	..	2	1	..	3	8	1	149
	14	Kumbharwada—Total ..	..	55	..	302	174	8	3	4	1	6	7	30	32	62	1	685
			1	32	..	112	63	4	2	..	1	2	4	6	11	21	..	258
			2	6	..	116	56	4	1	1	..	3	2	11	17	20	..	237
			3	10	..	39	88	..	..	..	..	..	..	10	2	7	1	107
			4	7	..	35	17	..	..	3	..	1	1	3	2	14	..	83
	15	Khara Talao—Total ..	..	14	1	132	258	1	1	2	..	12	3	13	58	42	5	542
			1	2	..	44	19	..	..	..	..	2	1	..	11	14	2	95
			2	1	1	18	17	..	..	..	..	3	2	1	3	4	..	50
			3	4	..	1	97	..	1	2	..	3	..	8	18	4	2	140
			4	4	..	..	97	..	..	..	..	4	..	..	18	10	..	133
			5	3	..	69	28	1	..	..	..	..	..	4	8	10	1	124
D		Grand Total for D Ward ..	..	2,309	488	1,447	1,031	20	35	565	5	147	134	130	394	2,087	38	8,830
	16	Khetwadi—Total ..	..	333	33	347	261	2	12	59	..	30	49	55	101	301	3	1,591
			1	63	13	15	34	1	6	18	..	2	7	7	7	63	1	237
			2	55	3	33	50	..	..	8	..	4	4	4	14	44	..	219
			3	65	2	72	26	1	2	2	..	2	13	5	5	54	..	249
			4	54	14	34	29	..	1	18	..	6	9	4	30	43	1	243
			5	35	1	42	23	..	..	1	..	3	..	3	2	19	..	129
			6	41	5	39	18	..	3	..	..	4	7	4	6	11	1	139
			7	15	..	54	31	..	..	5	..	4	3	3	4	20	..	139
			8	5	..	58	50	..	..	7	..	5	6	25	33	44	..	233
			B.B.C.I.	..	..	..	..	..	..	..	..	..	..	..	..	3	..	3

Ward.	Serial No. of section.	Name of Section.	Serial No. of circle.	Residential Buildings.								Non-Residential Buildings.						Total number of buildings.
				Bungalows and dwelling houses.	Servant's quarters.	Chawls.	Factories, shops, offices, etc. combined with dwellings.	Dharmashalas.	Institutions.	Huts.	Others and unclassifiable.	Places of worship.	Institutions and places of amusements.	Factories, Mills and Works.	Offices and shops.	Godowns, stables, garages, sheds and cowsheds.	Others and unclassifiable.	
	17	Girgaum—Total ..	..	268	2	484	185	6	5	55	2	33	22	29	84	164	12	1,351
			1	39	1	92	33	1	..	16	..	4	6	23	19	52	10	296
			2	33	..	46	21	..	..	4	..	1	..	1	12	5	1	124
			3	21	..	84	32	3	3	2	..	9	5	..	10	16	..	185
			4	12	..	25	8	2	1	3	1	..	..	..	3	6	..	61
			5	29	1	97	24	..	..	8	1	2	2	2	4	8	..	178
			6	117	..	113	46	..	1	15	..	13	5	3	21	58	1	393
			7	17	..	27	21	..	..	7	..	4	4	..	14	19	..	113
			B.B.C.I.	..	..	..	..	..	..	..	..	..	..	..	1	..	..	1
	18	Chaupaty—Total ..	..	258	20	61	147	..	2	62	1	5	18	8	45	189	..	816
			1	26	5	2	23	..	1	5	1	..	6	1	5	47	..	122
			2	71	6	17	20	..	..	19	..	1	3	1	7	31	..	176
			3	38	5	11	11	..	..	6	..	..	..	..	3	23	..	97
			4	35	..	10	26	..	..	12	..	1	..	2	1	34	..	121
			5	77	..	17	33	..	1	14	..	3	3	1	13	25	..	187
			6	11	4	4	34	..	..	6	..	..	6	3	16	27	..	111
			B.B.C.I.	..	..	..	..	..	..	..	..	..	..	..	..	2	..	2
	19	Walkeshwar—Total ..	..	752	219	234	235	9	11	101	1	53	27	17	39	637	6	2,341
			1	149	27	58	51	5	10	12	1	7	7	7	10	136	3	483
			2	134	12	43	44	..	1	18	..	8	2	..	7	69	..	338
			3	111	25	84	39	..	..	19	..	2	3	3	12	109	1	408
			4	24	14	14	9	..	..	3	..	1	..	..	..	19	..	84
			5	42	42	7	11	..	..	4	..	..	6	..	1	60	..	173
			6	162	19	19	45	4	..	29	..	33	5	..	6	95	..	417
			7	84	80	9	36	..	..	16	..	2	1	7	1	127	..	363
			Government House.	46	..	..	..	..	..	..	..	..	3	..	2	21	2	74
			Customs	..	..	..	..	..	..	..	..	..	..	..	..	1	..	1
	20	Mahalaxmi—Total ..	..	698	209	321	203	3	5	288	1	26	18	21	125	796	17	2,731
			1	183	76	32	40	..	1	23	1	1	6	2	8	174	10	557
			2	54	10	22	8	2	1	21	..	10	..	..	3	49	..	180
			3	59	54	15	13	..	..	14	..	..	1	..	3	67	..	226
			4	81	43	49	32	..	..	125	..	2	2	..	30	210	3	586
			5	47	1	32	31	1	..	20	..	4	..	1	11	31	..	179
			6	94	5	19	33	..	..	8	..	1	2	1	12	42	..	217
			7	43	7	47	8	..	..	6	..	1	2	10	15	68	1	208
			8	14	1	34	9	..	..	8	..	1	..	3	8	43	..	121
			9	101	9	69	29	..	1	59	..	4	3	4	17	90	1	387
			Government House.	13	2	..	..	..	2	..	..	2	..	..	1	6	..	26
			B.B.C.I.	9	1	2	..	..	..	4	..	..	2	..	8	16	2	44
E		Grand Total for E Ward	..	1,944	117	2,011	780	16	74	754	2	140	145	373	716	3,015	32	10,119
	21	Tardeo—Total ..	..	189	9	234	110	4	3	82	..	13	24	49	95	223	7	1,042
			1	76	..	35	22	..	1	23	..	2	8	4	11	42	1	225
			2	70	4	54	43	2	1	14	..	1	6	10	24	37	3	269
			3	23	1	64	19	2	1	19	..	7	9	16	30	70	2	263
			4	20	4	79	26	..	..	26	..	3	1	19	24	56	1	259
			B.B.C.I.	..	..	2	..	..	..	..	..	..	..	..	6	18	..	26
	22	Kamathipura—Total ..	..	629	..	163	128	2	..	16	..	28	4	13	27	84	2	1,096
			1	132	..	39	32	..	..	6	..	12	1	1	11	33	2	269
			2	464	..	32	61	..	..	7	..	7	2	4	6	33	..	616
			3	33	..	92	35	2	..	3	..	9	1	8	10	18	..	211
	23	First Nagpada—Total ..	..	18	13	58	5	..	4	22	..	11	1	2	6	25	2	167
			1	18	13	29	5	..	4	12	..	8	1	2	6	24	2	124
			2	..	..	29	..	..	..	10	..	3	..	..	..	1	..	43
	24	Second Nagpada—Total ..	..	150	..	100	169	..	..	3	1	2	3	24	17	45	1	515
			1	9	..	24	41	..	..	..	..	1	..	12	5	16	..	108
			2	46	..	2	54	..	..	1	..	..	1	8	12	14	1	139
			3	72	..	36	48	..	..	1	..	1	..	1	..	10	..	169
			4	23	..	38	26	..	..	1	1	..	2	3	..	5	..	99
	25	Byculla—Total ..	..	313	12	979	112	..	22	148	1	34	45	114	227	828	10	2,845
			1	166	9	277	65	..	6	38	1	3	18	55	63	305	4	1,010
			2	56	..	83	20	..	15	16	..	8	10	10	28	99	2	342
			3	29	2	212	9	..	1	24	..	7	4	23	36	166	1	514
			4	2	..	163	6	..	..	12	..	5	1	8	14	65	..	276
			5	4	..	21	1	..	..	4	..	8	..	4	15	16	..	68
			6	31	..	68	6	..	..	26	..	3	3	8	19	81	..	245
			7	8	..	84	4	..	..	10	..	7	4	..	9	15	1	142
			8	7	1	62	1	..	..	6	..	3	3	4	7	36	..	130
			B.B.C.I.	2	..	3	..	..	..	4	..	..	..	2	7	3	2	23
			G. I. P.	8	..	6	..	..	..	8	..	..	2	..	29	42	..	95

Ward.	Serial No. of section.	Name of Section.	Serial No. of circle.	Residential Buildings.								Non-Residential Buildings.						Total number of buildings.
				Bungalows and dwelling houses.	Servant's quarters.	Chawls.	Factories, shops, offices, etc. combined with dwellings.	Dharmashalas.	Institutions.	Huts.	Others and unclassifiable.	Places of worship.	Institutions and places of amusements.	Factories, Mills and Works.	Offices and shops.	Godowns, stables, garages, sheds and chowkies.	Others and unclassifiable.	
	26	Tarwadi—Total ..	..	234	67	228	146	4	39	187	..	18	49	100	137	809	6	2,024
			1	23	18	39	26	..	28	16	..	5	25	13	28	105	2	328
			2	160	24	70	83	3	7	47	..	8	9	37	53	383	2	886
			3	42	16	118	35	1	4	110	..	5	14	49	47	287	2	780
			G. I. P.	9	9	1	2	..	..	14	..	..	1	1	9	34	..	80
	27	Mazgaon—Total ..	..	411	16	249	110	6	6	296	..	34	19	71	207	1,001	4	2,430
			1	27	3	44	20	..	..	19	..	6	2	3	15	65	..	204
			2	89	1	14	34	..	3	11	..	1	1	1	11	41	..	207
			3	41	..	21	13	..	..	40	..	8	3	4	20	51	1	197
			4	139	..	48	22	2	..	42	..	6	1	10	23	43	..	336
			5	106	12	113	21	4	..	155	..	18	10	39	99	580	2	1,159
			B.P.T.	3	..	9	..	..	3	..	..	..	1	1	8	70	..	95
			Customs	5	..	..	..	..	..	29	..	..	1	13	25	124	1	198
			G. I. P.	1	..	..	..	..	..	..	..	..	..	..	6	27	..	34
F		Grand Total for F Ward	..	1,344	79	1,421	384	4	25	1,225	1	89	69	266	480	2,051	32	7,470
	28	Parel—Total ..	..	276	24	431	98	..	7	277	..	25	14	120	127	658	8	2,065
			1	10	..	31	1	..	..	1	..	1	..	..	..	2	..	46
			2	5	3	43	2	..	2	15	..	2	..	18	32	109	1	232
			3	20	1	61	12	..	..	21	..	2	3	10	20	81	..	231
			4	6	..	28	1	..	..	..	..	..	..	..	1	3	1	40
			5	..	..	50	2	..	..	4	..	3	..	20	8	37	2	126
			6	95	15	72	49	..	8	16	..	4	..	2	11	80	1	348
			7	6	..	38	4	..	..	5	..	4	1	21	13	39	..	131
			8	39	5	68	22	..	2	190	..	8	6	37	21	223	3	624
			9	76	..	33	4	..	..	10	..	..	3	..	6	15	..	147
			G. I. P.	19	..	7	1	..	..	15	..	1	1	12	15	69	..	140
	29	Sewri—Total ..	..	209	22	286	94	2	1	426	1	15	6	57	119	593	2	1,833
			1	21	4	70	31	2	..	150	..	3	2	20	21	159	1	484
			2	9	..	48	29	..	..	187	1	2	..	29	16	133	..	454
			3	70	..	38	14	..	..	23	..	..	..	..	5	22	..	172
			4	88	..	79	9	..	1	46	..	8	2	2	22	34	..	291
			5	1	1	24	2	..	..	2	..	..	..	..	6	24	..	60
			6	..	2	1	..	..	..	2	..	..	..	..	1	10	..	16
			7	2	2	16	..	..	..	7	..	..	..	..	6	34	..	67
			B.P.T.	18	13	10	9	..	..	9	..	2	2	6	42	176	1	288
			Customs	..	..	..	..	..	..	..	..	..	..	..	..	1	..	1
	30	Sion—Total	..	859	33	704	192	2	17	529	..	49	49	89	234	800	22	3,572
			1	52	1	55	24	..	2	9	..	5	4	3	29	70	2	256
			2	34	..	45	15	..	..	23	..	1	2	4	13	49	1	187
			3	53	1	141	25	..	1	27	..	6	10	..	34	47	..	345
			4	15	2	85	11	..	1	24	..	2	1	13	12	40	2	208
			5	94	1	52	14	..	..	53	..	3	..	4	9	30	..	260
			6	184	3	12	19	1	3	49	..	9	10	28	36	121	4	479
			7	75	4	70	18	..	2	62	..	8	7	14	22	80	7	309
			8	84	2	37	5	..	6	19	..	2	5	1	6	89	1	257
			9	85	..	34	20	..	..	21	..	4	1	2	4	23	1	195
			10	37	1	45	15	..	..	120	..	3	5	1	10	27	1	265
			11	122	..	13	8	1	2	53	..	6	..	..	3	24	..	232
			G. I. P.	7	6	24	2	..	..	38	..	..	..	..	30	84	2	199
			B.B.C.I.	..	..	..	..	..	..	..	..	..	..	..	1	1	..	2
			B.P.T.	16	11	90	5	..	..	24	..	..	4	19	19	109	1	298
			Customs	1	1	1	11	..	..	..	..	..	..	..	..	6	..	20
G		Grand Total for G Ward	..	1,917	27	2,084	390	9	40	2,615	5	128	54	423	518	2,546	54	10,810
	31	Mahim—Total ..	..	1,102	27	635	273	5	21	1,263	5	51	30	163	199	797	18	4,584
			1	44	1	5	8	3	..	13	..	..	2	20	2	82	3	183
			2	209	..	133	29	..	2	263	..	2	6	3	17	177	2	843
			3	53	4	99	26	1	4	214	..	8	5	19	23	90	3	549
			4	160	15	12	36	..	5	96	5	5	2	1	6	87	1	431
			5	240	3	74	120	1	3	73	..	17	5	9	13	94	1	653
			6	243	..	112	17	..	..	286	..	6	3	11	17	124	..	819
			7	94	..	27	15	..	..	40	..	3	2	37	14	58	3	293
			8	34	..	162	22	..	..	277	..	10	3	57	17	61	..	643
			Customs	..	1	..	..	..	..	..	..	..	..	..	1	..	..	2
			G. I. P.	15	2	4	..	..	7	..	..	..	2	6	72	..	..	108
			B.B.C.I.	10	1	7	..	..	..	1	..	..	..	..	17	24	..	60
	32	Worli—Total ..	..	815	..	1,449	117	4	19	1,352	..	77	24	260	319	1,749	41	6,226
			1	37	..	78	1	4	..	55	..	19	5	14	25	194	20	452
			2	35	..	148	15	..	13	34	..	7	10	38	48	277	8	628
			3	15	..	78	7	..	..	33	..	1	..	4	15	26	1	180
			4	3	..	27	2	..	..	1	..	..	..	2	3	9	..	47
			5	31	..	161	34	..	..	42	..	11	..	59	65	407	1	811
			6	359	..	6	21	..	..	214	..	9	1	2	2	22	2	638
			7	48	..	437	12	..	3	328	..	13	5	75	53	414	6	1,394
			8	273	..	493	22	..	3	640	..	17	3	38	47	268	2	1,801
			9	..	..	1	..	..	..	1	..	..	..	1	12	35	..	50
			10	2	..	5	..	..	..	3	..	..	..	4	17	37	..	68
			B.B.C.I.	12	..	17	2	..	..	1	..	..	..	19	28	33	1	108
			G. I. P.	..	..	3	1	..	..	..	..	..	..	4	9	30	..	47
			Customs	..	..	..	..	..	..	..	..	..	..	..	..	1	..	1
			B.P.T.	..	..	..	..	..	..	..	..	..	..	..	..	1	..	1
		Military—Total ..	..	98	74	11	5	..	63	3	..	1	20	9	30	158	6	473
A	1	Upper Colaba ..	..	75	61	11	3	..	30	1	..	..	15	8	20	67	2	293
	3	Fort South	..	7	..	..	..	..	..	..	..	..	1	..	6	16	..	30
	5	Esplanade	..	6	11	..	2	..	24	2	..	1	2	1	3	24	..	70
D	20	Mahalaxmi	..	..	..	..	..	..	8	..	..	..	..	..	..	..	..	8
		Harbour Islands ..	..	10	2	..	..	..	1	..	..	..	2	..	1	51	4	71

Classification of Buildings by the Number of Floors contained in each.

This Table explains itself. It is in the same form as in 1921. The Buildings included in this Table are the same as in Housing Table I.

Ward.	Section No.	Name of Section.	Circle No.	Number of Buildings with: Ground floor only.	One upper floor.	Two upper floors.	Three upper floors.	Four upper floors.	Five or more upper floors.	Total number of buildings.
1	2	3	4	5	6	7	8	9	10	11
		Grand Total, Bombay City	..	30,342	7,296	5,599	4,322	2,489	785	50,833
A		Grand Total for A Ward	..	1,987	455	397	429	426	192	3,886
	1	Upper Colaba	1	111	6	1	..	..	..	118
	2	Lower Colaba—Total	..	565	154	155	94	45	5	1,018
			1	83	32	43	13	4	..	175
			2	123	16	17	13	5	1	175
			3	14	26	30	19	..	..	89
			4	20	16	14	3	..	..	53
			5	57	15	20	5	2	..	99
			6	115	26	23	14	1	..	179
			7	10	8	3	1	1	..	32
			8	69	9	5	26	32	4	145
			Customs	2	..	..	..	..	..	2
			B. B. C. I.	61	6	..	..	..	..	67
			B. P. T.	2	..	..	..	..	..	2
	3	Fort, South—Total	..	132	76	64	62	33	13	380
			1	6	8	13	19	9	3	58
			2	26	22	19	18	7	3	95
			3	13	11	11	7	8	4	54
			4	4	4	10	14	6	2	40
			5	19	6	4	2	3	..	34
			6	12	5	..	..	..	1	18
			Customs	..	1	2	1	..	..	4
			B. P. T.	4	2	..	..	..	..	6
			R. I. M.	48	17	5	1	..	..	71
	4	Fort, North—Total	..	317	95	89	211	300	171	1,183
			1	31	6	6	41	46	17	147
			2	24	15	11	13	13	6	82
			3	20	10	17	24	50	28	149
			4	15	9	4	21	34	26	109
			5	24	9	16	31	28	14	122
			6	19	12	10	33	63	41	178
			7	23	7	6	19	29	26	110
			8	105	25	18	26	36	13	223
			Customs	33	1	1	1	1	..	37
			B. P. T.	23	1	..	2	..	..	26
	5	Esplanade—Total	..	862	124	88	62	48	3	1,187
			1	141	45	27	18	10	..	241
			2	55	13	19	14	21	1	123
			3	231	20	21	15	14	1	311
			4	165	16	11	9	3	1	205
			Customs	88	8	7	2	..	..	105
			B. P. T.	69	4	..	..	..	..	73
			G. I. P.	45	3	3	4	..	..	55
			B. B. C. I.	68	6	....	..	..	..	74
B		Grand Total for B Ward	..	1,292	545	454	585	544	190	3,610
	6	Chakla—Total	..	74	102	103	147	188	81	695
			1	2	8	8	17	42	13	90
			2	14	30	18	26	34	20	142
			3	2	3	14	28	30	9	86
			4	10	7	15	27	26	23	108
			5	11	7	11	20	29	6	84
			6	23	30	28	16	13	6	116
			7	12	17	9	13	14	4	69
	7	Mandvi—Total	..	426	200	131	189	197	69	1,212
			1	12	8	18	26	20	2	86
			2	3	1	3	3	12	..	22
			3	19	9	6	16	8	1	59
			4	5	15	10	14	24	8	76
			5	3	5	2	10	12	12	44
			6	2	5	6	9	11	10	43
			7	11	25	19	17	15	7	94
			8	12	20	9	15	12	9	86
			9	31	33	17	39	29	12	161
			10	10	23	25	19	36	6	119
			11	60	14	9	15	14	..	112
			12	177	20	2	3	4	2	208
			Customs	16	2	..	..	..	..	18
			B. P. T.	63	10	4	3	..	..	80
			G. I. P.	2	1	1	..	..	..	4

Ward.	Section. No.	Name of Section.	Circle No.	Number of Buildings with: Ground floor only.	One upper floor.	Two upper floors.	Three upper floors.	Four upper floors.	Five or more upper floors.	Total number of buildings.
1	2	3	4	5	6	7	8	9	10	11
	8	**Umarkhadi—Total**	..	**273**	**184**	**170**	**222**	**144**	**32**	**1,025**
			1	30	12	9	11	12	2	76
			2	6	4	19	28	27	7	91
			3	21	11	8	13	5	..	58
			4	6	9	9	20	17	4	65
			5	9	5	10	10	19	..	53
			6	14	26	32	39	19	2	132
			7	32	29	28	39	34	11	173
			8	87	32	14	27	8	5	173
			9	68	56	41	35	3	1	204
	9	**Dongri—Total**	..	**519**	**59**	**50**	**27**	**15**	**8**	**678**
			1	12	3	2	6	14	7	44
			2	52	4	2	15	..	1	74
			3	17	10	19	2	..	..	48
			4	194	20	14	4	1	..	233
			Customs	114	1	..	..	..	..	115
			B. P. T.	15	12	5	..	..	..	32
			G. I. P.	115	9	8	..	..	..	132
C		**Grand Total for C Ward**	..	**1,264**	**786**	**1,054**	**1,232**	**964**	**330**	**5,630**
	10	**Market—Total**	..	**184**	**134**	**128**	**192**	**269**	**163**	**1,070**
			1	30	7	16	27	21	10	111
			2	29	12	11	12	15	8	87
			3	15	30	8	10	12	11	86
			4	16	4	8	5	22	10	65
			5	31	17	27	40	47	39	201
			6	19	21	30	38	43	28	179
			7	35	24	13	16	33	17	138
			8	9	19	15	44	76	40	203
	11	**Dhobi Talao—Total**	..	**266**	**192**	**242**	**240**	**191**	**62**	**1,193**
			1	60	32	50	80	56	9	287
			2	28	17	8	18	11	9	91
			3	58	40	51	21	10	..	180
			4	16	12	21	18	22	10	99
			5	24	8	21	33	24	8	118
			6	37	37	45	32	28	6	185
			7	38	46	46	38	40	20	228
			B. B. C. I.	5	..	..	..	..	..	5
	12	***Fanaswadi—Total***	..	***388***	***153***	***212***	***162***	***77***	***16***	***1,008***
			1	201	45	66	71	35	8	426
			2	112	58	89	47	20	3	329
			3	75	50	57	44	22	5	253
	13	**Bhuleshwar—Total**	..	**184**	**138**	**199**	**320**	**244**	**47**	**1,132**
			1	28	24	33	31	41	11	168
			2	20	27	28	34	18	2	129
			3	57	27	23	22	7	1	137
			4	41	26	62	96	72	8	305
			5	28	22	36	91	52	15	244
			6	10	12	17	46	54	10	149
	14	***Kumbharwada—Total***	..	***136***	***98***	***191***	***182***	***69***	***9***	***685***
			1	55	41	63	61	33	5	256
			2	44	29	64	76	22	2	237
			3	17	12	40	31	6	1	107
			4	20	16	24	14	8	1	83
	15	**Khara Talao—Total**	..	**106**	**71**	**82**	**136**	**114**	**33**	**542**
			1	20	11	20	38	4	2	95
			2	12	4	10	11	12	1	50
			3	26	26	17	26	28	17	140
			4	25	23	15	35	32	3	133
			5	23	7	20	26	38	10	124
D		**Grand Total for D Ward**	..	**4,880**	**1,446**	**1,276**	**833**	**338**	**57**	**8,830**
	16	**Khetwadi—Total**	..	**710**	**225**	**216**	**277**	**143**	**20**	**1,591**
			1	145	28	14	27	19	4	237
			2	78	21	35	63	20	2	219
			3	91	35	45	55	20	3	249
			4	138	44	19	22	18	2	243
			5	32	26	22	32	15	2	129
			6	37	18	14	20	35	6	139
			7	52	18	31	26	12	..	139
			8	134	35	36	23	4	1	233
			B. B. C. I.	3	..	...	..	..	..	3

Ward.	Section No.	Name of Section.	Circle No.	Ground floor only.	One upper floor.	Two upper floors.	Three upper floors.	Four upper floors.	Five or more upper floors.	Total number of buildings.
				Number of Buildings with						
1	2	3	4	5	6	7	8	9	10	11
	17	**Girgaum—Total**	..	**470**	**222**	**401**	**198**	**52**	**8**	**1,351**
			1	162	54	51	17	9	3	296
			2	25	15	48	28	7	1	124
			3	57	30	68	28	2	..	185
			4	10	13	19	8	10	1	61
			5	30	25	84	32	7	..	178
			6	138	71	99	71	12	2	393
			7	47	14	32	14	5	1	113
			B. B. C. I.	1	..	..	..	..	..	1
	18	**Chaupati—Total**	..	**348**	**151**	**170**	**104**	**38**	**7**	**816**
			1	74	14	13	14	5	2	122
			2	70	28	60	16	2	..	176
			3	46	21	18	9	3	..	97
			4	51	30	15	15	8	2	121
			5	60	35	45	36	11	..	187
			6	44	22	19	14	9	3	111
			B. B. C. I.	1	1	..	..	..	..	2
	19	**Walkeshwar—Total**	..	**1,435**	**433**	**302**	**128**	**42**	**6**	**2,341**
			1	245	70	127	26	12	3	483
			2	211	63	44	16	3	1	338
			3	246	93	31	22	14	2	408
			4	54	14	7	8	1	..	84
			5	122	29	15	5	2	..	173
			6	249	75	54	31	8	..	417
			7	250	80	20	11	2	..	363
			Government House.	57	9	4	4	..	..	74
			Customs	1	..	..	..	..	..	1
	20	**Mahalaxmi—Total**	..	**1,919**	**415**	**187**	**131**	**63**	**16**	**2,731**
			1	870	121	44	12	9	1	557
			2	120	38	12	9	..	1	180
			3	140	49	24	5	5	3	226
			4	451	64	27	21	18	5	586
			5	116	24	15	15	7	2	179
			6	100	36	27	43	10	1	217
			7	140	49	13	3	1	2	208
			8	99	14	6	2	..	..	121
			9	322	10	15	17	13	1	387
			Government House.	26	..	..	..	..	..	26
			B. B. C. I.	35	1	4	4	..	..	44
E		**Grand Total for E Ward**	..	**6,256**	**1,600**	**1,309**	**760**	**182**	**12**	**10,119**
	21	**Tardeo—Total**	..	**564**	**223**	**107**	**92**	**50**	**6**	**1,042**
			1	105	57	28	20	13	2	225
			2	102	53	38	45	30	1	269
			3	160	70	18	8	4	3	263
			4	174	40	23	19	3	..	259
			B. B. C. I.	23	3	..	..	..	..	26
	22	**Kamathipura—Total**	..	**236**	**211**	**431**	**190**	**27**	**1**	**1,096**
			1	97	59	80	30	3	..	269
			2	71	106	290	130	18	1	616
			3	68	46	61	30	6	..	211
	23	**First Nagpada—Total**	..	**76**	**18**	**48**	**25**	**5**	..	**167**
			1	63	15	26	18	2	..	124
			2	13	3	17	7	3	..	43
	24	**Second Nagpada—Total**	..	**100**	**98**	**118**	**150**	**46**	**3**	**515**
			1	33	43	23	9	..	..	108
			2	37	28	39	31	4	..	139
			3	19	10	39	74	26	1	169
			4	11	17	17	30	16	2	90
	25	**Byculla—Total**	..	**1,842**	**493**	**349**	**142**	**19**	..	**2,845**
			1	625	203	132	44	6	..	1,010
			2	228	54	41	13	6	..	342
			3	327	77	64	42	4	..	514
			4	190	25	37	23	1	..	276
			5	52	8	5	1	2	..	68
			6	192	33	17	3	..	..	245
			7	80	31	29	2	..	..	142
			8	75	25	19	11	..	..	130
			B. B. C. I.	13	5	5	..	..	..	23
			G. I. P.	60	32	..	3	..	..	95
	26	**Tarwadi—Total**	..	**1,523**	**259**	**123**	**98**	**19**	**2**	**2,024**
			1	213	46	29	33	7	..	328
			2	660	112	54	52	6	2	886
			3	584	90	39	13	4	..	730
			G. I. P.	66	11	1	..	2	..	80

Ward.	Section No.	Name of Section.	Circle No.	Number of Buildings with: Ground floor only.	One upper floor.	Two upper floors.	Three upper floors.	Four upper floors.	Five or more upper floors.	Total number of buildings.
1	2	3	4	5	6	7	8	9	10	11
	27	Mazagaon—Total	..	1,915	298	188	63	16	..	2,430
			1	141	34	12	11	6	..	204
			2	102	43	39	21	2	..	207
			3	149	20	17	7	4	..	197
			4	197	90	32	14	3	..	336
			5	1,021	95	33	9	1	..	1,159
			B. P. T.	85	9	..	1	..	..	95
			Customs	187	6	5	..	..	..	198
			G. I. P.	33	1	..	..	..	..	34
F		Grand Total for F Ward	..	5,730	936	560	218	25	1	7,470
	28	Parel—Total	..	1,421	309	181	135	18	1	2,065
			1	8	12	17	7	2	..	46
			2	185	29	6	9	3	..	232
			3	152	35	20	19	4	1	231
			4	13	8	16	3	..	..	40
			5	65	5	19	35	2	..	126
			6	186	75	43	39	5	..	348
			7	94	25	7	4	1	..	131
			8	550	33	22	18	1	..	624
			9	44	79	23	1	..	..	147
			G. I. P.	124	8	8	..	..	..	140
	29	Sewri—Total	..	1,638	142	35	17	1	..	1,833
			1	451	21	11	..	1	..	484
			2	432	17	3	2	..	..	454
			3	135	31	6	..	..	..	172
			4	221	53	14	3	..	..	291
			5	45	2	1	12	..	..	60
			6	16	..	..	..	..	..	16
			7	63	4	..	..	..	..	67
			B. P. T.	274	14	..	..	..	..	288
			Customs	1	..	..	..	..	..	1
	30	Sion—Total	..	2,671	485	344	66	6	..	3,572
			1	171	57	23	4	1	..	256
			2	128	33	19	5	2	..	187
			3	211	44	37	51	2	..	345
			4	163	33	10	2	..	..	208
			5	207	48	4	1	..	..	260
			6	283	53	142	1	..	..	479
			7	332	34	3	..	..	..	369
			8	141	53	61	1	1	..	257
			9	103	49	42	1	..	..	195
			10	245	18	2	..	..	..	265
			11	211	21	..	..	..	..	232
			G. I. P.	185	13	1	..	..	..	199
			B. B. C. I.	2	..	..	..	..	..	2
			B. P. T.	271	27	..	..	..	..	298
			Customs	18	2	..	..	..	..	20
G		Grand Total for G Ward	..	8,550	1,464	525	249	9	3	10,810
	31	Mahim—Total	..	3,608	730	206	36	4	..	4,584
			1	149	27	6	..	1	..	183
			2	608	177	49	8	1	..	843
			3	461	58	25	5	..	..	549
			4	305	94	26	6	..	..	431
			5	390	172	76	14	1	..	653
			6	665	130	21	3	..	..	819
			7	264	29	..	..	..	..	293
			8	614	28	..	..	1	..	643
			Customs	2	..	..	..	..	..	2
			G. I. P.	96	9	3	..	..	..	108
			B. B. C. I.	54	6	..	..	..	..	60
	32	Worli—Total	..	4,942	734	329	213	5	3	6,226
			1	415	29	3	2	1	2	452
			2	492	63	34	39	..	..	628
			3	92	27	54	7	..	..	180
			4	17	22	7	1	..	..	47
			5	643	78	77	13	..	..	811
			6	578	54	5	1	..	..	638
			7	1,072	134	49	136	3	..	1,394
			8	1,406	287	96	11	1	..	1,801
			9	46	3	..	..	..	1	50
			10	57	11	..	..	..	..	68
			B. B. C. I.	80	25	3	..	..	..	108
			G. I. P.	42	1	1	3	..	..	47
			Customs	1	..	..	..	..	..	1
			B. P. T.	1	..	..	..	..	..	1
		Military—Total	..	383	64	14	16	1	..	478
A	1	Upper Colaba	..	227	42	9	14	1	..	293
	3	Fort, South	..	19	8	3	..	..	..	30
	5	Esplanade	..	60	14	1	1	..	..	76
D	20	Mahalaxmi	..	8	..	..	..	..	..	8
		Harbour Islands	..	69	..	1	1	..	..	71

Details of Buildings with more than five Upper Floors.

Ward.	Section number.	Name of Section.	Number of Buildings with		
			Six upper floors.	Seven upper floors.	Eight upper floors.
A	3	Fort, South	1	....	....
	4	Fort, North	21	....	....
		Total ..	22	....	....
B	6	Chakla	1	....	....
		Total ..	1	....	....
C	10	Market	24	....	....
	11	Dhobi Talao	4	....	....
	12	Fanaswadi	1	....	....
	13	Bhuleshwar	4	....	....
	14	Kumbharwada	1	....	....
		Total ..	34	....	....
D	20	Mahalaxmi	1	....	....
		Total ..	1	....	....
		Grand Total ..	58	....	....

RESIDENTIAL BUILDING CLASSIFIED ACCORDING TO THE NUMBER OF TENEMENTS CONTAINED IN EACH.

This Table deals with Residential Buildings only, for the definition of which see the Notes to Housing Table I. This Table excludes Military buildings and buildings under construction and demolition. The number of residential buildings treated in this Table falls short of those treated in Tables I and II as explained in the Statement below :—

Ward.	Residential buildings as per Tables I and II.	Residential buildings in Table III.	Difference.	Military buildings and buildings under construction and demolition.	Excess + deficit — in the figure in column 3.
1	2	3	4	5	6
Total City	32,225	31,743	—482	604	+122
A	2,515	2,257	—258	275	+ 17
B	2,104	2,069	— 35	34	— 1
C	4,417	4,388	— 29	37	+ 8
D	5,921	5,871	— 50	88	+ 38
E	5,698	5,659	— 39	72	+ 33
F	4,483	4,451	— 32	42	+ 10
G	7,087	7,048	— 39	56	+ 17

The difference in column 6 is due to the fact that the information for Tables I and II was compiled long before the date of final Count and that of residential buildings entered in Table III was actually compiled from the enumeration books.

All Residential Buildings not under construction or demolition are included, whether occupied at the time of the Census or not. In the same way all tenements are counted, whether occupied or vacant.

Tenement means so much of a building as from the records is shown as occupied (or in the case of vacancies as normally occupiable) by a separate family—

Provided that since it is not possible to consider a single room as constituting more than one tenement, such single rooms as at the Census were occupied by more than one family are counted as one tenement each.

Residential Buildings classified according to the number of Tenements contained in each.

Residential Buildings by the Number of Tenements.

Ward.	Section No.	Name of section.	Circle Number.	Number of Building containing: Ten tenements and under.	Eleven to twenty tenements.	Twenty-one to thirty tenements.	Thirty-one to forty tenements.	Forty-one to fifty tenements.	Fifty-one tenements and over.	Total No. of Buildings.
		Grand Total, Bombay City	..	23,161	4,353	1,774	986	496	978	31,743
A	..	**Grand Total for A Ward**	..	1,763	302	92	42	23	35	2,257
	1	**Upper Colaba—Total**	1	71	2	1	..	..	..	74
	2	**Lower Colaba—Total**	..	529	78	35	8	5	9	664
			1	99	15	4	2	1	..	121
			2	69	8	9	2	1	2	91
			3	61	18	4	..	..	..	83
			4	36	5	2	..	..	..	43
			5	77	2	2	1	1	..	83
			6	81	8	6	1	1	1	98
			7	11	3	2	1	1	1	19
			8	70	18	6	1	..	5	100
			B. P. T.	1	..	..	..	..	..	1
			B. B. C. I.	24	1	..	..	..	..	25
	3	**Fort, South—Total**	..	119	25	3	1	2	..	150
			1	27	3	1	..	..	..	31
			2	33	5	..	..	1	..	39
			3	10	8	..	1	..	..	19
			4	17	4	1	..	..	..	22
			5	12	4	1	..	1	..	18
			6	3	..	..	..	..	..	3
			Customs	..	1	..	..	..	..	1
			R. I. M.	17	..	..	..	..	..	17
	4	**Fort, North—Total**	..	605	160	42	25	15	10	857
			1	114	12	2	3	..	..	131
			2	52	2	1	1	..	..	56
			3	104	22	2	..	1	..	129
			4	58	20	7	5	..	..	90
			5	63	20	1	2	1	..	87
			6	103	36	14	1	2	..	156
			7	38	35	7	6	4	2	92
			8	61	12	8	7	7	8	103
			Customs	9	1	..	..	..	..	10
			B. P. T.	3	..	..	..	..	..	3
	5	**Esplanade—Total**	..	439	87	11	8	1	16	512
			1	152	4	1	1	..	..	158
			2	63	..	..	1	..	..	64
			3	144	13	3	4	..	14	178
			4	51	16	4	2	1	2	76
			Customs	8	..	2	..	..	..	10
			B. P. T.	4	..	..	..	..	..	4
			G. I. P.	7	1	1	..	..	..	9
			B. B. C. I.	10	3	..	..	..	..	13
B	..	**Grand Total for B Ward**	..	1,050	525	234	120	69	71	2,069
	6	**Chakla—Total**	..	331	113	38	13	8	4	507
			1	56	15	6	..	1	1	79
			2	79	13	6	2	..	..	100
			3	46	23	7	3	3	..	82
			4	53	22	7	3	2	..	87
			5	42	18	3	2	1	..	66
			6	34	12	5	2	..	3	56
			7	21	10	4	1	1	..	37
	7	**Mandvi—Total**	..	285	170	77	39	25	12	608
			1	41	15	9	1	..	..	66
			2	2	4	6	3	2	1	18
			3	19	8	..	2	..	1	30
			4	14	25	7	5	3	..	54
			5	7	13	6	4	1	1	32
			6	9	12	5	2	3	..	31
			7	12	17	7	4	2	..	42
			8	17	8	8	1	2	1	37
			9	60	24	10	2	..	..	105
			10	28	33	8	2	4	2	77
			11	15	8	6	10	6	5	50
			12	49	2	1	1	2	1	59
			Customs	2	..	..	..	..	..	2
			B. P. T.	1	1	1	2	..	..	5

Ward.	Section No.	Name of section.	Circle Number.	Number of Buildings containing						Total No. of Buildings.
				Ten tenements and under.	Eleven to twenty tenements.	Twenty-one to thirty tenements.	Thirty-one to forty tenements.	Forty-one to fifty tenements.	Fifty-one tenements and over.	
	8	**Umarkhadi—Total**	..	**333**	**220**	**97**	**54**	**26**	**31**	**761**
			1	31	5	8	5	3	5	57
			2	10	40	11	8	3	1	82
			3	19	5	3	4	2	6	39
			4	18	22	10	..	3	..	53
			5	15	12	6	9	..	1	43
			6	48	41	11	3	4	1	108
			7	57	41	22	12	4	1	137
			8	51	23	9	5	..	11	99
			9	75	31	17	8	7	5	143
	9	**Dongri—Total**	..	**101**	**22**	**22**	**14**	**10**	**24**	**193**
			1	3	6	9	4	3	6	31
			2	19	3	6	1	1	7	37
			3	9	5	2	9	4	4	33
			4	50	3	1	..	2	7	63
			Customs	1	..	..	..	..	..	1
			B. P. T.	6	1	..	..	..	..	7
			G. I. P.	13	1	4	..	..	..	21
C	..	**Grand Total for C Ward**	..	**2,537**	**996**	**413**	**221**	**105**	**117**	**4,388**
	10	**Market—Total**	..	**418**	**206**	**81**	**60**	**19**	**31**	**815**
			1	48	25	7	7	2	3	92
			2	38	11	4	5	..	5	63
			3	28	7	2	1	3	5	46
			4	14	15	8	6	2	4	49
			5	63	44	20	14	6	6	153
			6	82	35	18	10	4	4	153
			7	39	19	9	14	2	2	85
			8	106	50	13	3	..	2	174
	11	**Dhobi-Talao—Total**	..	**639**	**192**	**63**	**30**	**15**	**26**	**965**
			1	209	23	8	1	1	1	243
			2	34	13	2	4	2	6	61
			3	116	26	6	4	1	1	154
			4	41	23	9	1	2	8	84
			5	50	23	11	7	4	2	97
			6	93	33	7	6	1	1	141
			7	96	51	20	7	4	7	185
	12	**Fanaswadi—Total**	..	**476**	**135**	**56**	**26**	**16**	**19**	**728**
			1	214	43	18	4	2	2	283
			2	154	56	18	12	6	6	252
			3	108	36	20	10	8	11	193
	13	**Bhuleshwar—Total**	..	**564**	**196**	**93**	**43**	**23**	**14**	**933**
			1	83	31	16	12	3	2	147
			2	60	21	6	11	7	6	111
			3	37	11	10	5	3	4	70
			4	152	66	28	7	4	..	257
			5	156	38	17	3	1	..	215
			6	76	29	16	5	5	2	133
	14	**Kumbharwada—Total**	..	**258**	**140**	**68**	**40**	**19**	**15**	**540**
			1	126	48	17	11	5	4	211
			2	75	59	20	14	6	7	181
			3	35	18	19	5	0	3	80
			4	22	15	12	10	2	1	62
	15	**Khara-Talao—Total**	..	**182**	**127**	**51**	**22**	**13**	**12**	**407**
			1	26	19	7	8	2	2	64
			2	17	7	4	1	1	7	37
			3	42	38	14	5	4	1	104
			4	54	25	14	3	4	1	101
			5	43	38	12	5	2	1	101
D	..	**Grand Total for D Ward**	..	**4,719**	**654**	**250**	**119**	**52**	**77**	**5,871**
	16	**Khetwadi—Total**	..	**729**	**177**	**67**	**37**	**18**	**23**	**1,046**
			1	110	17	6	5	1	5	144
			2	84	37	9	11	3	5	140
			3	133	20	7	6	2	2	170
			4	130	12	3	2	..	3	150
			5	76	16	5	1	3	1	102
			6	79	16	5	4	..	2	106
			7	60	24	14	3	2	2	105
			8	57	35	18	5	2	3	120

Ward.	Section No.	Name of section.	Circle Number.	Number of Buildings containing						Total No. of Buildings.
				Ten tenements and under.	Eleven to twenty tenements.	Twenty-one to thirty tenements.	Thirty-one to forty tenements.	Forty-one to fifty tenements.	Fifty-one tenements and over.	
	17	**Girgaum—Total**	..	**728**	**139**	**65**	**26**	**23**	**23**	**1,004**
			1	127	25	11	4	8	7	182
			2	68	23	11	..	1	1	104
			3	86	26	18	6	3	9	148
			4	47	4	1	..	..	..	52
			5	118	27	8	3	4	..	160
			6	229	27	17	9	5	4	291
			7	53	7	4	4	2	2	72
	18	**Chaupati—Total**	..	**421**	**72**	**20**	**15**	**9**	**13**	**550**
			1	48	10	1	1	2	1	63
			2	112	9	4	3	..	5	133
			3	55	9	4	..	2	1	71
			4	62	13	..	3	2	3	83
			5	110	18	5	4	3	2	142
			6	34	13	6	4	..	1	58
	19	**Walkeshwar—Total**	..	**1,401**	**112**	**31**	**6**	**1**	**6**	**1,557**
			1	260	35	14	2	..	2	313
			2	238	5	6	..	1	..	250
			3	257	20	1	..	..	..	278
			4	64	..	..	..	..	..	64
			5	96	10	..	..	..	..	106
			6	241	24	6	3	..	1	275
			7	209	14	1	..	..	1	225
			Government House	36	4	3	1	..	2	46
	20	**Mahalaxmi—Total**	..	**1,440**	**154**	**67**	**35**	**6**	**12**	**1,714**
			1	343	6	2	3	..	..	354
			2	115	3	..	..	..	..	118
			3	143	4	4	..	..	..	151
			4	288	19	14	7	2	..	330
			5	102	18	9	2	..	..	131
			6	116	25	10	6	..	1	158
			7	76	15	4	10	2	4	111
			8	37	16	7	5	..	1	66
			9	197	45	14	2	2	2	262
			Government House.	14	3	..	..	..	..	17
			B. B. C. I.	9	..	3	..	..	4	16
E	..	**Grand Total for E Ward**	..	**8,735**	**903**	**893**	**239**	**181**	**258**	**5,859**
	21	**Tardeo—Total**	..	**376**	**114**	**45**	**31**	**13**	**47**	**626**
			1	108	23	7	7	2	8	155
			2	118	48	14	6	2	5	188
			3	62	26	14	11	8	6	127
			4	87	21	10	7	1	28	154
			B. B. C. I.	1	1	..	..	..	..	2
	22	**Kamathipura—Total**	..	**581**	**213**	**75**	**29**	**13**	**21**	**932**
			1	131	49	16	6	3	4	209
			2	387	131	32	7	1	3	561
			3	63	33	27	16	9	14	162
	23	**First Nagpada—Total**	..	**58**	**23**	**13**	**10**	**9**	**7**	**120**
			1	43	14	9	3	6	6	81
			2	15	9	4	7	3	1	39
	24	**Second Nagpada—Total**	..	**232**	**111**	**42**	**17**	**7**	**11**	**420**
			1	28	13	15	9	3	6	74
			2	55	28	11	4	1	3	102
			3	103	38	12	1	..	1	155
			4	46	32	4	3	3	1	89
	25	**Byculla—Total**	..	**952**	**231**	**136**	**93**	**67**	**86**	**1,565**
			1	379	62	37	19	14	43	554
			2	145	25	11	6	1	2	190
			3	142	38	36	20	28	11	275
			4	93	31	18	17	9	14	182
			5	21	7	1	..	1	..	30
			6	78	20	13	7	3	4	125
			7	48	26	8	6	5	9	102
			8	21	19	12	17	5	2	76
			B. B. C. I.	5	3	..	1	..	..	9
			G. I. P.	20	..	..	..	1	1	22

Ward.	Section No.	Name of section.	Circle Number.	Number of Buildings containing						Total No. of Buildings.
				Ten tenements and under.	Eleven to twenty tenements.	Twenty-one to thirty tenements.	Thirty-one to forty tenements.	Forty-one to fifty tenements.	Fifty-one tenements and over.	
	26	**Tarwadi—Total**	..	**674**	**79**	**41**	**44**	**18**	**51**	**902**
			1	89	11	10	11	4	25	150
			2	307	42	15	10	6	11	391
			3	214	26	16	22	3	15	326
			G. I. P.	34	..	..	1	..	..	35
	27	**Mazagaon—Total**	..	**862**	**132**	**41**	**15**	**9**	**35**	**1,094**
			1	77	13	6	2	3	12	113
			2	117	22	6	2	..	5	152
			3	89	17	3	1	..	5	115
			4	210	23	7	4	2	7	25
			5	327	50	18	6	4	6	411
			B. P. T.	8	6	1	..	..	..	15
			Customs	33	1	..	..	..	..	34
			G. I. P.	1	..	..	..	..	..	1
F	..	**Grand Total for F Ward**	..	**3,463**	**490**	**161**	**114**	**53**	**170**	**4,451**
	28	**Parel—Total**	..	**697**	**141**	**87**	**75**	**34**	**71**	**1,105**
			1	9	7	15	6	1	5	43
			2	37	2	4	12	2	12	69
			3	58	21	7	3	3	23	115
			4	8	7	7	7	2	3	34
			5	17	14	9	9	2	5	56
			6	145	44	23	19	7	11	249
			7	26	6	5	4	7	5	53
			8	263	16	14	13	8	7	321
			9	100	18	2	1	2	..	123
			G. I. P.	34	6	1	1	..	..	42
	29	**Sewri—Total**	..	**876**	**98**	**25**	**12**	**2**	**17**	**1,030**
			1	228	22	8	7	1	2	268
			2	237	24	9	..	..	3	273
			3	133	12	..	..	..	..	145
			4	188	27	7	5	1	..	223
			5	16	2	..	..	..	12	30
			6	4	1	..	..	..	..	5
			7	19	7	1	..	..	..	27
			B. P. T.	56	3	..	..	..	..	59
	30	**Sion—Total**	..	**1,890**	**251**	**49**	**27**	**17**	**82**	**2,316**
			1	95	18	14	5	5	2	139
			2	89	8	6	6	3	3	115
			3	138	28	11	7	3	61	248
			4	92	29	7	1	..	8	137
			5	197	15	1	..	..	1	214
			6	245	20	1	2	..	1	269
			7	219	8	..	1	..	1	229
			8	128	12	3	4	3	2	152
			9	137	13	4	..	2	3	159
			10	142	75	1	..	..	..	218
			11	197	2	..	..	..	..	199
			G. I. P.	75	1	..	..	1	..	77
			B. P. T.	122	22	1	1	..	..	146
			Customs	14	..	..	..	..	..	14
G	..	**Grand Total for G Ward**	..	**5,89}**	**483**	**232**	**131**	**63**	**245**	**7,048**
	31	**Mahim—Total**	..	**3,004**	**193**	**56**	**26**	**9**	**15**	**3,303**
			1	72	..	..	..	1	..	73
			2	560	44	12	10	5	4	635
			3	337	37	13	5	1	3	396
			4	319	5	1	..	..	2	327
			5	452	36	10	5	1	4	508
			6	600	28	11	5	1	2	647
			7	167	5	2	..	..	..	174
			8	455	35	4	1	..	..	495
			Customs	1	..	..	..	..	..	1
			G. I. P.	25	1	2	..	..	..	28
			B. B. C. I.	16	2	1	..	..	..	19
	32	**Worli—Total**	..	**2,890**	**290**	**176**	**105**	**54**	**230**	**3,745**
			1	158	9	6	4	2	..	174
			2	147	24	14	11	5	37	238
			3	59	10	16	16	2	28	132
			4	9	5	3	6	6	4	33
			5	148	35	20	15	5	35	267
			6	585	7	5	2	..	1	600
			7	573	73	51	21	9	101	828
			8	1,184	111	50	29	25	26	1,425
			9	2	..	..	..	..	..	2
			10	8	2	..	..	..	..	10
			B. B. C. I.	21	8	2	1	..	..	32
			G. I. P.	1	..	..	..	..	3	4

CLASSIFICATION OF RESIDENTIAL BUILDINGS BY THE NUMBER OF OCCUPANTS.

This Table, as at the last Census, is prepared primarily for Residential Buildings only. The figures in the main Table exclude buildings which were empty at the time of the Census.

But Supplement No. 1 gives the Number of Unoccupied Buildings by Sections.

Supplement No. 2 shows by Sections the number of persons enumerated in Non-residential Buildings. Persons enumerated otherwise than in a building are not considered at all.

Table III has excluded Military buildings.

In Table IV, occupied residential Military buildings are shown at the end. These are 221. 33 are military residential but unoccupied buildings. These together added to 31,743 shown in Table III give a total residential buildings 31,997. Of these 28,357 are shown in this table to have been occupied and 3,640 are shown in the Supplement No. 1 to have been unoccupied.

HOUSING TABLE IV—BOMBAY TOWN AND ISLAND.

Classification of Residential Buildings by the Number of Occupants.

Ward.	Section Number.	Section.	Circle No.	Number of buildings containing												Total No. of Buildings.
				20 Persons and under.	21 to 40 Persons.	41 to 60 Persons.	61 to 80 Persons.	81 to 100 Persons.	101 to 150 Persons.	151 to 200 Persons.	201 to 250 Persons.	251 to 300 Persons.	301 to 350 Persons.	351 to 400 Persons.	401 Persons and over.	
1	2	3	4	5	6	7	8	9	10	11	12	13	14	15	16	17
		Grand Total for Bombay City ..	..	**14,986**	**5,703**	**2,733**	**1,532**	**938**	**1,241**	**562**	**290**	**128**	**92**	**61**	**91**	**28,357**
A	..	**Grand Total for A Ward** ..	..	**1,151**	**465**	**170**	**87**	**39**	**44**	**26**	**6**	**6**	**4**	..	**3**	**2,001**
	1	**Upper Colaba—Total** ..	1	56	4	..	..	..	..	..	..	..	..	..	..	60
	2	**Lower Colaba—Total** ..	..	318	137	62	32	19	12	8	2	2	3	..	1	596
			1	71	21	15	5	1	1	..	..	..	..	..	..	114
			2	47	14	4	4	2	4	5	..	1	2	..	..	83
			3	36	26	8	7	3	..	..	..	..	..	..	..	80
			4	18	17	4	..	2	..	1	..	..	..	..	..	42
			5	59	15	1	3	2	1	..	1	..	..	..	..	82
			6	47	11	11	4	2	4	1	..	..	..	..	1	81
			7	8	3	2	..	2	3	..	1	1	..	..	..	19
			8	30	29	17	9	5	..	1	..	..	1	..	..	92
			B. B. C. I.	1	1	..	..	..	..	..	..	..	..	..	..	2
			B. P. T.	1	..	..	..	..	..	..	..	..	..	..	..	1
	3	**Fort, South—Total**	..	101	30	3	2	2	3	..	..	..	..	..	..	141
			1	27	4	..	..	..	..	..	..	..	..	..	..	31
			2	29	4	1	..	..	1	..	..	..	..	..	..	35
			3	12	6	..	1	..	..	..	..	..	..	..	..	19
			4	13	6	1	..	..	1	..	..	..	..	..	..	21
			5	7	4	1	1	2	1	..	..	..	..	..	..	16
			6	2	..	..	..	..	..	..	..	..	..	..	..	2
			R. I. M.	11	6	..	..	..	..	..	..	..	..	..	..	17
	4	**Fort, North—Total**	..	411	224	75	40	10	20	13	2	2	1	..	..	798
			1	78	35	7	1	..	..	1	..	..	..	..	..	122
			2	33	8	7	1	..	..	..	..	..	..	..	..	49
			3	64	38	9	2	2	..	1	..	..	..	..	..	116
			4	39	27	10	8	..	4	..	..	..	..	..	..	88
			5	46	28	6	1	1	1	1	..	..	..	..	..	84
			6	78	46	14	9	1	..	1	..	1	..	..	..	150
			7	23	24	11	10	2	7	3	1	..	..	..	..	81
			8	44	17	11	7	4	8	6	1	1	1	..	..	100
			Customs	3	1	..	1	..	..	..	..	..	..	..	..	5
			B. P. T.	3	..	..	..	..	..	..	..	..	..	..	..	3
	5	**Esplanade—Total**	..	265	70	30	13	8	9	5	2	2	..	..	2	406
			1	78	19	10	4	..	2	1	..	..	..	..	..	114
			2	39	12	2	..	..	1	..	..	..	..	..	..	54
			3	95	30	8	5	5	4	4	2	1	..	..	2	156
			4	42	8	5	2	1	2	..	..	1	..	..	..	61
			Customs	1	..	..	1	1	..	..	..	..	..	..	..	3
			B. P. T.	1	..	2	..	..	..	..	..	..	..	..	..	3
			B. B. C. I.	7	1	2	1	..	..	..	..	..	..	..	..	11
			G. I. P.	2	..	1	..	1	..	..	..	..	..	..	..	4
	..	**Grand Total for B Ward** ..	..	**630**	**467**	**313**	**182**	**108**	**147**	**60**	**26**	**11**	**8**	**8**	**7**	**1,962**
	6	**Chakla—Total**	..	202	131	73	30	26	15	1	..	..	..	..	1	479
			1	32	21	10	5	4	3	..	..	..	..	..	..	75
			2	52	20	14	3	1	4	..	..	..	..	..	..	94
			3	41	18	7	7	3	3	..	..	..	..	..	..	79
			4	28	22	22	4	5	3	..	..	..	..	..	..	84
			5	18	23	12	5	5	..	..	..	..	..	..	..	63
			6	20	14	5	4	4	1	1	..	..	..	..	1	50
			7	11	13	3	2	4	1	..	..	..	..	..	..	34
	7	**Mandvi—Total**	..	155	138	85	66	39	53	26	12	2	5	2	1	584
			1	21	20	9	5	5	4	1	..	..	..	..	..	65
			2	3	..	3	4	2	3	2	..	..	..	1	..	18
			3	11	7	3	3	1	..	..	..	..	..	..	1	26
			4	5	11	8	7	7	8	3	2	1	1	..	..	53
			5	4	8	7	5	1	3	..	2	..	1	..	..	31
			6	6	3	6	7	1	4	3	..	..	..	..	..	30
			7	6	10	11	8	6	5	..	..	..	1	..	..	42
			8	4	7	7	3	3	4	3	2	..	1	..	..	34
			9	25	42	13	12	1	3	..	..	..	..	..	..	96
			10	15	14	14	12	6	5	3	2	..	1	1	..	73
			11	13	5	2	2	4	11	8	4	1	..	..	..	50
			12	40	11	1	3	1	..	3	..	..	..	..	..	59
			Customs	2	..	..	..	..	..	..	..	..	..	..	..	2
			B. P. T.	..	..	1	..	1	3	..	..	..	..	..	..	5

Ward.	Section Number.	Section.	Circle No.	Number of buildings containing: 20 Persons and under.	21 to 40 Persons.	41 to 60 Persons.	61 to 80 Persons.	81 to 100 Persons.	101 to 150 Persons.	151 to 200 Persons.	201 to 250 Persons.	251 to 300 Persons.	301 to 350 Persons.	351 to 400 Persons.	401 Persons and over.	Total No. of Buildings.
1	2	3	4	5	6	7	8	9	10	11	12	13	14	15	16	17
	8	**Umarkhadi—Total**	..	**200**	**179**	**135**	**78**	**33**	**63**	**17**	**9**	**5**	**1**	**1**	**4**	**725**
			1	25	9	2	2	2	4	2	2	..	..	..	..	48
			2	9	26	24	8	2	10	2	..	..	..	..	..	81
			3	18	9	2	..	..	5	4	..	1	..	1	4	39
			4	4	15	16	10	3	4	..	..	..	..	..	..	52
			5	7	11	7	7	3	4	3	1	..	..	..	..	43
			6	30	30	20	12	4	9	1	..	..	..	..	..	106
			7	35	37	20	12	8	9	..	..	..	..	..	..	130
			8	32	16	15	10	4	5	..	6	2	1	..	..	91
			9	45	26	20	17	7	13	5	..	2	..	..	..	135
	9	**Dongri—Total**	..	**73**	**19**	**20**	**8**	**10**	**16**	**16**	**5**	**4**	**2**	..	**1**	**174**
			1	2	4	9	2	3	7	4	..	..	..	..	..	31
			2	16	4	1	1	3	3	2	2	4	..	..	..	36
			3	7	2	5	3	2	2	6	2	..	2	..	1	32
			4	37	7	..	2	1	4	4	1	..	..	..	..	56
			Customs	1	..	..	..	..	..	..	..	..	..	..	..	1
			B. P. T.	3	..	..	..	..	..	..	..	..	..	..	..	3
			G. I. P.	7	2	5	..	1	..	..	..	..	..	..	..	15
C	..	**Grand Total for C Ward** ..	..	**1,408**	**1,127**	**577**	**374**	**206**	**259**	**100**	**49**	**7**	**10**	**9**	**14**	**4,140**
	10	**Market—Total**	..	**264**	**203**	**91**	**72**	**38**	**54**	**17**	**11**	**3**	**1**	**1**	**3**	**758**
			1	33	18	11	7	8	5	1	2	..	..	..	..	85
			2	24	10	4	3	3	5	..	1	..	1	..	1	52
			3	17	6	7	4	..	4	3	..	1	..	..	..	42
			4	8	15	3	4	2	10	3	1	..	..	..	1	47
			5	53	36	18	16	7	6	2	4	..	..	..	1	143
			6	50	43	15	18	5	6	2	1	2	..	..	..	142
			7	33	24	7	3	5	4	2	1	..	..	1	..	80
			8	46	51	26	17	8	14	4	1	..	..	..	..	167
	11	**Dhobi Talao—Total**	..	**323**	**258**	**134**	**69**	**44**	**43**	**20**	**14**	**1**	**4**	**2**	**4**	**916**
			1	92	85	28	13	7	7	3	1	..	..	..	..	236
			2	20	10	12	2	2	4	1	1	..	1	2	3	58
			3	60	36	15	11	3	5	2	1	..	..	..	..	133
			4	26	12	15	10	4	5	1	1	1	1	..	1	77
			5	26	27	14	8	9	7	3	2	..	..	..	..	96
			6	42	41	20	13	6	6	4	2	..	2	..	..	136
			7	57	47	30	12	13	9	6	6	..	..	..	..	180
	12	**Fanaswadi—Total**	..	**253**	**174**	**82**	**56**	**34**	**41**	**19**	**10**	..	**2**	**2**	**1**	**674**
			1	105	74	39	20	16	11	1	3	..	..	..	1	270
			2	79	63	28	16	9	17	5	4	..	1	..	..	222
			3	69	37	15	20	9	13	13	3	..	1	2	..	182
	13	**Bhuleshwar—Total**	..	**356**	**258**	**124**	**64**	**29**	**28**	**12**	**6**	..	..	**1**	**3**	**881**
			1	59	34	19	12	4	4	2	1	..	..	1	..	136
			2	43	26	10	5	3	3	3	5	..	..	..	2	100
			3	27	14	8	4	6	2	4	..	..	..	..	..	65
			4	91	81	41	21	6	8	2	..	..	..	..	..	250
			5	91	67	32	10	5	4	1	..	..	..	..	..	210
			6	45	36	14	12	5	7	..	..	..	..	..	1	120
	14	**Kumbharwada—Total**	..	**132**	**123**	**72**	**54**	**40**	**60**	**21**	**6**	**2**	**2**	**3**	**2**	**516**
			1	72	53	25	15	10	15	2	1	..	..	..	2	195
			2	32	48	26	20	11	21	8	3	1	2	2	..	174
			3	16	16	16	12	8	9	8	1	..	..	..	..	86
			4	12	6	5	7	11	15	3	1	1	..	..	..	61
	15	**Khara Talao—Total**	..	**80**	**111**	**74**	**59**	**21**	**33**	**11**	**2**	**1**	**1**	**1**	**1**	**395**
			1	12	14	7	15	2	4	2	1	..	1	..	..	58
			2	9	14	2	8	2	1	3	1	1	..	..	1	37
			3	21	28	18	11	6	14	4	..	..	..	..	..	101
			4	19	31	24	12	8	5	1	..	..	..	..	..	100
			5	19	24	23	18	4	9	1	..	..	..	1	..	99

Ward.	Section Number.	Section.	Circle No.	Number of buildings containing: 20 Persons and under.	21 to 40 Persons.	41 to 60 Persons.	61 to 80 Persons.	81 to 100 Persons.	101 to 150 Persons.	151 to 200 Persons.	201 to 250 Persons.	251 to 300 Persons.	301 to 350 Persons.	351 to 400 Persons.	401 Persons and over.	Total No. of Buildings.
1	2	3	4	5	6	7	8	9	10	11	12	13	14	15	16	17
D	..	**Grand Total for D Ward**	..	**2,894**	**1,004**	**480**	**214**	**128**	**151**	**65**	**25**	**7**	**2**	**3**	**9**	**4,982**
	16	**Khetwadi—Total**	..	**398**	**248**	**142**	**74**	**26**	**42**	**11**	**6**	..	**1**	**1**	**7**	**956**
			1	52	31	17	7	3	6	2	4	..	1	..	..	123
			2	42	39	23	14	6	9	2	1	..	..	1	3	140
			3	66	42	20	16	5	0	1	..	..	..	..	1	157
			4	68	26	22	9	2	3	2	..	..	..	..	1	133
			5	40	32	14	2	..	4	1	1	..	..	..	1	95
			6	51	26	7	6	2	4	1	..	..	..	..	1	98
			7	30	29	13	8	4	5	..	..	..	..	..	..	08
			8	40	23	26	12	4	5	2	..	..	..	..	..	112
	17	**Girgaum—Total**	..	**451**	**210**	**100**	**42**	**38**	**55**	**29**	**10**	**4**	**1**	**2**	..	**942**
			1	89	30	11	7	7	13	7	3	..	1	2	..	170
			2	44	24	15	7	4	3	1	1	1	..	..	..	100
			3	49	34	17	7	7	10	7	3	3	..	..	..	137
			4	20	9	10	2	1	..	2	..	..	..	..	..	44
			5	73	35	16	7	5	8	4	..	..	..	..	..	148
			6	140	61	22	10	11	14	7	2	..	..	..	..	273
			7	30	17	9	2	3	7	1	1	..	..	..	..	70
	18	**Chaupati—Total**	..	**291**	**104**	**50**	**21**	**10**	**16**	**6**	**4**	**1**	..	..	**2**	**505**
			1	37	10	6	3	..	1	1	1	..	..	..	..	59
			2	72	24	7	..	3	4	2	2	..	..	..	2	116
			3	43	9	8	5	..	2	1	..	..	..	..	..	68
			4	48	17	8	3	1	1	1	..	..	..	..	..	79
			5	68	37	12	7	3	3	..	1	1	..	..	..	132
			6	23	7	9	3	3	5	1	..	..	..	..	..	51
	19	**Walkeshwar—Total**	..	**892**	**254**	**87**	**23**	**11**	**3**	**5**	**1**	..	..	..	..	**1,256**
			1	131	105	26	13	7	2	2	..	..	..	..	..	286
			2	148	35	12	1	1	..	2	..	..	..	..	..	199
			3	168	48	13	3	1	..	..	..	..	..	..	..	233
			4	51	6	1	..	..	..	..	..	..	..	..	..	58
			5	78	10	5	..	..	..	..	..	..	..	..	..	93
			6	174	24	6	1	1	1	..	..	..	..	..	..	207
			7	117	21	4	2	..	..	..	..	..	..	..	..	144
			Government House	25	5	..	3	1	..	1	1	..	..	..	..	36
	20	**Mahalaxmi—Total**	..	**862**	**188**	**121**	**54**	**43**	**35**	**14**	**4**	**2**	..	..	..	**1,323**
			1	166	24	6	2	1	2	..	..	..	..	..	..	201
			2	61	6	5	..	..	2	..	..	..	..	..	..	74
			3	98	8	3	5	2	..	..	..	..	..	..	..	116
			4	200	29	18	8	0	7	4	..	..	..	..	..	275
			5	53	19	15	6	9	3	1	..	..	..	..	..	106
			6	64	29	29	9	6	3	1	..	1	..	..	..	142
			7	53	16	9	6	3	8	5	2	..	..	..	..	102
			8	30	10	12	5	4	2	..	..	..	..	..	..	63
			9	119	44	22	12	8	8	..	1	1	..	..	..	215
			Government House	12	2	1	..	1	..	..	..	..	..	..	..	16
			B. B. C. I.	6	1	1	1	..	..	3	1	..	..	..	..	13
E	..	**Grand Total for E Ward** ..	..	**2,276**	**1,019**	**564**	**331**	**249**	**296**	**146**	**99**	**41**	**28**	**15**	**36**	**5,100**
	21	**Tardeo—Total**	..	**234**	**186**	**71**	**44**	**27**	**28**	**25**	**8**	**11**	**6**	..	**1**	**591**
			1	63	42	13	8	4	2	8	..	..	..	..	..	140
			2	70	53	30	15	7	8	1	..	..	..	..	..	184
			3	42	15	13	12	9	10	4	4	5	1	..	..	115
			4	58	25	15	9	7	8	12	4	6	5	..	1	150
			B. B. C. I.	1	1	..	..	..	..	..	..	..	..	..	..	2
	22	**Kamathipura—Total**	..	**397**	**238**	**106**	**66**	**33**	**34**	**15**	**8**	**1**	**1**	**1**	**5**	**903**
			1	100	36	26	17	7	10	4	1	..	..	..	..	201
			2	262	163	64	33	12	0	2	1	..	..	..	1	547
			3	35	37	16	16	14	15	9	6	1	1	1	4	155
	23	**First Nagpada—Total**	..	**46**	**11**	**22**	**3**	**9**	**11**	**8**	**3**	..	..	**1**	**1**	**115**
			1	33	7	15	3	6	4	4	3	..	..	1	1	77
			2	13	4	7	..	3	7	4	..	..	..	..	..	38

Ward.	Section Number.	Section.	Circle No.	Number of buildings containing												Total No. of Buildings.
				20 Persons and under.	21 to 40 Persons.	41 to 60 Persons.	61 to 80 Persons.	81 to 100 Persons.	101 to 150 Persons.	151 to 200 Persons.	201 to 250 Persons.	251 to 300 Persons.	301 to 350 Persons.	351 to 400 Persons.	401 Persons and over.	
1	2	3	4	5	6	7	8	9	10	11	12	13	14	15	16	17
	24	**Second Nagpada—Total**	..	**90**	**132**	**84**	**25**	**32**	**28**	**4**	**6**	**1**	..	**1**	..	**403**
			1	16	8	12	6	11	11	1	4	1	..	..	..	70
			2	20	34	18	5	8	8	2	1	..	..	..	..	96
			3	38	64	31	7	6	5	..	..	..	..	..	..	151
			4	16	26	23	7	7	4	1	1	..	..	1	..	86
	25	**Byculla—Total**	..	**559**	**242**	**134**	**103**	**92**	**119**	**61**	**47**	**18**	**11**	**5**	**8**	**1,399**
			1	261	80	35	25	25	34	16	19	5	5	1	..	506
			2	66	25	9	10	8	8	9	5	1	..	..	..	141
			3	82	48	29	21	21	33	8	5	5	..	2	2	256
			4	35	58	27	9	12	18	9	4	3	1	1	6	178
			5	16	2	3	3	2	1	1	..	..	..	..	..	28
			6	45	11	7	13	9	4	3	4	1	..	1	..	98
			7	26	12	18	9	8	7	6	3	2	4	..	..	95
			8	13	7	5	10	6	13	9	7	1	1	..	..	72
			B. B. C. I.	1	1	1	1	..	1	..	..	..	..	..	..	5
			G. I. P.	14	3	..	2	1	..	..	..	..	..	..	..	20
	26	**Tarwadi—Total**	..	**440**	**108**	**66**	**33**	**28**	**40**	**20**	**16**	**5**	**6**	**2**	**10**	**777**
			1	52	16	10	3	4	10	8	9	2	5	2	4	125
			2	182	53	33	22	10	9	5	2	2	1	..	3	322
			3	177	38	23	13	14	21	6	4	1	..	..	3	298
			G. I. P.	29	1	..	..	..	..	1	1	..	..	..	..	32
	27	**Mazagaon—Total**	..	**510**	**156**	**81**	**52**	**28**	**36**	**13**	**11**	**5**	**4**	**5**	**11**	**912**
			1	37	14	13	12	2	4	2	3	..	..	3	8	98
			2	66	34	14	9	4	4	2	2	..	1	..	..	136
			3	60	17	3	6	4	8	2	1	1	..	..	1	103
			4	136	41	19	14	5	6	4	3	2	1	..	1	232
			5	187	47	27	9	11	11	8	2	2	2	2	1	304
			B. P. T.	4	..	1	2	2	3	..	..	..	..	..	..	12
			Customs	19	3	4	..	..	..	..	..	..	..	..	..	26
			G. I. P.	1	..	..	..	..	..	..	..	..	..	..	..	1
F	..	**Grand Total for F Ward** ..	..	**2,293**	**816**	**348**	**170**	**95**	**156**	**74**	**42**	**25**	**23**	**17**	**15**	**4,069**
	28	**Parel—Total**	..	**458**	**176**	**95**	**68**	**49**	**87**	**47**	**18**	**14**	**6**	**9**	**8**	**1,035**
			1	2	3	7	5	1	12	7	1	2	..	2	1	43
			2	22	7	3	2	4	7	8	2	3	1	1	3	63
			3	40	14	15	5	6	7	8	4	6	3	3	2	108
			4	7	4	2	3	8	6	1	2	..	..	..	1	34
			5	8	8	10	9	6	9	1	1	1	..	..	1	54
			6	89	53	22	22	15	22	10	1	1	1	1	..	237
			7	16	7	4	6	1	3	4	5	..	..	1	..	47
			8	163	58	20	12	5	17	18	2	1	1	1	..	293
			9	84	18	10	1	2	3	..	..	..	..	..	..	118
			G. I. P.	27	4	2	3	1	1	..	..	..	..	..	..	38
	29	**Sewri—Total**	..	**603**	**182**	**75**	**26**	**18**	**19**	**6**	**7**	**2**	**5**	**2**	**2**	**942**
			1	148	52	22	5	4	8	4	4	..	..	..	..	247
			2	172	52	12	9	4	2	1	1	..	..	1	..	254
			3	98	22	11	2	..	1	..	..	..	..	..	..	134
			4	115	46	20	8	5	3	1	..	..	..	..	..	198
			5	9	6	3	..	..	..	..	2	2	5	1	2	30
			6	2	..	..	1	..	..	..	..	..	..	..	..	3
			7	11	1	7	1	..	5	..	..	..	..	..	..	25
			B. P. T.	48	3	..	..	..	..	..	..	..	..	..	..	51
	30	**Sion—Total**	..	**1,232**	**458**	**173**	**76**	**33**	**50**	**21**	**17**	**9**	**12**	**6**	**5**	**2,092**
			1	53	24	17	12	5	7	4	2	1	..	..	..	125
			2	65	14	9	6	2	4	..	..	..	..	..	1	101
			3	92	35	16	16	4	22	13	10	5	9	6	4	232
			4	50	35	18	10	4	3	1	3	2	3	..	..	129
			5	129	46	13	2	1	4	..	1	..	..	..	..	196
			6	112	93	27	3	2	3	1	..	..	..	..	..	241
			7	166	32	3	2	2	1	1	..	..	..	..	..	207
			8	73	38	10	5	4	2	..	1	..	..	..	..	133
			9	75	27	7	6	4	..	..	..	1	..	..	..	120
			10	105	45	35	11	4	4	..	..	..	..	..	..	204
			11	154	25	3	..	..	..	..	..	..	..	..	..	182
			G. I. P.	56	8	4	..	1	..	..	..	..	..	..	..	69
			B. P. T.	88	36	11	3	..	..	1	..	..	..	..	..	139
			Customs	14	..	..	..	..	..	..	..	..	..	..	..	14

MO-II Bk Ra Cs 3—78

Ward.	Section Number.	Section.	Circle No.	Number of buildings containing: 20 Persons and under.	21 to 40 Persons.	41 to 60 Persons.	61 to 80 Persons	81 to 100 Persons.	101 to 150 Persons.	151 to 200 Persons.	201 to 250 Persons.	251 to 300 Persons.	301 to 350 Persons.	351 to 400 Persons.	401 Persons and over.	Total No. of Buildings.
1	2	3	4	5	6	7	8	9	10	11	12	13	14	15	16	17
G	..	**Grand Total for G Ward** ..	..	**4,164**	**780**	**278**	**168**	**109**	**184**	**89**	**43**	**30**	**16**	**14**	**7**	**5,882**
	31	**Mahim—Total**	..	**2,220**	**400**	**102**	**48**	**25**	**31**	**11**	**1**	**2**	..	**2**	..	**2,842**
			1	36	5	..	..	..	..	1	..	..	..	..	..	42
			2	445	72	27	7	7	12	6	1	1	..	..	..	578
			3	250	60	20	10	5	7	1	..	..	..	2	..	355
			4	218	24	2	2	1	2	..	..	..	..	..	..	249
			5	334	72	13	4	2	4	..	..	1	..	..	..	430
			6	475	61	14	12	5	5	1	..	..	..	..	..	573
			7	125	21	1	3	3	1	..	..	..	..	..	..	154
			8	310	78	23	10	2	..	1	..	..	..	..	..	424
			Customs	1	..	..	..	..	..	..	..	..	..	..	..	1
			G. I. P.	12	5	1	..	..	..	..	..	..	..	..	..	18
			B. B. C. I.	14	2	1	..	..	..	1	..	..	..	..	..	18
	32	**Worli—Total**	..	**1,944**	**380**	**176**	**120**	**84**	**153**	**78**	**42**	**28**	**16**	**12**	**7**	**3,040**
			1	85	24	5	8	4	2	1	..	..	..	..	..	129
			2	72	38	15	10	10	11	10	7	8	8	3	2	194
			3	43	23	5	9	6	17	13	2	5	2	2	..	127
			4	6	1	5	3	4	8	2	1	1	..	..	..	31
			5	109	27	17	22	15	16	16	9	5	2	3	3	244
			6	466	14	2	1	1	3	..	..	1	..	..	..	488
			7	361	84	42	25	13	52	18	18	4	3	2	2	624
			8	779	162	84	39	29	41	18	5	4	1	2	..	1,164
			9	1	..	..	..	..	..	..	..	..	..	..	..	1
			10	6	..	..	2	1	..	..	..	..	..	..	..	9
			B. B. C. I.	15	7	1	1	1	..	..	..	..	..	..	..	25
			G. I. P.	1	..	..	..	..	3	..	..	..	..	..	..	4
		Military—Total	..	**170**	**25**	**8**	**6**	**4**	**4**	**2**	..	**1**	**1**	..	..	**221**
A	1	**Upper Colaba**	..	129	16	6	4	3	4	1	..	1	1	..	..	165
	3	**Fort, South**	..	3	3	..	..	..	..	..	..	..	..	..	..	6
	5	**Esplanade**	..	21	6	1	2	1	..	1	..	..	..	..	..	32
D	20	**Mahalaxmi**	..	8	..	..	..	..	..	..	..	..	..	..	..	8
		Harbour Islands	..	9	..	1	..	..	..	..	..	..	..	..	..	10

NUMBER OF UNOCCUPIED RESIDENTIAL BUILDINGS BY SECTIONS.

Ward.	Section.	Civil Area.	*Customs.*	Royal Indian Marine.	G. I. P. Rly.	B. B. & C. I. Rly.	B. P. T.	Military Area.
A	Upper Colaba	14	..	..	..	..	..	..
A	Lower Colaba	45	..	..	..	23	..	..
A	Fort, South	8	1	..	..	..	..	..
A	Fort, North	54	5	..	..	..	..	..
A	Esplanade	91	7	..	5	2	1	..
B	Chakla	28	..	..	..	..	..	..
B	Mandvi	24	..	..	..	..	..	..
B	Umarkhadi	36	..	..	..	..	..	..
B	Dongri	9	..	..	6	..	4	..
C	Market	57	..	..	..	..	..	..
C	Dhobi Talao	49	..	..	..	..	..	..
C	Fanaswadi	54	..	..	..	..	..	..
C	Bhuleshwar	52	..	..	..	..	..	..
C	Kumbharwada	24	..	..	..	..	..	..
C	Khara Talao	12	..	..	..	..	..	..
D	Khetwadi	90	..	..	..	..	..	..
D	Girgaum	62	..	..	..	..	..	..
D	Chaupati	45	..	..	..	..	..	..
D	Walkeshwar	301	..	..	..	..	..	..
D	Mahalaxmi	388	..	..	..	3	..	..
E	Tardeo	35	..	..	..	..	..	..
E	Kamathipura	29	..	..	..	..	..	..
E	First Nagpada	5	..	..	..	..	..	..
E	Second Nagpada	17	..	..	..	..	..	..
E	Byculla	160	..	..	2	4	..	..
E	Tarwadi	122	..	..	3	..	..	..
E	Mazagaon	171	8	..	..	..	3	..
F	Parel	66	..	..	4	..	..	..
F	Sewri	80	..	..	..	..	8	..
F	Sion	209	..	..	8	..	7	..
G	Mahim	450	..	..	10	1	..	..
G	Worli	698	..	..	..	7	..	..
	Military	..	..	..	..	..	..	33
	Total ..	3,485	21	..	38	40	23	33
	Grand Total ..	3,640	..	..	..	..	..	..

TOTAL POPULATION RECORDED IN NON-RESIDENTIAL BUILDINGS.

Ward.	Section.	Civil Area.	Customs.	Royal Indian Marine.	G. I. P. Rly.	B. B. & C. I. Rly.	B. P. T.	Military Area.
A	Upper Colaba	18	..	..	..	..	..	..
	Lower Colaba	571	..	..	..	5	..	..
	Fort, South	749	9	..	..	..	..	..
	Fort, North	472	32	..	..	..	5	..
	Esplanade	901	68	..	70	101	..	..
B	Chakla	399	..	..	..	..	..	..
	Mandvi	2,226	572	..	..	..	..	..
	Umarkhadi	446	..	..	..	..	..	..
	Dongri	319	5	..	523	..	38	..
C	Market	913	..	..	..	..	..	..
	Dhobi Talao	246	..	..	..	18	..	..
	Fanaswadi	161	..	..	..	..	..	..
	Bhuleshwar	489	..	..	..	..	..	..
	Kumbharwada	212	..	..	..	..	..	..
	Khara Talao	397	..	..	..	..	..	..
D	Khetwadi	1,116	..	..	..	4	..	..
	Girgaum	735	..	..	..	1	..	..
	Chaupati	351	..	..	..	4	..	..
	Walkeshwar	455	1	..	..	..	..	..
	Mahalaxmi	971	..	..	..	37	..	..
E	Tardeo	811	..	..	..	47	..	..
	Kamathipura	577	..	..	..	..	..	..
	First Nagpada	77	..	..	..	..	..	..
	Second Nagpada	129	..	..	..	..	..	..
	Byculla	4,959	..	..	9	23	..	..
	Tarwadi	1,239	..	..	13	..	..	..
	Mazagaon	1,405	72	..	748	..	44	..
F	Parel	2,192	..	..	339	..	..	..
	Sewri	514	2	..	..	..	86	..
	Sion	771	8	..	338	7	2	..
G	Mahim	1,639	..	..	35	15	..	..
	Worli	2,210	..	..	4	..	6	..
	Military	..	..	..	..	..	..	142
	Total	**26,670**	**769**	..	**2,079**	**262**	**181**	**142**
	Grand Total	**30,108**	..	..	..	..	..	..

Distribution of Persons by Rooms in Residential Buildings.

This table is prepared for Residential buildings precisely on the lines of the last Census Table. Unoccupied Residential buildings and Military residential buildings are not included. (Table IV—28,357 – 221 Military residential buildings =28,136. Total number of buildings treated in this Table.)

The population shown in the ninth column is the persons actually enumerated in Residential buildings specified above. It does not include (*i*) persons enumerated in Non-residential buildings (see Supplement to Housing Table IV) and (*ii*) persons not enumerated in any building at all but included in City Table I in the population of Sections (see Note to City Table I).

MO-II Bk Ra Cs 3—79

Distribution of Persons by Rooms in Residential Buildings.

Ward.	Serial Number of section.	Name of Section.	Circle Number.	Total number of persons living in rooms each occupied by				Total population.	Number of occupied buildings.	Average population per inhabitted building.
				5 Persons and under.	6 to 9 Persons.	10 to 19 Persons.	20 Persons and over.			
1	2	3	4	5	6	7	8	9	10	11
		Grand Total, Bombay City	..	719,967	256,379	80,133	15,490	1,071,969	28,136	38·10
A	..	**Grand Total for A Ward**	..	39,953	12,513	4,301	1,480	58,247	2,001	29·11
	1	**Upper Colaba —Total**	1	267	134	27	..	418	60	6·97
	2	**Lower Colaba—Total**	..	13,484	4,181	1,358	259	19,282	596	32·35
			1	2,385	270	103	..	2,758	114	24·19
			2	2,106	1,094	480	..	3,680	83	44·34
			3	1,620	449	247	..	2,316	80	28·95
			4	691	308	163	..	1,162	42	27·67
			5	868	834	111	..	1,813	82	22·11
			6	1,955	552	137	239	2,883	81	35·59
			7	866	224	23	..	1,113	19	58·58
			8	2,954	444	94	20	3,512	92	38·17
			B. P. T.	5	..	..	..	5	1	5·00
			B. B. C. I.	34	6	..	..	40	2	20·00
	3	**Fort, South—Total**	..	1,504	713	372	21	2,610	141	18·51
			1	274	135	12	..	421	31	13·58
			2	386	158	62	..	606	35	17·31
			3	176	107	71	21	375	19	19·74
			4	235	194	78	..	507	21	24·14
			5	407	97	54	..	558	16	34·88
			6	..	7	20	..	27	2	13·50
			R. I. M.	26	15	75	..	116	17	6·82
	4	**Fort, North—Total**	..	6,817	5,166	1,737	388	24,108	798	30·21
			1	1,609	406	207	26	2,248	122	18·43
			2	639	204	59	..	902	49	18·41
			3	1,990	542	144	..	2,676	116	23·07
			4	2,064	609	207	..	2,880	88	32·73
			5	1,385	522	174	..	2,081	84	24·77
			6	3,151	586	89	206	4,032	150	26·88
			7	2,693	897	314	59	3,963	81	48·93
			8	3,233	1,380	517	75	5,205	100	52·05
			Customs.	48	20	11	22	101	5	20·20
			B. P. T.	5	..	15	..	20	3	6·67
	5	**Esplanade—Total**	..	7,891	2,319	807	812	11,829	406	29·14
			1	1,776	214	276	29	2,295	114	20·13
			2	349	117	145	222	833	54	15·43
			3	3,965	1,545	319	561	6,390	156	40·96
			4	1,424	188	20	..	1,632	61	26·75
			Customs	140	36	..	..	176	3	58·67
			B. P. T.	26	49	34	..	109	3	36·33
			G. I. P.	96	57	..	..	153	4	38·25
			B. B. C. I.	115	113	13	..	241	11	21·91
	..	**Grand Total for B Ward**	..	72,339	22,310	7,190	1,558	103,397	1,962	52·70
	6	**Chakla—Total**	..	11,449	3,151	1,508	807	16,915	479	35·31
			1	1,500	696	340	52	2,588	75	34·51
			2	1,753	629	327	22	2,731	94	29·05
			3	1,977	404	98	..	2,479	79	31·38
			4	2,562	512	94	..	3,168	84	37·71
			5	1,688	335	205	41	2,269	63	36·02
			6	1,031	326	302	692	2,351	50	47·02
			7	938	249	142	..	1,329	34	39·09
	7	**Mandvi—Total**	..	22,753	8,860	3,167	235	35,015	584	59·96
			1	1,874	503	223	..	2,600	65	40·00
			2	1,000	527	130	..	1,717	18	95·39
			3	794	378	54	..	1,226	26	47·15
			4	2,570	1,210	481	94	4,355	53	82·17
			5	1,320	802	197	..	2,319	31	74·81
			6	1,634	382	55	..	2,071	30	69·03
			7	1,655	692	337	..	2,684	42	63·90
			8	1,338	822	585	..	2,745	34	80·74
			9	2,699	480	178	29	3,386	96	35·27
			10	3,272	1,493	222	..	4,987	73	68·32
			11	3,425	1,103	291	44	4,863	50	97·26
			12	814	358	311	68	1,551	59	26·29
			B. P. T.	282	110	103	..	495	5	99·00
			Customs.	16	..	..	..	16	2	8·00

Ward.	Serial Number of section.	Name of Section.	Circle Number.	Total number of persons living in rooms each occupied by: 5 Persons and under.	6 to 9 Persons.	10 to 19 Persons.	20 Persons and over.	Total population.	Number of occupied buildings.	Average population per inhabitted building.
1	2	3	4	5	6	7	8	9	10	11
	8	**Umarkhadi—Total**	..	**29,710**	**7,822**	**1,988**	**491**	**40,011**	**725**	**55·19**
			1	1,654	411	103	..	2,168	48	45·17
			2	3,224	945	179	..	4,348	81	53·68
			3	3,203	916	176	55	4,350	39	111·54
			4	2,206	385	140	..	2,731	52	52·52
			5	1,902	521	205	59	2,687	43	62·49
			6	3,508	830	290	188	4,825	106	45·52
			7	4,634	841	118	114	5,707	130	43·00
			8	4,128	1,518	558	75	6,279	91	69·00
			9	5,251	1,446	219	..	6,916	135	51·23
	9	**Dongri—Total**	..	**8,427**	**2,477**	**527**	**25**	**11,456**	**174**	**65·84**
			1	1,999	366	87	..	2,452	31	79·10
			2	2,102	548	107	25	2,782	36	77·28
			3	2,434	1,066	177	..	3,677	32	114·91
			4	1,481	439	156	..	2,076	56	37·07
			Customs	6	..	..	..	6	1	6·00
			B. P. T.	24	..	..	..	24	3	8·00
			G. I. P.	381	58	..	..	439	15	29·27
C	..	**Grand Total for C Ward**	..	**133,573**	**48,188**	**16,049**	**2,214**	**200,024**	**4,140**	**48·31**
	10	**Market—Total**	..	**23,794**	**10,561**	**2,249**	**590**	**37,187**	**758**	**49·06**
			1	2,568	952	260	42	3,822	85	44·06
			2	2,244	575	32	..	2,851	52	54·83
			3	1,429	555	282	..	2,266	42	53·95
			4	2,553	1,056	51	..	3,660	47	77·87
			5	4,855	1,568	340	..	6,763	148	47·29
			6	3,896	2,063	354	20	6,333	142	44·60
			7	2,666	706	121	..	3,493	80	43·66
			8	3,583	3,086	802	528	7,999	167	47·90
	11	**Dhobi Talao—Total**	..	**32,718**	**7,786**	**2,813**	**683**	**44,000**	**916**	**48·03**
			1	5,435	1,631	736	206	8,008	236	33·93
			2	4,252	491	216	..	4,959	58	85·50
			3	3,284	1,000	396	20	4,700	133	35·34
			4	3,635	764	272	111	4,782	77	62·10
			5	3,755	876	242	26	4,899	96	51·03
			6	4,391	1,512	509	220	6,632	136	48·76
			7	7,966	1,512	442	100	10,020	180	55·67
	12	**Fanaswadi—Total**	..	**22,210**	**6,701**	**2,673**	**170**	**31,754**	**674**	**47·11**
			1	7,014	2,604	1,355	98	11,071	270	41·00
			2	8,091	1,760	302	..	10,153	222	45·73
			3	7,105	2,337	1,016	72	10,530	182	57·86
	13	**Bhuleshwar—Total**	..	**23,551**	**7,169**	**2,736**	**432**	**33,888**	**881**	**38·47**
			1	4,311	825	154	222	5,512	136	40·53
			2	4,154	1,198	331	..	5,683	100	56·83
			3	2,198	515	82	22	2,817	65	43·34
			4	5,668	2,074	978	116	8,836	250	35·34
			5	3,840	1,586	631	72	6,129	210	29·19
			6	3,380	971	560	..	4,911	120	40·93
	14	**Kumbharwada—Total**	..	**18,619**	**9,387**	**3,287**	**195**	**31,488**	**516**	**61·02**
			1	5,856	2,407	690	20	8,973	195	46·02
			2	6,594	4,104	1,186	22	11,906	174	68·43
			3	3,657	1,554	428	..	5,639	86	65·57
			4	2,512	1,322	983	153	4,970	61	81·48
	15	**Khara-Talao—Total**	..	**12,681**	**6,584**	**2,298**	**144**	**21,707**	**395**	**54·29**
			1	2,103	1,131	308	..	3,542	58	61·07
			2	1,628	800	237	48	2,713	37	73·32
			3	3,300	1.541	778	21	5,640	101	55·84
			4	2,512	1,538	438	22	4,510	100	45·10
			5	3,138	1,574	537	53	5,302	90	53·56
D	..	**Grand Total for D Ward**	..	**111,586**	**26,136**	**9,139**	**1,842**	**148,703**	**4,982**	**29·85**
	16	**Khetwadi—Total**	..	**26,813**	**7,325**	**2,982**	**738**	**37,858**	**956**	**39·60**
			1	3,955	898	229	46	5,128	123	41·65
			2	4,844	1,714	965	209	7,732	140	55·23
			3	3,627	1,231	866	172	5,896	157	37·55
			4	3,[illegible]58	609	214	73	4,454	133	33·49
			5	2,545	506	82	98	3,231	95	34·01
			6	2,429	666	229	29	3,353	98	34·21
			7	2,555	679	188	111	3,533	98	36·05
			8	3,300	1,027	209	..	4,536	112	40·50

Ward.	Serial Number of section.	Name of Section.	Circle Number.	Total number of persons living in rooms each occupied by: 5 Persons and under.	6 to 9 Persons.	10 to 19 Persons.	20 Persons and over.	Total population.	Number of occupied buildings.	Average population per inhabitted building.
1	2	3	4	5	6	7	8	9	10	11
	17	**Girgaum—Total**	..	**29,319**	**6,634**	**1,525**	**229**	**37,707**	**942**	**40·03**
			1	5,800	1,439	292	41	7,578	170	44·58
			2	2,450	1,173	182	..	3,805	100	38·05
			3	6,235	879	89	168	7,371	137	53·80
			4	1,176	209	143	20	1,548	44	35·18
			5	3,683	1,284	185	..	5,152	148	34·81
			6	7,569	1,259	548	..	9,376	273	34·34
			7	3,400	391	86	..	2,877	70	41·10
	18	**Chaupati—Total**	..	**14,422**	**1,282**	**186**	**26**	**15,916**	**505**	**13·52**
			1	1,510	144	23	..	1,677	59	28·42
			2	3,930	412	70	..	4,412	116	38·03
			3	1,670	88	22	..	1,780	68	26·26
			4	1,797	118	49	..	1,964	79	24·86
			5	3,468	449	22	26	3,965	132	30·04
			6	2,041	71	..	..	2,112	51	41·41
	19	**Walkeshwar—Total**	..	**15,860**	**3,802**	**2,134**	**478**	**22,274**	**1,256**	**17·73**
			1	4,452	1,845	1,321	280	7,898	286	27·62
			2	1,913	629	525	115	3,182	199	15·99
			3	3,281	486	110	32	3,909	233	16·78
			4	598	25	12	..	635	58	10·95
			5	1,053	191	11	..	1,255	93	13·49
			6	2,202	271	44	..	2,517	207	12·16
			7	1,487	206	111	51	1,855	144	12·88
			Government House	874	149	..	..	1,023	36	28·42
	20	**Mahalaxmi—Total**	..	**25,172**	**7,098**	**2,312**	**371**	**34,948**	**1,323**	**26·42**
			1	1,921	615	381	196	3,113	201	15·49
			2	798	275	62	..	1,135	74	15·34
			3	1,494	191	30	..	1,715	116	14·78
			4	4,157	1,508	637	..	6,302	275	22·92
			5	2,478	738	359	..	3,575	106	33·73
			6	4,063	621	142	..	4,826	142	33·99
			7	3,271	1,068	282	22	4,643	102	45·52
			8	1,594	427	10	31	2,062	63	32·73
			9	4,394	1,382	388	122	6,286	215	29·24
			Government House	162	84	11	..	257	16	16·06
			B. B. C. I.	840	184	10	..	1,034	13	79·54
E	..	**Grand Total for E Ward**	..	**164,135**	**69,047**	**21,901**	**5,022**	**260,105**	**5,100**	**51·00**
	21	**Tardeo—Total**	..	**23,027**	**5,348**	**1,963**	**196**	**30,534**	**591**	**51·66**
			1	4,265	505	293	..	5,063	140	36·16
			2	5,905	567	86	..	6,558	184	35·64
			3	4,965	1,832	899	42	7,738	115	67·29
			4	7,848	2,444	685	154	11,131	150	74·21
			B. B. C. I.	44	..	..	..	44	2	22·00
	22	**Kamathipura—Total**	..	**24,173**	**8,449**	**3,739**	**660**	**37,021**	**903**	**41·00**
			1	4,494	1,791	760	197	7,242	201	36·03
			2	12,105	3,530	1,182	153	16,970	547	31·02
			3	7,574	3,128	1,797	310	12,809	155	82·64
	23	**First Nagpada—Total** ..	..	**5,348**	**1,261**	**365**	**90**	**7,064**	**115**	**61·43**
			1	3,877	652	223	43	4,795	77	62·27
			2	1,471	609	142	47	2,269	38	59·71
	24	**Second Nagpada—Total**	..	**12,350**	**5,003**	**2,188**	**1,067**	**20,608**	**403**	**51·14**
			1	3,095	1,515	467	48	5,125	70	73·21
			2	2,989	930	587	338	4,844	96	50·46
			3	3,618	1,631	556	256	6,061	151	40·14
			4	2,638	927	578	425	4,578	86	53·23
	25	**Byculla—Total**	..	**53,150**	**25,427**	**5,852**	**944**	**85,373**	**1,399**	**61·02**
			1	17,464	5,433	1,843	339	25,079	506	49·56
			2	2,958	2,766	962	498	7,184	141	50·95
			3	10,972	4,539	1,140	40	16,691	256	65·20
			4	9,182	4,044	721	37	13,984	178	78·28
			5	576	442	81	..	1,099	28	39·25
			6	3,635	1,633	254	..	5,522	98	56·35
			7	4,451	3,190	406	30	8,077	95	85·02
			8	3,471	3,225	344	..	7,040	72	97·78
			B. B. C. I.	204	100	10	..	314	5	62·80
			G. I. P.	287	55	91	..	433	20	21·65

Ward.	Serial Number of section.	Name of Section.	Circle Number.	Total number of Persons living in rooms each occupied by: 5 Persons and under.	6 to 9 Persons.	10 to 19 Persons.	20 Persons and over.	Total population.	Number of occupied buildings.	Average population per inhabited building.
1	2	3	4	5	6	7	8	9	10	11
	26	**Tarwadi—Total**	..	**27,116**	**9,513**	**2,154**	**71**	**38,354**	**777**	**50·00**
			1	7,252	3,847	911	..	12,010	125	96·08
			2	9,865	2,588	704	71	13,228	322	41·08
			3	9,799	2,836	430	..	13,065	298	43·84
			G. I. P.	200	242	109	..	551	32	17·22
	27	**Mazagaon—Total** ..	..	**18,971**	**14,046**	**5,640**	**1,994**	**40,651**	**912**	**44·57**
			1	2,957	4,239	2,386	1,305	10,887	98	111·09
			2	2,338	1,718	737	197	4,990	136	36·69
			3	2,454	1,419	282	151	4,306	103	41·81
			4	4,654	3,388	927	82	9,051	232	39·01
			5	6,106	2,657	1,214	236	10,213	304	33·60
			B. P. T.	215	482	94	23	814	12	67·83
			Customs	246	143	..	..	389	26	14·90
			G. I. P.	1	..	..	..	1	1	1·00
F	..	***Grand Total for F Ward*** ..	..	**95,303**	**41,689**	**12,846**	**2,700**	**152,038**	**4,069**	**37·36**
	28	**Parel—Total** ..	..	**38,775**	**16,482**	**3,676**	**1,130**	**60,063**	**1,035**	**58·03**
			1	2,815	2,386	382	..	5,583	43	129·84
			2	4,363	1,962	475	75	6,875	63	109·13
			3	7,514	1,947	173	..	9,634	108	89·20
			4	2,128	618	151	41	2,938	34	86·41
			5	3,080	964	119	21	4,184	54	77·48
			6	7,680	2,816	803	548	11,847	237	49·99
			7	2,540	1,415	142	..	4,097	47	87·17
			8	6,250	3,409	1,299	422	11,380	293	38·84
			9	1,837	723	112	23	2,695	118	22·84
			G. I. P.	568	242	20	..	830	38	21·84
	29	***Sewri—Total*** ..	..	**15,530**	**8,052**	**2,354**	**102**	**26,038**	**942**	**27·84**
			1	4,254	2,374	479	102	7,209	247	29·19
			2	3,132	1,724	689	..	5,545	254	21·83
			3	1,429	777	158	..	2,364	134	17·64
			4	3,250	1,335	310	..	4,901	198	24·75
			5	2,670	1,294	449	..	4,413	30	147·10
			6	65	6	..	..	71	3	23·67
			7	461	472	253	..	1,186	25	47·44
			B. P. T.	269	70	10	..	349	41	8·84
	30	**Sion—Total** ..	..	**40,998**	**17,155**	**6,316**	**1,468**	**65,937**	**2,092**	**31·52**
			1	3,423	1,617	611	44	5,695	125	45·56
			2	2,307	537	109	..	2,953	101	29·24
			3	11,946	5,913	2,243	72	20,174	232	86·96
			4	3,327	2,181	577	76	6,161	129	47·76
			5	1,932	1,084	606	575	4,197	196	21·41
			6	5,391	662	74	..	6,127	241	25·42
			7	1,584	776	380	370	3,110	207	15·02
			8	2,444	670	297	22	3,433	133	25·81
			9	2,166	380	116	157	2,819	120	23·49
			10	2,855	2,011	717	20	5,603	204	27·47
			11	1,141	543	291	132	2,107	182	11·58
			G. I. P.	588	172	141	..	901	69	13·06
			B. P. T.	1,830	609	154	..	2,593	139	18·65
			Customs	64	..	..	..	64	14	4·57
G	..	**Grand Total for G Ward** ..	..	**103,078**	**36,496**	**9,207**	**674**	**149,455**	**5,882**	**25·41**
	31	**Mahim—Total** ..	..	**35,167**	**9,229**	**2,419**	**260**	**47,075**	**2,842**	**16·56**
			1	554	79	..	..	633	42	15·07
			2	9,073	1,761	294	..	11,128	578	19·25
			3	5,325	2,122	244	..	7,691	355	21·66
			4	2,235	426	189	20	2,870	249	11·53
			5	5,600	978	159	65	6,702	430	15·59
			6	6,567	1,454	284	43	8,348	573	14·57
			7	1,305	628	379	72	2,384	154	15·48
			8	4,192	1,670	696	60	6,618	424	15·61
			Customs	9	..	..	..	9	1	9·00
			G. I. P.	241	49	24	..	314	18	17·44
			B. B. I. C.	166	62	150	..	378	18	21·00
	32	***Worli—Total*** ..	..	**67,911**	**27,267**	**6,788**	**414**	**102,380**	**3,040**	**33·68**
			1	1,990	851	101	..	2,942	129	22·81
			2	9,661	4,735	1,340	48	15,824	194	81·57
			3	7,183	2,220	447	74	9,924	127	78·14
			4	2,191	481	88	..	2,760	31	89·03
			5	11,626	3,669	677	44	16,016	244	65·64
			6	2,945	1,101	212	..	4,258	488	8·73
			7	19,292	6,689	1,507	89	27,577	624	44·19
			8	12,065	7,292	2,302	119	21,868	1,164	18·79
			9	1	..	..	..	1	1	1·00
			10	157	93	24	..	274	9	30·44
			B. B. C. I.	421	94	..	..	515	25	20·60
			G. I. P.	379	42	..	..	421	4	105·25

MO II Bk Ra Cs 3—80

Tenements By Rooms and Population.

This table is prepared for occupied Residential Buildings only—Military buildings are not included. For definition of "Tenement" see Notes to Housing Table III.

Ward.	Serial No. of section.	Name of Section.	Tenements with	Total number of occupied tenements of each class.	Percentage of each class of tenements to total tenements.	Total number of occupants of each class of tenements.	Percentage borne by population in each class of tenements to total population.	Average number of occupants per room in each class of tenements.
1	2	3	4	5	6	7	8	9
			Total ..	244,121	....	1,071,969	....	....
		Grand Total for Bombay City	1 Room ..	197,516	81	791,762	74	4·01
			2 Rooms ..	26,231	11	131,872	12	2·51
			3 ,, ..	7,416	3	44,821	4	2·01
			4 ,, ..	6,169	2	42,018	4	1·70
			5 ,, ..	2,953	1	22,302	2	1·50
			6 ,, and over.	3,836	2	39,199	4	....
			Total ..	13,726	....	58,247	....	....
A	..	Grand Total for A Ward ..	1 Room ..	10,436	77	39,091	67	3·75
			2 Rooms ..	1,612	12	7,630	13	2·37
			3 ,, ..	459	3	2,694	5	1·96
			4 ,, ..	646	4	3,991	7	1·54
			5 ,, ..	178	1	1,280	2	1·44
			6 ,, and over.	305	3	3,561	6	....
			Total ..	106	....	418	....	....
	1	Upper Colaba	1 Room	80	81	343	82	3·99
			2 Rooms ..	9	8	23	6	1·28
			3 ,, ..	3	3	6	1	·67
			4 ,, ..	3	3	17	4	1·42
			5 ,, ..	1	1	7	2	1·40
			6 ,, and over.	4	4	22	5	....
			Total ..	4,375	....	19,282	....	....
	2	Lower Colaba ..	1 Room ..	3,132	72	11,416	59	3·64
			2 Rooms ..	352	8	1,932	10	2·74
			3 ,, ..	195	4	1,089	6	1·86
			4 ,, ..	421	10	2,631	14	1·56
			5 ,, ..	90	2	645	3	1·43
			6 ,, and over.	185	4	1,569	8	....
			Total ..	523	....	2,610	....	....
	3	Fort South ..	1 Room ..	401	77	1,792	69	4·47
			2 Rooms ..	55	10	339	13	3·08
			3 ,, ..	28	5	132	5	1·91
			4 ,, ..	21	4	166	6	1·97
			5 ,, ..	10	2	74	3	1·48
			6 ,, and over.	13	2	107	4	....
			Total ..	5,977	....	24,108	....	....
	4	Fort North ..	1 Room ..	4,610	77	17,535	73	3·80
			2 Rooms ..	999	16	4,377	18	2·19
			3 ,, ..	178	3	990	4	1·85
			4 ,, ..	118	2	674	3	1·43
			5 ,, ..	41	1	311	1	1·52
			6 ,, and over.	31	1	221	1	....
			Total ..	2,745	....	11,829	....	....
	5	Esplanade ..	1 Room ..	2,207	81	8,005	68	3·63
			2 Rooms ..	197	7	959	8	2·43
			3 ,, ..	60	2	477	4	2·65
			4 ,, ..	83	3	503	4	1·51
			5 ,, ..	36	1	243	2	1·35
			6 ,, and over.	162	6	1,642	14	....
			Total ..	23,487	....	103,397	....	....
B	..	Grand Total for B Ward	1 Room ..	18,238	78	71,811	69	3·94
			2 Rooms ..	3,295	14	17,739	17	2·69
			3 ,, ..	900	4	5,718	6	2·12
			4 ,, ..	540	2	3,754	4	1·74
			5 ,, ..	200	1	1,538	1	1·55
			6 ,, and over.	264	1	2,837	3	....
			Total ..	3,871	....	16,915	....	....
	6	Chakla ..	1 Room ..	2,338	69	10,278	61	4·40
			2 Rooms ..	579	18	3,116	18	2·69
			3 ,, ..	214	7	1,459	9	2·27
			4 ,, ..	146	4	1,079	6	1·83
			5 ,, ..	49	1	396	2	1·65
			6 ,, and over.	45	1	587	4	....

Ward.	Serial No. of section.	Name of Section.	Tenements with	Total number of occupied tenements of each class.	Percentage of each class of tenements to total tenements.	Total number of occupants of each class of tenements.	Percentage borne by population in each class of tenements to total population.	Average number of occupants per room in each class of tenements.
1	2		4	5	6	7	8	9
			Total ..	6,888	....	35,015	....	....
	7	Mandvi	1 Room ..	5,027	73	22,857	65	4·55
			2 Rooms ..	1,102	17	7,201	20	3·02
			3 ,, ..	310	4	2,075	6	2·23
			4 ,, ..	180	3	1,331	4	1·85
			5 ,, ..	71	1	540	2	1·52
			6 ,, and over.	108	2	1,011	3	....
			Total ..	10,066	....	40,011	....	....
	8	Umerkhadi	1 Room ..	8,075	80	28,805	72	3·57
			2 Rooms ..	1,306	13	6,430	16	2·46
			3 ,, ..	338	3	1,993	5	1·96
			4 ,, ..	181	2	1,160	3	1·60
			5 ,, ..	65	1	510	1	1·57
			6 ,, and over.	101	1	1,113	3	....
			Total ..	3,112	....	11,456	....	....
	9	Dongri	1 Room ..	2,798	90	9,871	86	3·53
			2 Rooms ..	218	7	992	9	2·28
			3 ,, ..	38	1	191	2	1·68
			4 ,, ..	33	1	184	1	1·39
			5 ,, ..	15	1	92	1	1·23
			6 ,, and over.	10	....	126	1	....
			Total ..	41,942	....	200,024	....	....
C	..	Grand Total for C Ward	1 Room ..	32,629	77	138,374	69	4·37
			2 Rooms ..	5,276	13	28,722	14	2·72
			3 ,, ..	1,711	4	11,600	6	2·26
			4 ,, ..	1,149	3	9,152	5	1·99
			5 ,, ..	529	1	4,589	2	1·67
			6 ,, and over.	648	2	7,587	4	....
			Total ..	7,567	....	37,187	....	....
	10	Market	1 Room ..	5,653	75	24,373	66	4·31
			2 Rooms ..	1,091	14	6,047	16	2·77
			3 ,, ..	309	4	2,088	6	2·25
			4 ,, ..	214	3	1,663	4	1·94
			5 ,, ..	98	1	849	2	1·73
			6 ,, and over.	202	3	2,167	6	....
			Total ..	8,873	....	44,000	....	....
	11	Dhobi Talao	1 Room ..	5,882	66	23,421	58	3·98
			2 Rooms ..	1,526	17	8,363	19	2·74
			3 ,, ..	594	7	4,074	9	2·29
			4 ,, ..	421	5	3,522	8	2·09
			5 ,, ..	241	3	2,075	5	1·72
			6 ,, and over.	209	2	2,545	6	....
			Total ..	6,713	....	31,754	....	....
	12	Fanaswadi	1 Room ..	5,145	77	21,659	68	4·21
			2 Rooms ..	774	11	3,787	12	2 45
			3 ,, ..	311	5	1,927	6	2·07
			4 ,, ..	258	4	1,939	6	1·88
			5 ,, ..	97	1	862	3	1·78
			6 ,, and over.	128	2	1,580	5	....
			Total ..	7,717	....	33,888	....	....
	13	Bhuleshwar	1 Room ..	6,234	81	25,076	74	4·02
			2 Rooms ..	951	12	4,944	15	2·60
			3 ,, ..	273	3	1,775	5	2·17
			4 ,, ..	139	2	992	3	1·78
			5 ,, ..	54	1	409	1	1·51
			6 ,, and over.	66	1	692	2	....
			Total ..	6,412	....	31,488	....	....
	14	Kumbharwada	1 Room ..	5,542	87	25,596	81	4·62
			2 Rooms ..	587	9	3,488	11	2·97
			3 ,, ..	147	2	1,060	4	2·40
			4 ,, ..	72	1	593	2	2·06
			5 ,, ..	33	1	350	1	2·12
			6 ,, and over.	31	....	401	1	....

HOUSING TABLE VI-A—*contd.*

Ward.	Serial No. of section.	Name of Section.	Tenements with	Total number of occupied tenements of each class.	Percentage of each class of tenements to total tenements.	Total number of occupants of each class of tenements.	Percentage borne by population in each class of tenements to total population.	Average number of occupants per room in each class of tenements.
1	2	3	4	5	6	7	8	9
			Total ..	4,660	....	21,707	....	....
	15	Khara-Talao	1 Room ..	4,173	89	18,249	84	4·37
			2 Rooms ..	347	8	2,093	10	3·02
			3 ,, ..	77	2	676	3	2·93
			4 ,, ..	45	1	443	2	2·46
			5 ,, ..	6	....	44	....	1·47
			6 ,, and over	12	....	202	1	....
			Total ..	31,421	....	148,703	....	....
D		Grand Total for D Ward	1 Room ..	20,463	65	80,930	[illegible]	3·95
			2 Rooms ..	4,881	16	23,974	16	2·46
			3 ,, ..	1,808	6	10,349	7	·91
			4 ,, ..	1,629	5	10,986	7	·69
			5 ,, ..	1,075	3	7,516	5	·40
			6 ,, and over	1,570	5	14,948	10	...
			Total ..	8,343	....	37,858	....	....
	16	Khetwadi	1 Room ..	6,239	75	24,772	66	3·97
			2 Rooms ..	868	10	4,230	11	2·44
			3 ,, ..	363	4	2,013	5	1·85
			4 ,, ..	378	5	2,601	7	1·72
			5 ,, ..	248	3	1,872	5	1·51
			6 ,, and over	247	3	2,370	6	....
			Total ..	7,563	....	37,707	....	....
	17	Girgaum	1 Room ..	3,969	52	16,278	43	4·10
			2 Rooms ..	2,252	30	11,666	31	2·59
			3 ,, ..	542	7	3,181	8	1·96
			4 ,, ..	381	5	2,917	8	1·91
			5 ,, ..	185	3	1,285	4	1·39
			6 ,, and over	234	3	2,380	6	....
			Total ..	3,372	....	15,916	....	....
	18	Chaupati	1 Room ..	1,458	43	4,742	30	3·25
			2 Rooms ..	701	21	2,895	18	2·06
			3 ,, ..	359	11	1,901	13	1·85
			4 ,, ..	382	11	2,489	16	1·63
			5 ,, ..	187	6	1,386	8	1·43
			6 ,, and over	285	8	2,463	15	....
			Total ..	4,432	....	22,274	....	....
	19	Walkeshwar	1 Room ..	3,042	69	12,347	56	4·06
			2 Rooms ..	392	9	1,919	9	2·45
			3 ,, ..	151	3	877	4	1·94
			4 ,, ..	167	4	1,001	4	1·50
			5 ,, ..	178	4	1,165	5	1·31
			6 ,, and over	592	11	4,965	22	....
			Total ..	7,711	....	34,946	....	....
	20	Mahalaxmi	1 Room ..	5,755	75	22,791	65	3·96
			2 Rooms ..	668	9	3,264	9	2·44
			3 ,, ..	388	5	2,287	7	1·96
			4 ,, ..	321	4	1,978	6	1·54
			5 ,, ..	277	3	1,858	5	1·34
			6 ,, and over	302	4	2,770	8	....
			Total ..	60,045	....	260,105	....	....
E	..	Grand Total for E Ward	1 Room ..	53,241	89	219,776	85	4·13
			2 Rooms ..	3,895	6	19,291	7	2·48
			3 ,, ..	1,024	2	5,872	2	1·91
			4 ,, ..	925	1	5,827	2	1·57
			5 ,, ..	580	1	4,238	2	1·46
			6 ,, and over	380	1	5,101	2	....
			Total ..	7,365	....	30,534	....	....
	21	Tardeo	1 Room ..	5,399	78	20,534	67	3·80
			2 Rooms ..	915	12	8,541	11	1·93
			3 ,, ..	289	4	1,472	5	1·70
			4 ,, ..	455	6	2,752	9	1·51
			5 ,, ..	174	3	1,134	4	1·30
			6 ,, and over	133	2	1,101	4	....

Ward.	Serial No. of Section.	Name of Section.	Tenements with	Total number of occupied tenements of each class.	Percentage of each class of tenements to total tenements.	Total number of occupants of each class of tenements.	Percentage borne by population in each class of tenements to total population.	Average number of occupants per room in each class of tenements.
1	2		4	5	6	7	8	9
			Total ..	9,128	....	37,021	....	....
E.—contd.	22	Kamathipura	1 Room ..	8,113	89	31,262	85	3·85
			2 Rooms ..	814	9	4,175	11	2·56
			3 ,, ..	129	1	801	2	2·07
			4 ,, ..	41	1	388	1	2·37
			5 ,, ..	10	....	135	....	2·70
			6 ,, and over	21	....	260	1	....
			Total ..	1,981	....	7,064	....	....
	23	First Nagpada	1 Room ..	1,677	85	5,384	76	3·21
			2 Rooms ..	175	9	932	13	2·66
			3 ,, ..	33	2	170	2	1·71
			4 ,, ..	85	4	495	7	1·46
			5 ,, ..	5	....	38	1	1·32
			6 ,, and over	6	....	50	1	....
			Total ..	4,652	....	20,808	....	....
	24	Second Nagpada ..	1 Room ..	4,221	91	17,869	87	4·23
			2 Rooms ..	334	7	1,958	10	2·93
			3 ,, ..	52	1	372	2	2·38
			4 ,, ..	33	1	283	1	2·14
			5 ,, ..	6	....	48	....	1·60
			6 ,, and over	6	....	78	....	....
			Total ..	19,877	....	85,373	....	....
	25	Byculla	1 Room ..	18,439	93	76,774	90	4·16
			2 Rooms ..	780	4	4,346	5	2·79
			3 ,, ..	230	1	1,353	2	1·96
			4 ,, ..	167	1	985	1	1·48
			5 ,, ..	142	1	897	1	1·26
			6 ,, and over.	119	....	1,018	1	....
			Total ..	9,348	....	38,854	....	....
	26	Tarwadi	1 Room ..	8,144	87	32,048	82	3·94
			2 Rooms ..	581	7	2,637	7	2·27
			3 ,, ..	232	2	1,127	3	1·62
			4 ,, ..	106	1	620	2	1·46
			5 ,, ..	220	2	1,743	4	1·52
			6 ,, and over	56	1	670	2	....
			Total ..	7,694	....	40,651	....	....
	27	Mazagaon	1 Room ..	7,248	93	35,905	88	4·95
			2 Rooms ..	296	4	1,702	4	2·88
			3 ,, ..	59	1	577	1	3·26
			4 ,, ..	38	1	304	1	2·00
			5 ,, ..	14	....	248	1	3·54
			6 ,, and over	39	1	1,915	5	....
			Total ..	35,467	....	152,038	....	....
F	..	Grand Total for F Ward	1 Room ..	31,326	88	129,649	85	4·14
			2 Rooms ..	2,471	7	12,289	8	2·49
			3 ,, ..	632	2	3,469	2	1·83
			4 ,, ..	665	2	3,801	3	1·43
			5 ,, ..	135	....	831	1	1·23
			6 ,, and over	238	1	1,999	1	....
			Total ..	14,384	....	60,063	....	....
	28	Parel	1 Room ..	12,998	91	53,073	88	4·08
			2 Rooms ..	795	6	3,899	7	2·45
			3 ,, ..	181	1	833	1	1·53
			4 ,, ..	317	2	1,664	3	1·31
			5 ,, ..	44	....	241	....	1·10
			6 ,, and over	49	....	353	1	....
			Total ..	5,855	....	26,038	....	....
	29	Sewri	1 Room ..	5,395	92	23,183	89	4·30
			2 Rooms ..	352	6	1,938	8	2·75
			3 ,, ..	53	1	371	1	2·33
			4 ,, ..	35	1	308	1	2·20
			5 ,, ..	6	....	25	....	·83
			6 ,, and over	14	....	213	1	....

Ward.	Serial No. of Section.	Name of Section.	Tenements with	Total number of occupied tenements of each class.	Percentage of each class of tenements to total tenements.	Total number of occupants of each class of tenements.	Percentage borne by population in each class of tenements to total population.	Average number of occupants per room in each class of tenements.
1	2	3	4	5	6	7	8	9
			Total ..	15,228	....	65,937	....	....
F—contd.	30	Sion	1 Room ..	12,933	85	53,393	81	4·18
			2 Rooms ..	1,324	9	6,452	10	2·44
			3 ,, ..	398	3	2,265	3	1·90
			4 ,, ..	313	2	1,829	3	1·40
			5 ,, ..	85	....	565	1	1·33
			6 ,, and over	175	1	1,433	2	....
			Total ..	38,083	....	149,455	....	....
G	..	Grand Total for G Ward	1 Room ..	31,183	82	112,131	75	3·60
			2 Rooms ..	4,801	12	22,227	15	2·31
			3 ,, ..	887	2	5,119	3	1·92
			4 ,, ..	615	2	4,502	3	1·83
			5 ,, ..	256	1	2,310	2	1·80
			6 ,, and over	341	1	3,166	2	....
			Total ..	10,929	....	47,075	....	....
	31	Mahim	1 Room ..	7,643	70	29,260	62	3·83
			2 Rooms ..	2,232	20	9,896	21	2·22
			3 ,, ..	403	4	2,314	5	1·91
			4 ,, ..	323	3	2,504	5	1·94
			5 ,, ..	126	1	1,028	2	1·63
			6 ,, and over	202	2	2,073	5	....
			Total ..	27,154	....	103,380	....	....
	32	Worli	1 Room ..	23,540	87	82,871	81	3·52
			2 Rooms ..	2,569	9	12,831	12	2·40
			3 ,, ..	484	2	2,805	3	1·93
			4 ,, ..	292	1	1,998	2	1·71
			5 ,, ..	130	....	1,282	1	1·97
			6 ,, and over	139	1	1,093	1	....

Details of One-Roomed Tenements containing more than one Family.

Ward.	Serial No. of Section.	Name of Section.	One-roomed tenements containing: 2 Families.	3 Families.	4 Families.	5 Families.	6 Families.	7 Families.	8 Families and over.	Total.
1	2	3	4	5	6	7	8	9	10	11
		Grand Total, Bombay City ..	**646**	**184**	**28**	**23**	**10**	**12**	**94**	**997**
A	..	**Total for A Ward** ..	**127**	**21**	**3**	**6**	..	..	**2**	**159**
	1	Upper Colaba	..	..	..	..	..	..	..	..
	2	Lower Colaba	45	14	2	6	..	..	1	68
	3	Fort South	17	..	..	..	..	..	..	17
	4	Fort North	49	5	1	..	..	..	1	56
	5	Esplanade	16	2	.	..	..	..	..	18
B	..	**Total for B Ward** ..	**116**	**8**	..	**3**	**4**	**2**	**27**	**160**
	6	Chakla	8	1	..	2	3	2	27	43
	7	Mandvi	106	5	..	1	1	..	..	113
	8	Umerkhadi	2	2	..	..	..	..	..	4
	9	Dongri	..	..	..	..	..	..	..	..
C	..	**Total for C Ward** ..	**52**	**9**	**3**	**5**	**3**	**7**	**9**	**88**
	10	Market	13	1	..	4	3	6	9	36
	11	Dhobi-Talao	9	2	..	..	..	..	..	11
	12	Fanaswadi	7	..	..	1	..	1	..	9
	13	Bhuleshwar	2	..	..	..	..	..	..	2
	14	Kumbharwada	9	..	..	..	..	..	..	9
	15	Khara-Talao	12	6	3	..	..	..	..	21
D	..	**Total for D Ward** ..	**85**	**19**	**5**	**2**	..	..	**11**	**122**
	16	Khetwadi	18	6	3	2	..	..	2	31
	17	Girgaum	3	1	1	..	..	..	2	7
	18	Chaupati	3	..	..	..	..	..	..	3
	19	Walkeshwar	52	12	1	..	..	..	2	67
	20	Mahalaxmi	9	..	..	..	..	..	5	14
E	..	**Total for E Ward** ..	**221**	**123**	**15**	**7**	**3**	**3**	**45**	**417**
	21	Tardeo	1	..	..	..	..	..	..	1
	22	Kamathipura	26	7	4	2	..	..	..	39
	23	First Nagpada	..	..	..	..	..	..	..	..
	24	Second Nagpada	12	3	..	1	2	3	3	24
	25	Byculla	9	2	2	1	..	..	3	17
	26	Tarwadi	162	108	8	3	1	..	3	285
	27	Mazagaon	11	3	1	..	..	..	36	51
F	..	**Total for F Ward** ..	**24**	**3**	..	..	..	..	..	**27**
	28	Parel	23	3	..	..	..	..	..	26
	29	Sewri	..	..	..	..	..	..	..	..
	30	Sion	1	..	..	..	..	..	..	1
G	..	**Total for G Ward** ..	**21**	**1**	**2**	..	..	..	..	**24**
	31	Mahim	3	..	..	..	..	..	..	3
	32	Worli	18	1	2	..	..	..	..	21

TENEMENTS BY ROOMS AND

This is an amplification of Housing Table VI-A the

Name of ward.	Serial No. of Section.	NAME OF SECTION.	Total number of buildings.	Total number of persons.	RELIGION.	Total number of separate tenements occupied by persons of each religion with: One room.	Two rooms.	Three rooms.	Four rooms.	Five rooms.	Six rooms and over.
1	2	3	4	5	6	7	8	9	10	11	12
					Total ..	197,516	26,231	7,418	6,169	2,953	3,836
		Grand Total for Bombay City ..	28,136	1,071,969	Christian	10,106	1,831	829	956	469	740
					Zoroastrian	4,003	2,440	1,699	1,832	1,007	908
					Muslim	37,197	4,265	1,104	748	307	458
					Hindu	143,552	17,138	3,631	2,519	1,110	1,642
					Jain	1,052	228	54	25	20	29
					Jew and others	1,546	329	99	89	40	59
					Total ..	10,436	1,612	459	646	178	395
A	..	Grand Total, A Ward ..	2,001	58,247	Christian	1,654	298	174	354	76	208
					Zoroastrian	1,009	500	131	147	39	85
					Muslim	1,240	128	23	53	22	28
					Hindu	6,445	650	118	78	38	51
					Jain	24	1	..	..	..	..
					Jew and others	64	35	13	14	3	23
					Total ..	86	9	3	3	1	4
	1	Upper Colaba	60	418	Christian	15	2	1	..	..	1
					Zoroastrian	..	..	..	..	1	1
					Muslim	8	2	..	1	..	..
					Hindu	63	5	2	2	..	2
					Jain	..	..	..	..	..	..
					Jew and others	..	..	..	..	..	..
					Total ..	3,132	352	195	421	90	185
	2	Lower Colaba ..	596	19,282	Christian	710	127	123	310	53	108
					Zoroastrian	62	34	35	67	16	36
					Muslim	349	25	7	15	10	11
					Hindu	1,980	142	19	18	9	14
					Jain	19	1	..	..	..	..
					Jew and others	12	23	11	11	2	16
					Total ..	401	[illegible]	23	21	10	13
	3	Fort South ..	141	2,610	Christian	184	21	13	10	4	4
					Zoroastrian	13	2	..	1	..	..
					Muslim	26	8	2	5	3	3
					Hindu	104	18	7	5	3	6
					Jew and others	14	6	1	..	.	..
					Total ..	4,610	999	178	118	41	31
	4	Fort North	798	24,108	Christian	473	82	11	6	1	2
					Zoroastrian	872	447	86	62	13	14
					Muslim	510	62	7	7	3	1
					Hindu	2,732	406	74	42	24	14
					Jain	4	..	..	..	..	..
					Jew and others	19	2	..	1	..	..
					Total ..	2,207	197	60	88	36	162
	5	Esplanade	406	11,829	Christian	272	66	26	28	18	93
					Zoroastrian	62	17	10	17	0	34
					Muslim	347	31	7	25	6	13
					Hindu	1,506	79	16	11	2	15
					Jain	1	..	..	..	..	..
					Jew and others	19	4	1	2	1	7
					Total ..	18,238	3,295	900	540	200	264
B	..	Grand Total, B Ward ..	1,962	103,397	Christian	141	63	9	10	7	1
					Zoroastrian	18	10	1	..	..	1
					Muslim	7,989	1,717	557	334	131	161
					Hindu	9,649	1,374	307	186	58	96
					Jain	209	20	5	..	2	1
					Jew and others	232	111	21	10	2	4
					Total ..	2,338	579	214	146	49	45
	6	Chakla	479	16,915	Christian	..	3	..	2	..	..
					Zoroastrian	7	5	..	..	..	..
					Muslim	1,467	409	156	98	32	26
					Hindu	862	162	58	46	16	19
					Jew and others	2	..	..	..	1	..

POPULATION BY RELIGION.

statistics being given separately for the different Religions.

Total number of tenements of all kinds occupied by members of each religion.	Total number of members of each religion occupying tenements with						Total number of members of each religion occupying tenements of all kinds.	Percentage of total population of each religion occupying each class of tenements with					
	One room.	Two rooms.	Three rooms.	Four rooms.	Five rooms.	Six rooms and over.		One room.	Two rooms.	Three rooms.	Four rooms.	Five rooms.	Six rooms and over.
13	14	15	16	17	18	19	20	21	22	23	24	25	26
244,121	**791,762**	**131,872**	**44,821**	**42,013**	**22,302**	**39,199**	**1,071,969**	**74**	**12**	**4**	**4**	**2**	**4**
14,931	40,304	10,146	5,507	6,868	3,745	8,499	75,069	54	14	7	9	5	11
11,949	16,760	10,398	8,717	10,734	6,862	7,793	61,264	27	17	14	18	11	18
44,079	140,692	22,556	7,384	5,560	2,550	4,983	183,725	77	12	4	3	1	3
169,592	583,536	85,855	22,284	18,061	8,757	16,989	735,482	79	12	3	3	1	2
1,408	4,132	1,114	203	155	137	347	6,178	67	18	5	2	2	6
2,162	6,338	1,803	636	635	251	588	10,251	62	18	6	6	2	6
13,726	**39,091**	**7,680**	**2,694**	**3,991**	**1,280**	**3,561**	**58,247**	**67**	**13**	**5**	**7**	**2**	**6**
2,764	5,501	1,469	1,029	2,206	596	1,713	12,514	44	12	8	17	5	14
1,911	3,670	2,116	721	927	254	709	8,397	44	25	9	11	3	8
1,494	4,771	696	133	336	152	342	6,430	74	11	2	5	3	5
7,380	24,836	3,093	719	429	256	540	29,873	83	10	2	2	1	2
25	78	8	..	..	..	..	86	91	9	..	..	..	..
152	235	248	92	93	22	257	947	25	26	10	10	2	27
106	**343**	**28**	**6**	**17**	**7**	**22**	**418**	**82**	**6**	**1**	**4**	**2**	**5**
19	60	2	1	..	..	8	71	85	3	1	..	..	11
2	..	..	..	..	7	9	16	..	..	..	..	44	66
11	30	3	..	8	..	..	41	73	7	..	20	..	..
74	253	18	5	9	..	5	290	87	6	2	3	..	2
..	..	..	..	..	..	..	....	..	..	..	..	..	..
..	..	..	..	..	..	..	....	..	..	..	..	..	..
4,375	**11,416**	**1,932**	**1,089**	**2,631**	**645**	**1,569**	**19,282**	**59**	**10**	**6**	**14**	**3**	**8**
1,431	1,881	625	637	1,921	427	808	6,299	30	10	10	30	7	13
250	220	186	218	443	108	318	1,493	15	12	15	30	7	21
417	1,134	120	40	92	64	74	1,524	74	8	3	6	4	5
2,182	8,090	837	110	103	30	191	9,361	86	9	1	1	1	2
20	66	8	..	..	..	..	74	89	11	..	..	..	..
75	25	156	84	72	16	178	531	5	29	16	14	3	33
523	**1,792**	**339**	**132**	**166**	**74**	**107**	**2,610**	**69**	**13**	**5**	**6**	**3**	**4**
236	808	116	94	91	41	33	1,188	68	10	8	8	3	3
16	50	5	..	2	..	..	57	88	9	..	3	..	..
47	187	12	9	34	14	32	288	65	4	3	12	5	11
203	698	140	28	39	10	42	966	72	15	3	4	2	4
21	49	66	1	..	..	..	116	42	57	1	..	..	..
5,977	**17,535**	**4,377**	**990**	**674**	**311**	**221**	**24,108**	**73**	**18**	**4**	**3**	**1**	**1**
575	1,951	444	72	40	6	19	2,532	77	18	3	2	..	..
1,494	3,230	1,856	443	392	88	116	6,129	53	30	7	6	2	2
590	1,996	394	39	41	27	3	2,500	79	16	2	2	1	..
3,292	10,274	1,676	436	193	195	83	12,857	80	13	3	2	2	..
4	9	..	..	..	..	..	9	100	..	..	..	..	..
22	66	7	..	8	..	..	81	81	9	..	10	..	..
2,745	**8,005**	**959**	**477**	**503**	**243**	**1,642**	**11,829**	**68**	**8**	**4**	**4**	**2**	**14**
503	801	282	225	154	122	845	2,429	33	12	9	6	5	35
149	161	69	60	90	56	206	702	23	10	9	12	8	38
429	1,424	167	45	161	47	233	2,077	69	8	2	8	2	11
1,629	5,521	422	140	85	12	219	6,399	86	7	2	1	..	4
1	3	..	..	..	..	..	3	100	..	..	..	..	..
34	95	19	7	13	6	79	219	43	9	3	6	3	36
28,437	**71,811**	**17,739**	**5,718**	**3,754**	**1,538**	**2,887**	**103,397**	**69**	**17**	**6**	**4**	**1**	**3**
231	540	271	43	55	35	9	958	57	28	4	6	4	1
30	53	37	5	..	..	8	103	51	36	5	..	..	8
10,889	30,245	8,947	3,625	2,307	1,072	1,815	48,011	63	19	7	5	2	4
11,670	39,345	7,830	1,897	1,293	409	957	51,731	76	15	4	2	1	2
237	671	84	21	..	15	9	800	84	10	3	..	2	1
380	957	570	127	90	7	99	1,799	53	32	7	6	..	2
3,371	**10,278**	**3,116**	**1,459**	**1,079**	**396**	**587**	**16,915**	**61**	**18**	**9**	**6**	**2**	**4**
5	..	14	..	12	..	..	26	..	54	..	46	..	..
12	13	24	..	..	..	..	37	35	65	..	..	..	..
2,188	6,446	2,228	1,138	763	287	313	11,178	57	20	10	7	3	3
1,163	3,816	852	321	296	109	274	5,668	67	15	6	5	2	5
3	3	..	..	8	..	..	11	27	..	..	73	..	..

MO-III Bk Ra Cs 3—82

Name of ward.	Serial No. of Section.	NAME OF SECTION.	Total number of buildings.	Total number of persons.	RELIGION.	Total number of separate tenements occupied by persons of each religion with One room.	Two rooms.	Three rooms.	Four rooms.	Five rooms.	Six rooms and over.
1	2	3	4	5	6	7	8	9	10	11	12
					Total ..	**5,027**	**1,192**	**310**	**180**	**71**	**108**
B—contd.	7	Mandvi ..	[illegible]	35,015	Christian	31	1	2	1	..	1
					Zoroastrian	4	..	..	..	..	..
					Muslim	912	250	92	52	35	44
					Hindu	4,042	928	213	122	34	61
					Jain	18	1	..	..	1	..
					Jew and others	20	12	3	5	1	2
					Total ..	**8,075**	**1,306**	**338**	**181**	**65**	**101**
	8	Umerkhadi	725	40,011	Christian	89	56	6	5	5	..
					Zoroastrian	5	4	1	..	..	1
					Muslim	5,165	981	291	162	53	86
					Hindu	2,620	176	23	11	7	11
					Jain	42	9	3	..	..	1
					Jew and others	154	80	14	3	..	2
					Total ..	**2,798**	**218**	**38**	**33**	**15**	**10**
	9	Dongri	174	11,456	Christian	21	3	1	2	2	..
					Zoroastrian	2	1	..	..	..	..
					Muslim	445	77	18	22	11	5
					Hindu	2,125	108	13	7	1	5
					Jain	149	10	2	..	1	..
					Jew and others	56	19	4	2	..	..
					Total ..	**32,629**	**5,276**	**1,711**	**1,149**	**529**	**648**
C	..	**Grand Total, C Ward** ..	**4,140**	**200,024**	Christian	1,022	360	133	124	47	51
					Zoroastrian	467	527	400	251	160	97
					Muslim	6,095	716	161	95	17	42
					Hindu	24,681	3,581	991	672	296	448
					Jain	356	89	26	7	9	8
					Jew and others	8	3	..	..	..	2
					Total ..	**5,653**	**1,091**	**309**	**214**	**98**	**202**
	10	Market	758	37,187	Christian	128	43	16	12	5	7
					Zoroastrian	8	6	3	2	..	..
					Muslim	412	97	26	17	4	16
					Hindu	4,866	884	245	179	82	175
					Jain	236	60	19	4	7	4
					Jew and others	3	1	..	..	..	..
					Total ..	**5,882**	**1,526**	**594**	**421**	**241**	**209**
	11	Dhobi Talao	916	44,000	Christian	793	268	106	84	88	31
					Zoroastrian	327	419	288	176	135	76
					Muslim	201	38	9	8	3	3
					Hindu	4,544	791	188	151	64	97
					Jain	16	10	3	2	1	1
					Jew and others	1	..	..	..	..	1
					Total ..	**5,145**	**774**	**311**	**258**	**97**	**128**
	12	Fanaswadi	674	31,754	Christian	81	42	10	28	4	12
					Zoroastrian	100	89	100	69	22	19
					Muslim	88	10	..	..	..	2
					Hindu	4,869	633	200	161	70	95
					Jain	7	..	1	..	1	..
					Total ..	**6,234**	**951**	**273**	**139**	**54**	**66**
	13	Bhuleshwar	881	33,888	Christian	5	4	..	..	..	..
					Zoroastrian	29	10	9	3	3	2
					Muslim	1,919	256	53	31	5	11
					Hindu	4,231	669	209	104	46	51
					Jain	50	11	2	1	..	2
					Jew and others	..	1	..	..	..	..
					Total ..	**5,542**	**587**	**147**	**72**	**33**	**31**
	14	Kumbharwada	516	31,488	Christian	11	1	..	..	..	..
					Zoroastrian	2	2	..	1	..	..
					Muslim	386	84	7	4	..	..
					Hindu	5,114	543	139	67	33	29
					Jain	25	7	1	..	..	1
					Jew and others	4	..	..	..	..	1

Total number of tenements of all kinds occupied by members of each religion.	Total number of members of each religion occupying tenements with						Total number of members of each religion occupying tenements of all kinds.	Percentage of total population of each religion occupying each class of tenements with					
	One room.	Two rooms.	Three rooms.	Four rooms.	Five rooms.	Six rooms and over.		One room.	Two rooms.	Three rooms.	Four rooms.	Five rooms.	Six rooms and over.
13	14	15	16	17	18	19	20	21	22	23	24	25	26
6,888	22,857	7,201	2,075	1,331	540	1,011	35,015	65	20	6	4	2	3
36	118	5	15	3	..	9	150	79	3	10	2	..	6
4	14	..	..	..	..	..	14	100	..	..	..	..	..
1,385	3,943	1,317	660	360	278	405	6,963	57	19	9	5	4	6
5,400	18,609	5,798	1,388	922	247	579	27,543	68	21	5	3	1	2
20	76	6	..	..	8	..	90	84	7	..	..	9	..
43	97	75	12	46	7	18	255	38	29	5	18	8	7
10,066	28,805	6,430	1,993	1,160	510	1,113	40,011	72	16	5	3	1	3
161	324	232	26	30	29	..	641	50	36	4	5	5	..
11	7	12	5	..	..	8	32	22	37	16	..	..	25
6,738	18,463	5,018	1,724	1,051	430	995	27,676	67	18	6	4	2	3
2,848	9,227	724	135	51	51	80	10,268	90	7	1	1	1	..
55	148	37	12	..	..	9	206	72	18	6	..	..	4
253	636	412	91	28	..	21	1,188	53	35	8	2	..	2
3,112	9,871	992	191	184	92	126	11,456	86	9	2	1	1	1
29	98	20	2	10	6	..	136	72	15	2	7	4	..
3	19	1	..	..	..	..	20	95	5	..	..	..	..
578	1,393	391	103	133	77	102	2,199	63	18	5	6	3	5
2,259	7,693	456	53	24	2	24	8,252	93	6	1	..	..	..
162	447	41	9	..	7	..	504	89	8	2	..	1	..
81	221	83	24	17	..	..	345	64	24	7	5	..	..
41,942	138,874	28,722	11,600	9,152	4,589	7,587	200,024	69	14	6	5	2	4
1,737	4,632	2,835	1,471	1,764	743	1,398	12,843	36	22	11	14	6	11
1,902	1,479	2,385	2,060	1,556	1,170	843	9,493	16	25	22	16	12	9
7,126	26,066	4,316	1,267	913	144	689	33,305	78	13	4	3	..	2
30,669	104,335	18,636	6,613	4,887	2,459	4,559	141,489	74	13	5	3	2	3
495	1,838	542	189	32	73	80	2,754	67	20	7	1	2	3
13	24	8	..	..	..	18	50	48	16	..	..	..	36
7,567	24,373	6,047	2,088	1,663	849	2,167	37,187	65	16	6	5	2	6
211	716	246	98	163	96	158	1,477	48	17	7	11	6	11
19	23	22	14	13	..	..	72	32	31	19	18	..	..
572	1,949	560	157	182	24	317	3,189	61	18	5	6	..	10
6,431	20,226	4,815	1,671	1,284	672	1,658	30,326	67	16	6	4	2	5
330	1,450	400	148	21	57	34	2,110	69	19	7	1	3	1
4	9	4	..	..	..	..	13	69	31	..	..	..	..
8,873	23,421	8,363	4,074	3,522	2,075	2,545	44,000	53	19	9	8	5	8
1,320	3,525	2,184	1,242	1,172	516	833	9,472	37	23	13	12	6	9
1,421	1,086	1,909	1,553	1,128	1,006	894	7,466	15	27	21	15	13	9
262	730	210	55	45	26	19	1,085	67	19	5	4	3	2
5,835	18,031	3,930	1,207	1,170	516	983	25,837	70	15	5	5	2	3
33	47	40	17	7	11	6	128	37	31	13	5	9	5
2	2	..	..	..	..	10	12	17	..	..	..	..	83
6,713	21,659	3,787	1,927	1,939	862	1,580	31,754	68	12	6	6	3	5
177	316	389	129	429	131	404	1,798	18	22	7	24	7	22
390	272	311	461	388	139	136	1,707	16	18	27	23	8	8
100	305	60	..	..	..	36	401	76	15	..	..	..	9
6,028	20,736	3,027	1,334	1,122	587	1,004	27,810	75	10	5	4	2	4
9	30	..	3	..	5	..	38	79	..	8	..	13	..
7,717	25,076	4,944	1,775	992	409	692	33,888	74	15	5	3	1	2
9	15	8	..	..	..	..	23	65	35	..	..	..	..
56	92	35	32	14	25	13	211	43	17	15	7	12	6
2,275	8,274	1,600	429	322	56	129	10,810	77	15	4	3	..	1
5,810	16,533	3,231	1,207	652	328	513	22,554	74	14	6	3	1	2
66	162	68	17	4	..	37	288	56	24	6	1	..	13
1	..	2	..	..	..	..	2	..	100	..	..	..	..
6,412	25,596	3,488	1,060	593	350	401	31,488	81	11	4	2	1	1
12	47	5	..	..	..	..	52	90	10	..	..	..	..
5	5	17	..	13	..	..	35	14	49	..	37	..	..
431	1,477	156	52	26	..	..	1,711	86	9	3	2	..	..
5,925	23,965	3,278	1,004	554	350	390	29,541	81	11	4	2	1	1
34	89	32	4	..	..	3	128	70	25	3	..	..	2
5	13	..	..	..	..	8	21	62	..	..	..	..	38

Name of ward.	Serial No. of Section.	NAME OF SECTION.	Total number of buildings.	Total number of persons.	RELIGION.	Total number of separate tenements occupied by persons of each religion with					
						One room.	Two rooms.	Three rooms.	Four rooms.	Five rooms.	Six rooms and over.
1	2	3	4	5	6	7	8	9	10	11	12
					Total ..	4,173	347	77	45	6	12
C—contd.	15	Khara Talao	395	21,707	Christian	4	2	1	..	..	1
					Zoroastrian	1	1	..	..	..	..
					Muslim	3,089	281	66	35	5	10
					Hindu	1,057	61	10	10	1	1
					Jain	22	1	..	..	..	..
					Jew and others	..	1	..	..	..	..
					Total ..	20,463	4,881	1,808	1,629	1,075	1,570
D	..	Grand Total, D Ward ..	4,982	148,703	Christian	909	178	68	85	92	197
					Zoroastrian	1,405	492	502	579	443	499
					Muslim	1,357	136	49	37	34	86
					Hindu	16,678	4,066	1,179	910	494	763
					Jain	68	7	2	8	6	14
					Jew and others	46	2	3	10	6	11
					Total ..	6,239	868	363	378	248	247
	16	Khetwadi	956	37,858	Christian ..	125	15	9	4	..	2
					Zoroastrian	623	136	181	220	124	131
					Muslim	797	52	8	11	4	3
					Hindu	4,688	663	165	138	117	105
					Jain	4	2	..	4	3	5
					Jew and others	2	..	..	1	..	1
					Total ..	3,969	2,252	542	381	185	234
	17	Girgaum	942	37,707	Christian	50	39	16	13	13	37
					Zoroastrian	25	35	10	6	2	11
					Muslim	50	13	6	..	2	5
					Hindu	3,829	2,163	510	360	166	181
					Jain	15	2	..	1	2	..
					Jew and others	..	..	..	1	..	..
					Total ..	1,458	701	359	382	187	285
	18	Chaupati	505	15,916	Christian	53	15	13	16	9	10
					Zoroastrian	17	12	10	64	42	39
					Muslim	43	10	10	4	9	10
					Hindu	1,339	664	315	297	125	223
					Jain	2	..	2	..	1	1
					Jew and others	4	..	..	1	1	2
					Total ..	3,042	392	151	167	178	502
	19	Walkeshwar	1,256	22,274	Christian	305	52	16	29	37	98
					Zoroastrian	229	47	21	71	95	178
					Muslim	205	32	16	9	13	47
					Hindu	2,241	258	96	50	32	164
					Jain	30	2	..	3	..	7
					Jew and others	23	1	2	5	1	8
					Total ..	5,755	668	388	821	277	302
	20	Mahalaxmi	1,323	34,948	Christian	376	57	14	23	33	50
					Zoroastrian	511	262	271	218	180	140
					Muslim	262	29	9	13	6	21
					Hindu	4,581	318	03	65	54	90
					Jain	8	1	..	..	..	1
					Jew and others	17	1	1	2	4	..
					Total ..	53,241	3,895	1,024	925	580	380
E	..	Grand Total, E Ward ..	5,100	260,105	Christian	3,234	350	154	186	146	114
					Zoroastrian	643	311	347	400	301	135
					Muslim	15,100	1,093	198	140	68	68
					Hindu	33,063	1,987	272	155	38	50
					Jain	201	16	4	6	1	1
					Jew and others	1,000	138	49	88	26	12
					Total ..	5,399	915	289	455	174	133
	21	Tardeo	591	30,534	Christian	273	54	15	36	7	8
					Zoroastrian	232	223	190	313	148	100
					Muslim	1,158	208	34	32	7	12
					Hindu	3,654	407	47	69	7	10
					Jain	60	11	2	2	..	1
					Jew and others	22	12	1	3	5	2

Total number of tenements of all kinds occupied by members of each religion.	Total number of members of each religion occupying tenements with						Total number of members of each religion occupying tenements of all kinds.	Percentage of total population of each religion occupying each class of tenements with					
	One room.	Two rooms.	Three rooms.	Four rooms.	Five rooms.	Six rooms and over.		One room.	Two rooms.	Three rooms.	Four rooms.	Five rooms.	Six rooms and over.
13	14	15	16	17	18	19	20	21	22	23	24	25	26
4,660	**18,249**	**2,093**	**676**	**443**	**44**	**202**	**21,707**	**84**	**10**	**3**	**2**	..	**1**
8	13	3	2	..	..	3	21	62	14	10	..	..	14
2	1	1	..	..	..	..	2	50	50	..	..	..	..
3,486	13,331	1,790	574	338	38	188	16,199	82	11	4	2	..	1
1,140	4,844	355	100	105	6	11	5,421	89	7	2	2	..	..
23	60	2	..	..	..	..	62	97	3	..	..	..	..
1	..	2	..	..	..	..	2	..	100	..	..	..	..
31,421	**80,930**	**23,974**	**10,349**	**10,986**	**7,516**	**14,948**	**148,703**	**55**	**16**	**7**	**7**	**5**	**10**
1,529	3,613	920	403	570	636	1,501	7,643	49	12	5	7	8	19
3,920	6,696	2,114	2,828	3,658	2,973	4,446	22,615	30	9	13	16	13	19
1,099	4,852	856	323	213	305	893	7,442	65	12	4	3	4	12
24,090	65,273	20,038	6,762	6,526	3,539	7,816	109,954	59	19	6	6	3	7
105	289	38	9	66	30	222	654	44	6	1	10	5	34
78	207	8	24	53	33	70	395	52	2	6	14	8	18
8,343	**24,772**	**4,230**	**2,013**	**2,601**	**1,872**	**2,370**	**37,858**	**66**	**11**	**5**	**7**	**5**	**6**
155	554	54	67	86	..	9	770	72	7	9	11	..	1
1,415	2,663	595	949	1,379	925	1,297	7,808	34	8	12	18	12	16
875	2,531	342	73	78	28	50	3,102	81	11	2	3	1	2
5,876	19,008	3,229	924	1,029	897	981	26,068	73	12	4	4	3	4
18	13	10	..	22	22	29	96	14	10	..	23	23	30
4	3	..	..	7	..	4	14	21	..	..	50	...	29
7,563	**16,278**	**11,666**	**3,181**	**2,917**	**1,285**	**2,380**	**37,707**	**43**	**31**	**8**	**8**	**4**	**6**
168	207	285	124	84	63	307	1,070	19	27	11	8	6	29
89	66	165	86	35	15	84	451	15	36	19	8	3	19
70	193	52	21	..	10	43	319	61	16	7	..	3	13
7,209	15,766	11,140	2,950	2,782	1,192	1,946	35,785	44	31	8	8	3	6
20	46	15	..	9	5	..	75	61	20	..	12	7	..
1	..	..	..	7	..	..	7	..	..	..	100	..	..
3,372	**4,742**	**2,895**	**1,991**	**2,489**	**1,336**	**2,463**	**15,916**	**29**	**18**	**13**	**16**	**8**	**16**
116	145	66	89	134	65	79	578	25	11	16	23	11	14
193	44	53	103	410	352	319	1,281	3	4	8	32	27	26
86	121	61	61	22	79	96	440	27	14	14	5	18	22
2,963	4,407	2,715	1,729	1,915	830	1,943	13,539	33	20	13	14	6	14
6	5	..	9	..	3	16	33	15	..	27	..	9	49
8	20	..	..	8	7	10	45	44	..	..	18	16	22
4,432	**12,347**	**1,919**	**877**	**1,001**	**1,165**	**4,965**	**22,274**	**56**	**9**	**4**	**4**	**5**	**22**
537	1,249	245	75	155	266	709	2,699	46	9	3	6	10	26
641	1,463	192	147	409	547	1,596	4,354	34	4	3	9	13	37
322	1,109	225	106	59	129	543	2,171	51	10	5	3	6	25
2,841	8,208	1,240	526	318	214	1,972	12,478	65	10	4	3	2	16
51	206	11	..	35	..	89	341	61	3	..	10	..	26
40	112	6	23	25	9	56	231	48	3	10	11	4	24
7,711	**22,791**	**3,264**	**2,287**	**1,978**	**1,858**	**2,770**	**34,948**	**65**	**9**	**7**	**6**	**5**	**8**
553	1,458	270	48	111	242	397	2,526	58	10	2	4	10	16
1,582	2,460	1,109	1,543	1,323	1,134	1,150	8,721	28	13	18	15	13	13
340	898	176	62	54	59	161	1,410	64	13	4	4	4	11
5,201	17,884	1,705	633	482	406	974	22,084	81	8	3	2	2	4
10	19	2	..	..	..	88	109	17	2	..	..	..	81
25	72	2	1	6	17	..	98	74	2	1	6	17	..
60,045	**219,776**	**19,291**	**5,872**	**5,827**	**4,238**	**5,101**	**260,105**	**85**	**7**	**2**	**2**	**2**	**2**
4,184	14,090	2,034	1,048	1,131	1,152	2,682	22,137	64	9	5	5	5	12
2,137	2,702	1,124	1,567	2,322	2,067	1,057	10,839	25	10	15	21	19	10
16,667	55,997	5,678	1,277	1,092	575	719	65,338	86	9	2	1	1	1
35,565	142,211	9,666	1,647	985	255	494	155,258	92	6	1	1	..	..
229	590	49	11	29	11	5	695	85	7	2	4	1	1
1,203	4,186	745	322	268	178	144	5,843	72	13	5	5	3	2
7,365	**20,534**	**3,541**	**1,472**	**2,752**	**1,134**	**1,101**	**30,534**	**67**	**11**	**5**	**9**	**4**	**4**
393	906	241	71	213	45	66	1,542	59	16	5	13	3	4
1,206	708	786	886	1,860	926	801	5,967	12	13	15	31	16	13
1,451	3,977	974	231	220	88	168	5,658	71	17	4	4	2	3
4,194	14,742	1,464	280	421	46	55	17,008	87	9	2	2	..	..
76	132	32	2	9	..	5	180	73	18	1	5	..	3
45	69	44	2	20	29	6	179	39	25	1	16	16	3

Name of ward.	Serial No. of section.	NAME OF SECTION.	Total number of buildings.	Total number of persons.	RELIGION.	Total number of separate tenements occupied by persons of each religion with					
						One room.	Two rooms.	Three rooms.	Four rooms.	Five rooms.	Six rooms and over.
1	2	3	4	5	6	7	8	9	10	11	12
					Total ..	8,113	814	129	41	10	21
E—contd.	22	Kamathipura	903	37,021	Christian	83	10	5	1	2	6
					Zoroastrian	17	..	..	1	..	..
					Muslim	2,120	148	24	14	1	2
					Hindu	5,728	620	92	25	4	10
					Jain	35	..	..	..	..	..
					Jew and others	131	27	8	..	3	3
					Total ..	1,677	175	33	85	5	6
	23	First Nagpada	115	7,064	Christian	179	24	5	33	3	2
					Zoroastrian	7	1	..	..	1	..
					Muslim	464	35	3	12	..	2
					Hindu	778	67	11	18	..	1
					Jain	11	1	..	..	1	..
					Jew and others	238	47	14	22	..	1
					Total ..	4,221	334	52	33	6	6
	24	Second Nagpada ..	403	20,608	Christian	33	4	1	2	..	..
					Zoroastrian	15	1	1	..	..	..
					Muslim	3,168	281	43	25	3	5
					Hindu	864	32	4	1	1	..
					Jain	29	1	..	..	..	..
					Jew and others	112	15	8	5	2	1
					Total ..	18,439	780	230	167	142	119
	25	Byculla	1,399	85,373	Christian	1,331	94	50	64	56	51
					Zoroastrian	79	52	18	22	18	16
					Muslim	5,949	304	79	49	46	36
					Hindu	10,651	304	65	22	19	14
					Jain	47	2	2	4	..	..
					Jew and others	382	24	16	6	8	2
					Total ..	8,144	581	232	106	229	56
	26	Tarwadi	777	38,854	Christian	777	80	54	25	67	23
					Zoroastrian	102	16	134	57	138	15
					Muslim	1,030	74	9	6	10	8
					Hindu	6,137	401	32	16	6	9
					Jain	11	..	..	..	..	..
					Jew and others	87	10	3	2	8	1
					Total ..	7,248	296	59	38	14	39
	27	Mazagaon	912	40,651	Christian	559	84	24	25	11	24
					Zoroastrian	191	18	4	7	1	4
					Muslim	1,211	43	6	2	1	3
					Hindu	5,251	147	21	4	1	6
					Jain	8	1	..	..	..	..
					Jew and others	28	3	4	..	..	2
					Total ..	**31,326**	**2,471**	**632**	**665**	**135**	**238**
F		**Grand Total, F Ward** ..	**4,069**	**152,038**	Christian	1,799	179	52	41	36	59
					Zoroastrian	408	461	278	417	41	67
					Muslim	2,789	184	42	11	8	22
					Hindu	26,117	1,592	254	190	48	85
					Jain	82	39	2	..	..	2
					Jew and others	131	16	4	6	2	3
					Total ..	12,998	795	181	317	44	49
	28	Parel	1,035	60,063	Christian	811	79	17	14	25	16
					Zoroastrian	217	91	80	245	1	11
					Muslim	843	48	9	..	..	2
					Hindu	11,027	571	74	58	18	20
					Jain	33	1	..	..	..	..
					Jew and others	67	5	1	..	..	..
					Total ..	5,395	352	53	35	6	14
	29	Sewri	942	26,038	Christian	124	27	7	3	..	6
					Zoroastrian	6	2	1	..	1	..
					Muslim	588	32	6	4	1	1
					Hindu	4,660	269	38	28	4	6
					Jain	6	20	1	..	..	1
					Jew and others	11	2	..	..	..	..

Total number of tenements of all kinds occupied by members of each religion.	Total number of members of each religion occupying tenements with						Total number of members of each religion occupying tenements of all kinds.	Percentage of total population of each religion occupying each class of tenements with					
	One room.	Two rooms.	Three rooms.	Four rooms.	Five rooms.	Six rooms and over.		One room.	Two rooms.	Three rooms.	Four rooms.	Five rooms.	Six rooms and over.
13	14	15	16	17	18	19	20	21	22	23	24	25	26
9,128	**31,262**	**4,175**	**801**	**388**	**185**	**260**	**37,021**	**85**	**11**	**2**	**1**	..	**1**
106	297	44	23	2	44	55	465	64	10	5	..	9	12
18	66	..	..	5	..	..	71	93	..	..	7	..	..
2,309	7,678	736	164	191	25	14	8,808	87	9	2	2	..	..
6,488	22,670	3,299	534	190	49	133	26,875	84	12	2	1	..	1
35	110	..	..	..	..	..	110	100	..	..	..	..	..
172	441	96	80	..	17	58	692	64	14	12	..	2	8
1,981	**5,384**	**932**	**170**	**495**	**33**	**50**	**7,064**	**76**	**13**	**2**	**7**	**1**	**1**
246	490	107	49	171	17	15	849	58	12	6	20	2	2
9	8	2	..	..	5	..	15	54	13	..	..	33	..
516	1,372	197	20	86	..	23	1,698	81	11	1	6	..	1
875	2,524	314	60	106	..	7	3,011	84	10	2	4	..	..
18	21	5	..	..	11	..	37	57	18	..	..	30	..
322	969	307	41	132	..	5	1,454	67	21	3	9	..	..
4,652	**17,869**	**1,958**	**372**	**283**	**48**	**78**	**20,608**	**87**	**10**	**2**	**1**	..	..
40	147	19	6	9	..	..	181	81	11	3	5	..	..
17	38	4	3	..	..	..	45	84	0	7	..	..	..
3,525	12,184	1,556	271	206	24	71	14,312	85	11	2	1	..	1
902	4,907	284	63	13	6	..	5,273	93	6	1	..	..	..
30	105	2	..	..	..	..	107	98	2	..	..	..	..
138	488	93	29	55	18	7	690	71	13	4	8	3	1
19,877	**76,774**	**4,346**	**1,353**	**985**	**897**	**1,018**	**85,373**	**90**	**5**	**2**	**1**	**1**	**1**
1,646	6,053	777	307	344	323	367	8,171	74	10	4	4	4	4
200	433	166	76	114	56	110	955	45	17	8	12	6	12
6,463	21,778	1,683	476	349	348	365	24,999	87	7	2	1	1	2
11,075	46,669	1,574	366	116	109	158	48,992	97	3	..	..	..	..
53	171	7	9	20	..	..	207	83	3	4	10	..	..
438	1,670	139	119	42	61	18	2,049	81	7	6	2	3	1
9,348	**32,048**	**2,637**	**1,127**	**620**	**1,743**	**679**	**38,854**	**82**	**7**	**3**	**2**	**4**	**2**
1,026	3,119	335	280	166	493	461	4,854	64	7	6	3	10	10
462	477	94	576	311	1,077	111	2,046	18	3	22	12	41	4
1,137	3,594	308	60	25	83	50	4,120	87	8	1	1	2	1
6,601	24,428	1,852	197	108	37	55	26,677	92	7	1	..	..	..
11	32	..	..	..	..	..	32	100	..	..	..	..	..
111	398	48	14	10	53	2	525	76	9	3	2	10	..
7,694	**35,905**	**1,702**	**577**	**304**	**248**	**1,915**	**40,651**	**88**	**4**	**1**	**1**	**1**	**5**
727	3,078	511	312	226	230	1,718	6,075	51	8	5	4	4	28
225	972	72	26	32	3	35	1,140	85	7	2	3	..	3
1,266	5,414	219	55	15	7	28	5,738	94	4	1	..	..	1
5,430	26,271	879	147	31	8	86	27,422	96	3	1	..	..	..
9	19	3	..	..	..	..	22	86	14	..	..	..	..
37	151	18	37	..	..	48	254	59	7	15	..	..	19
35,467	**129,649**	**12,289**	**3,469**	**3,801**	**831**	**1,999**	**152,038**	**85**	**8**	**2**	**3**	**1**	**1**
2,106	6,743	866	284	197	217	450	8,757	77	10	3	2	8	5
1,672	1,664	2,188	1,346	2,140	263	542	8,143	20	27	17	26	3	7
3,056	9,760	886	261	85	47	111	11,150	88	8	2	1	..	1
28,286	110,706	8,077	1,548	1,340	294	851	122,810	90	7	1	1	..	1
125	278	170	10	..	..	16	488	58	37	2	..	..	3
162	498	93	20	39	10	29	689	72	14	3	6	1	4
14,384	**52,073**	**3,899**	**833**	**1,664**	**241**	**353**	**60,063**	**88**	**7**	**1**	**3**	..	**1**
962	2,779	358	77	62	140	77	3,493	80	10	2	2	4	2
645	671	334	308	1,130	2	97	2,542	26	13	12	45	..	4
902	2,897	266	28	..	..	12	3,203	91	8	1	..	..	..
11,768	46,326	2,911	414	472	98	167	50,389	92	6	1	1	..	..
34	100	2	..	..	..	..	102	98	2	..	..	..	..
73	300	28	6	..	..	..	334	90	8	2	..	..	..
5,855	**23,183**	**1,938**	**371**	**308**	**25**	**213**	**26,038**	**89**	**8**	**1**	**1**	..	**1**
167	425	151	42	24	..	62	704	60	22	6	3	..	9
10	37	8	5	..	2	..	52	71	15	10	..	4	..
632	2,148	167	39	58	3	9	2,419	89	7	2	2	..	..
5,005	20,514	1,486	280	231	20	136	22,667	90	7	1	1	..	1
28	28	112	5	..	..	6	151	19	74	3	..	..	4
13	31	14	..	..	..	..	45	69	31	..	..	..	..

Name of ward.	Serial No. of section.	NAME OF SECTION.	Total number of buildings.	Total number of persons.	RELIGION.	Total number of separate tenements occupied by persons of each religion with					
						One room.	Two rooms.	Three rooms.	Four rooms.	Five rooms.	Six rooms and over.
1	2	3	4	5	6	7	8	9	10	11	12
					Total ..	**12,933**	**1,324**	**398**	**313**	**85**	**175**
F—contd.	30	Sion	2,092	65,937	Christian	864	73	28	24	11	37
					Zoroastrian	185	368	197	172	39	56
					Muslim	1,358	104	27	7	7	19
					Hindu	10,430	752	142	104	26	59
					Jain	43	18	1	..	..	1
					Jew and others	53	9	3	6	2	3
					Total ..	**31,183**	**4,801**	**887**	**615**	**256**	**341**
G		**Grand Total, G Ward** ..	**5,883**	**149,455**	Christian	1,347	403	239	156	65	110
					Zoroastrian	113	139	40	38	23	24
					Muslim	2,027	291	74	78	27	51
					Hindu	26,019	3,888	510	328	138	149
					Jain	112	56	15	4	2	3
					Jew and others	65	24	9	11	1	4
					Total ..	**7,643**	**2,232**	**403**	**323**	**126**	**202**
	31	Mahim	2,842	47,075	Christian	601	224	118	88	35	61
					Zoroastrian	26	8	6	17	7	13
					Muslim	1,126	160	49	55	16	37
					Hindu	5,855	1,809	221	160	68	88
					Jain	32	26	9	3	..	2
					Jew and others	3	5	..	..	..	1
					Total ..	**23,540**	**2,569**	**484**	**292**	**130**	**139**
	32	Worli	3,040	102,380	Christian	746	179	121	68	30	40
					Zoroastrian	87	131	34	21	16	11
					Muslim	1,501	131	25	23	11	14
					Hindu	21,064	2,079	289	168	70	61
					Jain	80	30	6	1	2	1
					Jew and others	62	19	9	11	1	3

Total number of tenements of all kinds occupied by members of each religion.	Total number of members of each religion occupying tenements with: One room.	Two rooms.	Three rooms.	Four rooms.	Five rooms.	Six rooms and over.	Total number of members of each religion occupying tenements of all kinds.	Percentage of total population of each religion occupying each class of tenements with: One room.	Two rooms.	Three rooms.	Four rooms.	Five rooms.	Six rooms and over.
13	14	15	16	17	18	10	20	21	22	23	24	25	26
15,228	**53,393**	**6,452**	**2,265**	**1,829**	**565**	**1,433**	**65,937**	**81**	**10**	**3**	**3**	**1**	**2**
1,037	3,539	357	165	111	77	311	4,560	77	8	4	2	2	7
1,017	956	1,846	1,033	1,010	259	445	5,549	17	33	19	18	5	8
1,522	4,715	453	194	32	44	90	5,528	85	8	3	1	1	2
11,513	43,866	3,680	854	637	175	548	49,760	88	8	2	1	..	1
63	150	65	5	..	..	10	230	65	28	2	..	..	5
76	167	51	14	39	10	29	310	54	16	5	13	3	9
38,083	**112,131**	**22,227**	**5,119**	**4,502**	**2,310**	**3,166**	**149,455**	**75**	**15**	**3**	**3**	**2**	**2**
2,320	5,185	1,751	1,229	945	366	746	10,222	51	17	12	9	4	7
377	496	434	190	231	135	188	1,674	30	26	11	14	8	11
3,148	9,001	1,182	198	614	255	414	11,964	75	10	4	5	2	4
31,932	96,830	18,515	3,098	2,601	1,545	1,772	124,361	78	15	3	2	1	1
192	388	214	53	28	8	15	706	55	30	8	4	1	2
114	231	131	51	83	1	31	528	44	25	9	16	..	6
10,929	**29,260**	**9,896**	**2,314**	**2,504**	**1,028**	**2,073**	**47,075**	**62**	**21**	**5**	**5**	**2**	**5**
1,127	2,548	961	610	565	229	459	5,372	47	18	11	11	4	9
77	102	38	53	105	47	99	444	23	9	12	23	11	22
1,443	4,062	675	339	390	153	324	5,943	68	11	6	7	3	5
8,201	22,442	8,076	1,277	1,422	599	1,165	34,981	64	23	3	5	2	3
72	94	112	35	22	..	11	274	34	41	13	8	..	4
9	12	34	..	..	..	15	61	20	56	..	..	..	24
27,154	**82,871**	**12,331**	**2,805**	**1,998**	**1,282**	**1,093**	**102,380**	**81**	**12**	**3**	**2**	**1**	**1**
1,193	2,637	790	619	380	137	287	4,850	54	16	13	8	3	6
300	394	396	137	126	88	89	1,230	32	32	11	10	8	7
1,705	4,930	507	159	224	102	90	6,021	82	8	3	4	2	1
23,731	74,388	10,439	1,821	1,179	946	607	89,380	83	12	2	1	1	1
120	294	102	18	6	8	4	432	68	24	4	1	2	1
105	219	97	51	83	1	16	467	47	21	11	13	..	3

The definition of "Building" adopted at Karachi for the 1931 Census is as follows :—

"House" means—

Premises under one undivided roof whether let off into tenements or not (one such tenement would be given a number, thus 12, and the other tenements 12—1, 12—2, 12—3, etc.).

Provided—that in the case of a terrace of dwellings or semi-detached bungalow, each such dwelling with separate access to the public street, divided off by party walls and occupied by one family from the ground upwards shall be considered to be a separate house although the roof of the terrace, or semi-detached bungalow, may be a continuous one ; such cases will include dwellings of ground floor only, and of two or more floors, and each house to be given a separate number.

Note.—In the case of blocks of buildings forming servants' quarters to a bungalow, each of such blocks shall be classified as one house, the separate tenement being numbered as above for premises under one undivided roof, according to the number of separate families occupying the same.

Otherwise the Tables follow the Bombay Housing Tables, and all definitions there given apply.

The Tables are for the Municipal Area only, and do not include the Cantonments.

HOUSING TABLE I—KARACHI CITY.

General Classification of Buildings by uses.

GENERAL CLASSIFICATION

Serial No. of Quarter.	Name of Quarter.	Residential Buildings.						
		Buildings and Dwelling Houses.	Servants' Quarters.	Chawls.	Factories, shop offices, etc., combined with dwelling.	Dharmashalas.	Institutions.	Huts.
1	2	3	4	5	6	7	8	9
	Grand Total for Karachi City ..	**15,481**	**477**	**135**	**3,298**	**16**	**179**	**6,635**
1	Old Town	718	..	..	187	7	3	..
2	Lea	30	..	..	8	1	3	1
3	Napier	227	..	22	406	..	..	..
4	Market	180	..	22	270	..	..	..
5	Bunder	22	..	..	98	..	1	4
6	Machi Meani	141	..	..	161	3	..	..
7	Queen's Road	17	..	..	5	..	..	..
8	Railway	47	..	..	25	..	..	..
9	Serai	318	..	..	271	..	..	..
10	Rambaugh	319	..	..	111	1	4	18
11	Jail	122	..	21	181	1	..	..
12	Ranchoro	997	..	..	288	..	..	..
13	Ramswami	225	..	14	86	1	..	2
14	Herchandrai Vishendas	526	..	..	20	1	2	1
15	Soldier Bazar	200	..	..	21	..	1	1
16	New Jail	21	..	..	3	..	36	49
17	Preedy	138	..	23	28	..	1	..
18	Saddar Bazar	371	..	..	335	..	..	12
19	Civil Lines	446	23	..	14	..	..	..
20	Frere Town and Bath Island ..	96	173	..	4	..	..	3
21	Clifton	32	49	..	..	..	..	50
22	Gizri	23	..	..	1	..	..	185
23	Garden (East and West)	696	..	17	147	..	3	644
24	Tahilram	96	..	..	74	..	..	52
25	Lawrence	573	..	16	80	..	1	93
26	Lyari	5,625	..	..	246	..	1	3,715
27	Jamshed	304	1	..	29	..	..	1
28	Artillery Maidan	40	..	..	20	..	..	16
29	Trans-Lyari	451	..	..	..	..	..	1,033
30	Tatta Naka, Goda Village and Labour Corps..	103	..	..	4	..	..	..
31	Quarry Nos. 1 and 2 and other quarries.	108	..	..	1	..	..	..
32	Scattered Hamlets behind Cantonment station and Chinaser and Vagri Villages	199	..	..	1	..	..	..
33	Baba Islands	104	..	..	6	..	..	197
34	Bhit Island	59	..	..	1	..	..	113
35	Shamspir and Goth Mahomed ..	32	..	..	1	..	..	78
36	Bunker Island	..	..	—	..	..	..	7
37	Port Keamari with other Port area (viz. Thole Produce Yard, Mansfield Import Yard and West Wharf)	182	1	..	160	1	123	40
38	Maurypur	160	..	..	1	..	..	231
39	Railway area including City, Bunder and Cantonment Stations and Reception and Hump Yard and Platform population	1,533	230	..	4	..	..	89

OF BUILDINGS BY USES.

Other and Unclassifiable.	Total number of residential buildings.	NON-RESIDENTIAL BUILDINGS. Places of worship.	Institutions and places of Amusement.	Factories, Mills and works.	Offices and shops.	Godowns, Stables, Carriages and sheds and Chowkies.	Other and Unclassifiable.	Total number of Non-residential Buildings.	Total number of Buildings.
10	11	12	13	14	15	16	17	18	19
368	**26,589**	**328**	**261**	**144**	**1,799**	**1,301**	**10**	**3,843**	**30,432**
..	915	40	2	....	122	73	..	237	1,152
..	43	..	7	....	4	3	..	14	57
..	655	21	7	11	362	75	..	476	1,131
..	472	14	7	7	79	25	..	132	604
..	125	4	3	....	33	10	..	50	175
..	305	8	7	....	39	70	..	124	429
..	22	..	....	....	....	2	..	2	24
..	72	1	1	4	29	54	..	89	161
..	589	7	13	14	40	192	1	267	856
..	453	15	12	6	18	15	2	68	521
..	325	7	20	18	20	31	..	96	421
..	1,285	15	47	8	32	33	6	141	1,426
..	328	1	7	2	6	8	..	24	352
..	550	4	1	2	7	7	..	21	571
..	223	2	2	....	44	22	..	70	293
..	109	1	....	....	20	3	..	24	133
..	190	2	6	14	15	39	..	76	266
..	718	6	17	....	93	27	1	144	862
..	483	3	7	15	28	36	..	89	572
..	276	..	1	....	4	7	..	12	288
..	131	4	....	....	3	2	..	9	140
..	209	3	3	....	10	....	..	16	225
..	1,507	15	5	10	34	76	..	140	1,647
..	222	7	1	1	7	27	..	43	265
..	763	5	13	4	23	39	..	84	847
368	9,955	87	41	5	403	207	..	743	10,698
..	335	1	5	5	6	6	..	23	358
..	76	2	....	....	28	12	..	42	118
..	1,484	20	8	....	40	10	..	78	1,562
..	107	1	....	....	3	....	..	4	111
..	109	..	....	....	4	....	..	4	113
..	200	1	1	....	7	1	..	10	210
..	307	2	2	....	6	4	..	14	321
..	173	1	1	....	1	5	..	8	181
..	111	1	1	....	4	10	..	16	127
..	7	..	....	....	....	1	..	1	8
..	507	5	7	11	92	101	..	216	723
..	392	6	3	....	16	....	..	25	417
..	1,856	16	3	7	117	68	..	211	2,067

Classification of Buildings by the Number of Floors contained in each.

Serial No. of Quarter.	Name of Quarter.	Number of Buildings with: Ground Floor only.	One Upper Floor.	Two Upper Floors.	Three Upper Floors.	Four Upper Floors.	Total number of Buildings.
1	2	3	4	5	6	7	8
	Grand Total for Karachi City ..	**23,455**	**3,963**	**2,167**	**593**	**29**	**30,207**
1	Old Town	204	374	484	57	7	1,126
2	Lea	31	15	9	2	..	57
3	Napier	432	371	223	89	6	1,121
4	Market	109	197	233	63	2	604
5	Bunder	45	44	64	20	..	173
6	Machi Meani	154	103	110	54	3	424
7	Queen's Road	10	14	....	....	..	24
8	Railway	108	47	5	1	..	161
9	Serai	414	236	149	53	1	853
10	Rambaugh	205	158	95	56	4	518
11	Jail	160	93	113	51	4	421
12	Ranchore	601	463	295	66	1	1,426
13	Ramswami	87	104	113	46	..	350
14	Harchandrai Vishendas	557	11	3	....	..	571
15	Soldier Bazar	256	32	2	1	..	291
16	New Jail	129	1	....	....	..	130
17	Preedy	212	39	12	....	..	263
18	Saddar Bazar	347	359	135	20	1	862
19	Civil Lines	332	224	14	2	..	572
20	Frere Town and Bath Island ..	141	142	4	....	..	287
21	Clifton	100	39	1	....	..	140
22	Gizri	225	....	....	....	..	225
23	Garden (East and West)	1,280	307	9	1	..	1,597
24	Tahilram	185	62	16	2	..	265
25	Lawrence	795	40	11	1	..	847
26	Lyari	10,226	320	46	5	..	10,597
27	Jamshed	302	54	....	....	..	356
28	Artillery Maidan	110	7	1	....	..	118
29	Trans-Lyari	1,562	....	....	....	..	1,562
30	Tatta Naka, Goda Village and Labour Corps	111	....	....	....	..	111
31	Quarry Nos. 1 and 2 and other quarries.	113	....	....	....	..	113
32	Scattered Hamlets behind Cantonment Station and Chinaser and Vagri Villages	209	....	....	....	..	209
33	Baba Islands	319	....	....	....	..	319
34	Bhit Island	175	....	....	....	..	175
35	Shamspir and Goth Mahomed ..	125	....	....	....	..	125
36	Bunker Island	8	....	....	....	..	8
37	Port Keamari with other Port area (viz. Thole Produce Yard, Mansfield Import Yard and West Wharf) ..	608	91	20	3	..	722
38	Maurypur	415	2	....	....	..	417
39	Railway area including City, Bunder and Cantonment Stations and Reception and Hump Yard and Platform population	2,053	14	....	....	..	2,067

Residential Buildings by the Number of Tenements.

Serial No. of Quarter.	Name of Quarter.	Number of Buildings containing				Total number of Buildings.
		One to five tenements.	Six to ten tenements.	Eleven to twenty tenements.	Twenty tenements and over.	
1	2	3	4	5	6	7
	Grand Total for Karachi City ..	**23,163**	**1,889**	**1,017**	**327**	**26,396**
1	Old Town	841	39	7	3	890
2	Lea	33	5	4	1	43
3	Napier	402	136	82	27	647
4	Market	329	94	41	8	472
5	Bunder	52	32	22	17	123
6	Machi Meani	148	65	64	24	301
7	Queen's Road	16	6	....	....	22
8	Railway	62	9	1	....	72
9	Serai	357	141	61	29	588
10	Rambaugh	274	108	55	13	450
11	Jail	137	88	75	25	325
12	Ranchore	838	229	146	72	1,285
13	Ramswami	178	83	47	18	326
14	Harchandrai Vishendas	537	7	4	2	550
15	Soldier Bazar	217	3	....	1	221
16	New Jail	103	3	3	....	109
17	Preedy	158	19	9	1	187
18	Saddar Bazar	522	126	61	9	718
19	Civil Lines	315	126	37	5	483
20	Frere Town and Bath Island ..	213	58	11	....	282
21	Clifton	119	11	1	....	131
22	Gizri	209	....	....	....	209
23	Garden (East and West)	1,370	74	17	....	1,461
24	Tahilram	137	38	33	14	222
25	Lawrence	566	104	71	22	763
26	Lyari	9,640	133	71	17	9,861
27	Jamshed	262	72	3	....	337
28	Artillery Maidan	69	5	1	1	76
29	Trans-Lyari	1,484	....	....	....	1,484
30	Tatta Naka, Goda Village and Labour Corps	103	4	....	....	107
31	Quarry Nos. 1 and 2 and other quarries	109	....	....	....	109
32	Scattered Hamlets behind Cantonment Station and Chinaser and Vagri Villages	199	....	....	....	199
33	Baba Islands	305	....	....	....	305
34	Bhit Islands	167	....	....	....	167
35	Shamspir and Goth Mahomed ..	109	....	....	....	109
36	Bunker Island	7	....	....	....	7
37	Port Keamari with other Port area (viz. Thole Produce Yard, Mansfield Import Yard and West Wharf) ..	341	65	86	15	507
38	Maurypur	392	....	....	....	392
39	Railway area including City, Bunder and Cantonment Stations and Reception and Hump Yard and Platform population	1,843	6	4	3	1,856

HOUSING TABLE IV—KARACHI CITY.

RESIDENTIAL BUILDINGS BY THE NUMBER OF OCCUPANTS.

Serial No. of Quarter.	Name of Quarter.	Number of Buildings containing					Total number of Buildings.
		20 persons and under.	21 to 40 persons.	41 to 60 persons.	61 to 80 persons.	81 to 100 persons.	
1	2	3	4	5	6	7	8
	Grand Total for Karachi City ..	**21,996**	**1,477**	**485**	**191**	**248**	**24,397**
1	Old Town	725	70	6	1	2	804
2	Lea	19	9	4	3	2	37
3	Napier	395	116	35	8	8	562
4	Market	352	81	15	1	1	450
5	Bunder	62	25	16	4	7	114
6	Machi Meani	126	82	39	10	22	279
7	Queen's Road	22	....	....	....	..	22
8	Railway	60	2	....	....	..	62
9	Serai	367	89	57	18	24	555
10	Rambaugh	232	95	49	21	26	423
11	Jail	163	68	38	16	9	294
12	Ranchore	937	215	48	26	43	1,269
13	Ramswami	190	82	26	9	7	314
14	Harchandrai Vishendas	425	6	2	3	1	437
15	Soldier Bazar	187	8	....	....	1	196
16	New Jail	77	8	7	3	..	95
17	Preedy	164	8	3	1	1	177
18	Saddar Bazar	497	113	29	11	6	656
19	Civil Lines	382	39	7	....	1	429
20	Frere Town and Bath Island ..	241	13	2	....	..	256
21	Clifton	96	....	....	....	..	96
22	Gizri	208	....	....	....	..	208
23	Garden (East and West)	1,215	20	9	2	2	1,248
24	Tahilram	143	38	12	10	10	213
25	Lawrence	549	95	29	11	11	695
26	Lyari	9,020	132	31	10	13	9,206
27	Jamshed	273	12	....	....	..	285
28	Artillery Maidan	46	1	....	1	1	49
29	Trans-Lyari	1,384	1	....	....	..	1,385
30	Tatta Naka, Goda Village and Labour Corps	98	2	1	....	..	101
31	Quarry Nos. 1 and 2 and other quarries	102	....	....	....	..	102
32	Scattered Hamlets behind Cantonment Station and Chinaser and Vagri Villages	187	....	....	....	..	187
33	Baba Islands	283	....	....	....	..	283
34	Bhit Islands	159	....	....	....	..	159
35	Shamspir and Goth Mahomed ..	106	....	....	....	..	106
36	Bunker Island	2	....	....	....	..	2
37	Port Keamari with other Port area (viz. Thole Produce Yard, Mansfield Import Yard and West Wharf) ..	335	44	20	19	47	465
38	Maurypur	390	....	....	....	..	390
39	Railway area including City, Bunder and Cantonment Stations and Reception and Hump Yard and Platform population	1,777	3	....	3	3	1,786

Distribution of Persons by Rooms in Residential Buildings.

Serial No. of Quarter.	Name of Quarter.	Total number of persons living in Rooms each occupied by				Total population.	Number of occupied buildings.	Average population per inhabited building.
		5 persons and under.	6 to 9 persons.	10 to 19 persons.	20 persons and over.			
1	2	3	4	5	6	7	8	9
	Grand Total for Karachi City ..	**175,410**	**50,270**	**13,026**	**2,067**	**240,773**	**24,397**	**9·87**
1	Old Town	7,621	817	254	21	8,713	804	10·84
2	Lea	705	173	..	56	934	37	25·24
3	Napier	7,662	1,887	351	22	9,922	562	17·65
4	Market	5,295	1,162	52	..	6,509	450	14·46
5	Bunder	2,278	707	151	35	3,171	114	27·82
6	Machi Meani	6,084	2,108	532	53	8,777	279	31·46
7	Queen's Road	153	..	..	..	153	22	6·95
8	Railway	252	58	..	38	348	62	5·61
9	Serai	10,685	1,756	363	183	12,987	555	23·4
10	Rambaugh	11,077	352	42	..	11,471	423	27·12
11	Jail	6,668	610	188	21	7,487	294	25·47
12	Ranchore	19,382	4,989	553	..	24,924	1,269	19·64
13	Ramswami	6,742	296	..	..	7,038	314	22·41
14	Harchandrai Vishendas	1,944	124	137	46	2,251	437	5·15
15	Soldier Bazar	1,321	147	20	..	1,488	196	7·59
16	New Jail	273	133	62	672	1,140	95	12·0
17	Preedy	1,591	158	33	..	1,782	177	10·07
18	Saddar Bazar	7,241	1,983	884	85	10,193	656	15·54
19	Civil Lines	3,254	989	121	..	4,364	429	10·17
20	Frere Town and Bath Island ..	1,926	292	20	..	2,238	256	8·74
21	Clifton	346	48	21	..	415	96	4·32
22	Gizri	421	419	160	24	1,024	208	4·92
23	Garden (East and West)	5,605	1,890	476	29	8,000	1,248	6·41
24	Tahilram	3,090	1,273	214	..	4,577	213	21·49
25	Lawrence	7,135	2,490	542	..	10,167	695	14·63
26	Lyari	30,987	20,118	7,002	709	58,816	9,206	6·39
27	Jamshed	2,108	35	12	..	2,155	285	7·56
28	Artillery Maidan	479	59	..	..	538	49	10·98
29	Trans-Lyari	3,535	1,792	294	52	5,673	1,385	4·10
30	Tatta Naka, Goda Village and Labour Corps	413	330	117	..	860	101	8·51
31	Quarry Nos. 1 and 2 and other quarries	270	144	10	..	424	102	4·16
32	Scattered Hamlets behind Cantonment Station and Chinaser and Vagri Villages	446	329	84	..	859	187	4·59
33	Baba Islands	1,066	113	21	..	1,200	283	4·24
34	Bhit Islands	631	165	..	..	796	159	5·0
35	Shamspir and Goth Mahomed ..	449	15	..	..	464	106	4·38
36	Bunker Island	4	..	..	..	4	2	2·0
37	Port Keamari with other Port area (viz. Thole Produce Yard, Mansfield Import Yard and West Wharf) ..	10,129	1,076	246	21	11,472	465	24·67
38	Maurypur	1,059	319	22	..	1,400	390	3·59
39	Railway area including City, Bunder and Cantonment Stations and Reception and Hump Yard and Platform population	5,083	914	42	..	6,039	1,786	3·38

HOUSING TABLE, VI-A—KARACHI CITY.

TENEMENTS BY ROOMS AND POPULATION.

Serial No. of Quarter.	Name of Quarter.	Tenements with	Total number of tenements of each class.	Percentage of each class of tenements to total tenements.	Total number of occupants of each class of tenements.	Percentage borne by population in each class of tenements to total population.	Average number of occupants per room in each class of tenements.
1	2	3	4	5	6	7	8
	Grand Total for Karachi City ..	Total ..	57,046	....	240,773	....	....
		1 Room	37,708	66	140,838	58	3·74
		2 Rooms	12,683	22	57,527	24	2·27
		3 Rooms	3,646	6	20,194	8	1·85
		4 Rooms	1,469	3	9,801	5	1·67
		5 Rooms	450	1	3,517	1	1·56
		6 Rooms and over	1,090	2	8,896	4	....
1	Old Town	Total ..	1,485	....	8,713	....	....
		1 Room	387	26	1,418	16	3·66
		2 Rooms	513	34	2,693	31	2·62
		3 Rooms	261	18	1,748	20	2·23
		4 Rooms	120	8	868	10	1·81
		5 Rooms	68	5	610	7	1·70
		6 Rooms and over	136	9	1,376	16	....
2	Lea	Total ..	132	....	934	....	....
		1 Room	46	35	200	21	4·35
		2 Rooms	49	37	351	38	3·58
		3 Rooms	12	9	108	12	3·00
		4 Rooms	20	15	165	18	2·06
		5 Rooms	1	1	12	1	2·40
		6 Rooms and over ..	4	3	98	10	....
3	Napier	Total ..	2,163	....	9,922	....	....
		1 Room	1,336	62	4,560	46	3·41
		2 Rooms	556	26	3,021	30	2·72
		3 Rooms	100	4	707	7	2·36
		4 Rooms	88	4	722	7	2·05
		5 Rooms	17	1	147	2	1·73
		6 Rooms and over	66	3	765	8	1·93
4	Market	Total ..	1,380	....	6,509	....	....
		1 Room	742	54	2,656	41	3·58
		2 Rooms	421	30	2,159	33	2·57
		3 Rooms	101	7	658	10	2·17
		4 Rooms	53	4	441	7	2·08
		5 Rooms	25	2	188	3	1·50
		6 Rooms and over	38	3	407	6	....
5	Bunder	Total ..	806	....	3,171	....	....
		1 Room	577	72	2,068	65	3·58
		2 Rooms	153	19	718	22	2·33
		3 Rooms	60	7	244	8	1·36
		4 Rooms	8	1	52	2	1·62
		5 Rooms	5	1	64	2	2·56
		6 Rooms and over	3	....	30	1	....
6	Machi Meani	Total ..	1,896	....	8,777	....	....
		1 Room	1,014	53	4,170	48	4·11
		2 Rooms	765	40	3,595	41	2·35
		3 Rooms	53	3	345	4	2·17
		4 Rooms	21	1	163	2	1·94
		5 Rooms	10	1	67	1	1·34
		6 Rooms and over	33	2	437	4	....
7	Queen's Road	Total ..	49	....	158	....	....
		1 Room	33	67	86	56	2·61
		2 Rooms	12	25	44	29	1·83
		3 Rooms	....	....	....	....	....
		4 Rooms	....	....	....	....	....
		5 Rooms	1	2	9	6	1·80
		6 Rooms and over	3	6	14	9	....

Serial No. of Quarter.	Name of Quarter.	Tenements with	Total number of tenements of each class.	Percentage of each class of tenements to total tenements.	Total number of occupants of each class of tenements.	Percentage borne by population in each class of tenements to total population.	Average number of occupants per room in each class of tenements.
1	2	3	4	5	6	7	8
8	Railway	Total ..	115	....	348	....	....
		1 Room	94	82	280	80	2·98
		2 Rooms	12	10	42	12	1·75
		3 Rooms	1	1	4	1	1·33
		4 Rooms	....	....	....	....	....
		5 Rooms	2	2	2	1	·20
		6 Rooms and over	6	5	20	6	....
9	Serai	Total ..	2,639	....	12,987	....	....
		1 Room	1,294	49	4,758	37	3·67
		2 Rooms	927	35	4,955	38	2·67
		3 Rooms	255	10	1,628	13	2·13
		4 Rooms	85	3	703	5	2·07
		5 Rooms	26	1	249	2	1·92
		6 Rooms and over	52	2	699	5	....
10	Rambaugh	Total ..	2,331	....	11,471	....	....
		1 Room	524	23	1,698	15	3·24
		2 Rooms	1,075	46	4,854	42	2·25
		3 Rooms	353	15	2,129	19	2·01
		4 Rooms	244	10	1,506	13	1·55
		5 Rooms	43	2	506	4	2·35
		6 Rooms and over	92	4	778	7	....
11	Jail	Total ..	1,679	....	7,487	....	....
		1 Room	527	31	1,736	23	3·29
		2 Rooms	881	53	3,814	51	2·16
		3 Rooms	142	8	958	13	2·25
		4 Rooms	91	6	659	9	1·75
		5 Rooms	13	1	77	1	1·18
		6 Rooms and over	22	1	243	3	....
12	Ranchore	Total ..	6,543	....	24,924	....	....
		1 Room	5,001	76	18,382	74	3·68
		2 Rooms	1,279	20	5,151	21	2·02
		3 Rooms	188	3	849	3	1·51
		4 Rooms	49	1	292	1	1·49
		5 Rooms	5	....	76	....	3·04
		6 Rooms and over	21	....	174	1	....
13	Ramswami	Total ..	1,855	....	7,088	....	....
		1 Room	464	25	1,197	17	2·58
		2 Rooms	1,143	62	4,497	64	1·97
		3 Rooms	190	10	902	13	1·58
		4 Rooms	40	2	306	4	1·91
		5 Rooms	5	....	22	....	·88
		6 Rooms and over	13	1	114	2	....
14	Harchandrai Vishendas	Total ..	682	....	2,251	....	....
		1 Room	262	38	757	34	2·89
		2 Rooms	396	58	1,347	60	1·70
		3 Rooms	13	2	53	2	1·36
		4 Rooms	7	1	53	2	1·89
		5 Rooms	1	....	16	1	3·20
		6 Rooms and over	3	1	25	1	....
15	Soldier Bazar	Total ..	319	....	1,488	....	....
		1 Room	90	28	333	22	3·70
		2 Rooms	169	53	792	53	2·34
		3 Rooms	40	13	232	16	1·93
		4 Rooms	13	4	81	5	1·56
		5 Rooms	4	1	38	3	1·90
		6 Rooms and over	3	1	12	1	....

Serial No. of Quarter.	Name of Quarter.	Tenements with	Total number of tenements of each class.	Percentage of each class of tenements to total tenements.	Total number of occupants of each class of tenements.	Percentage borne by population in each class of tenements to total population.	Average number of occupants per room in each class of tenements.
1	2	3	4	5	6	7	8
16	**New Jail**	**Total** ..	**179**	....	**1,140**	....	....
		1 Room	175	97	1,127	90	6·44
		2 Rooms	2	1	7	1	1·75
		3 Rooms	1	1	5	....	1·67
		4 Rooms	1	1	1	....	·25
		5 Rooms	....	....	....	....	....
		6 Rooms and over	....	....	....	....	....
17	**Preedy**	**Total** ..	**457**	....	**1,782**	....	....
		1 Room	290	64	918	52	3·17
		2 Rooms	45	10	162	9	1·80
		3 Rooms	29	6	157	9	1·80
		4 Rooms	35	8	185	10	1·32
		5 Rooms	20	4	97	5	·97
		6 Rooms and over	38	8	263	15	....
18	**Saddar Bazar**	**Total** ..	**2,191**	....	**10,193**	....	....
		1 Room	1,309	60	5,476	54	4·18
		2 Rooms	611	28	3,214	31	2·63
		3 Rooms	141	6	630	6	1·49
		4 Rooms	75	3	500	5	1·67
		5 Rooms	11	1	87	1	1·58
		6 Rooms and over	44	2	286	3	....
19	**Civil Lines**	**Total** ..	**1,742**	....	**4,364**	....	....
		1 Room	1,399	80	3,161	72	2·26
		2 Rooms	131	8	457	10	1·74
		3 Rooms	50	3	158	4	1·05
		4 Rooms	46	3	151	3	·82
		5 Rooms	21	1	67	2	·64
		6 Rooms and over	95	5	370	9	....
20	**Frere Town and Bath Island** ..	**Total** ..	**873**	....	**2,238**	....	....
		1 Room	601	69	1,382	62	2·30
		2 Rooms	56	6	181	8	1·62
		3 Rooms	98	11	267	12	·91
		4 Rooms	62	7	214	10	·86
		5 Rooms	21	3	78	3	·74
		6 Rooms and over	35	4	116	5	....
21	**Clifton**	**Total** ..	**133**	....	**415**	....	....
		1 Room	118	89	306	74	2·59
		2 Rooms	1	1	8	2	4·00
		3 Rooms	1	1	9	2	3·00
		4 Rooms	....	....	....	....	....
		5 Rooms	....	....	....	....	....
		6 Rooms and over	13	9	92	22	....
22	**Gizri**	**Total** ..	**208**	....	**1,024**	....	....
		1 Room	208	100	1,024	100	4·92
		2 Rooms	....	....	....	....	....
		3 Rooms	....	....	....	....	....
		4 Rooms	....	....	....	....	....
		5 Rooms	....	....	....	....	....
		6 Rooms and over	....	....	....	....	....
23	**Garden (East and West)**	**Total** ..	**1,886**	....	**8,000**	....	....
		1 Room	1,294	69	4,452	56	3·44
		2 Rooms	209	11	1,050	13	2·51
		3 Rooms	87	5	399	5	1·53
		4 Rooms	62	3	423	5	1·71
		5 Rooms	34	2	312	4	1·84
		6 Rooms and over	200	10	1,364	17	....

Serial No. of Quarter.	Name of Quarter.	Tenements with	Total number of tenements of each class.	Percentage of each class of tenements to total tenements.	Total number of occupants each class of tenements.	Percentage born by population in each class of tenements to total population.	Average number of occupants per room in each class of tenements.
1	2	3	4	5	6	7	8
24	Tahilram	Total ..	1,221	....	4,577	....	....
		1 Room	1,101	90	3,966	87	3·60
		2 Rooms	112	10	534	12	2·38
		3 Rooms	4	....	38	1	3·17
		4 Rooms	1	....	12	....	3·00
		5 Rooms	2	....	23	....	2·30
		6 Rooms and over	1	....	4	....	....
25	Lawrence	Total ..	2,681	....	10,167	....	....
		1 Room	2,183	81	7,965	78	3·65
		2 Rooms	442	17	1,788	18	2·02
		3 Rooms	31	1	235	2	2·52
		4 Rooms	14	1	83	1	1·48
		5 Rooms	3	....	37	....	2·47
		6 Rooms and over	8	....	59	1	....
26	Lyari	Total ..	12,929	....	58,816	....	....
		1 Room	11,243	87	49,178	84	4·37
		2 Rooms	1,267	10	6,869	12	2·71
		3 Rooms	215	2	1,284	2	1·99
		4 Rooms	148	1	1,073	2	1·81
		5 Rooms	15	....	91	....	1·21
		6 Rooms and over	41	....	321	....	....
27	Jamshed	Total ..	404	....	2,155	....	....
		1 Room	129	32	266	12	2·06
		2 Rooms	32	8	137	6	2·14
		3 Rooms	54	13	299	14	1·85
		4 Rooms	82	20	557	26	1·69
		5 Rooms	61	15	494	23	1·62
		6 Rooms and over	46	12	402	10	....
28	Artillery Maidan	Total ..	168	....	588	....	....
		1 Room	116	69	317	59	2·73
		2 Rooms	40	24	141	26	1·76
		3 Rooms	7	4	30	6	1·42
		4 Rooms	1	1	17	3	4·25
		5 Rooms	1	1	2	....	·40
		6 Rooms and over	3	1	31	6	....
29	Trans Lyari	Total ..	1,487	....	5,673	....	....
		1 Room	1,435	100	5,660	100	3·94
		2 Rooms	2	....	13	....	3·25
		3 Rooms	....	....	....	....	....
		4 Rooms	....	....	....	....	....
		5 Rooms	....	....	....	....	....
		6 Rooms and over	....	....	....	....	....
30	Tatta Naka and Goda Village and Labour Corps.	Total ..	204	....	860	....	....
		1 Room	204	100	860	100	4·22
		2 Rooms	....	....	....	....	....
		3 Rooms	....	....	....	....	....
		4 Rooms	....	....	....	....	....
		5 Rooms	....	....	....	....	....
		6 Rooms and over	....	....	....	....	....
31	Quarry No. 1 and 2 and Other Quarries ..	Total ..	106	....	424	....	....
		1 Room	106	100	424	100	4·00
		2 Rooms	....	....	....	....	....
		3 Rooms	....	....	....	....	....
		4 Rooms	....	....	....	....	....
		5 Rooms	....	....	....	....	....
		6 Rooms and over	....	....	....	....	....

Serial No. of Quarter.	Name of Quarter.	Tenements with	Total number of tenements of each class.	Percentage of each class of tenements to total tenements.	Total number of occupants of each class of tenements.	Percentage born by population in each class of tenements to total population.	Average number of occupants per room in each class of tenements.
1	2	3	4	5	6	7	8
32	Scattered Hamlets, behind Cantonment station and Chinaser and Vagri Villages.	Total ..	191	....	859	....	....
		1 Room	191	100	859	100	4·49
		2 Rooms	....	....	....	....	....
		3 Rooms	....	....	....	....	....
		4 Rooms	....	....	....	....	....
		5 Rooms	....	....	....	....	....
		6 Rooms and over	....	....	....	....	....
33	Baba Islands	Total ..	317	....	1,200	....	....
		1 Room	146	46	529	44	3·62
		2 Rooms	141	44	532	44	1·89
		3 Rooms	25	8	116	10	1·55
		4 Rooms	5	2	23	2	1·15
		5 Rooms	....	....	....	....	....
		6 Rooms and over	....	....	....	....	....
34	Bhit Islands	Total ..	192	....	796	....	....
		1 Room	106	55	431	54	4·07
		2 Rooms	75	30	313	39	2·08
		3 Rooms	11	6	52	7	1·58
		4 Rooms	....	....	....	....	....
		5 Rooms	....	....	....	....	....
		6 Rooms and over	....	....	....	....	....
35	Shampir and Goth Mahomed ..	Total ..	124	....	464	....	....
		1 Room	43	34	149	32	3·47
		2 Rooms	53	43	190	41	1·79
		3 Rooms	23	19	94	20	1·36
		4 Rooms	5	4	31	7	1·55
		5 Rooms	....	....	....	....	....
		6 Rooms and over	....	....	....	....	....
36	Bunder Island	Total ..	3	....	4	....	....
		1 Room	3	100	4	100	1·33
		2 Rooms	....	....	....	....	....
		3 Rooms	....	....	....	....	....
		4 Rooms	....	....	....	....	....
		5 Rooms	....	....	....	....	....
		6 Rooms and over	....	....	....	....	....
37	Keamari with other Port Area (viz. Thole Produce Yard and West Wharf).	Total ..	2,673	....	11,472	....	....
		1 Room	606	23	2,026	18	3·34
		2 Rooms	847	32	2,949	26	1·74
		3 Rooms	1,052	39	5,569	48	1·76
		4 Rooms	78	3	462	4	1·48
		5 Rooms	30	1	125	1	·83
		6 Rooms and over	60	2	341	3	....
38	Maurypur	Total ..	377	....	1,400	....	....
		1 Room	304	81	1,032	74	3·39
		2 Rooms	64	17	302	22	2·36
		3 Rooms	5	1	52	4	3·47
		4 Rooms	1	....	6	....	1·50
		5 Rooms	3	1	8	....	·53
		6 Rooms and over	....	....	....	....	....
39	Railway Area including City Bunder and Cantonment Stations and reception and Hump Yard and Platform Population.	Total ..	2,276	....	6,039	....	....
		1 Room	2,007	88	5,032	83	2·51
		2 Rooms	202	9	652	11	1·61
		3 Rooms	43	2	235	4	1·82
		4 Rooms	11	1	52	1	1·18
		5 Rooms	2	....	13	....	1·30
		6 Rooms and over	11	....	55	1	....

Details of one-Roomed Tenements containing more than one Family.

Serial No. of quarter.	Name of Quarter.	One-roomed tenements containing			Total.
		2 Families.	3 Families.	4 Families and over.	
1	2	3	4	5	6
	Grand Total for Karachi City	**1,104**	**198**	**118**	**1,420**
1	Old Town	8	3	....	11
2	Lea	....	....	....	....
3	Napier	84	10	23	117
4	Market	20	....	....	20
5	Bunder	4	....	....	4
6	Machi Meani	38	4	3	45
7	Queen's Road	2	....	....	2
8	Railway	1	....	....	1
9	Serai	18	2	1	21
10	Rambaugh	42	3	1	46
11	Jail	10	4	1	15
12	Ranchore	55	6	....	61
13	Ramswami	6	....	....	6
14	Harchandrai Vishendas	17	3	2	22
15	Soldier Bazar	....	2	....	2
16	New Jail	....	....	....	....
17	Preedy	3	....	2	5
18	Saddar Bazar	9	....	21	30
19	Civil Lines	78	16	10	104
20	Frere Town and Bath Island	12	....	1	13
21	Clifton	1	....	....	1
22	Gizri	9	1	....	10
23	Garden (East and West)	14	....	1	15
24	Tahilram	43	11	10	64
25	Lawrence	43	6	2	51
26	Lyari	395	97	35	527
27	Jamshed	7	....	....	7
28	Artillery Maidan	1	....	....	1
29	Trans Lyari	22	1	....	23
30	Tatta Naka and Goda village and Labour Corps ..	30	2	....	32
31	Quarry No. 1 and 2 and other Quarries	....	....	....	....
32	Scattered Hamlets, behind Cantonment Station and Chinaser and Vagri villages	2	....	....	2
33	Baba Islands	9	2	....	11
34	Bhit Islands	9	....	....	9
35	Shamspir and Goth Mahomed	3	....	....	3
36	Bunker Island	1	....	....	1
37	Keamari with other Port Area (viz., Thole Produce Yard and West Wharf)	14	....	....	14
38	Maurypur	6	2	....	8
39	Railway Area including City Bunder and Cantonment Stations, and Reception and Hump Yard and Platform Population	88	23	5	116

TENEMENTS BY ROOMS AND

This is an amplification of Housing Table VI-A—

Serial No. of Quarter.	Name of Quarter.	Total No. of buildings.	Total number of persons.	Religion.	Total number of separate tenements occupied by persons of each religion with					
					One room.	Two rooms.	Three rooms.	Four rooms.	Five rooms.	Six rooms and over.
1	2	3	4	5	6	7	8	9	10	11
				Total ..	**37,708**	**12,683**	**3,646**	**1,469**	**450**	**1,090**
	Grand Total for Karachi City .	24,397	240,773	Hindu	17,239	7,645	1,902	823	242	491
				Muslim	19,289	4,241	1,370	386	86	321
				Jain	3	17	16	1	..	1
				Zoroastrian ..	102	121	114	52	27	62
				Christian ..	801	458	174	186	87	194
				Jew and others ..	184	145	67	17	7	20
				Sikh	94	56	3	4	1	1
				Tribal	2	..	..	..	..	..
				Total ..	**387**	**513**	**261**	**120**	**68**	**136**
1	Old Town	804	8,713	Hindu	360	468	243	117	65	128
				Muslim	17	45	18	3	3	8
				Jew and others ..	1	..	..	..	..	..
				Total ..	**46**	**49**	**12**	**20**	**1**	**4**
2	Lea	37	934	Hindu	41	48	12	19	..	4
				Muslim	2	1	..	..	..	..
				Christian ..	1	..	..	..	..	..
				Jew and others ..	2	..	..	1	1	..
				Total ..	**1,336**	**556**	**100**	**88**	**17**	**66**
3	Napier	562	9,922	Hindu	1,084	392	54	48	11	48
				Muslim	250	160	46	40	6	18
				Jew and others ..	2	4	..	..	..	..
				Total ..	**742**	**421**	**101**	**53**	**25**	**38**
4	Market	450	6,509	Hindu	683	348	81	42	19	28
				Muslim	59	70	19	11	6	9
				Jain	..	..	1	..	..	..
				Jew and others ..	..	3	..	..	..	1
				Total ..	**577**	**153**	**60**	**8**	**5**	**3**
5	Bunder	114	3,171	Hindu	540	130	32	7	5	3
				Muslim	30	22	28	1	..	..
				Jew and others ..	7	1	..	..	..	..
				Total ..	**1,014**	**765**	**53**	**21**	**10**	**33**
6	Machi Meani	279	8,777	Hindu	429	452	27	6	3	12
				Muslim	585	307	26	14	7	21
				Christian ..	..	..	..	1	..	..
				Jew and others ..	..	6	..	..	..	..
				Total ..	**33**	**12**	..	..	**1**	**3**
7	Queen's Road	22	153	Hindu	20	9	..	..	..	1
				Muslim	7	..	..	..	..	..
				Zoroastrian ..	1	..	..	..	1	..
				Christian ..	4	3	..	..	..	2
				Jew and others ..	1	..	..	..	..	..
				Total ..	**94**	**12**	**1**	..	**2**	**6**
8	Railway	62	348	Hindu	69	10	1	..	..	1
				Muslim	22	2	..	..	..	2
				Christian ..	1	..	..	..	2	3
				Jew and others ..	2	..	..	..	..	..
				Total ..	**1,294**	**927**	**255**	**85**	**28**	**52**
9	Serai ..	555	12,987	Hindu	1,161	766	207	63	13	38
				Muslim	126	149	41	19	5	13
				Zoroastrian ..	2	9	..	..	1	1
				Christian ..	2	1	1	3	7	..
				Jew and others ..	3	2	6	..	..	..

POPULATION BY RELIGION.

the statistics being given separately for the different Religions.

Total number of tenements of all kinds occupied by members of each religion.	Total number of members of each religion occupying tenements with						Total number of members of each religion occupying tenements of all kinds.	Percentage of total population of each religion occupying each class of tenements with					
	One room.	Two rooms.	Three rooms.	Four rooms.	Five rooms.	Six rooms and over.		One room.	Two rooms.	Three rooms.	Four rooms.	Five rooms.	Six rooms and over.
12	13	14	15	16	17	18	19	20	21	22	23	24	25
57,046	**140,838**	**57,527**	**20,194**	**9,801**	**3,517**	**8,896**	**240,773**	**59**	**24**	**8**	**4**	**1**	**4**
28,336	58,155	33,798	11,109	5,669	2,105	4,494	115,330	50	29	10	5	2	4
25,698	78,838	20,216	7,684	2,832	700	3,035	113,165	69	18	7	2	1	3
38	9	100	76	7	..	7	199	4	50	38	4	..	4
478	380	525	492	297	186	404	2,284	17	23	21	13	8	18
1,900	2,592	2,022	630	839	467	815	7,365	35	27	9	12	6	11
440	560	664	341	90	51	123	1,847	31	36	18	5	3	7
159	292	202	12	58	8	18	590	49	34	2	10	1	4
2	3	....	..	..	..	..	3	100	..	..	..	..	..
1,485	**1,418**	**2,693**	**1,748**	**868**	**610**	**1,376**	**8,713**	**16**	**31**	**20**	**10**	**7**	**16**
1,390	1,346	2,452	1,610	850	582	1,276	8,116	17	30	20	10	7	16
94	69	241	138	18	28	100	594	12	40	23	3	5	17
1	3	..	..	..	..	..	3	100	..	..	..	..	..
132	**200**	**351**	**108**	**165**	**12**	**98**	**934**	**21**	**38**	**12**	**18**	**1**	**10**
124	186	350	108	161	..	98	903	20	39	12	18	..	11
3	3	1	..	..	..	..	4	75	25	..	..	..	..
1	3	..	..	..	..	..	3	100	..	..	..	..	..
4	8	..	..	4	12	..	24	33	..	..	17	50	..
2,163	**4,560**	**3,021**	**707**	**722**	**147**	**765**	**9,922**	**46**	**30**	**7**	**7**	**2**	**8**
1,637	3,688	2,031	361	404	96	556	7,137	52	28	5	6	1	8
520	868	968	346	318	50	209	2,759	31	35	13	12	1	8
6	4	22	..	..	..	..	26	15	85	..	..	..	..
1,380	**2,656**	**2,159**	**658**	**441**	**188**	**407**	**6,509**	**41**	**33**	**10**	**7**	**3**	**6**
1,201	2,371	1,648	497	335	137	301	5,289	45	31	9	6	3	6
174	285	498	160	106	51	101	1,201	24	42	13	9	4	8
1	..	..	1	..	..	..	1	..	..	100	..	..	..
4	..	13	..	..	..	5	18	..	72	..	..	..	28
806	**2,068**	**713**	**244**	**52**	**64**	**30**	**3,171**	**65**	**22**	**8**	**2**	**2**	**1**
717	1,950	588	144	46	64	30	2,822	69	21	5	2	2	1
81	100	124	100	6	..	..	330	30	38	30	2	..	..
8	18	1	..	..	..	..	19	95	5	..	..	..	..
1,896	**4,170**	**3,595**	**345**	**163**	**67**	**437**	**8,777**	**49**	**39**	**4**	**2**	**1**	**5**
929	1,563	1,953	162	56	41	141	3,916	40	50	4	1	1	4
960	2,607	1,627	183	99	26	296	4,838	54	33	4	2	1	6
1	..	..	..	8	..	..	8	..	..	..	100	..	..
6	..	15	..	..	..	..	15	..	100	..	..	..	..
49	**86**	**44**	..	..	**9**	**14**	**153**	**56**	**29**	..	..	**6**	**9**
30	48	36	..	..	..	5	89	54	40	..	..	..	6
7	11	..	..	..	..	..	11	100	..	..	..	..	..
2	5	..	..	..	9	..	14	36	..	..	..	64	..
9	9	8	..	..	..	9	26	35	30	..	..	..	35
1	13	..	..	..	..	..	13	100	..	..	..	..	..
115	**280**	**42**	**4**	..	**2**	**20**	**348**	**80**	**12**	**1**	..	**1**	**6**
81	202	35	4	..	..	3	244	83	14	2	..	..	1
26	70	7	..	..	..	6	83	84	9	..	..	..	7
6	1	..	..	..	2	11	14	7	..	..	..	14	79
2	7	..	..	..	..	..	7	100	..	..	..	..	..
2,639	**4,753**	**4,955**	**1,628**	**708**	**249**	**699**	**12,987**	**37**	**38**	**13**	**5**	**2**	**5**
2,248	4,347	4,211	1,365	557	118	319	10,917	40	39	12	..	1	3
353	396	712	242	136	83	369	1,938	21	37	12	7	4	19
18	2	9	..	..	7	11	29	7	31	..	..	24	38
14	3	15	1	10	41	..	70	4	22	1	14	59	..
11	5	8	20	..	..	..	33	15	24	61	..	..	..

Serial No. of Quarter.	Name of Quarter.	Total No. of buildings.	Total number of persons.	Religion.	Total number of separate tenements occupied by persons of each religion with One room.	Two rooms.	Three rooms.	Four rooms.	Five rooms.	Six rooms and over.
1	2	3	4	5	6	7	8	9	10	11
				Total ..	**524**	**1,075**	**353**	**244**	**43**	**92**
10	**Rambaugh**	423	11,471	Hindu	366	765	301	224	33	77
				Muslim	136	244	29	12	5	10
				Zoroastrian ..	4	20	13	2	3	2
				Christian ..	7	7	1	3	1	2
				Jew and others ..	1	4	9	1	..	..
				Sikh	10	35	..	2	1	1
				Total ..	**527**	**881**	**142**	**94**	**13**	**22**
11	**Jail**	294	7,487	Hindu	403	699	84	62	5	15
				Muslim	115	148	46	30	7	6
				Jain	1	10	1	..	..	..
				Zoroastrian ..	..	1	..	..	..	..
				Christian ..	3	14	8	2	1	1
				Jew and others ..	5	9	3	..	..	..
				Total ..	**5,001**	**1,279**	**188**	**49**	**5**	**21**
12	**Ranchore**	1,269	24,024	Hindu	3,943	1,089	104	30	..	8
				Muslim	1,038	161	30	18	2	12
				Zoroastrian ..	..	9	54	..	..	..
				Christian ..	8	8	..	1	3	..
				Jew and others ..	..	12	..	..	..	1
				Sikh	12	..	..	..	..	..
				Total ..	**464**	**1,148**	**190**	**40**	**5**	**18**
13	**Ramswami**	314	7,038	Hindu	414	944	132	22	5	6
				Muslim	30	116	28	14	..	8
				Jain	..	7	14	1	..	1
				Zoroastrian ..	1	..	..	..	..	..
				Christian ..	..	10	6	..	..	..
				Jew and others ..	19	66	10	3	..	3
				Total ..	**262**	**396**	**13**	**7**	**1**	**3**
14	**Harchandrai Vishandas** ..	437	2,251	Hindu	104	135	3	6	..	..
				Muslim	148	254	9	1	..	2
				Christian ..	7	2	..	..	..	1
				Jew and others ..	3	5	1	..	1	..
				Total ..	**90**	**169**	**40**	**13**	**4**	**3**
15	**Soldier Bazar**	196	1,488	Hindu	55	80	14	7	3	2
				Muslim	34	88	26	5	1	..
				Zoroastrian ..	..	1	..	..	..	1
				Christian ..	1	..	..	1	..	..
				Total ..	**175**	**2**	**1**	**1**	..	..
16	**New Jail**	95	1,140	Hindu	61	1	1	1	..	..
				Muslim	101	1	..	..	..	..
				Zoroastrian ..	2	..	..	..	..	..
				Christian ..	5	..	..	..	..	..
				Jew and others ..	6	..	..	..	..	..
				Total ..	**290**	**45**	**29**	**35**	**20**	**38**
17	**Preedy**	177	1,782	Hindu	181	18	4	1	..	5
				Muslim	62	7	1	1	1	3
				Zoroastrian ..	8	6	14	17	4	18
				Christian ..	38	14	10	16	15	12
				Jew and others ..	1	..	..	..	..	..
				Total ..	**1,309**	**611**	**141**	**75**	**11**	**44**
18	**Saddar Bazar**	656	10,193	Hindu	439	145	21	18	1	15
				Muslim	562	182	73	17	3	13
				Jain	1	..	..	..	..	..
				Zoroastrian ..	69	45	17	18	4	6
				Christian ..	228	234	28	21	3	10
				Jew and others ..	2	5	2	..	..	..
				Sikh	8	..	..	1	..	..

Total number of tenements of all kinds occupied by members of each religion.	Total number of members of each religion occupying tenements with One room.	Two rooms.	Three rooms.	Four rooms.	Five rooms.	Six rooms and over.	Total number of members of each religion occupying tenements of all kinds.	Percentage of total population of each religion occupying each class of tenements with One room.	Two rooms.	Three rooms.	Four rooms.	Five rooms.	Six rooms and over.
12	13	14	15	16	17	18	19	20	21	22	23	24	25
2,331	**1,698**	**4,854**	**2,129**	**1,506**	**506**	**778**	**11,471**	**15**	**42**	**19**	**13**	**4**	**7**
1,766	1,287	3,501	1,790	1,319	430	637	8,964	14	39	20	15	5	7
436	342	1,096	214	120	49	109	1,930	18	56	11	7	2	6
44	18	96	65	10	17	11	217	8	44	30	5	8	5
21	14	26	3	8	2	3	56	25	47	5	14	4	5
15	1	12	57	10	..	..	80	1	15	71	13	..	..
49	36	123	..	30	8	18	215	17	57	..	14	4	8
1,679	**1,736**	**3,814**	**958**	**659**	**77**	**243**	**7,487**	**23**	**51**	**13**	**9**	**1**	**3**
1,268	1,347	3,024	627	427	27	170	5,622	24	54	11	8	..	3
352	371	600	283	225	44	68	1,591	23	38	18	14	3	4
12	1	71	7	..	..	..	79	1	90	9	..	..	..
1	..	3	..	..	..	..	3	..	100	..	..	..	..
29	11	56	25	7	6	5	110	10	51	23	6	5	5
17	6	60	16	..	..	..	82	7	73	20	..	..	..
6,543	**18,332**	**5,151**	**849**	**292**	**76**	**174**	**24,924**	**74**	**21**	**3**	**1**	**..**	**1**
5,174	14,427	4,479	540	188	..	47	19,690	73	23	3	1	..	..
1,261	3,876	527	134	101	65	125	4,828	80	11	3	2	1	3
63	..	27	166	..	..	..	193	..	14	86	..	..	..
20	23	42	..	3	11	..	79	29	53	..	4	14	..
13	..	76	..	..	..	2	78	..	97	..	..	..	3
12	56	..	..	..	..	..	56	100	..	..	..	..	..
1,855	**1,197**	**4,497**	**902**	**306**	**22**	**114**	**7,038**	**17**	**64**	**13**	**4**	**..**	**2**
1,523	1,072	3,561	612	182	22	60	5,509	20	65	11	3	..	1
191	65	537	138	97	..	14	851	8	63	16	11	..	2
23	..	29	68	7	..	7	111	..	26	62	6	..	6
1	1	..	..	..	..	..	1	100	..	..	..	..	..
16	..	42	20	..	..	..	62	..	68	32	..	..	..
101	59	828	64	20	..	33	504	11	65	13	4	..	7
682	**757**	**1,347**	**53**	**53**	**16**	**25**	**2,251**	**34**	**60**	**2**	**2**	**1**	**1**
248	355	502	9	48	..	..	914	30	55	1	5	..	..
414	323	793	37	5	..	18	1,176	28	67	3	..	..	2
10	72	20	..	..	..	7	99	73	20	..	..	..	7
10	7	32	7	..	16	..	62	11	52	11	..	26	..
319	**388**	**792**	**232**	**81**	**38**	**12**	**1,488**	**22**	**53**	**16**	**5**	**3**	**1**
161	197	379	80	43	29	3	731	27	52	11	6	4	..
154	135	410	152	30	9	..	736	18	56	21	4	1	..
2	..	3	..	..	..	9	12	..	25	..	..	..	75
2	1	..	..	8	..	..	9	11	..	..	89	..	..
179	**1,127**	**7**	**5**	**1**	**..**	**..**	**1,140**	**99**	**1**	**..**	**..**	**..**	**..**
64	355	5	5	1	..	..	366	98	1	1	..	..	..
102	753	2	..	..	..	..	755	100	..	..	..	..	..
2	2	..	..	..	..	..	2	100	..	..	..	..	..
5	11	..	..	..	..	..	11	100	..	..	..	..	..
6	6	..	..	..	..	..	6	100	..	..	..	..	..
457	**918**	**162**	**157**	**135**	**97**	**263**	**1,782**	**52**	**9**	**9**	**10**	**5**	**15**
209	644	71	20	8	..	41	784	82	9	3	1	..	5
75	135	23	4	1	1	26	190	71	12	2	1	1	13
67	28	26	77	94	32	128	385	7	7	20	25	8	33
105	105	42	56	82	64	68	417	25	10	14	20	15	16
1	6	..	..	..	..	..	6	100	..	..	..	..	..
2,191	**5,476**	**3,214**	**630**	**500**	**87**	**286**	**10,193**	**53**	**32**	**6**	**5**	**1**	**3**
630	1,697	635	138	97	3	82	2,562	64	24	5	4	..	3
850	2,423	1,088	269	135	18	107	4,040	60	27	7	3	..	3
1	6	..	..	..	..	..	6	100	..	..	..	..	..
159	274	249	111	115	37	51	837	33	30	13	14	4	6
524	1,036	1,223	104	133	29	46	2,571	40	48	4	5	1	2
9	17	19	..	..	..	..	44	39	43	18	..	..	..
9	23	..	..	20	..	..	43	53	..	..	47	..	..

Serial No. of Quarter.	Name of Quarter.	Total No. of buildings.	Total number of persons.	Religion.	Total number of separate tenements occupied by persons of each religion with One room.	Two rooms.	Three rooms.	Four rooms.	Five rooms.	Six rooms and over.
1	2	3	4	5	6	7	8	9	10	11
				Total ..	116	40	7	1	1	3
28	Artillery Maidan ..	49	538	Hindu	74	18	5	1	..	1
				Muslim	29	8	2	..	1	..
				Zoroastrian ..	2	14	..	..	..	1
				Christian ..	2	7	..	..	..	1
				Sikh	9	8	..	..	..	..
				Total ..	1,435	2	..	..	..	..
29	Trans Lyari	1,385	5,678	Hindu	51	..	..	..	..	..
				Muslim	1,384	2	..	..	..	..
				Total ..	204	..	..	..	..	..
30	Tatta Naka and Goda Village, and Labour corps.	101	800	Hindu	82	..	..	..	..	..
				Muslim	108	..	..	..	..	..
				Christian ..	1	..	..	..	..	..
				Jew and others ..	13	..	..	..	..	..
				Total ..	106	..	..	..	..	..
31	Quarry Nos. 1 and 2 and other quarries.	102	424	Hindu	3	..	..	..	..	..
				Muslim	103	..	..	..	..	..
				Total ..	191	..	..	..	..	..
32	Scattered hamlets behind cantonment station and Chinaser and Vagri villages.	187	859	Hindu	46	..	..	..	..	..
				Muslim	145	..	..	..	..	..
				Total ..	146	141	25	5	..	..
33	Baba Islands	283	1,200	Hindu	8	1	..	1	..	..
				Muslim	138	140	25	4	..	..
				Total ..	106	75	11	..	..	..
34	Bhit Islands	159	796	Hindu	..	1	2	..	..	..
				Muslim	106	74	9	..	..	..
				Total ..	43	53	23	5	..	..
35	Shamspir and Goth Mahomed	106	464	Hindu	..	1	..	..	..	..
				Muslim	43	52	23	5	..	..
				Total ..	3	..	..	..	..	..
36	Bunker Islands	2	4	Hindu	1	..	..	..	..	..
				Muslim	2	..	..	..	..	..
				Total ..	606	847	1,052	78	30	60
37	Port Keamari with other port area (viz.. Thole produce yard, Mansfield import yard and west wharf).	465	11,472	Hindu	313	475	423	37	9	8
				Muslim	271	334	574	18	5	13
				Zoroastrian ..	1	1	..	..	2	6
				Christian ..	16	25	32	20	14	29
				Jew and others ..	5	12	23	3	..	4
				Total ..	304	64	5	1	3	..
38	Maurypur	390	1,400	Hindu	88	8	..	..	..	..
				Muslim ..	210	54	5	1	3	..
				Christian ..	3	2	..	..	..	.
				Jew and others ..	3	..	..	..	..	..
				Total ..	2,007	202	43	11	2	1[illegible]
39	Railway area including City bunder and Cantonment stations and receptions and hump yard and platform population.	1,786	6,039	Hindu	1,057	77	26	..	..	1
				Muslim	872	84	11	..	..	8
				Zoroastrian ..	1	1	..	..	..	..
				Christian ..	16	31	1	9	1	7
				Jew and others ..	61	9	5	2	1	..

Total number of tenements of all kinds occupied by members of each religion.	Total number of members of each religion occupying tenements with						Total number of members of each religion occupying tenements of all kinds.	Percentage of total population of each religion occupying each class of tenements with					
	One room.	Two rooms.	Three rooms.	Four rooms.	Five rooms.	Six rooms and over.		One room.	Two rooms.	Three rooms.	Four rooms.	Five rooms.	Six rooms and over.
12	13	14	15	16	17	18	19	20	21	22	23	24	25
168	**317**	**141**	**30**	**17**	**2**	**31**	**588**	**59**	**26**	**6**	**8**	..	**6**
94	204	35	22	17	..	11	289	71	12	7	6	..	4
35	72	14	8	..	2	..	96	75	15	8	..	2	..
17	6	64	..	..	..	13	83	7	77	..	..	..	16
10	12	14	..	..	..	7	33	36	42	..	..	..	22
12	23	14	..	..	..	..	37	62	38	..	..	..	..
1,437	**5,660**	**13**	..	..	..	..	**5,673**	**100**	..	..	..	..	..
51	150	..	..	..	..	..	150	100	..	..	..	..	..
1,386	5,510	13	..	..	..	..	5,523	100	..	..	..	..	..
204	**860**	..	..	..	..	..	**860**	**100**	..	..	..	..	..
82	296	..	..	..	..	..	296	100	..	..	..	..	..
108	501	..	..	..	..	..	501	100	..	..	..	..	..
1	1	..	..	..	..	..	1	100	..	..	..	..	..
13	62	..	..	..	..	..	62	100	..	..	..	..	..
106	**424**	..	..	..	..	..	**424**	**100**	..	..	..	..	..
3	12	..	..	..	..	..	12	100	..	..	..	..	..
103	412	..	..	..	..	..	412	100	..	..	..	..	..
191	**859**	..	..	..	..	..	**859**	**100**	..	..	..	..	..
46	193	..	..	..	..	..	193	100	..	..	..	..	..
145	666	..	..	..	..	..	666	100	..	..	..	..	..
317	**529**	**532**	**116**	**23**	..	..	**1,200**	**44**	**44**	**10**	**2**	..	..
10	13	3	..	5	..	..	21	62	14	..	24	..	..
307	516	529	116	18	..	..	1,179	43	45	10	2	..	..
192	**481**	**313**	**52**	..	..	..	**796**	**54**	**39**	**7**	..	..	..
3	..	3	6	..	..	..	9	..	33	67	..	..	..
189	431	310	46	..	..	..	787	55	39	6	..	..	..
124	**149**	**190**	**94**	**31**	..	..	**464**	**32**	**41**	**20**	**7**	..	..
1	..	3	..	..	..	..	3	..	100	..	..	..	..
123	149	187	94	31	..	..	461	32	41	20	7	..	..
3	**4**	..	..	..	..	..	**4**	**100**	..	..	..	..	..
1	1	..	..	..	..	..	1	100	..	..	..	..	..
2	3	..	..	..	..	..	3	100	..	..	..	..	..
2,673	**2,026**	**2,949**	**5,569**	**462**	**125**	**341**	**11,472**	**18**	**26**	**48**	**4**	**1**	**3**
1,265	1,021	1,721	2,293	204	30	54	5,323	19	32	43	4	1	1
1,215	949	1,114	3,062	131	35	87	5,378	18	20	57	2	1	2
10	1	2	..	..	5	32	40	2	5	..	..	13	80
136	42	81	114	102	55	142	536	8	15	21	19	10	27
47	13	31	100	25	..	26	195	7	16	51	13	..	13
377	**1,032**	**302**	**52**	**6**	**8**	..	**1,400**	**74**	**21**	**4**	..	**1**	..
96	171	23	..	..	..	..	194	88	12	..	..	..	..
273	852	275	52	6	8	..	1,193	71	23	4	1	1	..
.. 5	4	4	..	..	..	..	8	50	50	..	..	..	..
3	5	..	..	..	..	..	5	100	..	..	..	..	..
2,276	**5,032**	**652**	**235**	**52**	**13**	**55**	**6,039**	**83**	**11**	**4**	**1**	..	**1**
1,161	2,579	258	152	..	..	6	2,995	86	9	5	..	..	..
970	2,254	264	51	..	..	15	2,584	87	10	2	..	..	1
2	1	2	..	..	..	..	3	33	07	..	..	..	..
65	87	104	7	43	5	34	230	16	45	3	19	2	15
78	161	24	25	9	8	..	227	71	10	11	4	4	..

* HOUSING TABLE No. I—SHOLAPUR.

General Classification of Buildings.

[" Building " or " House " in Sholapur City means the units which would in ordinary parlance be call a " house " and corresponds roughly with the unit having a separate entrance or entrances from t common way and partitioned off from other adjacent structures by dividing walls.]

Ward No.	Total No. of buildings.	Residential buildings.	Residential and Commercial buildings.	Commercial buildings.	Public buildings.	Huts and other small buildings of a temporary kind.
1	2	3	4	5	6	7
1 ..	1,198	1,010	59	77	51	1
2 ..	1,264	1,196	2	54	12	....
3 ..	1,927	955	100	251	67	554
4 ..	1,493	699	68	234	61	431
5 ..	1,605	1,270	1	193	68	73
6 ..	1,194	948	118	36	50	42
7 ..	2,153	1,941	....	34	65	113
8 ..	695	599	....	17	66	13
9 ..	2,127	1,388	....	18	78	643
10 ..	1,238	691	68	107	38	334
11 ..	5,736	4,066	4	419	232	1,015
Total ..	20,630*	14,763	420	1,440	788	3,219

* A few uncertain buildings have been excluded.

HOUSING TABLE No. II—SHOLAPUR.

Classification of Buildings by the Number of Floors.

Ward No.	Total No. of buildings.	Ground floor only.	One upper floor.	Two upper floors.	Three upper floors.
1	2	3	4	5	6
1 ..	1,198	852	325	21	....
2 ..	1,264	1,036	215	13	....
3 ..	1,927	1,477	392	57	1
4 ..	1,493	1,131	341	20	1
5 ..	1,605	1,200	375	30	....
6 ..	1,194	881	302	11	....
7 ..	2,153	2,038	110	5	....
8 ..	695	549	143	3	....
9 ..	2,127	2,037	90	....	....
10 ..	1,238	1,148	83	7	....
11 ..	5,736	5,421	300	13	2
Total ..	20,630†	17,770	2,676	180	4

† A few uncertain buildings have been excluded.

HOUSING TABLE No. III—SHOLAPUR.

Distribution of Buildings by the Number of Rooms.

Ward No.	Total No. of buildings.	Number of rooms.														
		1	2	3	4	5	6	7	8	9	10	11 to 15	16 to 20	21 to 30	31 to 40	41 and over.
1	2	3	4	5	6	7	8	9	10	11	12	13	14	15	16	17
1 ..	1,186	295	175	112	106	96	69	66	42	43	32	89	32	21	7	1
2 ..	1,263	200	214	237	181	101	109	57	41	36	21	51	8	5	2	..
3 ..	1,926	745	390	198	153	87	78	68	50	31	36	63	16	8	1	2
4 ..	1,493	545	270	173	160	65	68	54	49	26	21	54	5	3	..	..
5 ..	1,584	534	433	209	119	76	57	28	33	19	31	31	7	5	2	..
6 ..	1,189	100	198	170	198	149	135	57	57	40	31	45	8	1	..	..
7 ..	2,134	1,065	419	244	136	99	70	34	25	14	12	14	2	..	..	..
8 ..	690	215	116	101	75	41	38	23	26	12	14	22	5	2	..	..
9 ..	2,127	1,371	384	157	75	48	34	16	8	8	6	14	5	..	..	1
10 ..	1,230	263	324	228	169	105	65	18	24	15	7	6	2	3	..	1
11 ..	5,721	2,218	2,582	281	207	46	171	18	61	8	34	72	7	9	4	3
Total ..	20,543	7,551	5,505	2,110	1,579	913	894	439	416	252	245	461	97	57	16	8

HOUSING TABLE No. IV—SHOLAPUR.

Classification of Buildings by the Number of Families.

(Unoccupied Buildings are excluded.)

Ward No.	No. of buildings.	Number of families.												
		1	2	3	4	5	6	7	8	9	10	11 to 15	16 to 20	21 and over.
1	2	3	4	5	6	7	8	9	10	11	12	13	14	15
1 ..	1,164	593	170	108	78	51	40	36	24	18	10	30	4	2
2 ..	1,242	583	196	148	100	47	51	35	21	17	12	25	5	2
3 ..	1,357	1,420	169	97	63	37	23	15	9	6.	5	6	2	5
4 ..	1,415	1,060	124	68	64	39	20	13	11	4	7	5	..	..
5 ..	1,424	1,081	151	82	40	25	14	10	6	5	3	4	..	3
6 ..	1,142	529	238	148	73	55	31	14	17	10	9	13	3	2
7 ..	2,016	1,389	286	145	80	54	23	16	10	3	5	3	2	..
8 ..	523	398	68	27	13	6	4	3	3	1	..	..	..	..
9 ..	1,990	1,753	150	46	16	7	7	2	2	4	1	2	..	.
10 ..	1,128	699	200	108	56	24	12	8	11	4	1	1	3	1
11 ..	5,143	4,854	140	51	40	29	10	3	5	2	3	6	..	..
Total ..	19,044	14,359	1,892	1,028	623	374	235	155	119	74	56	95	19	15

MO-: Bk Ra Cs 3—90

BOMBAY: PRINTED AT THE GOVERNMENT CENTRAL PRESS.